PENGUIN BOOK

THE QUEST FOR SHER. ...ES

Owen Dudley Edwards is Reader in Commonwealth and American History at the University of Edinburgh, where he has been on the teaching staff since 1969. He has also taught at the Universities of Oregon, Aberdeen, South Carolina, California State University at San Francisco, and has been lecturer, writer, journalist, broadcaster in the British Isles and North America for over twenty years. Born in Dublin in 1938, he is married and has three children. His books include *Burke and Hare*; *P. G. Wodehouse*; *The Mind of an Activist – James Connolly* and *The Sins of Our Fathers: Roots of Conflict in Northern Ireland*.

Owen Dudley Edwards

THE QUEST FOR SHERLOCK HOLMES

A Biographical Study of Sir Arthur Conan Doyle

Penguin Books

Penguin Books Ltd, Harmondsworth, Middlesex, England
Penguin Books, 40 West 23rd Street, New York, New York 10010, U.S.A.
Penguin Books Australia Ltd, Ringwood, Victoria, Australia
Penguin Books Canada Ltd, 2801 John Street, Markham, Ontario, Canada L3R 1B4
Penguin Books (N.Z.) Ltd, 182–190 Wairau Road, Auckland 10, New Zealand

First published by Mainstream Publishing Company (Edinburgh) Ltd 1983
Published in Penguin Books 1984

Made and printed in Great Britain by
Hazell Watson & Viney Limited,
Member of the BPCC Group,
Aylesbury, Bucks
Set in Plantin

"*Honestly, I cannot congratulate you upon it. Detection is, or ought to be, an exact science, and should be treated in the same cold and unemotional manner. You have attempted to tinge it with romanticism, which produces much the same effect as if you worked a love-story or an elopement into the fifth proposition of Euclid.*"
"*But the romance was there*", I remonstrated. "*I could not tamper with the facts.*"
"*Some facts should be suppressed . . .*"

—The Sign of Four, *Chapter 1.*

For Colin Affleck,
     Richard Lancelyn Green,
     Graham Richardson,
     Graham Sutton,
     Timothy Willis—
      This Sign.

Contents

List of Illustrations

A Note for the Penguin Edition

Because I made a blunder, my dear Watson . . .
— A. Conan Doyle, "Silver Blaze"

To be a Penguin is to fulfil a lifelong ambition, and it seems sensible to clean a flipper or two.

The most important point to be made is that Richard Lancelyn Green and John Michael Gibson have now brought out their admirable work, *A Bibliography of A. Conan Doyle*, published in Oxford by the Clarendon Press as No. XXIII in the great series of Soho Bibliographies founded by Rupert Hart-Davis; and that in any differences in matters of fact between that work and this, it takes precedence. It points out that the story *"The Confession"* was originally published in the *Star* on 17 January 1898 before it appeared in the *Universal*, as discussed on pp. 92–95 below; the argument there acquires additional force when it is realised the story was written very shortly after Conan Doyle found himself to be in love with Jean Leckie. (Richard Lancelyn Green had told me of the earlier date and I very stupidly forgot it.) Arthur Guitermann's doggerel was published in 1912, not 1915 as stated by me on p. 142, and was entitled "To Sir Arthur Conan Doyle", not "The Case of the Inferior Sleuth" as I had concluded from Peter Haining's anthology. *"The Story of the Club-Footed Grocer"* was in fact printed in the volume *Round the Fire Stories* and was dropped from the author's subsequent collection of his works: the argument on p. 30 on Conan Doyle's possible reasons for disliking it would still apply, but the error is inexcusable.

The most contemptible blunder of the lot is perhaps that on p. 352 where I have ascribed to Lecoq the conduct of Père Tabaret, nicknamed Tirauclair, who in *L'Affaire Lerouge* is the great detective instructing Lecoq although Lecoq is the hero of many more of Gaboriau's works. This piece of idiocy arose because Holmes and Watson discuss Lecoq in *A Study in Scarlet*; it was Tirauclair, and not Lecoq, who had in fact been the really significant unconscious influence.

Further foolishness was exhibited by placing Shaw's residence as Conan Doyle's neighbour to Norwood, not, as it should have been, to Hindhead (p. 14): this was the more absurd as I had known for some thirty years about Conan Doyle, Shaw and Grant Allen going on walks together when neighbours, and Allen was in Hindhead for the reason Conan Doyle's wife Louise was, the belief the climate would be good for the tubercular illness which ultimately killed both of them.

Blackwood's was published from George Street, not Queen Street; and the friend who persuaded Conan Doyle to write his first story for publication was Rupert Hoare Hunter, nephew of Reginald Hoare, as Richard Lancelyn Green and John Michael Gibson point out in their valuable *Uncollected Stories* of Conan Doyle. But I hold to the opinion that the unpublished *"Haunted Grange at Goresthorpe"* is the oldest surviving Conan Doyle story, despite their preference for *"Sasassa Valley"*; years of reading undergraduate essays would make me fairly confident in stating what is second-year work and what third-year: a student may do worse work in his later year but not work which is less mature.

Conan Doyle went to his grave believing he had sat on Thackeray's knee, as I quote on p. 36; but he could not have done, as Thackeray's last visit to Edinburgh was in 1857, so it must have been Annette who so honoured the novelist and the family later misremembered in favour of the boy, as so often happens. The vivisection theme should have been extended to take in the fate of the dog in *A Study in Scarlet*.

My indebtedness in preparing this work must also be acknowledged to my old friend Joan Bakewell for some very helpful biographical information and to Michael and Lesley Heale for their kindness and hospitality while I was engaged in research. And my revisions now were particularly aided by Trevor Royle, V. G. Kiernan, Roger Savage, Graham Sutton, Richard Lancelyn Green and Leila Dudley Edwards, as well as by Bill Campbell and Peter McKenzie of Mainstream Press and Donald McFarlan of Penguin Books. It is a pity that such reviewers as disliked the book did not use their space for the discovery and denunciation of these errors instead of merely repeating one another's aesthetic preferences.

September 1983   *O.D.E.*

Introduction

Arthur Ignatius Conan Doyle was born on 22 May 1859 in Edinburgh to an Irishwoman and the son of a famous London caricaturist of Irish birth. He grew up in near-poverty, being one of ten siblings, seven of whom lived to maturity. His father, Charles Altamont Doyle, was a civil servant in the Office of Works at Edinburgh until he lost his post when Arthur was about eighteen. Thereafter he declined steadily into alcoholism and epilepsy, and was institutionalised for the last ten years of his life, dying in 1893. Meanwhile Arthur had been educated at home, in a local school, and ultimately, from 1868 to 1875, at the Jesuit preparatory school Hodder, in Lancashire, and its secondary school, Stonyhurst, a few miles distant. He then spent a year at the Jesuit school in Feldkirch, Austria, after which he returned to Edinburgh, studying medicine at the University from 1876 to 1881. During that time he took various minor assistantships, chiefly serving several short terms with Dr Reginald Ratcliff Hoare, in general practice in Birmingham. In 1880 he followed the example of other Edinburgh medical students and served for a season as ship's doctor aboard a Greenland whaler. Immediately after graduation he occupied a similar position on a trading vessel on a voyage to the West Africa coast. He had a brief experience as partner in a medical practice at Plymouth, culminating in a bitter break with his colleague, George Turnavine Budd, and thence moved to Southsea, a suburb of Portsmouth, where he built up a medical practice during his residence there from 1882 to 1890. His younger and only brother Innes shared his household there initially, until he married Louise Hawkins, then a Southsea resident, in 1885. In the same year he obtained a doctorate in medicine from Edinburgh for a dissertation on aspects of syphilis.

During these years he commenced the career which was to obliterate his medical profession: writing. His first attempt on a publisher with a story which still survives, "*The Haunted Grange at Goresthorpe*", took place between 1877 and early in 1879; his first publication, "*The Mystery of Sasassa Valley*", appeared in *Chambers's Journal*, an Edinburgh weekly, on September 6, 1879. Thereafter he found outlets slowly, but with growing success, in *London Society*, *All the Year Round* and other journals. His first really outstanding short stories were "*The Captain of the 'Pole-Star'*", published in *Temple Bar* in February 1883, and "*J. Habakuk Jephson's*

Statement", in the *Cornhill* in January 1884. The latter, a fictional solution to the mystery of the derelict *Mary Celeste* (the disappearance of whose crew and passengers is still unsolved) won celebrity and was widely taken to be an allegedly authentic document. Meanwhile he was making many photographic expeditions in Scotland and later in England, and publishing articles on the results. He was also writing modest but impressively professional articles on aspects of medical science for the learned journals. He commenced work on a manuscript apparently called *The Narrative of John Smith* which may or may not have been fictional and certainly reflected political interest: but his only copy was entrusted to the post and disappeared. From 1884 onward he worked on a novel about business turpitude and the abduction of an heiress, *The Firm of Girdlestone:* after many rejections it was published in 1890. By that time he had obtained considerable success with an historical novel on the Duke of Monmouth's insurrection of 1685, *Micah Clarke*, which appeared in 1889, and he had obtained a small but growing audience for a detective story, *A Study in Scarlet*, published initially in *Beeton's Christmas Annual* in 1887 and the next year on its own. It introduced the characters of Sherlock Holmes and Dr Watson.

Conan Doyle gave up work as a general practitioner and moved to London to specialise on the eye, but his arrival in the metropolis coincided with several great advances in his career as a writer and he shortly afterwards abandoned medicine completely. His historical novel *The White Company* which appeared in 1891 brought to life the medieval world of military adventure, social disorder and anti-clericalism, its action taking the reader into England, France and Spain during the later years of Edward III. Fifteen years later he would write a sequel about the early life of its principal hero, *Sir Nigel.* Together with *Micah Clarke* these books entitle him to be acknowledged as the finest historical novelist between his own day and that of Sir Walter Scott, at least of those who wrote in the English language. He was also to write several others which, while flawed, are rich in their presentation of the social history of their period and in their narrative skill: *The Refugees* (1893) on the expulsion of the French Protestants, the Huguenots, from the France of Louis XIV, and on the adventures of some of them in America; *Rodney Stone* (1896), a tale of boxing and mystery in the Regency period, whose weakness probably arises from its failure in the end to include the account of the Trafalgar campaign he seems originally to have intended for it; *Uncle Bernac* (1897), a story of murder and intrigue in Napoleonic France, in this instance weakened by the original story's being fleshed out with scenes at the court of Napoleon; and a slighter work with interesting Scottish content and a vivid account of Waterloo, *The Great Shadow* (1892). But his major success was by now in the short story, and it was here he produced his most popular historical work, the *Exploits* and *Adventures* of his Napoleonic officer Brigadier Gerard, whose pace and comedy are outstanding, and whose theme is ably summed up by Napoleon at the close of the first of them, "*The Medal of Brigadier Gerard*", that if Gerard "has the thickest head he has also the stoutest heart in my army".

But at the same time as *The White Company* was finding its public, Conan Doyle's reputation was taking off in another field of literature. He had produced a sequel to *A Study in Scarlet*, *The Sign of Four*, commissioned by the Philadelphia magazine *Lippincott's* simultaneously with Oscar Wilde's only novel *The Picture of Dorian Gray*. The *Strand* magazine, founded in January 1891, badly needed material for the mass reading public it sought, its catchment area ranging from dukes to housemaids, professors to schoolboys. In July 1891 it began to run *"Adventures of Sherlock Holmes"* and in this format the Holmes stories, still to that date largely unknown, became world famous. The idea of a series of short stories based on two well-established characters with a hero blending science and romance and a narrator exactly reflecting the probable reactions of the reader, proved an extraordinary success. The triumph was made the more evident when a large field of imitators of both magazine and detective began to appear.

Conan Doyle was somewhat annoyed by identification with a cult so widespread that it quickly became a caricaturist's and music-hall joke; and, partly to achieve recognition for work more akin to his literary ambitions, partly because he feared the need to provide Holmes incessantly would make the stories mechanical and unsatisfactory, he sought to "kill" Holmes in *"The Final Problem"* (published in the *Strand* in December 1893). As a detective story it is weak; as a miniature epic it is a work of art of extraordinary power, possibly the best short story he ever wrote. It completed the conquest of the reading public by Holmes and Watson, as is shown by the fact that with it Conan Doyle gave a third name to the common speech of the English language, that of the master-criminal Professor Moriarty. Holmes was left in abeyance by his creator until the new century, when he brought him back firstly in a novel, *The Hound of the Baskervilles*, and then in further short stories, *The Return of Sherlock Holmes*, following the revelation that he had not been killed after all. The "return" was partly prompted by the success and nature of the "return" of the gentleman criminal, A. J. Raffles, who had been created by Conan Doyle's brother-in-law, E. W. Hornung, left with his fate unknown at the end of his first book, and then resurrected to commence his second.

But Conan Doyle had made good use of the time he had won away from Holmes's domination. In addition to the historical novels, he produced in the 1890s several contemporary works, ranging from an amusing idyll of suburban life, *Beyond the City*, which salutes and occasionally gently mocks the new feminism, to a thrilling account of the adventures of a party captured by African rebels during the Mahdist wars of the 1890s, *The Tragedy of the "Korosko"*. His humour was never far away from any of these enterprises: the *"Korosko"* novel is distinguished by having a hero, Colonel Cochrane Cochrane, who dyes his hair and wears corsets in order to maintain the appearance as well as the character of an English military gentleman. Arthur Conan Doyle was also pouring out a vast flood of short stories involving adventure, mystery, the supernatural, piracy, boxing and medical life, for some of which very high claims may be made. In fact it is true to say that in structure, control, scientific and emotional content he placed the modern short story on its first truly professional footing, although he was always insistent that he was inferior to his masters Poe and Maupassant. This may be so, but his discipline was infinitely superior to the first, and his range to the second. Conan Doyle was also a modest but highly perceptive literary critic, as he showed in scattered essays and notably in his volume on his favourite writers, *Through the Magic Door* (1907).

He toured the U.S.A. in 1894 with his brother Innes and proved a popular lecturer and reader of his own works. He invested the proceeds of the lecture-tour in *McClure's Magazine*, the brainchild of the syndicator of many of his stories, and it is clear that the association of *McClure's* with the creator of the most famous scientific professional detective ultimately led to its adoption of investigative techniques among its reporters, with consequent effects for the "muckraking" movement and the Progressive era in the United States for the first decade of the twentieth century. But his wife Louise ("Touie") developed what was then called galloping consumption, and her life was despaired of. Nevertheless by careful nursing and the movement of the family to a country house in the salubrious air of Hindhead, she was enabled to survive until 1906. There were two children of this marriage, Mary (born 1889) and Kingsley (born 1892).

Meanwhile his mother Mary Foley Doyle, had lived since 1882 or 1883 at Masongill Cottage, on the estate of Dr Bryan Charles Waller and remained there until 1917 or shortly previous to that date. Several daughters were very close to their brother, including the youngest, Mrs Cyril Angell, who wrote two stories of detective interest the publication of which Conan Doyle encouraged: Mrs Angell chose the pseudonym "H. Ripley Cromarsh". Apart from occasional arguments he also maintained close links with his sister Connie, who married Hornung. Hornung's first Raffles book, *The Amateur Cracksman*, published in 1899, was dedicated "to A.C.D.—this form of flattery", thereby acknowledging its imitation of the Holmes stories. Conan Doyle was touched by this, but concerned about the moral implications of the "Raffles" series: he thought it dangerous to make a criminal a hero. He was much amused by Hornung's comment on his own most famous creation: "Though he might be more humble, there's no p'lice like Holmes." Presumably it was rendered as a song.

During this period ACD was close to a number of writers in addition to Hornung. Robert Louis Stevenson he never met, but they corresponded, and Stevenson deeply admired his work, while having himself more influence on Conan Doyle's literary formative years than any other contemporary writer. Rudyard Kipling Doyle knew slightly, their first meeting being in America in 1894: Kipling said that Conan Doyle's remarkable "*Lot No. 249*" gave him a nightmare for the first time in years, as well it might. His fellow-Scot J. M. Barrie became one of his dearest friends, and they collaborated on an unsuccessful comic opera called "*Jane Annie*". George Bernard Shaw was a neighbour of his in South Norwood before he removed to Hindhead; the kindly Conan Doyle was repelled by the streak of cruelty in Shaw, but the two men were much closer in thought than is generally realised, especially in their analyses of social gradations achieved in the Sherlock Holmes stories, and imitated in Shaw's *Pygmalion*. H. G. Wells he knew since he attended the proprietor of the draper's shop in which Wells was employed when Conan Doyle was a doctor in Southsea: he disliked his materialism and described the *Outline of History* as "a body without a soul". Jerome K. Jerome he knew as editor of the *Idler* for whom he wrote many of his medical tales before they were collected as *Round the Red Lamp* (the best single fictional volume on medical life written since Trollope's *Doctor Thorne*, and much better informed). The forgotten Canadian popular scientist Grant Allen he knew well from Hindhead: Allen was a remarkable analyst of culture and society, and wrote several social novels. When he was dying Conan Doyle promised to finish his uncompleted serial about a woman detective *"Hilda Wade"*, the earlier instalments of which were then running in the *Strand*. This he gallantly did, following plot outlines given him by Allen. The final episode, which like the rest said nothing about the circumstances of composition, happened to be entitled *"The Story of the Dead Man who Spoke"*.

W. E. Henley he knew and his poetry he admired, disposing of his bullying by feeling he "seemed to belong to the roaring days of Marlowe of the mighty line and the pot-house fray". With Rider Haggard he had less in common than might be expected; they knew each other through the literary world, though they ultimately came to differ rather oddly about the Salvation Army which Rider Haggard championed against Conan Doyle's advice. Oscar Wilde he met when *Lippincott's* were commissioning their work, and was much delighted by his admiration of *Micah Clarke*, but he was later repelled by Wilde's apparent conviction of the magnificence of his own plays, which shows a limit to Conan Doyle's sense of humour. He thought Wilde's imprisonment unjust. With A. E. W. Mason he played cricket, but Mason seems to have been jealous of him: no doubt many people in his circle were, for his financial rewards were exceptional for a writer. Of the younger writers, his greatest single influence was probably on P. G . Wodehouse, who played cricket for his team, interviewed him for a magazine in 1903, and revered him to the end of his life. Both men shared many things in common, above all the desire to write for the widest possible public, coupled with a distaste for literary élitism and highbrow pretentiousness.

Conan Doyle's politics were peculiar. He seems to have been a Liberal—indeed a radical Liberal—in early life. He became a Liberal Unionist when Gladstone took up Home Rule in 1885-86, but for different reasons than most: believing in the mingling of the English-speaking peoples he disliked anything which would set a barrier between them. Although he fell away from Catholicism at Stonyhurst, and left Edinburgh University more or less an agnostic, he was very hostile to anti-Catholicism and prevailed on the authorities to remove a famous anti-Catholic passage from the Coronation Oath. He was naturally hostile to Irish physical force separatism, but wrote rather a moving story, *"Touch and Go"*, in the mid-1880s about some Scottish children being rescued from a watery grave in the Irish Sea by the

Fenian leader James Stephens fleeing from the British authorities, and his more famous story, *"The Green Flag"*, commemorates the stand of a number of disaffected Irish soldiers rallied around a green flag against a Muslim army. He wrote eloquently, both in poetry and prose, about the Irish brigades in Europe after their members had been driven into exile following the defeat in the Williamite wars. He vigorously endorsed the British action against the Boers, wrote a highly successful pamphlet in defence of it, and also an official history of the Boer War. He served as a doctor in the fighting and reluctantly accepted a knighthood in 1902.

He knew various politicians, liked Balfour, also liked Asquith probably less well, and thought Haldane was most cruelly and unjustly treated in World War I when lies about his alleged pro-Germanism drove him from office. He stood as a Liberal Unionist in Edinburgh in 1900 and on the Scottish borders in 1906, losing both times. But his support for Roger Casement's campaign against the cruelties of King Leopold's régime in the Congo drew him closer to Casement, whom he seems to have portrayed as Lord John Roxton in *The Lost World*, and Casement converted him to Irish Home Rule about 1912. The Unionist readiness to employ physical violence against the working of a Home Rule Act absolutely disgusted him. When World War I came his path and Casement's diverged, he insisting this was Ireland's opportunity to prove herself and win British gratitude, Casement choosing a solitary diplomatic line for Ireland which he tried to implement by treating with the Germans. But Conan Doyle subscribed most of the money for Casement's defence when he was captured and tried for treason; and he contemptuously repelled the emissaries of the British Government who came touting the pornographic homosexual diaries ascribed to Casement—and, as he (and he alone) said, these could have no bearing on a charge of treason which was graver than anything they might contain. In this refusal to drop Casement's defence when the diaries were produced he was unique among public figures of his time who had good standing with the Government. He himself absolutely supported the war effort, reported it and wrote an official account of the British campaign in France and Flanders. His suspicion of German war aims was quite late in the years before the war, and he showed little of the violent jingoism prevalent while the war was in its course. After the war in which he lost his son Kingsley and his brother Innes, he became a missionary for Spiritualism and ultimately was prepared to throw his support to any party which would campaign against the archaic witchcraft acts under which Spiritualists were prosecuted. His political detachment may be summed up by his statement to his daughter Mary that while not prepared to call himself a Socialist, he thought he might well be one. (By this he meant Socialism in the theoretical sense, not in the modern jargon which identifies it with the Labour Party.) In fact, politics meant much less to him than to most people; he thought of people, especially individual people, and issues, rather than parties.

In 1907 he married Jean Leckie, and they had three children, Denis, Adrian and Jean. After his second marriage he continued to produce stories about Sherlock Holmes, much more sporadically than had been the case with the *Adventures, Memoirs* and *Return*. But in 1911 he turned his attention to a new theme, and a new hero, Professor George Edward Challenger, who leads three comrades—one of them bitterly critical of him, Professor Summerlee—to a plateau where prehistoric monsters and apemen survive. The book was called *The Lost World*, and represents something of a break in style for him, beginning with a tawdry romance on the part of the journalist-narrator, and convulsed throughout by hilarious academic controversies. He followed this up with a less satisfactory novel, *The Poison Belt*, where the comrades witness the threatened extinction of life on Earth, and in the 1920s by a highly autobiographical novel, *The Land of Mist*, in which Challenger and his surviving friends become converted to Spiritualism. This last has received severe criticism, but there are passages of remarkable power, and the generous wrath of the author at the persecution of the Spiritualists lends great dignity to it. Two very late stories, "*The Disintegration Machine*" and "*When the World Screamed*" complete the Challenger cycle: the last looks very like a comic but nonetheless heartfelt statement on the irresponsibility of scientists in pursuit of an experiment. Another very late work, *The Maracot Deep*, is concerned with the discovery of human survival in an undersea Atlantis. It was also subsequent to his second marriage that he embarked on a series of brief sketches in historical fiction in which he showed some imaginative insights on great historical events: most are published in his anthology *The Last Galley*. They proved his favourite short stories perhaps because they represented the fruit of more detailed scholarly reflection than most of the work in that form he produced with such skill and speed.

Despite his belittlement of his great achievement in the Sherlock Holmes stories, he maintained them for the rest of his life. A final novel, *The Valley of Fear*, appeared in 1914. It involves a more theatrical, facetious Holmes than the earlier work, although the detective part itself is unusually complex in its analysis of human relationships. In fact, Conan Doyle's use of the Sherlock Holmes stories turned increasingly on psychological problems in their final appearances. The last collection, *The Case-Book of Sherlock Holmes*, has been attacked for a decline in standards from the first three volumes and the fourth, *His Last Bow*, but it enters more deeply into psycho-sexual crisis than any of his other work. His medical research into syphilis had meant that his knowledge of sex as a human factor had a far deeper scholarly basis than most writers of his generation could possess, and the greater freedom of expression in the 1920s was utilised by him to some effect. He had dealt with sexual obsession and its destructive effects in some of his early work such as the short stories "*The Winning Shot*" and "*John Barrington Cowles*" and the short novel *The Parasite*, but late Victorian conventions had necessarily obliged him to be rather more reticent. He also showed a capacity for understanding the self-absorption, sensation-hunting and cruelty of the younger generation of the 1920s in his late story "*The Parish Magazine*", whose ironies bring him surprisingly close to Evelyn Waugh. In sum, he is a far more modern writer than he has been taken to be.

He wrote a vigorous and engaging autobiography, *Memories and Adventures*, partly founded on articles written by him over the years: it came out in 1924, and reappeared with additional material in 1930. There is a slight autobiographical element in some of his fiction, especially *The Stark Munro Letters* (1895), which draws heavily on his early life in medical practice, *A Duet with an occasional Chorus* (1899), a romance on the first months of a marriage, and *Three of Them* (1923), sketches based on the early life of his second family. His verse, for which he made no great claims, also throws light on his personality and outlook. It appeared in three volumes and was largely but not entirely brought together in his *Poems*. Several of his volumes on Spiritualism contain an important autobiographical element, and he also published volumes on his Spiritualist lecture-tours in the 1920s in Africa and America. He wrote several polemical works on the subject, as well as a *History of Spiritualism*. Many friends cooled after he had vehemently taken up the Spiritualist cause, although it was far from inconsistent with his earlier thought. He had never been easy with the scientific dismissal of the spiritual fashionable in the Darwinian world of his youth, and his literary imagination came back to the theme again and again from his early, delicate, ghost story of the Arctic, "*The Captain of the 'Pole-Star'* " onward through his career. Sometimes he could play with the theme scientifically, as in "*The Brown Hand*", sometimes satirically as in "*Playing with Fire*", sometimes with an unexpected surprise at the reader's expense as in "*How it Happened*". Spiritualism certainly did not weaken this aspect of his literary genius: one of his best ghost stories, also concerned with a favourite enthusiasm, boxing, was published in 1921, "*The Bully of Brocas Court*". It is the only story known to the present writer in which a ghost can box, and extremely painfully too: indeed it is made clear from the lack of impact of the opponent's blows on the ghost that this is probably the desirable condition for any pugilist.

Conan Doyle's Sherlock Holmes stories reflect a sympathy for the accused in the hands of official authorities whose zeal to obtain a conviction often leads to premature adverse judgment. This was exhibited in his own life, when he campaigned against the unjust sentences on George Edalji and Oscar Slater, respectively accused of cattle mutilation and murder. Between them these cases spanned most of the first thirty years of the twentieth century: Slater was convicted in 1909 and only released in 1928. The criminologist William Roughead, whose first edition of Slater's trial became an important document for the defence, gave the honour for the crusade and ultimate acquittal where he felt it was due when he dedicated his work to Conan Doyle. Slater probably owed his release to Conan Doyle's vehement renewal of the case in the late 1920s.

His literary powers showed no sign of decline towards the end of his life. "*The Veiled Lodger*", the penultimate Sherlock Holmes story to be published, in its action contains only Holmes's reminiscence of the crime and points in criticism of the police theory, and the confession of one of the participants, but is in fact a work of admirable reasoning, excitement, horror and compassion. It also shows the progress from the coldly scientific and materialistic Holmes of *A Study in Scarlet*; at the conclusion of "*The Veiled*

Lodger" he persuades the tragically mutilated Eugenia Ronder not to take her own life because of the spiritual testimony her courage could give to others. It is doubtful if a work could be produced to show so much beauty on a theme of so much horror. Conan Doyle's polemics, too, were in good shape, as he demonstrated in a vigorously controversial work on the Roman Catholic church, some of whose votaries had attacked his Spiritualism: his standpoint had more strength than that of most ex-Catholics, especially since he had retained his admiration for certain parts of Roman Catholic doctrine such as the cult of the Virgin Mary. Strangely enough, his lifelong love of cricket only produced one story amid all his fine celebrations of sport: "*The Story of Spedegue's Dropper*", which came out two years before his death.

On 7 July 1930, at the home in Crowborough, Sussex, where he had been living since his second marriage, Arthur Conan Doyle died.

He has been the subject of several biographies, and while it is tempting to follow the example of Sherlock Holmes's sneers at Poe's Dupin and Gaboriau's Lecoq, none of them are quite good enough to put into a comparative category with such work. They also involve some curious controversies of their own, such that John Dickson Carr pretended Hesketh Pearson's life did not exist and Pierre Weil-Nordon described Pearson without explanation as "pseudo-biography". Actually, Pearson's biography (1943), while given to a schoolboy facetiousness and conceit, could probably only be answered in kind by kicking, but essentially a friendly kicking. He is worth arguing with, and his insights are frequently thought-provoking. His worst crime was laziness: the Conan Doyle MSS were made available to him, but manuscripts were never his forte, he being at his best among printed memoirs and oral testimony, and he left much of Conan Doyle's published work unread. Finding *The Stark Munro Letters* he took it to be absolute fact as opposed to fiction founded to an unclear extent on autobiography, and even reproduces its conversations as actual occurrences. This still leaves Pearson in a more respectable position than Dickson Carr, who has chosen to invent his own conversations in his *Life* (1949), without any statement that he is so doing. Pearson's conversations, being founded on Conan Doyle's fictionalisation, make at least better reading than Dickson Carr's, based on his own. The Carr book is in addition embarrassingly redolent of the reverence of the American tourist for the real, authentic English. Nordon or Weil-Nordon (he signs various works differently) is much more painstaking than either, and prints important quotations from many documents in the French edition (*Sir Arthur Conan Doyle L'Homme et L'Oeuvre* (1964)) but is plodding and easily misled. All of these books are important, in that they drew on the Conan Doyle papers which a legal action has now closed to scholars. *The Adventures of Conan Doyle* by Charles Higham (1976), was based on rather dubious research, and showed some understanding of certain of Conan Doyle's neglected works, but it is careless in the extreme (such as using *The Firm of Girdlestone* quite correctly to describe Edinburgh University in Conan Doyle's day and then going on to credit him with his hero's address), and is mildly dotty on the subject of sex. Ronald Pearsall's

Conan Doyle (1977) wants its readers to know its author is more worthy of admiration than its subject, and despite its enthusiasm for this enterprise, fails: it might have included information of value if the author could have forgotten the importance of his opinions long enough to deliver it. Oh, for the showiness and superficiality of Dupin, the energy of Lecoq!

There is a certain advantage in being cut off from the easy option. Dickson Carr's biography lists the collection now closed to scholars. It was very clear to me that if I wished to get anywhere, it would have to be with what I could find myself. Accordingly I began work on a biography of Conan Doyle with what I could find in two areas of his life known to me, Edinburgh and Catholicism. As it happened, what I found proved far bigger than I had imagined, and produced a book covering his first twenty-three years, to which I have added an epilogue taking his literary life some five years later to the production of his first two published novels, *A Study in Scarlet* and *Micah Clarke*. Perhaps it is not very surprising that the view from Edinburgh and from Stonyhurst proved to be very different from that in earlier works, and a fortunate discovery about his West African voyage brought a further difference still. As a result, I am presenting a new story, and a new character.

1

First Impressions

"You'll be with him as much as possible, won't you?" again asked the baronet, after lying quite silent for a quarter of an hour.

"With whom?" said the doctor, who was then all but asleep.

"With my poor boy; with Louis."

"If he will let me, I will," said the doctor.

"And, doctor, when you see a glass at his mouth, dash it down; thrust it down, though you thrust out the teeth with it. When you see that, Thorne, tell him of his father—tell him what his father might have been but for that; tell him how his father died like a beast, because he could not keep himself from drink."

—Anthony Trollope, *Doctor Thorne*

The cab-horse clip-clops its way down the Brixton Road just after midnight; the murderous cabman puffs at a Trichinopoly cigar, and seems to descry, smiling at him from the rain-spattered darkness, the forms of the old man and girl whose deaths twenty years before he is about to avenge; within the cab his victim lies, in a huddled, drink-sodden mass, scarcely aware of the movement and wholly ignorant of the imminence of his doom.

Sherlock Holmes involuntarily flicks on the raw the family pride and shame of Dr Watson, as he deduces from a watch that Watson's elder brother was a man of advantages who threw away his opportunities, had a brief burst of reform and finally died a drunkard.

Colonel Elias Openshaw hurls himself screaming from his own door on the last of the drunken sallies in which he defies his former comrades in the Ku Klux Klan, comrades who this time will leave him dead in a green-scummed pool at the end of his own garden.

Mr Henry Baker, grizzled student normally working in the British Museum Reading Room, sits with a buttoned coat masking the absence of jacket or shirt as he vocally tells Holmes of the loss of his Christmas goose, and shaking hand and red nose silently tell of the cause of his own decline.

Jim Browner, having broken his total abstinence pledge and tortured himself into a mania of jealousy against his wife, thus feeding the alienation of affection he feared, crushes in her skull and that of her lover and sends an ear of each to her sister.

Sherlock Holmes as a student, staying with Victor Trevor, is unpleasantly impressed when his friend's father rushes into the house to swig brandy on the appearance of a mysterious sailor and after a brief conversation with the man is found an hour later stretched dead drunk on the drawing-room sofa.

Black Peter Carey is reported as having flogged his wife and daughter through the park until the village rang with their screams, during his drunken bouts at midnight, and after he has been transfixed by a harpoon his daughter blesses the hand that struck him down.

Sir Eustace Brackenstall, half drunk, drenches his wife's dog with petroleum and sets it on fire.

Eugenia Ronder's face is clawed away by a lion in her efforts to disguise her murder of the husband who used to assault her with such savagery in the course of his incessant drinking.

These are explicit references to alcoholism and alcoholic dependence in the Sherlock Holmes stories, from *A Study in Scarlet* written in 1886, to "*The Veiled Lodger*" which appeared in February 1927. They represent the author's personal imprint rather than mere conveniences of construction; examples of the use of drink to turn a writer's corner would be the drunkenness of the manservant, Toller, in "*The Copper Beeches*", to keep him off the scene of action, or the necessity to have Hugo Baskerville flown with insolence and wine in order to pursue the maid with dogs and hence unleash the hound of the Baskervilles for his first appearance.

The stories also abound in implicit references to drink. Arthur Conan Doyle as a student of medicine gave attention to drugs and their effects, but it is not hard to transpose the drug-crazed Isa Whitney in "*The Man with the Twisted Lip*" to a husband sinking deeper and deeper into drink while his wife flees, weeping, to friends with the story that he has now been away for three days. Similarly the conduct of Professor Presbury, in "*The Creeping Man*", where the great academic is superseded by the gibbering, spiteful, idiotic monkey, is reminiscent of the effects of alcohol as well as evocative of the side-effects of age-reducing monkey-gland serum. The degradation of a distinguished professor is also pictured by Conan Doyle in non-Holmes stories: directly by drink following an exchange of personalities in "*The Great Keinplatz Experiment*", and by a form of remote thought control in *The Parasite*.

Yet Conan Doyle's use of alcoholism is very varied. He brings his readers into hells that reveal the horror of women at the mercy of ferocious, drunken sadists, for whose murderers the reader is led to seek forgiveness without punishment. But he also could make a very amusing little narrative, "*The King of the Foxes*", about a huntsman swearing off drink for life after imagining himself to have *delirium tremens* because the fox he was chasing turned out to be a runaway wolf.

Victorian writing about alcoholics was normally obsessional and ferociously moralistic. Conan Doyle, as a medical man, writes of drink with much more clinical detachment. But his concern with it is pre-eminent. He knew a great deal about it and its effects, and he employed it with all of the shrewdness of the good literary economist who knows how to deploy his richest material. His reasons for knowing about it were simple enough: his youth from his birth in 1859 until his family quitted Edinburgh forever in 1882-83 was dominated by his father's conquest by alcohol; indeed the shadow remained a menacing one after that father, Charles Altamont Doyle, had been institutionalised from 1883 to 1893, when he died.

The truth about Charles Doyle's alcoholism and institutionalisation remained hidden until 1978 when Mr Michael Baker edited a surviving diary of his. Mr Baker made something of Victorian respectability in Conan Doyle's concealment of what happened. It is a harsh construction, and an unnecessary one. Mary Foley Doyle had married her husband when she was seventeen, in 1855, and she was then faced with a deepening misery as she struggled to keep the house together, bring forth ten children, see the dwindling and ultimate disappearance of his income, and be dragged into Heaven alone still knows what labyrinth of endless sordid attempts to maintain some standards of decency. She finally could take no more, and after some twenty-seven years she institutionalised her husband and broke with her church in the process. She had provided as best she could for her children, and all of those surviving were by now embarked on their education, or on their careers. It would be too much to ask of her that the world be invited to pry into the grief and shame of past years where she had battled so bravely.

There was a much more obvious temptation hanging over Arthur Conan Doyle than Victorian respectability: the readiness to appear a hero or martyr in the eyes of enthusiastic readers. Charles Dickens and George Bernard Shaw gave themselves that compensation for their former miseries. But Arthur was not a whiner, not even in the bantering tone in which Shaw told Ellen Terry of his "devil of a childhood". Alcohol is a major theme in Conan Doyle's writing, and one which gives it power, strength and authority; but he never actually discusses the impact of a father's drinking on a small boy. The sole, momentary, cry of pain in his writing is a passing mention in the earliest, magazine-published, version of *Through the Magic Door*, that his money-box was broken into. The pity of his audience is marshalled entirely for the service of injured women: Mrs Charpentier and her daughter in *A Study in Scarlet;* the girl abducted and pursued by Hugo Baskerville; Violet Smith likewise pursued and abducted—if with less fatal results—by the drunken Woodley in "*The Solitary Cyclist*"; Peter Carey's daughter and his wife "whose gaunt and deep-lined face, with the furtive look of terror in the depths of her red-rimmed eyes, told of the years of hardship and ill-usage which she had endured"; Lady Brackenstall with "two vivid red spots" standing out on "one of the white, round limbs" following her husband's attentions in "*The Abbey Grange*".

Where boys or young men are present, they can cope fairly easily: young Openshaw recalls his uncle simply as being kind to him, if the enemy of all the world. The closest we come to vulnerability of a small boy is Holmes's fury with the Duke of Holderness for wantonly leaving his son in the custody of a murderous publican in "*The Priory School*", but the publican's homicidal tendencies are not in fact presented as side-effects of the medical hazards of his profession. In fact *Rodney Stone* mixes with the romance of the Regency a vignette in which a boy, although a powerful, tall and well-developed one, Boy Jim, comes to know a woman far gone in drink and slowly cures her: she later proves to be his mother. Boy Jim in physique and pugilistic prowess is a little closer to his creator than is the somewhat negative Rodney Stone. The honest realism in depicting the drunken Polly Hinton takes no short cuts: Conan Doyle neither wallows in the squalor shown by what the beautiful actress has become nor hurries the reader to her redemption. But, with a remarkable switch of the identity of the drunken parent of distinguished origin from father to mother, it is clearly a yearning by Arthur for what he wished he could have achieved.

He did not, then, resent his father's tragedy for his own sake: if anything he regretted that he himself, boy though he was, proved unable to cure his father. On the other hand, while his fiction includes cures, above all self-cures, of alcoholism, experience in his family and in his professional life told him how unusual such cures were: the broken engagements and repulsive collapse of Captain Whitehall in the partly autobiographical *Stark Munro Letters* give something closer to the reality he knew than does the escapism of *Stone*. Whitehall, with his friendliness and hospitality, his generosity in material and spiritual matters, his half-destructive attempts to be of assistance, his attempts at assertion of dignity which disintegrate in miserable wreckage, at once wins the doctor's affection and disgust, but can never accept his cure. He also represents an important link between Charles Doyle and his son's historical fiction: by making a sailor of him, indeed possibly by basing him in part on a sailor as well as on Charles Doyle, Arthur Conan Doyle created enough to be redeployed in his use of drunken soldiery in stories of the Napoleonic wars.

On the other hand, his horrific witness to the effects of alcoholism on family life did not prevent his use of irony at the expense of the theme in literature. "*A Case of Identity*", the third of the Holmes short stories to appear in the *Strand* and evidently the second to be written, opens with a dialogue between Holmes and Watson in which Holmes insists that Life is stranger than Art. (This was certainly inspired by ACD's acquaintance Oscar Wilde whose "*The Decay of Lying*" had recently asserted the contrary: it is a reminder that the Holmes-Watson dialogues, one of the strongest features of the stories, derive in part from Wilde's *Intentions*, which revived the Platonic dialogue with wit, paradox and modern sophistication.) Watson dissents, citing a newspaper story "A Husband's Cruelty To His Wife":

> ". . . There is half a column of print, but I know without reading it that it is all perfectly familiar to me. There is, of course, the other woman, the drink, the push, the blow, the bruise, the sympathetic sister or landlady. The crudest of writers could invent nothing more crude."
>
> "Indeed, your example is an unfortunate one for your argument," said Holmes, taking the paper, and glancing his eye down it. "This is the Dundas separation case, and, as it happens, I was engaged in clearing up some small points in connection with it. The husband was a teetotaller, there was no other woman, and the conduct complained of was that he had drifted into the habit of

winding up every meal by taking out his false teeth and hurling them at his wife, which you will allow is not an action likely to occur to the imagination of the average storyteller. Take a pinch of snuff, doctor, and acknowledge that I have scored over you in your example."

It is a fine example of the spirit of the 1890s, and Wilde would have welcomed a brother artist in the notion of proving the superiority of Life to Art by self-assertion of the incomparable quality of his own imagination. In paradox as in pride Holmes was a very 'nineties figure. As to the satire on conventional stories of alcoholism, Conan Doyle is being very amusing, although his background reminds us the humour is the bitter sweetness of Maupassant, whom ACD did not salute as his master for nothing.

Alcoholism at one stage looked like a line of inspiration whichever way Arthur Conan Doyle might take his literary career. While serving briefly as a medical assistant in Ruyton, Shropshire in 1878 he composed an essay—never published—on alcoholism and its prevalence in Britain: it was an unsuccessful competition entry. His very earliest surviving story intended for publication must date from about 1878 also, and it involves the ghost of a homicidal alcoholic who murdered his wife and family. (It was sent to *Blackwood's* who forgot to return it; most likely the author, being a resident of *Blackwood's* own city, delivered it by hand without the precautionary envelope.) The story is much more jejune in style than ACD's first published work, "*The Mystery of Sassassa Valley*", which appeared in October 1879, and its use of alcohol is simply to supply a natural basis for the horror of mass family murder it intended to serve as a suitable origin for ghostly perambulation. But it does have two singular features: one is having a heavily down-to-earth narrator swept off his feet by a friend of unbelievable but soundly-based observations, and the other a dénouement where a horrific mass-murderer's ghost flies in abject terror when about to be confronted by the ghost of the gentle wife he murdered.

That principle, the murderous spirit's fear of being haunted by his victim, was resurrected by Conan Doyle more than forty years later, for his story "*The Bully of Brocas Court*", where the ghost of Hickman the "Gasman", having severely mauled a living pugilist in a contest, flies screaming from the ghost of the little white dog he had maimed and killed almost as his last action before being himself killed in an accident. The Gasman is perhaps the most fearful of all Conan Doyle's murderous drunkards, more so than Black Peter or Eustace Brackenstall or Ronder: their physical brutality dies with them even if its indirect consequences remain, but the Gasman's ghost remains physically able to do grievous bodily harm to anyone foolish enough to give him a fight and is now invulnerable to any blows landed on him.

This long-germinating horror-story device of the writer's youth must seem a very long way from the gentle and artistic Charles Altamont Doyle. Yet it is not completely separate from him. There seems to have been a propensity for violence when he became drunk. Mr Baker's discoveries make it clear that after his first institutionalisation Charles Doyle succeeded in getting hold of drink illicitly and broke out of the home with some violence. The evidence of the writings has to be handled with great care, but there is a frequent, and sometimes contextually slightly irrelevant, stress on the drunkard in question having been mild enough when sober. In *"The Abbey Grange"*, for instance, Inspector Stanley Hopkins tells Holmes and Watson that the late Sir Eustace Brackenstall was "a good-hearted man when he was sober, but a perfect fiend when he was drunk, or rather when he was half drunk, for he seldom really went the whole way. The devil seemed to be in him at such times, and he was capable of anything": certainly this reputation in sobriety weighs little enough with Lady Brackenstall as she piles up the evidence against herself:

> ". . . To be with such a man for an hour is unpleasant. Can you imagine what it means for a sensitive and high-spirited woman to be tied to him for day and night? It is a sacrilege, a crime, a villainy to hold that such a marriage is binding. I say that these monstrous laws of yours will bring a curse upon the land—Heaven will not let such wickedness endure."

And Arthur Conan Doyle became a very vigorous campaigner for reform of the divorce laws.

"The Abbey Grange" also raises the question of the merits of a good appearance in sobriety. "He was all honey when first we met him," affirms the maid Theresa Wright of Sir Eustace. "He won her with his title and his money and his false London ways." Here the reference is to Lady Brackenstall having come from Australia; but certainly the London-born Charles Doyle must have had a powerful impact on the seventeen-year-old Irish-born girl in the Edinburgh New Town. On the other hand the wholly tragic figure of Jim Browner, in *"The Cardboard Box"*, is that of a genuinely gentle soul, although "stark, staring mad" when in drink, and driven back to drink by the tangle of intrigue and jealousy in which his marriage was trapped by the machinations of his frustrated and revengeful sister-in-law. *"The Japanned Box"* from the *"Round the Fire"* series describes the converse case: a reformed alcoholic, who maintains his reform by the use of a recording of his dead wife's voice encouraging him to keep up his resolution, and who is described in his drinking days as "The greatest rip and debauchee in England!":

> ". . . He had got so far that his own fast set had thrown him over. There is a world of difference, you know, between a man who drinks and a drunkard. They all drink, but they taboo a drunkard. He had become a slave to it— hopeless and helpless. Then she stepped in, saw the possibilities of a fine man in the wreck, took her chance in marrying him, though she might have the pick of a dozen, and, by devoting her life to it, brought him back to manhood and decency. You have observed that no liquor is ever kept in the house. There never has been any since her foot crossed its threshold. A drop of it would be like blood to a tiger even now."

It was a converse case in more ways than one. Mary Foley had hardly the pick of a dozen or half a dozen, and probably knew little or nothing of her husband's weakness—at that point, in 1855, there may have been little to see beyond the effects of socialisation. Clearly attempts were made to break Charles Doyle of alcohol before he was institutionalised, and clearly they failed. "*A Sordid Affair*", a story published in 1891, tells a pathetic narrative of a woman's attempts to break her husband of his drinking, and his reversion to it by deceit and theft. In any case the periods of reform may have been trying enough: Sir John Bollamore in "*The Japanned Box*" becomes almost maniacal when dismissing an unfortunate charwoman for alleged spying on him (" 'I've lost my place, and glad I am for it, for I would never trust myself within reach of 'im again' ").

The most detailed portrait of an alcoholic in all of Conan Doyle's writing is that of old McIntyre in *The Doings of Raffles Haw*, written over fifteen days in Vienna in January 1891, and it brings in a further quality—the avarice and scheming of the drunkard in pursuit of his dram. The philosophy behind the novel deserves note: it is a protest against the money-hunger of his age, arguing that even with aesthetic priorities and philanthropic intentions, Midas is self-destroyed by his Golden Touch. It uses chemistry ably: in the most literal sense Conan Doyle was a pioneer of science fiction. But in terms of character it suffers through a conflict between the fairy-tale assumptions on the part of the philanthropist billionaire Raffles Haw himself, and the unheroic realities, and the author never seems quite clear whether his judgments should be in accord with reality or illusion. The one exception lies in the father of Raffles Haw's false friends, an old and ruined drunkard, who never deceives Haw and who hence is directly perceived by the reader throughout. Here is old McIntyre as we first meet him, his "life now one long wail over his misfortunes, and who alternately sought comfort in the Prayer-book and in the decanter for the ills which had befallen him":

> "I think, Robert, . . . that I will have a drop, just the very smallest possible drop, of brandy. A mere thimbleful will do; but I rather think I have caught cold during the snowstorm to-day."
>
> Robert went on sketching solidly in his folding book, but Laura looked up from her work.
>
> "I'm afraid there is nothing in the house, father", she said.
>
> "Laura! Laura!" He shook his head as one more in sorrow than in anger. "You are no longer a girl, Laura; you are a woman, the manager of a household, Laura. We trust in you. We look entirely towards you. And yet you leave your poor brother Robert without any brandy, to say nothing of me, your father. Good heavens, Laura! what would your mother have said? Think of accidents, think of sudden illnesses, think of apoplectic fits, Laura. It is a very grave res— a very grave respons— a very grave risk that you run."
>
> "I hardly touch the stuff", said Robert curtly; "Laura need not provide any for me."
>
> "As a medicine it is invaluable, Robert. To be used, you understand, and not to be abused. That's the whole secret of it. But I'll step down to the Three Pigeons for half an hour."
>
> "My dear father", cried the young man, "you surely are not going out upon such a night. If you must have brandy could I not send Sarah for some? Please let me send Sarah; or I would go myself, or—"
>
> Pip! came a little paper pellet from his sister's chair on to the sketch-book in front of him! He unrolled it and held it to the light.
>
> "For Heaven's sake let him go!" was scrawled across it.

> "Well, in any case, wrap yourself up warm", he continued, laying bare his sudden change of front with masculine clumsiness which horrified his sister. "Perhaps it is not so cold as it looks. And it is not more than a hundred yards."

Old McIntyre goes out:

> "He gets worse—he becomes intolerable", said Robert at last. "We should not have let him out; he may make a public exhibiton of himself."
> "But it's Hector's last night", pleaded Laura. "It would be dreadful if they met and he noticed anything. That was why I wished him to go."

The narrative is anything but sympathetic to the children, and the meannesses of their motives are clinically set forward. We are nevertheless given reason to suspect the insidious effect of their father's alcoholism in the debasement of their own characters, while we are also invited to see the family resemblance. The speciousness of the arguments of father and son have such similarities, set almost with the precision by which we are invited to see the resemblance between the handwriting of old Cunningham and his son in "*The Reigate Squires*". In fact the realistic analysis of these side-effects of alcoholism ultimately weakens *Raffles Haw* in that it means that Haw will entrust his confidence to vehicles warped by reasons external to his production of wealth.

The touch of avarice in the father, again to be all too faithfully reflected in his children, comes into its own a little later in the story, before the McIntyres have met Raffles Haw but after Laura's departing fiancé has asked her to take in trust for its owner a fifty-pound note mysteriously handed to him:

> "Tut! tut!" said old McIntyre. "How is this, Laura? I know nothing of this. What do women know of money or of business? Hand the note over to me and I shall relieve you of all responsibility. I will take everything upon myself."
> "I cannot possibly, papa", said Laura, with decision. "I should not think of parting with it."
> "What is the world coming to?" cried the old man, with his thin hands held up in protest. "You grow more undutiful every day, Laura. This money would be of use to me—of use, you understand. It may be the corner-stone of the vast business which I shall reconstruct. I will use it, Laura, and I will pay something—four, shall we say, or even four and a-half—and you may have it back on any day. And I will give security—the security of my—well, of my word of honour."

The counterpoint between the passages is instructive. When the drunkard is in pursuit of his drink, the status of the woman forced to look after him is varied absolutely as it suits his immediately acquisitive needs. At one moment she has the widest responsibilities, at another she cannot be permitted responsibility. Conan Doyle was to ridicule male attempts to block the advance of women in the professions fairly savagely. He may have arrived at his position from knowledge of the squalid basis such arguments could have.

Avarice and alcohol ultimately send old McIntyre mad, and he is certified insane after an attempt to murder Raffles Haw. The immediate antecedent of that attempt shows conspiracy mania well advanced:

> "Well, Robert", he began, "I suppose that, as usual, you have spent the morning plotting against your father?"
>
> "What do you mean, father?"
>
> "I mean what I say. What is it but plotting when three folk—you and she and this Raffles Haw—whisper and arrange and have meetings without a word to me about it? What do I know of your plans?"
>
> "I cannot tell you secrets which are not my own, father."
>
> "But I'll have a voice in the matter, for all that. Secrets or no secrets, you will find that Laura has a father, and that he is not a man to be set aside. I may have my ups and downs in trade, but I have not fallen so low that I am nothing in my own family. What am I to get out of this precious marriage?"

There is no reason to believe that Charles Altamont Doyle was avaricious, save when the craving for alcohol attacked him. But the idea of avarice opened up Conan Doyle's imagination. In *"Our Midnight Visitor"*, set in one of the less discovered Hebrides and written about the same date, a father also driven by avarice, though not in this instance by drink, likewise attempts murder. The theme even invades the historical novel *The Great Shadow*, of 1892, this time with complete irrelevance to the plot of the work:

> When I came down in the morning I found that he had been beforehand with me, for he was seated opposite my father at the window-table in the kitchen, their heads almost touching, and a little roll of gold pieces between them. As I came in my father looked up at me, and I saw a light of greed in his eyes such as I had never seen before. He caught up the money with an eager clutch, and swept it into his pocket.

This time the greed has no murderous sequel, but in an English context Conan Doyle had presented an avaricious and murderous father as early as 1885 in *"The Lonely Hampshire Cottage"*: the intended victim proves to be the would-be murderer's son. The antecedents of the story may be Scottish, Scots-Irish or American folklore: Robert Penn Warren's *"Ballad of Billie Potts"* records a similar folk-tradition of Kentucky, with the differences that there the boy is killed and the mother is a party to the crime. The theme had become sufficiently widespread by 1910 for Stephen Leacock to satirize it unmercifully in his *"Caroline's Christmas"*, one of the famous *Nonsense Novels*.

But sons as well as fathers are led into murder and violence against their own kin, in Conan Doyle's writing. In his *Round the Fire* series of the late 1890s the sottish, bestial James McCarthy tortures his father and is only prevented by a hairsbreadth from murdering his defender in his voracity for money (the story being *"The Latin Tutor"*, reissued as *"The Usher of Lea House School"*). Nor is there any particular identification of avarice with Scotsmen, however much the Doyles might see themselves as aliens in Caledon: in *"The Striped Chest"*, late in the 1890s, it is not the Scottish mate, Allardyce, who proves avaricious, but his colleague, Armstrong, whose lust for the presumed golden hoard of the mysterious chest destroys him in the process.

Sometimes the author seems to have been later repelled by his own success: there is an extraordinary portrait in *"The Story of the Club-Footed Grocer"* of Nemesis overtaking a grotesque embodiment of avarice, and in its effects, with mystery, solitude, siege, capture, confrontation and the bitter last testament of fidelity to the man destroyed by his own grasping treachery, it is worthy of its author. Yet ACD declined to include it in the volume *Round the Fire Stories* published in 1908, although it had appeared in the series of that name in the *Strand* ten years earlier. It was the only story so to be dropped, and its quality in the eyes of Greenhough Smith, the *Strand's* editor, had been signalled by its being given the honour of "lead" story with frontispiece. Arguably, Conan Doyle's life-long detestation of avarice induced both the production of the story and the distaste for reprinting it.

While Conan Doyle often presents the effects of alcohol with horror, there is a coolness of observation in his remarks on the subject which bespeak the medical student. It was a disease, and needed to be treated as such. Avarice, on the other hand, whether related to alcoholism or not, he held in utter contempt. His personal generosity was proverbial. Inevitably avarice supplies motive for many crimes, but Conan Doyle managed to throw its viciousness into a relief quite independent from the detective or other main theme of the plot. Major Sholto acknowledges it in *The Sign of Four*:

> " '. . . The cursed greed which has been my besetting sin through life has withheld from her the treasure, half at least of which should have been hers. And yet I have made no use of it myself—so blind and foolish a thing is avarice. The mere feeling of possession has been so dear to me that I could not bear to share it with another . . .' "

It deepens the odium of Charles Augustus Milverton's crime:

> ". . . I have said that he is the worst man in London, and I would ask you how could one compare the ruffian who in hot blood bludgeons his mate with this man, who methodically and at his leisure tortures the soul and wrings the nerves in order to add to his already swollen money-bags?"

It can be made a matter of comedy, as it is in *"The Missing Three-Quarter"* when Lord Mount-James's repulsive economics prompt Holmes to revenges reminiscent of Ben Jonson or Molière, but we are not allowed to forget that avarice is what has forced Godfrey Staunton to meet his tragedy in shameful hiding. Conan Doyle eagerly followed up the implications of Stevenson's *"The Rajah's Diamond"* with its unsparing depiction of human shame under the temptation of avarice,—compare Holmes's remarks on *"The Blue Carbuncle"*—and he reached perhaps, the supreme moment of horror in exhibiting in Mortimer Tregennis in *"The Devil's Foot"* the avaricious man who sends his brothers mad and kills his sister with the most unimaginable mental tortures, for the sake of some wrangle about property. Here something of a reversal of roles takes place again. Conan Doyle's father was institutionalised because of mental illness, one of whose effects may have been avarice, but Mortimer Tregennis ensured that his brothers would be institutionalised through the avarice himself. The theme persists to the end: one of the most nauseating and evil of all his misers appears in *"The Retired Colourman"*, the last story printed in the collected Holmes volumes and the third last to be written.

"The Retired Colourman" hints at alliance between avarice and

insanity, as *Raffles Haw* had done. "*A Sordid Affair*" only involves avarice and alcohol, much on the *Raffles Haw* lines but much more cruelly, as the woman denounced by her drunken husband is a courageous and altruistic figure, trying to keep her family and respectability by dressmaking:

> "We have fifteen pounds here", said she turning out a small heap of gold. "We'll make it twenty soon, and then I think I may afford to take on another assistant."
>
> Her husband looked wistfully at the gold. "It seems hard that you should put away all that money, and I should go about without a half-crown in my pocket", said he.
>
> "I don't want your pocket to be empty, John, but you don't need more than sixpence. It is only putting yourself in the way of temptation."
>
> "Well, anyway, I ought to be head in my own family. Why don't you give me the key, and let me have the keeping of the money."
>
> "No, no, John; it is my earning and I'll have the keeping. What you want I'll buy for you, but what I save I must have in my own hands."
>
> "A pretty thing, too!" He went back to his painting with a snarl . . .

Eventually the woman's efforts are faced by John's pawning for drink the dress commissioned by her client, and her inability to recover it without the ticket, so that she is forced to purchase the model she was seeking to undercut in price for her customer, and ultimately finds on the road home

> a horrid crawling figure, a hatless head, and a dull, vacant, leering face. In an instant she had called a cab.
>
> "It's my husband", said she, "he is ill. Help me to get him into the cab, policeman. We live quite close to here."
>
> They thrust him into a four-wheeler, and she got in beside him, holding him up in her arms. His coat was covered with dust, and he mumbled and chuckled like an ape. . . .

But the ape-like or monkey-like analogy frequently appears in the context of insanity, most notably in the obvious instance of Professor Presbury's metamorphosis after his consumption of his monkey-gland ration. There is a brief glimpse of either Owen or George Tregennis on the way to the asylum in "*The Devil's Foot*" where a simian analogy immediately suggests itself, and old McIntyre is found crooning and muttering over a gold ingot at the point when his insanity declares itself. More general analogies with beasts slip in at other contexts. In "*The Beetle-Hunter*", which carries the interesting touch of a madman being certified by two doctors, one of whom is a near relative, the climax involves a curious mixing of metaphors between tiger and deerhound. The madman, Sir Thomas Rossiter, makes a "tiger spring" at the bed to make an attack with a hammer on his brother-in-law, Lord Linchmere, whom he thinks to be in it, and then little Linchmere flings himself on him from behind "holding bravely on to him like a game bull-terrier with its teeth into a gaunt deerhound": the narrator, Dr Hamilton, then comes to Linchmere's rescue. Selden, the murderous convict in the *Hound*, whose sanity is very doubtful, is likened by Watson to a "crafty and savage animal", although not such an animal that the doctor will shoot him when he is running away. Brackenstall, although his sanity is not directly questioned, is called both madman and beast by his killer. The retired colourman, Amberley, is revealed as a hideous bird of prey at his moment of discovery as the murderer of his wife and her presumed lover.

Now, none of the foregoing can do more than tell us that these themes of alcoholism, avarice and insanity had made a severe imprint on Conan Doyle's youthful mind, forcing themselves inexorably into his artistic expression. We cannot make any firm assertion as to fact arising from these fictions; some details are decidedly suggestive, certainly, and we do know that Conan Doyle might weave a moment of autobiography directly into his narrative. But the main point is that this was his unavoidable inheritance.

Why should it be that Conan Doyle struggled so hard and so successfully to hide the tragedy of his father, while clearly reflecting it in so much of his best-selling fiction? The obvious answer is that he could not escape these themes, and if he used and used again material arising out of the cruelty of his youth, he disguised his hand very effectively. Certainly his refusal to allow certain stories to go beyond magazine publication was not always connected, or not only connected, with immaturity of quality. The treatment of homicidal mania in "*The Silver Hatchet*" or "*A Pastoral Horror*" he may simply have ruled out afterwards as excessively melodramatic, the former especially; "*The Surgeon of Gaster Fell*" is so vivid as to suggest his father may have initially gone to Masongill with his mother at her departure from Edinburgh, and had to be removed when he became impossible to guard. It was republished—but not for a quarter-century after its appearance in *Chambers's Journal* in 1890, when its revisal involved severe cutting, some but not all being fat-trimming, and its obloquy was permanent. My impression is that he would feel the urge to produce a story, would block and hammer it out with professional care, and would send it to appropriate periodicals without much thought as to what it might reveal. He saw book publication as a much more formal matter, and here he certainly worried as to its effects on his mother.

The Doings of Raffles Haw is rather an exception to any care Conan Doyle took about book publication, but it was in fact commissioned by Harmsworth for serialisation in *Answers*, and was simply permitted to slip out and earn its small recompense. After all its year of birth, 1891, was that in which the first Holmes short stories won *Strand* publication, and the urgency of maintaining the flow, to say nothing of watching over a comsumptive wife, would leave little reason to worry about self-censorship. Where self-censorship really was expressed was in the formally autobiographical writings such as *The Stark Munro Letters* (published in 1895, though possibly written as much as a decade earlier), *Memories and Adventures* (much of which appeared in article form in the author's later life, but the whole was finally assembled and streamlined in 1924), *A Duet* and *Three of Them; Stark Munro* and the *Duet* are fictionalised, and the others not, but the same principles apply.

We may now examine the meagre facts which help us to see the shell of the experience of which we have witnessed such striking evidence as to the core. Again, it must be stressed that Charles Altamont Doyle is not being assessed for himself in deploying that evidence: all it does is to convey something of the effects of his condition on the artistic consciousness of his son. As is usually the case, his alcoholism was probably less unpleasant for acquaintances than for his family, although it was likely ultimately to result in his being avoided and ostracised. His obituary in the *Scotsman* conveys an impression of a convivial soul, known for dropping in on the houses of literary friends in pursuit of pastime and good company, and it added, slightly ominously, that there were few houses of Edinburgh's *literati* whom he had not visited from time to time. On the other hand, this seems to have been recalled wryly rather than bitterly, especially after the Doyles had left Edinburgh. The speed with which the *Scotsman* and the *Glasgow Herald* leaped to hail the appearance of *A Study in Scarlet*, shrouded as it was in the obscurity of *Beeton's Christmas Annual*, suggests a reservoir of goodwill, and perhaps sympathy, for the family of the once-roistering artist. We can take it further and say that genuine affection for Charles Doyle might well have been one of the causes of such solicitude for Arthur. Of course a critic worthy of his salt should have recognised the genius evident in the first appearance of Sherlock Holmes; but how may critics, of whatever salt, were going to concern themselves with the contents of *Beeton's* without some extra-literary motivation? ACD's confidence in sending his early work to the great *Blackwood's*, and actually winning publication in *Chambers's*, do not suggest that he had reason to be unsure of his welcome in literary Edinburgh. Charles Doyle would have resembled many literary Scotsmen in fondness for the bottle, and while Edinburgh literary society had become slightly more sober since the days of Boswell and Burns in the previous century, few sneered at victims of "the national failing". Ironically one of the few who had was Charles Doyle himself, who in his letters home shortly after his arrival in Edinburgh in the late 1840s, expressed contempt for the Scottish aggrandisement of alcohol.

In preparing his *Memories and Adventures* for publication in 1924 Arthur Conan Doyle examined some of his father's letters to London in the 1850s, and found them full

> of interesting observations on that Scottish society, rough, hard-drinking and kindly, into which he had been precipitated at a dangerously early age, especially for one with his artistic temperament . . . his salary as a Civil Servant was not more than about £240. This he supplemented by his drawings. Thus matters remained for practically all his life, for he was quite unambitious and no great promotion ever came his way. His painting was done spasmodically, all the family did not always reap the benefit, for Edinburgh is full of water-colours which he had given away. It was one of my unfulfilled schemes to collect as many as possible and to have a Charles Doyle exhibition in London, and this has now been done. The critics were surprised to find what a great and original artist he was—far the greatest, in my opinion, of the family. Bernard Shaw, I remember, expressed the opinion that the pictures should have a room to themselves in a national collection. His brush was concerned not only with fairies and delicate themes of the kind, but with wild and fearsome subjects, so that his work had a very peculiar style of its own, mitigated by great natural humour. He was more terrible than Blake and less morbid than Wiertz. His originality is best shown by the fact that one hardly knows with whom to compare him. In prosaic Scotland, however, he excited wonder rather than admiration, and he was only known in the larger world of London by pen and ink book-illustrations which were not his best mode of expression. The prosaic

outcome was that including all his earnings my mother could never have averaged more than £300 a year on which to educate a large family.

In fact, the problem was that Charles Doyle as an artist needed scope to express his originality, and Charles Doyle as a wage-earner needed artistic commissions in addition to his bureaucratic work, and his genius was very badly adapted to commercial artistry. One of his son's biographers describes Charles Doyle as the "changeling" in the brilliant artistic family of John Doyle: the word is only justifiable if we are to suggest that Charles Doyle carried with him an air of not being entirely of this world. His mind soared and dipped among giant animals, strange sprites, confrontations of the grotesque and mundane. Compared to his work, his brothers and father seem mundane, remarkable though their work was. Arthur rightly singled his father out among his siblings, James, the master of ornate, elegant and profuse artistry in book design and illustration, Henry, Director of the National Gallery of Ireland, Dicky, the first great artist of *Punch* which he ultimately left in reproach for its anti-Catholicism. Their artistic sensibilities were profound, but their artistic achievements were lucrative.

Their father, John Doyle, had done more: art had won him both fortune and status. As "HB", John Doyle's political cartoons in the era of the First Reform Bill of 1832 revolutionised the whole style of political iconography. His predecessors were largely dependent on coarseness in design: the protagonists were accoutered with lengthy, illegible utterances, the analogies were gross with more than a hint of obscenity, the moral standpoint of the artist one leaning towards an assumption of Man's essential venality. At its peak the style reached the heights attained by Hogarth, but the mass of his imitators followed his concentration on squalor without appreciating his balance of tone in presenting it. Above all, caricature in the late eighteenth and early nineteenth centuries was embattled; the artist was as fully a footsoldier in the political wars as the poetaster or the pamphleteer. John Doyle asserted the place of political caricature as recording angel. He could hit hard, far harder than his cluttered and laboured predecessors, but no side could claim him as its mercenary or certain ally. A whole political world for the first time saw itself portrayed with something close to how it actually was. John Doyle's position as an educated Irish Catholic, first of his family to settle in London, gave him a curious objectivity in bringing London's politics to life. In some ways his origins declared themselves: he might ridicule Daniel O'Connell for his pretensions, or smile at him for his mingling of public principle and private bargain, or satirise the style of classical oratory which the Irish tribune thundered in the house of Rimmon, but he never saw him as less than a very great man. English satirists and artists of the same day differed markedly in their treatment of O'Connell from that they dealt out to English political opponents: their English adversaries were merely wrong, O'Connell was subhuman. Equally, Doyle was fascinated by the emergence of the English public during the Reform Bill crisis, and instead of portraying John Bull as one of élitist power, made him the spokesman for the English masses.

Arthur Conan Doyle, Irish by ancestry, Scots by birth, came to love the English among whom the last fifty years of his life were passed, and in his praise of the English soldier in *The White Company* or *Sir Nigel,* he reflected his grandfather's perspective. He employs it in many Holmes stories, nowhere more so than in the famous epilogue, *"His Last Bow",* when the German spy, Von Bork points out to his employer

> a dear old ruddy-faced woman in a country cap. She was bending over her knitting and stopping occasionally to stroke a large black cat upon a stool beside her.
> "That is Martha, the only servant I have left."
> The secretary chuckled.
> "She might almost personify Britannia", said he, "with her complete self-absorption and general air of comfortable somnolence. . . ."

But when Sherlock Holmes has overpowered Von Bork:

> "We need not hurry ourselves, Watson. We are safe from interruption. Would you mind touching the bell? There is no one in the house except old Martha, who has played her part to admiration. I got her the situation here when first I took the matter up. Ah, Martha, you will be glad to hear that all is well."

Significantly, Holmes's last exchange with Von Bork on the subject of English public opinion is pointedly iconographic:

> "Well, you realize your position, you and your accomplice here. If I were to shout for help as we pass through the village—"
> "My dear sir, if you did anything so foolish you would probably enlarge the too limited titles of our village inns by giving us 'The Dangling Prussian' as a signpost. The Englishman is a patient creature, but at present his temper is a little inflamed, and it would be as well not to try him too far. No, Mr Von Bork, you will go with us in a quiet, sensible fashion to Scotland Yard . . ."

Indeed it is noteworthy that the Sherlock Holmes stories in the *Strand* are agreed to have owed some part of their celebrity to the Sidney Paget illustrations of *Adventures, Memoirs, Return* and *Hound.* But the influence of John Doyle on his grandson invites us to look more closely at this proceeding: ACD met Sidney Paget some distance along the way in the fine visual sense his writing showed. In particular, the character groupings of several Holmes scenes are works of art in themselves, and inspirations to artist and reader, from Dr Grimesby Roylott's curving of the poker as a Parthian shot in his exit from Baker Street, to Dr Thorneycroft Huxtable's collapse on the floor following the arrival of the card laden with the weight of his degrees. Charles Doyle, on the other hand, lacked skill or interest in his father's field. When confined to a mental home, he was given the commission to illustrate the first book publication of *A Study in Scarlet,* but apart from his interesting endowment of Holmes with his own features and (despite the text) beard, the work is memorable only for its feebleness. Yet at the same time, as we know from his surviving diary, his fantasy was reaching some of its finest heights. Charles Doyle was an independent artistic mind. John Doyle, on the other hand, showed that he could speak for the reading public, much as his grandson was to do. Grandfather and grandson credited their public with considerable intelligence and breadth of reference. The readers of Sherlock

Holmes were presumed ready to appreciate citations from Goethe or Hafiz. The observers of HB were expected to grasp classical, biblical and general literary references without difficulty.

John Doyle was described by his grandson as "a gentleman, drawing gentlemen for gentlemen, and the satire lay in the wit of the picture and not in the misdrawing of faces. . . . He exerted, I am told, quite an influence upon politics, and was on terms of intimacy with many of the leading men of the day. I can remember him in his old age, a very handsome and dignified man with features of the strong Anglo-Irish, Duke of Wellington, stamp. He died in 1868." The point was of importance: by the use of his talent, the elder Doyle had won his own place among the politicians, instead of doing so on the backs of others. The sense of art as the means for status and independence, despite all disadvantages of place, race and faith, was a significant lesson. The effects of that status impinged on the young Arthur:

> When my grandfather's grand London friends passed through Edinburgh they used, to our occasional embarrassment, to call at the little flat "to see how Charles is getting on". In my earliest childhood such a one came, tall, white-haired and affable. I was so young that it seems like a faint dream, and yet it pleases me to think that I have sat on Thackeray's knee.

Behind that gentle and uncomplaining word "embarrassment" we can discern the sudden, fresh economic pressures to provide satisfactory hospitality (both Doyles and Foleys would have religiously followed the Irish principle that it was better to starve for a week than to deny a guest); the fears that Charles might drink too much before—or with—the visitor; the anxiety to keep the growing family under control in other rooms while the intruder saw only calm and benignity under his eye. There would be the anxiety not to demean the status which as Irish in Britain the Doyles had so painfully won; William Makepeace Thackeray, for one, had given all too much proof, via the Mulligan of Ballymulligan and others of his more repulsive creations, what depths he found as natural habitats for certain of the Irish in Britain.

John Doyle's own impact on his grandson may well have been formidable enough when the old gentleman made his way up to Edinburgh some months before his death. The patriarch made his authority felt over all of his descendants, at whatever age. The contrast, even to an eight-year-old boy, must have been sharp enough. On the one hand there was the Wellingtonian figure—and the analogy was well taken, for Wellington had carved his way from an Irish background almost as obscure as that of John Doyle. On the other, there was Charles Doyle, son and father:

> My father's life was full of the tragedy of unfulfilled powers and of undeveloped gifts. He had his weaknesses, as all of us have ours, but he had also some very remarkable and outstanding virtues. A tall man, long-bearded and elegant, he had a charm of manner and a courtesy of bearing which I have seldom seen equalled. His wit was quick and playful. He possessed, also, a remarkable delicacy of mind which would give him moral courage enough to rise and leave any company which talked in a manner which was coarse. When he passed away a few years later I am sure that Charles Doyle had no enemy in the world, and that those who knew him best sympathized most with the hard fate which

had thrown him, a man of sensitive genius, into an environment which neither his age nor his nature was fitted to face. He was unworldly and unpractical and his family suffered for it, but even his faults were in some ways the result of his developed spirituality. He lived and died a fervent son of the Roman Catholic faith.

But did that artistry of the fantastic influence his son, as the artist of the realistic affected his grandson? If John Doyle would have saluted, say, the splendid impression of Gladstone (as Lord Bellinger) in "*The Second Stain*", what would Charles Doyle recognise in Arthur's work? One direct influence is in the horror-fiction. The brilliant account of the air-jungle and its denizens in "*The Horror of the Heights*", or the terrifying revelation of the enormous underground cave-bear with its huge, sightless eyes in "*The Terror of Blue John Gap*", reflect Charles Doyle's concerns. *The Lost World* is more scientifically based, but its juxtaposition of the conventions of Edwardian academic bickering with prehistoric monsters is reminiscent of the father's work. Anyone might think of a pterodactyl, but it was the enjoyment of father and son in the incongruity of mingling convention and fantasy which has one resolving the argument of two professors by swooping away with their dinner, or has another causing a duke to fall into the orchestra-well of the Queen's Hall.

Charles Doyle also, apparently, recognised himself in Sherlock Holmes. Now, it is the thesis of this book that Holmes's origins are numerous, and it is the fate of successful authors to find many persons looking at mirrors in which they discover those authors' most famous creations. But Charles Doyle was only making the claim privately, as it were. Of those who saw the illustrations to *A Study in Scarlet*, second edition, only a few would connect Holmes with the artist's appearance, more especially as that artist was now firmly if unwillingly secluded from the world. It is evident that Charles felt strongly constrained to make the identification, at the cost of relevance to the clean-shaven Holmes of the text. He hardly suggests Holmes's dogmatism, or science, or dialogue, or reasoning. The cocaine may have owed something to Charles Doyle, particularly with reference to its consumption during periods of enforced idleness: "*A Sordid Affair*" involves the drunken artist dropping back into his discarded alcoholic habits because of his failure to get a commission. But this had nothing to do with whatever Charles recognized in *A Study in Scarlet:* Holmes is not presented as a drug-taker until *The Sign of Four,* and Watson specifically rules out such a possibility in the earlier book. In any case Charles Doyle would not necessarily have seen in a depiction of drug-taking an idea possibly partly prompted by his own alcoholism, and he would hardly have wished to underline such an association. But Charles may well have been attracted by the role in which Holmes is pictured as the story concludes—a genius unknown, whose credit is taken by others, whose wisdom is left to flourish anonymously, whose art is recognised for its greatness only by his intimates. And it would be good to believe that Arthur Conan Doyle comforted Charles Altamont Doyle, who so bitterly resented his sequestration, with the lines Watson spoke to Holmes "you must make yourself contented by the consciousness of success, like the Roman miser—

" 'Populus me sibilat, at mihi plaudo Ipse domi simul ac nummos contemplar in arca.' "

There was nothing insincere in that, for whether or not Arthur had been one of the main influences in his father's institutionalisation, he also remained to the end one of the most enthusiastic votaries of his genius. And he did acknowledge a place for his father in the origins of Sherlock Holmes by having Holmes take the name "Altamont" as an alias in "*His Last Bow*". It was only an assertion of one facet, but an important one, and it contributed importantly to the overall picture, in that this essentially private Holmes supplies his greatest personal charm. The Holmes of Baker Street, as opposed to the Holmes of the chase, or of the public, is fundamental to understanding his appeal. And it is in that Holmes that we may find preserved something of the wit and charm of Charles Altamont Doyle.

2

The Hero as Woman

This is the story of what a Woman's patience can endure, and a Man's resolution can achieve.

—Wilkie Collins, *The Woman in White*

The childhood of Charles Doyle and that of his son Arthur differed profoundly, and their contrast must have increased Charles's sense of inadequacy. John Doyle may well have had moments of doubt, and even despair, in the early days of his family but by the arrival of his youngest son he was firmly established as a force in London culture and society. Charles Doyle grew up in comfortable, increasingly opulent circumstances, protected not only by an authoritative father, but by female servants and a quiverful of elder brothers and sisters. The London that was growing with them excited them: their father had trained them to watch all epiphanies of life, from the human face, to the sweep of terrain, and they were perpetually going on long walks during childhood and adolescence—in Kensington Gardens, Hyde Park, Hampstead Heath, Woolwich, Blackheath.

Baby Charles, plump and eager, half-tried to compete with his elder brothers, half-depended on their guidance and tutelage. He was not over-protected. Indeed on intellectual terms the presence of his elder brothers spurred him on; he could draw with vigour if not yet with delicacy by his tenth birthday, and he could write tolerable appreciations of Turner's art and Ruskin's early criticism. His interest in the macabre asserted itself even at that age: watching a sheep-shearing, he waited in near-expectation the head would be removed with a stroke of the shears. But his was a world of firm security without responsibility in a city he loved, and from which he was to be exiled at seventeen for the remaining forty-four years of his life.

That childhood may not only have been vivid in Charles Doyle's recollection as a reproach to the poverty in which his own children were growing up; it was also there as a mournful ghost whose charms mocked his own present life and surroundings. This may have been a very telling influence on young Arthur—indeed, it almost certainly was. One of the greatest paradoxes of Sherlock Holmes, a figure synonymous with Victorian London, is that at the moment of his creation his creator had virtually no acquaintance with London at all. *A Study in Scarlet* and *The Sign of Four* were written after fleeting visits, and the "*Adventures*" were being spun from the whirring brain with absolute confidence in the omnipresent allusions to a London where Arthur Conan Doyle had only just taken up residence. But from his youth when Charles Doyle told the names of the streets and parks of Paradise whence he was forever excluded, Arthur would be able to recall Kensington, where Watson would have a practice (his other was near Paddington); and Blackheath, where Holmes would be so careful to begin his investigations of the supposed death of the Norwood builder before coming to Norwood; and Hampstead Heath, across which Holmes and Watson were to flee from the pursuit of the domestics of the murdered Charles Augustus Milverton; and Woolwich, where Cadogan West was to vanish and whence the Bruce-Partington Plans would be stolen. Only the visitors—John Doyle, Richard Doyle, Thackeray—brought their well-intentioned if socially and spiritually disruptive presences to reassure Charles his losses had been flesh and blood.

Arthur in Edinburgh grew up in a house where security was sinking rather than rising. Instead of a sure and single establishment at 17 Cambridge Terrace, Regent's Park, with occasional visits to premises at Blackheath for a change of air, Charles Doyle's family fled from flat to flat in mid-Victorian Edinburgh, with a declining rental and a rising number of children, so long as it was possible for Charles to pay the rent at all. Charles had been the youngest; Arthur, save for his sister Annette (and a baby who died at six months, before he was born), was the eldest. John Doyle sought to be mother and father to his children after the death of his wife Marianna Conan, whom Charles could not remember; Charles increasingly became neither father nor mother, so far as reliable concerns went. John Doyle required his offspring to write him continual letters and sketches, intended for his perusal and correction; Charles Doyle, sinking deeper and deeper into a pattern of outside journeyings in search of conviviality, left it to wife and teachers to inspire in Arthur the craft of story-telling from his earliest years.

In some ways, time warred against Charles's efforts to replay past charms to give his children the same pleasure that had been his. Military reviews were fewer in number in Edinburgh, though the Scottish regiments might be more colourful than many of their English counterparts and the hills of Edinburgh might make for more drama than the Thames basin, but the notables and Royalty of London had little counterpart in the Scottish capital. Arthur's childhood coincided with Queen Victoria's years of mourning for her lost Albert, so that Holyrood and the Royal Mile had no means of echoing the triumphs of Windsor and The Mall during the rejoicings of the Queen's courtship and marriage which Charles could remember. Edinburgh could hardly even run to decent funeral spectacles, what with the aristocracy and socially pretentious fleeing to London salons and cemeteries; how Charles and his brothers had enjoyed the obsequies when illustrious Royal profligates such as the Duke of Sussex finally ceased to be charges on the public exchequer! Certainly Edinburgh attracted visitors who might be touring the

island: if Charles as a boy was brought to several meetings when the great
Irish temperance crusader, Father Mathew, appeared in London, and, as his
brother Henry remarked, nearly had his plump form crushed thin in the
process, infant Irish Catholics in Edinburgh would have had the same
privilege at the same date, although it is to be hoped Father Mathew had
more influence on them. Little Arthur in Edinburgh would have been made
even more conscious than Little Charles in London of his identity with and
his separation from his fellow-Hibernians. The correspondence of Charles
and his brothers reveals a pride in their country of origin, above all its
religion and literature; but they also learned to make jokes about Irish
workers and refer to them as "Pat" as easily as any condescending
Englishman of unimpeachably Anglo-Saxon antecedents. In one way the
need to assert class differentials against the ethnic proximity of "Pat" was
even greater in Edinburgh than in London; the John Doyles might encounter
the masses at huge demonstrations for Father Mathew, but their normal
Sunday resort to spiritual refreshment would be in congenially better-class
surroundings. Edinburgh, with only four Catholic churches during Arthur's
youth, could make no such allowances for social distinction or pretension, and
it was a choice as a rule between the Jesuits of Lauriston Place, across the
sweep of the Meadows, or the more commodious but less salubrious St
Patrick's in the Cowgate, whither the Irish ghetto injected its hordes making
up in piety for what they lacked in hygiene, or the Cathedral, increasingly
remote after they had left the wealthy New Town. What made it even more
irritating was that the Scots Presbyterians, whom Charles Doyle despised as
bigoted, unimaginative Philistines to the end of his days, would have despised
him and his family as fundamentally little different from their most
odoriferous co-religionist in the Cowgate.

Arthur at the age of sixty-three would publish a sketch, "*A Point of
Contact*", reflecting on the irony of great men existing at the same moment of
time without the slightest awareness of one another, and fancifully illustrated
the point—for many of his *Tales of Long Ago* were historical propositions
teaching by example—by postulating a meeting between Odysseus and David.
There were such moments in his own life—we will encounter a striking case
of it during his first visit to Africa—but one could lyricise on the possibility of
one such encounter. It is a Sunday morning, and the Irish of all classes are
leaving the last Mass in St Patrick's; a four-year-old boy, in the family of a
poor Irish carter, stumbles over the feet of the tall schoolboy home on
summer vacation from Stonyhurst and is helped to his feet. In some such
fashion Arthur Conan Doyle might have met James Connolly: the originator
of the most famous figure in English fiction of the last hundred years
certainly crossed the path of the most distinguished Left-wing political
thinker of these islands to have emerged within the same period. They were
separated by class, by street-level—the Connollys being condemned to the
subterranean Cowgate—and by nine years; they had less dividing them in
blood, religion and income, even though in the case of the latter there was
still a chasm between the genteel poverty of the Doyles and the extreme

poverty of the Connollys. But if Conan Doyle's literary preoccupations were to be primarily middle-class, while James Connolly's were to be working-class, there is a literary point of contact between them also. *The White Company* and *Sir Nigel* are far more deeply conscious of the class struggles of the reign of Edward III than one finds in the writings of historians and fictionists of the same period; Edinburgh could show, and almost certainly had shown enough poverty and enough opulence to Conan Doyle for him to see the likelihood of rebellion from have-nots whom insult might rouse where deprivation alone could not. In particular the Cowgate, with its stench and its darkness, its misery and its cold, ran its ugly length below the wealthy thoroughfares of the mighty Bridges where the flower of Edinburgh society spent on its trivialities sums it would never vouchsafe to a hundred beggars. Poverty was also a strong enough common factor in the two families for Arthur to know the desperate scrapings and savings for survival where luxurious life-styles unjustified by any personal effort could be seen within a stone's throw. The brooding deprivation of the Cowgate was to produce the black humour and ruthless analysis of Connolly's polemics; it would not be surprising if to it we also owe the remorseless depiction of the sources of class hatred in *The White Company*. Conan Doyle did not prettify the Jacquerie, but he was if anything even more remorseless to the social cruelty which gave rise to it.

Charles Doyle was probably less fortunate than his brothers in one respect. The evidence of their letters suggests that the elder boys easily crossed the dividing-point between filial duty and affectionate friendship as far as their father was concerned, but that by the time his youngest son was ripe for education his father was too much a pattern of Victorian *paterfamilias* to be other than formidable in his eyes. Richard ("Dicky"), in particular, must have helped John Doyle during those critical years of the 1820s and early 1830s when he shuttled between Dublin and London, ventured on many enterprises before settling on and conquering in his chosen art, and sustained the loss of his wife; it is clear from the letters that a deep camaraderie existed between the young artist and the old. Richard shared John's devotion to his religion, his pride in the richness of Catholic culture, his excitement in the new trends in intellectual development taking place before their eyes. Given Richard's visits to Charles's family in Edinburgh, and Charles's own efforts to recall something of his childhood joys for the benefit of his children, it is important to notice that the Doyle boys were encouraged to read the latest Charles Lever novel: it celebrated their Irish heritage, while giving them a view of France during the Napoleonic wars. Arthur, the future author of the Brigadier Gerard stories and other evocations of Napoleon's Europe, is unlikely to have missed that family heirloom. Richard also shared with Charles—and Arthur—a fascination with the preternatural, although he was more conventional in his use of it than either. Richard, like his French-educated sister-in-law Mary Foley Doyle, was fascinated by French culture: from childhood he was an enthusiast, for instance, for the *Mémoires* of the French minister Sully who served Henri IV so ably, and this cult of a

Huguenot statesman in a profoundly Catholic artist gives us a direct line to his nephew's *The Refugees*. Even the childhood reflections of Dick at the menagerie on the similarity of men to monkeys seem to anticipate the passages in *The Lost World* where Challenger's companions are so struck by his resemblance to the King of the Ape-men, while the origin of that quest in the book of drawings by the deceased Maple White testifies to the sense of artistic heritage lying at its root. Richard as a progenitor of artistic fantasy in his nephew would be a lesser influence than his brother Charles, but nevertheless an important one.

The most curious point of Richard's effect on Arthur, either through Charles's recollection or through the relations of uncle and nephew during Edinburgh visits, lies in Richard's consciousness of being inspired by the "genius", as he described it, of Horace Vernet. In its appeal it seems to have been decidedly macabre: what particularly delighted him, he told his father, was Vernet's realisation of a ballad by the poet Burger in which the ghost of a dead bridegroom elopes on horseback with his bride on the wedding-day. ACD enjoyed toying with this form of literary conceit—his "*De Profundis*" has the corpse of a newly-married man float to the surface as his wife is leaning over the edge of a ship crossing the spot where the deceased has been confined to the waves—but enthusiasts for Holmes will recall a more celebrated association with the artist. Holmes in "*The Greek Interpreter*" tells Watson that he may owe his remarkable powers to his being the grandson of "the sister of Vernet, the French artist. Art in the blood is liable to take the strangest forms". The aphorism is eminently characteristic of Conan Doyle in the 'nineties: Holmes is speaking of his detective-powers, but simultaneously his creator is speaking of the stories in which Holmes is speaking. Vernet is made to do duty for the Doyles he inspired.

The other point lies in Richard himself. Dicky Doyle was a very interesting character in his own right, possessed of much resource and moral courage. He imperilled his status and income by resigning from *Punch*, whose cover he had designed and whose most distinguished cartoonist he was, when it entered into a violent No-Popery phase on the eve of Pius IX's restoration of the Roman Catholic hierarchy and Lord John Russell's contemptible efforts to make cheap political gains by crusading against it. In a way Arthur showed a comparable courage when he resolved in the interest of his art to kill off his own sure money-producer among his creations, Sherlock Holmes, or, equally, when he declined Dicky's use of Roman Catholic contacts during his early struggling days as a General Practitioner and could no longer accept Catholicism. In his discussion of artistic subjects, Dicky leaned to the fantastic, but having excited himself with the drama, power and mystique of a theme, he then enjoyed coldly demolishing its illogicality. In particular, he liked the old French folk-tale of the hound who guarded his master's body, thundered his accusations against his murderer, and was ultimately awarded trial by combat against the murderer, who confessed to end the implacable savagings he sustained from his canine adversary. Dicky pondered the possibilities of this with great delight—and then told his father that the story itself clearly broke down, since the dog so signally failed to save its master's life. If it knew so well where its master's corpse was, and who had killed him, and ultimately proved itself so desperate a threat to the murderer, how did the murder ever happen? This blend of fascination with the preternatural, and demolition of its absurdities after initially going along with them, is very much akin to his nephew's methods. It requires initially the inducement to the reader willingly to suspend his disbeliefs, and then, once that seduction has been convincingly made, to pull the carpet and leave him flat on his back on the cold floor of rationality. One of its most signal expressions in Conan Doyle, curiously enough, is also with reference to a hound:

> Holmes considered for a little time.
> "Put into plain words, the matter is this", said he. "In your opinion there is a diabolical agency which makes Dartmoor an unsafe abode for a Baskerville—that is your opinion?"
> "At least I might go to the length of saying that there is some evidence that this may be so."
> "Exactly. But surely, if your supernatural theory be correct, it could work the young man evil in London as easily as in Devonshire. A devil with merely local powers like a parish vestry would be too inconceivable a thing."

We will find that the scientific scepticism which formed so significant a strain in Conan Doyle owed much to Edinburgh University Medical School, but in Richard Doyle it coexisted most impressively with the romantic atmosphere against which it made so much warfare.

The disparity between Charles and his brothers was not immediately to assert itself, but by October 1849 John Doyle seems firmly to have decided that his youngest son would have to obtain a fixed position. This was to be a berth in the Civil Service, in its days when influence still could play its critical part as opposed to competitive examinations. It was a harsh decision given that Charles was only seventeen; but his ancestors had been earning their bread with far more labour and much less reward at decidedly younger ages. One point where Arthur was more fortunate than Charles was that in Edinburgh entrance to the University was the norm for reasonably well educated Scottish boys. England in the 1840s still assumed that university was a privilege for the Protestant élite, graduates of public schools, sprigs of the aristocracy or gentry. Charles might have had some hopes of artistic training, and indeed it may have been some controversy arising from the training he, like his brothers, was receiving from his father, which led to John Doyle's decision for his exile. At fifty-seven the great caricaturist may have felt his powers for continuing as father, mother and professor were no longer fit to control a wayward boy of seventeen. In any case, it was agreed that the post of clerk in H.M. Office of Works, Edinburgh, would be temporary: in fact, it would last until 1877, when John Doyle was dead, competitive examinations were in, and Charles Doyle was simply dismissed.

Charles Doyle started work under Robert Mathieson, the surveyor for Scotland, in November 1849 and shortly afterwards moved from temporary lodgings to 8 Scotland Street, where his landlady was Mrs Catherine Foley. It seems most likely that he found the quarters through St Mary's Catholic pro-Cathedral, as it then was. He had, no doubt following paternal instructions, started at once to interest himself in local Catholic philanthropy, quickly becoming secretary of the Edinburgh branch of the St Vincent de Paul Society. Its purpose was in part somewhat similar to that which Sherlock Holmes tells Dr Watson in "*The Crooked Man*" preoccupied Mrs Barclay on the Monday evening she met the crooked man, whose revelations then preoccupied her in a different direction. She "had interested herself very much in the establishment of the Guild of St George, which was formed in connection with the Watt Street Chapel for the purpose of supplying the poor with cast-off clothing". The secretary of such a body necessarily had to draw on the services of local ladies, and a landlady would have rather greater access to a variety of such material than would the average mother of a family. Traditionally, Catholic churches liked their flocks to gravitate around them, frequently to form the nucleus of a poverty-stricken ghetto, more rarely to supply a focal point in the fashionable districts. The Edinburgh New Town, solid, respectable, architecturally imposing, enshrined the taste of the late eighteenth century, the city's intellectual Golden Age, and while the Cathedral in Picardy Place was on the fringes rather than the heart of the New Town, the slightly lower rents in the apartment-houses there gave an added incentive to the better-class Catholics to settle as close as possible to their church doorstep.

Whether meeting Mrs Foley followed direct action by the Parish Priest, or a meeting arising from philanthropic questions, we do not know. Certainly St Vincent de Paul would have deepened the sympathy between landlady and tenant, and Charles Doyle's status as secretary, even more than his illustrious London connections, would have graced him in the eyes of Mrs Foley and her daughter Mary. The very close bonds of affection between Mrs Barclay and her friend Miss Morrison, in "*The Crooked Man*", conveys the intimacy produced by such a body. It was very conscious activity for the Catholic community in a hostile environment; but it was also a little psychologically rewarding in class terms, putting its participants firmly among the rulers rather than the ruled. That additional social advantage was dearly prized, and a St Vincent de Paul branch might well include on its committee persons more in need than many of their beneficiaries, but who would have died rather than admit the fact. On the other hand, the confidence induced by closeness within the community, and indeed the conditions of poverty which such workers witnessed, disposed of the pettier forms of social pretence. Mrs Foley saw no shame in being a landlady, nor her daughter in blacking a grate.

Scotland Street was hard by the pro-Cathedral. So was Abercromby Place, whence Charles Doyle was writing to a London friend later in 1850. Some two years later he had moved away from the New Town to Nicolson Street, near the University, still little more than ten minutes' walk from church. Whether Mrs Foley and her daughter were also making these moves is unclear. Edinburgh was a city where much "flitting" took place, and families often lasted only a couple of years in an apartment. At all events, Charles Doyle evidently became increasingly drawn to the young girl, twelve when he first knew her, seventeen when on 31 July 1855 they married. It was St Ignatius' Day, which may account for their eldest son, four years later, being named Arthur Ignatius Conan Doyle. The name, however, was never used, and remained unknown outside the family circle. It may have been imposed by the wish of a priest because of the common sacerdotal preference to have a saint's name given to each Catholic infant. Oddly enough, there is no St Arthur in the calendar, although early Irish Christian tradition certainly includes uncanonised holy men named Art, one an early convert of St Patrick. There was a St Conan, of whom the priest may not have known: he is patron saint of the Isle of Man. At all events the names asserted a sufficiency of Celticism, Welsh, Cornish, Manx, Breton, as well as Scottish birth and Irish ancestry.

Arthur's birth took place on 22 May 1859. By then the Doyles and Mrs Foley were settled at 11 Picardy Place with the Cathedral at their doorstep. But by then there had been two other children: Anne Mary Frances, afterwards known as Annette, was born almost exactly a year after her parents' marriage, and Catherine Emilia Angela, born on 22 April 1858. Arthur was never to see Catherine; she died at the age of six months, less than a year before his birth. Even before he was born, then, Arthur enjoyed a status of special protection in the eyes of his mother. The memory of the sibling who had died lay over his youth, particularly his earliest days. Catherine was evidently so ill from the first that the poor mite could not be brought to the church for baptism for three months: no doubt she was initially baptised very quickly for fear of death but the delay in the church ceremony implies six grim months until her death, especially for Mary Foley Doyle, faced with the horror of losing the child she had borne before she herself was 21 years of age. Arthur was healthier, and so was brought to church and baptised almost at once. His grand-uncle Michael Conan, brother-in-law of John Doyle, was godfather and in their haste the parents did not seek a godmother. This tells much of the fears for the boy's survival. A single godparent is very unusual in Catholic families, and unique among the ten children of Charles Altamont Doyle.

Two years later the fourth Doyle child arrived, Mary, another who would never survive infancy. But Arthur's first formal recollection of any kind was the death-bed of his grandmother, Catherine Foley, "the white waxen thing which lay on the bed". She died on 7 June 1862, at 6.55 pm., so the little boy would have been up. The family had removed by then from Picardy Place to 3 Tower Bank, Portobello, several miles away. The period must have been fraught with considerable difficulty for Charles and Mary. Catherine had been suffering from cancer of the uterus for two years before her death, as well as what was diagnosed as general dropsy: they had set in early as she was only 53 when she died. She had been an important contributor to the family finances during the early years of their marriage: that probably ended around Arthur's birth and was certainly finished by the removal to Portobello. She remains something of a mystery. Her grandson never discovered why she went to Edinburgh.

It is difficult to be precise about her origin, partly because Arthur's mother Mary Foley Doyle became accustomed to make high claims for her ancestry, as we shall see. But on the evidence of the death-certificate with information furnished by Charles Altamont Doyle on 23 June 1862, she was born in 1809 and her father, William Pack, was a landed proprietor. Conan Doyle claimed that Major-General Sir Denis Pack was her close relative and hence possibly his great-uncle: Pack had the career of a Charles Lever hero, serving in the Netherlands, Germany, Ireland (1798), the Cape of Good Hope, Buenos Aires, the Peninsular War and Waterloo. He is not a likely candidate for the status of great-uncle—there are over thirty years between Catherine Pack and himself—but he might have been William's brother. If so, William was of seventeenth-century planter stock and supposedly a descendant of the Cromwellian Lord Mayor of London. It would also make William quite definitely a Protestant; and however remote the relationship with Sir Denis, that seems probable enough for such a surname. Sir Denis was son of Thomas Pack, D.D., Dean of Ossory (born 1720), and he the son of Thomas Pack of Ballinakill, Queen's County (now Leix). Thomas's father is thus believed to be Simon Packe, son of Sir Christopher, the Mayor. The Ossory connection removed the Packs from central Ireland to the south-east, and hence to territory adjoining Waterford, the Foley country. William Foley, Catherine Pack's husband, is listed in *Alumni Dublinenses*, as admitted February 7 aged 17, son of Thomas Foley, Roman Catholic gentleman of Waterford; William is described as having been educated by the Rev. Mr Foley, presumably an uncle who was a priest. He graduated B.A. spring 1829, and M.A. summer 1834, presumably marrying in 1835 or so. Family tradition thereafter is clear enough: William Foley became a doctor, and died young. Why, then, was his widow reduced to running a lodging-house in Edinburgh twenty years after?

The important point here is that Mary Foley Doyle was brought up as a Catholic. Now in nineteenth-century Ireland, as distinct from the present century, the convention obtained whereby the boys followed the religion of the father, the girls that of the mother. Catherine apparently became a Catholic. The inference is that either because of this she was cut off by her family, or else that her family cut her off for marrying one, and she then embraced the faith of her husband. Catherine's case presents an interesting analogy to her grandson's creation of Effie in "*The Yellow Face*" who "cut myself off my own race" in order to marry the black man John Hebron, of Atlanta. Protestant-Catholic marriages did take place in Ireland in those times, indeed in some ways more easily than would be the case later, as the increasing power of the Catholic church led it to introduce more restrictions: but it would only be Catholic women marrying Protestant men that would be acceptable to the ruling Protestant episcopalian caste. The custom at that time as to the religion of children of mixed marriages kept inheritance firmly in Protestant hands provided the taboo against Protestant girls marrying Catholic boys was observed. In the previous century anti-Catholic legislation had prevented such alienation of Protestant property and affections; now

social sanction would have to do it. But in the case of Catherine Pack
apparently it did not. The result was that she found it preferable to migrate to
Edinburgh when her husband died, divided as she was from her husband's
family by birth, and her own by marriage. In the baptismal registers we find
evidence that the Charles Altamont Doyles cultivated their relatives as
godparents and ecclesiastical witnesses: there are Foleys at the wedding—
John Doyle and Ann Conan stood for Annette, Henry Doyle and Catherine
Foley stood for the lost little Catherine—and as the family grew larger there
would be sponsorship from Uncle James and Aunt Annette and Uncle Dick,
but the name Pack never appears, a further clue to the lost Protestant
heritage. But with Protestant forebears Mary clearly saw return to her
paternal ancestors' faith as an option, and one which she would ultimately
take.

There was one other member of the family when Catherine Pack Foley
died. She had two daughters, Mary and Catherine, and the latter continued to
make her home with her mother after the marriage of Charles and Mary. The
census of 1861 lists her as a governess by profession and 21 years of age. They
were still living at 11 Picardy Place in April, when it was taken. A curiously
human touch appears in the description of Grandmother Catherine: she is
initially listed as "invalid" and this is then stricken out and "no calling"
substituted. As she was dying of cancer, but as her life had shown her to be
independent, courageous and indomitable, we may presume the alteration
arose from her hearing her invalid status described to the census-taker and
her indignantly insisting on the correction. Such alterations are unusual in
the familiar particulars listed: there is something fine about her personality
thrusting itself into our vision between the inanimate meshes of Victorian
bureaucracy. If Arthur had no recollection of her living, she was nonetheless
the founder of his family and set the matriarchal pattern on it. Her life had
given her daughter Mary the training and example she would need so much.
Her daughter Catherine raises a different problem. How long did she live with
the family after her mother's death? She is included with them in the census
of 1871, this time as "Kate Foley", though now she is described as "visitor".
It was probably she who was the little Catherine's godmother. We are simply
left to speculate on whether her profession called her away from home, or
she really did reside with them for ten years, thus giving vital moral and
physical support to her elder sister. She would have added to Arthur's Irish
consciousness, and as a single woman probably helped to maintain the links
with Foley relatives in Waterford. The census also lists a maidservant, the
Irish-born 23-year-old Margaret Stafford. She had gone, and had no
successor, in 1871, although the improved circumstances of 1881 allowed for
a maid once more. If Margaret Stafford did stay for any length of time, she
must have been of importance in the baby eyes of Arthur.

Familial distinction clearly meant much to the *déclassé* Catherine Pack
Foley, as it would also mean to her daughter Mary, and Charles Doyle
had exactly what a mother in that position would seek—gentility of
class, Irishness of parentage and Catholicism of religion. Exactly what

financial arrangment was reached is unknown. Catherine still let rooms, and by 1858 had risen sufficiently well in status to place herself in the city directory as running lodgings for governesses. Charles is listed as paying the rent both for Picardy Place and for its predecessor, the slightly more expensive flat at 3 Nelson Street, which they occupied in 1858, but how far he was carrying the burden is a question. Catherine may have had a fairly sizeable shilling with which to be cut off from her Protestant relatives; she certainly seems to have been able to afford a journey to France for Mary who remained there for a year in her school days. Certainly the Foley relatives remained in touch and Arthur made several visits to them in Waterford in his youth. The critical factor is that at the point of her death she must still have been a vital symbol of social, economic and psychological protection to Mary and Charles.

This death formed the end of the governesses' institution: it would be impossible for Mary to operate as landlady, mother and chaperone altogether, and Kate was working. It probably eliminated lodgers in general for several years; our first firm evidence on their return is not until the mid-1870s. Catherine's decline seems to have decided Charles and Mary on removal to the sea-coast at Portobello, for the protection of the health of the five-year-old Annette, baby Mary and little Arthur, and there they remained from late 1861 to 1864 at Tower Bank House. Charles himself was so far manfully coping. A new periodical called *London Society* was starting, and he was retained for its early years to illustrate its stories; it remembered him sufficiently well to give a very early welcome to his son Arthur whose second story, "*The American's Tale*", would appear in its Christmas number for 1879 and who thereafter published much of his earliest work in it. Charles also was getting commissions for book illustration.

Nevertheless if Portobello gave the children some chance of health, particularly Arthur who grew up tall and strong, it probably was the downfall of their father. The journey from the offices of Works in Parliament Square was long, and the company of the clerks congenial. The work had interested him, involving such things as designing the fountain at Holyrood Palace, but it became less and less absorbing to him. Edinburgh also declined after Albert died and the Queen went into mourning: improvements at the palace of Mary Queen of Scots became less urgent. No doubt Charles enjoyed walking with his children in Holyrood park, as he had walked as a boy in London parks, and no doubt also it was pleasant to visit the palace and show the contributions he had made to it. In such visits Arthur would come to know the story of the ill-fated Mary Stuart, and hear in its excruciating detail the guide's account of the murder of Rizzio at the feet of the pregnant Queen by her husband Henry Lord Darnley, the ghastly and hollow-eyed Ruthven and their knife-hacking fellows, and see where the nobles had rushed in, and where Rizzio crouched, and where his murderers dragged him, and where the Queen stood. It would not be surprising if he saw visions of it in his dreams, much as he describes it appearing to an exhausted and over-wrought accountant in "*The Silver Mirror*", which he wrote for the *Strand* in 1908, forty years later. But everything began to pall for Charles once the parting glass and its sequels became necessary to bring him back to Portobello. "I always knew", says Mrs Raby in "*A Sordid Affair*" "that if you were to get away from those other clerks you would be all right." "Those other clerks" were probably credited with the cause of Charles returning late and drunk, or not at all, the ugly dilemma as to which was preferable taunting the unfortunate young wife as she waited. He began to abandon work for *London Society* and to seek, or to perform, less artistic work for publishers. The drink began to create its own destruction of will and achievement, and assert its own resentments and requirements.

And somewhere at this point Mary Foley had to face her loneliness and her terrible responsibility. Her mother had given her example in independence and contrivance, but she was gone. The children were increasing, yet if she were insufficiently vigilant, they would go the way of little Catherine. Already there must have been a problem in controlling the growing boy. And as she contemplated the claying feet of her husband, she resolved that come what may Arthur must be saved, from his father no less than from death.

Her grandson Adrian clothed her memory with suitably aristocratic lineaments and insisted on biographers doing the same, and the result is that Mary Foley Doyle has come down to us as a somewhat visionary autocrat, with high pretensions and an acute resemblance to Sir Nigel's grandmother in the book bearing his name. Above all, she is typified in the name "the Ma'am" with which the biographers signal her. In the 1860s she bore no such name; it was the Irish endearment "Mam" or "Mammy" by which her son called her. Arthur protected his father in his autobiography, but he said it all in the words "it was still my dear mother who bore the long, sordid strain" [that word "sordid" again]. "Often I said to her, 'When you are old, Mammie, you shall have a velvet dress and gold glasses and sit in comfort by the fire'. Thank God, it so came to pass." We must realise that the very Irishness of Arthur's way of putting it is its own clue. He grew up seeing her counting the pennies, making the economies, taking the decisions, losing the servants or perhaps never getting them, facing the physical exhaustion. She may have become a great lady by force of personality, but she seemed to have nothing between her and the gutter but a salary of £200 of which more and more vanished on drink, with less and less augmenting it from artistic commissions. It is this which accounts for her son's triumphant belief in the superiority of women, whether in the field of medicine (as he asserts in "*The Doctors of Hoyland*") or in defeating Sherlock Holmes (in "*A Scandal in Bohemia*"). The little Irish girl in her twenties gave him his first real taste of indomitable courage, resolution, and a love for her children, above all for him, that was ready to rise above the most cruel privation and degradation. "Oh, blind, angelic, foolish love of woman!" he cries at the end of "*A Sordid Affair*" in an apostrophe of a kind almost wholly alien to the rest of his work. "Why should men demand a miracle while you remain upon earth?"

Her capacity for transmitting her great qualities is one of the cardinal proofs of her nobility. His courage, his hatred of cruelty, his refusal to whine, his modesty, his gentleness in everyday life, his implacable fierceness against injustice, are all things that he drew initially from her example. The most telling proof is that despite her never-ending devotion to his interests above all others, he never showed the slightest sign of being spoiled. Her selfless love had gone out to him, but it was a wise love that trained him to be selfless in his turn. It did mean that he grew up with a far more realistic yardstick about human behaviour and its attendant regulations than most boys had. He was hostile to discipline at school, partly because he had grown up with a system of carefully worked out rules which were necessitated by specific and obvious needs. This practical relationship of conduct to necessity left him with a rooted objection to the notion of rules for their own sake. He showed this in Stonyhurst, and he showed it also in the way he publicly despised bureaucracy for bureaucracy's sake, whether in his fight against police misjudgment on the Edalji and Slater cases or in Sherlock Holmes's ever-present mockery at the expense of the official methods of criminal investigation. Bureaucracy made a drunk of his father; pragmatism had saved his father's family.

The little Irish girl was in certain ways very close to the condition of her fellow-countrywomen on the lower levels of Irish Catholic society in the eighteenth and nineteenth centuries. The husband was the breadwinner, when he remained with his family at all, but in so many instances alcohol became his permanent false friend. Alcohol gave him his illusions, whether in the extreme form shown by Sean O'Casey in *"Juno and the Paycock"* or in more moderate expression. Mothers needed their means of psychological support. Prayer formed one basis of it, with the Catholic cult of Mary, the mother of Jesus, who saw the death of the most glorious Son the world has ever known. Mary Foley had a spiritual dimension, but it seems to have grown away from her Catholic antecedents, possibly because of her husband's position as a prominent Catholic layman in the community. His religious fervour had done nothing to check his destructive effects on his family. There seems to have been some controversy with the local clergy on Mary's part— possibly she sought the aid of clerical acquaintances who answered her with male chauvinism disguised (to its reverend authors as well as those on whom they turned it) as spiritual instruction. Woman's place was to defer to her husband in all things, and if Charles took a drink too many, he had cares a foolish woman could not hope to understand and pressures she was unable to appreciate, much less to bear. We can only infer this from the family tradition of that conflict, but the portrait of Dame Ermyntrude in *Sir Nigel*, described to Adrian Conan Doyle by his father (and presumably his grandmother) as a portrait of Mary Foley Doyle, is at its most striking when she curses the clergy for their cruelty to her family. Clearly no priest extorted material wealth from the Doyles in the way the bursar of the encroaching Abbey of Waverley does from the impoverished Lorings, but there is a clear suggestion of very deeply-felt association between grinding poverty and clerical hostility.

In place of formal religious piety, Mary Doyle found her escapism in a cult of history, chivalry, ancestry. It may well have arisen in part from young

Arthur's hunger for stories, and it became an easy matter to identify herself and her ancestors with the stories of old times, often rooted in the French heritage of which she had learned in her European years. It was in its way the variant of another Irish tradition—the custody of a conviction that the ancestors of the most cruelly-oppressed Catholic labourer had been kings of Ireland. It is a family tradition that the ancestors of the Doyles had lost their estates, because of their adherence to religion. Mary herself, probably with that disenchantment with the Catholic clergy, stressed Protestant forebears on her side. "The Packs were a fighting family", recalled her son, "as was but right since they were descended in a straight line from a major in Cromwell's army who settled in Ireland. One of them, Anthony Pack, had part of his head carried off at the same battle [Waterloo], so I fear it is part of our family tradition that we lose our heads in action. His brain was covered over by a silver plate and he lived for many years, subject only to very bad fits of temper, which some of us have had with less excuse."

The smile of Arthur Conan Doyle may be inherited here also. Certainly Mary Foley Doyle wanted to entertain the boy and stimulate his historical enthusiasm, and would have known the rule that the best means of teaching is to raise a laugh in sympathy with the subject on the part of the pupil. John Dickson Carr's fictionalisations of her instructions to Arthur on heraldry, based on letters referring to it, suggest an obsessive and bullying snob, whatever his intentions: it is clear from Arthur's own account that the whole thing was great fun, and was intended to be so. If it came less naturally to her to become excited in accounts of battles, more naturally dear to the male heart, she allowed her ancestral enthusiasm to swing her into the action. Well might she identify with the derring-do of long dead and gone Percies, ascribed to her family tree; her own life was a struggle of probably much superior courage and gallantry to any of them. And despite the citation of Dame Ermyntrude, it seems to me that Arthur's first use of his mother in chivalric fiction was in the earlier work in which Sir Nigel appears, *The White Company*, written in 1890; set later in time than its sequel, Dame Ermyntrude does not appear in it but the obvious borrowing from Mary Foley Doyle is Sir Nigel himself. The concentration on analysis of ancestry in the midst of crisis and chaos is one example of it; the towering courage under the unassuming appearance and extreme smallness of stature is another; the gentleness of manner but absolute refusal to waver on a point of principle is a third. Certainly her absorption in ancestry became more and more of an end in itself as the years went by, but its origin in educational stimulation, and what her grandson Brigadier John Doyle has summed up as "keeping herself sane", is the critical point of departure in considering it. Indeed, there is some suspicion that whenever she wanted to whet her son's appetite for Waterloo —or Walter Scott—she obliged with yet another ancestor. She claimed kinship with Scott via her mother's mother Catherine Scott, for instance, and turned her son on Sir Walter's pages with profound results for *his* historical fictions. It gave it one remarkable quality: he possessed his material, yet he retained in his mastery of it a fairy-tale quality which made it at once familial and fantastic, above all in the Gerard stories.

He loved her with all the generosity of a great nature, and this love is critical to understanding his development, for it dominated his life. It thirsted for self-expression, never really finding it in his first marriage, triumphantly so doing in his second. It asserted itself in his patriotism, which for him was a profoundly personal matter, in which the cause of the Empire became analogous to the cause of his mother, all the more arising from those chivalric ideas she extolled. In the end, living humanity became too small to contain it, and he burst the bonds of contemporary life to embrace the "land of mist" beyond the bounds of mortality.

But it didn't prevent his being quietly very amused by her enthusiasm. Chivalry was Norman, and she convinced herself that she had married into a Norman family. The Doyles must be originally "D'Oil" (they were in fact of Viking, not of Norman, extraction, the name being the Gaelic for "dark foreigner", but the Vikings were a coarse and unheraldic crowd). Arthur duly repeated this, word-perfect as she liked him to be on heraldic matters (it was after all an excellent way of cultivating his powers of retention, and between her and the Jesuits—equal devotees of memory-work—he came to acquire one of the finest retentive memories of his time). He carefully reasserts it in *Memories and Adventures:* true, she was dead when he wrote it, but with his belief in spiritualism he would hold her to be aware of what he was writing. However in his early years as a writer, when he might well assume she would not see some of the work he was producing to improve his tiny income from medical practice, he wrote *"The Secret of Goresthorpe Grange"* in which the idiotic narrator, a self-made ex-grocer named Silas Dodd renamed Argentine (from the Latin, *argentium*=silver, a nice pre-Joycean pun) D'Odd, pursues ancient lineage with hilarious results, ultimately being swindled in his attempt to equip himself with a ghost:

> My habits are conservative, and my tastes refined and aristocratic. I have a soul which spurns the vulgar herd. Our family, the D'Odds, date back to a prehistoric era, as is to be inferred from the fact that their advent into British history is not commented on by any trustworthy historian. Some instinct tells me that the blood of a Crusader runs in my veins. Even now, after the lapse of so many years, such exclamations as "Br'r Lady!" rise naturally to my lips, and I feel that, should circumstances require it, I am capable of rising in my stirrups and dealing the infidel a blow—say with a mace—which would considerably astonish him.

The vulgar Argentine has nothing in common with Mary Foley Doyle, but she had equipped her irreverent son with the means of dissecting him from the outset, and he happily employed the patter learned from her instructions. The story is an early, cunning exercise in pure comedy, but he never reprinted it in his collections much though it merited it. His mother might have been hurt. On the other hand, she certainly would have seen the gentler though still very amusing, portrayal of an Irish genealogy-obsessed talker in Major Tobias Clutterbuck of *The Firm of Girdlestone*.

ACD did, more covertly, satirise the cult of ancestry in *"The Musgrave*

Ritual". His mother's insistence that the Irish Doyles were a cadet branch of the Staffordshire Doyles is recalled by the Musgraves of the ritual being a cadet branch of the Northern Musgraves—he had to give some explanation for them, as he had cheerfully extracted the name from the border reivers of whom he had heard so much from his mother, Sir Walter Scott, and Percy's *Reliques*. But Holmes's unkind comment, "You will excuse me, Musgrave, if I say that your butler appears to me to have been a very clever man, and to have had a clearer insight than ten generations of his masters" (" 'I hardly follow you', said Musgrave"), sets the priorities very nicely as between brains and lineage. Later on Mary Foley Doyle's emphasis on her Plantagenet ancestry inspires a naughty touch in *"The Noble Bachelor"*, where the aristocracy emerges in highly materialistic and ignoble colours, and the snobbish Lord Robert St Simon is described by Holmes as inheriting "Plantagenet blood by direct descent, and Tudor on the distaff side": the point is that the Tudors had no direct male descent and hence there was no way of inheriting blood from them save on the distaff side at some juncture.

One point where Mary Foley Doyle and her son largely disagreed was in the fashionable doctrine of heredity. Conan Doyle as a doctor knew about hereditary diseases: after all, he was to write his doctoral dissertation on an aspect of syphilis, and his *"The Third Generation"* deals with realism and horror on the longterm effects of G.P.I.. But he was very decidedly a believer, confirms his daughter Jean, in people making it their aim to do good in themselves, a far more important matter than priding themselves on their ancestry. In practical terms Mary Foley Doyle probably agreed with him. Her measures in his own case argue for a practical respect for environment as against heredity. But in theory she held out for heredity, and, in one Sherlock Holmes story only, her son went a little way in support of her. There was an excellent reason. She suggested to him the plot of *"The Copper Beeches"*. He was becoming worried about being enslaved to Holmes at that point, and worried, among other things, that the necessity to churn out instalments of Holmes would lead to the "forcing" of situations and the need to incorporate Holmes into plots which would do better without him. He argued for killing Holmes off. His mother indignantly protested. So he gave way at that point, such that Holmes would have twelve more stories before apparent destruction in *"The Final Problem"*, and the current series was ended with *"The Copper Beeches"*.

The story is important in our study of Mary Foley Doyle since no other case of her express influence is quite as clear-cut. Firstly, Conan Doyle was right: it really is not a Sherlock Holmes story apart (and it is a huge "apart") from the dialogue. Holmes makes no accurate deduction of any distinction, and the events of the story could comfortably resolve themselves without him (apart from his accidental influence on giving the villain a somewhat well-merited mauling by his pet mastiff, starved and fostered in order to maim or even kill his daughter's devoted swain). He fails to allow for the possible alliance between Mrs Toller and Alice Rucastle, and wholly incorrectly assumes from the evidence of Alice Rucastle's disappearance that her father had carried her off (for which Rucastle has no obvious motive, having an excellent prison for her, very elaborate means of its defence, and no knowledge of Holmes's impending arrival) when he has had a strong indication that if she has vanished there is another protagonist who is more likely to be the agent. But much more interesting are the clues to Mary Foley Doyle's priorities in outlining and influencing the story.

We may begin with the matter of heredity. There is the horrible child, half-brother to Alice Rucastle, of whom Holmes makes much although in fact he never appears and is mysteriously absent during the dénouement (despite Miss Violet Hunter's having to "look after" him during his parents' absence throughout the evening, a duty which disappears so completely from her agenda as to leave considerable doubts as to her fitness for her post). Rucastle says of him:

> " 'One Child—one dear little romper just six years old. Oh, if you could see him killing cockroaches with a slipper! Smack! smack! smack! Three gone before you could wink!' He leaned back in the chair and laughed his eyes into his head again.
>
> "I was a little startled at the nature of the child's amusement . . . "[comments Miss Hunter]

She meets him:

> " . . . I have never met so utterly spoilt and ill-natured a little creature. He is small for his age, with a head which is quite disproportionately large. His whole life appears to be spent in an alternation between savage fits of passion, and gloomy intervals of sulking. Giving pain to any creature weaker than himself seems to be his one idea of amusement, and he shows quite remarkable talent in planning the capture of mice, little birds, and insects . . . "

And Holmes comments later:

> " . . . The most serious point in the case is the disposition of the child."
>
> "What on earth has that to do with it?" I ejaculated.
>
> "My dear Watson, you as a medical man are continually gaining light as to the tendencies of a child by the study of its parents. Don't you see that the converse is equally valid? I have frequently gained my first real insight into the character of parents by studying their children. This child's disposition is abnormally cruel, merely for cruelty's sake, and whether he derives this from his smiling father, as I should suspect, or from his mother, it bodes evil for the poor girl who is in their power."

So firm an insistence is very much at variance with Holmes's procedure and outlook in most of his other cases. In *"The Boscombe Valley Mystery"* he actually encourages the marriage of the children of a blackmailer and a bushranger with apparently no doubt of its successful outcome. In *"The Naval Treaty"* he stakes everything on the integrity and reliability of Miss Annie Harrison, once having come to the conclusion that her brother Joseph is responsible for the crime. A real votary of theories of heredity would have been decidedly worried in either case. Admittedly he toys with a theory of heredity to account for Colonel Sebastian Moran in *"The Empty House"*:

> " . . . I have a theory that the individual represents in his development the whole procession of his ancestors, and that such a sudden turn to good or evil

stands for some strong influence which came into the line of his pedigree. The person becomes, as it were, the epitome of the history of his own family."

"It is surely rather fanciful."

"Well, I don't insist upon it. . . . "

But we will find a special reason for this passage when we meet George Turnavine Budd. Holmes did not speak with Doyle's voice, except when Doyle wanted him to. In my view he reflected various figures, mostly medical, whose views and manners suggested lines of developing him to his creator. Now, the hereditary theories are presented with the enthusiasm of the votary: Conan Doyle admired many doctors with whose views he did not in the least agree (his teacher Rutherford and his Mentor Bryan Charles Waller were both remorseless vivisectionists, and he was strongly critical of vivisectionism). In this case he uses one of his mother's enthusiasms to present a new facet of Holmes for his mother's story.

But *"The Copper Beeches"* reflects other concerns of Mary Foley Doyle. The figure of Mr Rucastle, with his charm and capacity to entertain masking an utter selfishness and hostility to the rights of his daughter, is a telling comment on some of the charming men Mary Doyle encountered during her marriage, companions vaunted for their ability to make the ladies laugh endlessly while selfishly keeping their husbands out drinking to the ruin of their character and family life. The image of good story-telling furthering destructiveness to family rights is highly suggestive, especially taken in context with the denunciation of "those other clerks" in *"A Sordid Affair"*. The fact that the story contains the famous passage on cruelty in the country as opposed to the ready availability of aid to the injured in a town is important. Conan Doyle, with memories of his own professional privations, made many allusions to the poor rewards of the industrious apprentice, notably in *"The Man with the Twisted Lip"*, *"The Engineer's Thumb"*, *"The Stockbroker's Clerk"*, *"The Musgrave Ritual"* (with respect to Holmes himself), and *"The Resident Patient"*, but in *"The Copper Beeches"* we see the harder fate of the professional woman. The nastiness of Miss Stoper, the administrator of the agency, when her commission looks like falling through because her client Miss Hunter declines to comply with a demeaning request on the part of the employer, underlines the peculiar defencelessness of women in the employment market-place, even members of her own sex being ready to be party to the injury of her interests. Mary Foley Doyle specifically produced the idea of that mysterious and demeaning request: that the governess's employment should depend on her long golden hair being shorn for some sinister purpose. By the time of that suggestion, 1891, three of her daughters had taken on the profession of governess, her sister Kate had earlier experience of it, she would have met other governesses among her mother's lodgers. The symbolism of the injury to human dignity so dictated by economic considerations, such that the employee can not even call her hair her own, showed that she knew enough about the ugly demands forced on young women in a profession with a large reservoir of available labour to replace them. To put it at its most obvious, a governess might have reason to suspect that her person was at risk in the household of a prospective employer, and yet how could she fight economic necessity purely on the basis of a mere intuition? Conan Doyle clearly took his mother's point—witness Holmes's frequent statements in the case that he would not like a sister of his to apply for such a job (the only time when the thought of a female relative crosses Holmes's mind). The governess, however unconsciously, is made an agent in a piece of extraordinary cruelty to an innocent person; how often might someone in such a position find themselves constrained to act against their best intentions in their hopeless dependence on the employer and his testimonial on their departure? And the mother's idea, acting on her receptive son's creative genius, gave the story such power and force that it easily transcended its basic irrelevance to Holmes and his normal procedures and methods. Mary Foley Doyle had had all too much opportunity of seeing the pitfalls for women in a man's world: it is noteworthy that she should suggest a theme not from her own personal misfortunes but from the possible dangers to her sister, her daughters and her friends.

She entertained herself and her son with her reflections on ancestry and heredity, leaving him to contemplate its relevance to art in the blood taking the strangest forms, as in his own case, but when a practical dilemma as to the future of her son arose, she acted very differently from her principles. Her disillusionment with her husband centred her love more and more on her son. Yet in her supreme unselfishness, she grasped at the opportunity to get him away from the squalor and misery being forced on his dawning consciousness by his father's degradation. The family had grown to know John Hill Burton, the historiographer-royal for Scotland, whose industry and range of investigative historical interests were only equalled by the diffuse nature of his presentation. Burton's wife Catherine or Katherine stood for Arthur's younger brother, born in 1873, and named "John Francis Innes Hay Doyle" after his godfather Robert Hay and his godmother's father, the antiquary Cosmo Innes: the boy would be known as Innes thereafter. Burton's sister Mary owned Liberton Bank, a house in the agreeably countrified atmosphere below Liberton Brae, free from the foetid airs of the town yet only a two-mile walk from the centre. Arthur was sent to live with her when he was seven or eight. It gave him a much more secure environment, apart from the terrible separation from his mother; it also won him the companionship of William K. Burton, John's son, to whom Arthur later dedicated *The Firm of Girdlestone*.

Burton went on to become an engineer, thereby supplying his friend with authentic detail for the background of another Holmes story with very little actual Holmes content, *"The Engineer's Thumb"*, and the tenure of a chair in the subject at Tokyo doubtless accounted for the authenticity of the "Anglo-Jap" in the account of the country in *"Jelland's Voyage"*. The story is a reminiscence of the 'sixties, of which presumably Burton heard his plenty during his stay and retailed it on his return home:

"The middle of the 'sixties was a stirring time out in Japan. That was just after the Simonosaki bombardment, and before the Daimio affair. There was a Tory party and there was a Liberal party among the natives, and the question they were wrangling over was whether the throats of the foreigners should be cut or not. I tell you, all politics have been tame to me since then. If you lived in a treaty port, you were bound to wake up and take an interest in them. And to make it better, the outsider had no way of knowing how the game was going. If the opposition won it would not be a newspaper paragraph that would tell him of it, but a good old Tory in a suit of chain mail, with a sword in each hand, would drop in and let him know all about it in a single upper cut.

"Of course it makes men reckless when they are living on the edge of a volcano like that. . . . "

It was thanks to Burton that Conan Doyle could set a story in Japan in 1892 and commence it with such assurance, in contrast to the weak settings of some of his narratives of the 1880s in Australia, New Zealand and South Africa, of which he knew nothing from first hand apart from Charles Altamont Doyle's occasional reflections on his chances at picking up a fortune on the gold diggings.

Yet his official reason for living in Liberton Bank was to attend a local school which he afterwards remembered with the utmost distaste, a hatred probably exacerbated at the time by his enforced separation from his mother. He encountered "a tawse-brandishing schoolmaster of the old type . . . From the age of seven to nine I suffered under this pock-marked, one-eyed rascal who might have stepped from the pages of Dickens. In the evenings, home and books were my sole consolation, save for week-end holidays. My comrades were rough boys and I became a rough boy, too."

The school was called Newington Academy. There were two such establishments, but the more likely candidate is that conducted in Salisbury Place by Patrick Wilson. His two names appear in *"Black Peter"*, where the murderer is Patrick Cairns, and the introduction alludes to the case immediately preceding, which resulted in the "arrest of Wilson, the notorious canary-trainer, which removed a plague-spot from the East-end of London". This would argue that "canary-trainer" symbolises a murderous ruffian training delicate, talented and vulnerable charges and that "plague-spot" was prompted by "pock-marked". In fact, Wilson's establishment became a hospital for incurables in 1879, as ACD would well know from his knowledge of the Edinburgh medical world as a student at that date—it is now the Longmore Hospital. Wilson also accords with the impression of seniority in the description of the headmaster; the other candidate, one McLauchlin, was decidedly younger.

Arthur returned to live at home when the family moved to Newington, about a mile from Liberton Bank but closer to town, at 3 Sciennes Hill Place: the excuse of distance from school would no longer obtain, and there were limits to the extent to which Mary Doyle could reveal her despair about her husband, even to her closest friends. "We lived", recalled her son, "in a *cul de sac* street with a very vivid life of its own and a fierce feud between the small boys who dwelt on either side of it. Finally it was fought out between two champions, I representing the poorer boys who lived in flats and my opponent the richer boys who lived in the opposite villas. We fought in the garden of one of the said villas and had an excellent contest of many rounds, not being strong enough to weaken each other. When I got home after the battle, my mother cried, 'Oh, Arthur, what a dreadful eye you have got!' To which I replied, 'You just go across and look at Eddie Tulloch's eye!' " It was his first taste of primary source-material which would go to provide the impetus and the personal identification in *"The Croxley Master"*, *"The Lord of Falconbridge"* and *"The Bully of Brocas Court"*—and, at a greater remove of identification, the fight in *Rodney Stone*. It is also rather pleasing to realise in his reply to his mother the very earliest version we possess of a line in the Holmes saga, one from *"The Solitary Cyclist"*: Holmes returns from his researches in the country pub "with a discoloured lump upon his forehead, besides a general air of dissipation which would have made his own person the fitting object of a Scotland Yard investigation. . ." " . . . 'I emerged as you see me. Mr Woodley went home in a cart. . . . ' "

The number of children had increased, but the amount of rent that was paid was by now falling drastically and ominously. The valuation rolls reveal £19 0s. 0d. where in Picardy Place days the payment was £30 9s. 0d. There were eight flats in the house, and the neighbourhood, while respectable, was far below the New Town in status. Even more ominously, one of Charles Doyle's two fellow-clerks at his place of business, Andrew Kerr, lived close at hand in Findhorn Place. What this meant in practical terms was that Charles could no longer be relied on to remain at home when he finally returned, but would be off with his colleague to discuss "business" in some nearby hostelry. There may also have been more pressure from him that drink be maintained in the house so that his colleague could be treated should they return together. Eventually Mary decided that the need to protect Arthur demanded even greater sacrifices from her than she had yet made. She enrolled him at Hodder, the preparatory college for the Jesuit school Stonyhurst, and close beside it, both of them near Preston in Lancashire, and she made an arrangement with the Jesuits—who faithfully kept her part in it from Arthur—that to protect him from his father he would return home only in Summer each year and that throughout his time there he would never join his family for Christmas or Easter vacations. He entered Hodder in 1868, and his next Christmas at home was in 1876. It was also Charles Doyle's last Christmas in salaried employment.

3

THE HERO AS JESUIT

He had the faith in him that moves mountains. Ten thousand souls won for God in a single month! That is a true conqueror, true to the motto of our order: ad majorem Dei gloriam: A saint who has great power in heaven, remember; power to intercede for us in our grief, power to obtain whatever we pray for if it be for the good of our souls, power above all to obtain for us the grace to repent if we be in sin. A great saint, Saint Francis Xavier! A great fisher of souls!
—James Joyce,
A Portrait of the Artist as a Young Man

Eddie Tulloch was the real name of the boy with the black eye: Conan Doyle was ready enough with pseudonyms in autobiographical narration, but a great fight like that, even more so at the distance of sixty years, demands identity on both sides. Physically, the incident was an inspirational precursor for the great fisticuffs in his writing; spiritually, it was rather more akin to the combat of Sir Nigel and Bertrand du Guesclin in *The White Company*, especially with that, too, being a draw, and it or its like was evidently in the mind of its creator when thinking of Eddie Tulloch, given his use of the word "champion". But what cause was he defending? That of the poorer against the richer in Newington is fair enough; also the defence of place, for the sides of the street were enfortressed with their separate names. Arthur fought for Sciennes Hill Place and its allies, Eddie Tulloch for Sciennes Grove. But there was more in it than class, economics or geography. Eddie Tulloch was the son of the local Baptist minister.

Conan Doyle said nothing of religion as a cause of the controversy; after he left the Catholic Church he regarded with particular disgust those ready to posture as its well-paid champions while secretly despising its cherished beliefs. He was in his rebellion against Catholicism something of a Cordelia in honourable reproof to the King Lear that the Roman Catholic Church so frequently seems to resemble. He repudiated with absolute horror any question of letters of introduction to the nucleus of Catholics who could have formed so satisfactory a foundation for a medical practice during his early days in Portsmouth. To the end of his life he sought to speak to the Catholic Church with a candour which showed a far greater love for it (without belief in it) than did the Gonerils and Regans who defended its excesses with an external zeal only matched by an internal indifference. In referring to Catholicism privately, Conan Doyle softly and affectionately alluded to it as "the old faith". But he was not prepared to give himself airs for his championship at the age of nine in the cause of beliefs he had abandoned by nineteen. Hence Eddie's name and approximation of address is all we learn from Conan Doyle's narrative. The rest emerges from city records.

The Rev. William Tulloch had risen fairly rapidly in the ranks of the Edinburgh Baptist church. He had emerged from small obscurity to the cure of the Tabernacle, on Leith Walk, by the mid-1850s, and from that frontier between port district and fashionable quarter had moved to the presumably quieter residential conventicle in Duncan Street. The strict abstinence from alcohol of the Baptists was in marked contrast to the self-indulgence of the Roman Catholics, and it may very well have been that a personal element entered into the conflict of the younger Tulloch and the younger Doyle, the Reverend William being the leader of teetotal sentiment in the neighbourhood, and the disreputable Charles Altamont probably being an all too well-known example of its converse. Schoolboy jeering can be very ugly; small neighbourhoods have little difficulty in identifying and disseminating the identity of late-night roisterers polluting their exemplary environment. Arthur noted in his memoirs the hard-drinking and kindly Scottish society which led his father astray, but neither its habits nor its charity would have had much in common with the Baptists of Newington. Apart from any other consideration, the old Calvinist notions of visible signs of salvation would survive in the contrast between the well-kept, prosperous house, respectable appearance and thrifty habits as contrasted with the families thrown on top of one another in large, decaying apartment-houses, with no sign of divine approval in their socio-economic circumstances. The Tulloch fortunes, to judge from the steady rise in the value of the property inhabited by the family, waxed as noticeably over the years as those of the Doyles waned. Yet after all it was of little good to the Tullochs, apart from the gratifying feelings of satisfaction it may have induced, for within another five years the Rev. William had retired from the ministry and his disappearance from the records some years after that suggests that his very promising career was cut so short by illness leading to early death. Eddie either emigrated from Edinburgh or died young or won little personal success, as the city directories have no reference to him in the lists of professionals and householders in the years to come, and the irony remains that he has only reached the attention of posterity because his eye was blacked by that wee Papish blackguard, Artie Doyle.

So Arthur had known, the hard way, what it was to be a member of a church in hostile surroundings. No doubt Charles Doyle, with his hostility to Scottish sanctimoniousness and his fears of Scottish bigotry (which he would later blame for his incarceration in a mental institution), left his family lively enough to the likelihood of Protestant discrimination or insult, and no doubt also they learned readily enough of the Protestant-Catholic brawls that took place in lower but not distant quarters of the city. The world Arthur encountered in Hodder and Stonyhurst was also highly conscious of being God's true church only just emerging from persecution at the hands of heretics and schismatics. But it was a more confident society. There were now Catholic bishops and sees in England whereas Scotland would still have Vicars-General and districts until 1878. The northern kingdom was taken to be without peer in its hatred of Rome.

Despite the respectability of Arthur's grandfather and uncles, without question the foremost family practitioners of the pencil in the English-speaking world, the boy's pointedly Irish name and immediate Irish ancestry were no passports to civility in the Britain of his day. He reached Hodder in 1868, and the weeping, little boy on his first solitary journey was discovering an England which may have been even more suspicious of his ethnic group than was the Scottish Protestantism he had left. Only a year previously the Fenian leader Colonel Thomas Kelly and his mate Deasy were rescued from a prison van at Manchester in the very shire to which the boy was now bound, and on November 23 Allen, Larkin and O'Brien were hanged for the death of the police-sergeant, Charles Brett, who was shot by the pistol-bullet intended to smash the lock of the van. Thereafter they were known to Irish nationalists as martyrs, and to English nationalists as murderers, and emotionalist discussion of the issue made nationalists of many moderates on both sides. It was the first execution of Irish nationalists in the United Kingdom since Robert Emmet in 1803, and the first time in history that Irish nationalists were put to death for actions committed on British soil. On December 13 a Fenian rescue attempt killed twelve people and wounded 120 in an explosion at Clerkenwell prison. On 15 January 1868 Fenians were arrested in Glasgow following an affray on the Green involving firearms. The whole south Lancashire area was a Fenian breeding-ground at this time, Liverpool being so active as to justify the police retention of the services of the leading professional informer of the day, the eminent Corydon, whose services in testimony against his former associates were hourly at the disposal of the police in consideration of their non-prosecution of him for the continued pursuit of love with such members of his own sex as attracted his aesthetic judgment.

Arthur can only have known a little of this, though Eddie Tulloch and other kindred spirits may have sought to enter into rather fuller discussion of the merits of the Manchester rescue with him. But it is likely that the beleaguered English, as opposed to the comparatively immune Scots (give or take the occasional rifle-flourish on Glasgow Green), would have looked with unusual reserve at the little stranger in their midst—a dark foreigner in more senses than the cognominal. In spite, and because, of the identification of Catholic so often with Irish, the English boys at Hodder and Stonyhurst would have been peculiarly sensitive to suspicions of Fenianism among their Irish-born, Irish-descended and Irish-surnamed schoolfellows. We cannot guess whether Arthur carried within him any personal opinions about the Fenians, whether the unexpectedly wide chorus of sympathy for the executed trio at Manchester resurrected some long-vanished strains of Hibernian self-identification from Charles Altamont Doyle's repertoire of ballads, if any, or reminded Mary Foley Doyle that her enthusiasm for chivalry owed something to the land which had borne both herself and Messrs Allen, Larkin and O'Brien, two of whom embraced on the scaffold and who were associated with the cry from the dock "God save Ireland!" (Mr Larkin does not appear in so heroic a light, having wept and cried a lot and taken an unconscionable time in dying, but then Mr Larkin was probably quite innocent, even of involvement in the rescue which cost Brett his life.) All we do know is that Arthur Conan Doyle's early writing is tinged with some affection for the Fenians, less in derring-do as in vestiges of their humanity despite their murderous reputation. In particular, his first really successful short story by his own and everyone else's judgment, *"That Little Square Box"*, written when he was just over 21 and retained in print throughout his life, is a savage satire on scaremongering about Fenianism.

Arthur's exposure to hostility to persons of Irish surnames because of the proximity of Fenian outrages—and the fears induced by an Irish name are critical to *"That Little Square Box"*—seems most likely in the years after Manchester and Clerkenwell. It seems very likely something did happen to him, whether mobbing in Edinburgh or hostility in England, because of an Irish name and perhaps a slow tongue in condemning the Fenians. All of Conan Doyle's best and most enduring work in his early years is based on some personal experience: *"The Captain of the 'Pole-Star' "* on his Arctic voyage; *"J. Habakuk Jephson's Statement"* on his meeting with the United States Minister to Liberia. Even his movement more directly into the world of imagination shows deep dependence on outside influences until he reached his thirtieth year: *A Study in Scarlet* would scarcely exist without Poe, Gaboriau and the Stevensons; *Micah Clarke* is homage to Macaulay, and Scott, very worthy homage too, but homage nonetheless. *"That Little Square Box"*, the very first indication of the mastery of the short story which he would reach, is not easy to accept as *sui generis*.

And the self-dissection of the narrator, deliberately, if largely unconsciously, portraying himself in colours as contemptible as Conan Doyle would ever use for a narrator, implies some bitterness in the episode which gave rise to it. The delay between the episode itself (presumably from the early 1870s) and its use in 1881 means nothing, apart from the maturing of the writer: some forty years elapsed between the invention of a contrivance in the unpublished *"Haunted Grange of Goresthorpe"* and its appearance in much more sophisticated form in *"The Bully of Brocas Court"*, and the autobiographical element in *The Lost World* is 35 years old.

But if Arthur encountered hostility to his name in England, even at Hodder and Stonyhurst, they and himself were necessarily both conditioned by the English hostility to Catholicism. Again, his first years in England were not a time of good Protestant-Catholic relations, what with the Protestant love of Garibaldi; the erosion of hope for the survival of the age-old Papal Rome; the first Vatican Council and the peculiar circumstances of asserting Papal infallibility; the withdrawal of Napoleon III's troops and the fall of the

Eternal City; the Papal self-immolation as Prisoner of the Vatican and the declaration of a siege mentality for the entire Church. Hodder and Stonyhurst have to be seen not so much as a public school training little English élitists as a dual fortress arming its children to withstand those élitists' enmity. It encapsulated several worlds within itself—Catholic boys from Europe and the Americas, British boys of Irish origin, scions of ancient Catholic recusant houses whose ancestors had been displaced by contemptible *arrivistes*, children of zealous and God-haunted converts, future wielders of power in a world where almost all anti-Catholic political barriers had fallen, future victims of discrimination in a world where almost all anti-Catholic social barriers were still standing. And the Jesuits themselves had much in common with their charges too, yet they differed deeply, and from the point of view of Conan Doyle's biographer, disastrously, from one another.

The first sight of Hodder preparatory school and the lovely country of witch-haunted Pendle may have been alien to Arthur, but how clean and open it must have seemed in contrast to the dark and grim Sciennes Hill Place, where after nightfall little light intruded save that accompanying the busybody's enquiries on the shortcomings of her neighbours. Baker Street is about three or four times as wide as Sciennes Hill Place; Holmes and Watson would have looked across the street into their old rooms from *"The Empty House"* with much greater difficulty than Eddie Tulloch and Co. could examine the interior of the Doyle residence with sundry deductions about the condition of the head of household. The memory of Sciennes Hill Place may well have given Conan Doyle the idea of silent watchers, of unobtrusive entries, of missiles hurled across streets on dark nights (certainly the antics of Colonel Sebastian Moran would seem to argue for a street with fewer likely passers-by than Baker Street, and a *cul-de-sac* is the one really reliable street for absence of pedestrian traffic). But the open country air of Lancashire, and the surroundings in which no rival small boys jeered at his family history, must have been a welcome change from the darkest corner of Newington. The new Catholic fortress was securer than the old.

But if Hodder and Stonyhurst left Arthur feeling less of an outsider on religious grounds, they were likely to induce alienation on a different ground. Arthur had never known the experience of widespread Catholicism in the upper and middle classes. Lancashire, throughout its history, had led the English shires in its fidelity to the old faith, and many of the richest families in the neighbourhood of Stonyhurst had been conspicuous among its members. Ireland, with its Catholic majority, had been savagely subjected to legislation leading to the forfeiture of land in Catholic hands, leaving Catholics by 1800 in possession of about 70% of the island's landowning total. Arthur, brought up to believe that his ancestors had been deprived of their place among the landed gentry because of their religious fidelity, now saw all around him the scions of Lancashire landed gentry whose Catholicism had had no such effect. At the point when the penal laws began to bite against Arthur's ancestors, in 1715, Lancashire Catholics owned 35% of the land. In 1870 the leaders of Lancashire Catholicism were rich by any normal standards: Professor John Bossy, the great modern historian of English Catholicism (and brother of the present Headmaster of Stonyhurst), notes that the Weld-Blundell fortune at that date was £36,000, the Clifton and Gerard wealth £40,000 each, the Scarisbrick brothers £30,000 each. Their association with the school was intimate in the extreme. The Welds had given it to the Jesuits, who had maintained a long connection with Lancashire even through the time of their suppression, and who had commenced the school by 1817. Father C. C. Martindale's biography of the famous preacher, Father Bernard Vaughan, who was a pupil at the school in the early 1860s and a novice on the teaching staff during Conan Doyle's time, remarks that it "was full of boys who were some sort of cousin to one another—Maxwells, Vavasours, Welds, Weld-Blundells, Cliffords, Tempests, Vaughans, Stourtons, de Traffords, and on Sundays, it was the custom for relatives to walk together" whence Vaughan and his relatives formed "a great clan, who patrolled the playground in a mass". There is no suggestion in any surviving account of the school, Conan Doyle's included, that the Jesuits showed any favouritism. But it would be hard for the lad from Edinburgh not to feel estranged when his own contemporaries among that formidable clan paraded in their proud patrol.

It was his first conspicuous exposure to the aristocracy and gentry, and it cannot be dismissed as one origin of the markedly critical sentiment on the subject of aristocracy which again and again appears in his work. As his mother's son he expresses fondness for old families, such as that of Nigel Loring in thirteenth-century England, but that is associated from the start of *Sir Nigel* with extreme poverty. Straitened times for aristrocrats who rescue themselves by financially advantageous marriages, a frequent feature of the last quarter of the nineteenth century, invite a gentle but nonetheless well-aimed ridicule in *"The Noble Bachelor"*, and the insufferable arrogance of the upper classes at their worst is coldly revealed and dissected by him again and again—notable in *"The Noble Bachelor"*, *"The Musgrave Ritual"*, *"The Priory School"* and even *"The Speckled Band"* in which Dr Grimesby Roylott's ancient lineage is clearly felt to account in part for his imperviousness either to the normal civilities or to the law of the land: his snobbery towards Holmes, and Holmes's anger at it, are particularly suggestive. Time and again the pretentious snobberies receive deflation at Holmes's hands: take the deduction opening *"The Noble Bachelor"* ("It is dated from Grosvenor Mansions, written with a quill pen, and the noble lord has had the misfortune to get a smear of ink upon the outer side of his right little finger") or the early dialogue with Lord Robert St Simon ("I understand that you have already managed several delicate cases of this sort, sir, though I presume that they were hardly from the same class of society." "No, I am descending." "I beg pardon?" "My last client of the sort was a king." "Oh, really! I had no idea. And which king?" "The King of Scandinavia." "What! Had he lost his wife?" "You can understand", said Holmes suavely, "that I extend to the affairs of my other clients the same secrecy which I promise to you in yours."). We have already noted the unfavourable contrast drawn between the intellect of ten generations of Musgraves and that of the butler dismissed by the latest of them. *"The Priory School"* is particularly famous for Holmes's rating of the "proud lord of Holdernesse . . . in his own ducal hall", on inexorable moral grounds.

From what we know of the Jesuits at Stonyhurst in Conan Doyle's day, they may have contributed to this facet of Holmes, in particular to his status as moral judge. When a disciplinary question was involved, lineage and wealth counted nothing with them, and the sardonic deflation of pretension we know to have been part of the stock-in-trade of the Prefect of Discipline at Stonyhurst, Father Thomas Kay, possesses something of the Holmes manner, although, as we shall see, Father Kay had even more in common with another famous creation of his pupil. Certainly the role of the priest as supreme on moral questions seems echoed both in that conversation with the Duke of Holdernesse ("To humour your guilty elder son you have exposed your innocent younger son to imminent and unnecessary danger. It was a most unjustifiable action"), and the equally famous demolition of the millionaire Neil Gibson in *"Thor Bridge"* ("Some of you rich men have to be taught that all the world cannot be bribed into condoning your offences."). In the Holdernesse case, so might have spoken a Stonyhurst Jesuit in confronting an aristocratic parent who had favoured an elder against a younger son in circumstances that justified clerical intervention; if it might seem improbable that Conan Doyle would know about it, we must remember that even with the great care about security, open windows and raised voices could make a story travel (and improve itself) in a small community. As for Senator J. Neil Gibson, the origin of his discomfiture, if Jesuit, might be not Stonyhurst, but a Stonyhurst man: Conan Doyle in *Memories and Adventures* recalled the "young novice, . . . whose handsome and spiritual appearance I well remember . . . Bernard Vaughan, afterwards the famous preacher". Holmes's attack on Gibson would have fitted very well into the great "Sins of Society" sermons preached by Vaughan to the well-to-do Edwardians.

The youthful Catholic gentry may have invited resentment on other grounds. Conan Doyle acknowledges his problems in fitting in with Stonyhurst discipline, and here it may be that the contrast between the tough young Scots boy and the elegant English recusants may have expressed itself in his resentment of the rituals which were second nature to them. Hodder and Stonyhurst were particularly conscious of their traditions, and to the descendants of the families who had first endowed them, these traditions would virtually have seemed family property. They had their own logic, just as the Musgrave ritual was to have, albeit to the outsider that logic might seem as impossible of discovery as the Musgrave ritual's. The Jesuits had their little ways, mastery of whose formulae could be a passort to good things. In Conan Doyle's time a small boy finding himself doing some additional service was advised by Bernard Vaughan that he might get the special tea, called the "good five o'clock", if he mentioned the service to the Rector, Father Purbrick, and then, prophesied Vaughan, Purbrick would say that the duty was its own reward, and the boy was to say that the labour would reward his soul, but Father Purbrick should reward his body, and so it fell out and the boy received temporal as well as spiritual gratification. But that sort of thing annoyed Arthur Conan Doyle: conformity at Stonyhurst irritated him, little ways to get advantages were never acceptable to him, and tips from the old families underlined the privileged position they asserted so pointedly. His attitude was closer to the young Nigel Loring, or to Hordle John in *The White Company*, with their tumultuous defiance of the easy way out of trouble. "I went out of my way to do really mischievous and outrageous things simply to show that my spirit was unbroken." ("The charges against the said brother John are . . . Item, that having been told by the master of the novices that he should restrict his food for two days to a single three-pound loaf of bran and beans, for the greater honouring and glorifying of St Monica, mother of the holy Augustine, he was heard by brother Ambrose and others to say that he wished twenty thousand devils would fly away with the said Monica, mother of the holy Augustine, or any other saint who came between a man and his meat.")

Yet the heart of the story of Conan Doyle's alienation at Stonyhurst lies not in a pattern of hostility, but in the inception of his school experience in joy, gratitude and love. He began not at Stonyhurst but at Hodder, and the two years he spent there may well have been the happiest so far in his life. His subsequent sorrows at Stonyhurst seem the product in part of having loved Hodder so well. For it was there that Arthur met the second hero to worship in his young life, and some part of the loss he sustained in parting from his mother was offset by the Rev. Francis Cassidy.

Hodder has been abandoned now, and hides its decaying walls, crazy doors and dark and cobwebbed interiors in the woods some distance away from the great house at Stonyhurst. It was still in use a century after Conan Doyle was there, but already the wilderness has reclaimed its own to such an extent that it is hard to see remnants of the vitality and happiness which characterised it. Stonyhurst itself won varying reactions among its former pupils, as do most boarding-schools, but while they viewed it from standpoints anywhere from the proprietorial to the alienated, Stonyhurst boys, like others of their age, would have recoiled with horror from anything that savoured of soppiness in their view of their institution. No person of mature years professes the objectivity associated with maturity nearly as earnestly as those on its threshold. Conan Doyle's disciple P. G. Wodehouse wrote in his *Mike* in 1908: "The average public-school boy *likes* his school. He hopes it will lick Bedford at Rugger and Malvern at cricket, but he rather bets it won't. He is sorry to leave, and he likes going back at the end of the holidays, but as for any passionate, deep-seated love of the place, he would think it rather bad form than otherwise. If anybody came up to him, slapped him on the back, and cried, 'Come along, Jenkins, my boy! Play up for the old school, Jenkins! The dear old school! The old place you love so!' he would feel seriously ill." This gives us a little perspective, in that it is not particularly removed from either the Bernard Vaughans or the Conan Doyles. But Hodder was different. No shame was attached to loving the first landfall from home; no sensible adult would think the worse of himself for having so loved it when he was so young. Hodder always seems to have had an understanding of the root of play in any approach to infant work: certainly it did so at either end of the century that begins with Conan Doyle's presence there and ends with its closure. And however much its pupils loved it, none did so more deeply than Arthur Conan Doyle. The Stonyhurst records themselves confirm that he found there the greatest figure of Hodder's existence in Francis Cassidy.

Francis Cassidy would return to Hodder in 1884 as priest and Superior and remain there for forty years: when Conan Doyle arrived he was still a youthful scholastic, and left Hodder the year after Arthur did, to complete his preparation for ordination. He may have paid special attention to Arthur, for the Jesuits knew he must be kept there throughout the year apart from Summer, and characteristically harder on themselves than on others (a quality their pupil always acknowledged), they ensured he would believe the ordinance was theirs and not his mother's. It was a very nice example of the Jesuitical method: one can imagine the reply to any remonstrance from Arthur, "I'm afraid, my boy, rules are rules", never indicating that the rule was Mary's, not theirs. They would have been at one with Mary in their insistence that her primacy in the boy's eyes must be protected at all costs. If their views were often very old-fashioned about the place of woman in the home, the cult of the Blessed Virgin (Bernard Vaughan prided himself on having the initials of her title) meant that they readily accepted the idea that a mother might be a far wiser, better and more reliable influence than a father, and her position in a boy's loyalties must be safeguarded at all costs. But where Francis Cassidy was so exceptional was in his capacity to translate that intellectual point into a brilliant and personal fulfilment of the emotional needs of the mother-deprived children under his care. Our evidence is that this remained true of him throughout his life, but on Conan Doyle's own showing it was present from the first. "I have always kept a warm remembrance of this man", he wrote in *Memories and Adventures,* "and of his gentle ways to the little boys—young rascals many of us—who were committed to his care."

It is always easy to exaggerate the personal qualities of a dearly-loved clergyman, but Cassidy really seems to have combined sanctity and affection to quite an extraordinary degree. His love of his charges became legendary. Wherever he was to go in the course of his life—and although his health was bad for most of it, he would live for some seventy years—the story was the same. Children when he was assigned to London thronged round him during catechism. All the little boys at Hodder seem to have adored him. "He seemed to live to make others happy", wrote a colleague afterwards. He loved to discover the potential of the young students and whet them into action, especially if their talents lay on the side of creative writing. "He", it was said by a Hodder fellow-priest, "could lead them on to success in their studies, and could tell them stories of adventure more wonderful than any they read in books." Conan Doyle agreed. "How well I can remember the stories which you used to read to us", he wrote Father Cassidy many years later, "and which I used to suck in as a sponge absorbs water until I was so saturated with them that I could still repeat them." Cassidy also encouraged Arthur's infant attempts at poetry, as his old pupil recalled in sending him a copy of *Songs of Action*, his first book of verse published in 1898. It was, he grinned, "a little more mature" than his early efforts but Cassidy should not "acknowledge it. You might find yourself in the dilemma which I was in lately when a young author sent me a volume of poems and essays (both very bad) with a direct request for my opinion of its merits. I told him in reply that 'He was equally at home in prose and in verse'." It would appear that the Jesuits in general, if not Father Cassidy in particular, had at least transmitted to their errant pupil the rudiments of that form of diplomacy traditionally ascribed to them.

Even the infant Arthur may have observed something which his later reflections as a doctor would confirm: the charismatic and eternally warm-hearted teacher was in fact fighting very unpleasant medical problems. Cassidy was not yet 25 when Conan Doyle came to Hodder—he had been born in London in 1845—yet even then he was a prey to blood-spitting and constant weakness which would ultimately force him out of the Rectorship of the Jesuits' other great English public school, Beaumont, in 1884, after seven years. (So early a promotion conveys something of the estimate entertained of him by his superiors.) It sounds tubercular, although its development seems to have been arrested. At all events, it may have had the advantage of bringing him back to the work which was his true calling. It was tragic that the pre-ordination requirements took him away from Hodder in 1871, when Arthur was up the road at Stonyhurst, so that the lonely young Scot could not wander back to his old Mentor in moments of emotional despondency or religious doubt. The hunger for love in Conan Doyle remained unfulfilled thereafter in all his years at Stonyhurst. But it is clear that his affection for Father Cassidy lasted until the end. When the headlines announced in 1909 that Conan Doyle was virtually at death's door, Father Cassidy sent his love and prayers, no doubt saying Mass for his old pupil, and before the month was out the slowly recovering patient was writing from his bed to thank him.

Mary Foley Doyle's capacity for entertaining her son with marvellous stories and drawing him into narration was followed in the latter by Cassidy. A curious reference in Conan Doyle's memoirs immediately following his tribute to Cassidy may give us a clue to one form this encouragement in story telling took. "I remember the Franco-German war breaking out at this period", he remarked, "and how it made a ripple even in our secluded backwater." It may be that the seeming *non sequitur* indicates that Cassidy invited the boys, particularly Arthur, to make up stories about the war, or discussed its progress with his customary vigour and capacity for fascination. We can have little doubt about the sides that would have been taken: whatever the Catholic misgivings about Napoleon III he had guarded the remnant of the Papal state in Rome against the armies of Victor Emmanuel I of Italy, whereas Prussia was the Protestant military state *par excellence*. Much might be expected to be made of the cruelty of the Prussians towards the demoralised and shattered French population, whose Catholic families supplied Stonyhurst with a few of its pupils and whose Catholic history included the eighteenth-century parent-house of Stonyhurst at St Omers. The siege of Paris would be less likely to be the object of attention—given the anti-clerical and communard features of its resistance—than the countryside where Catholicism survived in greater strength. At all events Conan Doyle, in 1894, would publish one of the very greatest pieces of historical fiction he ever wrote, *"The Lord of Chateau Noir"*, a dark, symbolic narrative of ancient aristocratic leadership of guerrilla activity against the Germans. Professor W. W. Robson of Edinburgh University has remarked how exceptionally biblical the narrative seems, with its itemised insistence on symbolic reparation for wrong after wrong, and—even more eerily—kindness after kindness. There may be something of Stonyhurst itself (Hodder would be too small) in the great building occupied by the German colonel whose eating and sleeping are watched from hidden passages by the eyes of his enemies until the time comes to strike. The newcomer to Stonyhurst, in particular, has the sense that the place has a thousand invisible windings and turnings, and the rush of boys' feet after silence might prompt the thoughts of a hidden band of warriors suddenly declaring its presence. Arthur transferred from Hodder to Stonyhurst while the terrible war was in full swing: indeed as its outbreak, in July 1870, seems to be associated in his mind with Father Cassidy it may be that in that particular summer conditions at home had kept him at Hodder until his remove to Stonyhurst.

Conan Doyle did write one other story about the war, but that was a light-hearted description of the effects of the outbreak of war on the London Stock Exchange—the *pièce de résistance* being a telegram reading "I am a bear of everything German and French. Sell, sell, sell, keep on selling" arising out of a horse-auction in rural Ireland. The author did not think too highly of this work, *"A Shadow Before"*, reprinting it in *The Green Flag* but dropping it from his later collections. It probably owed something to reminiscence by an Irish schoolmate returning to Stonyhurst in the autumn of 1870 with memories of the curious Hibernian consequences of war preparations; children of Irish landed families might be expected to know something of the change in the horse-dealing world caused by international crisis. It is a good story, but not to be compared with *"The Lord of Chateau Noir"*. If Cassidy inspired the latter he planted his young charge's feet on Parnassus.

But it is clear that even if his impact were more indirect, his place in the evolution of Conan Doyle as a literary artist is supreme. Apart from his direct influence on the story-telling, Cassidy implemented with outstanding effectiveness the Jesuit educational principle "What is written on the brain is far more important than what is written in an exercise-book". Memory-work was introduced to the boys as something delightful in itself, and hence something followed both within and without the formal limits of education. Arthur developed a prodigious memory, much as James Joyce of Belvedere, the Jesuits' Dublin college, would do in the next generation. Occasionally that admirable memory played him false. Throughout the 1880s his work was much more derivative than he realised, phrases and sentences reproducing themselves from inspirational sources where he intended his creative powers to be at full flow. Sometimes his passion for quotation transformed his characters: *A Study in Scarlet* shows that he had intended Holmes to be the scientific ignoramus with "Knowledge of Literature—Nil", but by *The Sign of Four* Holmes is off on his career as perhaps the least pretentious but most apposite master of the appropriate quotation, among the great detectives. Inevitably Conan Doyle's own ease in recollection led him, with his natural humility, to assume a far wider range of literary reference on the part of his readers. Clearly most of them were expected to know that Watson's farewell words to Holmes at the end of *"The Final Problem"* are the last words of Plato's *Phaedo,* on the death of Socrates, and in several other instances what might now seem plagiarism was the author's assumption of common literary heritage. We cannot give the Jesuits the primary credit for that marvellous memory; here again Mary Foley Doyle seems to have anticipated them. If Dickson Carr has read Charles Doyle's letters aright (which with his fictionalised conversations is uncertain), Arthur's mother weaned his memory on such demanding mnemonics as heraldry could supply. We can allow for some inheritance, art in the blood again taking its strange forms, for John Doyle could never have charted the course of English political development among its *dramatis personae* without a prodigious and most carefully trained memory for facial and physical details. But the Jesuits brought the matter as near to an exact science as education offered at the time, and the art of Francis Cassidy commenced the work with individual genius. It was Arthur's long literary apprenticeship which would finally enable him to unmask memory from its disguise as imagination.

Stonyhurst tradition supplied many points of origin for the Holmes saga in the personalities of individual Jesuit teachers. Probably more was read into them than the author had consciously inserted, although details doubtless added themselves unconsciously. With the exception of Father Kay, it is hard to be accurate in any ascriptions of such details to their vanished originals. But in the case of Father Cassidy, there seems one clear identification outside of the Holmes stories. The book is *The Refugees,* published in 1893, a tale of the Huguenots in France and the New World before and after Louis XIV's revocation of the Edict of Nantes. It is a somewhat undervalued work, although its author was delighted when his mother on a visit to Fontainebleau heard the guide announce that the "best and most accurate account" of Louis's Court was in an "Englishman's" book, *The Refugees.* It is hard-hitting about the cruelty of the fate of the Huguenots, although deeply and passionately concerned to vindicate the character and conduct of the great Catholic influence on Louis, Madame de Maintenon. The author says in his memoirs that a Reverend Mother in an Irish convent, having taken it to be the pious work of "Canon" Doyle, did not discover the error until the reading of it in public to the sisters was concluded. The inference is simple: the book is pro-Huguenot, but Conan Doyle was very concerned to do justice to their Catholic opponents.

Unusually for Conan Doyle's historical fiction, the interest of the work lies more in the historical characters—Louis, Madame de Montespan, Madame de Maintenon—than in his hero and associated friends, and the American section is episodic and somewhat inconsequential. Largely irrelevantly to the main plot, the exiled Huguenots at one point encounter a Jesuit missionary to the Indians, Ignatius Morat, who has been scalped, deprived of his fingers and of one eye. "The other, however, shot as bright and merry and kindly a glance as ever came from a chosen favourite of fortune. His face was flecked over with peculiar brown spots which had a most hideous appearance, and his nose had been burst and shattered by some terrific blow. And yet, in spite of this dreadful appearance, there was something so noble in the carriage of the man, in the pose of his head and in the expression which still hung, like the scent from a crushed flower, round his distorted features, that even the blunt Puritan seaman was awed by it."

The hero expresses horror at "how terribly you have been mishandled":

"Ah, you have observed my little injuries, then! They know no better, poor souls. They are but children—merry-hearted but mischievous. Tut, tut, it is laughable indeed that a man's vile body should ever clog his spirit, and yet here I am full of the will to push forward, and yet I must even seat myself on this log and rest myself, for the rogues have blown the calves of my legs off."

"My God! Blown them off! The devils!"

"Ah, but they are not to be blamed. No, no, it would be uncharitable to blame them. They are ignorant, poor folk, and the prince of darkness is behind them to urge them on. They sank little charges of powder into my legs and then they exploded them, which makes me walk slower than ever, though I was never very brisk. 'The Snail' was what I was called at school in Tours, yes, and afterwards at the seminary I was always 'the Snail'."

There follows an interview with the priest, who seems amusedly aware of their religious views and who finally concludes:

". . . And now, my children, if you must go, let me first call down a blessing upon you!"

And then occurred a strange thing, for the beauty of this man's soul shone through all the wretched clouds of sect, and, as he raised his hand to bless them, down went those Protestant knees to earth, and even old Ephraim found himself with a softened heart and a bent head listening to the half-understood words of this crippled, half-blinded little stranger.

"Farewell, then", said he, when they had risen. "May the sunshine of Sainte Eulalie be upon you, and may Sainte Anne of Beaupré shield you at the moment of your danger."

And so they left him, a grotesque and yet heroic figure staggering along through the woods with his tent, his pictures and his mutilation. If the Church of Rome should ever be wrecked it may come from her weakness in high places, where all Churches are at their weakest, or it may be because with what is very narrow she tries to explain that which is very broad, but assuredly it will never be through the fault of her rank and file, for never upon earth have men and women spent themselves more lavishly and more splendidly than in her service.

We can well see why Reverend Mother should have reposed such confidence in the word of "Canon" Doyle (and her mistake was not so great after all: Canons have their title between Christian name and surname). The author of that passage had not regarded himself as a Catholic for nearly twenty years, yet it would be impossible to miss the pride in the Church whence he had sprung which it declares. In part the passage, in common with much else in the book, picks up a continued involvement in Catholicism on its author's part which survived his formal rejection of his faith. He never quite lost the tribal sense: Holmes's range of cases from highest to lowest, as recalled by Watson in *"Black Peter"* for the year 1895 go "from his famous investigation of the sudden death of Cardinal Tosca—an inquiry which was carried out by him at the express desire of His Holiness the Pope—down to his arrest of Wilson, the notorious canary-trainer, which removed a plague-spot from the East-end of London". A Protestant writer would have been far less likely to see the Pope as the supreme client. At the same time the passage gives us the grin of the schoolboy with its parallel musical imagery ranging from Tosca to canaries. And while he became ex-Catholic, non-Catholic and (in defence of spiritualism) anti-Catholic, he retained the formidable Catholic quality of being anti-clerical. Even two of the most brilliant commentators on *The White Company* and *Sir Nigel,* Mary Renault and Anthony Burgess, miss this in assuming his rude remarks about the clergy to be some form of defence of the future advent of Protestantism. In fact, the clue to those passages is anti-clericalism: they express the anger of a Catholic who thinks that his Church should be better, not that it should be abolished. His invocation of Chaucer and his brief introduction of Langland (who appears on "the old, old road" in *Sir Nigel*) are direct assertions of his place in that great tradition of English Catholic literary anti-clericalism, a casualty of English (though not of Irish) writing after the Reformation. He had gone from Catholicism, but part of him was still thrusting to fight the battles within it for its cure. He always paid it the compliment of a fair fight. In this respect his Puritan and Huguenot heroes, Micah Clarke and the refugees, never won his identification in the same way. He viewed them as the persecuted, in part with the schoolboy satisfaction of cheering for the objects of official Catholic disapproval. Joyce, in similar fashion, made a hero of another victim of Catholic bigotry, Giordano Bruno of Nola. But Micah and the Huguenots were primarily intended as reproaches to Catholic bigotry, and to a Catholic form of history which downgraded their courage and sufferings. Hence in the end Conan Doyle does violence to their reality, as he never can to his Catholic subjects. Micah is obliged to tell his grandchildren how deeply he applauds the principle of freedom of religion now established, which is far from what might reasonably be expected from the son of an Ironside, himself the nearest miss of Judge Jeffreys's Bloody Assizes; and the Huguenots, in the passage just quoted, are similarly endowed with sentiments of ecumenism which have work to do in the cause of their author rather than in that of themselves.

As to the touching picture of Ignatius Morat, the source would certainly be from Francis Parkman's histories, to which Conan Doyle so warmly expressed his obligation; but in crediting Cassidy with the personal inspiration, certain individual touches suggest themselves. Morat is presented not only as holy but happy, genuinely triumphing over hideous physical afflictions. Cassidy's ailments were not of human origin, but all we know of him suggests that when his pupils did get brief sight of them, such as the blood-spitting, they were similarly dismissed by him. Conan Doyle, matured from infant schoolboy to doctor of medicine, could build on what he had deduced and heard to realise how bad the health of his beloved Mentor was. The image of the Indian as child is much abused nowadays, though it forms a pleasing contrast to the ravening savage as depicted in the mass of wild west literature, and in their exposure to the horrors of European invasion the Indians were children. I suggest that what happened here is that Conan Doyle inverted a passage where he heard Cassidy defend the children under his care, pitchforked as they were into an unfamiliar new world. There may have been some rough-house when Cassidy's young charges got involved in horse-play with him and, as children do, assumed an adult capable of sustaining assault from any number of infants; and the teacher collapsed. Authority intervened—Cassidy was form-master, not then headmaster, in Hodder—and the pupils were condemned as savages, and the teacher, as soon as he could speak, indignantly defended them as lovable children not knowing their own strength or the effects of their combined brutality. Conan Doyle's fleeting reference, "his gentle ways to the little boys—young rascals many of us were", gives a hint in support of some such thesis. One could see, too, the self-mockery as contrivance of an ill man to keep within control schoolboys on a walk with whose desire to stretch their legs he found hard to cope. But the real point which to me makes the origin of the incident inescapably his experience of Cassidy is the extraordinary love burning through the whole thing. Ignatius Morat has no more to do with the main plot than the sun or the moon, yet it is more vital than any other emotion in the book that the reader should admire and revere Ignatius Morat. Clearly the interest in the Jesuit martyrs would have been well instilled at school, by Cassidy, in all probability, among others. Any Jesuit boy emerges from Jesuit education well-grounded in the high points of the heroic history of the Jesuits. And boys latch on to bloody stories, gruesome martyrdoms always being popular even in the most irreverent class. But it is not the martyrdom which is Conan Doyle's preoccupation; it is the man. And by the use of his recollection of the one Jesuit he ever loved he pays exactly the tribute that Jesuit would most have wished, to be made a means of celebrating the nobility of one of his great predecessors.

"Your letter is the first word of any kind which has ever reached me from any old teacher or associate in Stonyhurst", wrote Conan Doyle gloomily to Father Cassidy, probably in response to his old teacher's congratulations on his knighthood in 1902. "It may very probably have been my own fault but I was never fortunate enough to make any friend except yourself during seven years at Stonyhurst, and I look back on no portion of my education there with any pleasure save only my two years with you in Hodder. If ever I should find myself in the north I should like above all things to see you again and to spend a day or two at Hodder." Now, this is not strictly accurate, nor was it intended to be so regarded. Arthur was not close to the future cartoonist Bernard Partridge who was a fellow-pupil at Stonyhurst, but they were close enough for him to give Partridge verses and parodies "on college personalities and happenings", as Partridge afterwards phrased it to Hesketh Pearson. More to the point, although neither of them said so, Conan Doyle, not Partridge, was known as the artist among his fellows with a gift for caricature: Partridge came late to his ultimate vocation, but when he did take his place as *Punch's* leading cartoonist he must have recalled having seen the work of the grandson and nephew of his great predecessors in the art. Both Partridge and Conan Doyle subsequently recalled one another as quiet and gentle, Partridge remembering Arthur's "curious furtive smile when he was visited with one of the school penalties, such as leaving his desk and kneeling in the middle of the classroom with his books." But they did have some close acquaintance in the early '90's, when both were associated with Jerome K. Jerome's magazine the *Idler*.

Conan Doyle is more memorably associated with the *Strand*, but it was the *Idler's* staff who won his social companionship, especially in the organisation of cricket fixtures. It was a good way for him to get over the embarrassment of obviously taking a younger writer under his wing, and Conan Doyle was enormously sensitive to what might embarrass less fortunately circumstanced writers. Young Wodehouse was one of his protégés via the *Idler* team and its successors. So Partridge saw something of him there. In any case, it was from Stonyhurst that he acquired his life-long devotion to cricket, which strangely enough only found literary expression in the last year of his life, in "*The Story of Spedegue's Dropper*", one of the funniest, tensest and most improbable cricket stories ever written, and a triumphant proof that his devotion to the game could in no way curtail his capacity for mordant satire of its high priests. For cricket at Stonyhurst was unique, even as Spedegue's form of bowling was unique. Not content with the normal season, the school engaged in its own variety of the game in March and April. "Stonyhurst cricket", as distinct from the orthodox variety played in summer and termed by the boys "London cricket", involved a single wicket, a club-shaped bat and a hard sheepskin ball. Herbert Thurston, who wrote it up for *The Times* of 12 September 1937, thought it possessed features of the game as played in the days of Elizabeth, and believed it was handed down from the parent Jesuit seminary at St Omers. This should have appealed to Arthur's rapidly developing fascination with history, and stimulated the enthusiasm for social history which was to dominate his historical novels. Certainly "London cricket" preserved his ties with the old school, despite his abandonment of its religion. In 1885 he went with an Old Stonyhurst cricket team to Dublin, combining it with an August honeymoon, and contributed a fine set of doggerel verses on the tour to the *Stonyhurst Magazine:* "The Wanderers' Irish Tour" (to the tune of "The Cork Leg").

> *My Stonyhurst lads, just listen awhile,*
> *And I'll sing you a song in right musical style,*
> *A song that will raise on your faces a smile,*

Concerning our trip to the Emerald Isles.
  Ri-tooral-rooral, etc.
    . . .
A finer team than then went o'er
Was never seen in the world before,
For we had eleven men and more
Who unless they got out might be reckoned to score.
    . . .
Oh, how can I tell of what fell to their lot,
Of the balls that they hit, and the balls they did not,
How the batsmen were cool and the bowlers were hot,
And the fielders were—well, goodness only knows what.
    . . .
The Phoenix came out with their heads in the air,
The Phoenix went back in a state of despair,
For Henry's performance it made them all stare,
And we won by an innings and fifty to spare.
    . . .
And Trinity, oh, but we walloped them well,
To George and the Doctor the honours there fell,
And Hatt's fast expresses dismissed them pell-mell,
And the heat was as great as in—Coromandel.
    . . .
In conclusion the Leinster their colours have struck,
Where the present composer compiled a round "duck".
There we fought against audience and players and luck,
And pulled off the match by sheer coolness and pluck.
    . . .
So fill up a bumper to one and to all,
Who handled the willow, the gloves and the ball,
May cricketers ever their prowess recall,
And may Stonyhurst flourish whatever befall.
    . . .
They may change the old College in whole or in part,
They may add a new wing, and a frontage so smart,
But in spite of all labours and science and art,
The place of the past is the place of my heart.
    . . .
And I just may remark at the end of my song
That the practical test is the best, and as long
As they turn out a breed as loyal and strong
As the boys of the past—they won't do very wrong.
  Ri-tooral.

"The Doctor", of course, was himself; resplendent with his brand-new doctorate awarded for his thesis the previous month by Edinburgh, he proudly signed his effusion "M.D." It is not his first essay in verse—Stonyhurst had seen many of those from him—and it is 'prentice in the extreme compared to the well-turned work he produced later—but it does in the "Phoenix" verse anticipate one of his very best battle poems, "*Cremona*", in which the heroics and mock-heroics are equally blended. Oddly enough, it commemorates an Irish victory:

The Grenadiers of Austria are proper men and tall;
The Grenadiers of Austria have scaled the city wall;
* They have marched from far away*
* Ere the dawning of the day*
And the morning saw them masters of Cremona . . .

Time and time they came with the deep-mouthed German roar,
Time and time they broke like the wave upon the shore;
* For better men were there*
* From Limerick and Clare,*
And who will take the gateway of Cremona?

Prince Eugène has watched, and he gnaws his nether lip;
Prince Eugène has cursed as he saw his chances slip:
* "Call off! Call off!" he cried,*
* "It is nearing eventide,*
And I fear our work is finished in Cremona."

What are we to make of the contrast between Conan Doyle's morose view of his old schooldays in his memoirs and correspondence to Father Cassidy, and the cheerful, sardonic but nonetheless enthusiastic paean of praise in his doggerel for the school magazine? He was under no obligation to write it, and his anxiety not to curry favour with the Catholic world he had left clearly induced his exuberant pseudonym and his limitation of his identity on the team to his title. In verses not quoted by me, he lists his team-mates, only one of whom seems to play any part thereafter in his life. The answer would seem to be that if he had no cause to celebrate people, he did rejoice in Stonyhurst's gift of cricket to him, and from that vantage-point he could celebrate the old school loudly enough. Apart from his letters to Cassidy, it was his last formal connection with it, however. The *Magazine* was subsequent to his day (although he had played a vigorous part in the unofficial predecessors produced in his time) and from time to time recalled him. He was proud of the part the old school played in the Boer War, and it was proud of him: "Several sketches and portraits of Dr Conan Doyle (O.S.) have been published lately in some of the weekly illustrated papers", noted the *Magazine* in July 1900. "One of the best entitled 'Doctor and Storyteller', represents him sitting at the foot of a wounded soldier's bed amusing the poor fellow by telling him stories. We can imagine that he must be a good companion for the hospital." A correspondent in the October issue of the same year gave an account of his work among the patients at the Bloemfontein Hospital. He evidently impressed others by his powers of sympathy and the trouble he took to entertain his patients. "Perhaps some of our readers will be interested to know that after disparaging professional critics he said, 'I want the boy critic, who will start a story and then chuck it down, and say "rot", or who will read a book through and say "ripping". That's the person I want to criticise my work.' " And in February, 1902, it gave an enthusiastic account of the success of his pamphlet *Causes and Conduct of the War*.

This belated reassertion of the school's ties with him was in fact based on another legacy he owed to it. The Jesuits were highly conscious of the historical treatment of English Catholics as security risks from the excommunication of Elizabeth I by Pope Pius V with concomitant release of her subjects from allegiance to her. The Jesuits themselves were always singled out as pernicious agents of alien powers, even as late as the twentieth century. Hence their education sought to compensate by instilling in the boys a particularly strong commitment to the ideal of military service. Stonyhurst boys in the armed forces, especially those who lost their lives, were extolled as examples to their successors. The romantic and high-flown patriotism which would distinguish so much of Conan Doyle's writing found initial inspiration here. His mother had given him a taste of the family heritage, accurate or not, in the service of the British colours, but at Stonyhurst he encountered a vast spread of celebration. Behind its formal professions of loyalty and devotion was a hard sociological point. Catholics could find honour in the army the most signal method of showing their title to full acceptance by the British people.

ACD maintained more individual contacts with his former associates than his letter to Cassidy implies, even encouraging young Jesuit poets such as Father Joe Keating (though we know of no point of contact between himself and the novice Gerard Manley Hopkins, near at hand in the Jesuit seminary of St Mary's during his Stonyhurst years). His work on the school magazine gave him his first sense of the importance of such a medium, which he personally would transform in Britain and America, and he evidently won deep respect from his fellow-workers, as Everard Digby's manuscript recollections preserved at Stonyhurst indicate. Digby assumes him to have been a very popular boy, and his expertise undoubtedly won the confidence of his inmates. His place as story-teller in his Stonyhurst days would have established such popularity in the initial instance. So would his presence in the Christmas plays of 1872, albeit in minor roles (farmers' boys in *The Omnibus* and the captain of a West Indiaman in *The Box of Mischief*). This may well have been the foundation of his references to the theatre in the Holmes saga, and it may account for the fact that such references in the early stories show an extraordinary optimism about the effectiveness of make-up as well as an odd inability to distinguish between the success of disguise in a bright room and on stage before a darkened school auditorium: Jefferson Hope's unnamed actor friend disguised as an old woman in *A Study in Scarlet*, Holmes's own disguises consistently imposing on Watson from *The Sign of Four* onwards, Neville St Clair's ability to conceal his identity from his wife in "*The Man with the Twisted Lip*".

Yet he was very clear, both in his memoirs and in his correspondence with Father Cassidy, that, apart from the master, he had but one friend in Stonyhurst. It is clear that he used the word "friend" in a very special way, having little use for the debasement of its coinage in modern speech where it was assigned to any political ally or close acquaintance. The letter quoted above denying any friend at all made that statement as an affectionate flourish, intended to be contradicted by the subsequent sentence: "I was down shooting with Ryan in Hertfordshire the other day and we had a long chat about the vanished days." Having elevated Father Cassidy to an altar of unique status, Conan Doyle felt called upon not to betray his other friend Ryan; but he did not wish to detract from the tribute (and, one suspects, the surrounding desolation) which he was drawing. The construction was one he had used for purposes of comedy in his favourite among his own works, *The White Company*—"Do not forget Sam Aylward, for his heart shall ever be thine alone—and thine, ma petite!"—this being the departing salutation of the bowman to the landlady of the "Pied Merlin" and her maid (although it is the landlady—or the inn—whom he ultimately marries). Stonyhurst was fairly clearly in his mind when he wrote *The White Company*, in any case, and the subsequent association of ideas, however unconscious, was natural.

James Paul Emile Ryan of Glasgow was in the year below Arthur at Hodder and Stonyhurst, and a common heritage of Scottish birth and Irish name and antecedents obviously did much to enhance this association. "A remarkable boy", he wrote in *Memories and Adventures*, "who grew into a remarkable man." Ryan's family were tea-planters in Ceylon, whither he ultimately returned. Victor Trevor in *"The Gloria Scott"* hardly has enough character for Ryan or anyone else to have constituted a model for him, but it is clear that the circumstances and nature of his friendship with Holmes are based on the relationship between Arthur Conan Doyle and James Ryan. The ultimate fate of Victor Trevor is particularly noteworthy in this connection: he "went out to the Terai tea-planting, where I hear that he is doing well". Holmes tells Watson that Trevor "was the only friend I made during the two years that I was in college". If by "college" we read "Hodder" it fits absolutely, since in such a student context Cassidy is irrelevant. It also accounts for the "two years" which so puzzle Holmesian commentators since the time is too short for a university degree and it is clear from *"The Musgrave Ritual"* that Holmes spent several years at University (he says "my last years" there—once again the author has his own experiences in mind, this time his five-year period at the Edinburgh medical school). "Trevor was the only man I knew", continues Holmes, again a statement belied by his acquaintance with Musgrave and others, but characteristic of the emphasis on personal solitude which Holmes in common with his creator liked to profess. Trevor and Holmes met "through the accident of his bull-terrier freezing on to my ankle one morning as I went down to chapel". Now, it is a bow at much more of a venture to see any real life antecedent in this, although the frequency of reference to bodily harm or the danger thereof from dogs in the Holmes saga might hint at some personal experience on the part of the youthful Conan Doyle. The references to "chapel" which so bedevil the rival proponents of Oxford and Cambridge as Holmes's university certainly would have every relevance to schooldays. If there is anything in it, the likely possibility was that the Ryan family had a bull-terrier, friendly to the children but difficult with strangers, that it grabbed Conan Doyle when he was on his way to the chapel at Hodder while James Ryan was taking his leave of family and bull-terrier (whose sense of emotional bereavement and unfamiliarity of surroundings might be allowed to account for his anti-social conduct) and that the smaller boy, possibly under orders from a concerned mother, made frequent inquiries as to the health of the victim in the infirmary. Mrs Ryan became a close friend of Mary Foley Doyle and of her son; a thoughtful enquiry as to the health of Arthur when the Glasgow lady was visiting Edinburgh would have been an obvious origin for it. The episode would account for the ripening of such a close friendship between boys of two separate years after Arthur's failure to make friends in his own first year. As Holmes would say, the reference to a bull-terrier as basis for a friendship is sufficiently *outré* to prompt the speculation that there was something in it.

Conan Doyle made many friends in the course of his life, but the friendship with Ryan is the only one which stands out from the mass by its situation. Nor does there seem to be another case of a special friendship taking precedence over all other forms of acquaintanceship. This in its turn raises the question of whether Ryan and the friendship with him supplied inspiration not only for the Holmes-Trevor association but also for that of Holmes and Watson. And at the outset a quite extraordinary coincidence hits us:

> "Let me see—what are my other shortcomings?. I get in the dumps at times, and don't open my mouth for days on end. You must not think I am sulky when I do that. Just let me alone, and I'll soon be right. What have you to confess now? It's just as well for two fellows to know the worst of one another before they begin to live together."
> I laughed at this cross-examination. "I keep a bull pup", I said . . .

Watson's bull pup, as opposed to Trevor's, is one of the most inexplicable references in the canon, as Sherlockians will acknowledge. It never appears, nor is mention ever again made of it. It is almost as though Conan Doyle, in accounting for a friendship between two solitary men, requires a bull terrier, pup or otherwise, as some sort of signature-tune. Another, equally inexplicable, Watsonian problem may also be allied to Ryan: that although known from *A Study in Scarlet* to be "John H. Watson" his wife in *"The Man with the Twisted Lip"* calls him "James". This is a great deal more conclusive than the bull pup, which, however interesting, is but a hypothesis based upon hypothesis. The intrusive "James" indicates that that Christian name came automatically to Conan Doyle's pen when casually referring to Watson. It surfaced in other contexts as well: Professor Moriarty is "James" in *The Empty House"* despite his brother's being Colonel "James" Moriarty in *"The Final Problem"*. But the latter is a simpler slip: Conan Doyle had accustomed his ear to the words "James Moriarty" and in the ten-year interval between the stories had forgotten that its initial use was for the Colonel, not the Professor. (In any case, as we will notice, Conan Doyle's initial problem with Moriarty was what Christian names to avoid.)

So it is to the meeting of the two boys, one ten, the other a little younger, that we must ascribe the remote cause of the most famous friendship in modern literature. It accounts in part for the extraordinary genius of Conan Doyle in writing for all ages

I have wrought my simple plan
If I give one hour of joy
To the boy who's half a man,
Or the man who's half a boy.

And so, forsaken Hodder may cherish the ghosts of two little Scots wandering around its environs or straying through the beautiful dale of the Ribble, the older, thick-set, already showing signs of future height and strength, talking animatedly as he tells the stories he is now beginning to coin on his own, the younger breaking in with a good, vigorous, slightly pretentious Scots emphatic "Amazing, Arthur!" And did Arthur reply "Elementary"? If so, it must have brought a guffaw from James, for while Arthur was in the senior class in Hodder, "Figures", James was in the junior. It was called "Elements".

4

The Hound of Heaven

I fled Him, down the nights and down the days;
I fled Him, down the arches of the years;
I fled Him, down the labyrinthine ways
Of my own mind; and in the mist of tears
I hid from Him, and under running laughter
  Up vistaed hopes I sped;
  And shot, precipitated,
Adown Titanic glooms of chasmed fears,
From those strong Feet that followed, followed after.
  —Francis Thompson, *"The Hound of Heaven"*

We had left the fertile country behind and beneath us. We looked back on it now, the slanting rays of a low sun turning the streams to threads of gold and glowing on the red earth new turned by the plough and the broad tangle of the woodlands. The road in front of us grew bleaker and wilder over huge russet and olive slopes, sprinkled with giant boulders. Now and then we passed a moorland cottage, walled and roofed with stone, with no creeper to break its harsh outline. Suddenly we looked down into a cup-like depression, patched with stunted oaks and firs which had been twisted and bent by the fury of years of storm. Two high, narrow towers rose over the trees. The driver pointed with his whip.

"Baskerville Hall", said he.

Its master had risen and was staring with flushed cheeks and shining eyes. A few minutes later we had reached the lodge-gates, a maze of fantastic tracery in wrought iron, with weather bitten pillars on either side, blotched with lichens, and surmounted by the boars' heads of the Baskervilles. The lodge was a ruin of black granite and bared ribs of rafters, but facing it was a new building, half constructed, the firstfruit of Sir Charles's South African gold.

Through the gateway we passed into the avenue, where the wheels were again hushed amid the leaves, and the old trees shot their branches in a sombre tunnel over our heads. Baskerville shuddered as he looked up the long, dark drive to where the house glimmered like a ghost at the farther end.

"Was it here?" he asked, in a low voice.

"No, no, the Yew Alley is on the other side."

The young heir glanced round with a gloomy face.

"It's no wonder my uncle felt as if trouble were coming on him in such a place as this", said he. "It's enough to scare any man. I'll have a row of electric lamps up here inside of six months, and you won't know it again, with a thousand candle-power Swan and Edison right here in front of the hall door."

The avenue opened into a broad expanse of turf, and the house lay before us. In the fading light I could see that the centre was a heavy block of building from which a porch projected. The whole front was draped in ivy, with a patch clipped bare here and there where a window or a coat-of-arms broke through the dark veil. From this central block rose the twin towers, ancient, crenellated, and pierced with many loopholes. To right and left of the turrets were more modern wings of black granite. A dull light shone through heavy mullioned windows, and from the high chimneys which rose from the step, high-angled room there sprang a single black column of smoke.

The Hound of the Baskervilles, apart from its London scenes, is set on Dartmoor. Probably no location is more famous in the Holmes saga apart from Baker Street itself, and it receives far more detailed description than Baker Street ever gets. And that is Baskerville Hall, as first seen by Dr Watson. It is also Stonyhurst, as first seen by Arthur Conan Doyle.

We may rid our minds of the image of the Hollywood producer who, having the need to film yet another version of the American Civil War campaign in the valley of the Shenandoah, in Virginia, decided he will obtain verisimilitude by filming on location in the valley of the Willamette, in Oregon. Conan Doyle, to set a story in Dartmoor, drew on his knowledge of Dartmoor. He visited it for the purpose, and knew it from his Plymouth days in 1882. He had previously used it for the location of the Holmes story "*Silver Blaze*". But in order to establish what it did not have, a mansion for the location of his principal indoor sequences, he returned to his old haunts.

Like a good cook, he did not limit himself to a single recipe. Baskerville Hall has touches of several real buildings, including the house Undershaw where Conan Doyle and his family lived in the middle and later 1890s. But the long straight drive, the two towers and the dark and menacing aspect are Stonyhurst as he first saw it, when coming to board within it, from the warmth and love in Hodder to this veritable symbol of a prison house about to close around the growing boy. It was not a symbol which long survived his presence behind its doors. As his poem on the Wanderers points out, drastic alterations were in progress shortly after his departure, and the cold and unwelcoming facade which had stood from the first occupation of the house by Jesuit seminarians in 1794 had given way to the gracious contours which command the long approach today. He became, therefore, its most famous memorialist.

But not all of the Stonyhurst transferred to *The Hound* has vanished. Only suggestions of the interiors accord with one another, the corridors and smaller staircases perhaps. The Baskerville Hall dining-room seems to share nothing with Stonyhurst's paved with white marble in diamond-shaped blocks, one and a half feet of slate covered marble wainscot, capped by oak for the remainder of the walls, all of which was no doubt daunting enough to the youthful Arthur, but too bright for the shade effects he was playing with in Baskerville Hall. The coats-of-arms Watson mentions are true of Stonyhurst, and with them the omnipresence of a striking heraldic device—the unicorn.

Stonyhurst really seems to have been very strongly in Conan Doyle's mind in 1900-01, perhaps in consequence of his awareness of a new bond between himself and his old school in their common commitment to the Boer War. In any event, the year previous to *The Hound* he had published in the *Strand* "*Playing With Fire*", what for a future spiritualist was a very comic, satiric though unquestionably menacing, story of occultists who succeed in materialising a unicorn. The initial appearance of the animal is in a picture, and one which from the fictional narrator's asinine comments sounds like a Charles Doyle work. ("I am not an expert in art, and I have never professed to understand what Harvey Deacon meant by his pictures; but I could see in this instance that it was all very clever and imaginative, fairies and animals and allegorical figures of all sorts.") The artist acknowledges the inspiration of his painting as heraldic ("Can't you see the horn in front? It's a unicorn. I told you they were heraldic beasts. Can't you recognize one?"). Possibly Conan Doyle failed to identify the unicorn when he reached Stonyhurst and encountered some mockery on that account, or heard laughter at the expense of some other neophyte who described it as a horse. Anyhow, Mary Foley Doyle's son might be expected to keep an eye on the heraldry of the place, and Stonyhurst abounded in that. In Conan Doyle's time Herbert Thurston collected crests and coats of arms, although over two year's seniority on Thurston's side prevented any such bond arising to bring them together. Given their bitter Spiritualism controversy in the closing years of Conan Doyle's life, it is a pity they did not make some effort at reconciliation over the literary spiritualistic adventures of Stonyhurst heraldry. To return to "*Playing With Fire*":

He flung open the door and we rushed in. She was there on the ground amidst the splinters of her chair. We seized her and dragged her swiftly out, and as we gained the door I looked over my shoulder into the darkness. There were two strange eyes glowing at us, a rattle of hoofs, and I had just time to slam the door when there came a crash upon it which split it from top to bottom.

"It's coming through! It's coming!"

"Run, run for your lives!" cried the Frenchman.

Another crash, and something shot through the riven door. It was a long white spike, gleaming in the lamp-light. For a moment it shone before us, and then with a snap it disappeared again.

"Quick! Quick! This way!" Harvey Deacon shouted. "Carry her in! Here! Quick!"

We had taken refuge in the dining-room, and shut the heavy oak door. We laid the senseless woman upon the sofa, and as we did so, Moir, the hard man of business, drooped and fainted across the hearthrug. Harvey Deacon was as white as a corpse, jerking and twitching like an epileptic. With a crash we heard the studio door fly to pieces, and the snorting and stamping were in the passage, up and down, up and down, shaking the house with their fury. The Frenchman had sunk his face on his hands, and sobbed like a frightened child.

"What shall we do?" I shook him roughly by the shoulder. "Is a gun any use?"

"No, no. The power will pass. Then it will end."

"You might have killed us all—you unspeakable fool—with your infernal experiments."

"I did not know. How could I tell that it would be frightened? It is mad with terror. It was his fault. He struck it."

Harvey Deacon sprang up. "Good heavens!" he cried.

A terrible scream sounded through the house.

"It's my wife! Here, I'm going out. If it's the Evil One himself I am going out!"

He had thrown open the door and rushed out into the passage. At the end of it, at the foot of the stairs, Mrs Deacon was lying senseless, struck down by the sight which she had seen. But there was nothing else.

I am not concerned with the Freudian possibilities of the passage, which readers, if they so desire, can investigate for themselves. It is decidedly possible, however, that this particular work originated in some story-telling occasion in the lower forms at Stonyhurst. Bereft of Francis Cassidy and of Mary Doyle he was thrown on his own resources, only to discover his schoolmates considered themselves on those resources as well. "On a wet half-holiday", he wrote in the *Idler* in January 1893, "I have been elevated on to a desk and with an audience of little boys squatting on the floor, with their chins upon their hands, I have talked myself husky over the misfortunes of my heroes. Week in and week out those unhappy men have battled and striven and groaned for the amusement of that little circle. I was bribed with pastry to continue these efforts, and I remember that I always stipulated for tarts down and strict business, which shows that I was born to be a member of the Authors' Society. Sometimes, too, I would stop dead in the very thrill of a crisis, and could only be set agoing again by apples."

We cannot tell how far his narrative powers on rainy days were immediately inspired by the *genus loci*, but there was certainly one part of the school grounds which made a powerful imprint on his mind.

"The facts of the case are simple. Sir Charles Baskerville was in the habit every night before going to bed of walking down the famous Yew Alley of Baskerville Hall. . . . The day had been wet, and Sir Charles's footmarks were easily traced down the Alley. Half-way down this walk there is a gate which leads out to the moor. There are indications that Sir Charles had stood for some little time here. He then proceeded down the Alley, and it was at the far end of it that his body was discovered. One fact which has not been explained is the statement of Barrymore that his master's footprints altered their character from the time that he passed the moorgate, and that he appeared from thence onwards to have been walking on his toes. One Murphy, a gipsy horse-dealer, was on the moor at no great distance at the time, but he appears by his own confession to have been the worse for drink. He declares that he heard cries, but is unable to state from what direction they came. . . ." . . .

". . . But one false statement was made by Barrymore at the inquest. He said that there were no traces upon the ground round the body. He did not observe any. But I did—some little distance off, but fresh and clear."

"Footprints?"

"Footprints."

"A man's or a woman's?"

Dr Mortimer looked strangely at us for an instant, and his voice sank almost to a whisper as he answered:—

"Mr Holmes, they were the footprints of a gigantic hound!"
. . .
"It is very bewildering."

"It certainly has a character of its own. There are points of distinction about it. That change in the footprints, for example. What do you make of that?"

"Mortimer said that the man had walked on tiptoe down that portion of the alley."

"He only repeated what some fool had said at the inquest. Why should a man walk on tiptoe down the alley?"

"What then?"

"He was running, Watson—running desperately, running for his life, running until he burst his heart and fell dead upon his face."

"Running from what?"

"There lies our problem. There are indications that the man was crazed with fear before he began to run."

"How can you say that?"

"I am presuming that the cause of his fears came to him across the moor. If that were so, and it seems most probable, only a man who had lost his wits would have run *from* the house instead of towards it. If the gipsy's evidence may be taken as true, he ran with cries for help in the direction where help was least likely to be. . . ."

The Yew Alley at Stonyhurst corresponds almost exactly to the particulars given by the coroner, by Dr Mortimer and by Holmes. It is indeed famous in the school's tradition. A century after Conan Doyle's sojourn the boys, unaware of the inspiration it had given their illustrious predecessor, would dare one another to race down it after nightfall braving imagined terrors from ghostly survivors of sixteenth- and seventeenth-century Pendle witchcraft. It is known as the "Dark Walk", and one side is indeed divided by a gate at its midsection. A very short lane leads from the alley to the gate which, being in Lancashire, does not give on to Dartmoor; on the other hand the mist-haunted, undulating countryside which is visible from the gate is almost as daunting. Little Stonyhurst boys might have seen witches there with as much conviction as Sir Charles saw the ghastly hound, if with somewhat less drastic consequences. In that connection the mist which rises at the end of *The Hound of the Baskervilles* and results in the mauling and the near-death of Sir Henry Baskerville, is very appropriate to a story whose opening tableau is at the alley-gate giving out to a landscape with mists thickening under the boys' eyes. It would be surprising if, with all that inspirational material, Arthur the storyteller did not use it to make his schoolfellows' flesh creep.

Never in the delirious dream of a disordered brain could anything more savage, more appalling, more hellish be conceived than that dark form and savage face which broke upon us out of the wall of fog.

A few minor notes may be added. Murphy would be a curious name for a gipsy on Dartmoor, but with Stonyhurst summoned up to Conan Doyle's memory he clearly put it in his text in tribute to his most unpleasant memory of the place—an obnoxious Irish Jesuit named Murphy who came to preach a retreat with sermons of the kind Joyce later made famous, in the course of which he noisily assured his youthful audience "that there was sure damnation for every one outside the Church". The deliverance of this performance may have been gratifying to Father Murphy; Conan Doyle claimed that it ultimately cost him his religion. "I looked upon him with horror, and to that moment I trace the first rift which has grown into such a chasm between me and those who were my guides". At Hodder under Cassidy's régime of love for his charges and for mankind Arthur had written his mother on 30 May 1869: "I am glad to say that I have made my first communion. Oh, mama [text from Nordon—original probably "Mam"], I cannot express the joy, that I felt on the happy day to receive my creator into my breast. I shall never though I live a hundred years, I shall never forget that day." If in after life Conan Doyle had seen his departure from the Catholic church as emancipation from superstition and that alone, he would have had no reason to hold a grudge against Father Murphy. But he did, most bitterly, resent what Murphy had done: he had torn from the boy something very dear to him, the religious faith for which Murphy was allegedly fighting. Hence Conan Doyle showed his contempt by writing Murphy into the passage in *The Hound* so carefully grounded on Stonyhurst, and by representing him as "by his own confession . . . the worse for drink". The word "confession" is important here, in its allusion to the Catholic sacrament. There may be a savage joy in making Murphy the worse for drink; the intoxication of his verbosity had produced something even more odious than scenes Charles Doyle's alcoholic bouts had visited on his family. On the other hand the reference to a gipsy is not a sneer, save that the respectable Murphy would not have liked it: Conan Doyle admired George Borrow, the great literary celebrant of the Romany, and several Holmes stories such as "*The Speckled Band*", "*Silver Blaze*" and "*The Priory School*" denounce the fashionable readiness to impugn gipsies for any crime under scrutiny.

Another source for *The Hound* emanating from Stonyhurst came with its observatory, of which the college was justly proud. In *The Hound* such an observatory is one of the obsessions of Mr Frankland, of Lafter Hall, eternal litigant, and unfeeling father of Laura Lyons. Frankland, one of the most shrewdly drawn of Conan Doyle's minor characters, is an admirable blend of the comic and the grotesque, and supplies the means for the dramatic discovery by Watson that Holmes is the mysterious man on the tor. Frankland unconsciously aids Watson in the quest for the unknown man by his hobby of searching the moor for the escaped convict by means of his telescope. It is doubtful if Frankland himself was based on a Stonyhurst original: there may have been something owing to the obsessiveness with which one of the Jesuits kept urging the charms and value of the telescope on the boys, and there may also be a suggestion that telescopes and litigation seemed to mean more to them than the boys under their care. Certainly the Rector, Father Purbrick, was largely preoccupied by his building programme and the problems caused by a vexatious legal dispute arising out of a will when Conan Doyle was there. The grasping sacrist in *Sir Nigel* whose interest in institutional wealth left him deaf and blind to human considerations might have reference to some administrator, but nothing in Arthur's contemporary references to Father Purbrick suggest any basis for such hostility. It may arise from some experience of a clerical bureaucrat with whom he had otherwise little connection. In fact, Purbrick's problems about the disputed will were wished upon him, rather than the reverse, and it is likely masters would have told the boys of the infamies distracting the Rector occasioned by vexatious litigation which seemed as unjust as it was unexpected. The Jesuits and the boys would thus have known that the law could be twisted to extraordinary lengths entirely contrary to the wishes of legislators and testators. From this standpoint, the initiator of the legal wrangle rather than any of the Jesuits seems a point of departure in the invention of Frankland. The legal action seems to have been thoroughly perverse, and probably stemmed from anti-Catholic prejudice on the part of a legal adviser. What strengthens the hypothesis that Frankland's original is the litigant against the Jesuits, is the fact that the Jesuits would have gone to law only for specific interests; Frankland strikes invariably for the hell of it.

> ". . . I mean to teach them in these parts that law is law, and that there is a man here who does not fear to invoke it. I have established a right of way through the centre of old Middleton's park, slap across it, sir, within a hundred yards of his own front door. What do you think of that? We'll teach those magistrates that they cannot ride rough-shod over the rights of the commoners, confound them! And I've closed the wood where the Fernworthy folk used to picnic. The infernal people seem to think that there are no rights of property, and that they can swarm where they like with their papers and their bottles. Both cases decided, Dr Watson, and both in my favour. I haven't had such a day since I had Sir John Morland for trespass, because he shot in his own warren."

Despite Conan Doyle's statement that Dr Watson never made a joke, he made a very good one about Frankland:

> . . . Dr Mortimer lunched with us. He has been excavating a barrow at Long Down, and has got a prehistoric skull which fills him with great joy. . . . there are rumours that [Frankland] intends to prosecute Dr Mortimer for opening a grave without the consent of the next-of-kin because he dug up the neolithic skull in the barrow on Long Down.

One might imagine some antecedent for that speculation in some Jesuit piece of sarcasm as to the lengths to which the litigious enemy might go next.

Other aspects of *The Hound* might also derive from Stonyhurst, such as nocturnal adventures and chases, Dr Mortimer's fascination with human skulls, and so forth, but the absence of evidence permits no further elaboration. In any case Mortimer's obsession would more likely have been prompted by an Edinburgh medical acquaintance than a schoolmaster. One character does invite a moment's further scrutiny—Stapleton, the murderer. He had been a schoolmaster and built an initial success on the use of a "consumptive tutor", who ultimately died "and the school which had begun well sank from disrepute into infamy". This recalls Conan Doyle's school days having begun well with the presumably consumptive Cassidy, and it is clear that from time to time at Stonyhurst the comments of his subsequent masters might imply he had progressed from disrepute into infamy. He recalled in his memoirs one man telling him he "would never do any good in the world, and perhaps from his point of view his prophecy has been justified" while another, hearing he was thinking of becoming a civil engineer, remarked "Well, Doyle, you may be an engineer, but I don't think you will ever be a civil one". It is all very common magisterial stock-in-trade to provide a safety-valve for personal irritation, or raise a laugh from the class at a dull moment, or, less defensibly, to pour scorn on a troublesome youth whose size, turbulence, alien accent and obstinacy were most easily answered by making him the butt of the class. As Conan Doyle noted, his bad experiences at Stonyhurst and his dislike of the mechanical application to classical texts, were simply part of the dehumanisation which characterised so much of British and Irish education at that time, and the Jesuits of Stonyhurst were no worse than any other educational authorities.

As to Stapleton, his conversation is certainly rather that of a schoolmaster than anything else—and a real schoolmaster, not just someone who took it up as a speculation for which he proved unfitted. If there was an original for him, it would only have been for his conversation. Whatever Conan Doyle may have thought of the Jesuits of Stonyhurst, he certainly did not credit them with parading around with alleged sisters but actually wives whom they flogged in private, or keeping large canine friends for the purpose of unleashing them on their next-of-kin. And Stapleton never appears save as the interested neighbour: his realisation that all is discovered, his flight and death, all happen off-stage. In this he is very unusual among Conan Doyle's villains. Either they exhibit themselves to Holmes and Watson in malignant colours throughout (Dr Grimesby Roylott, Moriarty (admittedly never speaking save as reported by Holmes), Bodymaster McGinty and the Scowrers, Charles Augustus Milverton), or else they ultimately appear in their true colours (James Windibank, Jephro Rucastle, the Cunninghams, Joseph Harrison (only as reported by Holmes), Colonel Moran, Jonas Oldacre, Culverton Smith, Killer Evans, Josiah Amberley). A few never appear at all save in the client's statement ("Colonel Lysander Stark", Biddle and Hayward, Latimer and Wilson Kemp), or in that of a minor villain (Oberstein, Eduardo Lucas). Once or twice, a villain, hitherto undetected although under suspicion, is murdered (Blessington alias Sutton, Mortimer Tregennis). One very distinguished group, Captain James Calhoun and fellow-graduates of the Ku Klux Klan, are never seen by any other protagonists in the story with the possible though by no means certain exceptions of the three deceased at the time of fatal encounter. Stapleton, then, presents unique features, and these may arise because Conan Doyle had so effectively realised him from some original impressions that he felt the revelation of the real man behind the façade would strike a note more false than the façade itself. The principle is an interesting one in terms of the deliberation of his literary execution, and his refusal to attempt a touch which might mar. One recalls Holmes's assertion in "*The Norwood Builder*" as to "that supreme gift of the artist, the knowledge of when to stop".

The Stapleton manner has this much in common with the Jesuits of

Stonyhurst as Conan Doyle recalled them—a good, and interesting, conversational capacity with a curiously dry manner. He has a violent temper, capable of exploding, but of the emotions which allow that temper to become uncontrollable we see nothing. Watson sees him lose his temper, ostensibly because he resents Sir Henry's attentions to his sister, actually because his use of her as a decoy cannot master the jealousy he feels for a rival in her affections since she is in fact his wife. Conan Doyle very ably develops the character of a man whose avarice is at times in alliance, at times in conflict, with his lust: it helps him that Laura Lyons is his mistress, believes him unmarried, and can be used as bait in bringing Sir Charles to his doom; it helps him that while his wife will not undertake that task, she acquiesces in pretending to be his sister, becoming friendly with Sir Henry and keeping silence about the hound. Yet these very advantages have the potential to destroy him, as is shown by the conduct of each woman as she learns he has deceived her with the other. Without overdoing it, Conan Doyle very nicely balances Stapleton's readiness for lust and for avarice to enjoy sexual mastery of both women (it is clear that this is the nature of the two sexual relationships) against his ungovernable fury, entirely against his economic interests, when his wife gives the impression he has asked her to give, of favouring the suit of Sir Henry. This question of Stapleton's emotional inability to control himself while basing a conspiracy on the emotions of others (Sir Charles, Sir Henry, Laura Lyons, Beryl Stapleton) is one of the things which lifts the book firmly into serious literature: another, as Edmund Wilson pointed out, is the writing itself.

But in structural terms Stapleton's emotions, though not always hidden, are never revealed directly through speech to the reader. Watson *sees* him doing it, but he does not *hear* him doing it. ("He was running wildly towards them, his absurd net dangling behind him. He gesticulated and almost danced with excitement in front of the lovers. What the scene meant I could not imagine, but it seemed to me that Stapleton was abusing Sir Henry, who offered explanations, which became more angry as the other refused to accept them.") All the reader ever knows of the expression of Stapleton's nature is in dumb-show: Conan Doyle had used the same technique very effectively in "*The Final Problem*" in which Professor Moriarty is only seen by Watson and the reader as "a tall man pushing his way furiously through the crowd and waving his hand as if he desired to have the train stopped" and "a man . . . walking very rapidly . . . his black figure clearly outlined against the green behind him". The precise methods are different: Stapleton in anger is wholly visible but inaudible, Moriarty is never more to Watson than a silhouette. All Watson ever discovers of Stapleton's emotional life is learned at second-hand, but it is not, as with Moriarty, wholly dependent on Holmes's account. The witnesses variously testifying as the plot grows deeper and darker each convey a further depth of revelation to Watson: in respective order they are Mrs (or as he thinks Miss) Stapleton, Sir Henry, Laura Lyons, Holmes, Laura Lyons again, Mrs Stapleton, and Holmes in summing up largely basing his remarks on still further interviews with Mrs Stapleton. In his anxiety to draw this concealed emotional complex Conan Doyle casually discards the principle of hiding the villain's identity until the end, and he does so very largely in the interest of this pattern of successive stages of revelation. Stapleton's guilt may be a surprise to the reader, but it is not one where any serious effort has been made at concealment. Watson, who represents the reader, is not surprised, as he normally is, by Holmes's announcement of the guilty party: he is surprised by Beryl Stapleton's being not sister but wife, but follows it with "All my unspoken instincts, my vague suspicions, suddenly took shape and centred upon the naturalist", and this is not meant to be vain-glory since he has in fact handled his end of the whole case in an excellently workmanlike fashion. What is wanted is that bit by bit Stapleton is revealed, not only as criminal, but as man. It is understandable and right, with Conan Doyle's particular horror at danger for women under the control of violent men, that the final revelation is "the clear red weal of a whiplash across" the neck of Mrs Stapleton, her arms "all mottled with bruises" and her cry "But this is nothing—nothing! It is my mind and soul that he has tortured and defiled." That is the novel's true heart of darkness and that also is why the author resolutely rejects a happy ending with Sir Henry marrying her.

Watson had seen, in dumb-show, the explosion of Stapleton against Sir Henry in spite of what Watson later learned to be his own better interests; yet Watson's last word on this is "this cold and cruel-hearted man". What he had heard was entirely against the first although not the second, adjective; Stapleton most evilly used the women in his life to entrap his Baskerville relatives but there is every indication he could not remain cold when they fulfilled his orders to flirt with his victims, for his anger at the thought of Laura Lyons being dependent on Sir Charles, although to his strategic advantage, is presumably intended to be as genuine as his anger at his wife's courtship by Sir Henry. In his hunger to possess women he is anything but cold. The point is that Watson has never heard the emotional side, and hence it is the repression of emotions he recalls in summing up Stapleton. And it is this repression of emotions, this coldness towards the boys in the wake of Francis Cassidy's warmth, which left such an unpleasant impression on Conan Doyle's mind at Stonyhurst.

It was a coldness which might explode into anger, and which was frequently peppered with irony, but it never seems to have broken through to affection. His word to contrast Cassidy from the rest is "human". It is not that we need take Conan Doyle's generalisations from his own experience too seriously: he himself clearly felt the Jesuits in North and South America and in China possessed qualities of warmth alien to those whom he knew other than Cassidy. He identifies himself with this aspect of Jesuit tradition in season and out, whether in his memoirs, in The Refugees, or in a remarkable digression in his unpretentious, magnificant volume of literary criticism, Through the Magic Door. According to several Jesuits of today, the consensus would seem to be that the repression of emotions was taken as the teaching of St Ignatius Loyola and was in fact the product of an unconscious insistence on conformity in all respects save doctrine to the Victorian norms. Ignatius was much closer to the spirit of the seventeenth-century missionaries and martyrs whom Conan Doyle admired to the end, and it was Cassidy, and not his colleagues, who typified that spirit. In any case I would advance Stapleton's disguise as a comment on the Jesuit clothing of emotions. His conversational habits, the quick range of comment, the ability to argue for both sides of a thesis, the cut through defences to force discussion of a point not suspected to be under scrutiny—all are very characteristic of what we know of the chief masters at Stonyhurst in Conan Doyle's day. So too is the instant recovery from an adverse blow, whether it be some schoolboy prank or the discovery that the latest victim of the hound is an irrelevant convict rather than the seigneur of Baskerville Hall.

> "Why, Dr Watson, that's not you, is it? You are the last man that I should have expected to see out on the moor at this time of night. But, dear me, what's this? Somebody hurt? Not—don't tell me that it is our friend Sir Henry!" He hurried past me and stooped over the dead man. I heard a sharp intake of his breath and the cigar fell from his fingers.
>
> "Who—who's this?" he stammered.
>
> "It is Selden, the man who escaped from Princetown."
>
> Stapleton turned a ghastly face upon us, but by a supreme effort he had overcome his amazement and his disappointment. He looked sharply from Holmes to me.
>
> "Dear me! What a very shocking affair! How did he die?"

The little tricks of speech, the acceptable but unrevealing commonplace, are eminently characteristic. No doubt when Arthur was discovered in one of numerous scrapes he was met by "don't tell me that it is our friend Doyle", admittedly delivered in a somewhat different tone of voice to Stapleton's but with the friendship not much stronger. Or the deflating response to crisis being a calm "Dear me! What a very shocking affair!" as who should say the same thing about a considerable rainstorm doing minor damage to the cricket-pitch.

The only work Conan Doyle ever wrote with a Jesuit as major protagonist dates from this selfsame period of 1900-01, in this case "The Confession", which appeared in the first number of the Universal magazine, published in March 1900. It was never reprinted. This is curious, for the time. Almost all of Conan Doyle's stories published after the '90's were reprinted by him in his short-story collections at least once. He may never have seen it in print: he sailed to play his part in the Boer War on February 18, 1900, and his complimentary copies might have been misplaced, given the illness of his wife Louise, although his agents, A. P. Watt, might have been expected to attend to such a matter. The Universal magazine, despite a pretentious launching in February 1900 with articles by Marie Corelli, the Countess of Warwick and the actor Charles Wyndham, and promises of future work by Lillie Langtry, Bret Harte, John Strange Winter and many others, did not last in its belated challenge to the Strand, the Windsor, Pearson's, Harmsworth's, the Royal and their fellows, and Conan Doyle seems to have written no more for it. The story is short, though in The Last Galley he reprinted work as brief. It is possible that he forgot about it, with the magazine's vanishing from his horizon. It is also possible that it seemed of less value to him after the experience of the South African war, although he cheerfully reprinted work of much more trivial character. And it could be that the mood in which he wrote it—and it is in some respects unlike anything he wrote—was one he did not wish to have recalled. If he excluded it from the canon on grounds of merit, he was being somewhat perverse, for it is a work of considerable power.

The story opens in a convent, rather charmingly described. The author shows a little unfamiliarity with the rivalry of Roman Catholic religious orders, for the convent is Dominican, and the subject is a retreat by a Jesuit: it is unlikely the nuns would have gone beyond the ranks of the Dominican priests, and it is likely that they would have heard about it if they did. (Conan Doyle's experience of Catholicism went little beyond the Jesuits.) In any event, Father Garcia gives his retreat. It is very clear from the outset that this is no act of revenge on Father Murphy: Garcia is one of Conan Doyle's heroes of Jesuit history.

> . . . Father Garcia was a priest whose name was famous through all Catholic Europe as being a worthy successor to those great men, the Xaviers and Loyolas, who founded the first company of Jesus. He was a preacher; he was a writer; above all he was a martyr, for he had carried the gospel into Thibet and had come back with splintered fingers and twisted wrists as a sign of his devotion. Those mutilated hands raised in exhortation had moved his hearers more than the exhortation itself. In person he was tall, dark and bent, worn to the bone with self-discipline, with a keen, eager face, and the curved predatory nose of the aggressive Churchman. Once that dark, deep-lined face had grace and beauty; now it had character and power; but in youth or age it was a face which neither man nor woman could look upon with indifference. A pagan swordcut, which had disfigured the cheek, gave it an additional grace in the eyes of the faithful. So warped, and worn, and haggard was the man's whole appearance, that one might have doubted whether such a frame could contain so keen and earnest a spirit, had it not been for those flashing dark eyes which burned in the heavy shadows of the tufted brows.
>
> It was those eyes which dominated his hearers, whether they consisted of the profligate society of Lisbon or of the gentle nuns of St Dominic. When they gleamed fiercely as he denounced sin and threatened the sinner, or when, more seldom, they softened into a serene light as he preached the gospel of love, they forced those who saw them into the emotion which they expressed.

So far Conan Doyle is taking care to give the totality of his Jesuit experience, the positive legacy he carried from Cassidy, the more negative from the others. He then moves to the nuns' confession which he describes with a good sense very different from anti-Catholic contributions to such a theme:

> One after another these white-gowned figures, whose dress was emblematic of their souls, passed into the confessional, whispered through the narrow grating the story of their simple lives, and listened in deep humility and penitence to the wise advice and gentle admonitions which the old priest, with eyes averted, whispered back to them.

And then at last the Abbess Monica, who has been very painfully moved by the retreat for all of her normal confidence and spirituality, comes to tell "the few trivial faults which still united her to humanity". And then she reveals that she cannot refrain from being reminded by his voice of a man she had loved before she entered the order. He absolves her, and then for the first time looks at her.

> She looked down at the grating, and shrank in terror from the sight. A convulsed face was looking out at her, framed in that little square of oak. Two terrible eyes looked out of it—two eyes so full of hungry longing and hopeless despair that all the secret miseries of thirty years flashed into that one glance.
> "Julia!" he cried.

So she at last recognises the man she loved, and they discover that where she thought he had left her and he that she had ordered him away, each of them had wished to marry the other.

> "Listen, Julia", said he "I saw you last upon the Plaza. We had but an instant, because your family and mine were enemies. I said that if you put your lamp in your window I would take it as a sign that you wished me to remain true to you, but that if you did not I should vanish from your life. You did not put it."
> "I did put it, Pedro."
> "Your window was the third from the top?"
> "It was the first. Who told you that it was the third?"
> "Your cousin Alphonso—my only friend in the family."
> "My cousin Alphonso was my rejected suitor."
> The two claw-like hands flew up into the air with a horrible spasm of hatred.
> "Hush, Pedro, hush!" she whispered.
> "I have said nothing."
> "Forgive him!"
> "No, I shall never forgive him. Never! never!"
> "You did not wish to leave me, then?"
> "I joined the order in the hope of death."
> "And you never forgot me?"
> "God help me, I never could."
> "I am so glad that you could not forget me. Oh, Pedro, your poor, poor hands! My loss has been the gain of others. I have lost my love, and I have made a saint and a martyr."
> But he had sunk his face, and his gaunt shoulders shook with his agony.
> "What about our lives!" he murmured. "What about our wasted lives!"

* * *

> The Sisters of St Dominic still talk of the last sermon which Father Garcia delivered to them—a sermon upon the terrible mischances of life, and upon the hidden sweetness which may come from them, until the finest flower of good may bloom upon the foulest stem of evil. He spoke of the soul-killing sorrow which may fall upon us, and how we may be chastened by it, if it be only that we learn a deeper and truer sympathy for the sorrow of our neighbour. And then he prayed himself, and implored his hearers to pray, that an unhappy man and a gentle woman might learn to take sorrow in such a spirit, and that the rebellious spirit of the one might be softened and the tender soul of the other made strong. Such was the prayer which a hundred of the sisters sent up; and if sweetness and purity can aid it, their prayer may have brought peace once more to the Abbess Monica and to Father Garcia of the Order of Jesus.

The story is certainly a protest against the strangling of love and human emotion, in however high a cause. It is also an argument, and a strong one, that many vocations are in fact expressions of emotional frustration rather than a straightforward entry into the religious life. The story militates against the potential pursuit of that theme into the cruelty to colleagues and subordinates that could follow such actions. Clearly Conan Doyle suspected that might lie at the root of some of the lack of sympathy he encountered among the Jesuits, but he was not going to foul his own nest. Medieval anti-clericalism was one thing; betraying his former tribe to its enemies was another. He might have abandoned the faith of his uncle Richard, but he would not abandon the principle which forbade him to collaborate in enmity to his Church. Garcia's recognition of the need to preach love animates him, whatever about Father Murphy (whose pre-ordination emotional history is fortunately beyond the scope of all enquiry), and Monica is described in heroic terms in her supremely compassionate reclamation of prostitutes. Garcia's cry of "our wasted lives" is left to stand, but equally, in the largest sense, their lives have been anything but wasted, much less so, perhaps than if they had found happiness in married life and absorption in one another. Yet Garcia's mutilation is meant to symbolise that their denial of their own emotions has made them less than whole, although it has also made them more.

The ambiguity is probably quite intentional. Conan Doyle on the eve of departure for medical service in a war which might well end his life may have been half-pondering on whether such might be the answer. For since 1897 he had been totally in love, grimly chaste love, with Jean Leckie. Neither would betray his invalid wife, dying for the previous ten years and yet destined to live for another six. "*The Confession*" is in part a heart-cry for the seemingly wasted lives hungering to unite with one another, and Garcia's prayer at the conclusion is in some degree Conan Doyle's own prayer for himself and Jean Leckie. His next collection of short stories was not brought out until Louise Doyle was dead, and by then the personal agony expressed in "*The Confession*" was at an end, and he had no wish to recall it. It is nevertheless of importance that his old religion apparently came to his aid, in that anti-clerical form which he had made his own, to give him some means of comfort and agony. In one way he never deviated in his hostility to the Jesuit repression of emotions: in another he was in closer sympathy to its adherents than at any other point in his life, as he was forced to repress his own. But "*The Confession*" makes its fine distinction. He could, and did, tell Jean Leckie he loved her, even if his and her honour forbade the pretence of a spiritual union justifying conjugal rights. He still opposed a spirit which would strangle all tenderness of speech and manner. Cassidy had taught him that the religious life did not necessitate that, and that personal sacrifice neither required nor justified the sacrifice of others. This episode may account for the Stonyhurst preoccupation of these years, triumphantly climaxing with *The Hound*. In battling against his own emotions, he was reconsidering the question which had concerned him about the Jesuits. The preoccupation wanes with subsequent years, although his letter to Cassidy of

1902 seems to show a yearning to recover the religious confidence of his infancy while knowing it to be impossible. Certainly the martial traditions of Stonyhurst also gave him some mild, and temporary, reconciliation with the memory of his old school. "I am told that the average of V.C.'s and D.S.O.'s now held by Stonyhurst boys is very high as compared with other schools", he said proudly in his memoirs.

Garcia, Ignatius Morat, Francis Cassidy and Arthur Conan Doyle had one thing in common among themselves which they shared with few of the priests at Stonyhurst: they were born into the faith. Most of the Stonyhurst teachers were converts. Conan Doyle saw the bigotry of Catholicism at war with emotional ties linking the convert to his pre-Catholic days. "The convert is lost to the family", he remarked in *Memories and Adventures*. The violence done to the natural fabric of family life—and it was very Catholic in him so to revere the institution of the family—increased the tendency to emotional repression. Having turned their backs on their own people, the converts had little love to spare for charges not even united to them by blood. And the converts also had turned their backs on the progress of a modern world which he was finding more and more fascinating to contemplate. The Rev. George Renerden Kingdon, S.J., the real spirit of Stonyhurst in his day, had won the Wix Prize for medicine at Bart's in 1846. But the Prefect of Lower Studies, as by Arthur's day he had become, had rejected modern science so vehemently on entering the religious life that he absolutely refused medical attention for his own ill-health and finally, in 1893, was discovered dead in his own chair. At the time when Conan Doyle's mind was turning more and more to medical life, Kingdon, son of a London physician, and the senior figure in the day-to-day running of the school, would have seen such ambitions as all too reminiscent of the world he had so rightly lost. Conan Doyle's dislike of mechanical learning ran directly counter to Kingdon's hatred of anything in the nature of experiment in education. Conan Doyle's frequent breaking of rules was *anathema* to him. "The world calls rules a burden", he would snap in his brusque manner made no softer by his increasing deafness. "It might as well call wings a burden to the bird." In a community hardly notable for its modernity he was singled out as resolutely old-fashioned.

Yet Kingdon had one outstanding intellectual effect on the rebellious mind at war with his prejudices. His hostility to modernism, his powerful personality, his identification with the Stonyhurst mind, his conservative manuals on the rules for Latin versification, classical grammar, and ways of assisting at Mass, all convinced Conan Doyle that the Catholic church was indissolubly wedded to obscurantism and enmity to objective scientific enquiry. Yet through all the writer's subsequent years of agnosticism, Kingdon's message kept tugging at Conan Doyle. Edinburgh University seemed to preach a science independent of, and indifferent to, the life of the spirit. But Conan Doyle was never able fully to accept the notion of science without religion, any more than he could rest content with Kingdon's insistence on religion without science. Kingdon, after all, was no ignoramus denouncing that of which he knew nothing: he had conquered his field before he abandoned it. And a Kingdon figure does seem to appear in certain of the Conan Doyle writings. The fourteenth-century Abbot of Beaulieu in *The White Company* is an obvious instance, one where the allusions to military life as opposed to religious are Conan Doyle's agreeable historical variation on what he saw as the nineteenth-century warrior caste, the medical world:

> His thin thought-worn features and sunken haggard cheeks bespoke one who had indeed beaten down that inner foe whom every man must face, but had none the less suffered sorely in the contest. In crushing his passions he had well-nigh crushed himself. Yet, frail as was his person, there gleamed out ever and anon from under his drooping brows a flash of fierce energy, which recalled to men's minds that he came of a fighting stock, and that even now his twin brother, Sir Bartholomew Berghersh, was one of the most famous of those stern warriors who had planted the Cross of St George before the gates of Paris. With lips compressed and clouded brow, he strode up and down the oaken floor, the very genius and impersonation of asceticism, while the great bell thundered and clanged above his head.

The passage, like all such passages, should not be wrested out of reality into a mere pen-portrait of a Victorian schoolmaster. The abbot reflected various facets of Conan Doyle's memory and imagination. It is even possible that the military reference could have a double significance, for the frail and ascetic Father Reginald Wellesley Colley, while much younger than Berghersh or Kingdon, could certainly have inspired so direct a reference to military and clerical kinship—his most distinguished kinsman was the Duke of Wellington, a link which must have delighted Arthur, who came under his form-mastership in the Sixth, his final Stonyhurst year. But Kingdon predominates. The rejection of science and progress is typified by him, and it was that which really drew the intellectual ire of Conan Doyle in his memoirs. Kingdon dominated the place, despite Purbrick's superiority of status: Purbrick was far younger, for one thing, and neither his preoccupations nor his character would have led him to challenge Kingdon's rule in the intellectual sphere. In long retrospect the period is known as Kingdon's time among Stonyhurst's custodians of tradition.

Indeed, the Prefecture of Studies is often far more important in immediate impact on the boys, physically and mentally, than is the Rectorship, in Jesuit schools. It is usually not so much the business of personal contact: form-masters and masters of subjects and prefects of discipline provided that, the last of them especially, given his power of corporal punishment. But the Prefect of Studies was omnipresent, and his personal rejection of the scientific life taunted Conan Doyle and forced upon him, he felt, a choice between intellectual development and religious fidelity. In his view, Kingdon had quite clearly abandoned his own scientific birthright for a mass of superstitious pottage, which he sought to impose on his charges. The portrait of Berghersh is kindly, in some ways suggesting deeper emotional commitment than Conan Doyle was prepared to concede to any Jesuit save Cassidy. When the Abbot gives his blessing to Alleyne Edricson and sends him out in the world, the scene is a tender one. He was not fitting Alleyne for that world, and yet for all of the need for Alleyne to put the years of innocence behind him as he comes to learn the realities, harsh and beautiful, the innocence he must lose is still very dear to him. Conan Doyle knew that his Parsifal would have to shed his guilelessness, but that integrity of purity before he did so was none the less admirable. On the other hand, he also saw it as involving much nonsense of a sort of super-nursery content in place of mental stimulation. He clearly saw Catholics as supporting themselves on fables instead of entering into the scientific arena, while wide in their cultural and philosophical range. "I have read Ockham, Bradwardine and other of the school-men, together with the learned Duns Scotus and the book of the holy Aquinas", Alleyne tells the Abbot. The diet would have sustained him for a good twenty years, one might feel, given the length of the *Summa Theologica* of St Thomas Aquinas, and the notion of the Benedictines encouraging their charges to wallow in the anti-Papal writings of William of Occam implies a liberalism on their part which is hardly consistent with *The White Company's* other evidence.

But if Conan Doyle was a little rusty on the contours of medieval intellectual achievements, he knew enough to testify to its extent and force. He was not prepared to subscribe to the Protestant delusion of the medieval clergy steeping the mind in darkness. The investigations of Bradwardine and the speculations of Scotus were no cul-de-sac. But the joke comes at the end, when we discover how profound is the innocent reverence of the Abbot for an authority the reader knows to be one of the foremost liars in human history:

"... Methinks the end of the world is not far from there [Jerusalem]."

"Then we can still find something to teach thee, Alleyne", said the Abbot complaisantly. "Know that many strange nations lie betwixt there and the end of the world. There is the country of the Amazons, and the country of the dwarfs, and the country of the fair but evil women who slay with beholding, like the basilisk. Beyond that again is the kingdom of Prester John and of the Great Cham. These things I know for very sooth, for I had them from that pious Christian and valiant knight, Sir John de Mandeville, who stopped twice at Beaulieu on his way to and from Southampton, and discoursed to us concerning what he had seen from the reader's desk in the refectory, until there was many a good brother who got neither bit nor sup, so stricken were they by his strange tales."

This particular passage has much work to do. It is at the start of *The White Company* and it is an important signal to the attentive reader that this is going to be an extremely funny romance of chivalry, will he but keep his eyes and ears going on more than conventional levels of response. The most remarkable quality of Conan Doyle's comedy is perhaps the seriousness of it, such that the reader is moving along with solemnity and respect, hearing the scholarly nature of the speech and the weights of its tone, and then suddenly finds himself looking at his narrator who is still apparently unchanged, moustache, pipe, smoke, voice, all unchanged, and the whole narration has slid into total hilarity. ACD never quite forgot the importance of keeping a straight face in doing a truly ludicrous imitation of a schoolmaster, or of allowing the opening to make sense the better to build up the final pillar of nonsense. The mood established has to be finely graded, since the story has to establish itself somewhere between Cervantes and Froissart, able to combine part of the spirit of Don Quixote with that of St Louis. Even Kingdon's war against science and progress is not wholly absurd; just as in real life a science without spirit proved to Conan Doyle to be as baseless as spirit without science, so the "complaisant" absurdities of the Abbot are founded on self-deception no greater than the chivalric spirit of Sir Nigel and his friends, for they ultimately lose lives, liberties and their company in the cause of Pedro the Cruel, a cause as unjust as its champions are noble. So the story ends, as it begins, in wonderful nonsense.

The irony is that in the tug-of-war of science against spirit which Kingdon opened for Conan Doyle, and whose other end would be supplied by the doctors and students of Edinburgh University, the writer's ultimate resolution was bitterly opposed by his former classmate Herbert Thurston, now an illustrious Jesuit priest. Conan Doyle's spiritualism was denounced by Thurston, and the controversy by the end had become very bitter, with Arthur making his greatest war against it; transubstantiation now moved his hardest ridicule as thoroughly as it once inspired his deepest piety. Even there his criticisms were much more positive than the norm, and his sensible anxiety about the wisdom of auricular confession administered by elderly celibates for adolescent girls deserved constructive attention instead of the idiotic defensiveness with which G.K. Chesterton assailed it in *The Thing*. In a way the crisis with Chesterton typified one problem of Conan Doyle at Stonyhurst; he, a Catholic by birth, always had an assurance about the realities of his faith which the exuberance, enthusiasm and indeed fanaticism of the converts who taught him could not have. Chesterton in denouncing his attack was simply running away from the problem of adolescent sex being treated by celibate old gentlemen who so seldom would know anything about it. Moreover, neither Thurston nor Chesterton really understood much about sex and were genuinely embarrassed by the subject; Conan Doyle, who won his doctorate for a dissertation on syphilis, did know what he was talking about. It is true that delicacy prevented his developing his argument fully: another cradle Catholic, Frank O'Connor, brought his objection into focus when in his short story *"News for the Church"* he described the psychological brutality of the celibate clerical conviction that sex was dirty, and that the procreative act was necessarily hateful.

But that whole controversy was based on Thurston's part on a misconception anyway. He denounced his old schoolmate for advocating spiritualism; in fact Conan Doyle's acceptance of spiritualism was a return to Kingdon in part. Science was not enough; spirit had to be acknowledged; man had to seek some explanation which materialism could not fulfil. But that narrowness of sect which ACD always denounced, and which unrealistically he would force Micah Clarke to denounce, demanded in its tribal greed that recognition of the role of the spirit had to be tied to a single code of interpretation. For all that, Conan Doyle in insisting on spiritualism had a larger common ground with Kingdon's position than had Thurston in simply denouncing spiritualism. "I wonder that so clever a man as Greeley [identified, rather oddly, as Horace Greeley of the *New York Tribune* in mid-nineteenth century America, by Father J.H. Crehan], and I may add as yourself, cannot see that the great thing in an age of materialism is to *prove* that there is anything outside the visible life", wrote Conan Doyle to Thurston in 1924: admittedly Thurston had in 1917 been somewhat mauled by action from Rome against his exploration of spiritualism up to then. Kingdon would certainly have denounced spiritualism also, but his reactionary critique still merits its place in keeping Conan Doyle's mind open to the call of the spirit. And that was what really mattered.

Kingdon won a great victory, but he neither knew it nor would have accepted it. The bent of Conan Doyle's mind was turning firmly against materialism through the 1880s and by the 1890s he, like Beardsley, Shaw, Wilde, Yeats and so many other major cultural giants of the decade, formally rejected it. Many of these men were to signal that rejection by the embrace of, or flirtation with, that Catholicism he had abandoned as a schoolboy, but whether they chose that or something else the religious commitment expressed in artistic terms provided several moments of supreme beauty and greatness: Wilde's *De Profundis* and *A Ballad of Reading Gaol*, Beardsley's drawing "St Rose of Lima", Shaw's *The Shewing-Up of Blanco Posnet*, Yeats's *A Vision*, the last two well after the 1890s but expressing conclusions whose initial rebellions were products of the decade. Conan Doyle's was a very startling affirmation indeed, put into the mouth of Sherlock Holmes on the eve of his destruction. It has the sense of natural wonder of Charles Altamont Doyle; but it also possesses Kingdon's insistence that science was not enough, that it was empty without soul. It was characteristic that Conan Doyle, so far from expressing it in Kingdon's rejection of science, made his statement in scientific terms, but its conclusion, while offering the reconciliation Kingdon rejected, triumphantly makes its own rejection of materialism.

> He walked past the couch to the open window, and held up the drooping stalk of a moss rose, looking down at the dainty blend of crimson and green. It was a new phase of his character to me, for I had never before seen him show any keen interest in natural objects.
>
> "There is nothing in which deduction is so necessary as in religion", said he, leaning with his back against the shutters. "It can be built up as an exact science by the reasoner. Our highest assurance of the goodness of Providence seems to me to rest in the flowers. All other things, our powers, our desires, our food, are really necessary for our existence in the first instance. But this rose is an extra. Its smell and its colour are an embellishment of life, not a condition of it. It is only goodness which gives extras, and so I say again that we have much to learn from the flowers."

The idiotic argument has been made that the work of the rose can be placed in wholly functional terms, but in fact the passage cannot be understood without the recognition of faith behind it, however deeply expressed in science. It is asking too much to assume that Conan Doyle would have known Kingdon's essay winning the Wix Prize was "On the connexion between Revealed Religion and Natural Science", although it is interesting that it was the hospital whence he won it, Bart's, which Conan Doyle chose for Watson's apprenticeship. It certainly is not impossible that Kingdon recalled one or two of its ideas in conversation with his young pupil on his medical ambitions, and what the boy might have dismissed as obscurantism he recalled later. He reaffirmed the connection which Kingdon after entering the church chose to ignore.

Conan Doyle's memoirs do not refer to Kingdon, though it is clear that his remarks on the hostility of Catholicism to science and progress are based on him more than anyone else. Neither does he refer by name to the other major figure whose rule in Stonyhurst would have directly affected him on a day-to-day basis, but the passage on corporal punishment had everything to do with the Rev. Thomas Kay, S.J., Prefect of Discipline, 35 when Conan Doyle first entered the college (Kingdon was then 49) and unusual in a group of schoolmasters with so many converts for having been born from the rich soil of Preston Catholicism. But if Kay resembled Cassidy in being born a Catholic, he lacked the common ground with Conan Doyle of the latter's Irish descent, and in place of Cassidy's affection he substituted a grim authoritarianism mildly redeemed by irony. For all his years at Stonyhurst save the last Conan Doyle was under the Rev. Cyprian Splaine as form-master, and Splaine's neurotic, gentle, lachrymose temperament (his career ended (after Conan Doyle's departure) in nervous prostration) almost certainly meant that the class received primary attention from the Prefect of Discipline. Kay kept order with what was called a "tolley", defined by his pupil as "a piece of india-rubber of the size and shape of a thick boot sole . . . One blow of this instrument, delivered with intent, would cause the palm of the hand to swell up and change colour. When I say that the usual punishment of the larger boys was nine on each hand, and that nine on one hand was the absolute minimum, it will be understood that it was a severe ordeal, and that the sufferer could not, as a rule, turn the handle of the door to get out of the room in which he had suffered. To take twice nine upon a cold day was about the extremity of human endurance."

Conan Doyle's account does not suggest Kay was sadistic. "I think", he wrote, "that it was good for us in the end, for it was a point of honour with many of us not to show that we were hurt, and that is one of the best trainings for a hard life." On the causes of his own punishments he says only "I went out of my way to do really mischievous and outrageous things simply to show that my spirit was unbroken". But Digby's account offers his early (and, it turned out, permanent) addiction to pipe-smoking as one cause. The Yew Alley was (and remained) notorious for offering attractions to smokers. Are we to deduce that at least investigation of the joys of tobacco ended by pursuit up the alley by Kay? It will be remembered that Sir Charles Baskerville had smoked until he saw the hound, after which he commenced his terrible flight. To wander into total speculation, Father Kay's fellow-Prestonian and exact contemporary of Conan Doyle, Francis Thompson, published his great poem *The Hound of Heaven* in 1893: certainly the imagery of Thompson's flight from the heavenly hound and Sir Charles's from the supposedly ghostly one have common features so strong as to suggest an influence. The word "hound" would have promptly suggested

Thompson in literary minds at the time Conan Doyle thought of his story and heard from his friend Fletcher Robinson the Devonshire legend of a spectre hound. Was all this the reason why the Yew Alley asserted itself so firmly at that point, and was Kay in a sudden resurrection of schoolboy reaction, prompted in Conan Doyle's mind by the inexorable footsteps of *"The Hound of Heaven"*? As we have seen, he himself was thinking a little about Catholicism in this period. Above all, the joke involved seems so like him, and his work contains many jokes for his own amusement as well as the countless ones for his readers. Quite apart from Thompson's poem, Conan Doyle is very strong about the Stoicism he required of himself with regard to Kay's punishments, but this does not mean that the boy on seeing the appearance of the wielder of inevitable punishment did not experience huge, sickening waves of fright. If the theory is true, then, Joyce's Jesuit schoolmasters described in the *Portrait* may have counted themselves fortunate: they appeared in immortal print as themselves, not as the hound of the Baskervilles.

One final little touch on the subject of smoking and the origins of the *Hound* may be found in its third chapter, where Watson enters after absence from Baker Street all day to find Holmes ruminating on the case:

> My first impression as I opened the door was that a fire had broken out, for the room was so filled with smoke that the light of the lamp upon the table was blurred by it. As I entered, however, my fears were set at rest, for it was the acrid fumes of strong coarse tobacco which took me by the throat and set me coughing. Through the haze I had a vague vision of Holmes in his dressing-gown coiled up in an arm-chair with his black clay pipe between his lips. . . .
> "Caught cold, Watson?" said he.
> "No, it's this poisonous atmosphere."
> "I suppose it *is* pretty thick, now that you mention it."
> "Thick! It is intolerable."
> "Open the window, then! .. . ... where do you think I have been?"
> "A fixture also."
> "On the contrary, I have been to Devonshire."
> "In spirit?"
> "Exactly. My body has remained in this arm-chair . . . ."

Two points arise, firstly, that Watson's reaction is very unusual for him. A fellow-smoker, he tells Holmes on their first meeting "I always smoke 'ship's' myself" in response to the query, "You don't mind the smell of strong tobacco, I hope?" Even when he sleeps in a bedroom in *"The Man with the Twisted Lip"* while Holmes in the same room goes through an ounce of tobacco (which should have caused Watson to wake up with a roaring headache), he says not a word of reproach. His description of the effects of the brooding on the Baskerville case sound not unlike the sarcasms of a schoolmaster finding pipe-smoking taking place in a loft, while his dialogue could well be that of a sarcastic investigator who abandons wit for testiness when his pretended fear of fire is met by repartee. If this, also, is another of the instances of Kay's discovery of Arthur smoking, it would presumably be in his later years, where brazen standing of ground had taken the place of flight. "If I was more beaten than others," comments ACD in *Memories and Adventures*, "it was not that I was in any way vicious, but it was that I had a nature which responded eagerly to affectionate kindness (which I never received), but which rebelled against threats and took a perverted pride in showing that it would not be cowed by violence . . . I deserved all I got for what I did, but I did it because I was mishandled." Holmes's dialogue, if that of a schoolboy being surprised at his pipe by Father Kay, would certainly fall into that category; and the more respectful demeanour of fellow-smokers could prompt the contrast Conan Doyle makes with the fate of the "others".

Secondly, the reference to Holmes's having been in Devonshire during Watson's absence is again an uncharacteristically fanciful form of talk for him. If the very passage itself is the result of the flight of the author's spirit across space and time to Stonyhurst while in the process of mentally transposing part of Stonyhurst to Devonshire, there is a very pleasing use of art to describe the process of its composition. On a straightforward level it is that in any case, but for the author to describe his own flight of spirit to Devonshire would be merely banal. It is the Stonyhurst contribution which makes it noteworthy, and such play with form and content is particularly evocative of the 'nineties whence he had just emerged.

Was Kay an inspiration for other work? Stonyhurst gossip when the Holmes short stories were published in the early 'nineties seemed fairly clear that he was, and he had left a very powerful memory in the place, having been Prefect of Discipline from 1869 to 1889. He favoured a particular sardonic style to "strike terror into a guilty breast", to borrow Holmes's phrase from *"The Three Students"* (employed after stage-management of a kind one suspects Kay would have recognised and respected). Kay was utterly indifferent to considerations of rank among his charges, and took particular pains—again, one thinks of Holmes—to deflate miscreants who sought to trade on their illustrious parentage. "My father is Prefect of the Seine", screamed a French student when told to fetch the tolley as a preliminary to its reception. "Then I", said Kay awfully, "must be Prefect of the Insane". This particular exchange, quoted by his obituarist in the Jesuit private publications on their Society, makes him the prime candidate for the remark quoted by Conan Doyle that he might become an engineer but never a civil one. But if there is a little of Kay in Holmes's dialogue, blended with the drier sarcasms of Edinburgh professors in the Medical School, Stonyhurst tradition saw much more evidence of the Prefect of Discipline when *"The Final Problem"* appeared in the *Strand* and the world learned for the first time of Professor Moriarty. (My source here is Father J.H. Crehan, S.J., who would in part have been basing himself on conversations with Conan Doyle's fellow-pupil Thurston as well as of former Stonyhurst staff.) It would seem that Kay had the capacity suddenly to materialise when least wanted before a group of students, and certainly the Holmes cycle has several striking epiphanies of awesome figures at the door of Holmes's room (although the only time a schoolmaster makes such an appearance it is, perhaps significantly, a preliminary to his collapsing at the feet of the detective in a dead faint—a

wild hope that might have flashed across the minds of the schoolboys when
Kay appeared, possibly with stage coughing on his part at the tobacco-smoke).
Presumably it was Moriarty's appearance before Holmes, the first presenta-
tion of him in the story, which conjured up the identification in the minds of
Kay's colleagues or former students:

> "My nerves are fairly proof, Watson, but I must confess to a start when I saw
> the very man who had been so much in my thought standing there on my
> threshold . . .
> " 'You have less frontal development that I should have expected', said he at
> last. 'It is a dangerous habit to finger loaded firearms in the pocket of one's
> dressing-gown.' "

Any actual antecedent of this would seem to suggest the line for Kay, "It is a
dangerous habit to dowse lighted pipes in the pocket of one's jacket", as
comment on a swift but vain attempt to conceal the evidence.

However, Kay was by no means the only Stonyhurst influence in the
making of Moriarty.

Cyprian Splaine was certainly not one of them. The form-master's gentleness might have been gratifying to Arthur, but its nature would have been
all too similar to that of Charles Altamont Doyle (not that there is any
evidence of Splaine being alcoholic). The gentleness in Cassidy had been
united to a very powerful, masculine spirit, all the readier to show love
because such a display was founded on innate strength. Had Kingdon and
Kay had some of Splaine's gentleness united to their own vigour of mind,
there would have been a basis for understanding with Conan Doyle. Splaine's
sensitivity resulted in introversion; he was in no way fitted to make a
conquest of the rapidly growing, masculine, sports-minded youth happiest
with authors of swashbuckling romance and thunderous prose, rapidly finding
Macaulay becoming his favourite author (an enthusiasm that, like the pipe,
would be lifelong). Splaine echoed the Jesuit fear of emotional expression,
apart from his propensity to tears. His aesthetic tastes led Gerard Manley
Hopkins at a later date to send him at his request a manuscript of the yet
unpublished *"Wreck of the* Deutschland", but he shuddered away from it. As
Arthur grew more and more doubtful about his own beliefs in Catholicism,
Cyprian Splaine continued to find his own solace in making detailed
investigations of intricate theological points, precisely the type of religious
enthusiasm least likely to answer the simple problems of the adolescent
Arthur. Arthur's increasing sourness against the Kingdon fascination with
rules would have been increased by Splaine as a teacher: the priest had little
inclination in pursuing the awkward questions of Greek and Roman ethics
which with his scholarly austerity he would find it necessary to deal, and
minute textual examination offered the retreat he sought. He may, indeed,
have taken his enthusiasm for Hebrew into the classroom, to be greeted, in
that event, with even less response from his pupil. Yet despite Arthur's
subsequent feeling that such methods robbed him of the grand presentation of
the totality of the classical world he needed, Splaine did give him the
apparatus for ready quotation, so much so that at the end of *A Study in*

Scarlet Watson can quote Plautus to Holmes and assume he will be able to understand it, for all of the literary agnosticism ascribed to him in that book and that one only. Any actual use of Splaine in the stories is hard to find, apart from the readiness of John Hopley Neligan in *"Black Peter"* and of Hilton Soames and Gilchrist in *"The Three Students"* to exhibit neurotic response to crisis. Neligan "sank his face in his hands and trembled all over"; Hilton Soames was "in a state of pitiable agitation . . . could hardly stand still . . . and he ran towards Holmes with two eager hands outstretched"; Gilchrist "with upraised hand, tried to control his writhing features" and then "had thrown himself on his knees beside the table and burst into a storm of passionate sobbing". But these instances could be founded on students less stoical than Arthur, although his statement suggests there were few of them.

Cyprian Splaine's successor in the unwelcome task of being form-master to Arthur was a man of very different stamp, but he arrived on the scene too late to affect the disposition of the disgruntled schoolboy very much. By that time Arthur seems to have articulated his doubts as to the validity of transubstantiation in speaking to a confessor, whose humane reaction was to arrange for him to serve Mass so that his failure to receive Communion (which he felt in conscience he could no longer worthily receive) would go unnoticed. (James Ryan's daughter told this story to Conan Doyle's.) The episode was characteristic of the invariable integrity of Arthur, and of his concern for not giving scandal. The latter point is important, as it is often confused with a search for respectability. Arthur never flinched at the odium which might result from an unpopular action—witness his championship of Slater, Edalji and Casement against the weight of élitist opinion, or his much-abused crusades for Spiritualism and allied causes—but he did most strongly retain the lessons of Jesuit teaching on the Christian duty to safeguard innocence. What Professor Emmet Larkin has termed the "devotional revolution" was then in full swing, in Britain as well as in Ireland; it was in fact a bourgeois form of asserting respectability by means of religious ostentation. It often went hand-in-hand with private indifference masked by calculated public expression of conformity. But for all of Arthur's denial of transubstantiation, he paid the doctrine the respect of absolutely refusing to receive Communion for appearance's sake: he was thus a far better friend to it than its nominal adherents. It is clear that the Jesuit to whom he spoke realised this. We do not know who he was, and Arthur's final year is perhaps a little late for it, but one candidate is the new form-master, the Rev. Reginald Edward Wellesley Colley, S.J., only eleven years Arthur's senior.

Certain qualities in him might have appealed to the boy, had they met earlier. Colley's relationship to the Iron Duke must have interested him, although Wellington's rejoinder in a Brigadier Gerard story after the Brigadier had been playing cards with British soldiers is rather more reminiscent of Kay:

> "See, my lord!" I cried, "I played for my freedom and I won, for, as you perceive, I hold the king."
> For the first time a slight smile softened his gaunt face.

"On the contrary", said he, as he mounted his horse, "it is I who won, for, as you perceive, my King holds you."

(Even the card-game may have a Stonyhurst original.) The gauntness of Wellington, apart from its iconographic antecedents, is certainly Colley rather than Kay. The young priest increased his ascetic appearance by his scorn for every form of self-indulgence, although he had ridden to hounds before his novitiate. Arthur might have got a story of a good run from him of the kind he would use in "*The King of the Foxes*" and, on a far higher level of comedy, "*The Crime of the Brigadier*": the latter dates from the period of Stonyhurst re-evocation, 1900, though Colley sounds an improbable source for its humour.

His manner was stiff and awkward with new acquaintances, and he drew his assignment to Arthur's class in his first year at Stonyhurst. He had even been a pupil in the school less than a decade before, which must have increased his lack of assurance. Yet he was of a type Conan Doyle would extol. It says much for his quality, and for the breadth of vision of the Jesuit authorities, that he was made Rector only ten years later, in his late thirties, winning particular renown for his selfless nursing of his boys during the terrible German measles and pneumonia epidemic of 1886 when four died. Here, as in his youthful promotion, there is an analogy with Francis Cassidy, who would put a boy with toothache in his own bed and himself sleep in a chair for fear the groans of the sufferer would arouse the others. But all we do know of this relationship with Arthur is that it seems to have been a very satisfactory one in scholarly terms so far as examinations are concerned. The boy had won some celebrity among the Jesuits as well as the boys when he brought his rising talent for versification to produce a poem about the Israelites' flight from Egypt, "*The Passage of the Red Sea*", completed in November 1873. Great things were now expected of him. The poem may seem absurd, and he grinned about it afterwards, but it showed very careful understanding of Virgil's *Aeneid*, to name but one source, the difficult and wonderful sixth book prompting particular touches. As Conan Doyle's earliest surviving work, it seems appropriate to include it here.

> Like to white daisies in a blooming wood,
> So round the sea the tents of Israel stood;
> To east and west, as far as eye could reach,
> The thronging crowds are seen along the beach.
> What host is this? Is it some savage band
> That bears destruction to a distant land?
> Is it some patriot army come to fight—
> To save their honour, and their nation's right?
> No army this. These girls who throng the plain,
> Would they e'er follow in an army's train?
> Behold these aged men, are their grey locks
> Fitted for war? Hark to the bleating flocks!—
> 'Tis but a nomad tribe who seek in flight
> Relief from bondage, and from Pharaoh's might.
> But lo! what shouts are these? What horrid sound

Which fills the air, and seems to shake the ground?
High on the summit of a mountain crest,
Hard by, a cloud of dust is seen to rest;
And higher still above the dust appears
The sheen of armour, and the gleam of spears!
And further off are heard the deafening peals
Of bugles, and the rush of chariot wheels:
In Israel's camp is frenzy and despair;
The women rave and tear their flowing hair;
The men by grief and disappointment cowed,
Around the standard of their leader crowd.
Then Moses spake:— "Behold my wondrous rod—
Think what its power has wrought, and think on God;
And say if He, the mighty God who boasts
To be the Lord of lords, and King of Hosts,
Cannot, although so mighty and so sage,
Free us from Egypt and from Pharaoh's rage."
He spake, and by the shore he took his stand.
And o'er the waters thrice he shook his wand.
Wonder of wonders! lo, the waves divide
And stand in dark green walls on either side!
Right through the midst the roaring sea is reft.
A slippery, dismal, weedy way is left!
There was no time for thought, no time for fear,
For Egypt's horse already pressed their rear.
On, on, they rush right through the sea, and reach,
Fatigued and tired, the rough opposing beach.
Then back they look, and see their daring foe
Still pressing through the yawning gulf below.
Once more did Moses shake his awful wand.
To his command the foaming waves respond.
One horrid shriek!—the tragedy is o'er,
And Pharaoh and his army were no more.

The ugly duckling had served notice of his graduation to swanlike plumage, although happily the song with which he did so began rather than ended his literary career. From thence he became a man to watch in a decidedly different sense to that Kay had assigned to him. He was put up for London University Matriculation, a passport for acceptance in Edinburgh University (which finance decreed was his only prospect in higher education). It was fortunate indeed that Colley was in charge of him; Splaine loathed the London Matric. Colley would probably have realised that Stonyhurst showing in such an examination would constitute a public triumph for Jesuit education. So, even more, did the Rector, Edmund Ignatius Purbrick, who now emerged from his vexatious legal dispute and building plans directly to inspire the drive for a major victory. And he got it. Conan Doyle and the other candidates were herded into his room in 1875 to see the smiling, spectacled, formidable, remote Rector waving the packet of London results aloft. Twelve of them, Arthur included, had made it, a tremendous personal triumph for Purbrick, who had been deprived of his Oxford studentship for entering the Roman Catholic church in 1850: he was sending his twelve little devils into the British university world whence he had been driven (to draw on a Scriptural text he assuredly did not employ). And he had another blessing to confer on Arthur. He was firmly ultramontane, and hostile to anything that looked like English particularism. Hence he encouraged recruits from Europe and the Americas to Stonyhurst, and thereby helped the growth of a strongly cosmopolitan influence on Arthur which would coexist thereafter with that patriotism also cherished at Stonyhurst. ACD was thus able to choose heroes from Napoleonic France as well as Plantagenet England with ease, sympathy and confidence, showing a brilliant sense of the cultural differences and prejudices involved not only in France but in the entirety of Napoleon-dominated Europe. The thing was clinched by Purbrick's decision to get a year for Arthur in the Jesuit institution at Feldkirch, in Austria near the Swiss border. It was a grand finale for the young scapegrace, even if it hardly compensated for the hunger of the heart along the road.

Looking back on his Stonyhurst years we must remind ourselves of much that is still missing from our knowledge, much that may include vital links in the story. Very many gaps still exist. On the most sublime level, we know of no meeting with Gerard Manley Hopkins, yet it would be absolutely fascinating to discover the boy had encountered the poet. St Mary's was close at hand, Cyprian Splaine is certainly a link in their stories, if an unpromising one. "A curious train of thought is started", wrote Conan Doyle in 1922, "when one reflects upon those great figures who have trod the stage of this earth, and actually played their parts in the same act, without ever coming face to face, or even knowing of each other's existence." He gave examples of Baber, the Great Mogul, and Hernando Cortez making their great conquests at the same moment, and added Caesar Augustus and the boy Jesus Christ for good measure. "It may be, however, that sometimes these great contemporary forces did approach, touch and separate—each unaware of the true meaning of the other." His remarks are the preface to the story, or more properly the fictional cameo, recounting a chance meeting between Odysseus on the eve of departure to Troy, and David accompanied by the boy Solomon, called "A Point of Contact".

In literary terms it would be hard to find such different worlds brushing one another as those of Hopkins's style and ACD's. Hopkins died of peritonitis at University College, Dublin, in 1889, and his poetic genius remained wholly unknown until 1918, when Robert Bridges published an edition of the poems: the Dictionary of National Biography knows nothing of him. Bridges's sponsorship made a ripple in Conan Doyle's circles, and he noted the critical interest aroused—nothing to what it became. The thought of the incongruity of the whole thing might have appealed to him, and could have worked its way through to "A Point of Contact" over the four years. If the phenomena are unconnected, it is a startling illustration of his opening irony.

There are clearly other questions. James Ryan's papers have so far not turned up, though he left a valuable library of Cingalese interest to

Stonyhurst, and it is not very easy to chart their friendship through the secondary school, beyond accepting ACD's insistence that it was pre-eminent. Mrs Ryan grew close to Mary Foley Doyle, and Arthur seems to have found his friend's mother a kindly correspondent himself, and one he needed outside of his family circle and free from its tensions. James Ryan went to Edinburgh University and acted as a laboratory assistant for Bryan Charles Waller, who shared rooms with the Doyles, but he did not graduate. He returned to Ceylon, kept in touch with Arthur and died in 1920 having disposed of his library in 1919. How they managed to retain contact during the year Arthur was in Stonyhurst and James in Hodder is problematic. Some Jesuits would have been a little doubtful about so close a friendship between boys of different years. ACD expressed deep respect in his memoirs for the Jesuits' vigilance— "The Jesuit teachers have no trust in human nature, and perhaps they are justified. We were never allowed for an instant to be alone with each other, and I think that the immorality which is rife in public schools was at a minimum in consequence. In our games and our walks the priests always took part, and a master perambulated the dormitories at night. Such a system may weaken self-respect and self-help, but it at least minimizes temptation and scandal." This, like his other absolutes, must be taken with reserve. Digby would hardly have built up so vivid an account of their feats as pipe-smokers over the years, and Father Kay's trick of miraculous appearance as recorded in his Jesuit obituary would be irrelevant, if there were always supervision. Newspapers got themselves written and edited, and sometimes, recalled Digby, their content was sufficiently anti-establishment to require secrecy in their composition and dissemination. Arthur's recollection that "In the last year I edited the College magazine" is about a manuscript and not a printed publication, and it may well have been *sub rosa*.

But the Jesuits could largely ensure that nothing like sexual adventure was happening. ACD is right in congratulating them, and modern sexual liberationists should agree: the sexual harassment of small boys, the hideous psychological effects of it, the acts of odious cruelty by senior to junior, were all consequences of magisterial incompetence or indifference in most of the major Protestant public schools, and a modern rhetoric which attacks sexual oppression could not justify the record. The fact that most Jesuits repressed their emotions did not mean lack of understanding: someone like Cassidy clearly knew the merits of friendship between an older and younger boy, and encouraged his young Irish Scots to associate at Hodder, while his Stonyhurst colleagues such as Splaine could have been more apprehensive. Kay would have discouraged association between Arthur and Jim Ryan because it would have invited Arthur's defiant ways to influence a younger boy and spread themselves to a lower form. Probably Arthur would have liked to have had more privacy with Ryan, but it does not seem to have rankled that he had so little of it. Of the Jesuit educational system *Memories and Adventures* concludes "On the whole it was justified by results, for I think it turned out as decent a set of young fellows as any other school would do".

One very important literary point resulted. Not only did the friendship with

Ryan remain in equipoise, Conan Doyle was left with the capacity to describe such a friendship. Holmes and Watson succeed as a friendship by an extraordinarily skilful use of emotion. The jokes about their relationship by subsequent commentators have been innumerable, and occasionally even funny, especially with the changes in language and perception since the time of writing. The achievement of the Holmes-Watson association is that it implicitly excludes a sexual content, and yet is shown over the years to be based on a very tender emotional association. We can see the Scylla and Charybdis facing the craftsman if we look at certain of Conan Doyle's precursors and imitators. Dupin and the narrator in Poe may be classed as an exception: the atmosphere of decadence might allow for the pursuit of strange passions had the narrator any personality worthy of notice. Gaboriau's Lecoq opens the line of detectives with Watsons so stupid as to lack any serious human association at all. On the other hand Conan Doyle's brother-in-law Ernest William Hornung produced in Raffles and Bunny an imitation of Holmes and Watson which is very obviously homosexual, and a mawkish, cloying, stifling business it is. This is particularly evident in the narrator, Bunny, who becomes very jealous whenever Raffles looks at girls, and fairly tense when any male rival for Raffles's attention is present also. Bunny is represented as having been in love with a woman when he became Raffles's assistant in the amateur cracksman business, but Raffles quite effectively drives that out of his mind. In any case the lady receives her first mention in the third book of the series which suggests Hornung thought his original version needed some cosmetic treatment. The relationship between Raffles and Bunny has begun in public-school, with Bunny as Raffles's fag, or conscript batman from a junior class, and this is constantly stressed as basic to all of their subsequent proceedings. Graham Greene very reasonably made the homosexuality explicit in his light-hearted play "*The Return of A. J. Raffles*", but even his genius could not quite sustain the atmosphere of schoolboy "crush" which radiates from Bunny. Curiously, the initial effort to sweeten the Raffles saga from the moralists' standpoint, when it was serialised, in *Cassell's* in 1898, resulted in a title "*In the Chains of Crime*", subtitled "Being the Confessions of a late Prisoner of the Crown, and sometime accomplice of the more notorious A. J. Raffles, Cricketer and Criminal, whose fate is unknown". This may have reminded everyone that Crime Did Not Pay And Was Wrong rather better than Hornung would succeed in doing, but it carried with it a picture, repeated each month, showing Bunny wearing evening-dress and chained by the neck being dragged by a skeleton in a monk's habit, possibly towards a pit but actually into the arms—and not very skeletal arms—of the skeleton who holds in his hand farthest from Bunny a confused bunch of leather possibly intended for punitive purposes.

Leaving the picture aside as a mere curiosity, the contrast between Holmes-Watson and Raffles-Bunny asserts itself most notably at the outset because of Conan Doyle's confidence in describing such a relationship and Hornung's wallowing in public-school sentimentality. To say this is not to question Hornung's artistry: if such a partnership as Raffles and Bunny were to exist, prolonged public-school idolisation was about the most likely basis for it. In any case, Hornung can claim much credit in facilitating the return of Sherlock Holmes. If Raffles owed much of his existence to the example of Holmes, Holmes owed much of the renewal of his to the example of Raffles. The fact remained that when ACD left Stonyhurst he carried with him a friendship whose literary consequences did not have to express themselves in hot-house terms.

Admittedly, its first literary expression, in the manuscript of about 1878, the earliest story of his to survive, went rather heavily in the other direction: "Tom Hulton was an old college chum of mine, and right glad I was to see his honest face beneath my roof. He brightened the whole house, Tom did, for a more good humoured hearty reckless fellow never breathed." Tom Hulton is not Jim Ryan, indeed the narrator and Hulton seem to express different aspects of the author's personality; but the companionship seems clearly based on a desire to record a friendship based on his association with Ryan. His success in doing so with Holmes and Watson is masterly in the almost mathematically calculated progress of a relationship. It should be borne in mind that despite the attempts to provide chronologies for the Holmes adventures, *The Sign of Four* as originally conceived is intended to follow *A Study in Scarlet* fairly rapidly in time, and for all the subsequent carelessness about dates, the location of Mrs Watson, residence in Baker Street and so forth, continuity is evident in most of the early stories. One or two, such as "*The Speckled Band*" and "*The Noble Bachelor*" are explicitly dated before Watson's marriage. But constant back references imply that once the short stories are launched there is a clear order among certain of them as follows: "*A Scandal in Bohemia*", "*A Case of Identity*", "*The Red-Headed League*", "*The Man with the Twisted Lip*", "*The Blue Carbuncle*", "*The Copper Beeches*". The order of Conan Doyle's composition weighed with him much more than any imaginary question of their date of occurrence or of Watson's time of narration. Hence on an overall basis we find the relationship very carefully graded. Watson learns a little of Holmes's work in *A Study in Scarlet*, rather more of the philosophy behind it in *The Sign of Four*, is still being called "Doctor" rather than the more intimate "Watson" in the early *Adventures*, is told it "is really very good of you to come" on the Boscombe Valley journey instead of any more casual not to say peremptory summons as in later years, is not told of Holmes's beginnings as a detective until the seventeenth short story, never hears of his brother until the twenty-second, and so progress is slowly made. Conan Doyle throughout his lifetime continued that process of gradation. Watson is deceived by Holmes as to his death in "*The Final Problem*" (and so was Conan Doyle) and that deception is rather oddly prolonged in "*The Empty House*", a further deception is practiced on him in "*The Dying Detective*", but Holmes deals with him as honestly as he can on the subject of his injuries in "*The Illustrious Client*". He specifically informs him in "*The Bruce-Partington Plans*" that he can disclose Mycroft Holmes's real employment now but that when he first introduced Watson to Mycroft for all of Holmes's and Watson's "long and intimate acquaintance" by that date, "I did not know you quite so well in those days. One has to be discreet when one talks of high matters of state".

Correspondingly, the emotional nature of their association is very sparingly revealed. Holmes's habits convey something of it, but so does Watson's married life: again, to leave the chronology out of account, in "*A Scandal in Bohemia*" Watson revisits Holmes apparently for the first time since buying a medical practice after his marriage (and Holmes rather oddly does not know he decided to do so), and Holmes takes him to have put on seven and a half pounds since he had last seen him. Holmes's first visit to Watson is not until the sixteenth short story. The first clear expressions of a very great deepening of the relationship are, naturally, those of Watson's grief in "*The Final Problem*"—it is not hard to imagine him fighting his tears as he writes its last paragraph and the foredoomed, anxious, haunted tone of the entire story is its own expression of love. We cannot take too much into account in "*The Final Problem*" as Conan Doyle intended it to be the last story, and its elegiac nature is partly to crown the existing cycle as it concludes; although the loose ends, such as the mention of the air-gun, which reappears in "*The Empty House*", leave some doubt as to whether all of Conan Doyle's mind consented in Holmes's death. "*The Empty House*" shows Watson fainting "for the first and the last time in my life" at Holmes's reappearance. The physical manifestations here are very ably done. Holmes opens Watson's collar-ends and gives him brandy, Watson grips Holmes twice, once by the arms and once again, as if to reassure himself that it is not a dream, "I gripped him by the sleeve and felt the thin, sinewy arm beneath it." Hornung may in fact have helped by giving Conan Doyle a reminder of what he did not want. After Raffles's return from disappearance which preceded Holmes's by a year or so, there is actually a brief and possibly fortunate interval between revelation and resumption of narrative, but Bunny's first words after the break are "Oh, my dear old chap, to think of having you by the hand again! . . ." which seems to imply, and may wish to imply, that they are holding hands throughout the ensuing dialogue. Hornung's intentions throughout the entire story ("*No Sinecure*") are ambiguous: Raffles, having returned disguised as an elderly invalid, takes an evil pleasure in humiliating the friend he had left to face trial and imprisonment in London, actually tormenting him with reference to his disgrace, before revealing his own identity. Conan Doyle, in monitoring his brother-in-law's story, evidently was very conscious of this exposure of a sadistic streak behind the public-school patronage and hero-worship. Certainly Holmes is by contrast more tender and sympathetic to Watson when he makes his return than he has ever been in the past.

But after the return he is more inclined to make fun of Watson than he has been in the past, though it is notable that actual ridicule always receives its Nemesis for himself in the same story (particularly in "*The Solitary Cyclist*" and "*The Disappearance of Lady Frances Carfax*"). There are arguments and verbal scorings-off in *The Hound of the Baskervilles* and *The Valley of Fear*, not always with Holmes as the winner. But after three books of short stories and three novels, Conan Doyle apparently decided in 1910 that he could allow very deep affection to express itself, although it does so at a moment of supreme danger and horror, when Holmes experiments with *Radix pedis diaboli* and Watson saves them both, roused to action by the sight of Holmes's face, not by his own fears:

> "Upon my word, Watson!" said Holmes at last, with an unsteady voice, "I owe you both my thanks and an apology. It was an unjustifiable experiment even for one's self, and doubly so for a friend. I am really very sorry."
>
> "You know", I answered with some emotion, for I had never seen so much of Holmes's heart before, "that it is my greatest joy and privilege to help you."
>
> He relapsed at once into the half-humourous, half-cynical vein which was his habitual attitude to those around him. "It would be superfluous to drive us mad, my dear Watson", said he. "A candid observer would certainly declare that we were so already before we embarked upon so wild an experiment. . . ."

And in *"The Three Garridebs"*, published in the *Strand* in 1925, fifteen years after *"The Devil's Foot"* appeared there, there is the moment when Killer Evans shoots Watson:

> . . . my friend's wiry arms were around me, and he was leading me to a chair.
>
> "You're not hurt, Watson? For God's sake, say that you are not hurt!"
>
> It was worth a wound—it was worth many wounds—to know the depth of loyalty and love which lay behind that cold mask. The clear, hard eyes were dimmed for a moment, and the firm lips were shaking. For the one and only time I caught a glimpse of a great heart as well as a great brain. All my years of humble but single-minded service culminated in that moment of revelation.
>
> "It's nothing, Holmes. It's a mere scratch."

To the end, Conan Doyle very carefully maintained the emotions in equipoise. Watson is far more moved by Holmes's love than by the killer's bullet, but he expresses his love by a dismissive comment fully equal to Holmes himself. Naturally Conan Doyle, for all his magnificent work in so carefully deepening the relationship over his forty years' work on it, was not simply still being programmed by a schoolboy friendship which had survived into college, was interrupted by thousands of miles, and maintained by correspondence and occasional meetings. Ryan had fairly recently died when he wrote *"The Three Garridebs"* but we must remember that death by now meant much less to Conan Doyle than most people, as he expected to hear from the departed loved ones, and had the liveliest expectation of joining them. What really enabled him to present the final expressions of love between Holmes and Watson is the fact that he had married Jean Leckie in September 1907. For the first time in his life he was really able to express to the full his love for another human being, not simply the good, generous regard of his first marriage, but an over-riding, supreme love which permeated every aspect of his life. Hence Holmes actually takes the initiative in affectionate expression in 1910, and writing *"The Three Garridebs"* in 1924 Conan Doyle evidently decided that his two old friends will not be allowed to perish without one triumphant release of their true love, Holmes to Watson, Watson to the reader. As a result, Conan Doyle has the distinction in that passage of having recorded love between male friends with more honour and more dignity than in any work in the language. It places us in debt to Stonyhurst, to Jim Ryan, to Jean Leckie, and above all to himself. It is a tremendous feat of artistic self-discipline, as great in its way as the absolute refusal on both his and Jean Leckie's parts to consummate their relationship during his first wife's lifetime.

The lifetime skill in slowly moving Holmes's and Watson's emotions is mirrored by the lifetime change in his own mental conflict about Stonyhurst and its message. He was angry about the outlawry of affection by master to boys; he was, possibly after anger at the time, grateful for emotional controls among schoolboys. In artistic terms, therefore, the Jesuits' work was well done, though with results they would hardly have anticipated. James Joyce's extraordinary, almost mathematical, direction over emotion as expressed in his work is a further indication of that achievement. The really remarkable thing in Conan Doyle's case was that he kept the momentum of emotional expression moving with such skill. That he established the notion of a series of separate stories about two fixed characters is long recognised. The joke that won respect far beyond its merit, that Holmes might not have been killed when he fell down the Reichenbach Falls but was never the same man afterwards, has one critical insight. There is a change in the Holmes of the *Return*, and there are further changes in later volumes. But Conan Doyle's statement "To make a real character one must sacrifice everything to consistency" is quite consistent with these changes. With characteristic modesty, the author simply did not make enough of his achievement, and where he found it worth a passing flicker of self-congratulation that he had kept his men as he had made them, neither he nor the public were ready enough to see just how delicately the development of association had been.

There are some problems about the great compass of years. The success of Holmes on the stage created the peril of a stagey Holmes. This obviously affects "*The Mazarin Stone*", which started life as a play, but seeps into some of the later stories, including *The Valley of Fear*. *The Case-Book of Sherlock Holmes* contains material much weaker than any of the preceding volumes, although only one story, "*The Three Gables*", is a failure—a failure in that case so total that it is hard to convince oneself Conan Doyle wrote it. But the *Case-Book* is undervalued in other respects. Purists dislike it, particularly because the detective element seems weaker than before. But it is actually much more powerful than the earlier work in a different degree. Conan Doyle's marriage, and the resolution of his religious dilemma, had released some quite new impulses in his writing. Because his knowledge of sex as a medical researcher had always been far greater than that of most of his contemporaries, he had been curbing his powers of expression in writing outside the Holmes cycle. The freedom of the 'twenties therefore was much more welcome to him than commentators who have blindly written him off as a Victorian prude could hope to understand. The *Case-Book* raises some much more fundamental human problems than any he had tackled before in "*The Veiled Lodger*", "*The Sussex Vampire*", "*Thor Bridge*", "*The Creeping Man*", "*The Illustrious Client*", "*The Retired Colourman*", and even in those unsuccessful attempts to make Holmes narrator, "*The Blanched Soldier*" and "*The Lion's Mane*". Not all of these stories are in themselves satisfactory, but he certainly showed his ability to respond to a climate accepting fuller expression of emotion than he encountered hitherto. Indeed one or two of his stories had met censorship at an earlier date: "*The Cardboard Box*", with its theme of adultery, was not published in book form after its *Strand* appearance until *His Last Bow* in 1917, and the *Idler* in 1893 prevented him from ending his remarkable story of a birth, "*The Curse of Eve*", with, as he had planned, the death of the mother and the father's attempt to kill the baby as its mother's murderer.

*   *   *

Surviving letters from Stonyhurst illustrate the contrast between the young Scot and his English associates. In July 1873, for instance, Arthur wrote home (text from Pearson):

> I hope you and the bairns are making the best of your vacation.
> I have never known a year pass so quickly as the last one, it seems not a month since I left you, and I can remember all the minutest Articles of furniture in the house, even to the stains on the wall.

The following year (probably, text from Carr) he wrote:

> I hope you all enjoy yourselves and have as fine weather as I have. On Shrove Monday we played the match, and we won a glorious victory. They got 111 runs and we got 276, of which I contributed 51. When I reside at Edinburgh, I would like to enter some cricket-club there. It is a jolly game, and does more to make a fellow strong and healthy than all the doctors in the world. I think I could take a place in the eleven of any club in Edinburgh.

(This, with the lack of Scottish enthusiasm for the English game, was no idle boast.) Now, let us look at a letter from his future opponent on spiritualism, Herbert Thurston, writing home at the same age, but in 1871 as he was two and a half years Arthur's senior:

> Mr Clayton, master of Syntax (our master) a very good fellow. I like him very much. . . . I have made enquiries about M. [name of son of family friends, presumably deleted by Thurston's biographer Father Joseph Crehan], and I discover him to be a tall lanky youth with a very large nose; he is about 6th in the class below me.

The inference would seem to be that to Arthur, he himself was a "fellow"; to Herbert Thurston, his teacher was one. Sherlock Holmes, whose creator had had to give considerable thought to the way the English used their language, employs the word about the commissionaire: ("About four o'clock on Christmas morning, Peterson, who, as you know, is a very honest fellow, was returning from some small jollification . . ."). Arthur, and Jim Ryan, probably weathered the superior manners and condescension of their English fellow-pupils with a mixture of reactions, much as Reginald Musgrave in "*The Musgrave Ritual*" is presented in curiously contrasting sequences. Holmes's first account of him is moderately sympathetic:

He was not generally popular . . . though it always seemed to me that what was set down as pride was really an attempt to cover extreme natural diffidence.

Yet as the story continues Musgrave emerges as stupid, tyrannical, insolent and inhumane. As Holmes is the narrator, it cannot be a case of Watson being mistaken on a first appearance. The origin of the ambiguity is probably at least two models, probably from Stonyhurst, one liked by Arthur, one not.

As to Arthur's more commonplace associations among his schoolfellows, information is, in most cases, too meagre to suggest direct influence on his writing life and career. They certainly gave one thing to his writing—their names. Not all coincidences can be construed as clues. We learn from "*The Dancing Men*" that Dr Watson never played billiards except with Thurston: however, Mr Michael Harrison's citation of Thurston's as a famous billiard-playing and manufacturing family in Newcastle Street, Strand, until 1900, which would have made them neighbours of the *Strand* magazine, may seem conclusive on that point of origin. It would have appealed to Conan Doyle's sense of humour to suggest that the unpretentious Watson declined to play billiards with anyone save a professional champion to the manor born. The identity with the name of an old schoolfellow might have been an additional incentive to make the private joke, but that is all. Henry Edmund Garcia sounds more conclusive, and it would be an obvious association of ideas for him to provide the name of the priest in "*The Confession*", and from that lodging of the name in Conan Doyle's creative mind, it reappeared as the name of the victim in "*Wisteria Lodge*". The character in "*The Confession*", on the other hand, sounds a little like Arthur's last form-master, Wellesley Colley, at the date of composition rising high in the Society of Jesus and about to become Provincial the following year. The original Garcia was admitted to Stonyhurst in 1867. Norbert Louis Moran reached Hodder two weeks after Conan Doyle, going into a higher class: promoted to a Colonelcy with the comparably unusual first name of Sebastian, after another saint, he was the "second most dangerous man in England" until captured by Holmes in "*The Empty House*" thus inaugurating the *Return*. There was a Watson, Alfred Aloysius, but he was five years senior to Conan Doyle: Edinburgh medical Watsons and Portsmouth acquaintances seem better candidates. But Patrick Sherlock of Co. Carlow can hardly be impeached. A year Arthur's senior, he arrived the same year, receiving the morose comment from the authorities, "can hardly read".

The awful thought crosses the mind that ACD amused himself by giving his great detective the name of possibly the most unpromising pupil among his own contemporaries, and indeed the Holmes of the first novel carried illiteracy into many fields. Patrick Sherlock may have been the case of an ignoramus on conventional levels who was famous for his talents in one direction: he was of sufficient quality as an actor to win the part of Tom Moore in the play of 1870, and Holmes's talents as an actor are notable, although not in the story which gave him birth. Early notes for *A Study in Scarlet* were available to former biographers, and reveal the first name put by Conan Doyle to paper was "Sherrinford" (and that Watson was originally

Ormond Sacker, a fact splendidly picked up in Gene Wilder's film *"Sherlock Holmes's Smarter Brother"* where the jealous younger brother of Holmes has a Watson named Ormond Sacker). This does not mean that "Sherrinford" came first to Conan Doyle's mind: it sounds like a composite. It may be that his impish sense of humour was struck by the thought of giving his detective the name of a pupil of proverbial stupidity, that he initially altered the name feeling that it was a bit unkind, and then that he sensibly told himself that no old schoolfellow would ever see *A Tangled Skein,* later renamed *A Study in Scarlet.* Then, when he had half-forgotten his first inspiration Holmes took hold of the public; the name of Sherlock was famous beyond recall. ACD would mention that there had been a Portsmouth cricketer named Sherlock, and persuaded himself that the idea of the name had come from there.

But names of classmates over so long a time in formative years are not obliterated so easily. Stonyhurst supplied Arthur with his first Sherlock. The "Holmes" part of the name was certainly intended to suggest wisdom and omniscience; ACD seems indisputable in insisting that it is taken from the famous American writer and doctor (and father of the Supreme Court judge) Oliver Wendell Holmes, author of the *Autocrat,* the *Professor,* and the *Poet* (each of *The Breakfast-Table*). Arthur Conan Doyle deeply admired the American Holmes, as well as being interested in his circle, and some of Sherlock Holmes derives directly from the Boston sage. The name "Holmes" was intended to offer a contrast with "Sherlock". Arthur's second experience of the name Sherlock would have been in the pages of Macaulay's *History* where the High Tory theoretician, who popped in to the Deanery of St Paul's after the Revolution of 1688 while men to his Left were sacrificing their sees in the nonjuror cause, cuts a somewhat ludicrous figure. Of course it was subsequently quite impossible to disclose the first Sherlock. It would have been wholly repugnant to Arthur to cause pain either to his former schoolmate or to his family.

On the other hand, his use of another Stonyhurst name sounds quite deliberate, and since it did not join the canon until Holmes was famous, it clearly cost its author no qualms of conscience at all. John Francis Moriarty won a Stonyhurst prize for Mathematics in 1873. Michael Moriarty won it in 1874. Michael's was the more remarkable achievement, as he obtained second prize in the entire school when a pupil in Grammar, in his first year at Stonyhurst proper. (Grammar was four classes away from the senior form, Rhetoric.) This is altogether too good for coincidence. Conan Doyle liked to have occasional jokes for himself, his people (and no doubt James Ryan) in his writings, and the comment on Professor Moriarty, "At the age of twenty-one he wrote a treatise on the binomial theorem, which has had a European vogue", acquires a particular charm in these circumstances. The binomial theorem was, perhaps, a rather jejune subject for a mathematician to make the keystone of his reputation and "on the strength of it" win his chair, but it would be a memorable feat for so junior a student in secondary school against overwhelming, indeed European, competition. I have discovered nothing more about Michael Moriarty save that he appeared in a minor part in the Christmas play in 1874.

But the other Moriarty, John Francis, would attain considerable, and not entirely inappropriate, celebrity. It is, as Holmes would say, singular that in listing his schoolfellows of distinction in his memoirs Conan Doyle recalls only Thurston, Partridge and Vaughan. Lord Justice John Moriarty of the Irish Bench is an odd, but understandable, omission. Michael's name might be used as a very kindly joke, John's name as a less kindly one, but when *Memories and Adventures* appeared in 1924 the Sherlockologists were well and truly in action and any allusion to a Moriarty among his schoolfellows would have led to some highly embarrassing research. We know little of Johnnie Moriarty's achievements at Stonyhurst, apart from his performance as Captain Middleton in the 1871 play, but if he had any resemblance to what he afterwards became, his memory gave his former schoolmate more than a name. In fact, the name probably came first. Having decided that Holmes was to be killed to prevent his stunting his author's further artistic development, Conan Doyle was casting round for an agent of destruction. The Horatian tag *"Dulce et decorum est pro patria mori"* was on his mind: in fact he used it in *"A Straggler of '15"* written about 1893, the year of *"The Final Problem"*. ("It is sweet and fitting to die for the fatherland" is the meaning: that Horace himself ran away from the battle of Philippi is a side-issue and need not detain us, any more than it detained him.) But Holmes was to die for his creator's art: *pro arte mori*. And that may very well have supplied the name. Moriarty. And up rushed the memories. The boy mathematical genius. And the older mathematician. Holmes said of his adversary that "his face protrudes forward and is forever slowly oscillating from side to side in a curiously reptilian fashion". When Johnnie Moriarty, K.C., rose to cross-examine a witness, "uncoiled" was the word which sprang to the mind of the observer. Maurice Healy tells numerous and disreputable anecdotes about him in his wonderful *The Old Munster Circuit* of which the most appropriate here is a case touching an hotel, whose landlady had dilated during her examination with pardonable pride on the merits of her establishment. Moriarty drew his person up to a crouching position, inserted an eyeglass, swung his head around and commenced cross-examination: "So you live in this earthly Paradise, ma'am? A regular garden of Eden, is it not? Tell me, ma'am, do you have any serpent there?" "Oh, no, Serjeant, but we'd always be delighted to see you."

If John Moriarty's appearance suggested that of the Professor, his other qualities were more those of the individual trickster and master-manipulator, but it is doubtful if they would have commended themselves to Conan Doyle. Moriarty was in religious attitudes a sceptic, but where Arthur went to great lengths to avoid the reception of Communion once plagued by intellectual doubt, Moriarty ostentatiously paraded his religious devotion. A Judge of known piety could always be sure of drawing some dreadful sign from Johnnie betokening his devotion to the One, Holy, Catholic Church, such as standing in mid-examination in statuesque silence for the Angelus, or slamming rosary-beads on the table if his religious credentials were called into question, or dilating on the admirable and public enthusiasm for Catholicism of a client at the slightest chance, or entering into elaborate mystifications of the Court under the guise of expounding some allegedly relevant piece of theological abstruseness. One can imagine similar antics at Stonyhurst in public, with possible statements of the utmost cynicism in private (of the kind he would make in his prime at the bar), and one can also imagine the curl of Arthur's lip in his personal crisis of faith about which he so passionately refused to lie. Moriarty's career was festooned from the first with opportunism and shady tricks. Arthur might have completely lost touch with him after Stonyhurst, but during the Irish tour of 1885 enquiry about old Stonyhurst contemporaries could well have won from barrister acquaintances and political observers the story of how Johnnie had won preferment by a judiciously commenced, and still more judiciously aborted, political campaign in a Mallow by-election in 1883 where his presence seemed likely to injure the prospects of the Government candidate; his tactical withdrawal won him another step up the professional ladder. As the seat was in fact won by the famous Parnellite journalist William O'Brien the incident was widely known.

Other Irish acquaintances could have supplied more in later years: T. P Gill, MP, who met Conan Doyle and Oscar Wilde on the famous occasion when the editor of *Lippincott's* commissioned *The Sign of Four* and *The Picture of Dorian Gray*, could have supplied further details. Johnnie's political trimming in search of promotion made him an object of execration in circles dominated by Gill's fellow-Parnellites. The stories abounded: how Moriarty would read three sentences from a document to a witness in successive questions, and prove their presence in the document, and then read a fourth from a concealed note which was not in the document at all, but would be assumed by the witness to be so. When "*The Final Problem*" appeared in the *Strand*, Moriarty may well have been called "Professor" by irritated colleagues, and it would hardly have dismayed Conan Doyle to hear they did so. He was quite safe from a libel action: it would simply have covered Moriarty with ridicule, the one commodity against which his life-style was not proof.

In any case, the Professor was many other people apart from his two namesakes (and in "*The Final Problem*" and *The Valley of Fear* he is equipped with two different brothers), Kay being one, the Jonathan Wild of Fielding and of reality another, and, insists Mr Charles Higham, the master-criminal of the 'sixties and 'seventies Adam Worth. Mr Higham also makes play with the possibility that Arthur on a visit to his relatives in London in December 1874 could have read the proceedings anent one George Moriarty, and perhaps such an event, even without the careful culling Mr Higham's thesis assumes, might have offered a pleasing association of the name of Moriarty and the world of crime. But none of these, apart from Kay, had the immediacy and the opportunity for detailed study and reflection of Arthur's protracted acquaintance with Johnnie. As for Johnnie himself, dark rumours undoubtedly continued to gather round him, although without the drastic effects on his career which similar comment had on academic status of the Professor. In his days of ill-fortune he had recourse to two weapons which seem to have eluded Moriarty—judicious marriage and bankruptcy. Ultimately, after an Odyssey through party politics such as would have excited the ridicule of the Vicar of Bray, he won his Lord Justiceship and is said to have breathed his last (in 1916) with the words "What won the three-thirty?" In retrospect he sounds amusing enough, but Maurice Healy's judgment of him as the "danger-spot" of the Irish Bar sums it up. His hypocrisy gave him something akin to the respectable disguise of the professor which so impressed Inspector MacDonald, and it would be easy to see how Arthur might regard him as "the organizer of half that is evil" in Stonyhurst. It is surely time that his name should be publicly coupled with its most outstanding artistic inspiration: a double inspiration, indeed, when one considers the influence of Moriarty on T. S. Eliot's cat Macavity:

> He shakes his head from side to side, with movements like a snake,
> And when you think he's fast asleep, he's always wide awake . . .

Finally, one last and very minor laugh. On the eve of the creation of Holmes and Watson, ACD wrote a story called "Uncle Jeremy's Household". It was almost finished by 18 May 1885, as he told his mother (Innes Doyle MSS), was rejected by Blackwood's, and finally serialised in the Boy's Own Paper in January and February 1887. A Study in Scarlet had been completed early in 1886 and accepted by Ward, Lock in October for publication at Christmas, 1887. Mr Peter Haining, reprinting it in his Final Adventures of Sherlock Holmes, draws attention to earlier work on it by the Sherlockian James Edward Holroyd. The narrator-hero Hugh Lawrence lives in Baker Street. He is summoned to the aid of a friend named John H. Thurston. Lawrence is a medical student while Thurston pursues chemistry, messing with test-tubes and solutions and even having an acid-stained finger. Lawrence goes in for character analysis on primitive Holmesian lines. Mr Haining is of course correct in seeing the story as birth-pangs of Holmes—he phrases it less medically—but it is amusing to see how Conan Doyle was switching attributes between his Holmes-type and Watson-type (he had in fact been doing it since "The Haunted Grange"). The medic-narrator in fact does the main work, while Thurston is largely required to bring Lawrence in, to provide the link with the mysterious household and be in mortal danger as its legatee, and to supply background briefing. Conan Doyle had yet to learn how best to split the companionship for maximum effectiveness. The hero-narrator is weakened in describing his methods, and strengths:

> It is proverbially easy to fall in love in a country house, but my nature has never been a sentimental one, and my judgment was not warped by any such feeling towards Miss Warrender. On the contrary, I set myself to study her as an entomologist might a specimen, critically, but without bias.

We can see the maturity achieved between 1885 and 1889, when The Sign of Four was written:

> "What a very attractive woman!" I exclaimed, turning to my companion.
> He had lit his pipe again and was leaning back with drooping eyelids. "Is she?" he said languidly. "I did not observe."

"You really are an automaton—a calculating machine", I cried. "There is something positively inhuman about you at times."

He smiled gently.

"It is of the first importance", he cried, "not to allow your judgment to be biased by personal qualities. A client is to me a mere unit, a factor in a problem. The emotional qualities are antagonistic to clear reasoning. I assure you that the most winning woman I ever knew was hanged for poisoning three little children for their insurance-money, and the most repellent man of my acquaintance is a philanthropist who has spent nearly a quarter of a million upon the London poor."

Later still, Holmes would recognise the importance of having his own litmus-paper for determining female attractiveness: "Now, Watson, the fair sex is your department". But *"Uncle Jeremy's Household"* is an important point in the development of a Holmes figure, and there is at least a laurel for Stonyhurst in providing an early version of a Watsonian name. "John H. Thurston", far more than "Ormond Sacker", is clearly the antecedent of "John H. Watson", and this particular antecedent can be firmly ascribed to Herbert Thurston: indeed it clears up the question of Dr Watson's middle name very nicely. Of course all of this had retreated fully into oblivion with *"The Dancing Men"* in which the name was brought back into play for entirely different reasons. It was indeed a singular irony that the man who had inspired the nomenclature of the earliest Watson should prove to be in the end the final antagonist of his creator. As for Inspector Stanley Hopkins and Gerard Manley Hopkins, there are some investigations even the most brazen biographer dares not undertake: the name may have stuck in Conan Doyle's memory as an inspiration for rhyme. After all, a possible meeting in Splaine's presence might have involved some mention of Arthur's infant poetic attempts. But I do not see much future in examining *"The Passage of the Red Sea"* as a source for *"The Wreck of the* Deutschland". We must leave some work for the Americans.

5

To Feldkirch and Back

The exiles departed, to learn in foreign camps that discipline without which natural courage is of small avail, and to retrieve on distant fields of battle the honour which had been lost by a long series of defeats at home.
—Thomas Babington Macaulay,
History of England, chapter XVII
(on the Irish after the treaty
of Limerick in 1691)

Far above the level of the Lake of Constance, nestling in a little corner of the Tyrolese Alps, lies the quiet town of Feldkirch. It is remarkable for nothing save for the presence of a large and well-conducted Jesuit school and for the extreme beauty of its situation. There is no more lovely spot in the whole of the Vorarlberg. From the hills which rise behind the town, the great lake glimmers some fifteen miles off, like a broad sea of quicksilver. Down below in the plains the Rhine and the Danube prattle along, flowing swiftly and merrily, with none of the dignity which they assume as they grow from brooks into rivers. Five great countries or principalities—Switzerland, Austria, Baden, Wurtemberg, and Bavaria—are visible from the plateau of Feldkirch.

Feldkirch is the centre of a large tract of hilly and pastoral country. The main road runs through the centre of the town, and then on as far as Anspach, where it divides into two branches, one of which is larger than the other. The more important one runs through the valleys across Austrian Tyrol into Tyrol proper, going as far, I believe, as the capital of Innsbruck. The lesser road runs for eight or ten miles amid wild and rugged glens to the village of Ladon, where it breaks up into a network of sheep-tracks. In this quiet spot, I, John Hudson, spent nearly two years of my life, from the June of '65 to the March of '67, and it was during that time that those events occurred which for some weeks brought the retired hamlet into an unholy prominence, and caused its name for the first, and probably for the last time, to be a familiar word to the European press. . . .

So opens "*A Pastoral Horror*", written by ACD some dozen years or more after his year at Feldkirch, 1875-76, thus making Feldkirch the first location he inhabited for any length of time to be formally honoured as the setting of one of his stories. He would use Edinburgh, had indeed done so before he wrote "*A Pastoral Horror*", but it was the Edinburgh he discovered after his return from Feldkirch to become a medical student. Stonyhurst locations he used under disguise. Feldkirch's importance lies in his growing unease with imaginary locations, the Commonwealth countries he summoned up so boldly for his early work, even the London he knew so slightly before his taking up residence there in 1891. The story itself is slight, and was never reprinted by him, but it gave him the basis for the confident use of European locations which he was to bring to a fine art in the Brigadier Gerard stories, in *The White Company, The Refugees, Uncle Bernac* and *Sir Nigel,* most of all in *"The Final Problem"* set in the Switzerland his young eyes first observed in 1875. He had capitalised vicariously on Feldkirch by the time of writing *"A Pastoral Horror"*—one story, which he did keep in print, being *"The Great Keinplatz Experiment"* of the mid-1880s, the other, which he did not, being *"The Silver Hatchet"*. The latter is theoretically placed in an unbelievably Teutonic Budapest, the former in the university town of Keinplatz, as ACD impudently termed his imaginary location. Keinplatz, no place: Arthur, greatly daring, had simply translated More's great Greek derivative Utopia into German. It was a nice assertion of his ambition to place himself among the literary giants.

Taken together they possess curious similarities of theme. *"A Pastoral Horror"* is about a kindly priest who proves a homicidal maniac; *"The Great Keinplatz Experiment"* concerns the transference of minds of a professor and a drunken student prolonged accidentally beyond the initial experiment; and *"The Silver Hatchet"* again deals with insanity, in the latter case caused by grasping a poisoned weapon which forces its wielder to murder those whom he loves most dearly. This is not to say that Arthur had some encounter with insanity in Feldkirch. His sources and contrivances for the stories went well beyond it. Even the inspiration for his protagonists' German names is not confined to his year there: the Keinplatz experimenter is Professor von Baumgarten—ACD's fundamental indifference to niceties of aristocratic title leading him to give a patent of nobility without qualm to as bourgeois a German name as could be found—and one of the users of the ghastly hatchet is Inspector Baumgarten: both came from his German master at Stonyhurst of whom he had written to his mother, "Father Baumgarten, talks to us in German always, while teaching us. I like it very much". As John Dickson Carr fairly acknowledged, the placing of Arthur in the first class for German clearly indicates that the Jesuits had long planned to place him at Feldkirch, and we may infer from it that they had more faith, hope and even charity for him than he realised. At sixteen Arthur was too young for University; a final Philosophy year in Stonyhurst would have been a mutually destructive anticlimax. Feldkirch offered safety from home and opportunity of cosmopolitan maturing.

His other notable story set in Germany, again not reprinted in his lifetime, *"An Exciting Christmas Eve"*, owes something also to Feldkirch, and its theme, an explosives expert kidnapped and forced to lecture to anarchists, at least deals with an unusual state of mind. It appeared in the *Boy's Own Paper* in 1883.

The balance of probability is clear enough. Charles Altamont Doyle's confinement in 1883 is the most obvious origin of the plots of the Feldkirch and Feldkirch-allied stories, *"Keinplatz"*, *"Hatchet"*, and the *"Pastoral Horror"*. *"Keinplatz"* brings this very close indeed, with the student's drunken habits continuing while he inhabits the professor's body and the professor in the student's body insults his own family by his natural familiarity to his wife and his spurning the advances of the daughter confronted, as she thinks, by the youth whom she loves and who (second to drink and brawling) loves her. Below this last point lies the ugly little thread suggesting that a man's own ways of addressing his family might seem very nasty indeed if employed by a stranger, although the professor himself is only a preoccupied and scholarly gentleman accustomed to treat his wife as though she were a food-producing machine. *"The Silver Hatchet"* underlines murderous attack being confined to dearest friends and loved ones very strongly, and the climax of the *"Pastoral Horror"* is a sermon by the homicidal priest mourning in the terms of deepest affection for the victims of the still unknown murderer. It is a way of writing out of his system how endangered the family felt by Charles Doyle in the later stages, and why they resorted to extreme measures. Yet for all the darkness of their inception, the stories are unable to fight against the author's humour. Oddly enough, *"Keinplatz"*, avowedly comic, is unexpectedly serious in its moments of revealing the shame of the apparent professor behaving like the drunken student and the real professor horrified by his treatment by intimates who see him as a student taking gross liberties. It is a comedy which remains very funny provided the reader does not identify too closely with any of the characters, a detachment easier to advocate than practise in reading Conan Doyle. On the other hand, *"The Silver Hatchet"*, in spite of being concerned with quite appalling murders by persons wholly devoted to their victims, breaks into total comedy of a kind closer to the work of Joe Orton than any contemporary of the author's:

> "Gentlemen", remarked the inspector, standing up and resuming his official tones, "this affair, strange as it is, must be treated according to rule and precedent. Sub-inspector Winkel, as your superior officer, I command you to arrest me upon a charge of murderously assaulting you. You will commit me to prison for the night, together with Herr von Schlegel and Herr Wilhelm Schlessinger. We shall take our trial at the coming sitting of the judges. In the meantime take care of that piece of evidence"—pointing to the parchment—"and, while I am away, devote your time and energy to utilising the clue you have obtained in discovering who it was who slew Herr Schiffer, the Bohemian Jew."

The experience of Conan Doyle among the Teutons therefore stimulated his mind very powerfully in one respect: it lent a strong discipline and direction to his sense of humour. Authority at Stonyhurst, even as satirised by him, is awesome in its "deliberate speed, majestic instancy", whether presented as Holmes, Moriarty, the Abbot Berghersh, or even the Hound. He could satirise the absurdities of priests laying a complaint, as he does in the first chapter of *The White Company*, but does not intend the judicial figures to seem ridiculous, and they are not. It is German bureaucracy, however he encountered it at Feldkirch, which lays itself open to his deft scalpel, and from that he obtained a theme that ran through both his writing and his public lives. The inspector's speech in itself is amusing as a reminder that the parodists of Sherlock Holmes had nothing to teach the creator: the jokes about Holmes detecting his own actions and ordering his own arrest in no case reach heights obtained by the forgotten and repudiated "*Silver Hatchet*". More significantly, we can see in this speech the origin of that implacable attack on the dangerous self-satisfaction of bureaucracy which dominates all of his critiques of the police in the Sherlock Holmes stories, as well as his devastating indictments of official incompetence and insistence on adherence to whatever quick solution has pleased the authorities. The immediately preceding passage has involved several pompous speeches from the inspector to the supposed miscreants, to be suddenly followed by his attempt to murder the sub-inspector when he grasps the hatchet himself. Certainly the story is at once a basis as well as a repository of irony. The solution refers to the use of mixtures "some of which, like the *aqua tofana* of the Medicis, would poison by penetrating through the pores of the skin".

Within a few months of its composition he was at work to dismember that sort of explanation in the splendid satire on the contemporary press which appears in *A Study in Scarlet*: "After alluding airily to the Vehmgericht, aqua tofana, Carbonari, the Marchioness de Brinvilliers, the Darwinian theory, the principles of Malthus, and the Ratcliff Highway murders, the article concluded by admonishing the Government and advocating a closer watch over foreigners in England." The passage as a whole—for that sentence, allegedly based on a leader in the *Daily Telegraph,* is but the close of one of three separate *tours-de-force*—follows the object of deflation in "*The Silver Hatchet*" by exhibiting the press as another example of the smugness of ill-informed bureaucracy. ACD maintained that crusade also to the end of his life, unkindly climaxing it in one of his very last stories, "*When the World Screamed*", when "an enormous spout of vile treacly substance of the consistence of tar" leaves "the unfortunate Press . . . so soaked and saturated, being in the direct line of fire, that none of them was capable of entering decent society for many weeks". Personal rancour had entered into it by that time, with the newspaper belittlement of his work by bad jokes about Sherlock Holmes followed up by perpetual sneers at his beloved Spiritualism. No doubt his friend George Bernard Shaw approved given the execution he did on journalistic modes of accuracy in the fourth act of *The Doctor's Dilemma,* which apparently owes much to ACD's personal reminiscences and published stories of medical life. This is not to say that he was instinctively hostile to the press. He had great admiration for certain editors and journalists—and became a fine journalist himself.

German academic life as exhibited in the stories has to be viewed with caution, since Edinburgh University experience was liable to intrude. The horror in "*Keinplatz*" of the supposed professor beer-swilling among students is a Scottish one: Conan Doyle knew nothing of the real tradition of professor-student fellowship in Stein-clinking, and any acquaintance on his part with university life in these German stories seems limited to literary

sources, of which his range was broad as his proficiency with the German
language increased rapidly and his voracity in reading led him to study
vernacular sources. This gave an odd development to his literary imagination.
German student life comes in, relevantly, to "*Keinplatz*", and "*The Silver
Hatchet*", the former in the necessary counterpoint of plot, the latter in that
one set of friends turned by the hatchet's properties into would-be murderer
and victim are medical students; and is irrelevantly but entertainingly used to
introduce the "*Christmas Eve*" story. "*The Silver Hatchet*" is set in December
1861, "*A Pastoral Horror*" as we have seen in 1865-67, and "*Kleinpatz*" is
appropriately in no time as well as no place. "*Christmas Eve*" is vaguer, but
the German narrator, a Heidelberg graduate now resident in Berlin, serves in
the Franco-Prussian war in which "I was stationed in an ambulance which
never even crossed the frontier, yet I succeeded in breaking my arm by
tumbling over a stretcher, and in contracting erysipelas from one of the few
wounds which came under my care. I got no medal or cross . . .", and that
seems to have been at some distance from the main events described, putting
it very nearly contemporary with the time of writing in the early 1880s.

Now, the accounts given of student life are a really odd amalgam from the
time standpoint. Obviously there is a basis in Edinburgh student life as
Conan Doyle knew it: indeed in "*Keinplatz*" the student, unaware of
inhabiting the professor's body, speaks of presiding and of taking the chair in
a gathering of drunken students, which are decidedly old Edinburgh formalities
of debauch. There is also some reminiscence of the student days in the
Feldkirch Jesuit school: "*An Exciting Christmas Eve*" recalls from Heidelberg
student days that "I was hurled out of a second-floor window by an English
lunatic because I ventured to quote the solemn and serious passage in
Schoppheim's 'Weltgeschichte' which proves Waterloo to have been a purely
Prussian victory, and throws grave doubts on the presence of any British
force nearer than Brussels!" This, minus the violence (which would have gone
no further than fisticuffs), sounds like a schoolboy argument: the defenestration
was doubtless owed to Conan Doyle's reading on the outbreak of the Thirty
Years' War. The likelihood of there having been some such dispute at
Feldkirch is strengthened by the consideration that Brigadier Gerard at
Waterloo sees virtually nothing of the British and is prevented from taking
part in the main battle because of an extraordinarily complicated series of
adventures with the Prussians. On the other hand some of the other material
sounds fairly "Student Prince" stuff, and in spirit is based on the roistering,
duelling, militaristic generation between Waterloo and 1848.

Arthur absorbed some of the German romantics at Feldkirch. One of the
students in "*The Silver Hatchet*" is called "von Schlegel", which sounds like
one way of acknowledging an influence, and there is a fine passage in "*How
the Brigadier Played for a Kingdom*" in which Gerard is defeated in his
attempts to hold "all Germany for the Emperor":

> Over went a table with a crash, and a young man had bounded upon one of the chairs.
> He had the face of one inspired—pale, eager, with wild haw eyes, and tangled hair. His
> sword hung straight from his side, and his riding-boots were brown with mire.

"It is Korner!" the people cried. "It is young Korner, the poet! Ah, he will sing, he will sing."

And he sang! It was soft, at first, and dreamy, telling of old Germany, the mother of nations, of the rich, warm plains, and the grey cities, and the fame of dead heroes. But then verse after verse rang like a trumpet-call. It was the Germany of now, the Germany which had been taken unawares and overthrown, but which was up again, and snapping the bonds upon her giant limbs. What was life that one should covet it? What was glorious death that one should shun it? The mother, the great mother, was calling. Her sigh was in the night wind. She was crying to her own children for help. Would they come? Would they come? Would they come?

Ah, that terrible song, the spirit face and the ringing voice! Where were I, and France, and the Emperor? They did not shout, these people—they howled. They were up on the chairs and the tables. They were raving, sobbing, the tears running down their faces. Korner had sprung from the chair, and his comrades were round him with their sabres in the air. . . .

The story was published in the *Strand* in 1895, and poor Gerard's last thought reads strangely indeed in view of events twenty years after, and Conan Doyle's part in them: "And I understood then that there was something terrible in this strong, patient Germany—this mother root of nations—and I saw that such a land, so old and so beloved, never could be conquered." ACD in the year before the Great War recorded in his profound essay "*Great Britain and the Next War*" how deeply he had cherished Anglo-German friendship and with what difficulty he had come to conclude that Germany's designs were no longer defensive but set on Napoleonic conquest in her turn.

He was particularly fitted by antecedents to respond to German romanticism. He was an enthusiastic reader of Carlyle, the great evangelist of German culture in the English-speaking world: indeed he would have Sherlock Holmes make the appropriate if unkind comment on the gulf he found between Carlyle's apostleship and Carlyle's sources:

". . . How small we feel with our petty ambitions and strivings in the presence of the great elemental forces of nature! Are you well up in your Jean Paul?"

"Fairly so. I worked back to him through Carlyle."

"That was like following the brook to the parent lake. He makes one curious but profound remark. It is that the chief proof of man's real greatness lies in his perception of his own smallness. It argues, you see, a power of comparison and of appreciation which is in itself a proof of nobility. There is much food for thought in Richter. You have not a pistol, have you?"

This is in *The Sign of Four*: the passage is the more remarkable in that it breaks consistency with *A Study in Scarlet* in the most drastic manner of the entire cycle, Holmes in the earlier work enquiring "in the naïvest way" in response to Watson's quoting Carlyle "who he might be and what he had done" (a *bétise* of Patrick Sherlock's perhaps? It is impossible to imagine an Edinburgh medic without such knowledge). *The Sign of Four* also involves Holmes quoting Goethe in the original as a specific against the effects of exposure to Athelney Jones's imbecilities. There is nothing casual about this. Having toyed with the idea of the specialist as Philistine, Conan Doyle angrily sweeps it away in the second book. If Holmes is to be a hero, he has to be endowed with his creator's zeal for German inquiry into mind and soul. The Jesuits' emphasis on spirit had now received a curious form of support. Science in the abstract would not suffice for anything worth doing.

In chronological terms, this mingling of reading and experiencing Germany tended to give Conan Doyle a strangely unified view of his own century, and one in which he would make surprisingly little allowance for change. He would have Holmes in the early 1880s carry out Robert Christison's experiments of the late 1820s. His imaginary German students are oscillating between Feldkirch in 1876 and Heidelberg in 1816. Some of his most notable symbolic figures are profoundly involved in spanning the century: Gerard telling his memoirs of Napoleonic Europe to café audiences of the France of Louis Philippe and of the Second Empire, the aged corporal in "*A Straggler of '15*" still alive in 1881 half-imagines he is at Waterloo and dies fully believing it. In his own turn this affected his work. The rowdy meetings in London in 1911 in *The Lost World* are really memories of Edinburgh thirty years earlier. Holmes begins as a figure in the very recent past, created in the mid-'eighties in episodes supposedly happening at the beginning of the decade, "*The Final Problem*" quite pointedly records in 1893 events of 1891, "*His Last Bow*" is published in 1917 and deals specifically with 2 August 1914, and yet all of the *Case-Book* deals with matters at least twenty or thirty years before publication. He was very conscientious about getting into period, although much less so with respect to specific dates (*The White Company* and *Sir Nigel* are quite inconsistent with one another as far as the events described and the stated interval between them are concerned).

But in other ways he was so much in love with the past as to be gathered into it, especially true of the recent past. This gives the curious sense of timelessness of so many of his narratives: but it is also the product of space displacement. In certain ways German romanticism made the Germany of the 1830s and 1840s no more foreign to him than the Germany he encountered in 1875-76. After all, German romanticism had much to tell a boy of Irish extraction. It had influenced the Young Ireland movement of the 1840s, it would influence much more powerfully the Gaelic revival and Irish Renaissance of the early twentieth century. Patrick Pearse would have no difficulty in appreciating Conan Doyle's sentiments of chronological unity: and the recovery of a vanished past variously extolled by Schlegel, Herder, Schiller, Goethe, Wagner, as well as by Scott, Macaulay and Carlyle, writers already encountered by Conan Doyle by the time of his sojourn in Feldkirch, was fundamental to Irish romantic nationalism from the 1840s to 1916. Where Conan Doyle differed profoundly from the Irish nationalist romanticists would be in the scientific development of his mind. If the Germans increased the intoxication of love for the search for the spirit of past ages, Edinburgh medicine would ensure that his historical writing was made rigorously dependent on factual source-material. Here, too, Scott was an excellent exemplar.

Hence his private war between science and spirit moved into a significant new phase in Germany. Stonyhurst began by increasing his private piety, under Cassidy, but soured him with public piety, such that he swung towards science in reaction against Kingdon, and swung to aggressively Protestant historians, Macaulay, John Lothrop Motley, and others, partly as an act of schoolboy rebellion. It would be this which gave such freshness to his writings like *Micah Clarke* and *The Refugees*. His contemporary writers of historical fiction took up Protestant themes with sureness and confidence, above all in their acceptability to their market: Conan Doyle set himself to work out Puritan and Huguenot dynamics as an act of intellectual dissent, thus bringing to what in Protestant writers was freshly laundered stock propaganda a tremendous sense of discovery, even of pioneering, of his own. The Jesuits may well have helped him along the road, for certain passages in Macaulay, notably the great essay on Ranke's *History of the Popes*, were much quoted in Jesuit schools. "The Jesuits", wrote Macaulay in that essay, "were to be found in the depth of the Peruvian mines, at the marts of the African slave-caravans, on the shores of the Spice Islands, in the observatories of China. They made converts in regions where neither avarice nor curiosity had tempted any of their countrymen to enter; and preached and disputed in tongues of which no other native of the West understood a word." Priest and pupil alike exulted in such sentences, so that we must realise the boy Arthur's rebellion was fuelled by the priests against whom it was taking place. Joyce's training resulted in a similar situation.

This sort of thing meant that Conan Doyle always took a *catholic* as opposed to a *Catholic* view of history. His highest praise for Protestant historians was always reserved for those who paid their tribute to the Catholics where it seemed due, even more to those who singled out the Jesuits for praise. The American Francis Parkman he singled out in his great work of literary celebration and criticism, *Through the Magic Door*, more particularly because of the volume on the Jesuits: "how noble a tribute is this which a man of Puritan blood pays to that wonderful Order!" Professional historians of today are less kind to Parkman on the Jesuits of New France, appreciating how he virtually transcribed the Jesuits' *Relations* for text without particular addition or analysis. Yet Conan Doyle's instinct still holds good: if Parkman could break so far from his background to honour the Jesuits (or endorse their honour to themselves) it was a fair index to his reliability on other matters (where in modern professional eyes his reputation remains far higher). And Conan Doyle, having rejected Catholic bigotry, had no interest whatever in adopting its Protestant counterpart: "I don't care what faith a man may profess, or whether he be a Christian at all, but he cannot read these true records without feeling that the very highest that man has ever evolved in sanctity and devotion was to be found among these marvellous men", continues his paean on Parkman's account of the Jesuits. If anything, German romanticism and Edinburgh science strengthened this attitude: it ecstatically proclaimed glory, it coldly assessed objectivity, and behind both of those sentiments it was his way of remaining true to the old colours.

His introduction to Parkman probably dates from this time, and from a Jesuit adviser or at least a Jesuit library. He would use Parkman for *The*

Refugees, but the relevant volumes cover a period subsequent to that of *The Jesuits in New France,* and the excitement with which he cites that work in *Through the Magic Door* suggests the shock of recognition very early in his discovery of the great historians: it is of course that volume he would be most likely to find, or to have found for him, in Stonyhurst or Feldkirch. Macaulay he definitely records in *Through the Magic Door* as coming to his acquaintance when he "was a senior schoolboy", in this case almost certainly at Stonyhurst. His copy of *Critical and Historical Essays* had been used by him so much that he had to replace it by the time of his voyage on an Arctic whaler in 1880. His mother and Macaulay combined drew him to Walter Scott, again before Feldkirch: he had been given a set of the Waverley Novels long before he had any interest in them, but Mary Foley Doyle's insistence on Sir Walter's triumphant recapture of the heroic past (and emphasis on her alleged kinship to him), and Macaulay's declaration that Scott had rescued social history from the mire where formal historians had left it, brought him to them "by surreptitious candle-ends in the dead of night, when the sense of crime added a new zest to the story". Whether he took up Carlyle before Feldkirch, thus finding the brook before the parent lake, is unclear: certainly he read him very early. Macaulay and Scott were in any case much more powerful, and significantly inter-reacted. "Perhaps it is that they both had so great an influence, and woke such admiration in me. Or perhaps it is the real similarity in the minds and characters of the two men. You don't see it, you say? Well, just think of Scott's 'Border Ballads', and then of Macaulay's 'Lays.' The machines must be alike, when the products are so similar. Each was the only man who could possibly have written the poems of the other."

The purpose of Macaulay's *Lays of Ancient Rome* (published in one volume with the *Essays* in many editions of Conan Doyle's time) was in part an extraordinary feat of historical creative imagination, the attempt to show what the lost songs of early Rome would have been like. The purpose is to establish the form in which myth is codified in popular terms. Macaulay was very consciously following on Scott's attempt to recover lost folklore and song of the Anglo-Scottish border, and both men were testifying to the role of folklore in developing the human historical sense. Conan Doyle was formally not concerned with this technical side, yet what he found in Feldkirch must have built on it. *Micah Clarke,* his first historical novel, written in the late 1880s is actually another attempt at recovery of a somewhat different oral narrative: in the long sub-title, discarded in later editions, it is made clear that the book is a "statement" from the old Puritan survivor of the Monmouth rebellion to his grandchildren. *Rodney Stone* implies a similar device to recall the Regency period. Even *The Hound of the Baskervilles* first has the theme of the ghostly persecution established by a document in which an otherwise unidentified eighteenth-century Baskerville puts the family story on paper for his sons (but not his daughter, an ironic side-thrust at eighteenth century male chauvinist obscurantism). And in Feldkirch itself he had ample means to see the results of Herder's attempts to uncover Slavic traditions, Schiller's excitement in past German glories as recounted in his histories as well as his plays, Wagner's unloosing of the deeps in divine myth.

The Germans were to provide him in miniature with ideas he later saw Tolstoy present on the gigantic canvas of *War and Peace:* the pettiness of mankind, the inability for true greatness to show itself save in a recognition of that pettiness, the absurdities of human self-congratulation against a universal yardstick. These thoughts also built on some lessons from the Jesuits, who stressed Man's absurdity in proclaiming his own greatness despite his unimaginable insignificance in the vastness of eternity, and in the divine perspective. Arguably, Wagner should have induced a different reaction, but there is no evidence of his having moved Conan Doyle from musical appreciation to ideological intoxication. A Conan Doyle hero, to the end, represented a rejection of the Carlylean and Wagnerian models: Holmes, Sir Nigel, Gerard, Challenger, always kept their feet on the ground by redeeming touches of the ridiculous. It meant a critical chain from the German inspiration through the author to the audience: by making the reader laugh at their absurdities, their heroism was tolerable against a Tolstoyan vastness, and the laugh moved imperceptibly from "at" them to "with" them. The sense of humour, built up in schoolboy days, remained one of the greatest strengths of Conan Doyle as man and writer to the end of his life. And science played its part also in stressing man's insignificance as well as the individual triumphs within that insignificance. The supermen would prove to be Gruners and Moriartys, both destined to fall victims to the powers of the scientific reasoner, and Wagner remained for Holmes a sedative rather than a stimulus, to be taken at the close rather than the outset of an investigation: ... "Well, Watson, you have one more specimen of the tragic and grotesque to add to your collection. By the way, it is not eight o'clock, and a Wagner night at Covent Garden! If we hurry, we might be in time for the second act."

Macaulay and Scott blended admirably with the new German influences, but also carried their own antidotes against them. If Macaulay's narratives swung into high romantic thunder, they were also splendidly restrained by rational argument and deflating irony. Scott, as Georg Lukacs has stressed, inspired a wave of romantic admirers across the North Atlantic, but he himself conceived his novels with marginal heroes, balancing between conflicting loyalties, and diminishing rather than increasing the novels' involvement in passionate crusade. Both writers liberated what was to prove one of Conan Doyle's greatest achievements, his use of the observer. Scott's effects are immensely heightened by keeping the reader at the side of an observer at some distance from the central protagonist, just as Watson was to keep the reader firmly with both feet on the ground. Macaulay's canvasses hardly permitted this, though Conan Doyle was to read his remarks on Boswell with the greatest attention, and with the significant positive criticism that Boswell's opinions on great public questions were usually sounder than Johnson's. His insistence on Boswell's good sense and taste, as a writer, affected his portrait of Watson profoundly. It is the caricaturish Watson of stage, screen and the imitators and parodists which recalls the poltroon depicted by Macaulay, not the Watson of Conan Doyle, who is in all moral respects a compliment to the reader who is to identify with him. Where a Macaulay original does come into play with respect to the observer it is not Boswell, save in inspiring Conan Doyle's contradiction, but George Savile, Marquess of Halifax, the great "trimmer" whom the *History of England* depicts as always leaning against the prevailing fashion. Halifax's tendency never goes to extremes, but his questions are taken by Macaulay as ensuring that acceptance is never won from him without clear justification.

Thus if Holmes simply had an imbecile friend, questioning his conclusions absurdly at the outset and then swallowing them uncritically, there would be very little of the effect of the dialogue. Absurd denunciation is left to the Scotland Yard bunglers and unappreciative clients. Conan Doyle certainly draws on Socrates's young friends, such as Glaucon in Plato's *Republic*, for Watson's sympathetic but uncomprehending questions; but the equality in age and status of Holmes and Watson demands some different inspiration than the youth of Glaucon and Boswell, or the class of Sancho Panza, could supply. By giving Watson the caution, if not the wit, of Halifax, against Holmes's apparently wilder flights, the perspective is maintained and the interest sustained. Holmes is perpetually forced to come down from his heights and justify his exotic conclusions, and thereby under Watson's questioning bring them into the realm of the possible. A Holmes without Watson would be as poor a thing as a Glorious Revolution without Halifax, and the *History* makes it clear that in Macaulay's view the moral strength of the event would have been infinitely less without Halifax.

This balance was asserted from the outset. The earliest surviving story, "The Haunted Grange of Goresthorpe", presents in its crude form the tension between romantic and observer that Conan Doyle found in his own war of science against spirit, in Macaulay's internal duel between reason and romance, and in the literary divergence of Scott's personal detachment as against the passionate involvement of his disciples. Of the Holmes-figure, "Tom Hulton", the narrator, Jack, tells his (non-existent) readers: "His only fault was that he had acquired a strange speculative way of thinking from his German education, and this led to continual arguments between us, for I had been trained as a medical student and looked at things therefore from an eminently practical point of view." This is Conan Doyle recognising and dissecting his own personality with its counter-pulls from Germany and Edinburgh (to say nothing of Jesuit piety versus Jesuit practicality). It is only one of the origins of Holmes and Watson, although an important one: and, crude as they are, neither Tom nor Jack are purely based on their founder, Jack clearly holding also something of Jim Ryan's role as auditor, while Tom is, like Jim Ryan, given a departure to Ceylon at the conclusion. (Ryan had probably not yet gone permanently to Ceylon when that story was written, given that its immaturity will not permit any date later for it than 1878, but it is clear he anticipated doing so: and there had probably been one separation caused by a return there.)

The speculative streak in Sherlock Holmes himself owed a good deal to Germany, as the citations of German authors are intended to assert, but the

Tom-Jack speculation-science dichotomies are reasserted within both Holmes and Watson, as well as in their counterposition to one another. Watson's speculations are much cruder than Holmes's and are usually about the case under discussion as Holmes's seldom are, although despite his warnings against such practices Holmes does produce some startling fruits of his imagination on individual cases from time to time. A nice example of the two varieties of speculation is given in *The Valley of Fear* in which Watson suggests that all the mysterious references to John Douglas's past may be invention:

> Holmes looked thoughtful. "I see, Watson. You are sketching out a theory by which everything they say from the beginning is false. According to your idea, there was never any hidden menace, or secret society, or Valley of Fear, or Boss MacSomebody, or anything else. . . ."

And then Holmes offers another explanation, which covers the known facts better but is even odder:

> "And yet there should be no combination of events for which the wit of man cannot conceive an explanation. Simply as a mental exercise, without any assertion that it is true, let me indicate a possible line of thought. It is, I admit, mere imagination; but how often is imagination the mother of truth?
>
> "We will suppose that there was a guilty secret, a really shameful secret in the life of this man Douglas. This leads to his murder by someone who is, we will suppose, an avenger, someone from outside. This avenger, for some reason which I confess I am still at a loss to explain, took the dead man's wedding ring. The vendetta might conceivably date back to the man's first marriage, and the ring be taken for some such reason.
>
> "Before this avenger got away, Barker and the wife had reached the room. The assassin convinced them that any attempt to arrest him would lead to the publication of some hideous scandal. They were converted to this idea, and preferred to let him go. . . ."

As Orwell argued in a different sense, it is the old Quixote-Sancho trick again, but with the far-fetched explanation having the advantage over the pedestrian. On Holmes's remarkably fair-minded expression of it, Watson's explanation, while imaginative, is convincing, rather more so than Holmes's although the evidence is more on Holmes's side than Watson's. But in this case both explanations are in fact wrong, and Holmes's disgusted description of himself for missing the truth reminds us that while closer than Watson's, his solution had been excessively speculative (" 'I say, Watson', he whispered, 'would you be afraid to sleep in the same room with a lunatic, a man with softening of the brain, an idiot whose mind has lost its grip?' ") It is also worth noting that Watson's deliberate scouting of the existence of the Valley of Fear throws the subsequent horror of the discovery of its existence and what it really entailed into starker relief, much as does Holmes's derisive "Boss MacSomebody" make Bodymaster McGinty all the more ominous when we encounter him. The discovery of a terror suspected, then discounted, and finally realized, is far greater than a mere movement from suspicion to certainty.

Germany stimulated Conan Doyle's imagination in a variety of ways, apart from the most direct one of imagining worthy citizens driven homicidal by clutching mysterious hatchets, or changing personalities with astonishing effects for their ignorant associates, or proving at once the public mainstay of sympathy at slaughter and the secret basis of its happening. One fairly clear point of investigation lies in race. Conan Doyle, as we shall see, was to show himself happily out of key with his contemporaries on racial questions, but his writing does reveal certain commonplace assumptions. As V. G. Kiernan points out, when the world is passing through the toxic atmosphere in *The Poison Belt*, its effects are described by Professor Challenger as initially greater on "the less developed races", although it is not absolutely clear whether the desirable development is cultural or physical. Macaulay, who defended the principle of inter-racial marriage, argued that economics and culture retarded racial development and that with the extinction of superstitious cultural antecedents and economic equality, all the races might co-exist and amalgamate with the greatest confidence. On the other hand, this view found much less favour in the late nineteenth century: the most that imperialists such as John Buchan were prepared to concede was that racial equality might be possible in the remote future. The key point in Challenger's recital is, curiously, his report on Austria, where "Slavonic population . . . is down, while the Teutonic has hardly been affected" (the Magyars, as in "*The Silver Hatchet*", appear to have eluded the vigilance of the author— perhaps he counted them as Slavs). This may be no more than reflections on excitability of temperament. Conan Doyle seems to have placed great respect in coolness and calmness, and resolution, and on the basis of that quality *The Tragedy of the Korosko* gives the Arabs the advantage over the dwellers of the North Mediterranean coasts. The Slav-German distinction may derive from contemplation of such excitable Slavs as Arthur encountered at Feldkirch, together with his evident impression of a Teutonic stolidity which his impish imagination subjected to startling metamorphoses. The last point may be telling: Conan Doyle may have seen, consciously or unconsciously, a reservoir of homicidal violence and irrationality lying far below the Teutonic exterior and his references to German madness rising to confound the appearance of benignity and tranquillity are frequent enough in these early works to suggest he may have observed some darkness beneath the surface. Certainly he must have contrasted the heady wine of the romantics whom he read with the bourgeois respectability that surrounded him. As to the Slavs, his few references in the early writings certainly argue a belief in their vehemence. "*A Night among the Nihilists*" produces a predictably violent clutch of conspirators, and the far more mature and impressive "*Man from Archangel*" plays exotically with the contrast between the Russian man sacrificing all for his love of the girl, the Russian girl seeking everywhere for sanctuary in her hatred of the man, and the malevolently scientific heir to the Scottish estate cursing the romantic drama in which he is remorselessly swept up. "*An Exciting Christmas Eve*" likewise contrasts the bourgeois self-absorption of the kidnapped German scientist with his noisy and homicidal audience of Slavic and Irish (though also of German) affiliation.

His own Irish antecedents left him less than wholly committed to any philosophy of Teutonic superiority in any case. The reports of Challenger on racial responses to imminent extinction, as with so much else in his writing, could well be largely satirical. His Edinburgh reminiscences are respectful of his great preceptors, but aware of their idiosyncracies of theory as well as of manner. He was always careful to refer to the inhabitants of the British Isles as "Anglo-Celtic", and differed from both his Irish and British contemporaries in correctly assuming a mingling rather than a separation of the original peoples of the two islands. This belief seems to have been at the root of his opposition to Home Rule, which led to his break with the Liberal Party in 1886 and his stand as a Liberal Unionist in the elections of 1900 and 1906, although following the growth of his friendship with Roger Casement over the Congo atrocities he became a Home Ruler before World War I.

His celebration of the Irish in his writing varied greatly. We are to assume that Edward Dunn Malone, narrator of most of the Challenger stories, is Irish, though not more so than would be consistent with a crude and external portrait of the artist as a young man. A clever and quizzical Irishman nicely offsets the extravagance of English, French and American protagonists in *The Tragedy of the Korosko:* it clearly amuses Conan Doyle to stress his being "strong, self-contained" and ultimately "obstinate" when it is a choice between his life and his Catholic faith. In fact, that particular book reads as though Conan Doyle had anticipated Bernard Shaw in contrasting the romantic English with the practical Irish. The English hero, Colonel Cochrane Cochrane, is gallant, but his military carriage he owes to stays and his raven locks to the dye-bottle, which looks like a cunning revenge on conventional fashions in national stereotyping. The Irishness of the murderous Scowrers in *The Valley of Fear* is carefully stressed, but so is that of their courageous opponent. In general, the evidence suggests that Conan Doyle tended to use his Irishness as Bernard Shaw used his, to strengthen his objective analysis of the English and occasionally to satirise them. "*The Heiress of Glenmahowley*" is an excellent demolition of the English fortune-hunting, snobbish, worthless narrator partly by the Irish landlord who sadly deplores the absence of agrarian outrage to amuse the visitors, while "*That Little Square Box*" also makes anti-Irish prejudice convict itself from the narrator's own silly mouth.

We cannot know whether Conan Doyle's Austrian experiences led to his application of his historical interest to his Irish antecedents, but there is some evidence for it. His poem "*Cremona*" chooses an Irish victory over the Austrians for its theme as opposed to the more usual subjects of the Irish actions in the battles of Ramillies or Fontenoy. The specific theme is hence decidedly suggestive. It would not be a question of the author's shrinking from commemorating an Irish action against the British: apart from the Gerard stories, *Uncle Bernac* has as its hero a young man who turns his back on his English hosts to join Napoleon's campaign against them, and nothing is said to question his return to national loyalty. Macaulay would certainly have supplied inspiration for treatment of the Irish exiles in European armies. His *History* contains a splendid paragraph on these "Wild Geese", and its treatment of the Irish Jacobite leader, Patrick Sarsfield, would have won no adverse reaction from the son of Mary Foley Dōyle. It was natural that Conan Doyle should have at one point attempted a *"History of the Irish Brigade in the Service of France"*, although it remained unpublished throughout his lifetime. His most famous Hibernian material is to be found in *"The Green Flag"*, a story whose title he also used for one of his short-story collections: it confronts the dichotomy of Irish gallantry in the field and Irish disaffection against Britain with a mutiny by Fenians and Land-Leaguers proving the heart of resistance to an Arab attack in battle when the mutineers rally behind a green flag. The last line is given to the Arab commander, describing the battle in which the Irish are wiped out: "In token of our victory I send you by this messenger a flag which we have taken. By the colour it might well seem to have belonged to those of the true faith, but the Kaffirs gave their blood freely to save it, and so we think that, though small, it is very dear to them." It would be very hard to deny the author's identification with that last sentence.

Yet Ireland offered *panache* more than pathos to Conan Doyle:

> *Said the king to the colonel,*
> *"The complaints are eternal,*
>   *That you Irish give more trouble*
>   *Than any other corps."*

> *Said the colonel to the king,*
> *"This complaint is no new thing,*
>   *For your foemen, sire, have made it*
>   *A hundred times before."*

D'Artagnan, in *The Three Musketeers,* counters Buckingham's line "proud as a Scotsman" with "proud as a Gascon", adding that the Gascons are the Scots of France. Conan Doyle, reading Dumas, would probably have accepted that, but he seems to have put a good deal of his impression of the Irish into his own Gascon, Brigadier Gerard, as well as the Scots pride. (In any case, Dumas gave the original remark to an odd person: the Scot whom Buckingham knew best, James VI and I, was anything but proud in his relations with him.)

Did Arthur draw involvement in the history of his ancestors' country from his discovery of the German romantics? Certainly they must have stimulated his zeal to recapture the past. But a Cornish holiday activated his Celtic consciousness in a more startling way: basing himself on the old tradition of Phoenician trades on the Cornish coast, he applied himself briefly in the early twentieth century to a quest he afterwards ascribed to Holmes in *"The Devil's Foot"*. "The ancient Cornish language had also arrested his attention, and he had, I remember, conceived the idea that it was akin to the Chaldean, and had been largely derived from the Phoenician traders in tin. He had received a consignment of books upon philology and was settling down to develop this thesis when . . ."—when *Radix pedis diaboli* drew itself somewhat forcefully to his attention. Finally: "And now, my dear Watson, I think we may dismiss the matter from our mind [sic] and go back with a clear conscience to the study of those Chaldean roots which are surely to be traced in the Cornish branch of the great Celtic speech." Conan Doyle would also employ something of the same principle to an Anglo-Scottish border ruined fort in *"Through the Veil"* where a man and his wife discover themselves to have been on distressingly opposed sides during a Pictish raid some thousand five hundred years earlier, although here the clue is psychological rather than philological.

In his memoirs Conan Doyle makes little enough of the intellectual significance of his Feldkirch stay, although it must have been a fine coping-stone on the internationalising influences which his European and American fellow-pupils at Stonyhurst had given him. But at least one impetus to his embrace of German romanticism came from home. One letter which reached him from a medical student then lodging with the Charles Altamont Doyles, a certain Waller (of whom more later) is worth noting for the topics apparently raised by Arthur in correspondence prompting it (text from fragments transcribed by Carr and Nordon):

> Absolve you to yourself and you shall have the suffrage of the whole world. If any one imagines that this law is lax, let him keep its commandment one day. Thus far, Emerson, in his never sufficiently to be extolled essay on Self Reliance. And here we put our finger on the weakness of all blind vicarious and fiducial trust in a hypothetical Providence, which forsooth is to help those who cannot or will not help themselves. Far truer and nobler is the teaching of the old proverb: heaven helps those who help themselves. This manful inward life is what theology would fain kill by making us hold ourselves vile, sinful, and degraded, which is a pestilent lie and cuts at the root of all that is best in our natures: for take away a man's self-respect and you do much towards making him a sneak and a scoundrel. . . . No truly self-reliant man can descend to the meanness of petty vanity: he knows himself far too truly to deem that he needs to have recourse to officious display; and in the end, he will make others know him too. Men of this mould die not with death: some of them write their names in the world's album: others influence an age or a generation: others but a smaller circle of personal friends. Yet when they pass away, their place remains empty. . . . Thus "Do" is a far finer word than "Believe": and "Action" a far surer watchword than "Faith". The one is male, the other female: the one active, progressive, developing; the other passive, stationary and decaying like the bloom of a cheek or the light of an eye. The one is stern and hard even to ruggedness but solid to the core: the other fair as the mirage but as deceitful and illusive. The one lulls us to slumber, the other wakes us rudely to action. Choose, then, whom ye will serve: the principle of Slumber and helpless despondence, draped in the rainbow decay, or that other standing erect and mighty with its face towards the sunrise and its great wings dispread for measureless and viewless flight. . . .

Professor Weil-Nordon sees this as prefiguring Nietzsche and imbued of neo-Kantianism. What Arthur Conan Doyle saw it as is an interesting question, since its author was less than six years older than himself. But however egregious, Bryan Charles Waller had the fascination for a verse-writing schoolboy which must be possessed by a close acquaintance already inscribed on the British Museum Catalogue as author of *The Twilight Land*, a substantial volume of his own verse published in 1875. He was also generous in the extreme, and was busily despatching to Arthur volumes of mathematics and chemistry. Clearly something of a common chord had been struck in German philosophy, and Arthur would have been interested enough in its application by Emerson. But the letter's noisy expostulation seems less an indication of an influence obligingly absorbed by Arthur, as previous biographers have assumed, so much as a recital in response to objections made by him to the writer's views.

It is hard to see Arthur responding enthusiastically to the male chauvinism of his correspondent. Mary Foley Doyle had left him with a very different sense of the strength of the female as against the male. Waller was not, as has been stated, an agnostic: he appears from his poetry to have been a deist at this point. This was strong meat for Arthur. Waller's forceful rejection of sectarianism as the cradle of bigotry was all well and good, and it is very likely that to Waller Arthur owed his introduction to Winwood Reade's *The Martyrdom of Man*, that brilliant summary of world history seeking to dissect religion's enslavement of humanity. "Let me recommend this book", Holmes adjures Watson, even more egregiously than Waller, given their preoccupation with Mary Morstan's problems, "one of the most remarkable ever penned", although Watson prefers thinking of Mary to Reade's "daring speculations". Why the book is suddenly thrust into the narrative of *The Sign of Four* is a good question, and it seems as though Conan Doyle knew it through someone's recommendation. Its date, 1875, makes Waller the most likely candidate, and with it follows the deduction that Waller supplied some of Holmes's force.

But admiration for Reade did not mean agreement with all of his views, and in turning from Catholicism Arthur would seem to have cherished the gentler aspects of the old religion in a way that found little sympathy in the lodger. To the end of his life he spoke with admiration for the Catholic "Angelus", recited at noon, with its chorus of "Ave Maria" and its successive stages in contemplation of the miracle of the incarnation of God the Son. As late as 1922 we find Conan Doyle writing in "*The Centurion*": "There was an old woman there, His mother, with her grey hair down her back. I remember how she shrieked when one of our fellows with his lance put Him out of His pain". It was, in fact, the female element in Roman Catholicism which maintained his affection, although not his allegiance, and while believing in self-reliance, he never put any faith in self-glorification of the type Waller extolled. He might agree with Waller's contempt for religion founded on an assumption of human degradation; he still differed from him in drawing from the Germans not their worship of man's greatness but their respect for his acknowledgment of his littleness. From this standpoint his spiritual Odyssey seems much more like a continuous evolution rather than a case involving the violent break which Waller urged. Even though he abandoned all formal religion after Feldkirch, his belief in God remained a positive one rather than in the remote and uncaring being whom Waller then acknowleged. The place of human suffering in a divine plan continued to perplex him but, as the close to "*The Cardboard Box*", and other passages written before his acceptance of Spritualism suggest, he could not be satisfied with the solution of a divine indifference rather than a divine plan. His whole anti-clerical tone in his writing speaks of anger against human shortcomings in God's work as opposed to any suggestion that the work in itself was futile.

There also remained the fact that Conan Doyle's rejection of orthodox theology as insisted on by his teachers would not make him much readier to submit to intellectual bullying by Bryan Charles Waller. He had many pulls on his spirituality. Visits at London to his uncles before he left Stonyhurst might simply have placed him in conflict with the old orthodoxy, but a visit to Paris after Feldkirch enabled him to grasp a little of the anti-clericalism of his old journalist godfather and great-uncle, Michael Conan, and if that anti-clericalism was to have any validity, it had to be concerned with serious debate, not warfare against a chimera. *Micah Clarke* was the fruit of this tendency, rather than of Waller's deism (Theism was what Arthur called his own faith): Micah's belief had to be comprehended and taken seriously, while not being accepted, and the very decision to come to terms with it was a further assertion of the importance of religion. Conan Doyle had grown up knowing of the bigotry of the Puritans, but he sought to show in his book the benefits to humanity which also resulted from their faith. Had he really followed Waller, he could never have had the interest in religion to make so much of the Puritans. Meantime, at Feldkirch, he encountered another new and exciting influence in Edgar Allan Poe.

Who sent him Poe is unclear: again, Waller seems a likely choice, including it as a leaven for the conic sections he also despatched. *The Twilight Land* is not conspicuously influenced by Poe, but some of Waller's later poetry is: possibly *The Twilight Land* was meant to be, but the tenebrous effects found it difficult to break through the rosy clouds of undergraduate complacency. The choice was an interesting alteration in the Anglo-Teutonic diet currently being absorbed by Arthur, and, with Poe's French locations and atmospherics, a welcome one to Mary Foley Doyle who was encouraging Arthur in Feldkirch to write her letters in French lest he be over-Teutonified. (But Poe's Dupin would have reinforced ACD's decision to have Holmes quote Goethe.) Poe played a critical part in that North Atlantic romanticism of which Arthur had been hearing the echoes, but whereas with the Germans the pattern is of Kant, Schlegel, Herder, Richter, Goethe and (another of Arthur's enthusiasms) Heine being picked up in Britain by Carlyle and lesser publicists and hence being transmitted to New England to charge Emerson and the transcendentalists with that peculiarly moral version of human self-realisation, Poe in Virginia was an original whose obsessive pursuit of death and flight from catalepsy made its pilgrimage in the reverse direction, to be picked up by Baudelaire and made the cornerstone of the great nineteenth-century decadence. The very word "decadence" supplies the radii of its own influence: decay, disintegration, rot, tomb, putrefaction (and any other facts in the case of M. Valdemar), but also decadence in the Latin sense of falling, human decline, destruction of antiquity, lineage, tradition, fall of the House of Usher, fall of the bottle-manuscript writer into the whirlpool, fall of the intellect of Dupin from social primacy, to travel onward in the century to the fall of Parnell, the fall of Wilde, the physical fall of Sherlock Holmes at Reichenbach. It seems to have struck particular response from Ireland, appropriately enough for a country which produced Charles Robert Maturin and Sheridan LeFanu. Of Conan Doyle's Irish contemporaries the young Wilde and the young Yeats are the most famous examples of Poe's influence. In Arthur's own case the discovery was profound. "I am sure", he wrote in *Through the Magic Door*, "that if I had to name a few books which have really influenced my own life I should have to put this one second only to Macaulay's Essays. I read it young when my mind was plastic. It stimulated my imagination and set before me a supreme example of dignity and force in the methods of telling a story." What dark responses it unleashed on him, perhaps realising themselves in the identification of Germany with loss of mental control, are implied by his next lines: "It is not altogether a healthy influence, perhaps. It turns the thoughts too forcibly to the morbid and the strange."

His sense of humour and love of people helped him in scaling the challenge of the misanthropic, morose Virginian down to the level where he might subject it to control. Poe even at his most terrible is not proof against a sense of humour, as was admirably proved by Messrs Vincent Price, Peter Lorre and Boris Karloff in their splendid satiric movie "*The Raven*". Conan Doyle seems to have judged this point well, and deployed that humour carefully, as may be seen by the comparison of the darkness of dialogue in the Dupin stories with the happy badinage of Holmes and Watson. "The reader must himself furnish the counteracting qualities", noted Conan Doyle, almost pharmacologically, "or Poe may become a dangerous comrade. We know along what perilous tracks and into what deadly quagmires his strange mind led him, down to that great October Sunday morning" in 1849 "when he was picked up, a dying man, on the side-walk at Baltimore, at an age which should have seen him at the very prime of his strength and manhood". Poe could induce in his young reader fears as to a doomed inheritance, an inescapable alcoholic curse, a yearning to fly beyond the repulsiveness of the known world by immersion in drug-laden dreams.

Arthur would in fact experiment with drugs for medical research, such as gelsemium and nitrate of amyl. Against any temptation to take drugs for pleasure, he carried within him the insurance given by a rugged, courageous, laughing mind. There was from his background a cloud somewhere at the back of his consciousness which could supervene. It fed his imagination, it encouraged his worship of solitude, it drew him into the contemplation of horror. "*The Devil's Foot*" sums up the problem brilliantly: we encounter a drug throwing the human mind into the uttermost pits of horror, yet drugs are intended by their users to be a release from the unendurable, whether unendurable fears and pressures, or unendurable tedium. As Martin Dakin points out, the dual perception of Conan Doyle is well expressed in that while

Holmes sees his drugs as a stimulus, Watson regards them as a sedative. The mind might reach heights of self-admiration, and with it the nadir of productivity.

Whatever the transient effects of Poe, his main impact on Conan Doyle was in the highest sense professional. He amused him greatly by the tricks he employed: "The mere suspicion of scientific thought or scientific methods has a great charm in any branch of literature, however far it may be removed from actual research. Poe's tales, for example, owe much to this effect, though in his case it was a pure illusion." It was for Arthur, then, to ask himself whether he with his new training could put Poe's methods to work with securer scientific bases. He applied the same consideration to Poe's art of the short story. So far as we can judge, Poe gave Arthur his first real experience with the short story, and this encounter cannot be illuminated too powerfully, for the short story's mechanics would be Conan Doyle's greatest professional achievement. In *Through the Magic Door* he hailed Poe as the master in deployment of "strength, novelty, compactness, intensity of interest, and a single vivid impression left upon the mind". He was "the supreme original short story writer of all time. His brain was like a seed-pod full of seeds which flew carelessly around, and from which have sprung nearly all our modern types of story. Just think of what he did in his off-hand, prodigal fashion, seldom troubling to repeat a success, but pushing on to some new achievement. To him must be ascribed the monstrous progeny of writers on the detection of crime—'quorum pars parva fui!' ". What the pious but not very modest Aeneas said to Dido about the Trojan war and its close was *"quorum magna pars fui"* (of which things I was a great part), and in substituting the words "small part" Conan Doyle was perhaps taking good manners too far, but he may have felt he had to counteract the boastfulness of Sherlock Holmes's ruderies at the expense of Dupin. On his arrival in the United States in 1894 he insisted to the New York *Herald* interviewer that Poe's detective, and not his own, was the greatest in literature—an unconsciously clever way of winning greater attention since he was at once marked out from the run of lecturers on the American circuit boosting their own wares with a zeal which made their hosts modest by comparison. In *A Study in Scarlet* Holmes tells Watson "No doubt you think that you are complimenting me in comparing me to Dupin . . . Now, in my opinion, Dupin was a very inferior fellow. That trick of his of breaking in on his friends' thoughts with an apropos remark after a quarter of an hour's silence is really very showy and superficial. He had some analytical genius, no doubt; but he was by no means such a phenomenon as Poe appeared to imagine" and then goes on to describe Gaboriau's Lecoq as "a miserable bungler . . . That book made me positively ill".

This passage was, like so much else in the portrait of Holmes, a clever satire on the self-glorification of scientists. One of the heartiest Edinburgh medical traditions was that of abuse of one's opponents. Bryan Charles Waller's doctoral thesis (on *Interstitial Nephritis*) began by describing some of his predecessors who "probably with a view to the conservation of energy, have adopted at second hand one or another of the plentiful stock of ready-made theories, dressing and bedizening the changeling in accordance with their several tastes, without troubling themselves in the least with superfluous enquiries into the legitimacy of its parentage. These, in too many cases, are blind men led by the blind; and it is to be feared that the ditch is but too often their ultimate, and perhaps not uncongenial, resting-place. Thus it is not to be wondered at, if a large percentage of the dissertations on the nature of the contracted kidney are worth precisely the paper they are printed on, and are valuable chiefly to the butterman as envelopes for his unctuous wares". It would be nicely Rolanding the Oliver if Waller had been responsible for the gift of Poe certainly sent to Arthur at Feldkirch, to have Holmes's comments on Poe conceived after Waller's own method of dealing with his predecessors. As the two men were still very close, particularly on literary matters, when *A Study in Scarlet* was written, it is a decided possibility.

Arthur continued to be intensely annoyed at the assumption that Holmes's views on Poe were his own. He deliberately made Holmes try out the Dupin trick of interrupting Watson's thoughts by showing what they were, partly as an exercise, partly to convict Holmes of the same showy superficiality he had ridiculed in Dupin: yet the response of commentators was to accuse him of pinching Poe's methods and then denouncing them. Arthur Guitermann's rocking-horse rhyme "The Case of the Inferior Sleuth" made the charge more amusingly than most, but no more perceptively:

> Holmes is your hero of drama and serial;
> All of us know where you dug the material
> Whence he was moulded—'tis almost a platitude;
> Yet your detective, in shameless ingratitude—
> Sherlock your sleuthhound with motives ulterior
> Sneers at Poe's Dupin as "very inferior!"
> Labels Gaboriau's clever "Lecoq", indeed,
> Merely 'a bungler', a creature to mock, indeed!
> This, when your plots and your methods in story owe
> More than a trifle to Poe and Gaboriau,
> Sets all the Muses of Helicon sorrowing.
> Borrow, Sir Knight, but be decent in borrowing!

Considering that by the time this was written, 1915, the devout tribute of *Through the Magic Door* had been in print for eight years, and the salutation on arrival at the U.S.A. on record for over twenty, Conan Doyle's response was understandably testy. Mr Peter Haining has unearthed it—"To an Undiscerning Critic"—to place after its target, in his *Final Adventures of Sherlock Holmes:*

> *Have you not learned, my esteemed commentator,*
> *That the created is not the creator?*
> *As the creator I've praised to satiety*
> *Poe's Monsieur Dupin, his skill and variety,*
> *And have admitted that in my detective work*
> *I owe to my model a deal of selective work.*
> *But is it not on the verge of insanity*

To put down to me my creation's crude vanity?
He, the created, would scoff and would sneer,
Where I, the creator, would bow and revere.
So please grip this fact with your cerebral tentacle:
The doll and its maker are never identical.

In fact, Conan Doyle owed very little in plotting to Poe. Dialogue and deduction in the early stories were under obligations to the great Virginian, and as with Conan Doyle's other work of the 1880s memory led to some actual regurgitation which the author took to be his own creation. But the one story really drawing on Poe, *"The Dancing Men"*, first published in the *Strand* in December 1903, is so obvious a variation on the Master's methods throughout that it is practically labelled as homage. It begins, quite inconsequentially, with the thought-reading trick, and goes on to an exposition of codes which is deliberately derived from Poe's *"The Gold Bug"*. When we find one story so overcharged with Poe in contrast to the rest, there can be no doubt of design in the matter, any more than Holmes in *"The Abbey Grange"* could doubt that two glasses deficient in beeswing and a third overcharged with it resulted from contrivance rather than an accident. In an earlier story, *"The Cardboard Box"*, when the thought-reading trick is also played, Poe is directly cited, and the passage was transposed to the opening of *"The Resident Patient"* after *"The Cardboard Box"* was dropped from the published *Memoirs of Sherlock Holmes*. In this instance, again, the use of the Poe device is wholly irrelevant to either of the ensuing stories, and clearly Conan Doyle intended that the Holmes stories pay tribute to their inspiration, in the only way in which Sherlock Holmes could be got to do so.

But if Edgar Allan Poe delighted and horrified Arthur at Feldkirch, from an early stage the American writer sharpened the critical instincts of the Scot. In *Through the Magic Door* he would give to only two of Poe's stories places among the greatest short stories of the language, although as a short-story writer he placed him above all others, even above Maupassant. "The great Norman never rose to the extreme force and originality of the American, but he had a natural inherited power, an inborn instinct towards the right way of making his effects, which mark him as a great master." Yet Conan Doyle's points in praise for Maupassant show precisely where Poe is weakest. Maupassant, he said, "produced stories because it was in him to do so, as naturally and as perfectly as an apple tree produces apples. What a fine, sensitive, artistic touch it is! How easily and delicately the points are made! How clear and nervous is his style, and how free from that redundancy which disfigures so much of our English work! He pares it down to the quick all the time." The generous celebration of Maupassant is not intended to weaken Poe, but a moment's reflection makes it clear that it does, and shows the value for himself of his critical examination of Poe. Exposition was the curse of the age. It dragged *"The Mystery of Marie Roget"* to its intolerable length, it turned Arthur's favourite ghost story, Lytton's *"The Haunted and the Haunters"*, from a brilliant progression of terror into a tutorial in mysticism, and, to draw on examples cited by Conan Doyle in the *Magic Door*:

There is, I admit, an intolerable amount of redundant verbiage in Scott's novels. Those endless and unnecessary introductions make the shell very thick before you come to the oyster. They are often admirable in themselves, learned, witty, picturesque, but with no relation of proportion to the story which they are supposed to introduce. Like so much of our English fiction, they are very good matter in a very bad place. Digression and want of method and order are traditional national sins. Fancy introducing an essay on how to live on nothing a year as Thackeray did in "Vanity Fair", or sandwiching in a ghost story as Dickens has dared to do. As well might a dramatic author rush up to the footlights and begin telling anecdotes while his play was suspending its action and his characters waiting wearily behind him. It is all wrong, though every great name can be quoted in support of it. Our sense of form is lamentably lacking, and Sir Walter sinned with the rest.

I know few better critics than Conan Doyle when he liked his subject, but I know none who was more of a gentleman. The lack of "Our" sense of form took with a pre-eminent courtesy the sin on his own shoulders which he of all writers had least reason to confess and had done most to eradicate. He was to take the short story, put it on a wholesome if far from stodgy diet, get it out for extensive exercise, threaten it with (and sometimes subject it to) invigorating operations, and never let it stop moving. Certainly his self-training was a long and painful process, and he had many unsuccessful experiments before he reached perfection. In Poe he had his first lesson: there was the originality, and all the rest of it. There was also endless self-indulgence, wallowing in atmosphere, incessant lecturing, ruthless discourse on whatever took the writer's fancy, longueurs, trivialisation, telegraphing of punch-lines, loss of plot in effect, loss of effect in plot. His two candidates for excellence are *"The Gold Bug"* and *"The Murders in the Rue Morgue"*, and it is worth noting that to neither is he putting a mechanical length-measurement. In each case he clearly feels the length justifies itself, as elsewhere the length—and sometimes even the brevity—does not. "These two have a proportion and a perspective which are lacking in the others, the horror or weirdness of the idea intensified by the coolness of the narrator and of the principal actor, Dupin in the one case and Le Grand in the other". In sum, what Poe lacked above all else was a sense of his reader. Conan Doyle strove all his writing life to retain that, and the result was what Agatha Christie in *The Clocks* rightly signalled as his supreme contribution: Watson. Holmes had his predecessors and successors, but Watson is a unique achievement in harnessing the reader. Hesketh Pearson's engagingly opinionated comments strike home perfectly here:

G.K. Chesterton once remarked that if Dickens had written the Holmes stories he would have made every character as vivid as Holmes. We may reply that if Dickens had done so he would have ruined the stories, which depend for their effect on the radiance of the central character and the relative glimmer of the satellites. True, Watson's glimmer amounts to genius, but it adds to the splendour of Holmes, and Dickens would have made a fearful mess of Watson.

In the most important respect the influence of Poe on Conan Doyle was akin to other major literary influences on him: it provided a challenge to which he responded. A striking illustration of this is to be found in *"The Resident Patient"* where the bogus Russian who calls on Dr Percy Trevelyan is actually anxious to murder Mr Blessington, but nominally to be treated for catalepsy. Catalepsy is one of the most permanent morbidities in Poe, from *"The Premature Burial"* to *"The Fall of the House of Usher"*; here it is introduced for entirely fraudulent purposes, Holmes remarking that "it is a very easy complaint to imitate. I have done it myself". It is the common sense of the Scottish doctor retorting to the Virginian neurotic, but he puts an additional twist by making a doctor the dupe of the pseudo-catalepsy! Again, the ever-present sense of humour in ACD enabled him at once to delight in the wonder of his masters and exploit their absurditites. Language too, fascinated him in Poe as elsewhere. It was probably thence that he took his pleasure in the adjective "singular" even if its meaning seems to change as it moves from the doom-laden tones of Poe's heroes to Holmes's dry, analytical voice.

Thus passed the Feldkirch year, of whose actual content we know virtually nothing beyond happiness, enjoyment of landscape, schoolboy pranks, playing in the band, and a few scattered letters to and fro, but whose imprint on Arthur's mind seems to have been decisive in his intellectual and artistic development. With its passing Arthur said farewell to his Jesuit training. He had rejected the fundamental orthodoxy implicit in that training, yet it had given him much. Even its hated emotional deprivation stimulated his imagination and thrust him more firmly into the world of books from which he was to garner and redeploy so much. The mental crisis and personal anguish to which his intellectual and religious rebellion would subject him gave a depth to him in his early years which made his belief in liberty of the mind so precious to him. The great range of writing and thought he devoured was all the more voraciously consumed because of being so dearly bought. Hence also he could embrace the concept of liberty with a fervour all the deeper that it was his own conquest, not simply the inheritance of a formal establishment tradition going back to 1688 and robbed of its meaning for most of those on whose lips it sat so lightly.

For this reason also, the German romantics' worship of liberty meant more to him than to most of their English readers. The idea was dearly bought for the Germans as well as him, whereas the British, mostly taking it for granted, celebrated it when, like him, they were closest to continental influence. And having made his rapturous discoveries, he put them to work with much more industry than did his contemporaries. Heine, for instance, he would make a source of his doctoral dissertation to describe the effects of syphilis. The parallel with Joyce in this sense of dearly-bought literary freedom is complete, and part of it relates to the economic circumstances of both boys. For all of the author's wealth by the time of his writing *Through the Magic Door* he is unable to conceal the excitement with which new literary acquisitions came his way, and the pride with which he prized them—the arrival of Poe at Feldkirch, the slow disintegration of the Macaulay *Essays* under incessant thumbing, the tragic immersion of *Ivanhoe* in a brook.

I first learned how in a time of scarce resources when the purchase of books, especially of fiction, was deemed an absurd luxury, Conan Doyle won his Irish following in the early twentieth century, as my mother told me of her luck as the daughter of a poor family in being allowed to rummage in the library of well-to-do neighbours indifferent to the treasures concealed in the numbers of the *Strand* on their shelves, and her friend Eileen MacCabe remembered for me how she cherished a copy of the *Adventures of Sherlock Holmes*, longing hopelessly for the sequel, and at last found a book tumbling down a waterfall, and brought it home, and dried it, and it was the *Memoirs*. I think of all the responses to his writings, those are the stories he would most like to have told, which is why I tell them.

The Jesuits had given him order, however much he disliked it, and it was that same concept of order he brought to his short-story writing with so much success. Yet in their own way they had given him a heritage of rebellion. It was not only that they were speaking for a Higher Kingdom as against a material culture, although this was important. Conan Doyle never forgot the case against worldly success, either as expressed by Sherlock Holmes in *"Thor Bridge"*, or as shown by himself in losing popularity for his championship of the ridiculed and despised Spiritualists. In fact, his crusade for Spiritualism owed everything to the inspiration of the Jesuits' readiness to risk all for their faith. They also gave him the message of man's duty to accept responsibility to a Higher Power under whatever temptation to end all in face of suffering, and this, too, is consistently vindicated in his work. The classic case is in *"The Veiled Lodger"*, but its counterpart is eloquently asserted in *"The Pot of Caviare"* (1908) where a benevolent Professor poisons himself and all of his companions rather than have them captured by the Chinese, only to discover that their relief is at hand and he is dying a suicide and mass-murderer, robbed even of the motivation of his action. Elsewhere protagonists in his writing contemplate suicide time and again, only to discover how foolish, even in materialist terms, such an action would have been.

In addition to these things, the boys at Stonyhurst had been educated to a denial that the existing social and governmental establishment, on which Kingdon had turned his back and which had dishonoured Purbrick, were automatically entitled to the airs it gave itself. The Sherlock Holmes stories are a consistent repetition of an argument that the existing authorities are insufficient, that their authors' status does not of itself justify administrative decisions, that humans are obliged to seek the best, and not just the safest, solution possible. The average public-school product was trained to accept society without question; the Jesuits might be pillars of orthodoxy, but at the heart of their teaching was the assumption that the authorities were critically wrong on one matter, and hence must be watched critically lest they prove so on others. Even the personal renunciation and asceticism of his teachers moved him, however little he wished to follow their methods of expressing it. He was to know great men: he had known men whom the world would never call great, but who might have been—Sir George Kingdon of Bart's, and Dr Purbrick of Oxford, and General Sir Reginald Wellesley Colley, M.F.H. And he had known, or at least would later learn he had been in the proximity of, Gerard Manley Hopkins, whose genius might have won recognition in his own lifetime had he remained in the world. Above all, he took away a belief in forgiveness and atonement expressed by Sherlock Holmes in story after story long before Chesterton's Father Brown practised it. If Arthur did not leave the Jesuits with a Catholic mind, he retained to the end of his life, in its finest sense, a Catholic heart. If he rejected formal Catholicism, he continued to believe in "the promptings of some beneficent force outside ourselves, which tries to help us where it can", as he wrote in *Through the Magic Door*. "The old Catholic doctrine of the Guardian Angel is not only a beautiful one, but has in it, I believe, a real basis of truth."

He was going to need that Guardian Angel. The tragedy of his Edinburgh home, from which his mother had striven so long to shield him, was now also to become his tragedy. Edgar Allan Poe may have had one special appeal to him then and later, in showing him the artist as self-destroyer who nevertheless produces work of sublimity and whose influence fires posterity; and the story of Poe was also one of a man bringing danger and grief to his closest friends and relatives, or so at least it was then believed from the versions of Poe's biography given to the world by his executor and bitter enemy. Poe, dead, could hurt others no more, apart from his more foolish readers; Charles Altamont Doyle, also brilliant, also unrecognized, was still alive and could still hurt a great deal. Behind Arthur lay the warmth of Hodder, the coldness but security of Stonyhurst, the adventure and escapism of Feldkirch, the enthusiastic congratulations of Michael Conan on the Feldkirch newspaper he had edited himself, the censorious but still reliable uncles and aunt in London. Before him was the city he was to rediscover in much larger scope than the backwaters he had so far known; before him also the fire, grief, courage and resource of his noble mother; before him the final disintegration of his brilliant, feckless, querulous, drink-ridden, dangerous father; before him the little group of siblings, one, Annette, older than himself and making her own terms with the family crisis, the rest looking up to their tall, powerful, far-travelled, heroic brother; before him the medical school with its murderous failure-rate and unknown pitfalls; before him—and now, as of Summer 1876, endowed with his Bacchalaureate of Medicine,—the formidable presence of Bryan Charles Waller.

6

The Resident Doctor

Artful Dodger: Consider yourself
          At 'ome!
        Consider yourself
          One of the family.
        We've taken to you
          So strong,
        It's clear
        We're
          Going to get along!
            —Song from the musical *Oliver*

What shall it profit thee when thou art old
If Glory gild thy record's closing page?
Will Fame relume Youth's fires too soon grown cold,
Transmute once more Life's piteous dross to gold,
Or touch with Spring the Winter of thy age?

What shall it profit thee when thou art dead,
Though nations build thy sepulchre, and raise
Fair sculptured stone above thy lowly bed,
Or wreathe about thy unregarding head
Cold marble mockeries of the deathless bays?

What shall it profit? Naught.—The souls that sing
Uncrowned, unwept, to death and darkness pass.
Shall oaten pipe, or tremulous silver string,
Break on the sleep that knows no wakening,
Or soothe dull ears beneath the daisied grass?

Nay, it shall profit nothing, verily
Sing if thou wilt, and if thou wilt, refrain;
Yet, if thou sing, it shall not profit thee,
And, if thou sing not, thou shalt surely see
The silence of thy soul shall turn to pain.

Sing not, if so thou list: the songs unborn
Within thy soul like kennelled hounds shall rave:
Sing,—and the world shall pay thy thanks in scorn,

Yea, deem thee overpaid, if men unborn
Turn and repent, and love thee in thy grave.

'Vanity!' saith the Preacher. — 'All is vain!' —
Yet still the lark renews his matins clear:
Still doth the nightingale's melodious pain
Fall soft as Love upon the listening ear. —
Men heed not. Peradventure God shall hear.

We do not know the date when Bryan Charles Waller wrote this poem: it was simply included without date in the collection of his unpublished poems *Echo, and Other Poems* published by his widow in 1936, four years after his death. It clearly was written long after his first volume of poems, *The Twilight Land, and other poems,* published by Bell in 1875: there is nothing in the earlier volume to touch it. One poem in *Echo* is dated: a poem to E.W. Hornung on the death of Hornung's mother, dated 6 June 1896. The inference is that most of the work is from the 1880s and 1890s.

"What shall it profit thee . . ." could probably take a comfortable place in the best five thousand poems in the language. Yet its fate is as ironic as its content: it has remained utterly unknown until now. The *Times Literary Supplement* welcomed the volume on its appearance, with perceptive if uneasy comments, noting that "poetry for him was clearly so much a condition of music that the more he could breath his

Soul upon the air
In wild Aeolian floods of sound,

independent of mundane matters, the better poet he was" but finding that "in his shorter lyrics, too, he cultivated rather too fluently and luxuriantly the music of grief" (28 March 1936).

What little mention of Waller that exists in the works of Dickson Carr and Weil-Nordon clearly implies him to be an elderly family friend. In *The Hound of the Baskervilles* when Watson tries to deduce the identity of Dr Mortimer from his walking-stick, Holmes corrects him:

"Now, you will observe that he could not have been on the *staff* of the hospital, since only a man well-established in a London practice could hold such a position, and such a one would not drift into the country. What was he, then? If he was in the hospital and yet not on the staff he could only have been a house-surgeon or a house-physician — little more than a senior student. And he left five years ago — the date is on the stick. So your grave, middle-aged family practitioner vanishes into thin air, my dear Watson, and there emerges a young fellow under thirty . . ."

Lacking the stick, we still have the *Medical Directory* with which Watson checked Holmes's conclusions, and thence from allied sources we find that Waller was also young, being born on a family estate at Masongill, in Yorkshire (actually on the borders of Yorkshire, Lancashire and Westmoreland), in 1853, that he graduated M.B. of Edinburgh University in 1876, followed by winning his M.D. with Gold Medal for his thesis in 1878, publishing it in 1881, producing learned articles in the *Edinburgh Medical*

Journal, the *Lancet* and elsewhere, becoming (like Mortimer) F.R.C.S., holding a post from 1879 to 1882 as Lecturer on Pathology at the Edinburgh University School of Medicine, and then returning to Masongill House where he remained until his death on 4 November 1932, two years after Conan Doyle. Like Dr Mortimer he was distinguished by giving up a promising career in the city—Edinburgh, as opposed to Mortimer's London. Holmes deduces of Mortimer that this proves him unambitious. Waller is less easy to be so described: his rapid publication suggests very considerable initial ambition. But the move back to Masongill ended his publication drive, and the brief biographical note in *Echo* mentions poetry and advanced mathematics as his chief preoccupation thereafter. Certainly Waller's experience provided Conan Doyle with the idea of Mortimer, the man of sophisticated urban-trained talents and intellectual interests, happily ministering to the people of a lonely countryside while maintaining a place in what better-class society it possessed. Probably Mortimer's eagerness and tactlessness, and obsessions with his hobby, owed something to Waller's inspiration, although the rounded portrait of Mortimer suggests a less forceful personality. It is hard to see Waller accepting relegation to the background of the story's action as Mortimer does in *The Hound*.

Although Waller's personality comes across with vigour from his medical writings, from the recollections of his tenants and servants, and his letter to Arthur, and with sensibility from his poetry, especially his later poetry, he remains in other respects a little shadowy. Did he simply return to Masongill from a sense of obligation to the estate he inherited from his father in 1877, did he come to the conclusion that his ambitions would not prosper further in Edinburgh (a new appointment to the Chair of Pathology after the continued illness of the Professor in Waller's years may have seemed firmly to block his further elevation), or was there some more personal reason connected with the Doyles? Arthur Conan Doyle might have helped us, but, apart from fleeting references in fiction, most of them by now probably hidden forever, he left no account of Waller. There were good reasons for that, apart from Waller's longevity. But the effect was to create a false Waller for some of the biographers, and for others to give an excessive significance to contemporaries like Dr George Budd, whom ACD did survive and hence described in his work. Budd, with whom he would briefly share a practice, was important, and clearly helped shape certain of his fictional creations; so was his teacher Joseph Bell, and other teachers. But Waller eclipses all of them by the nature of their association.

The Valuation Rolls preserved in the Scottish Record Office, the City Directory and the matriculation rolls of the university, taken together, convey the central fact. The Doyles remained in 3 Sciennes Hill Place, that ugly, dark cul-de-sac, until 1875. In 1875-77 they were in 2 Argyle Park Terrace, a far more agreeable domicile, with a bow window overlooking the great expanse of The Meadows, the Edinburgh park which remains the delight of countless pedestrians and (expressly contrary to the bye-laws) cyclists. It may well have been that bow window which accounts for the placing of a bow window in 221B Baker Street whence Watson observed the eccentric approach of the banker Alexander Holder in *"The Beryl Coronet"*: it has upset Sherlockologists, as Baker Street had and has no bow windows. The young Arthur could certainly have observed portly citizens, potentially of financial responsibility, describing weird gyrations in the snow which drives high on Argyle Park Terrace with a good wind behind it and no row of houses to hinder its approach from The Meadows, and the snow, of course, is a vital feature in *"The Beryl Coronet"*.

The rent of 2 Argyle Park Terrace was almost twice that of the previous domicile, being £35.00, but the additional cost was borne by Waller's joining the household in his final year as a medical student (or possibly towards the close of his fourth year). He remained as part of the household for the remainder of his time in Edinburgh, but the circumstances altered. Charles Doyle is still listed as the rent-payer for 1876-77, by which time Waller was licensed to practise (which the irreverent Arthur, when *he* acquired his M.B., described as "licensed to kill"), listed himself alongside Charles Doyle in the City Directory, and presumably put up his plate. The family was large, and the overcrowding must have been irritating. Then Charles's chief, the Surveyor of Scotland, died, and the advent of his successor seems to have involved a clean sweep of the Office of Works. Thereafter Charles is listed in the City Directory as an artist. The new surveyor may have had his own problems, quite apart from those he encountered among clerks whose bibulousness had been tolerated by his predecessor. He got rid of several of his new appointments with great speed. Meanwhile the Doyles transferred to a really impressive residence, 23 George Square, famous as perhaps the finest residential square in the city until the buildings on three sides were demolished in the 1960s by the official vandalism of Edinburgh University. The side on which 23 George Square stands survived, partly through the energy of the Dominicans, who now own it and its neighbour as the Catholic Chaplaincy under the Patronage of St Albert the Great. Hence, in the phrase of the Very Rev. Anthony Ross, O.P., Catholic Chaplain and later (1979-82) Lord Rector of the University, Arthur was the first Catholic student to live in the chaplaincy building, although he had ceased to be a Catholic and it was not yet a chaplaincy. The rent in 1877-81 was £85.00. The Valuation Rolls reveal that it was paid by Bryan Charles Waller.

23 George Square did not give the Doyles and Waller entire possession of the house. The basement remained in other hands, and so did the upper floor, known as 23A and 23B, a reminder of the origins of Arthur's use of addresses characteristic of Edinburgh and exceptional for London. It would be perilous to see the original 221B Baker Street as 23 George Square. What is suggestive is the presence of 23B on an upper storey, which accounts for the famous steps in the Sherlock Holmes narratives. Whether Mary Foley Doyle cooked for the upstairs and downstairs tenants, as Mrs Hudson does for Holmes and Watson is questionable: she may have done for David H. Gordon, M.D., but would have been less likely to do so for Edward Henry Roberts, Wool Broker. In any case, she clearly did see to the needs of Bryan Charles Waller, as well

as her family. Waller's work at the Royal Infirmary, five minutes' walk from the house, and his teaching, would have kept him away from the house for much of the day. On the other hand, he would have needed space and quiet for his writing, and he would have taken his patients at the house. The arrangement for a consulting-room may well have been as *ad hoc* as Holmes employed in *A Study in Scarlet*: "I found that he had many acquaintances, and these in the most different classes of society. . . . When any of these nondescript individuals put in an appearance, Sherlock Holmes used to beg for the use of the sitting-room, and I would retire to my bed-room. He always apologised to me for putting me to this inconvenience." The consulting-room, then, could be put to other purposes by the Doyle family when Waller did not need it. Charles, when artistic commissions had gained precedence over alcoholic temptations, would also have needed space, and Arthur, having embarked on his medical studies, probably shared the consulting-room with Waller for study during such times as Waller was not seeing patients. Since it seems clear that Waller really was the major influence dictating Arthur's decision to take up medicine, and no doubt took himself to be even more important in this respect than he was, his natural instincts for financial, intellectual and human generosity would have extended to room-space. In any case, the work was often integrated. Waller thanks Charles Doyle for transferring "two drawings to the wood" for his publication of his thesis *An Investigation Into the Microscopic Anatomy of Interstitial Nephritis*. He may have made Arthur a class assistant for a time; he certainly did bestow such patronage on James Ryan, who, however, did not complete his medical studies.

During these years Arthur had at his elbow a figure of outstanding success in the Medical School, with a deep knowledge of its personnel as student and faculty member, and few signs of restraint in the imparting of information. He would meet others later, such as George Budd, but Bryan Charles Waller was effectively the leader of any set there might have been. Budd, for instance, thanks him warmly for his "kindness and facilities given in experiment" when publishing his article on "*Amyloid Degeneration*" in the *Lancet* on 28 February 1880. The Conan Doyle memoirs record ACD's meeting with Budd as in his final year; Budd contracted his obligation to Waller in Arthur's fourth year, and probably that was the time of their early meeting, but the senior student in "*His First Operation*" must surely be Waller if the story is autobiographical at all. The opening certainly sounds as if recollection is feeding imagination. It would have been cumbersome, and perhaps unduly revealing, to have placed a first year in such clear collegiality to a postgraduate, and hence the division between the two students is made more commonplace. But the third year student pays for all the drinks as Waller would have done and an ordinary undergraduate would not.

> It was the first day of a winter session, and the third year's man was walking with the first year's man. Twelve o'clock was just booming out from the Tron Church.
>
> "Let me see", said the third year's man, "you have never seen an operation?"
> "Never."

"Then this way, please. This is Rutherford's historic bar. A glass of sherry, please, for this gentleman. You are rather sensitive, are you not?"

"My nerves are not very strong, I am afraid."

"Hum! Another glass of sherry for this gentleman. We are going to an operation now, you know."

The novice squared his shoulders and made a gallant attempt to look unconcerned.

"Nothing very bad—eh?"

"Well, yes—pretty bad."

"An—an amputation?"

"No, it's a bigger affair than that."

"I think—I think they must be expecting me at home."

"There's no sense funking. If you don't go today you must tomorrow. Better get it over at once. Feel pretty fit?"

"Oh, yes, all right."

The smile was not a success.

"One more glass of sherry, then. Now come on or we shall be late. I want you to be well in front."

"Surely that is not necessary."

"Oh, it is far better. What a drove of students! There are plenty of new men among them. You can tell them easily enough, can't you? If they were going down to be operated upon themselves they could not look whiter."

"I don't think I should look as white."

"Well, I was just the same myself. But the feeling soon wears off. You see a fellow with a face like plaster, but before the week is out he is eating his lunch in the dissecting rooms. I'll tell you all about the case when we get to the theatre."

The paternal solicitude of the older student seems more in keeping with a situation of patron and protégé than a simple acquaintanceship of students separated by two years would allow. Also the gossip is more authoritative than undergraduate gossip:

"There's Peterson", whispered the senior. "The big, bald man in the front row. He's the skin-grafting man, you know. And that's Anthony Browne, who took a larynx out successfully last winter. And there's Murphy the pathologist, and Stoddart the eye man. You'll come to know them all soon."

"Who are the two men at the table?"

"Nobody—dressers. One has charge of the instruments and the other of the puffing Billy. It's Lister's antiseptic spray, you know, and Archer's one of the carbolic acid men. Hayes is the leader of the cleanliness-and-cold-water school, and they all hate each other like poison."

Whether Arthur did faint during "his first operation" as the novice does, when with eyes down and ears stopped he imagines the hideous incision, we do not know. Certainly the Waller character responds as one might expect:

When he came to himself he was lying in the empty theatre with his collar and shirt undone. The third year's man was dabbing a wet sponge over his face, and a couple of grinning dressers were looking on.

"All right", cried the novice, sitting up and rubbing his eyes; "I'm sorry to have made an ass of myself."

"Well, so I should think", said his companion. "What on earth did you faint about?"

> "I couldn't help it. It was that operation."
> "What operation?"
> "Why, that cancer."
> There was a pause, and then the three students burst out laughing.
> "Why, you juggins", cried the senior man, "there never was an operation at all. They found the patient didn't stand the chloroform well, and so the whole thing was off. Archer has been giving us one of his racy lectures, and you fainted just in the middle of his favourite story."

But a fictionalised conclusion seems the more likely, possibly based on some other student's experience. The beginning has the sound of authentic memory, but Arthur showed few signs throughout his life of the total encapsulation by the world of neurotic imaginings which account for the downfall of the novice here. It is Waller, rather than Arthur, whose voice and conduct we catch.

The mode of speech is Waller's, "Hum! Ha!" being recalled by a former servant, and supplies a point of origin for the early manner of Holmes, one which later disappears. The notable instance is *"A Scandal in Bohemia"* when the client mentions Irene Adler:

> "Let me see!" said Holmes. "Hum! Born in New Jersey in the year 1858. Contralto—hum! La Scala, hum! Prima donna Imperial Opera of Warsaw—Yes! Retired from operatic stage—ha! Living in London—quite so! Your Majesty, as I understand, became entangled with the young person, wrote her some compromising letters, and is now desirous of getting those letters back."
> "Precisely so. But how—"
> "Was there a secret marriage?"
> "None."
> "No legal papers or certificates?"
> "None."
> "Then I fail to follow your Majesty. If this young person should produce her letters for blackmailing or other purposes, how is she to prove their authenticity?"
> "There is the writing."
> "Pooh, pooh! Forgery."
> "My private note-paper."
> "Stolen."
> "My own seal."
> "Imitated."
> "My photograph."
> "Bought."
> "We were both in the photograph "
> "Oh, dear! That is very bad! Your Majesty has indeed committed an indiscretion."

Although *"A Scandal in Bohemia"* was to be the basis of Holmes's fame, Conan Doyle was to drop this sort of dialogue very rapidly from the stories. As Mr Martin Dakin has observed, the boastful assurance of its logic is very different from the voice of experience in *"Charles Augustus Milverton"*, where Holmes is seriously aware of the danger of an indiscreet letter and makes no pretence that it can be dismissed as forged on stolen paper. His arrogance remains, but it is more subtle and elegant. We can speak with confidence on the presence of Waller in this early, unsophisticated self-admiration of Holmes, by recalling his comments on his precursors in his dissertation.

There is no reason to believe that ACD approved of the manners of this arrogant early Holmes, and much that he did not. In *Through the Magic Door* he makes one exception to his great panegyric in honour of Macaulay's *Essays:* "Only one would I wish to eliminate. It is the diabolically clever criticism upon Montgomery. One would have wished that Macaulay's heart was too kind, and his soul too gentle, to pen so bitter an attack. Bad work will sink of its own weight. It is not necessary to souse the author as well. One would think more highly of the man if he had not done that savage bit of work." The scruple does him honour, as Holmes said of Mr Sandeford's insistence on stating the purchase price of his Napoleonic bust, for all that Macaulay on Robert Montgomery has a ferocious charm to baser natures such as that of the present writer. But it does tell us something of the limitations of his receptivity to Waller, and reminds us that in portraying Holmes he wanted to describe aspects of the scholarly and specialist mind without necessarily endorsing them. Holmes, of course, speaks more informally than Waller in the thesis, but naturally Conan Doyle would have been drawing on Waller's conversation in Rutherford's of Drummond Street and in the consulting room at George Square, rather than on the thesis where even Waller was restrained by the necessity to clothe his diatribes in scholarly language. ACD does not, for instance, seem to have shared Waller's enthusiasm for vivisection, as may be noted by his comments in *Memories and Adventures* on the identical attitudes of Professor Rutherford, who helped inspire Challenger. Bryan Charles Waller's poetic soul expressed itself on vivisection in the *Lancet* on 16 April 1881: "At present, however, when the head of every tom-cat in the British Islands is held sacred as that of the bull Apis in ancient Egypt, it is to be feared that any and every thing pertaining to this subject [interstitial nephritis] must remain unsettled in the absence of experimental corroboration."

Waller had some reason for irritation. Under the Act passed in 1876 for the protection of animals from vivisection licences had to be sought by research specialists wishing to conduct experiments involving living animals. Edinburgh University medicine had been hostile to the Act from start to finish, refusing to accept the considerable indulgence it showed to scientific investigators despite the pressure of humanitarian sentiment. Professor Sir Robert Christison, Professor William Rutherford and others made no bones about their suspicion of a London-administered compromise. And they were sound in their judgment. The Home Secretary handled Edinburgh applications for licences roughly. To Bryan Charles Waller was given the distinction of being the first applicant actually refused a licence under the Act: he was turned down in January 1877. Only seven applications were rejected in the first three years of the Act. Professor Rutherford in January 1877 was refused certain certificates for vivisectional experiment, but he made several more attempts and was allowed three certificates after four years. Waller had no second chance. Nor had he reason to hope for a change of administration: Richard Assheton Cross, for the Tories, was milder than his Liberal successor, Sir William Venables Vernon Harcourt.

Arthur certainly heard much of Waller's opinions on his own fitness for research and his inability to practise his career as a researcher. Now, let us turn to *A Study in Scarlet*, which after the denunciations of Poe and Gaboriau, continues:

> I felt rather indignant at having two characters whom I admired treated in this cavalier style. I walked over to the window, and stood looking out into the busy street. "This fellow may be very clever", I said to myself, "but he is certainly conceited."
>
> "There are no crimes and no criminals in these days", he said, querulously. "What is the use of having brains in our profession? I know well that I have it in me to make my name famous. No man lives or has ever lived who has brought the same amount of study and of natural talent to the detection of crime which I have done. And what is the result? There is no crime to detect, or, at most, some bungling villainy with a motive so transparent that even a Scotland Yard official can see through it."
>
> I was still annoyed at his bumptious style of conversation. I thought it best to change the topic.

And the topic is changed, and Holmes deduces that a passer-by is a retired sergeant of Marines, and Holmes thereby moves from reflecting the influence of Bryan Charles Waller to that of Dr Joseph Bell, famed for his diagnoses of the social as well as the medical salient points of his patients. But the earlier passage is not Bell, who had no reason to complain. Waller, despite his scholarly successes, would encounter the disheartening setbacks opening before postgraduate medical students on the rise, anti-vivisection laws being only one of them, and he was not of the type to keep his professional woes to himself after the manner of the Spartan boy being gnawed by the fox he was concealing. Waller's fondness for classical allusion never led him into self-restraint. Look also at one significant sentence in the passage quoted: "What is the use of having brains in our profession?"—*our* profession. In the context it makes no sense. Holmes, especially at this point, does not take Watson to be a detective, licensed or trainee, and Watson has hardly heard of the calling. Holmes has just said he is the "only one in the world", of the profession of consulting detective. The real cause of the sentence is that an original piece of Waller complaint to Arthur, alluding to their joint profession, has crept into the Holmes text.

The harshness of the elder medical man seems, then, to have repelled the kindly instincts of the younger, but it continued to fascinate him, as both Holmes and Challenger bear witness, for Challenger, too, was the product of many human originals. But the other side of the Waller academic coin, the devotion to scientific observation and the insistence on grounding theses on personal investigation, supply facets of Holmes with which Conan Doyle was deeply in sympathy. Waller went in for literary analogy in medical exposition, larding his prose with quotations from the Greek, sometimes applied wildly out of context—but Conan Doyle's love of literature warmly responded to

Waller's belief that science must be presented with rich and compelling literary allusions and quotations. This, too, would be a trait he would share in common with Holmes, and one strengthened rather than weakened after the early work, especially when the cultural ignoramus of *A Study in Scarlet* had been superseded. Waller was inclined to overdo cultural allusion; Conan Doyle, with his growing self-mastery of literary economics, made cultural allusion do his work without swamping it. *Interstitial Nephritis* won awards which were never accorded to Conan Doyle's M.D. thesis on "Tabes Dorsalis", but the latter brings in Heine with astonishing effectiveness and the utmost relevance to his subject where Waller insists on dragging in Sophocles and Moschus with only the most tenuous justification. The fact that Arthur's were much more modest achievements at Edinburgh Medical School than were vouchsafed to his patron helped him to retain the modesty which kept his literary feet on the ground. The hare was kind to the tortoise, but the hare dropped out of the race, even if his work after his dropping out was far better than that accomplished when he was in.

The most remarkable impact of Bryan Charles Waller on Arthur Conan Doyle was directly literary. To have on the premises a man so devoted to the interests of the family who had at the tender age of twenty-two published a book of poems was exciting enough, but Waller through his family background brought Arthur in touch with a literary London far wider than he could discover even from his uncles and grandfather. Waller was fond of pointing out his descent from the poet Edmund Waller, singled out by Pope as the exemplar of sweetness in *"Essay on Criticism"*, and recalled rather less happily by political historians for the judicious vagaries of his allegiance during the English Civil War.

Not all the family's associations were literary, though: a Waller (Richard) was said to have captured at Agincourt Charles Duke of Orleans, first cousin of the French king and father of the future Louis XII. The slight uncertainty as to whether the prize was indeed Richard Waller's clearly supplies the origin of the dispute at the climax of *Sir Nigel* as to whether Nigel is the person responsible for the capture of King John of France at Poitiers (and hence is also an origin of Bertie Wooster's ancestors "who did dashed well at Crecy") but the Wallers boldly added the Royal Arms of France to their bearings, which no doubt interested Mary Foley Doyle. His descendants were parliamentarians in the English Civil War, General Sir William Waller commanding parliamentary troops in the west country up to 1645 when Cromwell served under his command on the expedition to relieve Taunton; as a leader of the Presbyterian party Waller later became alienated from his old subordinate and was secretly intriguing with the Royalists before Cromwell's death. But his cousin Hardress Waller supported the army against Parliament, signed Charles I's death-warrant and only narrowly avoided execution after the Restoration, dying in prison. These facts would be of service in giving Arthur a whiff of family folklore for the background to *Micah Clarke*, specifically for his perception of gentlemen of ancient nobility supporting the Puritan cause. The Masongill countryside had seen fighting during the war, a camp-site on Bryan Charles Waller's future estate being fortified and attacked there, as the people still point out to visitors. It was in the hands of the Wallers by the mid-eighteenth century and ultimately passed to the Rev. Bryan Waller, a Cambridge don, incumbent of Burton-in-Lonsdale in 1806. He was an indifferent poet, who dedicated individual poems and in 1796 a collected volume of verse to Edmund Burke in tribute to his crusade against the French Revolution, for which Burke made him a very kind reply: it made a pleasing contrast to the Irish statesman's local feuds in Beaconsfield about mud-ponds with the senior line of Edmund Waller's descendants. The Rev. Bryan, having inherited the Masongill estate, left it in 1842 to his nephew Nicholas Procter in consideration of the latter taking the surname "Waller". Nicholas, born in 1802, married Julia Perry, eleven years his junior, and Bryan Charles was born on 27 July 1853, their only child.

But Nicholas was not the oldest Procter of his generation. His brother, Bryan Waller Procter, fifteen years his senior, would naturally have been given the first refusal. The conditions of bequest demanded residence on the estate, and thus presumably account for his rejection of it. For by the time of the Rev. Bryan Waller's death in the 1840s Bryan Waller Procter had become a celebrity of literary London and had every incentive to remain one. As "Barry Cornwall" he was the author of plays, songs and stories, of a bad biography of the actor Edmund Kean and an excellent one of his friend Charles Lamb. He was at school with Peel and Byron at Harrow, studied boxing under Thomas Cribb (later to make fictional appearances in Conan Doyle's Regency stories particularly *The Lord of Falconbridge*"), became an intimate of Leigh Hunt, initiated Hazlitt into non-Shakespearean Elizabethan and Jacobean drama, guaranteed jointly with the poet Thomas Lovell Beddoes the publication of Shelley's posthumous poems, encouraged the early work of Browning and Swinburne, and married the stepdaughter of Basil Montagu whose biography and edition of Bacon proved the occasion for the longest of Macaulay's *Critical and Historical Essays*. Thackeray dedicated *Vanity Fair* to him, and Wilkie Collins *The Woman in White*. His daughter Adelaide Anne Procter won celebrity for her poems long before she acknowledged her true identity to her delighted editor, Charles Dickens, who contributed a memoir to her posthumous *Legends and Lyrics*. Much of her work would appear in his magazine *All the Year Round* which later published some of ACD's earliest stories, no doubt following Bryan Charles Waller's prompting to Arthur. Adelaide Anne Procter became a Roman Catholic, and her most famous poem *"The Lost Chord"* inspired one of Sir Arthur Sullivan's most famous sacred compositions. She died aged 39 in 1864, her father surviving her by ten years.

The young Bryan Charles Waller was enormously proud of this heritage. The rules at Edinburgh Medical School permitted him taking certain courses under recognised teachers elsewhere, a recognition he later obtained for himself. He took these courses in London in the early 1870s (having gone up to Edinburgh in 1871) and became intimate with his uncle who permitted the dedication of *The Twilight Land* to him or, as it proved, to his memory. Bryan

Charles Waller's epic poem, *Perseus and the Hesperides,* published in 1893, is dedicated to the memories of Edmund Waller, Bryan Waller Procter and Adelaide Anne Procter; his doctoral dissertation is dedicated to that of Thomas Lovell Beddoes, as another poet-doctor. It may even be that the decision to lodge with the Doyles stemmed from Procter's circle. Bryan Waller Procter had no resentment against his daughter's conversion, and befriended some of her Catholic admirers, such as Coventry Patmore, who edited his *Autobiography* with a memoir. The literary Catholic grape-vine would have known the Doyles of Edinburgh; for that matter so would other literary associates of Procter, such as Thackeray. In any event, Waller joined the Doyle household somewhere in 1875, at a time when he was probably in touch with Patmore about his uncle's memoir and he was doubtless making use of London literary acquaintances to advance the prospects of *The Twilight Land.* Thus he bore to the Doyle household the armigerous antiquity dear to the heart of Mary Foley Doyle, and the lively literary associations of the kind whence Charles Altamont Doyle had been exiled.

For the young Arthur this heritage was of enormous importance. It must have been like finding the great men and women of English literature in the back bedroom. Indeed it probably inspired his *"A Literary Mosaic"* in which a young author finds his room and table suddenly expanding to give room to the literary Titans, Lamb and Dickens among them. The presence on the scene of a senior man in medicine who had already published a book of poems was exciting enough, but the reminiscences he could impart from the uncle to whom he had dedicated it opened up literary battalions. Waller liked gossip, his uncle had known much, and what had been salvaged provided a personal glimpse of the heart of literary London from the Regency onward. The link with Cribb opened up boxing and its literature, whence Arthur went on to George Borrow, and, as he recorded in his delightful transposition of Borrow into ordinary life, *"Borrowed Scenes"*, Borrow's enthusiasms included Edmund Waller, making another point of inspiration or discussion from Bryan Charles. Waller's anxiety to ensure Arthur really did drop Roman Catholicism—a point on which he clearly did not share the views of his uncle—would have been alleviated by seeing so anti-Catholic a writer in his protégé's hands, but he hardly reckoned with Arthur's sense of humour—his passages on Borrow, either in *Through the Magic Door* or *"Borrowed Scenes"*, howl with laughter at the absurdity of his bigotry while paying deep tribute to his originality, folklore preservation, philology and roaring love of vigorous life.

There were disadvantages to Waller as a sponsor in making the acquaintance of the great literary dead. He was egocentric to a degree, and while this had good results in putting Arthur in close touch with the world of Bryan Waller Procter, it must have been very difficult to choke him off. But he did one great service for Arthur. *Through the Magic Door* reveals a remarkable sense of the authors as people. Great biographies by intimates made this possible for Johnson and Scott, yet in general ACD's appreciation of the writers who so deeply influenced him often seems almost a matter of physical acquaintance. Macaulay's portraits of his favourite writers are vivid in the extreme, but at all times they are limited by the book-learned contours of their personalities. Conan Doyle often seems to transcend biographical sources in looking at literary figures of the past. His method was to study men through their books, yet he had acquired the means of seeing human personality of which the books were but the most formal epiphany. It is this sense of life pulsing through the veins of his literary icons which enabled him to ensure that, say, his use of Johnson and Boswell to inspire Holmes and Watson concentrated on living character behind the wit and force of the dialogue, and produced figures of powerful identity fired by Johnson and Boswell yet far removed in nature from them. To bring Langland into *Sir Nigel* is not forced as Corneille and Racine are forced very unrealistically into *The Refugees*: there is a sense in which Langland, a flesh-and-blood Langland, told him part of the story. This sense of the flesh-and-blood writer he owed to Waller's self-importance and sense of his own significance as confidant of his uncle and hence observer of his circle. There was a little knowledge of flesh-and-blood writers before, but sitting on Thackeray's lap was much less valuable than looking though Bryan Waller Procter's eyes.

The family background of this association can be deduced in part. Charles Doyle's loss of his supposed sinecure, the Doyles' and Waller's move to George Square, and the death of Nicholas Waller are all very close in time. John Innes Hay Doyle had been born in 1873, and Jane Adelaide Rose Doyle ("Ida") in 1875. Now the family's sense of obligation to Bryan Charles Waller was shown when the tenth and youngest child, a girl, born on 2 March 1877, was named "Bryan Mary Julia Josephine", a decision probably taken between 12 March (when Nicholas died) and 20 March (when the baby's birth was registered). How deeply Bryan Charles Waller was moved by the death of his father is a question; the old gentleman was fifty years his senior, and it is his and his mother's names that were given the new daughter in compliment to him, not a version of his father's. The birth is registered from 2 Argyle Park Terrace, so that it was after his inheriting the property from his father that the move was made to George Square. The use of names of friends for the children was nothing new. The Burton-Innes connection was reflected in the naming of Arthur's brother, for instance. But it certainly symbolised the growth of dependence as well as friendship. Waller's inheritance relieved the Doyles of the immediate horror of financial disaster, though at a cost to their self-respect that must at times have been painful, especially to the fiercely self-reliant Arthur. Charles Doyle made efforts at self-redemption, but matters grew worse.

But Waller from 1876 to 1878 drove full-tilt for his doctorate, and his speed of accomplishment was noteworthy. From the first he "undertook only consulting practice, devoting all my leisure time to study and research in the domain of Pathology and Morbid Anatomy" (as he phrased it to the Court of Edinburgh University in January 1881 when he unsuccessfully applied for a post of Examiner in Pathology). Here is the origin of Holmes in *A Study in Scarlet*, insisting that he is a "consulting detective". A consultant status for doctors is not the rarity Holmes saw it as being for detectives, but the principle is the same. Of course Holmes dropped the principle of consultancy very quickly: Mary Morstan, in *The Sign of Four*, is not forwarded to him from any general practitioner of detective-work (the recommendation of a previous client hardly counts), nor is the King of Bohemia (though Waller would be more than likely to relax his rules in such a case), nor are most of their immediate successors. The odd business of Miss Turner's retention of Lestrade in "*The Boscombe Valley Mystery*", whence derives Holmes's brief, is a reversion to the earlier situation. It is, as Mr Martin Dakin has said, nonsensical in context: Scotland Yard men could not be retained by the defence after a police arrest has been made. But it would make sense for a Waller original, with a problem being referred to Waller from some assistant in a fog in the Royal Infirmary. The illness of the Professor of Pathology at Edinburgh University, William Rutherford Sanders, ultimately totally incapacitated him in the year before his death in February 1881, and seriously affected the performance of his duties as Professor and as private consultant at various times from 1874. At such times assistants, often very junior, were called on to meet his obligations, and Waller's contempt for such young hopefuls is predictable from his scornful comments on rivals and suggestive with respect to Lestrade and the other Scotland Yard men. Holmes shows little gratitude enough for such commissions from them, and *A Study in Scarlet* above all is very clear that they will appropriate such credit as comes to them: these also seem reactions highly consistent with Waller's arrogance, and with his defeat for the Examinership in 1881 where the post ultimately went to a former assistant of Sanders (after the initially successful candidate, William Smith Greenfield of London, was appointed to Sanders's chair on his death).

Waller's acquisition of his doctorate of Medicine with award of gold medal was followed by his purchase of part of the pathology collection of Daniel Rutherford Haldane of Edinburgh, a famous physician and pathologist who taught medicine at Surgeons' Hall, uncle to Lord Haldane and great-uncle to Professor J. B. S. Haldane. Simultaneously he set up his own museum for purposes of student instruction in New Minto House, Chambers Street, around the corner from Old College, and on the strength of his excellent instruments, preparations, drawings and commodious premises, for all of which he had clearly spared no expense, he was recognised as a Lecturer in Pathology by the University Court without any of its frequent reservations. Arthur, who by that stage had passed his Pathology during one of Professor Sanders's bouts of good health, was fortunately immune from the courtesy of taking the family friend's course, but no doubt he derived benefit in the subject from their association and was reminded of the fact.

Meanwhile Julia Perry Waller administered the Masongill estate. It was not a situation which could be prolonged permanently, and ultimately she became bed-ridden, some years before her death on 18 May 1887. She seems to have had a vigorous personality and a sense of humour. The daughter of the head gardener on the estate, himself a privileged person as the son of a previous head gardener, recalls her father telling her of a summons to the bedroom for instructions at a time when Julia Waller could no longer leave her chamber, and at the close of business the mistress of the house remarked in a tone of decided satisfaction "Kettlewell, I'm as ugly as a pig!" Her son shows little sign of comparable humour, but apart from his acid wit at the expense of precursors and rivals in research he also revealed a cool, agreeable, instructive wit under firm control in the presentation of his lectures, on the evidence of the one which has survived.

How he would propose in the event of winning his Chair to manage his obligations to his estate, where residence was assumed to be a qualification for ownership by his forebears and by himself in making his will, has to be as conjectural as Stapleton's intentions as to taking possession of the Baskerville estate should he be successful in his attempt to kill Sir Henry. He certainly listed himself in the *Medical Directory* with his Edinburgh and Masongill addresses, and perhaps he would have left it to a reliable steward and week-end commuting. He had no near relatives other than the disinherited Procters, the surviving male, son of Bryan Waller Procter, being an officer serving in India. In any event his ambitions crumbled after the loss of the Chair and the Examinership. His mother's condition made return a necessity, and Charles Doyle was becoming increasingly impossible. In 1881 they all moved to the quieter, but still conveniently situated 15 Lonsdale Terrace, on the other side of the Royal Infirmary. Charles may have made continued residence in the fashionable George Square no longer advisable. The new residence was less agreeable than the beautiful Georgian square they had left, but it had a pleasant prospect on The Meadows and its main artery to a thoroughfare was Lauriston Gardens, which would supply Arthur with the street of the murder in *A Study in Scarlet*. Once again the rent, which fluctuated around £60, was paid by Bryan Charles Waller, who continued to teach, to act as a consultant, and to engage in dispensary work at which he quarrelled bitterly with at least one of his colleagues.

The older children were by this stage slowly moving away from the nest. Arthur made several efforts at paying his own way by taking brief medical assistantships and then voyages as ship's doctor after graduation, in 1881. He did not leave for good until 1882 and then, as we will see, he was left with very little time for longterm planning when he took that decision. Annette took up a post as governess in Portugal in 1879, and was followed within the next three years by her next surviving sisters, Lottie and Connie. Connie was probably sent to school in Portugal at Annette's expense. The three youngest children, Innes, Ida and "Dodo" (Bryan Mary Julia Josephine) were all under ten by 1882. Innes was sent down to Arthur in the late summer. Bryan Charles Waller brought Mary and the two youngest to Masongill, and lodged them in Masongill Cottage, a sizeable house on his estate.

Charles's fate is a little uncertain, but ultimately he was placed in a series of homes, first for alcoholics, then, as epilepsy was diagnosed, for lunatics. It has to be presumed that some very bad outbreaks accompanied that decision. We do not yet know who certified Charles Altamont Doyle, as the certificates are not yet open for inspection if in fact they survive, but the probability is that Bryan Charles Waller and Arthur Conan Doyle were the signatories. "*The Beetle-Hunter*" is important here. Sir Thomas Rossiter is described as making a murderous attack on his wife before the action of the story, and it is stated that in his outbreaks "his inclination is always to attack the very person to whom he is most attached". "*The Beetle-Hunter*" also raises the phenomenon of a relative being cosignatory to certification, and while it is that relative, Lord Linchmere, who is small where the narrator, unacquainted hitherto with the protagonists, is bigger, the heights correspond with those of the six-foot Arthur and the short, bandy-legged Waller. That description of the little man hanging on to the tall madman while the narrator stands briefly bemused could be that of an actual incident. In any event, there is no avoiding the certainty that horror of some kind brought the residence at 15 Lonsdale Terrace to its end. Arthur had good reason for ghastly and melancholy associations with the neighbourhood of Lauriston Gardens. Of the depth of the tragedy for him no adequate word could be found. In his Stoicism he said nothing, so we have nothing to say.

But what motivated Bryan Charles Waller? Apart from his later poetry, which, while beautiful and sorrowful, is deeply self-obsessed, he does not shine in other respects as an altruist. In one matter we may make an exception. He was from first to last absolutely conscientious as a doctor and teacher, from all the evidence in hand. This was not merely self-seeking professionalism. He did not practise when he returned to Masongill, but he made it a rigid rule to be available to the neighbourhood without fee whenever the local practitioner could not be obtained. Masongill and Ingleton and Thornton-in-Lonsdale still contain men and women who can recall the aged little figure, with long white beard and tall hat, clad in Victorian greatcoat and system of capes, driving grimly into the night in his carriage in rain or snow to the home of some sufferer. It must have been a little galling to his brothers in the locality, for Waller's research brilliance was echoed by his reputation in folklore. Either in dispensary decisions, or in diagnosis, or in treatment, or in comfort, he remained on the heights that had once been his. Otherwise he was widely regarded in the neighbourhood as "a perfect snob", in the phrase of one of his former servants. Children of tenants were not permitted within sight of his windows. Acquaintance with them, Mary Foley Doyle alone excepted, was strictly financial and through his agents.

The bitterness of this reclusive life adds its own clue, and so does the poetry. Some terrible tragedy had also darkened the life of Bryan Charles Waller, and for all his outward show of pride he had sunk under it as his former protégé did not. But the tragedy was not that of Charles Altamont Doyle, for all that Waller had been his friend and thanked him warmly for his assistance in enabling the publication of medical sketches for Waller's dissertation. Waller as a medical man had seen far too many tragedies to be overcome by one even as close to him as that. Arthur, too, knew his father's fate to be but one of the omnipresent cases of human suffering, though there is a heartcry over such tragedies at the end of "*The Cardboard Box*", a

heartcry all the greater in its recognition that the dreadful fate of Jim
Browner is but one of a gigantic "circle of misery and violence and fear". It is
one indisputable case where Sherlock Holmes speaks for his creator. Waller's
tragedy is different. For one thing, its inception is very early. It is reasonable
to assume the decision to provide for the Doyles coincided with the news of
his father's death, and the naming of Dodo was a profound expression of
gratitude. Why did he undertake it? Certainly, in his own dominating, self-
aggrandising way, he liked them. He was not the world's easiest lodger. His
former maidservant recalls his special demands for endless oysters and the
hottest curries imaginable. Mary Foley Doyle knew the cooking he liked; after
his marriage, when she was over sixty and was living at Masongill, his wife,
left to cope with making dinner because of her difficulties in retaining
servants, noted in a bitter cry in her diary that Waller had left his meal to go
to Mary, no doubt for curry done as he wanted it. Curry makes its
appearances in the Holmes cycle: it appears for breakfast in "*The Naval
Treaty*" and the important deduction in "*Silver Blaze*" that the stable-boy
must have been doped by someone familiar with the household as the use of
powdered opium demanded a dish which would disguise its taste, turns on
curry being served for dinner. Oysters, too, appear as Holmes's choice for
dinner in *The Sign of Four,* and in "*The Dying Detective*" Holmes raves about
oysters covering the floor of the ocean although Watson and he have done
their part to keep the numbers down. Clearly, Bryan Charles Waller had
made his impact on the family diet.

The key figure seems to be a very important person in Arthur's life of
whom little is known because of her early death. Annette Doyle was three
years older than Arthur, and three years younger than Bryan Charles Waller.
Only one piece of evidence on the point survives, but it is telling. It is a poem
called "*Annette's Music*", one of the *Echo* collection. It is long, lyrical and
unspeakably mournful. It is dominated by the sense of a lost love, indeed the
utter rupture of the poet's relationship with Annette. It makes reference to
the breath of the South, and the South wind sighing, and intervening oceans,
and an unknown land where the music now is: Annette was in Portugal from
1879 until her death in 1889 of the influenza epidemic. When *Echo* appeared
in 1936 *The Times Literary Supplement* saw in it the conspicuous example of
the luxuriance of grief. Excerpted stanzas cannot give its cumulative effect,
but they tell much of Waller's love for Annette:

> *Oh! lost, lost, lost!*—
> *Oh perished glory of youth,*
> *Oh songs of love and of truth,*
> *Ye are silenced for ever and dead!*
> *Oh blackness of night overhead,*
> *Oh days that shall not dawn again,*
> *Though sought through a lifetime of pain,*
> *And priced at an empire's cost!*
>
> *Soft, soft and low,*
> *Soft as the dirge of Love,*—

Over the sandy floor
Of the moony inland bay,
Flooding the rockless shore,
The shimmering moonbeams stray,
And the midnight waters flow,
With never a ripple above
With never a billow below:—
While soft as the feathery snow,
Slow as the sad sea-roll,
Over my dreaming soul
Memories come and go.
. . .
Lo! on the winds and seas
The blasts and billows of song,
My soul like a white bird flees
Over the edge of the world,
Where the pale ghost-shadows throng.—
And the wind pipes shrill on the waves,
And the waves to the clouds are hurled,
And the vaporous moon, like a ghastly eye,
Glares through the veil of the misty sky,
While deep in the ocean caves
Mariners drown and die.
And strong through the tempest's roll
Rises a song on high,
And a wail of death in the soul.
. . .
'Twere good there were rest above,
For Life is labour and pain,
And Love is a grief, for those who love
Seldom are loved again.
Man wanders from birth to grave,
A wreck on the trackless wave,—
Sea-foam on the salt sea-spray;—
Earth's sweetest songs are sad;
The gayest is not so glad
But he hides some thought of pain;
The sun may shine for a day,
Then follows the wintry rain.
. . .

As we do not know the date of the poem, it is not clear that Annette was dead when it was written. She may simply have rejected Waller totally after initially giving him hope that his love was returned. She may not, of course, ever have loved him as he loved her; she may only have been polite to the family benefactor. On the other hand, his love for her would explain his sense of responsibility towards the family. Whatever her views on marriage with him during the Edinburgh days, she seems to have shared her brother Arthur's conviction that the children who could do so must make some contribution, independent of Waller, to the family's almost non-existent finances. Annette, says *Memories and Adventures* writing of 1880, "had already gone out to Portugal to earn and send home a fair salary, while Lottie and Connie were about to do the same". Waller may have offered marriage to Annette at an early juncture, and been refused: the role of beggar-maid to King Cophetua was hardly likely to appeal to the daughter of Mary Foley and the granddaughter of John Doyle. If there were such a proposal, it would have increased her need to get out. The continued proximity of both parties in the event of a refusal would have been highly embarrassing. On the other hand, Waller would not have taken "no" for an answer very easily, and his continued benevolence would have been intended, on his side, to maintain his status as a suitor in good standing. She might have been prepared to accept him after Lottie and Connie were established and she had built up enough money to give her parents some independence until Arthur had made himself financially strong enough as a practising doctor to take over.

If Annette's music haunted her family as well as her admirer, we may have a very tender memory of her in *"The Solitary Cyclist"*.

> . . . the story of the young and beautiful woman, tall, graceful, and queenly, who presented herself at Baker Street late in the evening, and implored his assistance and advice. . . .
>
> My friend took the lady's ungloved hand, and examined it with as close an attention and as little sentiment as a scientist would show to a specimen.
>
> "You will excuse me, I am sure. It is my business", said he, as he dropped it. "I nearly fell into the error of supposing that you were typewriting. Of course, it is obvious that it is music. You observe the spatulate finger-ends, Watson, which is common to both professions. There is a spiritual quality about the face, however"—she gently turned it towards the light—"which the typewriter does not generate. The lady is a musician."
>
> "Yes, Mr Holmes, I teach music."
>
> "In the country, I presume, from your complexion."
>
> "Yes, sir, near Farnham, on the borders of Surrey."
>
> "A beautiful neighbourhood, and full of the most interesting associations. You will remember, Watson, that it was near there that we took Archie Stamford, the forger. . . ."

No doubt Annette's complexion bore more signs of the Portuguese climate than Violet Smith's was likely to do of the Farnham air, given the relatively small time of her employment by the ambiguous and amorous Mr Carruthers. They differed also in that, as Arthur wrote to Mrs Hoare at the time of Annette's death, her life had been one of total self-sacrifice for her family.

Arthur in his memoirs never mentions Waller, but he makes one comment on the lodging arrangement: "My mother had adopted the device of sharing a large house, which may have eased her in some ways, but was disastrous in others." With Annette gone, and Arthur away so much, Bryan Charles Waller was necessarily the person other than Mary who had chiefly to cope with the disintegration of Charles Doyle. It may well have been that, apart from the financial incentive, Arthur also found continued sharing of quarters with, and sense of obligation to, the effervescent, self-absorbed and egregious Waller becoming too much to stand. In subsequent years he would be apt to describe himself in public writings and in private marginalia as a man with a deep love of solitude. He continually emphasises this trait in both Holmes and Watson, at points when each one is at his most sympathetic. In one letter he remarks of his having made several references in the text that his continued "I— I— I—" is beginning to sound like Waller. His removal to Southsea, shortly followed by taking Innes into his bachelor household, meant affectionate letters to "Dear Mam", but absence of reference to Waller is sometimes a little marked. The problem was that Waller probably could not understand what privacy meant, and certainly having to play his part over the years in coping with Charles's alcoholism and the Doyle finances, gave him a title for interfering impossible to deny and almost as impossible to grant. From the very first he had been thrusting his way into Arthur's mind, seeking to stock it and mould it. The stocking was deeply appreciated, the moulding probably much less so. In one way the results of Waller's activity was constructive, if irritating: Arthur learned under the barrage of exhortation to take what was good, leave what he did not accept, and judge critically if quietly that which was being offered to him to endorse without question. But the impact of Waller meant that Arthur had very little left to him which was his own, until he left Edinburgh: his family, his reading, his philosophy, his career were invaded—even his friends, for the appointment of James Ryan as Waller's class assistant meant that, from Waller's viewpoint, he had compounded his help to the Doyles by helping their friend, and, possibly, from Arthur's, that he could not even retain his oldest companions without Waller taking them over.

The probability exists that the move from Edinburgh was made by both Charles and Mary Doyle as well as the youngest daughters, and that all of them accompanied Waller to Masongill. Since Charles Doyle had become impossible to maintain in Edinburgh, and Waller had resolved on return to Masongill, the experiment of looking after the invalid in rural surroundings where Waller had a firm social base was open for trial. In the late Sherlock Holmes story "*The Blanched Soldier*" Holmes in his exposition goes into some detail on the question of such an arrangement, before discarding it in his approach to the solution as to Godfrey Emsworth's sequestration:

". . . There was the explanation . . . that he was mad and that they wished to avoid an asylum . . . The presence of the second person in the outhouse suggested a keeper. The fact that he locked the door when he came out strengthened the supposition and gave the idea of constraint. On the other hand, this constraint could not be severe or the young man could not have got loose and come down to have a look at his friend. You will remember, Mr Dodd, that I felt round for points, asking you, for example, about the paper which Mr Kent was reading. Had it been the *Lancet* or the *British Medical Journal* it would have helped me. It is not illegal, however, to keep a lunatic upon private premises so long as there is a qualified person in attendance and that the authorities have been duly notified. Why, then, all this desperate desire for secrecy? Once again I could not get the theory to fit the facts."

There are some slightly odd points about this. It is difficult to see why a normal private keeper of a lunatic, however qualified, would be more likely to be reading the *Lancet* or the *British Medical Journal* in preference to a more commonplace literary diet. An attendant of responsible standing, reasonable nursing credentials, strength and watchfulness, would not necessarily have medical ambitions of the kind reflected by those papers. In any case the reading matter would be even more applicable to Holmes's third and, as it turned out, correct, theory, that Emsworth was believed by his family to have contracted leprosy. But if the case of maintaining a lunatic on private premises most forcefully in Conan Doyle's mind was that of his father, and the attendant was Bryan Charles Waller of *Lancet* and *B.M.J.* publication, the matter becomes simple. It is also suggestive that such a clue should have been introduced under the lunatic theory rather than under the leprosy theory where it properly belonged. On the other hand, it is most unlikely that Charles Doyle was certified before leaving Scotland: his transference to Kirkby Lonsdale in general and Masongill House in particular would have involved leaving Scottish legal jurisdiction. Hence the fugitives from the horror which Edinburgh had become had not yet proceeded to invoking the state.

Even more pointed evidence is at hand in the short story "*The Surgeon of Gaster Fell*" published in 1890 but not reprinted in book form for almost thirty years. It is in very much the same country as Masongill, the action beginning in "the little town of Kirkby-Malhouse" in Yorkshire but from which the Morecambe sands "washed by the Irish Sea" are visible, and specific reference is made to what would be a perfect description of Masongill, "the wild and desolate region where Yorkshire borders on both Lancashire and Westmoreland". (Kirkby Lonsdale, a few miles from Masongill, contrasts markedly with its solitude of terrain.) The story tells of a lone observer who takes refuge in Gaster Fell (which even sounds like Masongill) from an unduly garrulous landlady, and falls in with a brother, the Surgeon of Gaster Fell, and a sister back from Brussels; after suspicions have been raised of the brother's ill-treatment of a prisoner the man and girl are proven to be guarding their father who has become a victim of dangerous homicidal mania, "intermittent in its nature, but dangerous during the paroxysms". The experiment of keeping the father in private custody collapses when he menaces the narrator's life, and he is removed to Kirkby Lunatic Asylum. The Surgeon's concluding letter to the narrator turns on a number of suggestive points:

"... My poor father's disease rapidly assumed both a religious and a homicidal turn, the attacks coming on without warning after months of sanity. It would weary you were I to describe the terrible experiences which his family have undergone. Suffice it that, by the blessing of God, we have succeeded in keeping his poor crazed fingers clear of blood. ... He has an intense dread of madhouses; and in his sane intervals would beg and pray so piteously not to be condemned to one, that I could never find the heart to resist him. At last, however, his attacks became so acute and dangerous that I determined, for the sake of those about me, to remove him from the town to the loneliest neighbourhood that I could find. ... He, poor fellow, was as submissive as a child, when in his right mind; and a better, kinder companion no man could wish for. ... Your arrival first upset his mental equilibrium. The very sight of you

in the distance awoke all those morbid impulses which had been sleeping. . . .
My sister Eva bids me to send you her kind regards. . . . You will understand
from what I have already told you that when my dear sister came back from
Brussels I did not dare to bring her home, but preferred that she should lodge
in safety in the village. Even then I did not venture to bring her in the presence
of her father, and it was only at night, when he was asleep, that we could plan a
meeting."

There is some important telescoping here. There is a little of Conan Doyle
in the narrator, particularly in his search for solitude, which is a theme of his
writing in the 1880s, sometimes worked out with outstanding comedy as in
the misanthropic narrator of "*The Man from Archangel*". As noted, this is
evidently a reaction to the claustrophobia of Argyle Park Terrace, George
Square and Lonsdale Terrace, especially with Waller thrown in. Waller also
has perhaps a touch of influence on the portrait of the landlady, especially
when meeting the girl: "I was conscious of . . . the harsh voice of my
landlady, loud in welcome and protestations of joy. From time to time, amid
her whirl of words, I could hear a gentle and softly modulated voice", but of
course he is also the Surgeon. At the same time ACD himself is partly present
in the Surgeon, possibly through the self-reproach that guarding his father
has had to be made over to a stranger. Mary Foley Doyle is present in part in
the sister, with her convent education and her Belgian (i.e. French)
sympathies, but Annette seems also there.

Arthur and Annette became close companions during her return journeys
to Britain; for instance, they explored the Isle of Wight together when she
visited him at Southsea. It is likely that on such an occasion they made a joint
journey to Kirkby Lonsdale, the situation being peculiarly terrible for Annette
for her having been cut off from it for so long and having come so directly
from a foreign country:

> . . . she was an admirable companion—sympathetic, well read, with the quick,
> piquant daintiness of thought which she had brought with her from her foreign
> training. Yet the shadow which I had observed in her on the first morning that
> I had seen her was never far from her mind, and I have seen her merriest laugh
> frozen suddenly upon her lips, as though some dark thought lurked within her,
> to choke down the mirth and gaiety of her youth.
> . . . "If I may read your life, I would venture to say that you were destined to
> fulfil the lot of women—to make some good man happy, and to shed around, in
> some wider circle, the pleasure which your society has given me since first I
> knew you."
> "I will never marry" said she, with a sharp decision, which surprised and
> somewhat amused me.
> "Not marry—and why?"
> A strange look passed over her sensitive features, and she plucked nervously
> at the grass on the bank beside her.
> "I dare not", said she in a voice that quivered with emotion.
> "Dare not?"
> "It is not for me. I have other things to do. That path of which I spoke is one
> which I must tread alone."
> "But this is morbid", said I. "Why should your lot, Miss Cameron, be

separate from that of my own sisters, or the thousand other young ladies whom every season brings out into the world? But perhaps it is that you have a fear and distrust of mankind. Marriage brings a risk as well as a happiness."

"The risk would be with the man who married me," she cried.

Eva Cameron is speaking about the fear of inheriting a homicidal trait in the blood. But the passage may well also relate to Waller's hopes and Annette's refusal, thus mixing Waller with Conan Doyle in the narrator. What it does not refer to is that Annette would not marry because she was in fact dead when "*The Surgeon of Gaster Fell*" was published; for she was still alive when it was offered to *Blackwood's* in November 1888.

The process may have been tried decidedly earlier than the final departure from Edinburgh. Bryan Charles Waller and Charles Altamont Doyle were both listed in the City Directory as the occupants of the apartment at 15 Lonsdale Terrace, for 1881 and 1882, and Waller is on the Valuation Rolls as paying the rent for both of those years; yet the Census for 1881 mentions neither of them. Mary J. E. Doyle aged 44, is listed as "Head of Household", the post assigned to Charles in the past, even when they had moved in on her mother. The Census allows for the head being absent at the time of census-taking, but Mary did not avail herself of that procedure. Apart from the Irish maidservant, the 17-year-old Mary Kilpatrick, the other persons listed are Arthur, aged 21, a "student of medicine", Constance, aged 13, a "scholar" (if the Victorians gave children less freedom they also gave them more dignity), John (i.e. Innes) aged 8, Jane (i.e. Ida) aged 6, and Bryan (i.e. Dodo) aged 4. Annette was already in Portugal and Lottie had evidently followed her. Coincidentally neither had appeared in the previous census, that of 1871, which includes of the children only Constance and the five-year-old Caroline (the third child to die young, and probably given the age she had attained, the hardest of the three deaths for the parents and siblings to bear). Annette and Lottie, like Arthur, had probably been sent away to school, if not into the custody of friends. But where were Charles Doyle and Bryan Charles Waller? The Census would take no account of temporary absences: if they were elsewhere when it was taken at the beginning of April 1881, they would be counted for wherever that was. The likelihood is that Waller had profited by the end of ten weeks of lectures and demonstrations since Christmas to return to Masongill and take Charles with him, possibly to dry out after an alcoholic bout, possibly to administer some intensive medical care and convalescence. The "surgery" at Masongill may thus have been built before Waller's final return in late 1882 or early 1883. (Alternatively, Charles may already have been in a nursing home.)

If these hypotheses be correct, and their only alternative is that "*The Surgeon of Gaster Fell*" is a piece of guesswork on Arthur's part on what might have happened had his father been brought to Kirkby Lonsdale—and taken in conjunction with "*The Blanched Soldier*" that is much less likely—then matters ended as happens to old Cameron in the story. Charles Altamont Doyle did break out, probably with some violence to persons, and was taken back to Scotland where he was placed first in a nursing home

called Fordoun House, fifteen miles north of Montrose, and then, after an
alcoholic breakout and an escape attempt, to Montrose Royal Lunatic
Asylum, where he was admitted in May 1885. (The Surgeon of Gaster Fell
writes to the narrator on 4 September 1885, from Kirkby Lunatic Asylum
where his father now is.) And since Waller would have been in charge of
arrangements at Masongill, the decision to certify Charles Doyle was almost
certainly his. (He actually built what he called a "surgery" near his house;
Charles Doyle might have been kept there.) Waller's toughness of mind, and
readiness to insist on harsh solutions where needful, would have overborne
the tender feelings of the family. It is this which solves the discrepancy which
has always lain between Arthur Conan Doyle's own gentleness and the
severity of the decision to place his father under public restraint. Waller in
charge, Waller full of stories of the danger to Mary Doyle, Waller perhaps
insisting that visits from Annette and Arthur threw his patient out of
equilibrium, Waller ultimately asserting on his medical qualifications and
high attainments that any further liberty to Charles Doyle meant disastrous
and unforgivable risk to Mary Foley Doyle—these things could not be easily
resisted by the young doctor far away in Southsea. The clear indication is
that Arthur signed his father's liberty away to preserve the life of his mother.
But the final decision of what must be done, and the intransigence in over-
ruling softer feelings, falls absolutely in tune with what we know of Bryan
Charles Waller.

And this, too, supplies a perfect explanation of the subsequent break with
Annette. If "The Surgeon of Gaster Fell" is correct in showing her responses
of overwhelming grief to the tragedy ("Even as I watched her, she burst
suddenly into wild weeping, and throwing down her bundle of flowers, ran
swiftly into the house.") her nature may well have recoiled at the severity of
the decision. There is some evidence that she sided with her father: she left all
her money for his care. She would have been away from the worst outbreaks
in the final years, and hence she might have felt the situation was tolerable,
where Waller had decided it was intolerable, Mary Foley Doyle with all too
much reason had agreed, and Arthur had at long distance more reluctantly
agreed; and in her love for her mother and brother the choice of a scapegoat
was not hard to make. This explains the poems, several more of which seem
to refer to Annette though not by name: the momentary anger at her rejection,
the more considered realisation that, with the best will in the world, Waller
had wrecked her life and that perhaps his entry into the Doyle household had
been the catalyst which had set the final chain of circumstance in motion,
deepened Charles Doyle's tendency towards suspicion, self-pity, alcoholic
dependence and recourse to violence, and finally forced the brutal solution.
Yet he had clearly been fond, in his turn, of Charles Doyle: the enlistment of
him into the artistic aspect of the publication of the doctoral thesis indicates
that. Is his "Threnody" a farewell to Charles, undoubtedly the man whose
acquaintance first led to his introduction into the household?

    Softly! wake him not;
    Low he lies,

Earth and all its cares forgot,—
Winds and skies,
Leaves and grasses round his grave,
And the far-off western wave
Chant their lullabies.

Gentlest sleep
Evermore his eyelids keep
Dreamless in the daisied ground,
While the timeless years roll round.

Fare thee well, true heart,
Thou art blest!
We amid the tempest's strife,
Battling with the storms of life,
Oftentimes would fain depart
To thy rest!

On thy grave
Dewlike tears
Fall from off the whispering trees
Whose mysterious branches wave
To the wild wind symphonies,
These shall lull thy soul asleep
Down the years.

If it is in memory of Charles it is kind to its author in its self-reassurance that all is for the best. Yet Waller had acted nobly according to his lights, in his financial munificence, in his genuine concern for others, and in his final gift of a cottage to Mary Foley Doyle for as long as she wished. If Arthur grimly said that the effect of taking in a lodger was "disastrous", and vouchsafed not a single public word more, privately he was deeply grateful for Waller's kindness to his mother, kept his portrait in his house and spoke of his generous friend. Masongill House, as well as Masongill Cottage, remained a major focal point for the Doyle family. Thither came Arthur for his first marriage, and he kept Christmas there from time to time—apparently in the house rather than in the little cottage—as may be seen from his letter to Alfred Harmsworth from there in 1890. The novel he wrote shortly afterwards, in answer to Harmsworth's commission, *The Doings of Raffles Haw*, may be important in that it portrays the disastrous impact of an outstandingly brilliant chemist and philanthropist on a family he wishes to help and love, although apart from the portrait of old McIntyre there is no shade of the Doyles themselves in the materialistic brother and sister. Raffles Haw is not Bryan Charles Waller, but the relevance of his philanthropy inducing his tragedy and those of his friends is notable. At that Christmas in particular, after Annette's death, it could not have been hard to see what the poems affirm with such eloquence, that Waller, as Sherlock Holmes would say of Neil Gibson in "*Thor Bridge*", had "learned something in that schoolroom of sorrow where our earthly lessons are taught".

To say this is not to deny that comedy continued alongside tragedy. Waller remained egregious. When Arthur was working on *"Uncle Jeremy's Household"* in 1885, Waller was evidently soliciting opportunities for improving the literary output of his former protégé. "Thug story finished but any hints of the Doctor's can be interpolated in clean copy", wrote Arthur to his mother on 18 May, and sure enough the published story concludes with a letter from a character hitherto unmentioned in the story, for the purpose of lecturing the readers on the properties of Indian Thugee, with which the action of the narrative had been concerned. The letter is signed "B. C. Haller", who is kindly described as "a man of encyclopaedic knowledge, and particularly well versed in Indian manners and customs. It is through his kindness that I am able to reproduce the various native words which I heard from time to time from the lips of Miss Warrender, but which I should not have been able to recall to my memory had he not suggested them to me". The letter which follows sounds Walleresque, bursting with information, shrewd in some of its detailed comments, but one penultimate sentence is either a joke by Arthur, or else indicates that Waller had reverted much more drastically to Christianity than even his later poetry suggests: "Truly the 'dark places of the earth are full of cruelty', and nothing but the Gospel will ever effectually dispel that darkness." The prose of the letter is a little too lacking in Lamb-like polysyllables for Waller: no doubt the *Boy's Own Paper* knew how to protect its readers from a surfeit of literacy.

In any case, while Waller's personal impact on the young Holmes was considerable, his editorial contributions did little to advance ACD's literary credentials. What the young writer needed was less matter and more art, and he showed it by making Holmes's final analyses firmly dependent on the case rather than on its more remote academic implications. Still, the shadow of Waller can be dimly discerned with the advance of Conan Doyle's literary prowess. If he never came as close as "Haller" again, he remained drawn to six-letter surnames ending in -er. Of these, the reference to Waller is most obvious in *"The Engineer's Thumb"*, where the murderous "Colonel Lysander Stark" lives with an Englishman called "Dr Becher" of whom the station-master says "there isn't a man in the parish who has a better-lined waistcoat": Dr B**** Ch***** ****er is too obvious a joke to be overlooked, and no doubt the references to him as "morose" and "silent" are inserted as suitable contradictions. But otherwise there are John Turner, John Horner, Helen Stoner, Alexander Holder, and Mr Fowler in the *Adventures;* Pinner, Colonel Hayter, Inspector Lanner in the *Memoirs*; Von Herder, James Wilder, Slater, Horace Harker and Captain Croker in the *Return;* Sir James and Colonel Valentine Walter in *His Last Bow;* and Baron Gruner, Kitty Winter, Grace Hunter and Eugenia Ronder in the *Case-Book.* As to an actual portrait, in the stories, Dr Leslie Armstrong in *"The Missing Three-Quarter"* with its tragic finale seems to have some features of Waller, with brilliance of research, harsh public manner and unswerving devotion regardless of his career interests to the cause of a friend in need.

After Annette's death, Mary Foley Doyle remained at Masongill Cottage, holding the common bond with Waller and their tragedies. Waller continued to use his surgery for experiments, whether or not it was built for Charles Doyle. Eventually he married in August 1896, when he was forty-three and Mary was sixty. He passionately believed in his line, and it is probable that his choice was partially dictated by the fact that his chosen bride was one of fourteen children. She had come to the neighbourhood as a governess, to a local Vicar. Waller, as a local magnate and the governor of a local school, whose children even made shirts for him, was now a pillar of the established church and invariable in his attendance at St Oswald's, Thornton-in-Lonsdale. Mary also attended that church now, and her daughters Ida and Dodo grew up in the Anglican faith: Dodo married the son of a local clergyman.

Ada Roberts, the governess, is locally said to have set her cap at the eligible bachelor of Masongill House, but she had some social claims on his attention. Her father, the Rev. Alexander Roberts, D.D., was made Professor of Humanity (Latin) at St Andrews, 1872, the appointment being in the gift of the then Duke of Portland. The Duke's successor was half-brother to Lord Henry Cavendish-Bentinck, MP, of Underley Hall, Kirkby Lonsdale, with whom Waller dined regularly. Roberts himself was a remarkable if eccentric figure most of whose works were an attempt to show that Greek was the habitual speech of Jesus Christ. Ada Roberts disappointed her husband, however, by miscarrying with her first child and then proving unable to have another. She seems to have resented his friendship with Mary Foley Doyle, and certainly the elderly lady of Masongill Cottage was loved for her warmth of nature and kindliness to the villagers where the chatelaine of Masongill House is remembered for a snobbery greater than that of her husband, and a habit of spying on servants which was entirely her own. Her meanness as a housekeeper became proverbial, and few servants would stay with her. Bryan Charles Waller showed little sign of affection for her, and with advancing years would keep her reading to him until the dawn was near.

Bryan Charles Waller kept up relations with Mary's children: the motor-car brought Arthur down in the early twentieth century and Hornung, to judge by the poem on his mother, seems to have become a friend. Mary remained there until about 1917. After she left, Waller drew increasingly in on himself, and towards the end seldom left his bed. The poems would seem to have been preserved in manuscript, and it is doubtful if Ada Waller, when she arranged for their publication, knew how intimately they referred to the Doyle family: Annette, after all, preceded Bryan to the grave by over forty years. It is noteworthy that despite Ada, Mary remained so long at Masongill Cottage until going down to live in West Grinstead near her daughter Connie Hornung. She kept up links with other friends, and visited her children from time to time. But Waller clearly meant a great deal to her, and she to him. It is probable that her first years at Masongill Cottage were partly preoccupied by nursing Julia Waller until she died in 1887.

Waller was buried in his parents' grave, and left instructions that the estate was to go to cousins provided they adopted the name and arms of Waller, but when Ada died there was no money left, and the estate was sold. The house passed into the ownership of tenants who as children had been excluded by the Wallers from the sight of it. Ada had wished her ashes to be scattered over the hills at Masongill where she used to walk, but in the end they were placed in her husband's tomb. To the end her status as a late intruder was symbolised: no mention of her appears on the stone. And the grass grows high over the grave of Bryan Charles Waller.

Yet for all of their unhappiness together, Ada did loyally bring together a noble memorial of her husband in *Echo*, and her choice of a final poem, to which she may have given the title "*L'Envoi*", captures something of his spirit of exultation before it grew bitter and old. It captures his egotism, generosity and confidence, and also his vitally important sense of his place in a great tradition. And it conveys something of the roaring enthusiasm which swept into the Doyle family, before it withered in the cruelty of the world.

> *"Singer of Songs forbear!*
> *The world is weary of Song."*
> *So sounds the voice of Despair,*
> *And the voice of the tuneless throng.*
> *"Dead is the ancient fire,*
> *Unlaurelled the poet's brow;*
> *The songs of the lyre from the heart of the lyre*
> *Expire unheeded now."*
>
> *"Why wilt thou spend thy breath*
> *In singing that none will hear,*
> *Till the pallid roses of Death*
> *Are white on thy nameless bier?*
> *The lot of the Singer is hard,*
> *His glory faded and fled:*
> *The flame of the Bard and the name of the Bard*
> *And the fame of the Bard are dead."*
>
> *Nay, nay, my soul, not so!*
> *Till the bright sun sink from the sky*
> *The fire of the Bard shall glow,*
> *His glory shall pass not by.*
> *While the fair sky, myriad-starred,*
> *Over the earth stands sure,*
> *Shall the name of the Bard and the fame of the Bard,*
> *And the flame of the Bard endure.*
>
> *From the hush of the natal sleep,*
> *From the ocean of life, that flows*
> *From the deep to the trackless deep*
> *Of Birth and of Death, arose,*
> *With the morning's earliest gleam,*
> *Radiant and clear and strong,*
> *The delight of the dream and the light of the dream*
> *And the might of the dream of Song.*

Born of the Spirit of Man,
Before the beginning of Time,
The fire of the Bard began,
His spirit fashioned the rhyme:
And while Earth and Heaven endure,
The moon and the stars and the sea,
The desire of the Bard and the fire of the Bard
And the lyre of the Bard shall be.

Fair as the rose in June,
Subtle as scents of May,
Wild as the mystic tune
Of the wind on woods astray;—
Never, till Spring grow old
And the scent of the roses die,
Shall the flower of the Song and the power of the Song
And the hour of the Song pass by.

Sweet were the strains that rang
From the choir of the Bards of old;
Mighty the songs they sang,
Deathless the tale they told.—
Ever while Fame shall fire,
Ever while Love shall lure,
Shall the days of the Bard and the lays of the Bard
And the praise of the Bard endure.

Great were the Bards of old,
Honoured of men and dear:
Nor less shall the praise be told
Of the Bards that the world shall hear.
They shall rise like the stars on high,
They shall shine, that the world may see
The light of the Songs, the delight of the Songs,
And the might of the Songs to be.

7

Athens or Sparta

"Doctors is all swabs."

—R. L. Stevenson, *Treasure Island*

Edinburgh University may call herself with grim jocoseness the "alma mater" of her students, but if she be a mother at all she is one of a very heroic and Spartan cast, who conceals her maternal affection with remarkable success. The only signs of interest which she ever designs to evince towards her alumni are upon those not infrequent occasions when guineas are to be demanded from them. Then one is surprised to find how carefully the old hen has counted her chickens, and how promptly the demand is conveyed to each one of the thousands throughout the empire who, in spite of neglect, cherish a sneaking kindness for their old college. There is symbolism in the very look of her, square and massive, grim and grey, with never a pillar or carving to break the dead monotony of the great stone walls. She is learned, she is practical, and she is useful. There is little sentiment or romance in her composition, however, and in this she does but conform to the instincts of the nation of which she is the youngest but the most flourishing teacher.

A lad coming up to an English University finds himself in an enlarged and enlightened public school. If he has passed through Harrow and Eton there is no very abrupt transition between the life which he has led in the sixth form and that which he finds awaiting him on the banks of the Cam and the Isis. Certain rooms are found for him which have been inhabited by generations of students in the past, and will be by as many in the future. His religion is cared for, and he is expected to put in an appearance at hall and at chapel. He must be within bounds at a fixed time. If he behave indecorously he is liable to be pounced upon and reported by special officials, and a code of punishments is hung perpetually over his head. In return for all this his University takes a keen interest in him. She pats him on the back if he succeeds. Prizes and scholarships, and fine fat fellowships are thrown plentifully in his way if he will gird up his loins and aspire to them.

There is nothing of this in a Scotch University. The young aspirant pays his pound, and finds himself a student. After that he may do absolutely what he will. There are certain classes going on at certain hours, which he may attend if he choose. If not, he may stay away without the slightest remonstrance from the college. As to religion, he may worship the sun, or have a private fetish of his own upon the mantelpiece of his lodgings for all that the University cares. He may live where he likes, he may keep what hours he chooses, and he is at liberty to break every commandment in the decalogue as long as he behaves himself with some approach to decency within the academical precincts. In every way he is absolutely his own master. Examinations are periodically held, at which he may appear or not, as he chooses. The University is a great unsympathetic machine, taking in a stream of raw-boned cartilaginous youths at one end, and turning them out at the other as learned divines, astute lawyers, and skilful medical men. Of every thousand of the raw material about six hundred emerge at the other side. The remainder are broken in the process.

The merits and faults of this Scotch system are alike evident. Left entirely to his own devices in a far from moral city, many a lad falls at the very starting-point of his life's race, never to rise again. Many become idlers or take to drink, while others, after wasting time and money which they could ill afford, leave the college with nothing learned save vice. On the other hand, those whose manliness and good sense keep them straight have gone through a training which lasts them for life. They have been tried, and have not been found wanting. They have learned self-reliance, confidence, and, in a word, have become men of the world while their *confrères* in England are still magnified schoolboys.

Arthur Conan Doyle commenced the fifth chapter of his novel *The Firm of Girdlestone* with these paragraphs: the chapter-title is "Modern Athenians". The verdict is particularly important for its time of writing: although *Girdlestone* was not published until 1890, it was originally commenced in 1884 and this passage, largely irrelevant to the plot if invaluable to the biographer, is almost certainly no later than that date, eight years after his matriculation and three after his graduation. His later comments are abridged, matured, but not substantially altered versions of these judgments. The writing is still somewhat mannered: the novel (as was remarked by the Edinburgh University *Student* of 10 February 1892) is heavily under Dickensian influence, the plot, as M. R. James emphasised, owes much to Sheridan LeFanu's *Uncle Silas*, and the passage quoted above is very firmly in the key of Macaulay.

In some respects its verdict is a little unduly rosy. About one student in eleven graduated in Conan Doyle's time. It was not only drink, or inability to progress without personal tutelage, or sheer loneliness—for the majority of undergraduates were non-Scots in a strange country, at its most alienating, perhaps, if they were English; but the Scots themselves came from enormously divergent cultural antecedents, highland and island, Gaelic and Lallans, Protestant and Catholic, rural and urban. Money dried up, or intermittent employment became necessary, or the failure of one of the annual examinations brought it home that economics could not justify the additional investment of another year in time and money: here, too, was a contrast from Oxbridge. The Macaulayism of the passage is an able exercise in Macaulay's method of throwing a situation into relief by an effective and artistic contrast, but within it lies a class-consciousness largely foreign to Macaulay. The Scottish tradition was austere, but it was also anti-élitist in the concept of student recruitment. Élites certainly dominated Scottish society, and the University itself was dominated by a deference to professorial intellect reflected in the writings of Conan Doyle so strongly as to repel his very English biographer Hesketh Pearson writing in the mid-twentieth century. To Pearson such reverence seemed ridiculous, "dons" to him, with his non-university background, being rather absurd and posturing establishment figures distinguished by pedantic pretension and archaic ritual from literary workmen such as himself.

In one respect Pearson was closer to Conan Doyle than he realised. Conan Doyle, as the child of a Scottish university, and a Scottish heritage, took very seriously the idea of knowledge diffused as widely as possible, and grew to hold the utmost contempt for "highbrows". Scott, Macaulay, Stevenson, wrote for a mass literate audience: what was praiseworthy about writing for a coterie in forms inaccessible to the multitude? Pearson's rejection of English academic stuffiness in his breezy popular biographies for popular markets was another, if less profound, assertion of the same principle. But where Pearson worked out his attitudes in a somewhat ham-handed if highly entertaining manner, Conan Doyle inherited them from his Edinburgh university education as well as from the writers he was devouring in his spare time. Within the university, the primacy of the lecture and the demonstration asserted the ideal of mass diffusion of knowledge. It put learning on a pedestal: the great man did not unbend, and seemed to make no friends; once again the affection-hungry boy was denied any successor to Francis Cassidy among his teachers. But it also put that learning at the disposal of those who were prepared to reach for it.

The position of Edinburgh University was not unique: it was closely akin to those of Glasgow University, and King's and Marischal Colleges, Aberdeen. It was fair in Conan Doyle to describe Edinburgh as the "most flourishing" of the Scottish universities, however, although its capitoline airs left it vulnerable to erosion of its cultural roots in ways from which the hardier and more representative institutions of Glasgow and Aberdeen remained better immunised. By the time Arthur was entering the portals of Edinburgh University, to say nothing of those of Rutherford's historic bar, the relative positions of town and university had altered from the early days. The cultivated and wealthy had fled northwards to the New Town, a brief distance, but pointedly divided by the great gulf spanned in Arthur's day by the North Bridge (the South, on which the Old College stood, merely crossed the narrow Cowgate). To the New Town also went most of the professoriate. The Old Town was given over to the poorer classes, mostly Irish: "The Bedouins camp within Pharoah's palace walls, and the old war-ship is given over to the rats", sneered Robert Louis Stevenson in his *Edinburgh: Picturesque Notes,* published when Conan Doyle was in his second year at the university. "Even in the chief thoroughfares Irish washings flutter at the windows, and the pavements are encumbered with loiterers." Unlike Stevenson, some years his predecessor as a student, Arthur would not drop out of university, but he can have had few illusions about anti-Irish sentiment being limited to dissolute conservatives who found in nostalgia a welcome rationale for indolence, as did Poe's Dupin. His favourite teacher, Joseph Bell, acknowledged his pet aversions to be "Polish Jews and Connaught Irish",

while praising as his favourites the "East-coast Scotch (Scandinavian)".
Arthur himself, indignantly conscious of his Scottish birth, English literary
affiliations and Irish antecedents, would condemn this sort of thing as
nonsensical separation of peoples whom the British experience had actually
fused, and fused with great success. Where Stevenson and Bell saw the people
of Edinburgh as divided, ACD to the end of his days asserted their unity. The
young Irish Scotsman would be allowing his own British identity to be called
into question if he admitted the separation of ethnic groups as automatic and,
by implication, desirable. He would never take the cheap way out, of
assimilating and denying his heritage: he retained his Scottish accent and his
pride in being "Anglo-Celt".

But if the immediate townsfolk, whether on the street or in the operating
theatre, were heterogeneous, so was the university, far more so than Glasgow
or the Aberdeen colleges, and yet it, like the townsfolk, had to possess a unity.
The teaching had to take account of the students' diversity of origin while
asserting their unity as a class, and indeed Edinburgh teaching has been at its
most valuable where it has continued so to do. Edinburgh drew on all of
Scotland, from Shetland to the Borders. In Arthur's fourth year, 1879, the
intake for the matriculating students would be 622 Scots. Yet in intake and in
graduation, Scots would be in a slight minority. 492 students entered from
England in 1879, 25 from Ireland, 89 from India, 174 from the British
colonies, and 40 from foreign countries. The cosmopolitanism which
surrounded Arthur at Stonyhurst was again evident here: a lesser percentage
of Irish and foreign fellow-students, a greater of fellow-Scots, but the total
effect would be again one stressing diversity of origin and unity of purpose.
Accordingly lectures and demonstrations aimed at diffusion of ideas and
methods across great geographical, ethnic, religious and cultural divides. John
Chiene, Professor of Surgery, junior surgeon at the Old and New Infirmaries
in Conan Doyle's day, told the graduating students in 1886 that of 2000
graduates who had left Edinburgh in the previous 20 years, 21% had come
from the Colonies and well over that percentage of graduates had found
employment in British overseas possessions. Such antecedents and such
expectations among Arthur's fellow-students naturally orientated his mind
towards colonial consciousness. This would express itself boldly if rashly in
his earliest published short stories, and much more impressively and subtly in
the use of colonial themes and origins in his mature work. The School of
Medicine, wealthiest, largest and proudest of Edinburgh's Faculties, was
representative of the University as a whole, and roughly accounted for half of
its students. On the other hand, the School of Medicine preserved stronger
links with its far-flung graduates than the university as a whole, most notably
in its extensive postgraduate programme. When ACD won his doctorate in
1885 he had over fifty fellow-recipients of the coveted M.D.

We know virtually nothing of the students with whom Arthur came into
close contact, apart from Waller, whom he knew before he started, Budd,
whom he came to realise he never understood until after they had graduated,
and Ryan, with whom his friendship renewed itself without difficulty but with

little information available to us. Another two mysterious "points of contact" came to his mind when writing drafts for *Memories and Adventures*: Stevenson, and J. M. Barrie. He was to become Stevenson's pen-friend and Barrie's personal friend in the 1890s, but had no recollection of meeting either of them when they overlapped at Edinburgh. "Strange to think that I probably brushed elbows with both of them in the crowded portal." Indeed, "the crowded portal" may not have been the university's. Barrie's correspondence has one hilarious but fictional recollection of crossing Princes Street, bumping into Stevenson (whom he did not know), being dragged away from his Latin class and hurried into Rutherford's historic bar, there to discourse "by the solid hour". The episode ends in Barrie breaking away, pursued by Stevenson through the streets with cries of "stop thief" and, Barrie insisted, descriptions of him to passers-by as "a man with a wooden leg and a face like a ham", though how Barrie managed to acquire the particulars given to him during the pursuit is problematic. Jenni Calder remarks that the anticipation of Long John Silver may simply be Barrie's transposition; alas, the whole thing was Barrie's imagination, although characteristic of Stevenson. The pub's primacy in the narrative is also from reality. But where the escapades of that nature meant release for Stevenson from his respectable, New Town, family, and for Barrie from his adored mother, they were a very two-edged form of escapism for Conan Doyle. No doubt he had his evenings roistering with fellow-students, yet any signs of excess must bring on his unfortunate mother the fear that the family curse would assert itself in the next generation from which so much was expected and needed.

Yet he had to have forms of escape during his undergraduate life, and the need for making money provided them: hence his career at Edinburgh was exceptional in the extent to which he took time off during the year. It was natural enough for Edinburgh students to take brief and badly paid assistantships in general practice, but the seven-month voyage to Greenland from March to October 1880 was less common; yet the fact that the commission came from a fellow-student who had had to drop out of his agreement to act as whaler's surgeon reminds us that even such inordinate absences existed easily within the scheme of things at Edinburgh. Conan Doyle's description of the university's remoteness and lack of concern with the students' use of their time is not a personal complaint, though the undercurrent of regret as to the absence of human interest in the students is; the arrangement suited his financial crusades to better his mother's situation and remove a little of the sting of her dependence on Waller. And again Waller, whatever his drawbacks, ensured that there would be a man of responsibility in the household in Arthur's absence. Indeed while with one part of him Arthur must have regretted being hurried into adult responsibility so brutally as his father's disintegration demanded, with another he must equally have resented that Waller's role prevented his meeting more of those unwelcome adult obligations. The role of absentee breadwinner went some way to remove him from these strains, a role, as he may have realised, in which countless Irish labourers in Scotland had preceded him, although often without his sense of preserving his gains and placing the family foremost.

Despite his absences from Edinburgh, he also found time to become a vigorous and valuable Rugby football player for his University, as he so splendidly commemorated in *The Firm of Girdlestone*. The mingling of sporting achievement and family tragedy makes a very haunting story of *"The Missing Three-Quarter"*. It gives us one important deduction: in any clash between the game and the dictates of family life, the latter came first.

On a more relaxed level he found escape also in his early literary efforts, the first to achieve publication, *"The Mystery of Sasassa Valley"*, reaching the readers of the Edinburgh weekly, *Chambers's Journal*, on Saturday, 6 September 1879. It was a great moment, for which he had been waiting some six months since he won acceptance; and he prized the issue and pored over the other contributions. The first article, a heavy but lucid discussion on land transfer, began with some discussion of "the Dimsdale frauds, which consisted in the manufacture of false titles to property and similar documents". One wonders if Dimsdale "now suffering the penalty due to the enormity of his crimes", ever realised that a side-effect of his peculations was that he gave Arthur Conan Doyle a surname for the hero of his first completed novel, *The Firm of Girdlestone*.

Publication in *Chambers's Journal* reminds us of the Edinburgh audience towards whom the student naturally first addressed himself. He had picked up the point that a light-hearted thriller in a South African setting about a demon who turned out to be a diamond, was exactly what the solid citizens of Edinburgh and beyond might require after paying their due meed to weighty issues of the day as represented by the Dimsdale frauds or whatever might form a text for the lay sermons of Messrs William and Robert Chambers in any given week. There was a decidedly Scottish character to the journal, in that it recognised the need to justify the expenditure of time and a penny and a half in its readers' conscience balance-sheets, by giving them heavy matter, and then a little frivolity might be slipped in provided always it was understood not to be there for its own sake. Meanwhile Conan Doyle was starting his career as a writer of romances by giving his readers the escapism he sought at the time himself. His stern sub-title, "A South African Story", carried the implication that colonial questions, and not mere fiction, would justify the reader's concentration on pp. 568-572, and it is fair to assume that the conversation of some South African students helped give the setting what small authenticity it had. It is very rough work, but already Arthur was progressing towards the establishment of a credible narrator, very different from himself but sufficiently realised to act as a conduit between prosaic reader and outlandish subject. It is also remarkably sophisticated, given its boundless ambition in subject and locale, for a youth of nineteen. Poe is an obvious influence, in content rather than style (the style is somewhere between Bret Harte's westerns and R.M. Ballantyne's *Masterman Ready*) the notable point being that where the hero of *"The Gold Bug"* locates his treasure by dropping the gold-bug through the eye of a skull, *"Sasassa Valley"* makes the eye of the demon prove to be the treasure itself. Already the principle of contructive variations on Poe was asserting itself.

There is some mystery about its composition. It may not have been written in Edinburgh, but during a stint as a Birmingham doctor's assistant in the spring of 1879. He was hard worked there, but the moments of quiet and room for work were probably more satisfactory than 23 George Square could offer. His memoirs simply say that "Some friend remarked to me that my letters were very vivid and surely I could write some things to sell . . . for my own part I never dreamed I could myself produce decent prose, and the remark of my friend, who was by no means given to flattery, took me greatly by surprise". This certainly sounds like Waller, who would have been getting, or at least seeing, letters from Arthur ever since Feldkirch (it is reasonable to assume he received an answer to his famous allocution to Feldkirch, for instance). Ryan might be a possibility, but the description does not suggest a friend slightly junior in age who had been a year's junior at school. W.K. Burton is again possible, but it is *Girdlestone* which ACD credited to his encouragement. From what we know of Arthur's anxiety about making a financial contribution, we might expect some self-reproach in speaking to Waller that the latter was making so great a gift to the family coffers and he, the son of the house, was wretched at doing so little, and Waller, fertile as ever with advice, produced a suggestion for which humanity should bless his name evermore. The evidence certainly would accord with Waller's being "by no means given to flattery", and the failure to mention the name of the godfather of the enterprise would be consistent with the absence of any reference to Waller in *Memories and Adventures*. Conan Doyle is generous in paying tribute to persons who did him far more minor services. Waller, too, with his family recollections of Procter's encouragement to budding poets and Dickens's publication of Adelaide's poems, would be the man to suggest *Chambers's*. Yet although the next sentence in the memoirs refers to *"Sasassa Valley"*, it does not specifically state that this is the first result of the conversation. In fact, as one might expect, the rough polish of *"Sasassa Valley"* followed earlier trial and error.

At some point before this, quite possibly as early in 1877, Arthur had written *"The Haunted Grange of Goresthorpe—a True Ghost Story"*, and seems to have gone down personally to *Blackwood's* with it: the style reads at least a year younger than *"Sasassa Valley"*. The MS was signed, but had no address or envelope that remained attached to it, if Arthur indeed in his innocence thought of that point. Hence *Blackwood's* never returned it; they were inefficient and dilatory, but not to that extent, and the permanent loss of the story in their files looks like the result of a visit to their Queen Street premises from an eager boy, ignorant of the conventions, who met with a courteous reception and left a manuscript to be read, rejected, and, lacking means for return, pigeonholed and forgotten. It was quite unusable, yet it deserved a much more constructive response than it received, and its reliance on ordinary narrator and adventurous friend is unquestionably the embryo of Holmes and Watson. In later correspondence with *Blackwood's* from Birmingham in 1882, Conan Doyle alluded to the former story "which did not come up to your standard". He gave 15 Lonsdale Terrace as his return address then, and enclosed *"The Actor's Duel"*, which was rejected, this time with much less justification; two years later *"The Fate of the* Evangeline" received another negative, and *"The Great Keinplatz Experiment"* was also declined about that time. Yet in 1885, sending *"Uncle Jeremy's Household"* (once more without success), it was the first manuscript which remained in his mind and, apparently oblivious of the three formal rejections, he recalls that "the only other MS I ever remember sending you" was lost.

Eventually *Blackwood's* did accept a story, *"A Physiologist's Wife"*, although it took some fifteen months to publish it before its appearance in 1890. Characteristically, once he had obtained acceptance and publication, Conan Doyle had triumphed in his twelve-year quest and never troubled *Blackwood's* further after the *Strand* opened its doors to him. It is clear that quite apart from his permanent literary and financial ambitions, Conan Doyle was going to tear an acceptance from his first choice of editor, and having done so, honour was satisfied. In fairness to *Blackwood's*, his reception at the time of his personal call at Queen Street must have been sufficiently encouraging to make it his continual target until the thing became a virtual obsession. *Chambers's* he seems to have gone back to seldom enough—it printed *"Gaster Fell"* after a *Blackwood's* rejection—but its rates were a little low (he got three guineas from *"Sasassa Valley"*). As for the lost manuscript, we have noted that the plot as well as the loss haunted Conan Doyle to re-emerge after forty years in *"The Bully of Brocas Court"*.

In all of this Charles Doyle should not be neglected. Mary Foley Doyle and Bryan Charles Waller were obviously making efforts to help him win back his self-respect, witness Waller's commission of the drawings; and from the evidence of his published diary he was obviously very proud of his son's literary achievement. Arthur's next successful attack, on *London Society*, with a very Hartean piece, *"The American's Tale"*, was almost certainly on his advice. He had drawn for it at its foundation, and he may well have supplied the name to whom a personal approach might be made; indeed it is possible that the choices of *Blackwood's* and *Chambers's* stemmed from his inspiration also. His work in the civil service would from time to time have necessitated informing local magazines as well as newspapers of the progress of improvements at Holyrood House and other sites, and with his popularity in the town (on which his obituary's geniality rings true) it would be natural for him to suggest a personal approach to Blackwood. Fortunately, to his fertility of ideas which Arthur inherited from him there was added the dogged spirit Charles lacked.

September 6, 1879, must have been a very happy day in the Conan Doyle home, at least in its morning, but Arthur still needed other ways of escape. He took up photography under the influence of the Burtons and made field trips to the Isle of May, Arran and elsewhere. But ordinary student life offered its breaks from the grind of work as well. Arthur developed the capacity for dividing his time between university study, financial quests and methods of escape, and he was sufficiently master of this form of economics to throw himself into certain activities whose demands in time imperilled the careers of students less self-regulated than himself. In particular, two contests for the office of Rector took place during his years at Edinburgh. He left no formal record of participation in these, but it is certain from another passage of fascination to the biographer and irrelevance to the plot of *The Firm of Girdlestone* that at least one of them made a substantial impression on him.

The Rectorship officially was a post whereby the students received representation on the University Court by electing a public figure not on the staff to chair its proceedings; in fact the Rector did nothing save deliver a public address sometimes rendered largely inaudible by the noise and horseplay of the students. (Lord Rosebery, victor of the second contest in Conan Doyle's time, delivered a belated oration in circumstances where the University Court had subsequently to compensate the Free Church of Scotland, owners of the hall, to the tune of several hundreds of pounds.) In general the contests were fairly evenly split between Liberal and Tory supporters, and as a rule the choice fell between one of the two camps. Gladstone won the Rectorship, and so did Thomas Carlyle; the latter might seem an unlikely Liberal, but in the struggle he defeated Disraeli so effectively that the latter declined the offer of a further contest. It seems unlikely that the 1880 contest took up much of Arthur's attention; he was newly back from Greenland, he was highly conscious of having found much more real life among the whalers than he could discover in Edinburgh student activities, and he had heavy work on which to catch up. Nor do we know whom he would have supported. Lord Rosebery, master-mind of the organization of Gladstone's Midlothian campaign in 1879, opposed the former Professor Sir Robert Christison, the last survivor of the giants of the Edinburgh Medical School of the mid-nineteenth century. Christison had calls on ACD's respect, but had fanatically opposed the admission of women to the Medical School some ten years previously, even to the point of haranguing a class against them, after which students from that class showered the women with mud and singularly unpleasant abuse. Although this was well before Arthur's time, Waller supplied him with a link to the controversies of the decade before the Rectorial election. The Burtons would have talked about it: Professor Cosmo Innes had been vehement in Sophia Jex-Blake's cause. ACD detested anything savouring of insult to women, and his short story *"The Doctors of Hoyland"* is a passionate defence of the value of women in the ranks of the medical profession.

Yet one wonders if Arthur would be attracted by Rosebery, with his ready oratory and luxurious life; his ambition was naked and somewhat repellent, and his academic credentials consisted of having declined to take his degree when the Oxford authorities objected to his owning a race-horse. There is some temptation to see in Rosebery the original of Lord Holdhurst, the Foreign Secretary in *"The Naval Treaty"*, who gets a job in the Foreign Office for his nephew and appears almost eager to throw him to the wolves on the threat of scandal. Holmes deduces his weak financial circumstances from the resoling of his boots, and it is certainly true that Rosebery shortly before

his inaugural found it advisable to make a financially advantageous marriage
to a Rothschild heiress. Student gossip and scandalmongering during
the Rectorial, which was guaranteed to show little charity to the reputations
of the candidates, doubtless exaggerated Rosebery's need for money. Lord
Robert St Simon's pressing urgency to wed an American heiress in *"The
Noble Bachelor"* may also be relevant here, as may his aristocratic
condescension, of which Rosebery had his fair share. But all of this could
have come Conan Doyle's way without his taking the part in that Rectorial
which was evidently taken in some contest by the author of *The Firm of
Girdlestone*. The medical students were very thoroughly split by the contest,
and he was bound to hear much from both sides, especially if his voting
loyalties were pulled in two directions.

On the other hand the 1877 election seems a certain candidate for his
involvement, and, although lacking definite knowledge, we can be fairly clear
as to his choice. When Gladstone introduced his first Bill for Irish Home Rule
in 1886, Conan Doyle opposed it, clearly in protest against its divisive
character as against the mingling of the population of the British Isles in
which he so deeply believed. He called himself a Liberal Unionist, and stood
for Parliament twice under that party label. Now, this implies that he had
previously been a Liberal of some considerable commitment. It would not
rule out support for a distinguished former professor from his old medical
school nominated on a non-partisan basis. But it would indicate that he was a
Liberal in a straight party fight, and there is nothing to suggest political
vicissitudes on his part between 1877 and 1886. Liberalism would also have
jelled easily with his growing rebellion against convention in theological
orthodoxies and their social application. Hence the Marquis of Hartington,
heir of the Duke of Devonshire and nominally leader of the Liberal party
during Gladstone's "retirement", seems to have been the obvious target for
his support, as opposed to the lack-lustre Tory nominee, the Right Hon.
Richard Assheton Cross, P.C., M.P., Disraeli's Home Secretary. Waller, with
Cross's recent rejection of licence to experiment, must have been high in
hostility to his candidacy. Where the contest becomes important for Conan
Doyle's writing is that the initial formal challenge was evidently the direct
origin of the rowdy meetings in *The Lost World* where Professor Challenger
meets his critics. The *Scotsman's* report of 5 November 1877 is the record of a
gathering at which Arthur was almost certainly present, as a second year
medical student:

> There was a crowded attendance of students, who, previous to the commence-
> ment of the proceedings, amused themselves in their wonted fashion, by singing
> snatches of favourite songs, rapping the desks with their sticks, throwing peas
> about the room, and playing on musical instruments. Mr Scott Lang, who acted
> as chairman of the meeting held on Friday evening in favour of Mr Cross, was
> called on to preside; and on approaching the chair, he was saluted with a
> shower of peas from the back benches. He proceeded to state the order of
> procedure it was proposed to follow; but the students refused to listen, and kept
> on shouting, howling, and yelling at the extreme pitch of their voices. The
> Chairman having invited nominations, Mr Atkinson, medical student, submit-

ted the name of the Right Hon. Richard Assheton Cross, the mention of which was greeted with cheers, hisses, howling, flourishing of sticks, and showers of peas. After quiet had been in some measure restored, Mr Atkinson went on to state the claims of Mr Cross to the suffrages of the students, affirming that the right hon. gentleman since his accession to office in 1874 had passed measures more numerous and more important than any other Minister. (Cheers, hisses, howling, and a voice—"Where did you learn your grammar?"). Mr Cross, moreover, was known, not only in England and Scotland, but throughout the world, as a man of sound judgment, as a philanthropist, and as an indefatigable worker—("Oh!")—and as a tribute to his many good works he thought the students should elect—(A Voice —"Lord Hartington", followed by loud cheers)—to the office of Lord Rector. Mr Arthur Gordon, Divinity student, who rose to second the nomination, was saluted with peas, and a variety of noises which continued for some minutes. The Chairman appealed to the meeting to give the speaker a fair hearing; but no heed was paid to the request, and three more cheers for Lord Hartington were given with much cordiality. Seeing, apparently, that there was no prospect of obtaining a hearing, Mr Gordon contented himself with remarking that Mr Cross was a singularly sagacious and successful statesman; that he was a good man, and would be Lord Rector of Edinburgh University. ("Oh, oh.") After waiting patiently till the noise had somewhat abated, Mr Watters [spoke for Hartington and was seconded] . . .

Mr Wilson Calder, an Arts student, afterwards proposed [the blind Radical] Mr Henry Fawcett, M.P., whose nomination was duly seconded. This "move" was characterised as a "Tory dodge" and, apparently as a set-off to it, the name of Sir Robert Christison [who had retired from his professorship that summer] was formally submitted, this nomination being seconded by Mr Phin, law student, and followed by shouts of "Hurrah for Dr Phin". Mr McKenzie, another law student, explained that Sir Robert Christison had already declined to stand, if for no other reason than that his health would not permit him to do so, and moved that Sir Robert's name be not brought forward. This proposal was received with cries of "Split the Tory votes", and "Withdraw". Mr McKenzie said that, if it was the will of the meeting, he should withdraw the motion—("Sit down")—but he put it to the meeting if it was right to bring forward a candidate who had declined to stand. The Chairman beckoned Mr McKenzie to take his seat, and ruled that it was quite competent for the students to nominate Sir Robert Christison if they liked. A student in one of the back seats wished to know if Mr Fawcett, as a Professor in Cambridge University, was eligible for the office. (Cries of "No, no".) The Chairman replied that if the students thought the professor was not eligible, they would not vote for him. (Hear, hear, and "Sold again".) [Votes were taken and Fawcett and Christison eliminated.] . . . The result was received with "three cheers for Lord Hartington", and a singing of a stave of "For he's a jolly good fellow".

The Chairman then asked for a show of hands as between the Marquis of Hartington and Mr Cross, and the result was declared as follows:—the Marquis of Hartington, 240; Mr Cross, 223—majority for the Liberal candidate, 17. Great cheering, beating of sticks, and twirling of hats, followed the announcement of the figures. Mr Atkinson, for the Conservative students, demanded a poll on behalf of Mr Cross, which will take place next Saturday. The proceedings, which lasted about an hour, terminated with three cheers for the chairman. As the students separated, there were cries for "a procession", and during the evening bands of youths, marching four abreast, paraded some of the principal streets.

The Firm of Girdlestone describes comparable scenes at the announcement of a Rectorial final election result in the "Old Quad" where the run-off returns were traditionally declared. The Liberal majority there is 241. Hartington's majority at the 1877 final Poll was 248; Rosebery's in 1880 was 30. So it was his first Rectorial which lodged so firmly in Conan Doyle's mind.

The Lost World is distinguished by being probably the funniest science fiction story ever written, much of its humour being the disputes between Professors Challenger and Summerlee, and the mingling of heroism and absurdity in Challenger himself, but the meetings at the inception and conclusion of the four comrades' mission to the prehistoric plateau are outstanding in their juxtaposition of excitement and chaos. Yet the meetings are fairly incredible for London in 1911; disturbances at such gatherings at that time and on such a scale were very improbable unless Home Rule, the suffragettes, or labour protests were responsible for them. The students have a cohesion in their interest and barracking which the scattered hospitals could hardly be expected to furnish. But the positive evidence for the roots of such meetings in Edinburgh is much stronger than negative. The last chapter supplies in its very title one proof: it is headed "A Procession! A Procession!" with reference to the cry which goes up at the end of the final meeting, and the crowds march off "in a dense phalanx, blocking the streets from side to side". They parade down Regent Street, Pall Mall, St James's Street, and Piccadilly. This would be hard to document from London annals, but would have every relevance to the parades after the Rectorial nominations and elections in Edinburgh in the 1870s and 1880s, when South and North Bridges, Princes Street, the Mound, George IV Bridge, and appropriate thoroughfares in the New Town would have traffic scattered by the noisy mobs. Again, at this point, the returned travellers are serenaded with "For they are Jolly Good Fellows". Turning to the initial meeting in the novel, parallels continue. The students sing at the slightest opportunity from the first. The chairman is inaudible, although in *The Lost World* partly for reasons of personal inability to project his voice. Challenger interrupts the speaker with his famous repetition of "Question!" and during his own remarks is heckled continually to the point when he sometimes cannot be heard.

(Cries of "Bosh!" "Prove it!" "How do *you* know?" "Question!") "How do I know? you ask me. I know because I have visited their secret haunts. I know because I have seen some of them." (Applause, and a voice, "Liar!") "Am I a liar?" (General hearty and noisy assent.)

Again, at the final meeting, when Dr Illingworth of Edinburgh insists on an amendment to the resolution of congratulation, which amendment demands more proof:

"It is difficult to describe the confusion caused by this amendment. A large section of the audience expressed their indignation at such a slur upon the travellers by noisy shouts of dissent and cries of 'Don't put it!' 'Withdraw!'

> 'Turn him out!' On the other hand, the malcontents—and it cannot be denied that they were fairly numerous—cheered for the amendment, with cries of 'Order!' 'Chair!' and 'Fair Play!' A scuffle broke out in the back benches, and blows were freely exchanged among the medical students who crowded that part of the hall. . ."

Mr McKenzie's intervention would seem to have supplied some of the incentive for the form of Dr Illingworth's intervention, and their reception would seem to be very similar. Naturally both the plot and the distance in time put the meetings in *The Lost World* on a somewhat different footing from the initial meeting to decide on the Hartington-Cross contest, but the parentage of the latter for the former seems hard to dispute. Even the fact that the Hartington-Cross initial engagement concludes with a challenge which requires a Rectorial election to resolve (a customary situation) foreshadows the structure of *The Lost World* with the initial meeting dictating the quest, and the final meeting affirming its successful conclusion.

Hartington's Rectorial address, which he did not deliver until 31 January 1879, seems to have involved less turbulent proceedings than most. If Conan Doyle was there, he had ample opportunity of assessing the strengths and weaknesses of the 45-year-old patrician. But Hartington's Rectorial and nominal Liberal suzerainty were eclipsed by Gladstone's increasingly certain return to the leadership on a wave of popular opinion. Gladstone exemplified the point by descending on Edinburgh in November of the same year for his famous Midlothian campaign. It is very unlikely that Arthur missed all of the Edinburgh meetings, although we know that he was there no more than we do that he attended Hartington's Rectorial. But while there is no obvious figure in Conan Doyle's fiction based on Hartington, apart from the useful sense it would have given the young student of the aristocratic style, Lord Bellinger in *"The Second Stain"* is so clearly a portrait of Gladstone that it strongly increases the case for Arthur's having seen him in action in his prime, almost certainly during Midlothian:

> Austere, high-nosed, eagle-eyed . . . The Premier's thin, blue-veined hands were clasped tightly over the ivory head of his umbrella . . .the Premier's shaggy eyebrows gathered in a frown. . . . The Premier sprang to his feet with that quick, fierce gleam of his deep-set eyes before which a Cabinet has cowered . . . Holmes turned away smiling from the keen scrutiny of those wonderful eyes.

There is also a nice line in gentle satire of Gladstonian evasion:

> Holmes considered for some little time.
> "Now, sir, I must ask you more particularly what this document is, and why its disappearance should have such momentous consequences?"
> The two statesmen exchanged a quick glance . . .
> "Mr Holmes, the envelope is a long thin one of pale blue colour. There is a seal of red wax stamped with a crouching lion. It is addressed in large bold hand-writing to—"
> "I fear, sir", said Holmes, "that, interesting and indeed essential as these details are, my inquiries must go more to the root of things. What *was* the letter?"
> "That is a state secret of the utmost importance, and I fear that I cannot tell

you, nor do I see that it is necessary. If by the aid of the powers which you are
said to possess you can find such an envelope as I describe with its enclosures,
you will have deserved well of your country, and earned any reward which it
lies in our power to bestow."

Sherlock Holmes rose with a smile . . .

Here again a long interval separates meeting and writing, this time almost a
quarter-century, but we hardly need remark by this time on the excellence of
Conan Doyle's recall of youthful impressions. One point may be added to
bear out his presence during the Midlothian campaign: had he witnessed
Gladstone in the House of Commons it would have been from a height, but in
the Midlothian campaign he could easily have surveyed him from eye-level or
something below the speaker's eye-line. This would appear an essential
ingredient in his personal impression.

Conan Doyle was away from Scotland when Rosebery gave his inaugural,
but the young Earl was on the platform for several of the Midlothian
speeches, and frequently took the chair. Were his boots resoled, Conan Doyle
could have noted the fact from a seat, or more likely a stance, below the level
of the platform. In passing, Rosebery's address at his Rectorial completely
threw Hartington's into the shade: it is doubtful if Conan Doyle would have
liked it much, as it was practically a clarion-call for Scottish nationalism.
Trelawney Hope of *"The Second Stain"* is too neurotic and lacking in self-
asurance for Rosebery, but his years and appearance are suggestive: "dark,
clear-cut, and elegant, hardly yet of middle age, and endowed with every
beauty of body and of mind . . . the most rising statesman in the country". It
is the proximity of Gladstone and Rosebery on the Midlothian platform
which might have prompted that juxtaposition in the story.

The only other clue to involvement in political meetings in Edinburgh
peters out very disappointingly. *"Crabbe's Practice"* was published in the
Boy's Own Paper in 1884, although not reprinted in book form for many
years, and is generally agreed to be a somewhat fantastic portrait of George
Budd. It begins "at one of the Bulgarian Atrocity meetings held in Edinburgh
in '78". The problem is that the Bulgarian Agitation was in 1876, not 1878,
and although Professor R.T. Shannon, the foremost historian of the episode,
mentions an early meeting in Edinburgh, he is in error. Scotland showed little
interest in the question and the meeting to which the professor alludes actually
took place in Glasgow. Yet the passage is vivid enough to invite the suspicion
of autobiography:

The hall was densely packed and the ventilation defective, so that I was not
sorry to find that owing to my lateness I was unable to get any place, and had
to stand in the doorway. Leaning against the wall there I could both enjoy the
cool air and hear the invectives which speaker after speaker was hurling at the
Conservative ministry. The audience seemed enthusiastically unanimous. A
burst of cheering hailed every argument and sarcasm. There was not one
dissentient voice. The speaker paused to moisten his lips, and there was a
silence over the hall. Then a clear voice rose from the middle of it: "All very
fine, but what did Gladstone—" There was a howl of execration and yells of
"Turn him out!" but the voice was still audible. "What did Gladstone do in

'63?" it demanded. "Turn him out. Show [Shove?] him out of the window! Put him out!" There was a perfect hurricane of threats and abuse. Men sprang upon the benches shaking their sticks and peering over each other's shoulders to get a glimpse of the daring Conservative. "What did Gladstone do in '63?" roared the voice; "I insist on being answered". There was another howl of execration, a great swaying of the crowd, and an eddy in the middle of it. Then the mass of the people parted, and a man was borne out kicking and striking, and after a desperate resistance was precipitated down the stairs.

Ultimately the narrator follows him out:

"Pardon my curiosity, but would you mind telling me what Gladstone *did* do in '63?"

"My dear chap", said Crabbe, taking my arm and marching up the street with me, "I haven't the remotest idea in the world. You see, I was confoundedly hot and I wanted a smoke, and there seemed no chance of getting out, for I was jammed up right in the middle of the hall, so I thought I'd just make them carry me out; and I did—not a bad idea, was it? . . ."

While the meeting seems authentic enough, Crabbe's intervention seems more a projection of how George Budd might have behaved in such circumstances. But the date we have assigned to the first meeting of Budd and Conan Doyle may be helpful. As Scotland remained politically fairly quiescent until the Midlothian campaign, the opening may be a reminiscence of the heat at one of those meetings, coupled with an irreverent thought of what would happen if anyone were to question the record of the Grand Old Man.

*   *   *

These were the more exotic means by which ACD furnished his storehouse of recollection. Yet the Medical School itself supplied the most important contributions to it. At the time when Arthur entered it, the first signs of relative decline were beginning to set in. The last of the giants were departing. James Syme, known in his day as the greatest living authority in surgery, died in 1870. So did James Young Simpson, discoverer of the anaesthetic properties of chloroform, pioneer in modern obstetrics and advocate of the cause of women doctors. Joseph Lister, the great apostle of antiseptics, left his Chair of clinical surgery in 1877 at the age of 50 for a corresponding Chair in London. Robert Christison retired at the age of 80 in the same year, having occupied one chair or another over 55 years and became world-famous for his achievements in toxicology. Lister's departure was an unpleasant signal that the future lay with London rather than with Edinburgh. Hitherto London had been emphatically second-best: Robert Liston had gone there after defeat in controversy and rivalry with his former friend Syme, Robert Knox had ended his days there after the ruin of his career by Burke and Hare, Syme had briefly held an appointment there and after the most cursory acquaintance with London students fled back to Edinburgh. But the city of Edinburgh had outgrown its enlightenment by the mid-century, and from the departure of Lister the university was no longer able to hold its own, in the fullest sense of the term.

Yet for all that Edinburgh was beginning to decline, it had much to teach Arthur even in its concentration on teaching as against practical experience. All depended on the excellence of the lecture, and hence for all of his life Arthur was conscious of the economics of presentation. Discipline in the arrangement of materials was vital, albeit supported by relaxing and illustrative anecdotes—such as "Archer's" "racy lectures" and "favourite story" in *"His First Operation"*. In his story of the bewitchment of a professor, *The Parasite*, ACD reveals that sense in a way which staggered Hesketh Pearson: the professor's enemy "uses her telepathic power to make him talk nonsense at his lectures. To anyone who has listened to professorial lectures the effect of this is extraordinary: he is suspended from his chair by the authorities of the university". This is funny, but Pearson is even more instructive in error than in humour. As an Englishman, he could not understand the notion of a university where so much depended on the power of the lecture. *The Parasite* is evidence of the status of lectures in the University's mind and in Conan Doyle's.

If the University was austere, it kept its bargain: the students, left so much on their own responsibility, could not be short-changed on what they were given by the university. In times past the badness of medical lectures, such as those of Professor Alexander Monro *tertius*, had forced students to make up the deficiency in extra-mural lectures, such as those of Dr Robert Knox; the extra-mural lectures had now been given status allowing classes with them to count towards a degree, and the internals had to look to their laurels.

In Arthur's own day, the most careful scrutiny of the illnesses of the Professor of Pathology was maintained by the Court, as Waller with his recognized extra-mural Lectureship in Pathology could well attest. Pearson's complaints about "Doyle's boylike belief in the superiority of dons" rest on his failure to realise that Doyle encountered "dons" who were superior. Even if the giants were gone or going, they were leaving figures of great stature behind them. In any case Arthur had opportunity to see a little of one or two of the giants. He may have known Lister, he most certainly came to know something of Christison.

Christison retired at the end of Arthur's first year and, as we have noted, was used as a Liberal stalking-horse in the 1877 Rectorial election to split Tory votes, for though his baronetcy had been conferred by Gladstone he was a Tory to his lean finger-tips. So Arthur missed taking Materia Medica from him, but Waller had taken the course, and although Arthur does not mention him in his memoirs—his concern is with his actual teachers—Christison was in and out of university circles, his son John being the Secretary to the University court, his son David, a classmate of Lister, rising to prominence as archaeologist and antiquarian. If Arthur took any interest in the Rectorial of 1880 he would certainly have seen the old man, and perhaps heard his final bitter speech complaining that his candidacy had been promised to him as non-partisan and then checkmated by a Liberal party political campaign. On a more pleasant note, the godlike status of Christison was well attested by his devout admirers at the University—Lister, until his departure, Turner, his

John Doyle caricatures Queen Victoria in 1837 between Lords Melbourne and Palmerston, with the title "Susanna and the Elders" (see the Douai Bible, Daniel, chapters 13-14).

Artist and subjects: Richard Doyle (bottom right) and his drawings of sister-in-law Mary (about the time of her marriage) and Arthur (about the ages of five and nine).

Charles Doyle with six-year-old Arthur; and his self-portrayal as Sherlock Holmes inspecting the Baker Street Irregulars.

A Stonyhurst cricket group; Arthur, with cricket ball in hand.

Arthur Conan Doyle graduating.

Bryan Charles Waller in old age.

The pterodactyl may have featured in medical orals, but it was one of the few signs of chaos not present at Rectorial elections.

Originals and products. James Syme (top left) on his dignity, Robert Christison (top right) on the alert, William Rutherford (bottom left) uneasy—and Challenger tells Summerlee "it is, in my opinion, the end of the world".

"HE RAN YOUNG ALEC SIMPSON, OF THE 'COURIER,' A MILE DOWN THE ROAD."

the little and obscure planetary system to which we belong. A third-rate sun, with its ragtag and bobtail of insignificant satellites, we float under the same daily conditions towards some unknown end, some squalid catastrophe which will overwhelm us at the ultimate confines of space, where we are swept over an etheric Niagara, or dashed upon some unthinkable Labrador. I see

Professor Challenger meets the Press.

The most famous Edinburgh father of Sherlock Holmes—Joseph Bell.

Doctor (Patrick Heron) Watson.

Three faces of Authority from the Strand: *Napoleon confronts Gerard, the charwoman flees from Sir John Bollamore, and Boy Jim restrains Polly Hinton from alcohol.*

The "Challenger" Expedition. Professor Wyville Thomson in white sits between Sub-Lieutenants Lord George Campbell and Herbert Swire (bearded).

Doctor Hamilton and Lord Linchmere restrain the mad Sir Thomas Rossiter, while their creator, in an early Southsea photograph, keeps his silence.

Henry Highland Garnet and Arthur Conan Doyle as they looked about the time they met.

At Masongill House about 1883: Mary Foley Doyle with her youngest daughters "Ida" and "Dodo", Julia Waller and her son Bryan, and two unidentified ladies.

Love and Hate in Paget's illustrations in the Strand. *Holmes and Watson rejoice in Grant Munro's embrace of his black step-child; and they are confronted by Doctor Grimesby Roylott.*

William Budd

[*facsimile of signature*]

. declare that the preceding statement is a true
. was born at **Clifton** on the
.all not, on the **2nd** day of **August**
, be under Articles of Apprenticeship to any

George Budd

Date) **April 23. /80**

Family resemblances: The faces of William Budd (left) and George Challenger,
the signatures of William and George Budd. Sherlock Holmes's views on family
characteristics in calligraphy ("The Reigate Squires") and its revelation of self-
esteem (The Sign of Four) find some basis here.

The Doctor at Southsea about the time of writing Micah Clarke.

'The noose placed round my neck with trembling fingers' (p. 368)

Micah Clarke captured by the Royal troops: title-page illustration from the fifth edition (1891).

follower on scholarship and the prevention of women doctors alike, Balfour, the botanist, for whose Botanical Society Christison's last work was done in a characteristically lucid, vigorous, aesthetic, systematic and detailed series of papers on the exact measurement of trees for which his field research took his long spare form around the rural environs of the city and around Tayside.

His wintry, sidewhiskered, austere and formal countenance was by now one of the most famous in the city, to say nothing of his tall profile beheld racing up Arthur's Seat with a speed which took no account of the supposed demands of eighty years. It is going very far afield to imagine that the fast-moving profile was to inspire the famous silhouette of Professor Moriarty in *"The Final Problem"* as Watson saw it, unaware of its identity, "walking very rapidly" towards Holmes whom the innocent Watson had just left in quest of the mission of charity to the mythical dying Englishwoman, but Hesketh Pearson is surely right in seeing Moriarty's professorial status as directly derivative of Conan Doyle's admiration for the Edinburgh professoriate. And Christison was certainly the great legendary figure of the University in Arthur's day. Holmes's comments on Moriarty in part quoted by Pearson on their Edinburgh relevance may have specific application to Christison: "He is a genius, a philosopher, an abstract thinker. He has a brain of the first order. He sits motionless, like a spider in the centre of its web, but that web has a thousand radiations, and he knows well every quiver of each of them. He does little himself. He only plans. But his agents are numerous and splendidly organised." Now this in fact is rather a good description of Christison's power in the university during his final years before retirement. Sophia Jex-Blake was to discover it as she fought him to gain entry for women into the Medical School. He used everything against her, from his position as Physician to the Queen which he ruthlessly employed to disseminate (no doubt with absolute truth) the opposition of Victoria to the idea of women doctors, to his hold over his undergraduates with what ugly results we know. His position would have been even stronger when his opponent on that question, Sir James Y. Simpson, died, although his other great enemy in the town, the *Scotsman,* had forgotten none of its animosity against him when he faced his final battle in the Rectorial of 1880. And with his professorial connections, administrative awareness through his son, outstanding links with the General Medical Council, British Medical Association, British Association (whose Presidency he declined in 1876), Royal College of Physicians, Oxford University, Volunteer Corps, and even Edinburgh University Musical Society, might not some irreverent student such as Waller readily think of him as a spider at the centre of his web, running the University and much of British medicine too, for as much or as little as it pleased him. He was supremely the Edinburgh establishment. His father had been Professor of Humanity (Latin) at the University from 1806 to 1820. He won his first Chair in 1825, at the University, the Crown Professorship of Medical Jurisprudence and Police, and then was elected to the Chair of Materia Medica in 1832, holding it for 55 years. His vigour, vitality and longevity seemed scarcely believable.

But his most powerful literary impact on Conan Doyle was not Moriarty but Holmes. Fortunately, we can be very precise. Stamford's famous warning to Watson before the latter meets Holmes at the beginning of *A Study in Scarlet* runs:

> "Holmes is a little too scientific for my tastes—it approaches to cold-bloodedness. I could imagine his giving a friend a little pinch of the latest vegetable alkaloid, not out of malevolence, you understand, but simply out of a spirit of inquiry in order to have an accurate idea of the effects. To do him justice, I think that he would take it himself with the same readiness. . . ."

Christison's outstanding achievement was in toxicology. Professor John Hutton Balfour, writing his obituary for the *Transactions and Proceedings of the Botanical Society* (Edinburgh, 1883), vol. XIV, wrote as follows:

> Professor Christison took a deep interest in poisons, as shown in his published volume, and he made many experiments on their action and preparation. He sometimes went too far in making experiments on himself, of which the following occurrence, in reference to the Calabar bean (*Physostigma*), furnishes a remarkable instance. In the course of some experiments which he was making on this bean, not at this time ascertained to be poisonous, he brought home with him a piece of a bean, and finding it to be neither bitter or acrid, he chewed a considerable portion. Soon, however, symptoms of poisoning came on, he immediately emptied his stomach by swallowing his shaving water, and he was only with difficulty saved by remedies applied by his friends Professors Simpson and Maclagan.

Balfour taught Arthur botany, and this episode seems almost certain to have illustrated one lecture. Its obvious relevance to Holmes's experiment on Watson and himself in *"The Devil's Foot"* needs no elaboration, although this must be qualified by remembering that ACD himself followed Christison's ruthless self-experimentation on his own researches, notably on nitrate of amyl, as his doctoral thesis bears witness. In passing, it is touching to think of Christison's life being saved by his great adversary on female medical students. To return to *A Study in Scarlet*:

> ". . . He appears to have a passion for definite and exact knowledge."
> "Very right too."
> "Yes, but it may be pushed to excess. When it comes to beating the subjects in the dissecting-rooms with a stick, it is certainly taking a bizarre shape."
> "Beating the subjects!"
> "Yes, to verify how far bruises may be produced after death. I saw him at it with my own eye."

Now, this proceeding in fact formed the basis of one of Christison's most famous experiments, for it was the root of a magnificent attempt to solve the Burke and Hare murders in 1828. What had happened was that Burke and Hare were discovered because of their last murder, but that before the body was obtained by the police it had been delivered to Dr Robert Knox though not as yet examined by him. Bruises were discovered on the body. Burke told a story of the old lady having died naturally and insisted that bruises found on the body emerged from packing it for delivery to Knox after death. As Christison testified at the trial, the state of the body suggested artificial suffocation but could be consistent with accidental suffocation caused by intoxication. The hope was that the experiments of beating dead bodies, human and animal, would show whether the bruises on the deceased excluded the possibility of natural death, in that they could not have been produced afterwards, and Christison conducted several experiments at various time-spans from moment of death. Having been unable to come to a final conclusion, he very firmly told the Lord Advocate, and later the Court, that his experiment failed to clear the matter up.

Throughout his life he remained absolutely unshakable in his insistence that a medical expert witness must be utterly free to give his evidence regardless of its effects on one side or on another, and he was famous for his terrific independence in the witness-box and utter refusal to be brow-beaten by counsel: and his evidence was given in many great cases, including Madeleine Smith and William Palmer. He wrote up his experiments of beating anatomical subjects for the *Edinburgh Medical Journal* in April 1829. Conan Doyle's library included the rare *West Port Murders*, a contemporary report of the Burke and Hare trial with accompanying (if frequently inaccurate) newspaper comment and report on the ramifications of the case. It is hardly surprising that with the West Port, where the murders had taken place, virtually on his doorstep at Lonsdale Terrace, and Burke's own skeleton still preserved in the custody of the Edinburgh Professor of Anatomy, ACD would take an early interest in it. Christison's detective-work was critical in the direction taken by the case, in that its failure led to the prosecution granting immunity to William Hare and his wife, although Hare was as fully responsible as Burke for fifteen murders. In the year of Christison's death, 1882, ACD wrote *"My Friend the Murderer"*, published in *London Society's* Christmas number of that year. The story is concerned with a figure such as Hare who is himself "the arch criminal" but has obtained immunity by giving evidence against his fellows, and the text even alludes to the Burke and Hare murders. The same phenomenon, expressed with far greater artistic subtlety, accounts for the origin of the murder in *"The Resident Patient"*: "This Blessington, or Sutton, who was the worst of the gang, turned informer. On his evidence, Cartwright was hanged and the other three got fifteen years apiece." What haunts both narratives is vengeance in pursuit of a criminal protected by the law although guilty of crimes equal to or greater than those of the persons whose lives were forfeit because of his evidence.

If Hare inspired Blessington alias Sutton and his crude antecedent, what of Burke? That seed took much longer to germinate, but the results were ultimately striking: *"The Disappearance of Lady Frances Carfax"*, and specifically its villain, Holy Peters alias the Rev. Dr Shlessinger. Unlike Burke, Peters is not Irish but Australian (a return to an association of ideas in *"My Friend the Murderer"*). Burke, while born and dying Roman Catholic, became interested in evangelicalism and used to take part in street religious meetings and seems to have done so with no motives of personal profit, but no doubt that supplied the idea of Peters's form of fraud. Peters's wife's statement when Holmes and Watson arrived that "my husband is not afraid to face any man in the world" is almost exactly what Burke's mistress Helen MacDougal said to the police when they arrived for the interview which concluded with Burke's arrest. Peters's first remarks are a little like Burke's on that occasion. Burke and Peters are both men of great charm with particular influence on ageing ladies. Burke's and Hare's major achievement was the committing of murder so skilfully that no murder could be proved to have been committed, against which Christison carried out his corpse-beating in vain; the attempted murder of Lady Frances Carfax is devised with similar intent. The claiming as a dependent a dying old lady to obtain a burial certificate, is a perfect inversion of the murder for which Burke was arrested: he disclaimed his continued association with an old lady whose son had walked out on her, and the disclaimer was to cover inducing her death for which no burial certificate would be required.

The sale of Lady Frances's jewels as means by which the crime is discovered follows the sale or giving away of property of Burke's and Hare's victims which subsequently proved one of the factors fatal to Burke. "The horrible den upstairs" is the language of the Burke trial (and a little out of context for Peters, whose motive for maintaining a room in a large Poultney Square house in such conditions is obscure). Holmes's remarks at the outset of the case are almost an epitaph for Burke's last victim, the old woman Docherty:

> "One of the most dangerous classes in the world . . . is the drifting and friendless woman. She is the most harmless and often the most useful of mortals, but she is the inevitable inciter of crime in others. She is helpless. She is migratory. . . . She is a stray chicken in a world of foxes. When she is gobbled up she is hardly missed. . . ."

What prevented the connection between the story and the case being made before now was Conan Doyle's shrewd analysis of the similarity between human conditions in the highest and the lowest classes in such a situation. The aristocratic Lady Frances and the destitute, alcoholic Mary Docherty may seem very different—in person Mrs Docherty was much closer to Lady Frances's coffin-mate—but their fate is absolutely similar. Much as the study of human illness leads to a sense of human equality in the face of disease, comparative criminology invites a similar response. But Conan Doyle's class-conscious readers lacked his scientific capacity to cut through artificial class distinction.

Christison supplies us with some more points in the making of Holmes. Holmes's activity, and insistence on testing conclusions by experiment, however dangerous or disgusting, recall Christison. The rather curious social deference Holmes receives from the Lestrades and the Gregsons, even when they are most contemptuous of his theories, would be that of the police in dealing with the professor. Henry Littlejohn as Police Surgeon in Arthur's day, and one of his lecturers, would have given him contemporary evidence as to the operation of such relations. Littlejohn could be very contemptuous of official evidence and theories when performing in the box.

Holmes's own insistence that his retention in a case can only mean that he will use his powers to find the truth, not simply to assist one side, is absolutely characteristic of the Christison principle and method. As for the extraordinary rudeness which characterises much of the relations between Holmes and the police, it will be remembered in addition to Waller's manner that Christison, Robert Knox, Liston, Syme, Simpson and the rest were distinguished by their arrogance and acerbity in controversy. It may also be an indirect product of Conan Doyle's awareness of Christison that the one case in which Holmes (*pace* his claim in *"The Final Problem"*) actually did use his powers "upon the wrong side" is *"A Scandal in Bohemia"* where he is employed against a woman whom he afterwards acknowledges to be in the right.

So Christison is vital to the development of Holmes, but it is the legend of Christison rather than the man himself as Arthur might have seen him. Is there any evidence of the latter? Here any ascription has to be much more tentative, but there is one figure who certainly seems founded on something very like the aged Christison. We have noted how deeply Edinburgh University was in Conan Doyle's mind in writing *The Lost World*, and on his own evidence we will observe yet more proof of this shortly. *A Study in Scarlet* makes it clear how strongly impressed he had been by the reputation of Christison: it would not be surprising to find some image of him in the work which of all others consciously owes so much to Edinburgh Medical School. And Christison is to be found, I suggest, in Professor Summerlee, not so much the Summerlee of *The Poison Belt* with his farmyard imitations (although the toxic theme is suggestive), and hardly the ghostly apparition at the beginning of *The Land of Mist*, but in his appearance in *The Lost World* from the moment that he enters the lists against Challenger at the first meeting. We have noted the origins of that meeting in the affray where Christison's name appeared after the initial confrontation of forces, and in *The Lost World* Summerlee comes to the fore only after Challenger has routed the initial lecturer, Mr Percival Waldron:

> Mr Summerlee, the veteran Professor of Comparative Anatomy, rose among the audience, a tall, thin, bitter man, with the withered aspect of a theologian. He wished, he said, to ask Professor Challenger whether the results to which he had alluded in his remarks had been obtained during a journey to the headwaters of the Amazon made by him two years before.
>
> Professor Challenger answered that they had.
>
> Mr Summerlee desired to know how it was that Professor Challenger claimed to have made discoveries in those regions which had been overlooked by Wallace, Bates, and the other previous explorers of established scientific repute.
>
> Professor Challenger answered that Mr Summerlee appeared to be confusing the Amazon with the Thames; that it was in reality a somewhat larger river; that Mr Summerlee might be interested to know that with the Orinoco, which communicated with it, some fifty thousand miles of country were opened up, and that in so vast a space it was not impossible for one person to find what another had missed.
>
> Mr Summerlee declared, with an acid smile, that he fully appreciated the difference between the Thames and the Amazon, which lay in the fact that any

assertion about the former could be tested, while about the latter could not. He would be obliged if Professor Challenger would give the latitude and the longitude of the country in which prehistoric animals were to be found.

Professor Challenger replied that he reserved such information for good reasons of his own, but would be prepared to give it with proper precautions to a committee chosen from the audience. Would Mr Summerlee serve on such a committee and test his story in person?

Mr Summerlee: "Yes, I will." (Great cheering.)

Later comments on Summerlee remain consistent with Christison:

The scientific attainments of Professor Summerlee are too well known for me to trouble to recapitulate them. He is better equipped for a rough expedition of this sort than one would imagine at first sight. His tall, gaunt, stringy figure is insensible to fatigue, and his dry, half-sarcastic and often wholly unsympathetic manner is uninfluenced by any change in his surroundings. Though in his sixty-fifth year, I have never heard him express any dissatisfaction at the occasional hardships which we have had to encounter. I had regarded his presence as an encumberance to the expedition, but, as a matter of fact, I am now well convinced that his power of endurance is as great as my own.

Recollections of Christison are particularly strong on the enthusiasm for mountain-climbing almost to the end of his life, on his devout religious beliefs, and on an "often wholly unsympathetic manner", while surviving photographs testify to the gauntness and "withered aspect of a theologian". Summerlee is bearded and while Christison wore long side-whiskers for most of his life, he grew a beard towards the end of it. Summerlee necessarily has to be younger than the Christison of Arthur's day: it would be asking too much to have an octogenarian going up the Amazon and joining issue with the pterodactyls. On the the other hand, Summerlee in controversy seems admirably fitted to represent the man who had once the very ugly duty of interviewing Robert Knox to determine how aware he might have been that he was in receipt of murdered bodies from Burke and Hare:

Last night Challenger said that he never cared to walk on the Thames Embankment and look up the river, as it was always sad to see one's eventual goal. He is convinced, of course, that he is destined for Westminster Abbey. Summerlee retorted, however, with a sour smile, by saying that he understood Millbank Prison had been pulled down.

And on another level:

I learned, however, that day once for all that both Summerlee and Challenger possessed that highest type of bravery, the bravery of the scientific mind. . . . It is decreed by a merciful Nature that the human brain cannot think of two things simultaneously, so that if it be steeped in curiosity as to science it has no room for merely personal considerations.

Turning briefly to *The Poison Belt*, it is notable that Summerlee is given pride of place in toxicological classification:

". . . I fancy, so far as my toxicology carries me, that there are some vegetable nerve poisons—"

"Datura", suggested Summerlee.

"Excellent!" cried Challenger. "it would make for scientific precision if we

named our toxic agent. Let it be daturon. To you, my dear Summerlee, belongs
the honour—posthumous, alas! but none the less unique—of having given a
name to the universal destroyer, the great Gardener's disinfectant. The
symptoms of daturon, then, may be taken to be such as I indicate. That it will
involve the whole world and that no life can possibly remain behind seems to
me certain, since ether is a universal medium. . . ."

And in an immediately preceding passage, after Summerlee has asked
Challenger to explain what is happening—to which the answer will be that
the earth is doomed—he concludes:

". . . You need not stand on ceremony with us, Challenger. We have all faced
death together before now. Speak out, and let us know exactly where we stand,
and what, in your opinion, are our prospects for our future."
   It was a brave, good speech, a speech from that staunch and strong spirit
which lay behind all the acidities and angularities of the old zoologist.

Finally, when it proves that the last cylinder of oxygen they have to sustain
them against immediate death is defective:

"So we are to be cheated out of the last hour of our lives", Summerlee
remarked, bitterly. "An excellent final illustration of the sordid age in which we
have lived. Well, Challenger, now is your time if you wish to study the
subjective phenomena of physical dissolution."

From the courage to the Conservatism, it is complete.
   In his valuable memoirs, *Mostly Murder*, Sir Sydney Smith, father of the
poet Sydney Goodsir Smith, comments on the strange fact that Holmes in the
stories does not use his laboratory skill, and his references to experiments (in,
for instance, *A Study in Scarlet*, and "*The Naval Treaty*") have nothing to do
with the cases with which the stories are concerned. This, I suspect, is more
deliberate than Sir Sydney realised, although he deserves all respect for
separating and classifying the phenomenon. If the arguments between Holmes
and the police, and between Challenger and Summerlee, have as their most
important human antecedent the controversies among Edinburgh scholars,
they do so in a strong spirit of comedy. Holmes's separation of experiment
from investigation, and still more Mycroft Holmes's indifference to checking
his conclusions in any respect, have to be seen as affectionate satires on the
academic world Conan Doyle had come to know. Christison is not involved
here: his experiments were undertaken, as we have seen, with every relevance
to cases in hand. Christison was, in fact, Arthur's first real experience of a
detective, and a detective of extraordinary genius and international celebrity.
   But the separation of theory from practice at Edinburgh which ACD
criticises in *Memories and Adventures* relate much more directly to the most
famous inspiration for Holmes he encountered there, Joseph Bell. Mycroft
is possibly based on a living model, and unlike Sherlock, conceivably a single
one: but I am unable to identify him. It *could* be Waller in part—"seven years
my senior" is not far from the actual six—but it seems very unassertive to be
so. It seems most likely founded on a teacher or researcher who eschewed the
practical altogether, rather after the manner of Chris Kingsley (in Professor
Fred Hoyle's *The Black Cloud*) whose success as an astronomer is maintained

without looking through a telescope for decades. Mycroft, of course, may simply be the principle of the separation of the theoretical from the practical carried to the extremes of absolute absurdity. As it is, the portrait is highly satirical, occasionally to the the point of savagery: in "*The Greek Interpreter*" Mycroft's cold-blooded interest in the case, as opposed to the human beings involved, directly results in the murder of Kratides and the attempted murder of Melas when the villains see the advertisement he has inserted in the newspapers. Sherlock Holmes is guilty of this to a lesser degree. He sends a client out of doors to his death in "*The Five Orange Pips*" instead of giving him a shakedown on the sofa, although the weather and the danger give every justification for such an action. His pursuit of the mystery of the identity of the two Pinners in one in "*The Stockbroker's Clerk*" instead of proceeding at once to discover who has taken Hall Pycroft's place at Mawson and Williams results in the death of the watchman. He sees danger for Hilton Cubitt in "*The Dancing Men*", but his failure to send a warning telegram because of his preoccupation with checking his conclusions on the spot also seems a probable contribution to the death of his client. In *The Hound of the Baskervilles* his dependence on the exact solution of affairs he has contrived leads to a nervous breakdown for his client and the considerable risk of his death. He expresses repentance in "*The Five Orange Pips*" and *The Hound* for his failure to avert danger to his client, but he shows no sign of amending his procedures.

Commentators have seen these lapses as inadequacies in Holmes: what they have not seen is the deliberate intention of the author. Here he is throwing into relief the inhumane attitudes towards patients he observed at Edinburgh, where the patient seemed to have no existence outside of his medical situation and where the discussion of his ailments, especially before a class, was carried on with utter indifference to his personal reactions. As a doctor, Conan Doyle laid great stress on human sympathy. It is the permanent theme of his medical stories in *Round the Red Lamp*. It was not a quality he found in abundance in the teaching faculty, either towards students or towards patients. Nor has it been particularly evident in medical teaching since his day. Richard Gordon, whose "Doctor" books are in danger of being generally devalued because of the soap-opera form of the later volumes, throws much light on comparable attitudes in his valuable *Doctor in the House:*

> "Now!" He tapped the abdomen with his pencil as if knocking for admission. "When we have cut through the skin what is the next structure we shall meet? Come on, you fellers. You've done your anatomy more recently than I have . . . what's that? Yes, subcutaneous fat. Then, gentlemen, we first encounter the surgeon's worst enemy." He glared at us all in turn. "What?" he demanded in general. There was no reply. "Blood:" he thundered.
>
> At that point the patient restored his personality to the notice of his doctors by vomiting.

Looked at from this standpoint, the famous deductions of Joseph Bell assume a more cold-blooded and less admirable character. Arthur clearly

admired him greatly, and was accepted as one of his favourite students. He
was still a comparatively young man when Arthur came under his direction in
surgery, having been born in 1837. ACD's later memoirs of him are
affectionate, and the author's readiness to support his old Mentor's belief that
he was Sherlock Holmes—he was known for proclaiming it at Edinburgh
dinner parties—are stronger testimony to that affection than to the accuracy
of the statement. But Conan Doyle's indictment of the Edinburgh University
faculty for its lovelessness does not except Bell. His encounter with Bell on
the Isle of Arran left him with a sense of amazement at such a figure doing
anything so human as taking a holiday, and Bell does not seem to have
responded by relaxing in honour of the fortuitous meeting off duty. There is a
note of slight suspicion in *Memories and Adventures*:

> For some reason which I have never understood he singled me out from the
> drove of students who frequented his wards and made me his out-patient clerk,
> which meant that I had to array his outpatients, make simple notes of their
> cases, and then show then in, one by one, to the large room in which Bell sat in
> state surrounded by his dressers and students. Then I had ample chance of
> studying his methods and of noticing that he often learned more of the patient
> by a few quick glances than I had done by my questions.

The question hangs in the air. Why did Bell take him up? For the matter of
that, why did Holmes make so much of Watson? Ultimately, as I have
suggested in another context, the latter question is resolved when Watson
learns very gradually how deeply fond of him Holmes has become. There is
no great evidence that Bell became similarly fond of Conan Doyle, save in
respect of the Holmes stories and the local lustre they gave Bell. He was
persistent in sending Conan Doyle unusable ideas for the stories, and as a
vigorous Tory he did turn out to support Conan Doyle's Liberal Unionist
candidature in 1900. He also liked to give his circle the notion that the
Holmes identification was somewhere between a public nuisance and a
pardonable, but irreverent, piece of cheek, but this is decidedly at variance
with his cultivation of the image and his readiness to write prefaces for *A
Study in Scarlet*, thereby gaining some financial returns where Conan Doyle
himself, having sold the copyright to Ward, Lock, for £25, never made
another penny from it.

Naturally Bell's friends, notably Mrs Jessie Saxby who threw together a
memoir of him, resented the less pleasant aspects of Holmes and asserted
Bell's superiority over the character. The Waller strain was hardly likely to be
one Bell would have wanted to own. There was much stress among his friends
on Bell's personal warmth; but here his pupil seems to have been faithful
enough to his own observation. There is obviously part of Conan Doyle in
Holmes and in Watson; but Bell clearly cast him for Watson. And it is not the
most pleasant part of Holmes's and Watson's relationship that Bell seems to
have inspired. The famous deductions are in part Holmes's scoring off
Watson, with rather small justification for it; and Bell's deductions seem to
have involved scoring off Conan Doyle. He noted that Conan Doyle admired
him, and was clearly prepared to take a good deal from him. Discipleship was

an Edinburgh tradition, for all of Edinburgh's coldness: Robert Knox had won the devotion of his pupils, notably the future Sir William Fergusson, and Thomas Wharton Jones, and Alexander Miller; Christison had a large following, among whom the future Sir William Turner was the most conspicuous; Syme had Bell and his own son-in-law Lister; and Simpson his own son who succeeded him. Bell was less distinguished than any of them, and he had need of disciples. Hence he was ready to take up Conan Doyle, who psychologically had need of an intellectual icon. But the relationship had a decided touch of ridicule about it. Bell seems particularly to have enjoyed diagnosing Irishmen, possibly with an eye cocked on the Irishness of his clerk. He gave an example in an interview to the *Pall Mall Gazette* after ACD and Sherlock Holmes had become household words:

> I recollect he was amused once when a patient walked in and sat down. "Good morning, Pat", I said, for it was impossible not to see that he was an Irishman.
> "Good morning, your honour", replied the patient.
> "Did you like your walk across the Links today, as you came in from the south side of the town?" I asked.
> "Yes", said Pat, "did your honour see me?"
> Well, Conan Doyle could not see how I knew that, absurdly simple though it was.
> On a showery day, such as that had been, the reddish clay at bare parts of the Links adheres to the boot, and a tiny part is bound to remain. There is no such clay anywhere else round the town for miles. . . .

It is all a little chilly in its condescension. The readiness to address the Irishman as "Pat", which deduction had certainly not told Bell was his name, begins the embarrassment. Some Irishmen are not called Pat. Curiously enough, the most famous Dr Watson on the Edinburgh medical scene was: Dr Patrick Heron Watson, surgeon at the Royal Infirmary and friend of Lister. Certainly Bell deserves credit for observation, although Bruntsfield Links, lying just beyond The Meadows and five minutes from the Infirmary, were not difficult to reconnoitre. Conan Doyle profited by the instance, whatever he thought of the condescension. The reddish clay is transferred to London at the commencement of *The Sign of Four*:

> ". . . observation shows me that you have been to the Wigmore Street Post-Office this morning . . ."
> "Right!" said I. ". . . But I confess that I don't see how you arrived at it. It was a sudden impulse upon my part, and I have mentioned it to no one."
> "It is simplicity itself", he remarked, chuckling at my surprise; "so absurdly simple that an explanation is superfluous; and yet it may serve to define the limits of observation and of deduction. Observation tells me that you have a little reddish mould adhering to your instep. Just opposite the Wigmore Street Office they have taken up the pavement and thrown up some earth which lies in such a way that it is difficult to avoid treading in it in entering. The earth is of this peculiar reddish tint which is found, so far as I know, nowhere else in the neighbourhood. . . ."

It forms an excellent illustration showing how dominated by Edinburgh Sherlock Holmes's London really was. Bell could speak with authority about

Edinburgh, especially its small vital centre. Holmes really could not answer for a vast metropolis. Yet much of the appeal of the stories lies on an intimate and *known* London, very much more of a comfortable unity than the city really was. By putting so much of the intimacy of Edinburgh into it, Conan Doyle gave a sense of place to the dismaying anonymity of London and thereby won readers' identification. The migrant, thinking of his own place of origin, hungers for some reproduction of the smallness which he has left but cannot lose from his heart. Conan Doyle supplied the means for showing how the lost home with its ready identification of its accidents can be found once more in the frightening greatness of the metropolis. The whole process came the more naturally because as late as *The Sign of Four* his only knowledge of London was as a visitor. It was Bell who made that transition peculiarly possible by supplying the human agency. Yet his craft of observation and deduction was not humane. The very next exchange between Holmes and Watson reveals the grossest of insensitivity on Holmes's part, when he diagnoses Watson's brother's alcoholism without the slightest consideration of the pain such brutal conclusions must give to Watson. There may be an indication here of the young out-patient clerk's alarm lest his master's skill in diagnosis might in some horrible fashion lay bare the tragedy of the Doyle family. It is even possible that there was some incident in which he did. If so, the evidence of *The Sign of Four* suggest that the revelation was exceedingly unpleasant for Arthur.

After Holmes gained celebrity, Bell necessarily found himself developing the science of deduction in detailed exposition where once he had merely done so in automatic observation. Syme, he remarks in his introduction to *A Study in Scarlet*, "had a favourite illustration which, as a tradition of his school, has made a mark on Dr Conan Doyle's method, 'Try to learn the features of a disease or injury as precisely as you know the features, the gait, the tricks of manner of your most intimate friend',", and Syme, he reminded his largely English audience, was "one of the greatest teachers of surgical diagnosis that ever lived". So, thanks to Bell, we can identify yet another Holmes in Syme—indeed Holmes's father, in that Syme pioneered what Bell was bringing to a fine art. Holmes's love of showmanship is more Bell than Syme; as an operator, for instance, Syme, recognised as the greatest of his day, went about his work so effectively and so economically that the business was robbed of any frills or flourishes or any unnecessary trimming whatsoever. Holmes on the scent gives the audience much more of a performance for their money. Yet Bell had a Scots appreciation of literary economics, and, while officially dealing with *A Study in Scarlet*, Ward, Lock's one Holmes possession to which they held on with the force of Mr Rucastle's mastiff, Bell showed himself a workmanlike critic of the short stories:

> Dr Conan Doyle in this remarkable series of stories has proved himself a born story-teller. He has had the wit to devise excellent plots, interesting complications; he tells them in honest Saxon-English with directness and pith; and, above all his other merits, his stories are absolutely free from padding. He knows how delicious brevity is, how everything tends to be too long, and he has

given us stories that we can read at a sitting between dinner and coffee, and we have not a chance to forget the beginning before we reach the end. The ordinary detective story, from Gaboriau or Boisgobey down to the latest shocker, really needs an effort of memory quite misplaced to keep the circumstances of the crimes and all the wrong scents of the various meddlers before the wearied reader. Dr Doyle never gives you a chance to forget an incident or miss a point.

At least one edition of the *Adventures* is dedicated "to my old teacher, Joseph Bell, M.D., &c, of 2, Melville Crescent, Edinburgh" (a very fashionable address in the west New Town), and Bell, both as inspiration and as critic, well justified it. His own remarks put to the utmost shame the absurd performances from popular literary names with which Cape and Murray disfigured a recent edition of the stories. One point gets to the heart of a literary problem to a depth that eluded even Edmund Wilson: Wilson asked himself why the Holmes stories are genuinely distinguished in a way most of their counterparts are not, but many years before, Bell had answered that they really are stories instead of puzzles requiring the reader to back-track and check up, conscious of being in a contest against the author.

It is Bell's public deductions which give us the delicious realisation that the words of Sherlock Holmes probably ought to be read in a Scottish accent; not only that, but, said ACD, "his voice was high and discordant". Bell was "thin, wiry, dark", recalls *Memories and Adventures*, "with a high-nosed acute face, penetrating grey eyes, angular shoulders and a jerky way of walking". On the other hand, even in the business of deduction Holmes seldom reaches the cool, insolent indifference to the embarrassment of the client invariably exhibited by Bell. "With women especially the observant doctor can often tell by noticing her, exactly what part of her body she is going to talk about": thus Bell to the *Pall Mall Gazette*. Even more, his method demanded that he be ready to inform students the patient was a liar. In the same interview he recalled:

> "A man walked into the room where I was instructing the students, and his case seemed to be a very simple one. I was talking about what was wrong with him. 'Of course, gentlemen', I happened to say, 'he has been a soldier in Highland regiment, and probably a bandsman.' I pointed out the swagger in his walk, suggestive of the piper; while his shortness told me that if he had been a soldier it was probably as a bandsman. In fact, he had the whole appearance of a man in one of the Highland regiments. The man turned out to be nothing but a shoemaker, and said he had never been in the army in his life. This was rather a floorer, but being absolutely certain that I was right, and seeing that something was up, I did a pretty cool thing. I told two of the strongest clerks (or dressers) to remove the man to a side room, and to detain him till I came. I went and had him stripped and . . . under the left breast I instantly detected a little blue 'D' branded on his skin. He was a deserter. That was how they used to mark them in the Crimean days and later, although it is not permitted now. Of course the reason for his evasion was at once clear."

"*This*" said Bell complacently to the interviewer, "struck me as funny at the time." It strikes the present writer as humiliating in the extreme for all

parties, and that a human tragedy of that kind, dragged into the light of day
with its rags of self-respect torn apart once more, should have amused Bell,
exhibits him in a remarkably unpleasing light. Mrs Saxby's memoir insists
that "his pity for a sinner was ever on the alert to help him out of the mire",
but pity in fact seems very foreign to his public conduct.

To Dr Graham Sutton, who cast a professional eye over Bell's *Manual of
the Operations of Surgery* at my request, must go the credit of the discovery
that Bell unquestionably brought for the first time before Conan Doyle the
juxtaposition of the names "Holmes" and "Watson" as well as the obvious
origin of "Mycroft". Dedicated to Syme, the *Manual* went through many
editions, and the fifth, published in 1883, gives us the clearest indication of
what material Arthur would have obtained from Bell. Pp. 132 and 135 are
respectively concerned with the excision of hip-joint and knee-joint, "Mr
Holmes" being given pride of place as the authority in the first case, "Dr P.
H. Watson" in the second. Watson, that is to say Patrick Heron Watson of
Edinburgh, is particularly complimented on his use of plaster-of-Paris
moulds: amusingly, the monograph making so much of plaster-of-Paris is
transferred in *The Sign of Four* from Watsonian to Holmesian authorship:
"Here is my monograph upon the tracing of footsteps, with some remarks
upon the uses of plaster of Paris as a preserver of impresses." Patrick Heron
Watson was certainly known to Conan Doyle personally: President of the
Royal College of Surgeons in 1878 (and again in 1903), he had been surgeon
to the Edinburgh Royal Infirmary since 1863, had served in the Crimean War
at the age of 23 and was generally known in Edinburgh as "Dr Watson" until
Edward VII knighted him in 1903, four years before his death. To say this is
not to say that Dr P. H. Watson supplied the sole identity of Dr J. H.
Watson, though that military service so soon after graduation (Heron Watson
graduated M.D. from Edinburgh in 1853) is decidedly suggestive. It is the
possibly unconscious association of Holmes and Watson that Bell's *Manual*,
and no doubt lectures, created in the mind of Conan Doyle. The name
Holmes arose, as we know, from conscious invocation of Oliver Wendell, yet
Oliver Wendell Holmes was, in addition to his famous essay-writing, a
Professor of Anatomy at Harvard (he had been briefly at Edinburgh in the
1830s, and studied with Dr Robert Knox, the autocrat of the dissecting-table).
The thought of Oliver Wendell Holmes, like ACD, doctor and writer,
naturally gave by association of ideas the name of Timothy Holmes the
surgeon; Timothy Holmes edited *A System of Surgery* in four volumes. Bell
was relying on his *Surgical Treatment of Diseases in Infancy and Childhood* in
conjunction with Watson's work on the excision of the knee-joint. It is
curious that the London and Edinburgh locations of the two men meant that
Timothy Holmes was cited, following London practice, as "Mr Holmes"
whereas the Scots did not believe in concealing doctorates when they had
them (the English had far fewer M.D.s) and Heron Watson was thus "Dr
Watson".

In the case of Mycroft, Dr Sutton points out that the passage on the hip-
joint commencing with a paragraph devoted to Holmes has as the subject of

its penultimate paragraph the work of "Mr Croft" and that in a rough note of a lecture that could very easily become "Mycroft". Croft was the Listerian surgeon of St Thomas's Hospital in London, famous for the introduction of "Croft's splints" for leg fractures. His paper on hip-joint excisions was read to the Clinical Society and published in its *Transactions* for 1879. In this case inspiration would clearly be much more conscious than in that of the Holmes-Watson juxtaposition. Mycroft Holmes, it will be remembered, does not appear until "*The Greek Interpreter*", published in the *Strand* for September 1893. ACD had by then retired from medical practice, and had no professional occasion to look at his copy of Bell's *Manual* or to look out his old lecture-notes. But if he found himself running a little short of examples of deduction and wished to refresh his memory of Bell's methods, the lecture notes would be a logical source of re-examination. Significantly, *Memories and Adventures* singles out a prime example of Bell's deductions.

In one of his best cases he said to a civilian patient: "Well, my man, you've served in the army."

"Aye, sir."

"Not long discharged?"

"No, sir."

"A Highland regiment?"

"Aye, sir."

"A non-com. officer?"

"Aye, sir."

"Stationed at Barbados?"

"Aye, sir."

"You see, gentlemen", he would explain, "the man was a respectful man but did not remove his hat. They do not in the army, but he would have learned civilian ways had he been long discharged. He has an air of authority and he is obviously Scottish. As to Barbados, his complaint is elephantiasis, which is West Indian and not British." To his audience of Watsons it all seemed very miraculous until it was explained, and then it became simple enough.

Now for "*The Greek Interpreter*":

"An old soldier, I perceive", said Sherlock.

"And very recently discharged", remarked the brother.

"Served in India, I see."

"And a non-commissioned officer."

"Royal Artillery, I fancy", said Sherlock.

"And a widower."

"But with a child."

"Children, my dear boy, children."

"Come", said I, laughing, "this is a little too much".

"Surely", answered Holmes, "it is not hard to say that a man with that bearing, expression of authority, and sun-baked skin is a soldier, is more than a private, and is not long from India."

"That he has not left the service long is shown by his still wearing his 'ammunition boots', as they are called", observed Mycroft.

"He has not the cavalry stride, yet he wore his hat on one side, as is shown by the lighter skin on that side of his brow. His weight is against his being a sapper. He is in the artillery."

"Then, of course, his complete mourning shows that he has lost someone very dear. The fact that he is doing his own shopping looks as though it were his wife. He has been buying things for children, you perceive. There is a rattle, which shows that one of them is very young. The wife probably died in child-bed. The fact that he has a picture-book under his arm shows that there is another child to be thought of."

The reference to death in child-bed is a nice touch: Bell was particularly celebrated for his work in paediatric surgery, and became chief surgeon at the Edinburgh Sick Children's Hospital. Our deduction that this story at least was written with a look back at the old lecture-notes throws an interesting light on Conan Doyle's methods of composition. That he did detailed research for the historical novels is well known. The Holmes stories are usually assumed to have involved little of that kind of preparation but in fact there must have been more of it than the author's casual allusions would lead us to assume. In passing, the craftsmanship of the passage is worthy of respect. In order to provide a dialogue Sherlock Holmes has to be presented as functioning decidedly below his best. Most of Mycroft's deductions are ones which would be commonplace for Sherlock as a rule. As the original shows, Bell would have achieved any of them, and had achieved variants. Conan Doyle gets over this by the subtle suggestion that Sherlock has something of an inferiority complex about Mycroft (a complex which, switched to the mythical "Siggy" Holmes on the topic of Sherlock, becomes the plot of the movie *Sherlock Holmes's Smarter Brother*). The repetitive and somewhat defensive "I perceive", "I see", "I fancy", do that work. One could follow the joke made by the film to suggest that Mycroft was never the intellect Sherlock thought he was, and indeed the comments of Mr Martin Dakin remind us of the fundamentally satiric basis to the entire portrait of Mycroft.

Mr Richard Lancelyn Green has pointed out that Conan Doyle's class marks, while generally a B average, are somewhat lower for Bell's subjects, surgery and practical surgery. So Bell did not play favourites, if indeed Conan Doyle meant more in his life than an enthusiastic disciple to be exploited and tantalised. He took pride in the fact that his demonstrations inspired Conan Doyle, and saw it as successful teaching. But it is not clear that he did prove successful in his transmission of powers of diagnosis. Conan Doyle became in his own right a good detective, as the Edalji and Slater cases were to show. But his detection did not depend on powers of personal observation and deduction about the life and habits of individuals on the basis of tiny fragments of evidence of the kind Bell employed. His tribute to Bell is one to a performer rather than a teacher. Watson is much too modest a figure to try to ape Holmes, and Holmes never really succeeds in teaching his methods to Watson. Nor is there any evidence that he seeks to do so, any more than to seek a vulgar triumph once again when Watson under his instruction tries to use the methods and proves mistaken. The sorcerer has no intention of making his apprentice a competitor.

The one episode where Watson does try to put Holmes's methods into

action, one so grief-laden that it is wholly lacking in any self-aggrandisement
on his part, is his reading of the clues in "*The Final Problem*" to show that
Holmes and Moriarty have indeed gone to their deaths: and when Conan
Doyle decided to resurrect Holmes he does so by use of an inversion, with
Holmes using Holmesian clues to deceive Watson and his associates into
thinking Holmes has died by the means the evidence suggests. Elsewhere
Watson does show powers as a detective, but they are entirely different from
Holmes's. In *The Hound*, he follows up the problem of Selden and Barrymore
with dogged persistence and the maximisation of qualities he has in much
stronger degree than Holmes, his humanity above all. He sees the evidence
that Mrs Barrymore has been weeping, because the sound of weeping has
máde him anxious that somewhere in Baskerville Hall a human being is
suffering. His human sentiment results in his sparing the fleeing Selden and
concealing the role of the Barrymores as accessories: it is a splendid
expression of human decency on his part, but Holmes, while justly
complimenting him on his contribution to the case, merely comments
cynically to Sir Henry Baskerville that the absence of marks on Selden's
clothing which might have shown that the suit had come from Baskerville via
Barrymore is "lucky for [Barrymore]—in fact, it's lucky for all of you, since
you are all on the wrong side of the law in this matter. I am not sure that as a
conscientious detective my first duty is not to arrest the whole household.
Watson's reports are most incriminating documents." This seems quite
deliberate on Conan Doyle's part. The reader's emotions have been
thoroughly drawn in to the charity animating all four actors—Watson,
Baskerville and the Barrymores. There is something very beautiful in Mrs
Barrymore's continued love for her brother and grief when he is dead despite
his bestial and homicidal nature and her towering respectability.

> ". . . to me, sir, he was always the little curly-headed boy that I had nursed and
> played with, as an elder sister would. . . . When he dragged himself here one
> night, weary and starving, with the warders hard on his heels, what could we
> do? We took him in and fed him and cared for him. . . . Every day we hoped
> that he was gone, but as long as he was there we could not desert him. That is
> the whole truth, as I am an honest Christian woman, and you will see that if
> there is blame in the matter it does not lie with my husband, but with me, for
> whose sake he has done all that he has."

And Barrymore, from the somewhat sinister figure, suspected as the
murderous enemy of the Baskervilles, suspected as a domestic tyrant
assaulting his wife, proves to be a noble and stoical hero ready to risk
dismissal and disgrace for the sake of his wife even to the point of trying to
silence her rather than let her save him at risk to her brother. Watson and
Baskerville show corresponding love and nobility in Baskerville's forgiveness
of the Barrymores for their deception of him in sheltering Selden, Watson's
refusal to shoot the defenceless Selden, and their agreement to silence and
concealment of their discovery. Holmes, alone, is flippant and indifferent to
the humanity exhibited by the protagonists.

Conan Doyle, conscious of the persistence of his own and his family's love for his father despite all the misery and disgrace to which he had reduced them, perhaps conscious above all of Annette's abiding affection for him, is very clearly in sympathy with the Barrymores. He represents, as Watson does, the doctor concerned about the human element in the medical cases he examines; Holmes, analogously to Bell, is concerned with the case only so long as it remains in his consulting-room, or under his treatment. This facet of Holmes is characteristic from beginning to end. And even when Watson carries through detective-work irrelevant to human considerations, notably in the very late adventure "*The Retired Colourman*", he does so by natural human mnemonics, recalling the theatre-ticket number because it was his old school number. For all their years together, Conan Doyle never intended to suggest Holmes shone as a teacher, or was even trying so to do. Yet teaching was supposed to be Bell's job.

Curiously enough, Bell's failure to communicate his art to his student is the subject of a detail in "*A False Start*", one of the stories in the medical collection *Round the Red Lamp*, the book being published in 1894, but the story, unusually for that collection, being dropped from Conan Doyle's later assemblage of his works. There is an element of autobiography in the episode, although the estimate of the doctor's mental powers is only relevant to self-portraiture as a wild and freakish caricature to enable the author assert his modesty:

> Doctor Wilkinson planted himself behind his desk, and, placing his finger-tips together, he gazed with some apprehension at his companion. What was the matter with the man? He seemed very red in the face. Some of his old professors would have diagnosed his case by now, and would have electrified the patient by describing his own symptoms before he had said a word about them. Doctor Horace Wilkinson racked his brains for some clue, but Nature had fashioned him as a plodder—a very reliable plodder, and nothing more. He could think of nothing save that the visitor's watch-chain had a very brassy appearance, with a corollary to the effect that he would be lucky if he got half-a-crown out of him. Still, even half-a-crown was something in those early days of struggle.
>
> Whilst the doctor had been running his eyes over the stranger, the latter had been plunging his hands into pocket after pocket of his heavy coat. The heat of the weather, his dress, and this exercise of pocket rummaging had all combined to still further redden his face, which had changed from brick to beet, with a gloss of moisture on his brow. This extreme ruddiness brought a clue at last to the observant doctor. Surely it was not to be attained without alcohol. In alcohol lay the secret of this man's trouble. Some little delicacy was needed, however, in showing him that he had read his case aright, that at a glance he had penetrated to the inmost sources of his ailments.
>
> "It's very hot", observed the stranger, mopping his forehead.
>
> "Yes. It is weather which tempts one to drink rather more beer than is good for one", answered Doctor Horace Wilkinson looking very knowingly at his companion from over his finger-tips.
>
> "Dear! dear! You shouldn't do that."
>
> "I! I never touch beer."
>
> "Neither do I. I've been an abstainer for twenty years."

This was depressing. Doctor Wilkinson blushed until he was nearly as red as the other.

"May I ask what I can do for you?" he asked, picking up his stethoscope and tapping it gently against his thumb-nail.

"Yes, I was just going to tell you. I heard of your coming, but I couldn't get round before—"

He broke into a nervous little cough.

"Yes", said the doctor encouragingly.

"I should have been here three weeks ago, but you know how these things get put off."

He coughed again behind his large, red hand.

"I do not think that you need say any more", said the doctor, taking over the case with an easy air of command. "Your cough is quite sufficient. It is entirely bronchial by the sound. No doubt the mischief is circumscribed at present, but there is always the danger that it may spread, so you have done wisely to come to me. A little judicious treatment will soon set you right. Your waistcoat, please, but not your shirt. Puff out your chest, and say ninety-nine in a deep voice."

The red faced man began to laugh.

"It's all right, doctor", said he. "That cough comes from chewing tobacco, and I know it's a very bad habit. Nine and ninepence is what I have to say to you, for I'm the officer of the Gas Company, and they have a claim against you for that on the meter."

The last part of the encounter is probably autobiographical, for a variant of it occurs in *The Stark Munro Letters,* although the Gas Company man probably never got off anything as Shavian as saying nine and ninepence instead of ninety-nine. On the other hand, the early part is almost certainly fictional: alcoholism was one complaint Arthur was not likely to diagnose in error, having all too much practical acquaintance with it from his earliest years. The whole extract is a nice blend of ACD's courage and humour, showing his capacity to draw laughter out of two of the saddest things in his own life, supposed alcoholism undergoing medical analysis, and economic privation as a young professional making his start. A thread of slightly more bitter mockery runs through it: pompous young Horace Wilkinson makes a fool of himself misdiagnosing alcoholism, having had a protected childhood which kept him free from seeing it at close quarters. There is, too, the Irish and Scots amusement at English pretension, and seeing the possibilities for mistaken confession in what was intended as the aristocratic usage "one". But it still shows how little Bell could transmit his most famous talent to his pupils, and stands as a nice Conan Doyle satire on the Holmes (and Bell) method.

Joseph Bell did have qualities as teacher which were independent of his showmanship, and these included aphorisms and epigrams of the type lending themselves to mental retention. Perhaps the profoundest of these he had inherited from Syme and others, and some of his ideas betray a mind enjoying a voyage on wings of philosophical speculation, where logic brings results at total variance with reality. Bell admired, and may even have originated, Holmes's dictum on the mind which Bell summarised as "A man should keep his little brain-attic stocked with all the furniture that he is likely to use, as the rest he can put away in the lumber-room of his library, where he can get it if he wants it" (Holmes phrases it much more memorably and coherently in the second chapter of *A Study in Scarlet*). As we know, the theory proved quite unworkable, and *The Sign of Four* has advanced to the point where cultural literacy is acknowledged as needful rather than wasteful to the mind of the specialist in deduction. But Bell preferred the first idea, with all of its denial of the value of knowing the Copernican theory, or the identity of Carlyle. He saw Holmes as possessing "perhaps the best gift of all—the power of unloading the mind of all the burden of trying to remember unnecessary details". Much of the importance of Joe Bell, then, would be that his weakness as well as his strength would give Holmes his most notable of features, transmitted so clearly by Conan Doyle that Stevenson in Samoa wondered if this could be "my old friend Joe Bell". It was, but it was also many more.

The one other very firm identification of character with original made in *Memories and Adventures* raises a different set of problems:

> Most vividly of all, however, there stands out in my memory the squat figure of Professor Rutherford with his Assyrian beard, his prodigious voice, his enormous chest and his singular manner. He fascinated and awed us. I have endeavoured to reproduce some of his peculiarities in the ficticious character of Professor Challenger. He would sometimes start his lecture before he reached the classroom, so that we would hear a booming voice saying: "There are valves in the veins", or some other information, when the desk was still empty. He was, I fear a rather ruthless vivisector, and though I have always recognized that a minimum of painless vivisection is necessary, and far more justifiable than the eating of meat as food, I am glad that the law was made more stringent so as to restrain such men as he. "Ach, these Jarman Frags!" he would exclaim in his curious accent, as he tore some poor amphibian to pieces. I wrote a students' song which is still sung, I understand, in which a curious article is picked up on the Portobello beach and each Professor in turn claims it for his department. Rutherford's verse ran:

> *Said Rutherford with a smile, "It's a mass of solid bile,*
>   *And I myself obtained it, what is more,*
> *By a stringent cholagogue*
> *From a vivisected dog,*
>   *And I lost it on the Portobello Shore."*

(The dog was in fact quite authentic. Rutherford read a paper on it on 18 June 1878 to the Edinburgh Medico-Chirurgical Society, stringent cholagogue and all. Arthur was either present or read the report in Waller's copy of the *Edinburgh Medical Journal*, for November 1878.)

The historian, and perhaps the critic, may lament that ACD did not preserve the other verses among the poetic literary work he afterwards published in volume form, but at least this verse gives us a welcome, if rare, flash of Arthur among his fellow-students, using his powers of composition to delight them, making his earliest literary vivisection of his professors, and knowing his craft like a good professional, such that his last line of each verse would give work to the chorus. We have to think of a happy, beer-swilling band, roaring the words "Portobello Shore" in Rutherford's of Drummond Street, or perhaps Stewart's bar opposite with its fine engravings in frosted glass. The Rutherford verse was probably the best, and lent itself to recollection and reproduction for that reason.

Yet in certain ways neither the fictional Challenger nor his fragment of memoir supplies the reality of Rutherford. Recognizable features of Christison and Bell, Waller and Syme, Conan Doyle and Oliver Wendell Holmes, flicker into life as we look at Sherlock Holmes, all the more so because Holmes was created when Conan Doyle was still a highly derivative writer greatly dependent on his models. Even the man Arthur had never known, Syme, lived on in his practical laws for the surgeon which Professor John Chiene and others still quoted as frequently as possible in part to keep the polish on the glitter of the fading Golden Age: "Never believe what you are told", "Be persuaded in your own mind", and so on—excellent laws for the historian as well as the surgeon or the detective. On the other hand, *The Lost World* was written when its author was well over fifty, and had been writing with full professional mastery for over twenty years. It was no longer a case of drawing character by a mosaic technique, fearful of going any distance from proven human material. By the time of *The Lost World* ACD could use human material or no as he wished. Hesketh Pearson shrewdly notes that it was really Rutherford's physical characteristics which contributed to Challenger, and he then continues that in idiosyncracies, "fiery energy and uncertain temper . . . [Challenger is] copied direct from George Budd." Budd is certainly present in Challenger, but there is more than that to it; Pearson, having discovered Budd, discovered him everywhere. There is also something of Conan Doyle's friend of the '90s, George Bernard Shaw, who particularly impressed him for his ruthlessness towards the feelings of others, for his insensitivity towards their natural right to self-respect, for his pleasure in being perverse. It is singular that Pearson, so heavily under Shaw's influence in the 1940s, did not see how much GBS there is in GEC, even to the public self-allusion by means of initials, but Shaw was kind to Pearson and knew on which side of the biographical bread to do his buttering.

Conan Doyle makes much of the Rutherford basis to Challenger in what I suspect to be a symbolic shorthand. Edinburgh University is deeply present in the book through the Rectorial contests, through Christison and, as we shall see, through the expedition itself: hence he picks out his use of Rutherford. Surviving portraits of Rutherford do suggest that Assyrian beard, and no doubt Conan Doyle's recollection of the voice is correct. All the same, Rutherford was in other respects quite staggeringly different from Challenger. He was extremely shy, remained unmarried throughout his life, and many of his tricks of manner arose from his fear of human society, not his rejection of it. Challenger prides himself on not teaching at all: Rutherford was a brilliant lecturer—many people thought him the best in the university—but his brilliance seems to have been partly owed to his nervousness and tremendous anxiety to do his work well. Good lecturing is not a natural art: the best work is often elicited from the lecturer by his fear that he will fail.

Is there anything of Challenger in Rutherford, then, apart from the appearance? Not even the appearance holds good, indeed, in that Rutherford's photograph suggest an alarmed, uneasy, almost hunted, appearance, the great beard serving as defence and concealment of a timorous disposition rather than an oriflamme of aggression. Certainly Rutherford's commitment to teaching, which he maintained to his death in harness in 1899 at the age of sixty, is nowhere echoed in Challenger. There is perhaps an echo in Challenger's retirement from London academic life: Rutherford resigned two London Chairs of Physiology before returning to Edinburgh in 1873. But Challenger's love of controversy and ferocious contentiousness make him less like Rutherford than almost anyone else Arthur might have encountered among the Edinburgh professors: *The Lost World* does give a marvellous, exotic and hilarious indication of the academic arena of Edinburgh medical and scientific scholarship, and the extraordinary range of expertise achieved by so many of the protagonists, but Rutherford left very little impression on the minds of observers of those battles of giants. The furious disputations which had animated almost all advances of Edinburgh medical scholarship find few echoes in him, and his published writing, when it finds it necessary to mention established writers on medicine, is almost invariably courteous and favourable to them. He was bitterly assailed from outside of the academic world, by the antivivisectionists, but his colleagues largely supported him there. Even the smile in Conan Doyle's rhyme conveys a man more anxious to persuade than to refute. The clue probably lies in the statement of the geologist John Smith Flett, who followed Arthur at Edinburgh by a decade, and whose recollections of the Edinburgh medical faculty include the sentence:

Rutherford was a strange man, indeed it was difficult to believe he was not rather demented.

And Rutherford did ultimately become insane for a time before the end of his life. This, probably, is the main point apart from the physical appearance.

Rutherford supplied the spectacle of a brilliant public performer, master of exposition of his subject, and apparently half-insane. This is much of Challenger's appeal. In Moriarty Conan Doyle had drawn the Bad Professor, now, with Challenger—and later, with Maricot—he was to draw the Mad Professor. Pearson's complaint about his undue respect for "dons" looks even weaker when we take into account the full implications of what Conan Doyle was doing. He was showing the impact of pure scientific reasoning on the enlargement of popular understanding using fictional devices, and yet doing so with the fullest possible resources of comedy. It requires singular greatness to celebrate academic genius while making it of the widest interest and the utmost hilarity. The fact that the Bad Professor and the Mad Professor, like the Great Detective, were subsequently cheapened by innumerable imitations does not gainsay the achievement of the original. Challenger in particular is splendidly poised between the heroic and the absurd and holds that position through to the end.

Challenger is certainly Scottish, although only his *curriculum vitae* as presented in *The Lost World* gives any sign of it, and the Scots news editor McArdle is far more anxious to have him done down than seems consistent with the record of the Scots in London journalism in dealing with the reputations of their fellow-countrymen in public life, a record of which Dr Johnson took sour note. Challenger, unlike McArdle, has no note of Scots accent: Rutherford's must have made his life a little miserable during his London sojourn. There might have been a touch of Rutherford's initial conversation with Conan Doyle in Challenger's first exchanges with Edward Dunn Malone after their initial fracas, if we omit the insulting portions:

> "I am going to talk to you about South America", said he. "No comments if you please. First of all, I wish you to understand that nothing I tell you now is to be repeated in any public way unless you have my express permission. That permission will, in all human probability, never be given. Is that clear?"
>
> "It is very hard", said I. "Surely a judicious account—"
>
> He replaced the notebook upon the table.
>
> "That ends it", said he. "I wish you a very good morning."
>
> "No, no!" I cried. "I submit to any conditions. So far as I can see I have no choice."
>
> "None in the world", said he.
>
> "Well, then, I promise."
>
> "Word of honour?"
>
> "Word of honour."
>
> He looked at me with doubt in his insolent eyes.
>
> "After all, what do I know about your honour?" said he.
>
> "Upon my word, sir", I cried, angrily, "you take very great liberties! I have never been so insulted in my life."
>
> He seemed more interested than annoyed at my outbreak.
>
> "Round-headed", he muttered. "Brachycephalic, grey-eyed, black-haired, with suggestion of the negroid. Celtic, I presume?"
>
> "I am an Irishman, sir."
>
> "Irish Irish?"
>
> "Yes, sir."
>
> "That, of course, explains it. . . ."

Preoccupation with the cephalic peculiarities of an interlocutor offers a workable means for a shy professor to avoid the need for direct human engagement. Somebody seems to have talked like this to Conan Doyle, if we compare Mortimer's preoccupation with the same subject in *The Hound,* and Edinburgh University seems the obvious place for him to have encountered them, but again Rutherford is far from being the only candidate.

We do find a case for Rutherford in a fairly odd place, though, and one generally written off as a bad watering down of the Challenger portrait: the fictionalised case against the persecution of Spiritualists, *The Land of Mist.* The novel is in many ways weak, episodic, and much too much the pamphleteer using fictional devices rather than the fictional artist integrating a crusade into his fiction. Yet there are important signs in *The Land of Mist* that, apart from the need to make a case for his religious beliefs and their defenders, Conan Doyle wants to probe much more deeply than before into what makes Challenger tick. Abstract devotion to science was all Conan

Doyle could discover of the motives of most of his preceptors in Edinburgh, with some refinements contingent on that devotion, such as college politics in Turner's case, lecturing mastery in Rutherford's, medical and socio-economic public diagnosis in Bell's. But his conversion to Spiritualism meant that he had formally rejected materialism, and with it a science whose practitioners might go to church on Sunday but whose scholarship showed no signs of it. Challenger is finally converted to Spiritualism in *The Land of Mist* when he receives a message that two men whom he had treated with a dangerous drug had died not, as he had feared throughout his life, from his remedy, but from their original disease. Clumsily perhaps, yet credibly, we are led to realise that his violence has been partly induced by self-reproach repressed over the years. It is not a bad piece of psychology. It certainly does seem consistent in character-analysis, if not in incident, with Rutherford's tremendous platform performance and Assyrian appearance masking profound diffidence and self-doubt. The self-doubt did not involve a doubt of science: it was himself Rutherford doubted, not his histology or physiology.

There may also be consistency in that Challenger has sought to repress a memory from his very early life as a young physician, whence he graduates to natural science without direct dealing with living medical subjects. Rutherford might have had memories that haunted him from his days as a medical student before he became a teacher and spent his energies in the vivisection of animals rather than in the restoration of humans. ACD himself may also have had a long, self-reproachful memory about some possible error in treatment of a patient on his part which might have led to that patient's death—with the problem forever insoluble thereafter. But we can be quite sure such a point would not in the least have worried Joe Bell, whose *Manual* abounds in cool examples where the cure was a success and the subsequent death of the patient a minor tailpiece to the case. To Watson, as to Conan Doyle, the sequel to a case seemed important; to Holmes, as to Bell, it did not. Perhaps once upon a time it had been important to Rutherford.

In the passage of *Memories and Adventures* before his memories of Rutherford, Conan Doyle furnishes a clue of a very different kind to the origins of *The Lost World:* he lists among the professors whom he heard and "managed to know . . . pretty well without any personal acquaintance . . . Wyville Thomson, the zoologist, fresh from his *Challenger* expedition". Behind this lies Arthur's first formal encounter with high adventure, in which science and romance were joined with almost dizzying interaction. *The Lost World*'s first chapter-heading "There are Heroisms All Round Us" acquires outstanding force when we think of Arthur commencing his University career to be told that the 46-year-old Professor of Natural History from whom he was to take lectures had been the leader of the most scientific expedition in the history of exploration, and had only returned from it the previous May having taken three and a half years and travelled 68,890 nautical miles. The *Challenger* expedition would ultimately supply Conan Doyle with the idea of a great and triumphantly successful expedition of scientists, as its name supplied that of the hero, to be realised in *The Lost World*, but there is even greater association with his last major scientific romance, *The Maracot Deep*, whose first version was drafted when he was in his late sixties.

As *The Maracot Deep* acknowledges, the *Challenger* had plumbed the deepest underwater "deeps" hitherto recorded, the deepest of all, 27,000 feet and 4,500 fathoms, at 11°24' North 143°16' East, being named after Herbert Swire, the lively young Navigating Sub-Lieutenant, who kept a cheerful, valuable and irreverent journal of the expedition published after his death in 1934. The invitation to the narrator of *The Lost World*, Malone, to name the central lake of the plateau (which he fatuously names Lake Gladys after the girl whose tawdry ambition to be known as the consort of a hero sends him on his adventures) seems a direct echo of this. In *The Lost World* the journalist Malone writes the lively reports sent home, seriatim, in journal-style reports. The fourth member is an aristocrat, Lord John Roxton, and Conan Doyle's writing had been distinguished for its deflation of aristocratic pretension. The origin of these facts would seem to be that the popular account of the *Challenger* expedition published in the year of its return was *Log-Letters from "The Challenger"* by Sub-Lieutenant Lord George Campbell, a younger son of Gladstone's most factious cabinet collegue in his first two Governments, the eighth Duke of Argyll. The Duke had some (exaggerated) literary credentials, and Lord George, in his mid-twenties during the voyage, showed himself an observer, writer and traveller of infectious boyish enthusiasm and charm. A very dull but widely-read account by Engineer Sub-Lieutenant W. J. J. Spry, *The Cruise of H.M.S. "Challenger"*, quickly followed Lord George's book; Wyville Thomson's volumes on the Atlantic phases of the voyage also appeared, severely academic though much of them is; his secretary J. J. Wild brought out his *At Anchor* in 1878; and the next year saw the naturalist H. N. Moseley add his *Notes* of the expedition to the rising pile of literature. Wyville Thomson, knighted as Sir Charles Wyville Thomson on his return, died in 1882 when no doubt the obituaries would have reawakened Arthur's interest in the whole affair, but between 1885 and 1895 some fifty volumes of a report appeared from his surviving scientific associates.

Exactly how much the whole story impinged on Arthur during the lifetime of Wyville Thomson is hard to say. It does not sound as if his first-hand information from the professor amounted to much more than what could be teased out of him at lectures, though it may have been hard for him to restrain himself in giving illustrations from his expedition relevant to his exposition of zoology, and harder to restrain the students' demand for them. Most of the explorers, especially the literary sub-lieutenants, were not Edinburgh-based, but ACD may have been luckier with Wyville Thomson's chief assistant, John Murray, who although by now in his late thirties had been a "chronic" medical student at Edinburgh so wayward in his studies as to earn the rebuke of Robert Louis Stevenson! Murray, of Scottish parents and Canadian birth, had studied under several of Arthur's future teachers, including the chemist Alexander Crum Brown, and the anatomist Turner, but his chief Mentor was the Professor of Natural Philosophy Peter Guthrie Tait at whose recommendation he was given a place on Wyville Thomson's team vacated at the last moment. It would be in a similar situation that Conan Doyle accepted the place of ship's surgeon to a Greenland whaler eight years later. Murray himself had also served as surgeon to a whaler for seven months in the Arctic Ocean in 1868. On his return after the *Challenger* expedition he briefly resumed activities as "chronic" medical student but quickly became indispensible in the Challenger Office when it was set up early in 1877 at 32 Queen Street, near at hand to *Blackwood's*. He constitutes the likeliest personal informant on the expedition Arthur might have met, possibly through the offices of Waller whose arrival in Edinburgh in 1871 would have enabled him overlap with Murray's last contemporaries as a student. Murray's work on the 50-volume *Report* was vital: he became its chief editor on Wyville Thomson's death. The parallels and overlap with Arthur's Edinburgh life suggest direct influence rather than continuance.

Conan Doyle uses the name Murray twice in his early work, both times as the name of a man who saves the life of the narrator—Watson's at the beginning of *A Study in Scarlet,* J. Habakuk Jephson's in the opening of his *"Statement"*. Murray certainly saved the life of the *Challenger* Report and hence the lasting reputation of the expedition. An obvious point where Arthur could have first seen Murray in action was his lecture on the expedition to the Edinburgh Literary Insitute. Hugh Robert Mill, writing in *British Rainfall,* 1913, described it (dating it 1878) and it would have been a useful support for Arthur's studies under Wyville Thomson:

> A thick-set man with a defiant air and a voice of tremendous power. . . . His was a style of speaking I had never heard before—not an echo of the learning of books, but the authoritative tone of one who described what he himself had seen and reasoned out. The account he then gave of the origin of deep-sea deposits was a revelation of the workings of Nature that can never be forgotten. Here was a man, as yet unknown to fame, who tore to pieces the beautiful theories of Maury, and showed beneath them raw facts just wrenched from the abysses of Nature, yet piled already into a cyclopean structure shining in the dawning light . . .

This also suggests a link with the inspiration for Challenger, as does Mill's remark that the atmosphere in the *Challenger* office under Murray was "that of a world where there was no such word as 'impossible' ". Murray, a forceful, rough diamond of Canadian birth, was known for his rudeness to subordinates while being ready to give belated acknowledgment of their sounder ideas. He was a convivial figure, singing with enthusiasm the shanties he had picked up on the *Challenger,* and he led research expeditions on the coastal waters of Scotland at points where Arthur was prospecting with his camera. Murray also turned his attention to the earth's crust, as Challenger was to do in *"When the World Screamed"*.

But Murray, in his turn, also shares an important experience in common with Sherlock Holmes. The account of Holmes's medical curriculum as given by Stamford reads very like Murray's:

> ". . . I have no idea what he intends to go in for. I believe he is well up in anatomy, and he is a first-class chemist; but, as far as I know, he has never

taken out any systematic medical classes. His studies are very desultory and eccentric, but he has amassed a lot of out-of-the-way knowledge which would astonish his professors. . . .

"He is sure to be at the laboratory. . . . He either avoids the place for weeks, or else he works there from morning till night.

". . . Heaven alone knows what the object of his studies are. . . ."

If Arthur was introduced to Murray during the latter's return to his "chronic" studies it was certainly with more information than this, as the *Challenger* naturally gave an identity to Murray's pursuits now. But Murray and Holmes were similar in their enormous range of specialisation, their contempt for prescribed degree curricula, their enthusiasm for the pursuit of one form of research for a period of time followed by movement elsewhere.

Even before the *Challenger* set sail Murray had a reputation; after the voyage he would certainly have been the most famous student of his time. Singularly, his overlap with Conan Doyle from Autumn 1876 to Spring 1877 was his very last manifestation as student, and after *A Study in Scarlet* Holmes visits the hospital laboratories no more. ACD had his doubts as to the value of the official degree curriculum, and it would hardly have escaped his notice that his most distinguished contemporary in the scientific world had pointedly ignored it: and Murray had taken over the *Challenger* office after Wyville Thomson's death, and begun rapidly to rise in celebrity, by the time *A Study in Scarlet* was written. So it would seem that to Bell, Christison, Syme, Waller and others John Murray must be added to the medical and scientific attendants on the birth of Sherlock Holmes.

One odd little pointer to the contemporary influence of the *Challenger* expedition on the pen of the young Conan Doyle is a curious item of nomenclature in *A Study in Scarlet*. The suspect wrongly arrested by Gregson for the murder of Drebber is "Arthur Charpentier, sub-lieutenant in Her Majesty's navy". Now the crew of the *Challenger* included two names remarkably similar to that. Sub-lieutenant Arthur Channer is recorded by Moseley as riding some sixty miles with him across the Falklands to Port Stanley (most of those they met on the way being Scottish shepherds), also explored Kerguelen with him, and became notable as one of the finest caricaturists of the expedition. Lieutenant Alfred Carpenter, who joined the *Challenger* at Hong Kong from the *Iron Duke* in January 1875, was awarded the Albert Medal for driving into a bitterly cold sea around the Falklands to rescue a sailor named Bush whom he recovered alive and brought to the *Challenger;* Bush died some hours later but Carpenter survived. ACD wrote *A Study In Scarlet* at a time when his imagination was still heavily saturated by his unconscious memory. Had he thought about it, he would never have given a murder suspect a name and profession so close to that of real-life persons, one of them likely to have won his utmost admiration. The imaginary Charpentier is chivalrous and rash, but puts himself in peril by a suspicious absence resultant on what looks like a roister with an old shipmate. But if Arthur had combed the accounts of the expedition, and perhaps talked with Murray in detail about it, the name would have swum readily into his mind when thinking about Navy Sub-Lieutenants.

Whether in later life Conan Doyle won more details of the expedition from survivors is conjectural. Lord George Campbell, who wore his monocle and brought his Newfoundland dog throughout the world, lived until 1915, and Captain Herbert Swire, the last survivor of the expedition, outlived ACD to die in December 1934. What makes such speculation of some minor importance is that the division in *The Lost World* between the professors, on the one hand, and Lord John Roxton and Malone, on the other, is decidedly marked. There is no such separation of Holmes and Watson, at any point. There is a touch of exhibiting the professors as fauna as remote from the human norm in their way as the prehistoric monsters. Lord John, who in birth, life-style and speech must be almost as alien to Malone, acts with him in a natural collegiality to circumvent the impracticality of Challenger and Summerlee. Now, the similar division between the ship's company, and Wyville Thomson and the scientists, is a very marked feature of the literature, but nowhere more so than in Herbert Swire's posthumously published account, where the academics are irreverently presented as "the philosophers". Two points obtain with respect to Swire's account in its sixty years of non-publication: Swire sent it to his family, but also permitted others to see it; Swire deleted in his final years with a view of publication the most unkind references to persons taking part in the expedition. Did Conan Doyle meet Swire and see the splendid journal? We do not know. But if he did, he would have seen the more ribald features of the irreverent comments on the scientists, features now lost to us. It would have supplied a valuable source for the tone of *The Lost World*. On the other hand, the accounts of all parties say little of academic controversy, and this was clearly directly imported into *The Lost World* not from any account of the *Challenger* expedition but for those they had left behind in Edinburgh. Christison alone, in presence and in reputation, would have supplied the source for any such controversial argument.

Wyville Thomson can hardly rank as a suitable father for Challenger, save very indirectly. Yet in one respect there is a closeness between Swire's view of him and Malone's of Challenger. Challenger's poise between heroism and absurdity, noted above, recalls Falstaff, and it was in fact Falstaff of whom the irreverent Swire was reminded in thinking of Wyville Thomson. One of his caricatures directly quotes Falstaff's description of himself while playing King Henry IV: "A good portly man, i' faith, and a corpulent; of a cheerful look, a pleasing eye, and a most noble carriage; and, as I think, his age some fifty, or, by'r lady, inclining to three-score; and now I remember me his name is . . ." On the whole, I incline to the belief Conan Doyle met Swire before 1911 and was shown the journal. His recollection of his student days would have supplied a credential for being given the privilege.

Arthur was brief about his other teachers in his recollections. Crum Brown he recalled as sheltering himself carefully "before exploding some mixture, which usually failed to ignite, so that the loud 'Boom!' uttered by the class was the only resulting sound. Brown would emerge from his retreat with a 'Really gentlemen!' of remonstrance, and go on without allusion to the abortive experiment." Yet Crum Brown resembled his colleagues in the disparity of his interests, something to which Conan Doyle paid tribute in indicating the extraordinary range of scholarly attainments on the finger-tips of Challenger, Summerlee and Sherlock Holmes. Crum Brown himself, for instance, learned the art of knitting, and knitted a perfect closed cylinder which still excites the admiration of historians of science.

John Hutton Balfour, aged 68 when Arthur arrived at the University, moved his annoyance for his "face and manner of John Knox, a hard rugged old man, who harried the students in their exams, and was in consequence harried by them for the rest of the year", and it may be he who inspired the cruel portrait of John Girdlestone with his Calvinist manner and his indifferent conscience. Yet Balfour was a cold but important link with the past, who had taught Botany to Wyville Thomson in 1850 as well as to Conan Doyle nearly thirty years later, and who lived to lament Christison in words which show how he could communicate in his subject what he could never do in person: "I cannot speak sufficiently of the happy days I have spent with him in the Botanic Garden. I have lost one who was also a kind physician to me during illness. *Requiescat in pace.*"

Arthur Conan Doyle graduated M.B. in 1881. Many years after his death, a film was brought out about a mentally disturbed man imagining himself Sherlock Holmes which, thinking of the great original for Holmes, *Don Quixote*, took as its theme the reflection that when Don Quixote attacked the windmills under the belief that they were giants, yet, said its title, *They Might Be Giants*. Of the University in which he studied and its attendant hospitals, some of the faculty remembered giants, and some still were. In his own distinctive fashion he remains their greatest celebrant. But for their coldness, which so closely reminded him of Sparta, he substituted that artistic warmth which elicited that somewhere concealed by Sparta, Athens survived.

8

The Long Voyage Home

Call me Ishmael.

> —Herman Melville,
> *Moby-Dick*.

A trader sailed from Stepney town—
Wake her up! Shake her up! Try her with the mainsail!
A trader sailed from Stepney town
With a keg full of gold and a velvet gown:
       Ho, the bully rover Jack,
       Waiting with his yard aback
Out upon the Lowland sea!

The trader he had a daughter fair—
Wake her up! Shake her up! Try her with the foresail!
The trader he had a daughter fair,
She had gold in her ears, and gold in her hair:
       All for bully rover Jack,
       Waiting with his yard aback,
Out upon the Lowland sea!

"Alas the day, oh daughter mine!"—
Wake her up! Shake her up! Try her with the topsail!
"Alas the day, oh daughter mine!
Yon red, red flag is a fearsome sign!"
       Ho, the bully rover Jack,
       Reaching on the weather tack,
Out upon the Lowland sea!

"A fearsome flag!" the maiden cried—
Wake her up! Shake her up! Try her with the jibsail!
"A fearsome flag!" the maiden cried,
"But comelier men I never have spied!"
       Ho, the bully rover Jack,
       Reaching on the weather tack,
Out upon the Lowland sea!

There's a wooden path that the rovers know—
Wake her up! Shake her up! Try her with the headsails!

> *There's a wooden path that the rovers know,*
> *Where none come back, though many must go:*
>   *Ho, the bully rover Jack,*
>   *Lying with his yard aback,*
> *Out upon the Lowland sea!*
>
> *Where is the trader of Stepney town?—*
> *Wake her up! Shake her up! Every stick a-bending!*
> *Where is the trader of Stepney town?*
> *There's gold on the capstan, and blood on the gown:*
>   *Ho for bully rover Jack,*
>   *Waiting with his yard aback,*
> *Out upon the Lowland sea!*
>
> *Where is the maiden who knelt at his side?—*
> *Wake her up! Shake her up! Every stitch a-drawing!*
> *Where is the maiden who knelt at his side?*
> *We gowned her in scarlet, and chose her our bride:*
>   *Ho, the bully rover Jack,*
>   *Reaching on the weather tack,*
> *Right across the Lowland sea!*
>
> *So it's up and it's over to Stornoway Bay,*
> *Pack it on! Crack it on! Try her with the stunsails!*
> *It's off on a bowline to Stornoway Bay,*
> *Where the liquor is good and the lasses are gay:*
>   *Waiting for their bully Jack,*
>   *Watching for him sailing back,*
> *Right across the Lowland sea.*

It sounds amusing, if you don't try to ask yourself what it means. Conan Doyle did want you to, and that supplies the keynote to all of his writing on the sea. He revered Robert Louis Stevenson, yet he could never bring himself to prettify a pirate as Long John Silver is prettified. Silver, for all of the murders of Alan and Tom—and the somewhat more justifiable killing of George Merry—is the hero of *Treasure Island*. Conan Doyle could not do that. For one thing, his sense of historical reality was too strong. It was not that he insisted villains must be villains, *per se*. The reader is allowed to admire the academic genius of Professor Moriarty, the military courage of Colonel Moran, the ape-man king's similarity to Professor Challenger, the diplomacy of Uncle Bernac, the ambiguities of Napoleon. Compassion is freely extended to villains in the eyes of the law, once repentance has been established: Ryder, Captain Croker, Dr Leon Sterndale. But evil was evil. He came not from a doubting Calvinism, like Stevenson, but from a rejected Catholicism, which he supported in embracing the sinner yet hating the sin. And mortal sin persisted in, marked the sinner as accursed. Hence Conan Doyle produced the most horrifying vision of the pirate leader shown to a popular audience: Captain Sharkey.

The four Sharkey stories, three from 1897, the fourth a decade later, are masterly studies in cruelty and its psychological effects, and reminders of how effortless Conan Doyle's writing could seem in throwing off a short story based on a weight of research. The stories themselves come from the last formal phase of piracy, around 1720 (although another story, *"The* Slapping Sal" gives a realistic theory as to an outbreak of piracy in the early nineteenth century, significantly close to the mutinies at the Nore and Spithead), but while ACD was at some pains to establish the distinction between earlier phases and that final one, exhibiting the degeneration of the latter, he endowed Sharkey with several of the more colourful attributes of seventeenth-century freebooters. In *"The Blighting of Sharkey"*, for instance, the pirate crew turn against their captain, initially for braining Bartholomew, the carpenter, with a bucket. Captain Kidd, unfairly tried even by the standards of the day, was found guilty on the first count of the murder of William Moore with a bucket valued at eightpence. However the main original for Sharkey seems to have been Captain Edward Low, of the *Good Fortune* (Sharkey's ship is the *Happy Delivery*). Conan Doyle actually mentions Low in an introductory passage as on the same level of "amazing and grotesque brutality" as Sharkey but Patrick Pringle, author of a cool re-evaluation of piracy, *Jolly Roger*, points out that the account of Low as "a ferocious brute . . . of unequalled cruelty" given by the standard early eighteenth century authority (perhaps in many senses), Captain Charles Johnson's *General History of the Robberies and Murders of the Most Notorious Pyrates*, is scarcely borne out by the memoirs of Captain George Roberts, who fell into Low's hands and found him civil and courteous: in any case Mr Pringle suspects that the account of Low owed something to earlier buccaneer stories in its turn. There was hard evidence enough of brutality of pirates on lines similar to those of Sharkey, whatever doubts might exist in the specific case of Low. Certainly Low was very much in Conan Doyle's mind: his name is actually present within that of Sharkey's quartermaster, Roaring *Ned* Gal*low*ay. Perhaps the Roberts case supplied Sharkey's antecedent for sparing Captain Scarrow in the first story *"How the Governor of Saint Kitt's Came Home"*.

All the same, what distinguishes the stories is their grace and movement in the water, much more than the historical basis of Sharkey's brutality. Take the elegance of the end of *"The Governor of Saint Kitt's"* when Sharkey, having captured Scarrow on his own ship, makes preparations for his own departure:

> "Now, Captain Scarrow, we must take our leave of you", said the pirate. "If I had half a dozen of my brisk boys at my heels I should have had your cargo and your ship, but Roaring Ned could not find a foremast hand with the spirit of a mouse. I see there are some small craft about, and we shall get one of them. When Captain Sharkey has a boat he can get a smack, when he has a smack he can get a brig, when he has a brig he can get a barque, and when he has a barque he'll soon have a full-rigged ship of his own—so make haste into London town, or I may be coming back, after all, for the *Morning Star.*"

And when after his departure Scarrow manages to get free, Sharkey and Galloway are away in a dinghy:

> Down splashed the long-boat and down splashed the gig, but in an instant the coxswains and crews were swarming up the falls on to the deck once more.
> "The boats are scuttled!" they cried. "They are leaking like a sieve."
> The captain gave a bitter curse. He had been beaten and outwitted at every point. Above was a cloudless, starlit sky, and neither wind nor the promise of it. The sails flapped idly in the moonlight. Far away lay a fishing-smack, with the men clustering over their net.
> Close to them was the little dinghy, dipping and lifting over the shining swell.
> "They are dead men!" cried the captain. "A shout all together, boys, to warn them of their danger."
> But it was too late.
> At that very moment the dinghy shot into the shadow of the fishing-boat. There were two rapid pistol-shots, a scream, and then another pistol-shot, followed by silence. The clustering fishermen had disappeared. And then, suddenly, as the first puffs of a land-breeze came out from the Sussex shore, the boom swung out, the mainsail filled, and the little craft crept out with her nose to the Atlantic.

And that is that: it is almost as though a painting of a seascape became animated, with immediate homicidal consequences. The sense of menace lurking under the appearance of peace is particularly well done as the once peaceful and now murderous little craft will move to the next point of prey, and its victim to the next, and all now clear to the reader without a further word being necessary. Or take the next story, *"The Dealings of Captain Sharkey with Stephen Craddock"*, where the vainglorious Craddock, trying to capture Sharkey, is captured himself and breaks free at the last moment to alert the awaiting British sloop that the craft now moving towards it is not commanded by his victorious self but by the murderous Sharkey:

> The dark head appearing on the crest of the roller, and then swooping down on the other side, was already half-way to the sloop. Sharkey dwelt long upon his aim before he fired. With the crack of the gun the swimmer reared himself up in the water, waved his hands in a gesture of warning, and roared out in a voice which rang over the bay. Then, as the sloop swung round her head-sails, and the pirate fired an impotent broadside, Stephen Craddock, smiling grimly in his death agony, sank slowly down to that golden couch which glimmered far beneath him.

Again the tempo is all-important here, the contrasts of fast and slow, the suggestion of water now increasing now retarding the human frame in movement. In his very last reprint of them, Conan Doyle gave these and other sea stories the title *Tales of Pirates and Blue Water*, but the blue water was much more important to the success of the writing than the pirates.

And the Greenland whaler voyage was at the heart of this success: it was its effects which won him his first literary triumph. The line from the cruise of the whaler *Hope* in 1880 to the Sharkey stories of 1897 is at its clearest in the tale of *"How Copley Banks Slew Captain Sharkey"*, for it concludes with Sharkey being overpowered by Banks and tied up to await the burning of a candle-flame until it detonates enough powder to blow up the ship, while upstairs their drunken crews are heard from time to time raised in musical salutation of the socio-economic relations between the trader of Stepney Town and the bully Rover Jack:

The words came clear to his ear, and just outside he could hear two men pacing backwards and forwards upon the deck. And yet he was helpless, staring down the mouth of the nine-pounder, unable to move an inch or to utter so much as a groan. Again there came the burst of voices from the deck of the barque.

> So it's up and it's over to Stornoway Bay,
> Pack it on! Crack it on! Try her with the stun-sails!
> It's off on a bowline to Stornoway Bay,
> Where the liquor is good and the lasses are gay . . .

The song is Conan Doyle's, only three verses being used to supply Sharkey with his hideously cheery death-knell, but the whole published in his *Songs of Action* in 1898. Good sculptor, he first wrote his song in full, then extracted enough of it to see Sharkey off without breaking up the story. The vernacular does not matter—he had no interest in getting in the way of his pirates and blue water by having Captain Sharkey talk like Sir Roger de Coverley—but the last verse is a little out of the way for the Captain and his associates in the West Indies. A simultaneous enthusiasm for the Isle of Lewis on the part of two pirate crews drawn from the scum of North American and Caribbean waters argues a spiritual imperialism for the Hebrides such as even the author of the *"Canadian Boat Song"* did not venture to imply. The origin is clear enough. On the *Hope* Arthur heard some sea-shanty from the crew which was about a Hebridean landfall, in their cases a reasonable choice enough, since many of them would be western islanders. Naturally the song would have a theme, indeed a seemingly separate theme, alluding to the work required on the sails. Equally naturally it would speak of an agreeable and nearby port. On the other hand the enthusiasm for the lassies of Stornoway would be the customary quest for what they might give, as opposed to Rover Jack's procedure which fairly clearly was one of what he chose to take. But as Arthur listened, perhaps to lines almost identical about Stornoway, the very first lines to be created in the Sharkey saga were beating themselves into being.

The chain of memory, at its most powerful with music and song, linked Sharkey to the *Hope*. In thematic terms the voyage is also linked to the Sherlock Holmes story *"Black Peter"*, in the *Return*—in that case an interval of over twenty years separating voyage and writing. But its links to literary achievement are even greater than that. It directly supplied inspiration for his first two really good stories, *"That Little Square Box"*, published in *London Society* in 1881, and *"The Captain of the 'Pole-Star' "*, which appeared in *Temple Bar* in January 1883. It was the sea which discovered the literary genius of Arthur Conan Doyle. These two stories were the very first he wished to preserve in making his own book collections of his work, and he retained them in the corpus of his work he wished to survive him.

His ideas on an author's methods, put forward thirty years after his voyage as *"Advice to a young Author"*, assert the whole business of writing in naval terms. The poem is exceedingly important, not only for ACD, but for a summation of a master literary workman's views on his trade, and as such claims comparison with Trollope's *Autobiography* and Wodehouse's *Performing Flea*.

First begin
Taking in.
Cargo stored,
All aboard,
Think about
Giving out.
Empty ship,
Useless trip!

Never strain
Weary brain.
Hardly fit,
Wait a bit!
After rest
Comes the best.
Sitting still,
Let it fill;
Never press;
Nerve stress
Always shows
Nature knows.

Critics kind,
Never mind!
Critics flatter,
No matter!
Critics curse,
None the worse!
Critics blame,
All the same!
Do your best.
Hang the rest!

Apart from conveying why ACD was not only a great author, but a *loved* author, the form of the poem carries its own message. It is fitting that the great economist of the short story should present his advice so economically. In autobiographical terms, he used the same metaphor of the ship. Speaking of the early 1880s, *Memories and Adventures* says, with over-finality, "though I was not drawing out I was taking in. I still have note-books full of all sorts of knowledge which I acquired during that time. It is a great mistake to start putting out cargo when you have hardly stowed any on board. My own slow methods and natural limitations made me escape this danger". The metaphor is its own inversion: it was going on board ship that gave him something really substantial to take on board his creative ship. *"That Little Square Box"* and, much more substantially, *"The Captain of the 'Pole-Star' "* are his first uses of material inspired by personal experience, and the distance between them and his first published work is the distance between literature and ephemera. Certainly even before his voyage on the *Hope* he had made excellent progress. From *"The Haunted Grange of Goresthorpe"*:

Looking back now at the events of my life that one dreadful night looms out like some great landmark. Even now, after the lapse of so many years, I cannot think of it without a shudder. All minor incidents and events I mentally classify as occurring before or after the time when I saw a Ghost.

Yes, saw a ghost. Don't be incredulous, reader, don't sneer at the phrase; though I can't blame you for I was incredulous enough myself once. However hear the facts of my story before you pass a judgement. . . .

Was it only one year, or two, before that gave way to *"The Mystery of Sasassa Valley"*?

Do I know why Tom Donahue is called "Lucky Tom"? Yes, I do; and that is more than one in ten of those who call him so can say. I have knocked about a deal in my time, and seen some strange sights, but none stranger than the way in which Tom gained that sobriquet, and his fortune with it. For I was with him at the time.—Tell it? Oh, certainly; but it is a longish story, and a very strange one; so fill up your glass again, and light another cigar while I try to reel it off. Yes; a very strange one; beats some fairy stories I have heard; but it's true sir, every word of it. There are men alive at Cape Colony now who will remember it and confirm what I say. Many a time has the tale been told round the fire in Boers' cabins from Orange State to Griqualand; yes, and out in the Bush and at the Diamond Fields too. . . .

And a few months later *"The American's Tale"* in which an Englishman is saved from lynching when his supposed victim proves to have been absorbed (temporarily) and killed (permanently) by the action of an Arizona "fly-catcher" ("Dianoea muscipula", as one character, no doubt with some inspiration from Wyville Thomson or Balfour, kindly points out) concludes:

"And what became of Scott?" asked Jack Sinclair.

"Why, we carried him back on our shoulders, we did, to Simpson's bar, and he stood us liquors round. Made a speech, too—a darned fine speech—from the counter. Somethin' about the British lion an' the 'Merican eagle walkin' arm in arm forever an' a day. And now, sirs, that yarn was long, and my cheroot's out, so I reckon I'll make tracks afore it's later"; and with a "Good-night!" he left the room.

"A most extraordinary narrative!" said Dawson. "Who would have thought a Dianoea had such power!"

"Deuced rum yarn!" said young Sinclair.

"Evidently a matter-of-fact, truthful man", said the doctor.

"Or the most original liar that ever lived", said I. I wonder which he was.

The last ironic interplay certainly represents an advance on the poor *"Haunted Grange"* with its pathetic little empty fraud of a sub-title "A True Ghost Story". But it is revealing that all three stories have preoccupation with their own veracity. Even the sub-title was revived when Arthur wrote *"The Gully of Bluemansdyke"* ("A True Colonial Story") for *London Society* to turn a few pennies in 1881: this may well have been the time "when a paper sent me a woodcut and offered me four guineas if I would write a story to correspond [and] I was not too proud to accept". So little impact did the true colonial narrative make on its author that when he played with the idea of the mass murderer turning informer in *"My Friend the Murderer"*, he used the same character who is described as so saving himself in the *"Gully"*, but accidentally based the reference to the events in the earlier story as having taken place in New Zealand and not, as he originally designed them, Australia. The ambiguity of the close of *"The American's Tale"*, however, is serious in its artistic purpose: is "the doctor", the name by which Arthur would afterwards refer to Waller in correspondence, a private joke here in that "the doctor" makes an emphatic, self-assured, infallible-sounding judgment, upholding the veracity of what is clearly a Munchausen fable? The story certainly meant more to its author than the *"Gully"* was to do (apart from the latter's introduction of the disciple of Hare and precursor of Blessington, Wolf[e] Tone Maloney).

Another story from 1880, *"That Veteran"*, also worries about the question of truth, but this time has a string of lies and stolen reminiscences being used by a thief with which to beguile and rob a violently anti-Welsh visitor to Wales who turns with relief to an English interlocutor. Both here and some years later in *"The Heiress of Glenmahowley"*, Conan Doyle showed himself very much alive to the bad manners of English visitors in Celtic regions, and seems thoroughly to enjoy the narrator being swindled by the one English man he finds among the supposedly dishonest Welsh. ("My opinions of the original Celt, his manners, customs, and above all his language, were very much too forcible to be expressed in decent society. The ruling passion of my life seemed to have become a deep and all-absorbing hatred towards Jones, Davis, Morris, and every other branch of the great Cymric trunk.") The finale shows that Arthur is developing his comedy satisfactorily:

> And so, reader, I present you with a string of military anecdotes. I don't know how you will value them. They cost me a good watch and chain, and fourteen pounds, seven shillings and fourpence, and I thought them dear at the price.

And yet by 1884 ACD would have mastered the technique of realistic narrative so well, that his publication of *"J. Habakuk Jephson's Statement"* in the *Cornhill* resulted in Mr Solly Flood, Advocate and Proctor for the Queen in Her Office of Admiralty at Gibraltar, Mr Horatio Sprague, U.S. Consul at Gibraltar, and Mr J.C. Bancroft Davis, U.S. Assistant Secretary of State, all taking the narrative to be an alleged statement of fact while insisting, respectively, it was "a fabrication from beginning to end", "replete with romance of a very unlikely or exaggerated nature" and that "The mystery . . . is in no wise satisfactorily explained in that statement". The mystery was that of the *Mary Celeste,* found derelict at sea with no passengers on 4 December 1872, and Arthur was simply writing a story inspired by the idea, using the real name of the ship as his beloved Scott used real events and people as a background to his fictional creations. As Dickson Carr, for once saying something worthy of note, points out, Poe's famous Balloon Hoax was taken seriously, but was written to be, with the names of the novelist William Harrison Ainsworth and others being used as protagonists to lend verisimilitude; whereas Conan Doyle was taken seriously with no such intention or apparatus. Nor is it enough to write off Solly Flood as an egregious ass (which he was); Sprague had held his position through several administrations, and Bancroft Davis was a very serious professional diplomat. Davis told Sprague that "the article to which you refer has been read with attention and much interest", and he certainly was capable of being nasty enough had it impinged on him that his subordinate was wasting his valuable time on a piece of popular fiction. There was a touch of Nemesis in it: from my encounters with his letters in 1882 on State Department intrigues and politics, he seems to have been so fond of weaving conspiracies against his rivals and opponents that he was most appropriately made a victim himself of a conspiracy set on foot by nothing more than the authentic intonation in the style of Conan Doyle. How, then, had Arthur's fictions leaped in so few years to this authenticity of voice, an authenticity that would presage the countless Sherlockians who would insist on the real existence of Watson and Holmes?

There is a special point on the content of "Jephson", but the growth in authority of the writer's voice seems the product of his exposure to real life adventure on the whaler. Certainly a maturing of voice and a growth in self-assurance is essential in a youth progressing from first-year medical student to general practitioner and M.D. Of all professions, that of the doctor requires the sound of authority from the first. A teacher may dispense with authority; if his mastery of material is good enough, he can carry his class without pulling rank. A doctor must impose the conviction that he has to be accepted and obeyed. But the voyage of the *Hope* meant that Arthur had now "taken on board" real human experience under testing physical and psychological conditions. After all, the only real basis for something like *"The American's Tale"* would have been a meeting between the young medical student and the United States Consul to Glasgow, Mr Bret Harte, to be appointed in 1880. As "the American" had to do most of the telling, a meeting with Mr Harte might have improved matters; not but what Mr Harte had become very European-ised in his manners since his great work of the late 1860s. Strangely, ACD's need to work by means of first-person narrators, even when he was making the wildly ambitious attempt to sound Australian (or New Zealandish), South African or Western American, contrasted with Harte's cool, almost demure and pedantic, style. But even if they did not meet, and Harte remains yet another lost "point of contact", Conan Doyle summed up his influence neatly in *Through the Magic Door*:

> Bret Harte, . . . one of those great short story tellers who proved himself incapable of a longer flight. He was always like one of his own gold-miners who struck a rich pocket, but found no continuous reef. The pocket was, alas, a very limited one, but the gold was of the best. *"The Luck of Roaring Camp"* and *"Tennessee's Partner"* are both, I think, worthy of a place among my immortals. They are, it is true, so tinged with Dickens as to be almost parodies of the master, but they have a symmetry and a satisfying completeness as short stories to which Dickens himself never attained. The man who can read these two stories without a gulp in the throat is not a man I envy.

The satisfying completeness of that piece of criticism is, in part, that it singles out Harte's real strength much more profoundly than do most commentaries. Harte has been applauded for his handling of great natural disasters within small compass: yet *"Tennessee's Partner"* contains no such thing, the only disaster being decidely man-made, a lynching, and it has the symmetry and the completeness lacking in good Harte pieces like *"The Outcasts of Poker Flat"* and *"How Santa Claus came to Simpson's Bar"*, for all of their splendid snowscapes. It may be that Conan Doyle did more, in those lines, for Harte than Harte ever did for him, if we think of "Alabama Joe" in *"The American's Tale"* or "Chicago Bill" in *"The Gully of Bluemansdyke"*. In any event, Harte kept his admirer's 'prentice hand in, until reality came to the rescue, and for that we are greatly in his debt.

Curiously enough, another "point of contact" presumably not made by Arthur in the Edinburgh of these years would be Charles Reade, who visited the city in July and August 1876, perhaps overlapping with Arthur's return from Feldkirch. He might have heard enough about the visit, for it was concerned with the novelist's libel action against the *Glasgow Herald*, and it very likely would have raised his interest in the writer or quickened it if he had already found him. Reade stayed with Blackwood while in Edinburgh: perhaps that could have inspired ACD's obsession with getting published by Blackwood. Arthur would come to classify Reade's *The Cloister and the Hearth* with Tolstoy's *War and Peace* as seeming to him "to stand at the top of the century's fiction". And Reade, after Scott, would be his great exemplar in his future historical romances:

> He takes the reader by the hand, and he leads him away into the Middle Ages, and not a conventional study-built Middle Age, but a period quivering with life, full of folk who are as human and real as a 'bus-load in Oxford Street. . . . It contains, I think, a blending of knowledge with imagination, which makes it stand alone in our literature . . . It is a good thing to have the industry to collect facts. It is a greater and a rarer one to have the tact to know how to use them when you have got them. To be exact without pedantry, and thorough without being dull, that should be the ideal of the writer of historical romance.
>
> Reade is one of the most perplexing figures in our literature. Never was there a man so hard to place. At his best he is the best we have. At his worst he is below the level of Surreyside melodrama. But his best have weak pieces, and his worst have good. There is always silk among his cotton, and cotton among his silk. But, for all his flaws, the man who, in addition to the great book of which I have already spoken, wrote "It is Never Too Late to Mend", "Hard Cash", "Foul Play", and "Griffith Gaunt", must always stand in the very first rank of our novelists.

Reade is in decline now, though Orwell was one of his most eloquent defenders (for everything except *The Cloister and the Hearth*) and makes the point that Reade was one of the few defenders of the Jews among English novelists. Conan Doyle is also distinguished in his generation for an absence of that anti-semitism which disgraces the literature of his time. Orwell is helpful, too, in reminding us how public-spirited Reade was, how ready to take on crusades against social abuses, and this also seems likely to have struck a chord with Arthur. The element in Holmes which makes him so much the defender and which was so vigorously carried out by Conan Doyle time and again in his own life, comes from here rather than any of the obvious literary antecedents: that it comes from Arthur's own character is obvious, but it was Reade that helped to make that character and formulate its sense of crusade.

His regard for Harte and Reade Arthur brought on board the *Hope*; Macaulay he literally brought on board physically, and fanatically commended the *Essays* to his mates on the voyage. "Honest Scotch harpooners have addled their brains with it", he grinned reminiscently in *Through the Magic Door*, "and you may still see the grease stains where the second engineer grappled with Frederick the Great." This was one of the things which directly developed his sense of criticism. He was to be a life-long believer in the universal appeal of great literature, and now he had his first opportunity of fighting for it. He was now tall, strong and fit. Although not required to take part, he made it his business to get involved in the work of sealing and whaling, for all that he often found his sympathies with the whales rather than the killing. He fell into the sea from a frozen rail and once nearly froze to death having slid into the water from an ice-floe while skinning a dead seal. He saw men shot overboard to their deaths by the unwinding cord of a harpoon, and heard the harpooner restrain a seaman wanting to cut the rope (uselessly, for the man was dead already hundreds of fathoms deep): "Haud your hand, mon, the fush [whale] will be a tine thing for the widdey." For one more whale successfully harpooned meant additional pay, and the loss of harpoon and whale would be the seaman's sacrifice made vain for his family. "It sounds callous", he remarked in his *"Life on a Greenland Whaler"*, "but there was philosophy at the base of it."

Jack Lamb, the steward, started him on the right footing when he helped him unpack and found his boxing-gloves. Lamb then knew nothing of boxing, but insisted on a bout. "Our contest was an unfair one, for he was several inches shorter in the reach than I, and knew nothing about sparring, although I have no doubt he was a formidable person in a street row. I kept propping him off as he rushed at me, and at last, finding that he was determined to bore his way in, I had to hit him out with some severity. An hour or so afterwards, as I sat reading in the saloon, there was a murmur in the mate's berth, which was next door, and suddenly I heard the steward say, in loud tones of conviction: 'So help me, Colin, he's the best surrr-geon we've had! He's blackened my e'e!' It was the first (and very nearly the last) testimonial I ever received to my professional abilities." They kept up the boxing, and Lamb became proficient, and delighted Conan Doyle with his store of "pathetic and sentimental songs, and it is only when you have not seen a woman's face for six months that you realize what sentiment means". After this first testimonial, Macaulay's champion had the credentials to justify advocating the reading of Macaulay, although not to Colin McLean, for the mate was illiterate and was brought on board as cook's assistant, while the man who appeared as mate was articled but beyond sailoring, so they automatically switched when at sea. It was a practical lesson on the limits of literacy, and the delusions of bureaucracy, as regards the business of seamanship. As Arthur put it, fresh from the Darwinism of Edinburgh, McLean "was an officer by natural selection, which is a higher title than that of a Board of Trade certificate". His one blemish, a white-hot temper, gave the ship's doctor reason to be thankful for his own height, as the six-foot mate had sometimes to be physically pulled off an opponent by ACD.

Macaulay's presence aboard ship illustrated one problem in Arthur's life, quite apart from the problems *"Frederick the Great"* may have posed to the second engineer. The great essay on Bacon, reviewing the edition by Bryan Charles Waller's uncle's father-in-law, is particularly famous for the great paragraph at the commencement on the solace of the great literary dead for the unhappy man, a passage believed to have been prompted by Macaulay's own desperate grief at the death of one beloved sister, and the marriage of another:

> The debt which he owes to them is incalculable. They have guided him to truth. They have filled his mind with noble and graceful images. They have stood by him in all vicissitudes, comforters in sorrow, nurses in sickness, companions in solitude. These friendships are exposed to no danger from the occurrences by which other attachments are weakened or dissolved. Time glides on; fortune is inconstant; tempers are soured; bonds which seemed indissoluble are daily sundered by interest, by emulation, or by caprice. But no such cause can affect the silent converse which we hold with the highest of human intellects. That placid intercourse is disturbed by no jealousies or resentments. These are the old friends who are never seen with new faces, who are the same in wealth and in poverty, in glory and in obscurity. With the dead there is no rivalry. In the dead there is no change. Plato is never sullen. Cervantes is never petulant. Demosthenes never comes unseasonably. Dante never stays too long. No difference of political opinion can alienate Cicero. No heresy can excite the horror of Bossuet.

Now, to these sentiments Arthur gave life-long adhesion, and as *Through the Magic Door* reveals so well he entered into the kingdom beloved by Macaulay and made his countless friends, headed by that greatest of all literary companions the incomparable historian himself. But there was a difference. Literature and history became the purest escapism to Macaulay, an escapism from which the world has reaped immortal benefit, and which indeed he re-routed into the writing of his *History* so that he might find in the admiration of the world the solace forever lost to him in his own life. There was a danger that this might happen to Arthur. His own home had become a tragic spectacle, to which his most useful contribution seemed to be that of going away and earning money. The responsibility he would have wished to discharge was out of his hands. He had seldom found outside of it that emotional warmth which had meant so much to him when he encountered it with Father Cassidy. His University offered him food for intellectual maturity, student companionship, laughter and casual friendship, but nothing like the real bonds he sought. His need to earn money that would be his mother's by right, and not by charity, meant that his absences dictated a far harder and more rigorous programme of study when he was there.

At first it seemed even the absences would be worthless. He worked for three weeks with a Dr. Richardson of Sheffield, in a practice among the city poor, but it proved impossible for him to measure up. "I dare say he was patient", wrote Arthur afterwards; but much recrimination may have lain behind that "I dare say" and the humiliation of the final departure must have left him wondering if his medical career was hopeless. He then went to London, stayed with his relatives, probably argued with them about religion, and found their staid, childless lives very different from his own propensity for rambling and devouring the heritage of the city: he was probably well used by now to the need for finding some cause to keep him out of his domicile. He thought very seriously of entering the army, and only his mother's conviction that he must not fail in his medical enterprise held him back. He did actually volunteer as a dresser for the English ambulances expected to be brought out under the Red Cross for the expected war against Russia, but following the diplomacy of Beaconsfield and Bismarck, the war was averted. (It was the anticipated war which gave the word "jingoism" to the language:

> We don't want to fight, but, by jingo!, if we do,
> We've got the ships, we've got the men, we've got the money, too.
> We've fought the Bear before, and while Britons shall be true,
>   The Russians shall not have Constantinople.

But Arthur did not volunteer as a jingoist, but as a healer.) Then an advertisement of his was answered by Dr Elliot of Ruyton, Salop., with Edinburgh Medical School connections. He helped there for four months, enjoying the countryside, reading and thinking, and at least once having to cope with an ugly emergency:

> The doctor was out [he recalled in *Memories and Adventures*] when there came a half-crazed messenger to say that in some rejoicings at a neighbouring great house they had exploded an old cannon which had promptly burst and grievously injured one of the bystanders. No doctor was available, so I was the last resource. On arriving there I found a man in bed with a lump of iron sticking out of the side of his head. I tried not to show the alarm which I felt, and I did the obvious thing by pulling out the iron. I could see the clean white bone, so I could assure them that the brain had not been injured. I then pulled the gash together, staunched the bleeding, and finally bound it up, so that when the doctor did at last arrive he had little to add. This incident gave me confidence and, what is more important still, gave others confidence.

The ghost of Syme, who had pioneered medical progress in the closing of wounds, would have had reason to be proud of him.

Then he obtained the assistantship with Mr Hoare, F.R.C.S., of Birmingham, "who had a five-horse City practice, and every working doctor, before the days of motors, would realize that this meant going from morning to night". Arthur was offered £2 a month, for hard and incessant work. The dating of this is a little difficult. Supposedly it followed the Elliot episode which ACD describes as a third year appointment; but the University Medical School records indicate that his work as a dispensary assistant was permitted to count in his degree and took place in his second year, 1877-78, as well as his third. The record may be inaccurate (it is elsewhere, putting Arthur's birth a year early with what seems an altered digit) but *Memories and Adventures* acknowledges that he twice returned to Birmingham after his first stint, and the record shows him taking midwifery with Hoare in 1878-79, and 1879-80; 20 cases are mentioned in 1880-81, which would argue a return to Birmingham after the *Hope* cruise, but these cases may not have been under Hoare. In any event, he had added experience and important degree qualifications to some financial contributing to the family needs. He was fundamentally very lucky in this arrangement, initially; he maintained it and returned to it because of his conscientiousness, progress, efficiency, and likeability. "Hoare was a fine fellow, stout, square, red-faced, bushy-whiskered and dark-eyed. His wife was also a very kindly and gifted woman, and my position in the house was soon rather that of a son than of an assistant." At last, his hunger for affection received some recompense, and it is clear that he earned that too by the gentleness, enthusiasm and humour which characterised him.

But beyond his Birmingham work, destined to produce some literary results in his use of the mythical "Birchespool" (*Bir*mingham, Man*ches*ter, Liver*pool*) for several of his England-based short stories of the 1880s, and beyond his enthusiasm for sport at the University, there lay the danger of succumbing to the urge to escape. He was going to see his course through, and win if he could, urged on, perhaps, because of the examples of defection. Ryan dropped out, apparently for reasons of health. Claud Augustus Currie, whose last-minute defection from the *Hope* won ACD his place, never graduated from Edinburgh. George Budd, whom he had now come to know, would graduate while Arthur was in the Arctic, but never paid his fee to the General Council. Conan Doyle hungered for friends, yet the disappointments and wounds of his life, and the need for money and medical recognition, made it less and less likely he would be attuned to making them. Macaulay's way offered the surest friends. Were there to be no others?

The *Hope* changed all that. The very fact that he was eagerly thrusting his Macaulay on unlikely targets argues that he had at last found the business of making friends a success and joy, as well as that his own need to retreat into Macaulay was diminishing. That black eye had won him the regard of Lamb in contrast to Eddie Tulloch. He clearly won McLean's goodwill: an infuriated six-footer does not take kindly to being manhandled away from the object of his wrath unless he respects the manhandler. And his position was one of which he could make everything or nothing. He could retreat to his books, or he could become the focal point of the ship. Protocol isolated the captain from everyone but the doctor. (The interchange of mate and cook's assistant probably did nothing to improve that.) He acknowledged in his memoirs that

> I should have found it intolerable if the captain had been a bad fellow, but John Gray of the *Hope* was really a splendid man, a grand seaman and a serious-minded Scot, so that he and I formed a comradeship which was never marred during our long *tête-à-tête*. I see him now, his ruddy face, his grizzled hair and beard, his very light blue eyes always looking into far spaces, and his erect muscular figure. Taciturn, sardonic, stern on occasion, but always a good just man at bottom.

As the surgeon was young and inexperienced, the captain kept him from the first day's sealing, but since he slipped off a thin sheet of ice which had formed on the bulwarks where he was sitting, he fell into the sea. Gray observed that since he was bound to fall into the sea in any case he might as well do it from the ice as from the ship; he duly fell in twice again that day and had to go to bed while all his clothes dried. The captain thought it a great joke, and they all called him "the great northern diver" for many a day. His ready enjoyment of the joke against him clearly made him a prime favourite. His insistence on taking part in the harpooning resulted in the Captain offering him double pay as harpooner and doctor if he would come on a second voyage. He refused—but it was as precious to him as another degree.

Harpooning was difficult enough, with the danger of sudden death from the line.

> But the lancing, when the weary fish [as, he explained, the whale was always termed] is killed with the cold steel, is a more exciting because it is a more prolonged experience. You may be for half an hour so near to the creature that you can lay your hand upon its slimy side. The whale appears to have but little sensibility to pain, for it never winces when the long lances are passed through its body. But its instinct urges you to keep poling and boat-hooking along its side, so as to retain your safe position near its shoulder. Even there, however, we found on one occasion that we were not quite out of danger's way, for the creature in its flurry raised its huge side-flapper and poised it over the boat. One flap would have sent us to the bottom of the sea, and I can never forget how, as we pushed our way from under, each of us held one hand up to stave off that great, threatening fin—as if any strength of ours could have availed if the whale had meant it to descend. But it was spent with loss of blood, and instead of coming down the fin rolled over the other way, and we knew that it was dead. Who would swap that moment for any other triumph that sport can give?

There were other whales. He reflected on them in an article for the *Idler* in 1892, "*The Glamour of the Arctic*":

> To play a salmon is a royal game, but when your fish weighs more than a suburban villa, and is worth a clear two thousand pounds, when, too, your line is a thumb's thickness of manilla rope with fifty strands, every strand tested for 36lb., it dwarfs all other experiences. And the lancing too, when the creature is spent, and your boat pulls in to give it the *coup de grâce* with cold steel, that is also exciting! A hundred tons of despair are churning the waters up into a red foam, two great black fins are rising and falling like the sails of a windmill, casting the boat into a shadow as they droop over it, but still the harpooner clings to the head, where no harm can come, and, with the wooden butt of the twelve-foot lance against his stomach, he presses it home until the long struggle is finished, and the black back rolls over to expose the livid, whitish surface beneath. Yet amid all the excitement—and no one who has not held an oar in such a scene can tell how exciting it is—one's sympathies lie with the poor hunted creature. The whale has a small eye, little larger than that of a bullock, but I cannot easily forget the mute expostulation which I read in one, as it dimmed over in death within hand's touch of me. What could it guess, poor creature, of laws of supply and demand, or how could it imagine that when nature placed an elastic filter inside its mouth, and when man discovered that the plates of which it was composed were the most pliable and yet durable things in creation, its death-warrant was signed.

It takes a very great man indeed to see beyond the excitement, glory and gain
to the tragedy beyond. They even came to know the whales personally, in
some cases:

> There was one, I remember, which was conspicuous through having a huge
> wart, the size and shape of a beehive, upon one of the flukes of its tail. "I've
> been after that fellow three times", said the captain, as we dropped our boats.
> "He got away in '61. In '67 we had him fast, but the harpoon drew. In '78 a fog
> saved him. It's odds that we have him now!" I fancied the betting lay rather the
> other way myself, and so it proved, for that warty tail is still thrashing in Arctic
> seas for all that I know to the contrary.

Inevitably the result of this was to bring a new sense of priorities to Arthur
as a literary critic. He was distinguished among his generation for his
admiration for Herman Melville, whose obscurity then was as complete as his
fame is now. He took it farther than *Moby-Dick,* however, and in *Through the
Magic Door* denounced the oblivion into which *Typee* and *Omoo* had fallen.
"What a charming and interesting task there is for some critic of catholic
tastes and sympathetic judgment to undertake rescue work among the lost
books which would repay salvage!" he said of them. Ironically, the critic who
finally arrived and rescued Melville was probably a little too catholic in his
tastes for Conan Doyle, although he must have been pleased with the revival
already evident by the end of his life following the publication of D. H.
Lawrence's *Studies in American Literature.* His sea experiences led him
enthusiastically to join in the welcome for Joseph Conrad and Jack London,
though he always retained a kind word for old favourites such as his
contemporary W. Clark Russell. Russell, in fact, was a somewhat insidious
influence on him. If he had admired Gray of the *Hope,* Russell's realism made
his portraits of brutal captains natural food for reflection and subsequent
literary development, and in "*Black Peter*" he himself would depict the
captain of a whaler (the *Sea Unicorn,* of Dundee; the *Hope* was from
Peterhead, Aberdeenshire), who for sheer horror is unbeatable. The *Hope,*
itself, showed him how easily a murder at sea could be covered up, for there
was loss of life on his expedition for more reasons than harpoon-ropes. Grave
danger was present even at the point of parting company with the harpooned
and stripped whale. In "*The Glamour of the Arctic*", he recalled

> Some years ago a man, still lingering upon the back, had the misfortune to have
> his foot caught between the creature's ribs at the instant when the tackles were
> undone. Some aeons hence those two skeletons, the one hanging by the foot
> from the other, may grace the museums of a subtropical Greenland, or astonish
> the students of the Spitzbergen Institute of Anatomy.

Macaulay *had* added his voice to the whaler's crew.
If the effect of the voyage was to turn Arthur firmly towards realism and
the use of experience in his literary work, it also left him sceptical about what
passed muster among landsmen:

> The gallant seaman, who in all the books stands in the prow of a boat, waving a
> harpoon over his head, with the line snaking into the air behind him, is only to
> be found now in Paternoster Row. The Greenland seas have not known him for

more than a hundred years, since first the obvious proposition was advanced
that one could shoot both harder and more accurately than one could throw.
Yet one clings to the ideals of one's infancy, and I hope that another century
may have elapsed before the brave fellow disappears from the frontispieces, in
which he still throws his outrageous weapon an impossible distance. The swivel
gun, like a huge horse-pistol, is a more reliable, but a far less picturesque,
object.

It was a pleasing inversion that the first literary use of which ACD would
put his maritime experiences on his return was in a story "*That Little Square
Box*", portraying a narrator as much of a poltroon as his creator had been a
hero. It is as though his imagination told himself how he would appear if he
shrank from the coarse company of his shipmates, the open-air wisdom of the
captain, the dangerous challenge of participating unasked in the whaling and
sealing. The voyage had been a triumph, in that he did not seal himself off
from reality. Suppose he had? The result was his first really good story, and
one of the finest comic characters he ever drew, the absurd Hammond with
his perpetual fears that the ship is about to be blown up. He also takes his
early interest in ghost-stories and inverts that. Hammond appears too farcical
to be believed as a prophet of disaster, as far as the sailors and passengers are
concerned, yet the reader cannot escape from a lingering doubt that he may
have powers beyond the normal since he is so clearly inadequate in the sphere
of normality itself:

> I have the misfortune to be a very nervous man. A sedentary literary life has
> helped to increase the morbid love of solitude which, even in my boyhood, was
> one of my most distinguishing characteristics. As I stood upon the quarter-deck
> of the Transatlantic steamer, I bitterly cursed the necessity which drove me
> back to the land of my fore-fathers. The shouts of the sailors, the rattle of the
> cordage, the farewells of my fellow-passengers, and the cheers of the mob, each
> and all jarred upon my sensitive nature. I felt sad too. An indescribable feeling,
> as of some impending calamity, seemed to haunt me. The sea was calm, and the
> breeze light. There was nothing to disturb the equanimity of the most
> confirmed of landsmen, yet I felt as if I stood upon the verge of a great though
> indefinable danger. I have noticed that such presentiments occur often in men
> of my peculiar temperament, and that they are not uncommonly fulfilled. I well
> remember that Herr Raumer, the eminent spiritualist, remarked on one
> occasion that I was ·the most sensitive subject as regards supernatural
> phenomena that he had ever encountered in the whole of his wide experience.

The story, then, keeps Hammond's credibility in play against all reason. The
parody of the Poe manner is kept skilfully at work, and if Hammond is a
poltroon, many a Poe hero carries his misanthropy, clairvoyance and macabre
concerns within a very unappetizing moral framework. Admittedly the cause
of terror proves earthly, as Hammond interprets a conversation to conclude
the ship is going to be blown up. By giving this a sufficiently sinister cast,
ACD can let himself go with its immediate sequel, remembering the candour
and courage of his shipmates:

> How long I remained sitting on that coil of rope I shall never know. The
> horror of the conversation I had just overheard was aggravated by the first

sinking qualms of sea-sickness. The long roll of the Atlantic was beginning to
assert itself over both ship and passengers. I felt prostrated in mind and body,
and fell into a state of collapse, from which I was finally aroused by the hearty
voice of our worthy quartermaster.

"Do you mind moving out of that, sir?" he said. "We want to get this lumber
cleared off the deck."

His bluff manner and his ruddy healthy face seemed to be a positive insult to
me in my present condition. Had I been a courageous or muscular man I would
have struck him. As it was, I treated the honest sailor to a melodramatic scowl
which seemed to cause him no small astonishment, and strode past him to the
other side of the deck. Solitude was what I wanted—solitude in which I could
brood over the frightful crime which was being hatched before my very eyes.

There is clever playing with his own emotions there. He was fond of solitude,
and from time to time lyricised about his love of it. Yet he had triumphed in
the Arctic by putting all such feelings firmly behind him.

From here on, however, a different theme emerges in *"That Little Square
Box"*, the use of a Watson-figure, Philistine, hearty, insensitive to the
perceptions and deductions of the neurotic narrator, and hence surely to be
confuted at the end? Taking Orwell's point that part of the brilliance of
Holmes and Watson is using the Quixote-Sancho relationship to create a set
of situations in which the Don Quixote figure proves to be right and the
Sancho Panza wrong, it is fascinating to see this early employment of it for
the alternative result. And so tension is built up through a series of
conversations apparently loaded with significance and in fact meaningless
small-talk, apart from the ghastly hints Hammond seeks to interject. Finally
arrives the crisis in which the infernal machine proves a device to release
racing-pigeons. The whole satire, controlled and very funny, holds its reader
strongly enough to force re-reading after tragedy has been so spectacularly
floored by comedy. It was also a firm realisation on Arthur's part that realism
could do his work better than fantasy, and that comedy could make a far
better ally to dramatic narration than he had realised. From this it was a
logical step to the Holmes formula, with its careful and studied intermingling
of humour and realism within the seemingly fantastic. Henceforward his use
of escapism was subject, when he could manage it, to firm controls.

Yet having used his shipboard experience so well to make nonsense of the
supernatural, he inverted the coin for his next experiment on what he had
witnessed. The Arctic continued to haunt him, and he ultimately found the
means of expressing it. On the haunting itself he would write in *Through the
Magic Door*

He who has once been within the borders of that mysterious region, which
can be both the most lovely and the most repellent upon earth, must always
retain something of its glamour. Standing on the confines of known geography I
have shot the southward flying ducks, and have taken from their gizzards
pebbles which they have swallowed in some land whose shores no human foot
has trod. The memory of that inexpressible air, of the great ice-girt lakes of
deep blue water, of the cloudless sky shading away into a light green and then
into a cold yellow at the horizon, of the noisy companionable birds, of the huge,

greasy-backed water animals, of the slug-like seals, startlingly black against the dazzling whiteness of the ice—all of it will come back to a man in his dreams, and will seem little more than some fantastic dream itself, so removed is it from the main stream of his life.

In *"Life on a Greenland Whaler"* he wrote:

> The peculiar other-world feeling of the Arctic regions—a feeling so singular, that if you have once been there the thought of it haunts you all your life—is due largely to the perpetual daylight. Night seems more orange-tinted and subdued than day, but there is no great difference. . . . After a month or two the eyes grow weary of the eternal light, and you appreciate what a soothing thing our darkness is. I can remember as we came abreast of Iceland, on our return, catching our first glimpse of a star, and being unable to take my mind from it, it seemed such a dainty little twinkling thing. Half the beauties of Nature are lost through over-familiarity.

And it was that memory, with some assistance from R. M. Ballantyne's *The World of Ice*, which supplied the beautiful, haunting title for his story "*The Captain of the 'Pole-Star'* ". It is a ghost story, and a very subtle and delicate one, in which a neurotic and possibly crazed Captain is mourning his lost love, and ultimately haunted by her so that he follows her spirit on to an ice-floe where he dies. But the atmosphere is brilliantly caught, partly by the use of a diary, partly by the fear throughout the story that the ship will be trapped by the increasing pack ice to the south and prove unable to return at all. The supernatural is thus firmly grounded on material anxieties which then go on to feed its impact. The journal is that of a medical student acting as ship's doctor, exactly Conan Doyle's position, and his relationship to the Captain, to whom he alone has full social access, again follows real life experience. The time, too, is September, precisely when the *Hope* was making her homeward journey, and the student at the beginning of the story sees his first star since May. The Captain's insistence on keeping the ship in dangerous ice-ridden waters is first explained by him in terms of profit, as so much was explained to Arthur on board the *Hope*. Little by little the evidence of the haunting begins to increase, and again the plot is kept firmly away from its being a mere delusion of the Captain by the initial accounts coming from members of the crew. Use of Arctic fauna serves both the needs of realism and of fantasy:

> Our only visitor was an Arctic fox, a rare animal upon the [ice-]pack, though common enough upon the land. He did not come near the ship, however, but after surveying us from a distance fled rapidly across the ice. This was curious conduct, as they generally know nothing of man, and being of an inquisitive nature, become so familiar that they are easily captured. Incredible as it may seem, even this little incident produced a bad effect upon the crew. "Yon puir beastie kens mair, ay an' sees mair nor you nor me!" was the comment of one of the leading harpooners, and the others nodded their acquiescence. It is vain to attempt to argue against such puerile superstition.

The narrator, the student John M'Alister Ray, is deliberately kept in the most severely scientific mould which experience of Edinburgh University could supply, and he shows a social condescension which Arthur, with his love of his shipmates and his enthusiasm for snapping their photographs and persuading them to try Macaulay, certainly did not share. On the other hand, the proximity of writing to the original voyage leads ACD to include things that seemed incongruous to him at the time, but which dimmed in importance when he wrote his factual accounts of the voyage, twelve, seventeen and forty-odd years afterwards after many years of English domicile:

> Divine service was read as usual by the chief engineer. It is a curious thing that in whaling vessels the Church of England Prayer-book is always employed, although there is never a member of that Church among either officers or crew. Our men are all Roman Catholics or Presbyterians, the former predominating. Since a ritual is used which is foreign to both, neither can complain that the other is preferred to them, and they listen with all attention and devotion, so that the system has something to recommend it.

Eventually the sceptical medical student is forced to acknowledge something, and the manner of the haunting suggests an antecedent in Arthur's experience on the *Hope*—sound:

> . . . It is only here in these Arctic seas that stark, unfathomable stillness obtrudes itself upon you in all its gruesome reality. You find your tympanum straining to catch some little murmur, and dwelling eagerly upon every accidental sound within the vessel. In this state I was leaning against the bulwarks when there arose from the ice almost directly underneath me a cry, sharp and shrill, upon the silent air of the night, beginning, as it seemed to me, at a note such as prima donna never reached, and mounting from that ever higher and higher until it culminated in a long wait of agony, which might have been the last cry of a lost soul. The ghastly scream is still ringing in my ears. Grief, unutterable grief, seemed to be expressed in it, and a great longing, and yet through it all there was an occasional wild note of exultation.

But the medical student remains a medical student, viewing the Captain with the eye of a doctor rather than a convert to his supernatural obsessions. The fear increasing in the story that the Captain is in fact going insane carries its own horror, and the judicious playing with alternative horrors owes something to Arthur's awareness of the progression of his father through alcoholism to insanity, for the story was written in 1882. One passage certainly seems autobiographical, although it is founded on the Captain's making a will. He is expecting his dead beloved to take him. Ray does not know that:

> The more I think of his conversation the less do I like it. Why should the man be settling his affairs at the very time when we seem to be emerging from all danger? There must be some method in his madness. Can it be that he contemplates suicide? I remember that upon one occasion he spoke in a deeply reverent manner of the heinousness of the crime of self-destruction. I shall keep my eye upon him, however, and though I cannot obtrude into the privacy of his cabin, I shall at least make a point of remaining on deck as long as he stays up.

Deduction here would lead to the assumption that such fears crossed Arthur's mind about his father's will, and, his own Catholicism discarded, he hoped against hope that his father's would remain strong and proof against any suicidal tendency. Catholicism (like Spiritualism) views suicide with particular horror. It may also be that what seem to Ray the signs of insanity in the Captain are in fact the signs Conan Doyle was observing in his father, or signs Waller was drawing to his attention. The Captain is variously morose, mystical, furious, laughing, switching moods and thrown into anger or depression by the most inexplicable phenomena. It does make sense once the fact of his being haunted by his lost love is accepted. In Charles Altamont Doyle's case there was no sense to be made.

The Captain's final race to the ice with a tender cry that he is coming is followed by fruitless search, and by his ultimate discovery. The science of Ray reveals a humanity in its scepticism which Arthur clearly longed to find at Edinburgh, and which he demanded for the rest of his life:

> He was lying face downwards upon a frozen bank. Many little crystals of ice and feathers of snow had drifted on to him as he lay, and sparkled upon his dark seaman's jacket. As we came up some wandering puff of wind caught these tiny flakes in its vortex, and they whirled up into the air, partially descended again, and then, caught once more in the current, sped rapidly away in the direction of the sea. To my eyes it seemed but a snow-drift, but many of my companions averred that it started up in the shape of a woman, stooped over the corpse and kissed it, and then hurried away across the floe. I have learned never to ridicule any man's opinion, however strange it may seem. Sure it is that Captain Nicholas Craigie had met with no painful end, for there was a bright smile upon his blue pinched features, and his hands were still outstretched as though grasping at the strange visitor which had summoned him away into the dim world that lies beyond the grave.

The journal concludes with the way clear through the ice-pack and a note from Ray's father describing his discovery that Craigie "had been engaged to a young lady of singular beauty residing upon the Cornish coast. During his absence at sea his betrothed had died under circumstances of peculiar horror." There it ends. Thirty years later *"The Devil's Foot"* records such a death in Cornwall, although on that occasion the bereaved fiancé seeks not death but revenge. It is a further striking example of ACD's capacity to work out an idea after an extraordinary interval of time between conception and execution.

As the great American horror-story writer H. P. Lovecraft said in his admirable survey *"Supernatural Horror in Literature"*, *"The Captain of the 'Pole-Star'"* "struck a powerfully spectral note". But its achievement was far from limited to the genre of the spectral. It is also a great sea story, a great work of psychological preoccupation, and an achievement of astonishing tenderness and delicacy. Its beauty remains typified by that last appearance of the lost love, and is as insubstantial. Certainly he put to good use what he had learned from W. Clark Russell, Herman Melville, Captain Marryat and his other favourite sea story writers. One or two of the most finely worked touches draw with professional skill on Edgar Allan Poe's *"The Narrative of A. Gordon Pym"*, a very obvious source for A. Conan Doyle (as from the first he signed those few magazine contributions for which a signature was permitted). The mysterious cry is all the more powerful in Conan Doyle for the absence of any attempt to reproduce its sound, as opposed to the indication of its content: it was probably inspired by the haunting "*Tekeli-li!*" with which the fearful savages at the close of *Pym* respond to whiteness and which is later echoed by the birds. Lovecraft himself made some use of "*Tekeli-li!*" in his "*At the Mountains of Madness*" and followed up the possibility that its frequent repetition derived from horrific antecedents. Conan Doyle pursued the contrary effect: by limiting the cry to one appearance he put everything into its description and rightly relied on that single impact, rather than on any later repetition, to make itself dominate the remnant of the action. The snow-vision above Craigie's body (with which illustrators of the book publication of the story would manfully do their best) was most likely suggested by the vision of the snow figure in the very last lines of "*The Narrative of A. Gordon Pym*". The close of *Pym* is in any case an invitation to Poe's disciples, since having brought on his final effect he leaves the resolution of the narrative in general and the vision in particular to the imagination of the unfortunate reader. The haunting effects of Poe's use of the ice are taken up in part by Conan Doyle, but in realism he very naturally outstrips his great predecessor, and he also bettered him in delicacy of treatment.

"*The Captain of the 'Pole-Star'* " is an astonishing achievement in human understanding for a boy of twenty-two or twenty-three, and it is irrefutable evidence for the change in his powers as an artist brought by the voyage of the *Hope*. If he had not rivalled the high protracted drama and the invaluable contributions to science of the *Challenger* expedition, he had effectively captured the material which was to make him one of the greatest artists of his day. In his memoirs he restricted his achievement to the physical: "I went on board the whaler a big, straggling youth. I came off it a powerful, well-grown man. I have no doubt that my physical health during my whole life has been affected by that splendid air, and that the inexhaustible store of energy which I have enjoyed is to some extent drawn from the same source." But he was very proud of the fruits. The first book of his stories he collected, not, to his annoyance, the first collection to be made, he entitled *The Captain of the "Pole-Star"*. As he says, he still remained very boyish, and, happily, always would. "I had . . . more money than I had ever possessed before. . . . I remember that I concealed gold pieces in every pocket of every garment, that my mother might have the excitement of hunting for them. It added some fifty pounds to her small exchequer." To his Mam it must have been worth fifty times its amount.

"Now I had a straight run in to my final examination, which I passed with fair but not notable distinction at the end of the winter session of 1881", recorded ACD briskly in rounding off that chapter for *Memories and Adventures*. Well, we all have chapters to finish. Perhaps he will forgive me for choosing a different ending. When he got off the *Hope* he devoured the current numbers of the magazines to which he was already laying siege. And in the September and October numbers of the *Cornhill* he found a story called "*The Pavilion on the Links*". Its author was Robert Louis Stevenson.

9

Blue Water, Black Man

Except a corn of wheat fall into the ground and die, it abideth alone: but if it die, it bringeth forth much fruit.

—John, xii. 24.

"**The** very model of dramatic narrative" wrote ACD of "*The Pavilion on the Links*" in *Through the Magic Door:*

That story stamped itself so clearly on my brain when I read it in *Cornhill* that when I came across it again many years afterwards in volume form, I was able instantly to recognise two small modifications of the text—each very much for the worse—from the original form. They were small things, but they seemed somehow like a chip on a perfect statue. Surely it is only a very fine work of art which could leave so definite an impression as that.

As with so much in *Through the Magic Door*, that most unpretentious piece of first-class criticism, the authorities are only beginning now to see what the enthusiastic Conan Doyle had perceived from his celebrationist pulpit long years ago. M. R. Ridley, in editing the work for Everyman's Library, has restored the *Cornhill* text, arguing that for all the sparsity of its amendments, the neglect of the work since its appearance in book form lies in its failure to establish rapport between narrator and audience, something achieved in the *Cornhill* version by making it clear the narrator is speaking to his children.

Ironically, the eccentricities of popular book production wreaked the same effect on one of Arthur's books, although less dangerously because it was not accompanied by his emendations. *Micah Clarke* in omnibus form is simply sub-titled "His Statement", in print small enough to be overlooked. On its first appearance in 1889 it boasted the sonorous full title *Micah Clarke His Statement As Made to his Three Grandchildren Joseph, Gervas, and Reuben During the Hard Winter of 1734 wherein is contained A Full Report of Certain Passages in his Early Life, together with some Account of his Journey from Havant to Taunton with Decimus Saxon in the Summer of 1685. Also of the Adventures that Befell them during the Western Rebellion and of their Intercourse with James Duke of Monmouth, Lord Grey, & Other Persons of Quality—Compiled Day by Day, from his Own Narration, by Joseph Clarke, & Never Previously set down in Print. Now for the First Time Collected Corrected and Rearranged from the Original Manuscript by A. Conan Doyle.* In part this is an imitation of late seventeenth-century book-titling, in part an opening blow at the convention which called attention to "persons of quality" (since Monmouth, in particular, comes very badly out of Clarke's statement). But it is really necessary to the story. *Micah Clarke* retains some of the effect of that title by its opening reference to the grandchildren, but the assertion of their identities in the original title gives an immediacy to the narrative which in later versions it lacks. It is singular that one of Stevenson's principal points of influence on Arthur should be one which he himself unwisely discarded, and which ACD's later publishers dramatically weakened.

The impact of Stevenson on Arthur, just back from six months' physical fruition and literary starvation on the *Hope*, was gigantic. That they were both Edinburgh men, separated by but a few years, was the greatest part of it; that, and the fact they never met. Thereafter Arthur knew that his birthplace still had the power to produce genius of a kind believed buried with Scott. It was true that the Edinburghs which brought them to maturity were very different. Arthur was never to assert Edinburgh as flesh of his flesh, bone of his bone, as Stevenson did. His father never accepted an Edinburgh identity, his mother was Edinburgh-born but her adult life there was perpetually clouded with shame and sorrow. Yet Edinburgh was the most protracted experience of his formative years, and Stevenson touched that awareness. If his Edinburgh origins cry less loudly to students of his work than Stevenson's did, it was because they offered him in retrospect a private more than a public pain. Edinburgh wove itself deeply into his artistic consciousness for all that.

Stevenson must have deepened that identification, showing him how much conquest was still possible for Edinburgh men, keeping that little distance in front of him to spur him to further effort: firstly in the *Cornhill,* RLS making that grade in January 1878, ACD six years later to the month, next with the success of a novel (RLS with *Treasure Island* in 1883, ACD with *Micah Clarke* at a similar interval—1889), and then, the gap closing dramatically, *The Strange Case of Dr Jekyll and Mr Hyde* reaching the public in 1886 and *A Study in Scarlet*, its initially much less successful counterpart, in December 1887. That thought of Stevenson always blazing the trail just before him haunted Conan Doyle, even to the unspoken physical realisation he immediately antedated him at Rutherford's. That establishment then (but alas not now) contained a series of little cubicles each with benches facing one another separated by a table and enclosed from the remainder of the public of the house by doors, one per booth and thus may have possessed them both within its walls, a thin partition alone keeping the man in the velvet coat from the tall, athletic, pipe-smoking Hiberno-Scot. Their ways during Arthur's student years were also from time to time as divided as when later they corresponded with ACD in London and RLS in Samoa, for when Arthur was on the coasts of Greenland Stevenson was in San Francisco. The consciousness of Stevenson working ahead of him was absolutely one of encouragement—never of rivalry. The older Edinburgh writer showed what was possible for one to do, and might be for another.

The one major Edinburgh literary figure Arthur did know, the historian John Hill Burton, died on 10 August 1881. Burton's writings, *The Scot*

Abroad, The Book Hunter, and, more generally, the *History of Scotland* and biography of David Hume, had shaped Arthur's intellectual development in a very different sense from Stevenson. Conan Doyle even used the old professor's name for Watson's alias "Dr Hill Barton" during what proved his fateful call on Baron Gruner in *"The Illustrious Client"*—a story written almost forty-five years after Burton's death. Burton's *History,* the work of an unsystematic antiquary rather than an historian, still provided some factual groundwork for what Walter Scott was giving ACD in his fiction, and, above all, *The Book Hunter* made Edinburgh for Arthur the great literary pearl-bed where innumerable raids were to be made. Threepenny stalls yielded incomparable treasures for him over the years, but it was in Edinburgh the foundation of the collection was built up. He seems to have remembered Burton's title in his story *"The Beetle-Hunter"*, and the fanaticism of the lunatic Sir Thomas Rossiter for his subject, recalled Burton's for his. The stories are also associated in that Rossiter subjects Dr Hamilton to an oral examination on coleoptera with special reference to Rossiter's own book, and Gruner does the same to Watson, becoming as annoyed when Watson does not know his as Rossiter is mollified when Hamilton proves well-versed. Arthur may have sustained such a quiz from the old antiquary about *The Book Hunter* when first he essayed to show his 'prentice work in book collecting, and it sounds like a formidable proceeding, in that the difference in time between the composition of the stories, 1897 for *"The Beetle-Hunter"* and 1924 for *"The Illustrious Client"* suggests that the association between Burton, his book, his hobby and a fairly gruelling cross-questioning persisted throughout Conan Doyle's adult life. Admittedly, however formidable the old man, he was linked to the boy by Arthur's friendship with his son and by his sister's friendship with Mary Foley Doyle. That would not prevent such an interview being somewhat shaking, but it would have been an excellent training for the oral examinations of the medical school, the last of which took place in the year of his death, 1881.

The old Edinburgh influence, Burton, held its own against the new, Stevenson, in certain ways. Ironically, in 1881 Stevenson applied (unsuccessfully) for Cosmo Innes's Chair at Edinburgh, which Burton did not seek when Innes died in 1874. Burton may have been more antiquary than historian, much as Cosmo Innes had been, but his factual knowledge was enormous, and Stevenson had virtually no historical sense at all. It was the point at which the twin Edinburgh literary influences on Conan Doyle, Scott and Stevenson, were at their most divergent. From Burton and Macaulay Arthur knew of Scott's tremendous achievement in rescuing and popularising social history, and to Scott he went for instruction in historical imagination. The Edinburgh he found in the *The Heart of Midlothian* offered him a real past, and Scott's journals which he later read with such delight rekindled his enthusiasm for the city's richness and diversity up to thirty years before his own birth. *The Black Arrow* came nowhere near *The White Company*—again the composition has a six-year interval and surely the adjectival contrast is more than coincidence—because Stevenson's concern with moral questions stands in the way of any sense of period whereas Conan Doyle raised such questions but kept them subordinate to his main business of conveying a narrative of historical events and its world. Stevenson did follow Scott, and Conan Doyle followed them both, in concentrating attention on narrators of marginal loyalties close to the reader, innocents whose doubts and questionings, half-deductions and problems of identification, throw into relief the bold and essentially alien standpoints of the figures larger than life with whom they are drawn into strange association. The Scott narrators do this work to bring the major actors and movements of the past into the realm of modern understanding; the Stevenson narrators do it to force attention on the gigantic figures who question so much of the convention on which the innocents rest their initial faith. Some of the latter is present in Scott also, but Stevenson, lacking the historical imagination, and essentially economical where Scott is profuse, makes it the pre-eminent factor. It is at its most vigorous in *Kidnapped*, where the alliance and opposition of Alan Breck and David Balfour keep David's affection for Alan and loyalty to his own heritage in fascinating interplay. It is suggested in the relations of Jim Hawkins and Long John Silver, but any idea of Jim's half-yielding to the temptations of piracy would be outrageous for Stevenson's Victorian schoolboy audience. He is realist enough to acknowledge a boy might do this, and hence we have the wretched Dick, seduced within our hearing during the apple-barrel episode, doomed in body by fever and in soul by the mutilation of his Bible, and finally marooned at the close—a piece of wholly unjustifiable cruelty, given his medical condition and harmlessness and the official excuse for the marooning being limited to security reasons. Again, in *Dr Jekyll and Mr Hyde* the maintenance of most of the story through the eyes of Mr Utterson does the same work, and he maintains a marginal position between Lanyon, who condemns Jekyll as he himself is dying, and Jekyll himself.

Conan Doyle picked up his legacy readily enough. Watson as a marginal figure, representing the reliable and the known, stands as the Scott-Stevenson narrator, as well as the closest of Socrates's friends in Plato, and Boswell in his *Life of Johnson*, but, most particularly in *A Study in Scarlet* and *The Sign of Four*, he has to be drawn away from his assurance. The remarkable thing is that Watson never sells out completely to Holmes. He resembles David Balfour in remaining the fount of common sense although finding time and again that what seemed solidly-based common sense proves the lesser part of wisdom in the new worlds inhabited by Alan Breck and Sherlock Holmes. He forces his own wisdom on Holmes in the matter of drug addiction, and in helping him understand more of human emotion and its expression, as Holmes testifies by masking his inadequacy in the almost unbearable facetiousness about the fair sex being Watson's department. Watson's marriage reasserts his world at the end of *The Sign of Four* as David Balfour's arrival outside the British Linen Bank reasserts his. As Jenni Calder, and ACD himself, have stressed, *Kidnapped* is stronger on historical consciousness than most of Stevenson's other work, although *The Master of Ballantrae* goes psychologically much deeper into the nature of divisions of loyalty in the post-Culloden period. Here, too, Conan Doyle was ready to learn. *The White Company* plays pleasantly with the various cultural standpoints in confrontation between the monastery-educated Alleyne, the anarchistic Hordle John, the rakish Samkin Aylward, and the devout and chivalric Sir Nigel. *The White Company* also turns the trick of the two boys, one secure, one doomed, although ACD greatly improved on Stevenson in making Ford, the doomed figure, a laughing, lovable, irreverent and witty companion, whose death is foul in execution, hideous in revelation, and all the more chilling for his anticipation of it by supernatural means.

In the case of *Micah Clarke* there is something of a different turn of loyalties. Here Micah Clarke himself goes on the Monmouth rebellion believing himself to be acting out his beliefs, only to discover extraordinary divergences in motivation on the part of his comrades. The cleverness of the story here is not one of formal crossing of cultural or ethnic barriers, as with Stevenson and Scott, but discovery of new barriers within an embattled force on one side. There is no question of finding challenges to Micah's allegiance among the followers of James II (and VII): the problems for Micah are caused by his discovery of cynicism, opportunism and cowardice on his own side, above all his being saved by a figure of such uncertain moral stature as Decimus Saxon. This last looks like Stevenson's example, but the contrast is that Conan Doyle had learned from Macaulay how deeply complex the mixture of motives and morals were in the superficially straightforward political confrontations under the later Stuarts. Hence the moral ambiguities, in Conan Doyle's hands, are serving a historical purpose rather than standing in the way of one.

If Stevenson's name did come before Conan Doyle's awareness as the aspirant for the chair of the revered Innes, it was not as the author of "*The Pavilion on the Links*" which the *Cornhill* ran with its usual insistence on anonymity. When ACD reached the *Cornhill* in his turn Stevenson was known to himself and the world as the author of *Treasure Island*, and he recalled in his "*My First Book*" in the *Idler* for January 1893 that "I saw with astonishment and pride that 'Habakuk Jephson's Statement' in the *Cornhill* was attributed by critic after critic to Stevenson, but overwhelmed as I was by the compliment, a word of the most lukewarm praise sent straight to my own address would have been of greater use to me". That gentle expression of resentment had its sting smoothed away in the best of all possible ways: in August 1894 the "*My First Book*" series in the *Idler* included RLS's account of writing *Treasure Island*, to the excellent fortune of his biographers and critics, and he told Arthur in a letter that he did so having been inspired by the Conan Doyle contribution of eighteen months before. ACD's impact was only just in time: by the end of 1894 Stevenson was dead. The footsteps that led before Conan Doyle had ceased, but only after paying him the superb compliment of pausing to walk briefly in ACD's own tracks. Arthur had been saluted as worthy to follow Stevenson whom he, perhaps, had once seen as unfit to follow Cosmo Innes.

The Edinburgh that Stevenson would have conveyed to Arthur's awareness was more geographical than historical: what there is of history in Stevenson's *Edinburgh: Picturesque Notes,* published in 1878, is largely highly dubious legend, assisted by use of Scott at his most publicity-minded. RLS and ACD took enormous delight in scrambling over the hills, Arthur with his camera, and exploring the Firth of Forth and its islands. Where ACD differs most profoundly from both Scott and Stevenson is in his sense of the unity of the city and its people where his great predecessors are haunted by the conflict in the Scottish tradition. Conan Doyle could fling bold, dark contours on a canvas to confront the reader with grotesque Scottish Goths such as the hilariously misanthropic Caithness-shire *savant* in *"The Man from Archangel"* or the homicidally avaricious father on the Western Isle in *"Our Midnight Visitor"*. James Hogg would have recognised them, and Stevenson would have acknowledged their kinship. *"Our Midnight Visitor"* is certainly a relative of *"The Merry Men"*. Other Stevenson counterparts are Northmour in *"The Pavilion on the Links"* (the Conan Doyle misanthrope, revealingly, having by contrast the engagingly nutritious name of M'Vittie), and *"A Lodging for the Night"*, where the murderous avarice is in the Paris of François Villon rather than the Edinburgh night-howffs RLS knew so well.

But to see the full implications of the unity of Conan Doyle's Edinburgh we have to look at it under other guises: like Stevenson, he could produce its most vigorous expression in a different identity. *"A Lodging for the Night"* is an obvious extrapolation from Stevenson's Edinburgh, *Dr Jekyll and Mr Hyde* a more subtle one. Pesumably ACD saw the Edinburgh omnipresence in the latter story when he read it, with its Scottish lawyer Utterson ("No modern English lawyer", observes Chesterton, "ever read a book of dry divinity in the evening merely because it was Sunday"); more fundamental is the Lanyon-Jekyll mutual criticism in no way inhibiting Jekyll's automatic turn to Lanyon in crisis (following Christison's summons to Simpson to save his life: Stevenson, like Conan Doyle, was drawing on the great scientists of his Edinburgh, and Christison was obviously the legendary case of auto-experimentalism). Oscar Wilde's remark in *"The Decay of Lying"* that "the transformation of Dr Jekyll reads dangerously like an experiment out of the *Lancet"* goes right to the heart of the story's root. Conan Doyle's Edinburgh was much less Calvinist-dominated than Stevenson's and so the controversy as to the theology of the story does not concern us; but he would have recognised the cold scientific ambition, and the readiness to sacrifice moral considerations to science, which are fundamental to Jekyll. The geography, too, is Edinburgh, with its characteristic, little shared by London, of a fashionable house backing on a small disreputable street. Mr John S. Gibson's study of Deacon Brodie notes this, particularly felicitously adding that Utterson's "mounting" a small street to the square where Jekyll lived clearly reflects the famous steep slopes of Edinburgh. Yet Stevenson firmly asserted the location of his work was in London.

This metamorphosis of location on Stevenson's part seems a vital origin of Conan Doyle's *Study in Scarlet* and subsequent works. If Stevenson could get away with it, why could not he? Hence scene after scene, name after name, trait after trait, of Sherlock Holmes's London can be found in Edinburgh rather than in London. The same juxtaposition of rich and poor streets obtains in the Sherlock Holmes stories. In *"The Man with the Twisted Lip"* Edinburgh is strongly asserted from the first. Opium dens are few enough for Mrs Isa Whitney to know exactly where her husband is, lacking the problems London would pose with a large choice at his disposal. Watson, at Holmes's suggestion, packs Whitney home in a cab, which was a natural arrangement in the small centre of an intimate town, but fairly risky for a huge city. The local police are amusedly ready to humour the idiosyncracies of prisoners held for trial rather than insisting on the application of prison regulations, and are also ready to oblige the local gentry—as, even more incredibly, for London, Athelney Jones and the authorities in *The Sign of Four* are to permit Watson to take recovered stolen property home to its alleged part-owner before it has even been processed. Mrs Neville St Clair walks from the customer service of a shipping office to her train which takes her through Swandam Lane with its opium den; London would find such a proceeding very unusual, but in Edinburgh a cut through any wynd or close would be a logical proceeding even for a fashionable lady going from the High Street to the railway station, and in so small an area her odds would be far better for making an accidental discovery of a husband supposedly at work. The names of the streets continue Edinburgh rather than London: Saxe-Coburg Square, as described, is far less elegant than the New Town's Saxe-Coburg Place, but its nearby streets seem appropriate locations for a declining pawn-broker.

The problems about London geography which bother the Sherlockologists have an obvious explanation in the author's thinking consciously or unconsciously of his Edinburgh. Mr Martin Dakin points out that Breckinridge in *"The Blue Carbuncle"* would not have a goosestall at Covent Garden, and would rather have been in Smithfield Market, but Edinburgh stall-markets would have been less specialist. The commissionaire in *"The Blue Carbuncle"* is an odd touch: 221B would hardly have had one, yet Holmes and Watson do not even trouble to identify him by his office, as they would do in a neighbourhood as well-supplied in such officials as the Baker Street area would be; but a University servitor in a building near at hand to 23 George Square would automatically supply his own identification without further parley. Mr Dakin (these are all his points) is particularly bothered about the poky quarters revealed in the sketch of the Foreign Office, but if Conan Doyle were thinking about an Edinburgh solicitor's office with a clerk kept in late to transcribe a critical document, it makes immediate sense; even the sketch resembles a New Town solicitor's office or perhaps bears some relation to the Office of Works where Charles Doyle, his superior and his two fellow-clerks, discharged their duties. The "Baker Street Irregulars" do not come from Baker Street, as they cost Holmes something in bus tickets when they report, and sound much more like products of a city in which the walker might readily get to know street-urchins: certainly in such a case they would not need bus fares, as they would likely come from places like the Cowgate, and could easily get from there to a fashionable residence. The bus fares would be a sensible attempt to transfer their location to London, but it then becomes unclear how Holmes could be so sure of them. Moreover, Holmes's use of them does testify to the "Democratic Intellect", as does John Buchan's *Huntingtower* with its "Gorbals Die-Hards", both men carrying a profound belief in the natural intellectual powers of proletarian youth demanding and deserving means of expression and encouragement. Holmes is too impersonal to become sentimental about the association as Dickson McCunn does, but in abstract argument he makes his position very clear. The *locus classicus* is "*The Naval Treaty*":

> . . . Holmes was sunk in profound thought and hardly opened his mouth until he had passed Clapham Junction.
>
> "It's a very cheering thing to come into London by any of these lines which run high and allow you to look upon the houses like this."
>
> I thought he was joking, for the view was sordid enough, but he soon explained himself.
>
> "Look at those big, isolated clumps of building rising up above the slates, like brick islands in a lead-coloured sea."
>
> "The Board schools."
>
> "Lighthouses, my boy! Beacons of the future! Capsules, with hundreds of bright little seeds in each, out of which will spring the wiser, better England of the future. . . ."

This is all quite irrelevant to the case, and clearly was inserted from deliberate motives of evangelisation. Conan Doyle was educating his English audience to the Scottish educational principle of learning being given the widest dissemination to maximise the intellectual resources of the country.

The sense of Edinburgh as a unity is powerfully reasserted in all of this transferrence of Edinburgh locations and persons to London. The very fact that Conan Doyle had abandoned his Catholicism reinforced that sense of unity, and all the more from that he would give no quarter at all to any Protestant anti-Catholicism, even to the extent of trying to rob Micah Clarke of much of it. It would be his work which would result in the removal of anti-Catholic matter from the King's Coronation oath. In so seeing it, he did not discount the existence of conflict, but succeeded in viewing it as an example of the unity in nature of contending figures, much as Challenger and Summerlee are never more akin to one another than when they are locked in ferocious opposition. Oddly enough, that great sense of humour transformed one last memory of Edinburgh University from the pain and anger that it evoked at the time to the grand comedy of the larger totality of which it formed part when symbolised by him in the battles of Challenger and Summerlee. It arose out of his final oral examination.

His orals had on the whole gone well. In *The Firm of Girdlestone* he recalled the 1878 group on Botany, Natural History and Chemistry, although he altered his own experience by having Dimsdale, his hero, fail Chemistry and thereby abandon his medical career. Wyville Thomson and another examiner took the Natural History oral. Neither description in *Girdlestone* sounds like the *Challenger* explorer, bearded and stout, but the subject was that put to Arthur in their examination:

. . . Tom found himself facing a great spider crab, which appeared to be regarding him with a most malignant expression upon its crustacean features. Behind the crab sat a little professor, whose projecting eyes and crooked arms gave him such a resemblance to the creature in front that the student could not help smiling.

"Sir", said a tall, clean-shaven man at the other end of the table, "be serious. This is no time for levity."

Tom's expression after that would have made the fortune of a mute.

"What is this?" asked the little professor, handing a small round object to the candidate.

"It's an echinus—a sea-urchin", Tom said triumphantly.

"Have they any circulation?" asked the other examiner.

"A water vascular system".

"Describe it."

Tom started off fluently, but it was no part of the policy of the examiners to allow him to waste the fifteen minutes allotted them in expatiating upon what he knew well. They interrupted him after a few sentences.

"How does this creature walk?" asked the crab-like one.

"By means of long tubes which it projects at pleasure."

"How do the tubes enable the creature to walk?"

"They have suckers on them."

"What are the suckers like?"

"They are round hollow discs."

"Are you sure they are round?" asked the other sharply.

"Yes", said Tom stoutly, though his ideas on the subject were rather vague.

"And how does this sucker act?" asked the taller examiner.

Tom began to feel that these two men were exhibiting a very unseemly curiosity. There seemed to be no satiating their desire for information. "It creates a vacuum", he cried desperately.

"How does it create a vacuum?"

"By the contraction of a muscular pimple in the centre", said Tom, in a moment of inspiration.

"And what makes this pimple contract?"

Tom lost his head, and was about to say "electricity", when he happily checked himself and substituted "muscular action".

"Very good", said the examiners, and the student breathed again. The taller one returned to the charge, however, with, "And this muscle—is it composed of striped fibres or non-striped?"

"Non-striped", shrieked Tom at a venture, and both examiners rubbed their hands and murmured, "Very good, indeed!" at which Tom's hair began to lie a little flatter.

"How many teeth has a rabbit?" the tall man asked suddenly.

"I don't know", the student answered with candour.

The two looked triumphantly at one another.

"He doesn't know", cried the goggle-eyed one decisively.

"I should recommend you to count them the next time you have one for dinner." As this was evidently meant for a joke, Tom had the tact to laugh, and a very gruesome and awe-inspiring laugh it was too.

Then the candidate was badgered about the pterodactyl, and concerning the difference in anatomy between a bat and a bird, and about the lamprey, and the cartilaginous fishes, and the amphioxus. . . .

The examiners' notes go into detail on the examination on the echinus, but suggest the remainder of the discussion was on amphibians. If the pterodactyl was really featured in the discussion, it is one of the few occasions known to science when a question at an oral examination gave rise to the climax of a great work of literature a third of a century later. Even if it did not, it is amusing to note that the identification of pterodactyls with the leader of the *Challenger* expedition had already lodged itself in Conan Doyle's mind by *Girdlestone,* and hence that it is indeed to Wyville Thomson we owe the famous emergence of the prehistoric monster in the Queen's Hall at the end of *The Lost World.* If the pterodactyl did not receive a glancing mention in the oral, then it must have been associated with one of his lectures: perhaps some student sarcastically inquired afterwards of his peers why the great man had not brought a pterodactyl back with him on the *Challenger* when he appeared to have brought virtually everything else. Hence came the natural decision to make an expedition of Challenger one concerned with prehistoric flora and fauna, which in any case was demanded in some form to provide something dramatic enough to outshine the huge wealth of material in the *Challenger* expedition. Once again, Conan Doyle kept his material on board for a fine long spell of maturation before putting it out.

As to the rabbit's teeth, again unmentioned in the examiners' note, it also seems an inspiration for the future, one classic instance of where it paid off being in "*A Scandal in Bohemia*":

> . . . "You see, but you do not observe. The distinction is clear. For example, you have frequently seen the steps which lead up from the hall to this room."
>
> "Frequently."
>
> "How often?"
>
> "Well, some hundreds of times."
>
> "Then how many are there?"
>
> "How many! I don't know."
>
> "Quite so! You have not observed. And yet you have seen. That is just my point. . . ."

If the matter rather than the person in the zoology oral in *Girdlestone* relates to Wyville Thomson's oral, it is the converse with John Hutton Balfour's Botany oral. Eighty years of age when he examined Arthur, he would retire the following year and would be treated by Christison, as we have seen, although surviving him and dying in 1884. *Girdlestone* seems at variance in the matter discussed during the oral from what can be deduced from the official note on Conan Doyle's transcript, and there is no reason to credit the idea that Arthur resembled Tom Dimsdale in passing because the second examiner wanted to help a local rugby football hero. But the portrait of Balfour in action seems credible enough:

> . . . As he moved to the botany table a grey-bearded examiner waved his hand in the direction of the row of microscopes as an intimation that the student was to look through them and pronounce upon what he saw. Tom seemed to compress his whole soul into his one eye as he glared hopelessly through the tube at what appeared to him to resemble nothing so much as a sheet of ice with the marks of skates upon it.

"Come along, come along!" the examiner growled impatiently. Courtesy is conspicuous by its absence in most of the Edinburgh examinations. "You must pass on to the next one, unless you can offer an opinion."

This venerable teacher of botany, though naturally a kind-hearted man, was well known as one of the most malignant species of examiners, one of the school which considers such an ordeal in the light of a trial of strength between their pupils and themselves. In his eyes the candidate was endeavouring to pass, and his duty was to endeavour to prevent him, a result which, in a large proportion of cases, he successfully accomplished.

"Hurry on, hurry on!" he reiterated fussily.

"It's a section of a leaf", said the student.

"It's nothing of the sort", the examiner shouted exultantly. "You've made a bad mistake, sir; a very bad one, indeed. It's the spirillae of a water plant. Move on to the next."

Tom, in much perturbation of mind, shuffled down the line and looked through the next brazen tube. "This is a preparation of stomata", he said, recognizing it from a print in his book on botany.

The professor shook his head despondingly. "You are right", he said; "pass on to the next". . . .

Girdlestone takes us no farther in the realm of authentic reminiscence, unless Dimsdale's subsequent misadventures in chemistry are those of some friend or acquaintance. Perhaps it should be added, in view of Mr Charles Higham's use of the book, that he is of course mistaken in stating "Luckily for the biographer, he left a detailed account of the rooms he occupied in Howe Street while he was a student", and subsequent commentators have accepted Mr Higham's word for it. Arthur lived at home all the time he was in Edinburgh. However, the Howe Street flat was not imaginary, although probably he never saw it. Howe Street was the first Edinburgh residence of Bryan Charles Waller.

We have no recollection of the orals of 14 April 1879 to equal *Girdlestone's* version of those of 6 April 1878. Arthur weathered Anatomy, Institutes of Medicine, Materia Medica and Pathology. Of his final orals, however, on 9 and 11 June 1881, we have a slight account in an indignant letter to Dr and Mrs Hoare of Birmingham, where he complained bitterly of unfair treatment at the hands of Professor James Spence in Surgery. Spence, then almost seventy and with only a year to live, was the original of "Hayes" mentioned in passing in *"His First Operation"* as "the leader of the cleanliness-and-cold-water school", and the relevance of the next line "they all hate each other like poison" had to do with Spence's protracted feud with Lister and the Listerians. It had conspicuously begun in 1864 when Lister put in for the Chair of Systematic Surgery, backed by Syme, his father-in-law, and by Christison. With one rival for the chair, Patrick Heron Watson, he was on tolerably friendly terms, but with the other, Spence, he was not, and Spence, with seniority on the faculty, won, by one vote. Spence, somewhat encouraged by Simpson, began to attack Lister publicly on his use of antiseptics, and early in 1880, with Lister in London, returned to the fray, openly accusing Lister of falsifying the statistics he had cited in favour of his argument. The violence of the exchanges was obviously an antecedent of the Challenger-

Summerlee duel, including Summerlee's implication that the fraudulency with which he charged Challenger came within the realm of the criminal. Spence in fact had tried Lister's method, specifically with respect to the use of catgut, and had failed.

Known to the students as "dismal Jimmie", Spence encased his feet in very tight patent leather boots, ultimately the cause of the senile gangrene from which he died: it may have accounted for the unfairness with which he treated Conan Doyle at the oral, for the pain must have been greatly advanced even by then. The fact that his vanity was his executioner did nothing to improve his temper. His pessimism was both incessant and infectious.

There was no particular reason why Conan Doyle should have fallen a victim to the wars among his seniors, envenomed though they were. Thomas Annandale, who succeeded Lister, used to refer to Arthur and his companions by snarling at some student, "Shut that door, and keep out the noise of Dr Bell's rabble", but ACD does not seem to have encountered him in an examination. Patrick Heron Watson never accepted Lister's antiseptic methods, but his memory remained green in the Listerian ranks. It was certainly from his Crimean experience, whence he returned home, believed certain to die, that Arthur drew the military fate of his Dr John Watson. But Bell supplied a target for Spence in place of the absent Lister, and more specifically Arthur as Bell's clerk, most conspicuous among his large following, and quite possibly becoming celebrated as a student short-story writer and whaler, was in for a very rough ride when he finally encountered Spence at the examination table. All the accumulated bitterness, pain and despair of years confronted the youthful and confident Arthur, now faced by his last hurdle, and whatever the details the episode seems to have been a singularly unpleasant one. There is little sign that ACD forgave Spence, either. Any use of his eccentricities in a work of fiction would have been impossible without Arthur's humour bubbling out, and there seems no equivalent of "Dismal Jimmie" in the Conan Doyle fiction. But at least Challenger and Summerlee enabled Conan Doyle to put to constructive use his wounds as a surrogate Bell, Lister and Syme. In the last analysis, however unwelcome, Spence's hatred was almost a compliment.

It was a sour note on which to end, and home conditions prevented any immediate permanent plan by which a career could be started in Edinburgh. Here Arthur's fate was the reverse of Stevenson's. His own health was excellent, his response to the town far less personally doom-laden, yet his family situation demanded short-term plans and preferably away from Edinburgh. He does not seem to have agonised about his departure, though it is clear from his articles in the *British Journal of Photography* that he had acquired a deep love of the Scottish countryside, especially for the islands whether in the Forth or in the west. The open air, the exercise, the challenge of the camera, the remoteness yet nearness to home, the simplicity of brief escape, all combined to woo him. Little enough remains in his fiction to perpetuate that happiness, and indeed the sense of his father's tragedy

looming over his head accounts for the doom-laden atmosphere of all three
of his major stories dealing with Scottish locations: *"John Barrington
Cowles"*, *"The Man from Archangel"* and *"Our Midnight Visitor"*. It was a
different doom from that which haunts Stevenson's work: conspicuously, in
none of the three stories is the narrator personally made part of the doom,
though in all three cases he is deeply drawn in by sympathy, Armitage by his
friendship for Cowles, the student in *"Our Midnight Visitor"* by his duty to
his father and even the ludicrously misanthropic M'Vittie winning
unexpected dignity in the end by his most reluctant sentiment for the
mysterious Russians embroiled in their love and hate.

Arthur rejoined the Hoares in Birmingham after his graduation, and he had
certainly returned there by March 1882 when he sent *"The Actor's Duel"* to
Blackwood's, although the transience of the arrangement was shown by his
giving Lonsdale Terrace as his return address. But in the interval he
commenced another adventure, with literary consequences more specific yet
in some ways also deeper and more far-reaching than his Greenland voyage.
He was thinking about "the Army, Navy, Indian Service of anything which
offered an opening". Then he obtained an unexpected response to an offer of
his to act as ship's doctor, and was appointed to the African Steam Navigation
Company's *Mayumba*. Once again, he was lucky in his captain. "Captain
Gordon Wallace was one of the best", he remembered affectionately in
Memories and Adventures. He received an early indication of it when the
ammonia he required for his photographic experiments exploded, reducing
the entire crew to tears through which the Captain parodied Thomas Moore
sardonically

> You may scowl at the surgeon, and swear if you will,
> But the scent of his hartshorn will hang round you still.

Nevertheless, it was one of his less happy memories. The weather was
initially diabolical, the crew was most unpleasantly seasick and in need of
much attention, and the surgeon's stomach was feeling by no means strong
enough to minister with that remoteness which characterised his former
instructors. At Lagos he fell a prey to fever, and was lucky to emerge from it
with his life. He also began to become worried by the relative luxury of the
life of a ship's doctor, and swore off drink for the rest of the voyage. "I drank
quite freely at this period of my life", he recalled in *Memories and Adventures*,
"having a head and a constitution which made me fairly immune, but my
reason told me that the unbounded cocktails of West Africa were a danger,
and with an effort I cut them out." The shadow of Charles Altamont Doyle
never left him, although his medical training helped him distinguish between
relaxation and actual danger. There is a sympathetic understanding of what
dragged his father down in his discovery of "a certain subtle pleasure in
abstinence, and it is only socially that it is difficult". On the other hand, he
found, with pleasure, an old Stonyhurst schoolmate, whom he calls "Tom" in
his photographic reminiscences, possibly the purser, Tom King.

But the great event of the journey, and perhaps the most momentous
encounter he had yet sustained in the course of his life, was when the

American Minister to Liberia came on board the ship for some three days. Arthur had met and seen great men before, at Edinburgh University, in his family circle and friends, possibly at Stonyhurst if in fact Gerard Manley Hopkins was called in to help adjudge his early efforts at poetry. But this was his first meeting of any intimacy with a man who had played a great part in the history of the world, outside of the purely cultural and intellectual spheres. It was indeed a point of contact. And, like his future imaginary meeting of David and Odysseus, it was one in which the participants only dimly realised the significance of what was taking place. Arthur came to appreciate that he was talking to a very remarkable man; his account in *Memories and Adventures* testifies to that. On the other hand, his new friend's name made no dent in his memory that he recorded. He never met him again. A month after Conan Doyle's return to Liverpool, the United States Minister to Liberia was dead. Arthur may have realised that was going to happen. He does not say that their talk was begun by a medical examination, but it was the most likely basis for it.

In any event, they quickly progressed to literature. "My starved literary side was eager for good talk, and it was wonderful to sit on deck discussing Bancroft and Motley, and then suddenly realize that you were talking to one who had possibly been a slave himself, and was certainly the son of slaves." This sounds a little vague on the basis of a three-day conversation: in fact it is absolutely correct. Henry Highland Garnet was born on December 23, 1815, in New Market, Kent County, Maryland, where his parents were slaves, but when he was nine they all escaped. Garnet left no record as to whether he was involved in slave labour himself, and his comments on the system seem to have related always to the sacrifices of his family and his people, not of himself. Hence Arthur's record is absolutely consistent with what we know of his friend. But he may well have heard some account from Garnet of his time on a schooner from New York to Washington, D.C., as cook and steward in 1829, a natural thing to talk about on board ship; no doubt Garnet was forced to remain on board ship as slavery and the slave-trade still existed in the District of Columbia, and his status was driven home to him when he discovered on return to New York that the slave-catchers, using the existing federal legislation for the return of fugitive slaves, had raided his home, stolen or destroyed the furniture, and dragged his sister Elizabeth back into slavery. His father had escaped by running through a neighbour's back yard on hearing the sound of his name pronounced by one of the catchers: it was not simple cowardice, necessarily, for his daughter had far more chance of proving her freedom than did he. Almost certainly in her early 'teens, she convinced the recorder of New York she had always been a resident, and even if it was suspected she had fled to New York as a child, that put her in a very different category from an adult male runaway slave whose continued defiance of white law and order would be a dangerous example to others. Garnet's mother was sheltered by friends, and meanwhile the returned fourteen-year-old bought a large clasp knife and prowled the city in search of his family's enemies. It was hard work for friends to convince him to give it up. The fact that the man whose name-dropping wrecked the slave-catching operation knew Garnet's father's name since he himself was a relative of the Maryland slaveowner from whom they had fled, was an additional incentive. The name of the slaveowner struck a chord in Arthur's mind: Colonel Spencer. The name was sufficiently close to that of the injurious "dismal Jimmie" whose punishment of students for his controversies with their teachers still rankled. They came together in *"The Copper Beeches"* to supply the name of Violet Hunter's original employer, and Mr Rucastle's observation, despite his detestable character and conduct, is illuminating:

" 'You are looking for a situation, miss?'

" 'Yes, sir.'

" 'As governess?'

" 'Yes, sir.'

" 'And what salary do you ask?'

" 'I had four pounds a month in my last place with Colonel Spence Munro.'

" 'Oh, tut, tut! sweating—rank sweating! . . . How could anyone offer so pitiful a sum to a lady with such attractions and accomplishments? . . . The point is, have you or have you not the bearing and deportment of a lady? There it is in a nutshell. . . . if you have, why, then, how could any gentleman ask you to condescend to accept anything under the three figures? . . . ' "

Conan Doyle's account of the unnamed Garnet in *Memories and Adventures* begins "The most intelligent and well-read man whom I met on the Coast was a negro gentleman". What was in his mind, as his mention of slavery makes clear, was that Garnet was so pre-eminently a man of culture, learning, wisdom and a gentleman, and yet the rights of Colonel Spencer were intended to ensure that the law doomed him to servitude. With his thoughts on his sisters, governesses in Lisbon, it was an easy transference to thinking how close their situation was to wage-slavery, and that they, also, could be all too easily at the mercy of selfish and possibly dangerous employers. ACD was throughout his life acutely sensitive to the thought of women in subjection at the mercy of men in positions of authority; it led him, for instance, to denounce the Roman Catholic practice of auricular confession, expressing his greatest horror at the thought of young girls confessing to celibate older men. He did not imagine sexual misconduct on the part of the clergy so much as fear the psychological implications, and the assumptions of the clergy of their fitness to pronounce on matters which were peculiarly the right of women to keep to themselves. In this he showed far more sensitivity than his Catholic critics, notably converts like Chesterton (in his book *The Thing*): it was not a reassertion of the idiotic old charges of clerical lechery of the Maria Monk kind but a very sensible response from a medical authority, and one which Roman Catholic authorities today should treat with the greatest of receptivity. The fate of Garnet's sister Elizabeth would naturally have prompted such a train of thought, all the more so because he regretted the voyage brought him so close to Lisbon without stopping there.

The second name of "Colonel Spence Munro" is also suggestive. Garnet's title was correctly that of Minister to Monrovia, the capitol of Liberia, named after the American President James Monroe. The name also reappears, again from mental association with Garnet, in *"The Yellow Face"*, the client John Grant Munro being the man who liberates his wife's black daughter from her life of disguise and sequestration.

On a somewhat more frivolous note, Mr Martin Dakin has noted that all colonels, apart from Watson's friend Hayter in *"The Reigate Squires"*, are invariably unpleasant in the Holmes cycle. It is not an anti-military prejudice, and such a thing would be absurd in the context of Conan Doyle's life. As he says,

> Think of the list. Colonel Sebastian Moran, 'the second most dangerous man in London'; Colonel Moriarty, who tried to whitewash his villainous brother by taking away Holmes's character; Colonel Barclay, who emulated David's sin; Colonel Valentine Walter, who stole the Bruce-Partington plans; Colonel Carruthers, whom Holmes locked up; Colonel Upcott [Upwood], of atrocious conduct; Colonel Ross, who was unpardonably rude to Holmes; and perhaps even Colonel Spence Munro, who extracted sweated labour from Miss Violet Hunter. For the sake of completeness I should mention also Colonel Lysander Stark, who wasn't really a colonel at all, and Colonel Emsworth, also rude to Holmes . . .

And even there the indefatigable Mr Dakin forgets Colonel Warburton, whose madness was drawn by Watson to Holmes's attention, admittedly an ambiguous case, and, most relevant to Garnet of all, Colonel Elias Openshaw, Negrophobe and participant in Ku Klux Klan atrocities. An instinctive coupling of colonels with evil may be grotesque, but, as Holmes put it, "there is but one step from the grotesque to the horrible". And the horror is Colonel Spencer and his slavecatchers, thirsting to drag the boy Henry Highland Garnet and his intellect, the sister Elizabeth and her virtue, back to degradation, dehumanization, dishonour, ignorance and darkness. It lent a deeper twist to *Uncle Tom's Cabin*. The famous episode of Eliza, the bloodhounds and the ice, is justly celebrated for its blazing assertion of precisely what the pursuit of slaves entailed, but Garnet, profound in his learning, inspiration and character, conveyed to Arthur exactly what loss to the world was taking place when intellect such as his was stunted in slavery.

The lessons ACD had learned from Scottish education as to the urgency of giving opportunity to intellect from any level of society naturally shaped themselves into assimilation of a further implication of the horror of slavery. Here the Scottish legacy shook hands with one of the cardinal motivations of modern American Negro thought. As Henry Highland Garnet and Arthur Conan Doyle were speaking, there was growing up in the United States a young man who would become famous for his demand that blacks readjust their aims to further "the talented tenth" of their number whose intellect could only serve their people by being given its opportunity to develop. And W. E. B. du Bois's priorities were accepted, as the great development of black education, historiography, sociology and culture in the early twentieth century bears witness. The blacks, in fact, proceeded from the Scottish principle which had played so conspicuous a part in leavening American education. But if it did, it was to do so on the principle Henry Highland Garnet had asserted throughout his life, that blacks must rely on their own efforts to win their true freedom.

Conan Doyle's evidence and that of his stories enables us to see that his conversations with Garnet involved the slavery experience. What else he learned has to be more inferential, and it is probable that he heard more of Garnet's views than any great detail on his career. He probably never realised that Garnet became one of the most famous black advocates of the abolition of slavery in the 1840s, second only to his rival Frederick Douglass. Mr Earl Ofari, to whose *"Let Your Motto be Resistance": The Life and Thought of Henry Highland Garnet* I am profoundly obliged, is rather too ready to see Garnet as the militant and Douglass as the conciliator. In fact Garnet associated himself with what was regarded as a more conciliatory wing of the anti-slavery movement, that of Lewis Tappan, Theodore Dwight Weld and James Gillespie Birney, who supported constitutional action and intervened in Presidential elections to considerable effect with their Liberty party. We may make allowance for geographical influence: Garnet followed a New York line in New York, black abolitionists in Massachusetts accepted the leadership of Garrison and his newspaper *The Liberator*. Yet Garnet's thought leads one to go beyond this materialistic explanation. The high-flown theology of such an argument as Garrison's repelled him in itself, an aspect of his character which would have appealed to Arthur. The Liberty party and the elections were there to be used, as were any means which might bring an end to slavery. Moreover, behind Garrison's terrific courage, marvellous eloquence and embattled intransigence was an element of patronage of the great black orator under his banner, and ultimately Douglass was forced out of self-respect to break with him. Garnet seems to have been decidedly quicker than Douglass in scenting the implications of white patronage. He had with difficulty won an education, and his struggles made learning all the dearer to him. In 1835 he went to classes in Noyes Academy at Canaan, New Hampshire, but a local mob dragged the school down with oxen demanding the black students be driven out of the state. When a students' boarding-house was fired on, Garnet fired back and their enemies in the darkness dispersed. As a result, Garnet never accepted the non-violence of Garrison and Douglass. Driven from New Hampshire and forced to ride on the tops of carriages and decks of river-boats because of the oppressive legislation in the north demanding segregation (in the slaveholding south slaves travelled inside carriages, being valuable property whose health needed protection), the students were assailed by abuse on their road and Garnet himself was suffering from fever. This again was possibly a talking-point with Conan Doyle. The *Mayumba's* doctor had just recovered from his own terrible experience with fever, and Garnet is described as having contracted fever "on his arrival" in Liberia. (He shook it off, but developed asthma, and died on February 12, 1882, aged sixty-six.)

Conan Doyle may have been treating him after an attack of fever, or prescribing against what might have been looking like an imminent attack. Clearly they would not have been talking incessantly to one another for three days if Garnet was actually in the throes of the illness which ultimately proved fatal to him. But as a doctor Conan Doyle would naturally have sought particulars of his history, especially with reference to previous attacks of fever: it was hardly a moment to play Joe Bell, and in any case Holmes, if not Bell, knew the advantage of inviting the client to indulge in auto-biography. Sitting on deck, the comfort of their quarters, the respect of the crew towards the American Minister (quite apart from the doctor's delight in his company) must have seemed grimly ironic to Garnet in any reminiscent vein.

In 1835 Garnet went to the great anti-slavery centre of higher education, the Oneida Theological Institute (which argues tremendous purpose on his part in having, with so much opposition and privation, somewhere acquired pre-university attainments). He graduated in 1840, moved to Troy, New York, where he obtained licence to preach from the Presbytery of Troy. He married Julia Williams, who had studied in the famous boarding-school for black girls run in the teeth of local opposition by Prudence Crandall in Connec-ticut—a futher illustration of his intellectual priorities—and in 1843 was ordained and appointed pastor of Liberty Street Presbyterian Church, Troy. He played a major part in the agitation for votes for blacks in the state, again a reminder of his pragmatism as opposed to the Utopianism of the Garrisonians, and he threw himself into several short-lived ventures in black abolitionist journalism. He became noted as an orator, and encountered much abuse.

Once a pumpkin was thrown at his head, he ducked, it deluged the stage as it crashed, and he said coolly "My good friends, do not be alarmed, it is only a soft pumpkin; some gentleman has thrown away his head, and lo! his brains are dashed out!" The sixty-six-year-old and twenty-two-year-old on the *Mayumba* had it also in common that they were crusaders of humour. Arthur's new-found adhesion to temperance for the voyage would also have won support from his friend, whatever social embarrassment it caused elsewhere. Garnet had crusaded in the 1840s to eliminate the use of alcohol by blacks, believing drink one cause of family breakup, crime, prostitution, vagrancy and other qualities whites reiterated against blacks to justify their degradation in the north and their enslavement in the south. On his way to Canada in 1848 to address a temperance meeting he was beaten and dragged from a Buffalo railway carriage for refusing to give up a seat declared to be in the "white section". Garnet reacted characteristically by pointing out in a letter to the sympathetic Buffalo *Propeller* that such crimes were character-istically Northern rather than Southern:

> In justice to the people of the South, whom the Northern dough-faces make the scape goats of their villainy and outrage, I would say that there is no evidence that they demand any such gratuitous servility and inhumanity.

But by now he was known as a highly extreme advocate of antislavery, whose critics within and outwith the abolitionist circles charged him with calling for a servile war. In August, 1843, he had stated in a major address at Buffalo, specifically breaking with antislavery tradition to address his remarks to the slaves themselves:

> Slavery has fixed a deep gulf between you and us, and while it shuts out from you the relief and consolation which your friends would willingly render, it

afflicts and persecutes you with a fierceness which we might not expect to see in
the fires of hell . . .

It is in your power so to torment the God-cursed slaveholders, that they will
be glad to let you go free. If the scale was turned, and black men were the
masters and white men the slaves, every destructive agent and element would
be employed to lay the oppressor low. Danger and death would hang over their
heads day and night. Yes, the tyrants would meet with plagues more terrible
than those of Pharaoh. But you are a patient people. You act as though you
were made for the special use of those devils. You act as though your daughters
were born to pamper the lusts of your masters and overseers. And worse than
all, you tamely submit while your lords tear your wives from your embraces
and defile them before your eyes. In the name of God, we ask, are you
men? Where is the blood of your fathers? Has it all run out of your veins?
Awake, awake; millions of voices are calling you! Your dead fathers speak to
you from their graves. Heaven, as with a voice of thunder, calls on you to arise
from the dust.

Let your motto be resistance! *resistance! resistance!* No oppressed people have
ever secured their liberty without resistance . . .

Very formidable qualities lay behind the charming, erudite black diplomat.
His striking figure was impaired by one deformity. After the sortie of Colonel
Spencer's agents Garnet had been sent to live secretly in Smithtown, Long
Island, where being employed as a contract labourer he lost his right leg in an
accident. As Simpson and his work had not yet advanced the science of
anaesthetics, the amputation would have been under the full horrors of
consciousness. An examination by Arthur involving study of the mutilated
limb could well have revealed some frightful side-effects, for the chances of
treatments of the sophistication of Syme and Liston were extremely small for
a poor Negro labourer.

But whatever his deformity, Garnet's eloquence and intellect charmed
Arthur. And the reference to discussion of George Bancroft and J. L. Motley
is extremely revealing. Both writers were charged, more than any of their
contemporaries, with exaltation of human liberty and the justice of violence
in its behalf. Motley might well have emerged if, as seems probable, the
Presbyterian minister Garnet asked whether the young Scottish doctor was of
his faith, whereof Scotland was honoured as the cradle. Arthur, in denying it,
would have had to explain his own position, and Motley, as the most popular
American historian of Europe, would be a natural point of discussion. Arthur,
the future author of *Micah Clarke*, would vehemently assure his friend that
he held no brief for the Inquisition. And from the due meed of applause, with
possible judicious reservations, for Motley's panegyric on William the Silent
and the sea-beggars, and discussion of the finer points of Bancroft's paean in
praise of the American Revolution as triumph of freedom, it was all too
natural for Garnet politely to move the discussion to the implications of
Motley's and Bancroft's doctrines for their enslaved black fellow-countrymen.
To acknowledge that both Arthur and Garnet would have hailed the doctrines
of freedom in the simplicity with which Motley and Bancroft extolled them is
obvious on the face of it; in neither case would this have meant a blanket
endorsement, for both of them had keen and critical intellects, and a lively

capacity to tease out the inconsistencies, failures in logic and crudity of portraiture in material under analysis.

And once turning the conversation to the blacks, Garnet would naturally have given his opinions in characteristic honest fashion. Arthur was very impressed by his capacity for neatly serving out sauce for the white gander in equal proportion to that normally reserved for the black goose. "The only way to explore Africa", he recorded Garnet saying in answer to his remarks on travel in the interior, "is to go without arms and with few servants. You would not like it in England if a body of men came armed to the teeth and marched through your land. The Africans are quite as sensitive." Conan Doyle, writing forty years later, cheered the recollection: "It was the method of Livingstone as against the method of Stanley. The former takes the braver and better man." Yet it would be logical to see exactly such treatment of the justice of the Dutch or the American cause: that it was only just if the cause of blacks in rebellion against slavery was just too. Garnet in September 1848 had regretted in print that a group of slaves had been recaptured without their giving a good account of themselves. "They ought to have been better prepared. One good cannon, well managed, would have crippled a dozen steamers. If white men were to undertake to run away from human blood-hounds, they would see to it, that the telegraph wires were cut the distance of every ten miles, in the direction of their flight. More than this they would do; they would pull up the rails of the railroads, and stop the speed of the iron horses. Do you think . . . it would be an unpardonable sin for slaves to do the same?"

"This negro gentleman did me good", remarked Conan Doyle in *Memories and Adventures*, "for a man's brain is an organ for the formation of his own thoughts and also for the digestion of other people's, and it needs fresh fodder." It had certainly found it. True to his principles, Arthur let the seed Henry Highland Garnet had sown lie in the soil for almost two years. Then he produced the second major work of his life, *"J. Habakuk Jephson's Statement"*, which gained him entry into the *Cornhill*, and is of the quality of the *"Captain of the 'Pole-Star'"*, but where the latter is a masterpiece of delicacy, this is one of strength, power and anger. It is also a historical source for us, in that it conveys that Henry Highland Garnet told Arthur far more than the quiet complimentary reminiscences in *Memories and Adventures* suggest, and that in so doing he gave him simultaneously a marvellous window into human history, into the relations of black and white, into the pitfalls of freedom, into the savagery induced by oppression. It explains how he could write with such understanding in *The White Company* of the miseries of a despised class, who creep through the story under oppression, contempt and outlawry, to blaze into light and slay when they can: very significantly one of the first "masterless men" Alleyne finds in *The White Company* is black, which is decidedly odd for fourteenth-century England but very helpful for a biographer in quest of historical symbolism.

But it is in *"Jephson"* that the evidence is richest. It comes in the great speech of Septimius Goring, who has massacred the whites in the *Marie*

Celeste, and is forced to help Jephson escape. Goring is not Garnet, although he is the product of part of Garnet's logic, as well as of the brutalisation Garnet saw as the inevitable result of slavery. His mutilation is a nice touch, indicating how Conan Doyle was inspired by the recollection of Garnet's lost leg, but very sensibly it is made the direct result of enslavement instead of the more casual consequence of the socio-economic degradation of the blacks in the North. The grandeur of the speech is that it defies white comment. Jephson has emerged as a somewhat patronising but decent man of excellent racial instincts which justly save his life: because he has given much to the cause of the freedom of the blacks he deserves the protection he gets in the story, where ordinary neutral figures perish, but he would never get that protection, whatever his virtues, from Septimius Goring. Nor does he seek an iota of forgiveness:

> "I wish you to carry a message back", he said, "to the white race, the great dominating race whom I hate and defy. Tell them that I have battened on their blood for twenty years, that I have slain them until even I became tired of what had once been a joy, that I did this unnoticed and unsuspected in the face of every precaution which their civilization could suggest. There is no satisfaction in revenge when your enemy does not know who has struck him. I am not sorry, therefore, to have you as a messenger. There is no need why I should tell you how this great hate became born in me. See this", and he held up his mutilated hand; "that was done by a white man's knife. My father was white, my mother was a slave. When he died she was sold again, and I, a child then, saw her lashed to death to break her of some of the little airs and graces which her late master had encouraged in her. My young wife, too, oh, my young wife!" a shudder ran through his whole frame. "No matter! I swore my oath, and I kept it. From Maine to Florida, and from Boston to San Francisco, you could track my steps by sudden deaths which baffled the police. I warred against the whole white race as they for centuries had warred against the black one. At last, as I tell you, I sickened of blood. Still, the sight of a white face was abhorrent to me, and I determined to find some bold free black people and to throw in my lot with them, to cultivate their latent powers, and to form a nucleus for a great coloured nation. The idea possessed me, and I travelled over the world for two years seeking for what I desired. At last I almost despaired of finding it. There was no hope of regeneration in the slave-dealing Soudanese, the debased Fantee, or the Americanised negroes of Liberia. I was returning from my quest when chance brought me in contact with this magnificent tribe of dwellers in the desert, and I threw in my lot with them. Before doing so, however, my old instinct of revenge prompted me to make one last visit to the United States, and I returned from it in the *Marie Celeste*. . . . "

One's first reaction has to be, I think, a sense of profound respect for the writer, at the time of composition in his twenty-fifth year. He had taken his material with outstanding success from Garnet. Indeed he had mastered so well what were the full horrors of slavery, from a black standpoint, and one ready to justify resistance, that he made Goring sound an eminently convincing avenger. He also did it with the artistry which more and more came to characterise his economics. The sentence on Goring's wife is one of pure horror, for what is not said, what even he cannot bring himself to say, glutted with blood though he is. The use of the word "young", with all its joy, innocence and love, conveying a sense of the foulest loss, does its work far better than any continued recital of the pornography that was slavery could be. There is a question as to whether Garnet in fact showed Conon Doyle his famous speech: he would likely have carried a text of it with him, for he did not expect to return from Africa. Ministers often remained after their term was concluded in the land of their assignment—Motley had done so after ceasing to be Minister to London, and died there, being buried in Kensal Green. Before he was appointed minister by the Arthur administration he had told friends he wished to be buried in Africa. Arthur succeeded Garfield on 19 September 1881, fired his enemy James G. Blaine from the State Department, and moved to put in his own men, coming as he did from a wing of the party hostile to Blaine and Garfield. Hence Garnet was not appointed until late in the year, and did not arrive in Monrovia until the beginning of 1882, and might be expected to bring many of his most precious possessions, seeing that he had an idea he might never return to the U.S.A. He presumably took ship to Lagos, and picked up the *Mayumba* on its return journey from Old Calabar (it was on the outward journey that fever struck Arthur in Lagos). So with ACD's obvious historical interests, and the historiographical basis for their initial association, it would have been natural to show him memorabilia of the antislavery struggle without asserting that he himself had done much more than make a speech or two.

He certainly did not share Septimius Goring's anti-Liberian views, but these were absolutely consistent with the latter's hatred of the whites. Conan Doyle intensely disliked the trader blacks he encountered on the coast, and contrasted them in his photographic reminiscences with those he met in the interior: for the latter he showed great affection. On the voyage he had gone ashore at one point, apparently before he met Garnet, and there he saw one of the foul dens to which captured Africans intended for the slave market were shackled. He told the readers of the *British Journal of Photography* that it made the Black Hole of Calcutta look like a salubrious resort, which sounds like a lesson applied from Garnet's teaching on the comparative history of liberty with reference to the persecution of blacks as set against that sustained by whites. He also spoke of the corruption of Africans by white commercial civilisation, and earlier by the slave trade (still active in the Red Sea) into which so many of them were brought as collaborators. The Africans of the interior he believed were best left to themselves, to prevent their corruption by white impacts and influences; again, this sounds like a sermon from Garnet. Garnet in the early 1840s had, like most extreme abolitionists, been wholly hostile to the idea of ending slavery by colonizing the slaves in Africa. The idea had had altruistic antecedents in many respects before it was discredited when slaveowners in economic difficulties exploited it to dispossess themselves advantageously of their stock.

But Garnet coupled that hostility to a tremendous pride in the idea of Africa, and the maintenance of American Negro consciousness in the African heritage. And by the end of the 1840s Garnet was moving away from the severely anti-colonisation line laid down by Garrison, Frederick Douglass and the custodians of abolitionist orthodoxy. Jamaica attracted him, and so later did Haiti, as places where blacks in fear of the even more stringent Fugitive Slave Law of 1851 might flee and show their capacity to the world by economic triumph. As early as 1848 he had produced an address denouncing the libels on the African past by white historians, praising its great traditions in antiquity, asserting its promise of future glory and coupling its fate at white hands with those of its scattered children. "If I might apostrophize that bleeding country I would say, O Africa! thou hast bled, freely bled, at every pore! Thy sorrow has been mocked, and thy grief has not been heeded. Thy children are scattered over the whole earth, and the great nations have been enriched by them. The wild beasts of thy forests are treated with more mercy than they." He was fond of the close of Herodotus's *Histories*, built up a great slogan from it, quoted it to Congress (as the first black to preach a sermon in the House of Representatives (12 February 1865)) in the form that Cyrus preferred that one should fight rather than be a slave; but the actual final lines of the *Histories* sum up his conclusion on the whole question of the merits of black American emigration to Liberia: "they [the Persians under Cyrus] chose rather to live in a rugged land and rule than to cultivate rich plains and be slaves". The problem was that the waning of the promise of freedom when Reconstruction was made a party political football, then eroded, and finally abandoned, renewed Garnet's fear that it was time for Liberia once more. Hence his mission to Liberia, and his intentions of renewing the idea of emigration there which he had courageously championed before the war in the teeth of abolitionist hostility. He shared with Goring the idea of salvation in Africa: but he would have agreed with him neither on the Fantee of the Gold Coast or the Liberians, however much he abominated the slave-trade of the Sudan.

Arthur's Scottish birth and Irish origins certainly woke a couple of chords in Henry Highland Garnet. He had visited Edinburgh and lectured there in 1851, and ultimately became affiliated to the United Presbyterian Church of Scotland, in whose interest he became a missionary to Jamica for the next four years. It may be that apart from his anxiety to build up the blacks in a society which had given an example to the United States by abolishing slavery, he feared for his own liberty under the new, stringent Fugitive Slave Law, of whose operations he heard dire things during his European lecture-tour. And his great Troy address in 1848 demanded that the blacks take example from "that giant of freedom, Daniel O'Connell", in whose cultivation of national symbols rather than metropolitan wealth he read a lesson to the American blacks. "A half penny's worth of green ribbon and a sprig of shamrock signified to the Irishman more than all the gaudy trappings of a Grand Master, or a Prince of Jerusalem." Arthur's attitude to Irish nationalism was somewhat mixed, but he clearly sympathised with hostility to anti-Irish sentiment and would have liked the identification of his ethnic origins with the inspiration of freedom.

Arthur afterwards saw Henry Highland Garnet as having saved him from intellectual sterility on the voyage, and his stimulus and invaluable information was of first-class value in firing him to major creative effort with *"Jephson"* and, as we will see, beyond. But he also had the effect of systematising his attitudes to Africa and the Africans. The voyage out had depressed ACD considerably. Death, above all, seemed to loom over the Africa coast, a sense he transferred with great skill in *"Jephson"* to the *Marie Celeste* itself. He kept meeting people who were dying, he himself had a brush with death, he was appallingly aware during his brief stay in Freetown of the alcoholism of the whites and the ravages of malaria and blackwater fever. "A year's residence seemed to be about the limit of human endurance", he wrote in *Memories and Adventures.* "I remember meeting one healthy-looking resident who told me that he had been there three years. When I congratulated him he shook his head. 'I am a doomed man. I have advanced Bright's disease', said he. One wondered whether the colonies were really worth the price we had to pay."

Yet it was the dying Garnet who injected into him a trimphant renewal of the creative urge, albeit the voyage itself probably added to his understanding of Conrad when the latter's works began to appear. *Heart of Darkness* seems prefigured in some of Conan Doyle's contemporary as well as permanent reactions. Before meeting Garnet, he was caught in a maze of ambiguities in response to the Africans. He was repelled by the stench when the trading blacks swarmed into the cabin, but in writing *Girdlestone* he nailed the sentiment by putting it into the mouth of a murderous, corrupt, drink-sodden captain whose compliance with the Girdlestones' avoidance of naval precautions brings him and them to a just doom. The skipper's methods of cornering coast trade depend on the exploitation of the blacks under the guise of equality:

> " . . . Now when I gets among 'em I has 'em all into the cabin, though they're black and naked, an' the smell ain't over an' above pleasant. Then I out with the rum and it's 'help yourself an' pass the bottle'. Pretty soon, d'ye see, their tongues get loosened, and as I lie low an' keep dark I gets a pretty good idea o' what's in the market. Then when I knows what's to be got, it's queer if I don't manage to get it. Besides, they like a little notice, just as Christians does, and they remembers me because I treat them well."

And *Girdlestone* also quickly links up the atmosphere of jollification prompting corruption to the cold, hypocritical profiteering of the merchants in whose interest the debasement is achieved:

> "The fellow's half a savage himself", his father said. "He's in his element among them. That's why he gets on so well with them."
>
> "He doesn't seem much the worse for the climate, either."
>
> "His body does not, but his soul, Ezra, his soul? However, to return to business. I wish you to see the under-writers and pay the premium of the *Black Eagle.* If you see your way to it, increase the policy; but do it carefully, Ezra, and with tact. She will start about the time of the equinoctial gales. If anything *should* happen to her, it would be as well that the firm should have a margin on the right side."

The voyage out had, of course, given him all too much experience of the equinoctial gales. He duly gave them their head at the end of *Girdlestone,* and

also in encompassing the doom of the Ku Klux Klan murderers at the end of
"The Five Orange Pips". He coupled the memory of his own suffering on the
voyage to Africa with doom for two kinds of enemy to the blacks.

Despite Garnet, he retained some ambiguities to the end. The *Case-Book*
contains some of the most remarkable of all the Holmes stories, where human
drama of emotion throws deduction to one side with most powerful results,
but it also contains the worst Sherlock Holmes story he ever wrote, and the
only one to be pronounced a total disaster. It may be that the distaste for the
ridicule of his literary genius which seemed to dog him by the endless
facetious imbecilities on the subject of Holmes resulted in his giving vent to
transient but almost homicidal moments of detestation of his all-conquering
hero. From time to time this showed itself in the decision to maintain the
standard but write finis to the series, and several groups of six show signs of
being the last he intends to do, the *locus classicus* of course being *"The Final
Problem"* followed by Holmes's eight-year silence and his best creative burst
to date. *"The Three Gables"* may be the one case where his fury with Holmes
bursts into the story. Holmes is given some of the most odious traits of the
captain from *Girdlestone,* such as cheap remarks to the Negro bruiser, Steve
Dixie, alluding to the smell of him, sneers about his lip, and so forth. Mr
Martin Dakin's damning verdict can hardly be bettered:

> Never has a feebler story insulted the memory of the great detective. In the
> final scene, after telling the fair Isadora Klein coldly that her fate is sealed, he
> gives in to her and lets her off with a contribution of £5000. The roguish
> badinage of his exchanges with the pretended maid Susan—'Oh, Susan!
> Language! . . . Good-bye, Susan. Paregoric is the stuff'—is . . . embarrassing . .
> . But the falsest note of all is struck in his cheap gibes at the Negro Steve Dixie.
> No admirer of Holmes can read these scenes without a blush. For Holmes was
> a gentleman; and one thing no gentleman does is to taunt another man for his
> racial characteristics. (The true attitude of Holmes—and Watson—to the
> African races is shown clearly in the closing incident of *The Yellow Face* . . .)

"The Three Gables" was published in the *Strand* in October 1926 as part of a
sequence of four of which the next two were *"The Blanched Soldier"* and
"The Lion's Mane", in which the formula of the Watson narrative or
(necessarily with the plot of *"His Last Bow"* and the translation from play of
"The Mazarin Stone") a third-person narrator, gives way to Holmes's
narrative, decidedly poorer than Watson's. Conan Doyle had become so
irritated by the cult of Holmes that he was now tinkering with him to a point
of real danger. This is the only answer I can give to the problem of *"The
Three Gables"*.

The ambiguities on Africa assert themselves in one important non-Holmes
story, *"The Fiend of the Cooperage"*, which dates from the early twentieth
century. It is a direct child of the cruise of the *Mayumba*, narrated by a
lepidopterist, who stays on a remote part of the Africa coast with two white
men on a trading station. There is a good use of swamp, fever, and the bad
jokes of the isolated men. What is noteworthy about the traders is their
contempt for the Africans. Walker fires his attendant for cowardice, although
the man is in fact giving him excellent advice about not staying in the

cooperage: but "White men don't run away", for which piece of pointless self-aggrandisement Walker pays with his life. The "fiend", for believing in which the black servant is ridiculed, turns out to be the great python of the Gaboon brought down to the station in a huge hollow tree swept into the environs in a freshet. Before his identity is discovered, by the sheer accident of the tree being carried out to the Atlantic, the survivors are in a dreadful panic, and their attempts to cling to the white man's status are looking dreadfully tawdry: "I wouldn't have had the niggers see me as I was just now for a year's salary", and then, when all is revealed, "The sooner we have breakfast and get back to the island the better, or some of those niggers might think that we had been frightened".

It is very cleverly using the conflict of black and white superstition to a result where the white self-regard is left looking far the more ridiculous. The terrain is most evocatively recalled despite the twenty-year interval, and perhaps an episode on the Old Calabar river in 1881 gave rise to the identity of the fiend. "Once, in an isolated tree", he recalled in *Memories and Adventures*, "standing in a flood, I saw an evil-looking snake, worm-coloured and about 3 feet long. I shot him and saw him drift down stream. I learned later in life to give up killing animals, but I confess that I have no particular compunctions about that one." In *"The Fiend of the Cooperage"* the corresponding passage runs:

> And at the same instant we saw it.
>
> A huge black tree trunk was coming down the river, its broad glistening back just lapped by the water. And in front of it—about three feet in front—arching upwards like the figure-head of a ship, there hung a dreadful face, swaying slowly from side to side. It was flattened, malignant, as large as a small beer-barrel, of a faded fungoid colour, but the neck which supported it was mottled with a dull yellow and black. As it flew past the *Gamecock* in the swirl of the waters I saw two immense coils roll up out of some great hollow in the tree, and the villainous head rose suddenly to the height of eight or ten feet, looking with dull, skin-covered eyes at the yacht. An instant later the tree had shot past us and was plunging with its horrible passenger towards the Atlantic.

But if Africa had supplied that inspiration it also remained in Conan Doyle's memory as the grave of white vain-glory. Small wonder he felt an instinctive affinity to Conrad. As for the blacks, ACD was ready enough to admit to conflict of emotions. He told the *British Journal of Photography* how he could look on a series of Africans heading down the side of a ship to a boat as monkeys, and one minute later see them at the paddles as black Apollos. His greatest perception of all, in *Girdlestone*, in the *"Fiend"*, in *"Jephson"* and, if you wish, in *"The Three Gables"*, is that black unattractiveness stems from the inadequacy of the eyes of the whites. In *"Jephson"* he played this really well, exhibiting the abolitionist Jephson as full of condescending comment, moments of physical revulsion, and monumental lack of perception. Garnet was the obvious man to convey to him precisely those qualities as he had seen them in so many of the white abolitionists, a point which it took modern white scholarship many decades to grasp.

"J. Habakuk Jephson's Statement" has been described as deriving from

Melville's *"Benito Cereno"*, but in fact, while allied in theme and comparable in quality, their strengths are very different. In both there is the phenomenon of a ship seeming to be under white control and actually under black, but Melville's effect is achieved by having some of the whites aware of what is happening while too terrorised to reveal it, while Conan Doyle's depends on the maintenance of general white ignorance until the moment of revelation is declared by the blacks. There are the clues in both instances which alert the reader and fail to alert the narrator. Perhaps this might be derivative; but it stems rather more directly from ACD's recollections of clues Bell told him he should have seen. Melville probably helped to point a few of them, and even there the main point is that the whole idea is brilliantly reversed for the Holmes cycle, the reader as represented by Watson missing the point and Holmes in command of it. The two architects of destruction, Babu and Septimius Goring, are starkly in contrast. Babu is small, apparently docile, and functioning through conversations which while reassuring to the newly-arrived Captain Delano are terrifying to Don Benito, who knows exactly what is meant by them. Goring is large, hideous, menacing, temporarily successful in allaying suspicion but increasingly conveying the impression that he is mad, which he probably is, though not in the way Jephson imagines. Goring's conversation is not only largely unrecorded, but it is simple deception, not loaded with special meaning for different auditors. The closest parallels are perhaps between Captain Delano and Jephson, with their assumption of the moral righteousness of their abolitionism, the cloud cast by their complacency over their powers of deduction, and their ultimate failure to begin to comprehend the logic behind the slaughter.

The difference lies in that Melville is playing with the ignorance but mental strength of the non-slave society as against the knowledge and mental sickness of the slaveholding one, where Conan Doyle is concerned to show the utter agony that lies at the back of atrocious crimes in avenging slavery. In one sense his demands on the reader are greater than those of Melville. Precisely because Babu speaks in two simultaneous tongues during the story and is silent after all is revealed, the reader is left numbed by the horror of slavery and the sickness of slaveowning which will kill Benito Cereno in the end. Septimius Goring, on the other hand, is robbed of all sympathy by Jephson's witness to several of his murders or their resultant corpses and his almost cynical confession to the rest of them. Yet his reasons, as quoted above, are an indictment of slavery from the black standpoint which are far more shattering in their effect than the ambiguities of *"Benito Cereno"*. Henry Highland Garnet had done an extraordinary thing for Conan Doyle. He had given him his first authentic voice outside his own range of experience, and the voice was black. As to the moral position of the story, it was that of Longfellow's poem on Custer's last stand, where his horror of the slaughter was if anything increased by his knowledge that it was the natural consequence of a century of oppression and dishonour.

As a work of artistry, *"Jephson"* succeeded in its day and deserved its long life which followed. Yet its success presaged the problems of the success of

Holmes: the real plaudits came for the wrong reasons. *"Jephson"* was in some ways far too early. Interest in authentic black voice was pretty dead by 1884, and when it revived it did so with ethnic tariff barriers which demanded that only blacks could be held capable of speaking with black voices. In 1884 Goring was dismissed as a simple monster. As white liberals washed their hands of concern with oppression of blacks, Goring's crime and its accomplishment dwarfed the real strength, the motivation. Nor was it in the least comforting to white liberals. Jephson himself is a classic white liberal, yet he has not the remotest awareness of the real meaning of slavery for all of his pride that "I managed, in spite of my professional duties, to devote a considerable time to the cause which I had at heart, my pamphlet 'Where is thy Brother?' (Swarburgh, Lister & Co., 1859) attracting considerable attention". Garnet's tutelage had opened Conan Doyle's eyes much wider to the ironies of white self-satisfaction in philanthropy. Even the scene in which the stone which will preserve Jephson's life is given to him is replete in mockery at white self-regard:

> "Massa", she said, bending down and croaking the words into my ear, "me die soon. Me very old woman. Not stay long on Massa Murray's plantation."
> "You may live a long time yet, Martha", I answered. "You know I am a doctor. If you feel ill let me know about it, and I will try to cure you."
> "No wish to live—wish to die. I'm gwine to join the heavenly host." Here she relapsed into one of those half-heathenish rhapsodies in which negroes indulge.
> . . .

This seems the fruit of a well-informed reading of *Uncle Tom's Cabin* at the moment in conclusion when George Shelby tells Uncle Tom he mustn't die as Shelby has bought him and will take him back to Kentucky and Uncle Tom, reasonably if brutally, replies that Heaven "is better than Kentuck". The significance of the fetish, too, is suggestive of Conan Doyle's new awareness of the strength of the African past under all the oppression of American slavery. Authorities have wrangled on this very point with dramatic confrontation, but Henry Highland Garnet's Africanism put Conan Doyle firmly on the side of the persistence of African consciousness.

It was, curiously, the device ACD employed to throw a captivating story around his lessons from Garnet which won him celebrity. He heard of the finding of the derelict *Mary Celeste* on December 4, 1872, possibly as a schoolboy, possibly from some of the *Challenger* people, it being a very fresh mystery when they put out to sea, possibly from Captain Gray, Captain Wallace or one of their crew. Wallace or a crewman of the *Mayumba* would be the most likely candidate: they were not far from the point where the ship was found drifting and it would be a natural moment for a sailor's yarn. This, too, would tie it in his mind contemporaneously with the dreadful revelations he received shortly afterwards from Henry Highland Garnet. The peculiar thing was that when he employed the mystery it had been forgotten, and in so employing it, in the words of the mystery's historian Macdonald Hastings, "he had launched, ten years after it had happened, the everlasting riddle of the *Mary Celeste*". He even got its name wrong, with an over-accurate sense of symmetry in the use of French names, and it was his version of the name that the world remembered thereafter.

Undoubtedly the strength of the story arose from what he had learned from Garnet and his magnificently dramatic method of using it, including a skilful movement of narration from introduction to journal to conclusion, as he would later do so well in *The Hound*. He tied the idea of the long silence to bitter resentment on Jephson's part at his not being believed, and thereby kept and if anything improved on the touches of authenticity with which Stevenson had buoyed up the *Cornhill* version of *"The Pavilion on the Links"* and subsequently foolishly discarded. But as the story persisted in the public consciousness there was initially the incredible assumption on noteworthy levels that claims of absolute truth were being made for *"J. Habakuk Jephson's Statement"*, claims ironically assisted by the *Cornhill* policy of anonymity and by the obvious narrative device that Jephson, as a medical man, knows himself to be dying—and hence, readers assumed, he would not be further heard from. It was from his version that flowered a series of absurd intentional hoaxes, carefully if over-dramatically charted by Mr Hastings. Most tragically of all the failure of the longterm public to grasp the real significance of the narration, to which the name of the actual ship was but a backdrop, meant that Mr Hastings in his dramatisation of the Conan Doyle version dropped Goring's explanation almost entirely.

Yet the story demands revival in its own right, wholly without reference to the unsolved mystery with which it was only marginally concerned. The evidence for recent occupancy of the ship, the domesticity of the captain's cabin, the existence on board of a child, the absence of any form of looting, were details very ably exploited by ACD to trick out his material. The child makes the humanity of the crew and of Jephson himself come into stronger relief, as well as making the murders even uglier than ordinary mass slaughter can be, while the avoidance of looting is used for Goring to make a dramatic point at the close of his narrative: "I also bargained that there should be no plunder. No one can say we are pirates. We have acted from principle, not from any sordid motive." Here was a point, with the success of *Treasure Island* in the year of composition, which should have won greater attention than it did. The mutilated Goring, minus the fingers of his right hand where Garnet had lost a leg, should have suggested Silver: it may be that ACD thought of his old friend's lost leg and rejected it as being too reminiscent of Long John. But for all that Goring, rather after the manner of Macaulay's view of Robespierre, would not have murdered for gain one of the vast number he murdered for philanthropy, and for all that he is proud of the ideological purity of his motives, Stevenson's mercenary and most justly-named Silver wins friends and Goring gained none. In a sense it was in character. In fiction Goring wanted nothing from the whites, except their extinction; in fact, he got nothing, and the ship he abandoned got everything. Nevertheless the assumption in some circles that the story was Stevenson's reminds us of ACD's awareness of following so closely in his fellow-citizen's footsteps. The difference lay in the much greater seriousness of the antecedents and intentions of his story.

Garnet's other literary legacies to Conan Doyle were much less ambiguous in their effect. To him we directly owe *"The Five Orange Pips"* and *"The Yellow Face"*. These clearly derive from Garnet's own disillusion with Reconstruction and bitterness at the destruction of its ideals. With his powerfully developed sense of the human savagery which had produced slavery and the human cruelty which had condoned it, the Ku Klux Klan can hardly have been a surprise. The story came so powerfully from ACD's heart that it constituted the first Sherlock Holmes story in which the detective was almost irrelevant—indeed his main contribution is his soulless indifference to his client's well-being. The Klan as represented is unspeakably nasty: never seen, all-powerful in deluding the authorities, fundamentally far more concerned with murder than with the recovery of the papers on which its title for vengeance is theoretically based. ACD follows Garnet in his assumption that divine retribution alone is likely to give its members their deserts: there is a stern deliberation in making all Holmes's final efforts ultimately pointless. The one member of the KKK of whom we get a detailed picture is Colonel Elias Openshaw. Here we receive some excellent insights. The point is made that involvement in such an organisation has nothing necessarily to do with immersion in the traditions and long folkways of the Old South, as Openshaw is an English immigrant. Garnet, as a good observer, had adverted to the fact that before the civil war crimes against blacks were a northern rather than a southern feature. Openshaw himself, steeped in drink, screaming with false readiness to defy his enemies, radiating virtual misanthropy towards his neighbours, is anything but a good advertisement for his former comrades. His one quality of value seems to be his ability to get on with his nephew, which in the event amounts to using that nephew as an unpaid steward. Not the slightest sign of sense of community is evident in him, although the KKK prided itself on seeking to preserve a community.

Holmes himself produces one or two armchair deductions which are more the authentic voice of Garnet than any conspicuous product of reasoning on his part. They are forceful and instructive enough. Firstly, there is a reading from the encyclopedia, with a version of the origin of the name more likely to emanate from a concerned black observer than from the nonsense about Greek circles ("kyklos") which the would-be cultural swanking of the original Southern bloods created:

> "Ku Klux Klan. A name derived from a fanciful resemblance to the sound produced by cocking a rifle. This terrible secret society was formed by some ex-Confederate soldiers in the Southern States after the Civil War, and it rapidly formed local branches in different parts of the country, notably in Tennessee, Louisiana, the Carolinas, Georgia, and Florida. Its power was used for political purposes, principally for the terrorising of the negro voters, and the murdering or driving from the country of those who were opposed to its views. Its outrages were usually preceded by a warning sent to the marked man in some fantastic but generally recognised shape—a sprig of oak-leaves in some parts, melon seeds or orange pips in others. On receiving this the victim might either openly abjure his former ways, or might fly from the country. If he braved the matter out, death would unfailingly come upon him, and usually in some strange and

unforeseen manner. So perfect was the organisation of the society, and so systematic its methods, that there is hardly a case upon record where any man succeeded in braving it with impunity, or in which any of its outrages were traced home to the perpetrators. For some years the organisation flourished, in spite of the efforts of the United States Government, and of the better classes of the community in the south. . . ."

And Holmes is utterly unimpressed by the encyclopedia's claims as to the Klan's social unacceptability to the élite. Perfectly correctly, he observes:

". . . You can understand that this register and diary may implicate some of the first men in the South, . . ."

Garnet had indeed informed his friend ably. Robert E. Lee, for all of his alleged sanctity, gave the Klan his blessing from his retreat in the Presidency of Washington College. General Nathan Bedford Forrest, the only notable user of guerrilla tactics in the Confederate Army, was the initial leader. Holmes's deductions as to the one document that has survived Openshaw's holocaust are equally chilling:

. . . It was headed, "March, 1869", and beneath were the following enigmatical notices:—
"4th. Hudson came. Same old platform."
"7th. Set the pips on McCauley, Paramore, and John Swain of St Augustine."
"9th. McCauley cleared."
"10th. John Swain cleared."
"12th. Visited Paramore. All well."
. . .
"Then the page which we have seen—"
"Is such as we might expect. It ran, if I remember right, 'sent the pips to A, B, and C',—that is, sent the society's warning to them. Then there are successive entries that A and B cleared, or left the country, and finally that C was visited, with, I fear, a sinister result for C. . . ."

And the Negrophobia behind the whole thing is asserted from the first, where we are told Colonel Openshaw "had made a very considerable fortune in the States, and his reason for leaving them was his aversion to the negroes, and his dislike of the Republican policy in extending the franchise to them". Garnet had firmly linked the profitability of slavery and repression of the blacks in Arthur's mind.

This was written in 1891. The next series, in book form called the *Memoirs*, placed Sherlock Holmes once more under obligation to Henry Highland Garnet—or perhaps Doyle more than Holmes, since once again the story is one in which it is the event, not the deduction, which is of significance. *"The Yellow Face"* in fact is acknowledged by Holmes as a signal failure in deduction, and, characteristically, it is with that he is concerned rather than with the human drama which so deeply moves Watson. Here the most extraordinary thing about the story is how little subsequent critics appreciated the phenomenally unusual nature of its content for that time. I placed it before Dean Willie Harriford, the dean of Black Students at the University of South Carolina in 1973, and he, with his knowledge of white hostility to his fellow-blacks in the 1890s, found it virtually incredible that a story so stoutly defending the marriage of white woman and black man could have won a mass audience in 1893. Mr Martin Dakin, admirable as ever in his ethical comment, cites some earlier Sherlockologists who went to excruciating length to argue such a marriage could not have happened. In fact, ACD was so much in advance of his time of writing and the next fifty years that his great gesture was passed over in silence. The only attempt to harmonise it with American prejudice was the Doubleday edition's wantonly putting Grant Munro's splendid decision to have the black child of the former marriage become part of his family as taken after "ten minutes" rather than the two in the original. But there could be no disguising where Conan Doyle's sympathies lay:

> . . . Holmes, with a laugh, passed his hand behind the child's ear, a mask peeled from her countenance, and there was a little coal-black negress with all her white teeth flashing in amusement at our amazed faces. I burst out laughing out of sympathy with her merriment, but Grant Munro stood staring, with his hand clutching at his throat.
> "My God!" he cried, "what can be the meaning of this?"
> "I will tell you the meaning of it", cried the lady, sweeping into the room with a proud, set face. "You have forced me against my own judgment to tell you, and now we must both make the best of it. My husband died at Atlanta. My child survived."
> "Your child!"
> She drew a large silver locket from her bosom. "You have never seen this open."
> "I understood that it did not open."
> She touched a spring, and the front hinged back. There was a portrait within of a man, strikingly handsome and intelligent, but bearing unmistakeable signs upon his features of his African descent.
> "This is John Hebron, of Atlanta", said the lady, "and a nobler man never walked the earth. I cut myself off from my own race in order to wed him; but never once while he lived did I for one instant regret it. It was our misfortune that our only child took after his people rather than mine. It is often so in such matches, and little Lucy is darker far than ever her father was. But, dark or fair, she is my own dear little girlie, and her mother's pet." The little creature ran across at the words and nestled up against the lady's dress.
> "When I left her in America", she continued, "it was only because her health was weak, and the change might have done her harm. She was given to the care of a faithful Scotchwoman who had once been our servant. Never for an instant did I dream of disowning her as my child. But when chance threw you in my way, Jack, and I learned to love you, I feared to tell you about my child. God forgive me, I feared that I should lose you, and I had not the courage to tell you. I had to choose between you, and in my weakness I turned away from my own little girl. For three years I have kept her existence a secret from you, but I heard from the nurse, and I knew that all was well with her. At last, however, there came an overwhelming desire to see the child once more. I struggled against it, but in vain. Though I knew the danger I determined to have the child over, if it were but for a few weeks. I sent a hundred pounds to the nurse, and I gave her instructions about this cottage, so that she might come as a neighbour without my appearing to be in any way connected with her. I pushed my precautions so far as to order her to keep the child in the house during the

daytime, and to cover up her little face and hands, so that even those who might see her at the window should not gossip about there being a black child in the neighbourhood. If I had been less cautious I might have been more wise, but I was half crazy with fear lest you should learn the truth.

"It was you who told me first that the cottage was occupied. I should have waited for the morning, but I could not sleep for excitement, and so at last I slipped out, knowing how difficult it is to awaken you. But you saw me go, and that was the beginning of my troubles. Next day you had my secret at your mercy, but you nobly refrained from pursuing your advantage. Three days later, however, the nurse and the child only just escaped from the back door as you rushed in at the front one. And now to-night you at last know all, and I ask you what is to become of us, my child and me?" She clasped her hands and waited for an answer.

It was a long two minutes before Grant Munro broke the silence, and when his answer came it was one of which I love to think. He lifted the little child, kissed her, and then, still carrying her, he held his other hand out to his wife and turned towards the door.

"We can talk it over more comfortably at home", said he. "I am not a very good man, Effie, but I think that I am a better one than you have given me credit for being."

It was a brave, fine story, and one which charted with the utmost fidelity the demeaning temptations thrust upon a woman in such circumstances, her initial act of courage bringing her deeper into situations where at last she found herself, with divided love, embarked on a course of cowardice and deception, and yet at the moment of revelation showing a dignity which wholly transcended her previous weakness. The time-lag from Garnet's presentations of such cases during the Reconstruction period is a problem here, as it is not in *"The Five Orange Pips"*, since there would be little chance of such a family as the Hebrons being permitted to survive in Atlanta beyond the end of Reconstruction in Georgia in the mid-seventies. But this is no more to us than a reminder than ACD was drawing again on what he learned from Garnet. It is again a story from the black standpoint, for such originals as it might have had would be remembered with respect among American blacks and banished from utterance among whites. And its ethical position showed a writer as fearless in saying what he had learned to believe as anyone could wish. He made jokes later about the dangers to his pocket-book when he killed off Holmes in *"The Final Problem"* but it was nothing to the risk he took in outraging the social taboos of his patrons on both sides of the Atlantic in *"The Yellow Face"*. A white husband's black wife might be permissible, if regarded as a somewhat demeaning piece of self-indulgence. or personal inadequacy; a black man's white wife was enough to send a lynch-mob into action without a moment's delay.

Henry Highland Garnet was a noble advocate of human freedom who courageously kept up the cause of his still enslaved people despite having won residence in a free state for himself. Yet his anger led him to call for a politics of confrontation more dangerous for them than for him. Inevitably, it made his position a harder one than that of his black fellow-abolitionists who followed the wiser and better, but more acceptable, argument of moral suasion. His belief in an African identity also angered white friends who demanded acceptances of purely American status as the *quid-pro-quo* for their advocacy of antislavery. But he remained true to his ideals. Yet it was appropriate and fitting that his last major literary legacy to Conan Doyle should not have been the rhetoric of the brutalised Septimius Goring, or the ruthless exposure of the crimes against freedom and humanity of the Ku Klux Klan, but a beautiful story of the love of a black man and a white woman in the past, destined to have as its sequel the love of two white people for their black child in the future. It was right that this should be the last word from that strangest of all friendships in the life of Arthur Conan Doyle, that of the United States Minister and Consul-General to Monrovia and the young Scottish bibliophile doctor whom he charmed and instructed so well for three days in the last six weeks of his life. For behind all of his life's battles Garnet's fundamental cause had been one of love between the races, and it was that love to which Arthur responded with such hunger and such greatness.

The Plymouth Brother

"He looked like a great man, and not like a bad man."
Thomas Babington Macaulay,
"Warren Hastings"
Critical and Historical Essays

Conan Doyle had shown very clearly to his future biographers how deeply he had been moved by his meeting with Henry Highland Garnet, but, with their own prejudices, they saw little reason to celebrate his intellectual debt to a black man, much less to discover his identity. The next adventure of his young life, however, is perhaps its most famous episode to date: his partnership in Plymouth with George Turnavine Budd. He devoted most of *The Stark Munro Letters* to an account of it, and in the chapter assigned to it in *Memories and Adventures* confirmed that "the whole history of my association with the man whom I called Cullingworth, his extraordinary character, our parting and the way in which I was left to what seemed certain ruin, were all as depicted". On the other hand he hardly intended every word of every conversation to be taken as the gospel truth, as Hesketh Pearson took it. Pearson did good work in affirming the vital significance of the Budd incident in the creative life of his subject, though he overstated his case; and he identified "Cullingworth" with Budd from the Conan Doyle papers. In fact the identification had already been made in a life of William Budd, George's father, published by the medical historian E.W. Goodall in 1936, but Pearson probably never saw it, and as for Messrs Dickson Carr, Weil-Nordon, Higham and Pearsall, they added so little to the subject that they proved incapable of transcribing Budd's first name. Goodall throws some light on Budd, while not questioning Conan Doyle's version of events, any more than anyone else.

But the story is in fact more complex than Conan Doyle indicated. Caution as to the law of libel restrained his account in one respect—George Turnavine Budd had died in 1889, but he left a widow and other relatives, and while the dead cannot be libelled, under English law, any statements which might reflect on surviving Budds had to be made with the utmost care. Nor would he have wished to cause pain to survivors. Again, even as late as 1924, the date of the first edition of *Memories and Adventures*, Conan Doyle was leaving many things unsaid: the fate of his father, the circumstances of his mother, the existence of Bryan Charles Waller. So with the best will in the world to tell the truth, it could not be the whole truth. In fact, on looking back over his memories he decided he had little to add to *The Stark Munro Letters*, yet the publication of that as early as 1895 meant that still other persons were alive requiring discretion apart from Budd relatives. To know what happened we have to look more closely at that book, and examine it in the context of such other evidence as survives.

The story of the Plymouth adventure is simply enough told. After a false start in Bristol where he briefly called in his former fellow-student Conan Doyle for moral support, Budd invited him to partnership in Plymouth early in 1882. They managed fairly well, Budd now having a very flourishing practice, induced by his eccentricity, bullying methods towards patients, free medical advice but with charges for medicine, and blatant self-advertisement. Conan Doyle found it hard to compete but little by little managed to make some money, he specialising in surgery and Budd on the physician's side. However, Budd and his wife showed curious exhibitions of suspicion, hostility, and in the husband's case flashes of savage temper. Eventually it was suggested that the partnership should dissolve, Conan Doyle start out in another town, and Budd provide him with funds, Budd offering this as compensation for the dissolution of the partnership, ACD accepting it only as a loan. Finally, ACD left Plymouth for Portsmouth and when he was well settled in at Southsea, Portsmouth, he received a letter from Budd claiming to have found torn-up fragments of a letter from Mary Foley Doyle alluding to himself as "the unscrupulous Budd" and "A bankrupt swindler". It was indeed true that Arthur's mother had written in very strong terms against his continued association with Budd, whom she particularly excoriated for not having paid tradesmen to whom he had owed money when in Bristol before starting in Plymouth. Arthur had disagreed with her, strongly, and Budd's action in cutting off all financial support for him for having been party to such a correspondence while under Budd's roof, ignored the obvious point that Mary Foley Doyle's letters were induced by her son's obviously having championed Budd against her. More, the so-called torn-up letter proved still to be in Conan Doyle's own possession, whence he deduced that Budd and his wife had been surreptitiously reading his correspondence while he was in Plymouth and slowly building up a plot to ruin him as punishment for his mother's harsh judgments. By persuading ACD to settle in Southsea and make certain arrangements with landlord and tradesmen in the expectation of an income from Budd which would not then materialise, Budd's plan was that Arthur himself would be convicted as "a bankrupt swindler".

Thus the account in *The Stark Munro Letters*, as supported by *Memories and Adventures*. But despite the claims of the latter for the veracity of the former, there was a clear breach at one point. *The Stark Munro Letters* ends with "Cullingworth" and his wife meeting "Stark Munro" (Conan Doyle) once again before they emigrate to South America; in fact on the evidence of the memoirs Conan Doyle never saw Budd again after his departure from Plymouth and their breach—and when Budd broke off relations, Conan Doyle thanked him for having resolved his only argument with his mother and doing so in a manner which showed, after all, that she had been right in attacking Budd and Arthur wrong in defending him. *Memories and Adventures* mentions Budd's early death, and expresses the fear that his wife was left poorly off. It is a safe inference that ACD's generosity was partly responsible for the authority of this statement, and that he made some contribution to the Budd widow and children, possibly anonymously through relations. He reaffirms his admiration for Budd's near-greatness, which indeed lends much interest to the pages of *Stark Munro*.

This version of events should have elicited more question than it did, even without examination of other evidence. The person whose conduct seems oddest in the story is Mary Foley Doyle. She had been distinguished for her forebearance in general in dealing with her son. He had taken several jobs, some involving risk to his life, he had taken up with many people, become part of the household of one set of them, the Hoares, he had even acknowledged other women of her age as second mother and greeted them as "mam" as he did her. She showed no sign of undue fussiness, jealousy or resentment: as for the "second mothers", such as Mrs Drummond of Edinburgh, Mrs Hoare of Birmingham, Mrs Ryan of Glasgow, it is clear that she herself became very close friends with all of them. If anything, she seems to have encouraged him to cultivate them. Why should she suddenly get so worked up about Budd? Apart from some questions about his financial history, to which Arthur sensibly pointed out that he could hardly be the judge of a man's conduct when he was not there and before their partnership had commenced, there seem to have been fears that Arthur was implicating himself with a person of dubious medical ethics which could prove very dangerous for his own career in the event of a scandal. Clearly, the correspondence was not a simple matter of mother and son, and with our knowledge of Bryan Charles Waller's presence in the Edinburgh home it is a reasonable deduction that he was the person concerned about medical ethics, and hence putting Mary Foley Doyle's indignation on the boil. And certainly Waller must have been involved, and certainly adversely to Budd: Mary would hardly have been mounting an attack on Budd against both Arthur and Waller. But the story, as we shall see, is more complex still.

But before proceeding to it in detail we should take a careful view of our fullest source, *The Stark Munro Letters*, and examine it in its larger context. The book is a curious one, being supposedly the letters of a young doctor, John Stark Munro, to his friend Herbert Swanborough, of Lowell, Massachusetts, who while American was apparently at University with him in Britain. There are sixteen of these letters, the first dated 30 March 1881 and the last, 4 November 1884. A note by Swanborough at the close states that on his way to his family for Christmas, 1884, Stark Munro and his newly-married wife were killed in a railway crash. Conan Doyle cancelled that final note in his own copy of one edition, perhaps with an intention of a somewhat less drastic ending; and he toyed with a sequel, *The Posthumous Papers of Stark Munro*, but it never went beyond a few draft pages. The dating of the letters themselves do not correspond with what is known of his own life. For instance, Stark Munro is settled at "Bradfield" (Plymouth) by 7 March 1882, but on that date Conan Doyle was still in Birmingham, where he had returned to work as Reginald Ratcliffe Hoare's assistant after his voyage to Africa, and a letter from him to Blackwood is sent from Hoare's address as late as 24 March. Again, the book implies that "Paul" (Innes Doyle) joined his brother at "Birchespool" (Southsea in this book, although used initially and subsequently as a disguise for Birmingham) about November 1882, but Innes was firmly settled in at Southsea by mid-August. We may be on safe ground in accepting the book's assumption that the Plymouth episode lasted three months: it can hardly have been much more.

The date of publication may also be misleading. Even with Arthur's excellent memory, so rich an amount of detail would tax his powers. The book may have been written long before 1895. It was not the sort of work to win acceptance by a publisher unless the author was established enough to carry it, for it is concerned deeply with theology and social questions, apart from interesting but not absorbing accounts of the early struggles of a young doctor. It could have been written as long ago as 1885: it is certainly no earlier, because it describes the marriage of "Stark Munro" in the last letter, and Arthur's own marriage to Louise Hawkins took place in August 1885. The wedding itself is not correctly described—the book implies that it happened in Southsea, whereas it was celebrated in reality in Thornton-in-Lonsdale with Bryan Charles Waller as best man. Stark Munro's letters to Swanborough act as a rather odd device; they do ensure that surprise will be sustained in charting the progress, if that is the right word, of relations with Cullingworth, but they do not enter the story as Munro's correspondence with his mother does. Conan Doyle never could make a document play a part in the story as well as recording it, in the way that Wilkie Collins does so effectively in the middle of *The Woman in White*, although he could use changes of narrative form to advance and retard the pace, as he does particularly ably in *The Hound of the Baskervilles*. The reader knows that four major letters about Cullingworth are sent off by Stark Munro to Swanborough while at Bradfield, yet Swanborough's "two long letters, which lie before me as I write" (on 23 April 1882) are apparently immune from Cullingworth's illicit surveillance of Stark Munro's incoming correspondence. It is a minor point but it puts the method of telling the story on an artificial level.

Yet the origin of the method may not be artificial at all. By way of a start, if Cullingworth, Stark Munro, their wives, Munro's mother, and others are intended to be seen as directly relating to originals, who is Swanborough? There is one very singular fact about him: Stark Munro addresses him as "Bertie". Now, not only is this form of intimacy entirely foreign to Stark Munro himself in dealing with everyone else, it is also very rare indeed elsewhere in the works of Conan Doyle. Holmes and Watson style each other by their surnames from start to finish, apart from one or two early occasions when Holmes varies it by calling Watson "Doctor". Only Mycroft calls Holmes "Sherlock" and only Mrs Watson uses Watson's first name (and then gets it wrong). Conan Doyle himself employed the same usages. He would sign himself often "ACD" and he was "Arthur" to the older ladies who mothered him, but he addressed most male friends by their surnames. Waller, who shared his family home for so long, is "Waller" or "the Doctor" in the very few epistolary references to him I have found, the latter even when writing to his mother. The likely exception is James Ryan. That friendship had long preceded the association with Waller, and being of preparatory school origin would not have involved the public-school habit of using surnames, although a casual reference to an old Stonyhurst acquaintance met again on the *Mayumba* also uses a first name, so Stonyhurst may have been less inclined to surnames than, say, Greyfriars.

Ryan seems a likely candidate for Swanborough for other reasons. He had by now returned to Ceylon; he had been at university with Arthur, moving to medical studies after initial enrolment in Arts; he seems to have used his University library borrowing to read literary works which would provide Arthur with common ground for discussion. (For instance, he borrowed Scott's *A Legend of Montrose* which in the character of Dugald Dalgetty gave some inspiration for Decimus Saxon in *Micah Clarke*.) Nothing would have been more likely than that Arthur maintained a lengthy correspondence with him. More, Stark Munro is represented as theistic but hostile to all organized religion and to sectarianism in general, whereas Swanborough is clearly attached to the faith of his fathers, and there is a clear implication that he and Stark Munro had initially been of the same sect. For fictional purposes that is said to be "Wesleyan". James Ryan certainly remained a practising and believing Catholic, and exemplified it by leaving his Cingalese library to Stonyhurst. Accordingly, *The Stark Munro Letters* seem very likely to have had a clear origin in fact, and possibly Arthur was enabled to examine his own letters to Ryan before writing the book. The preoccupation with religious argument is very powerful, and gives considerable intellectual depth to the work, although it also makes it rather difficult to classify, falling as it does between philosophy and autobiography.

The book is fictionalised on certain levels, and not all of the philosophising is necessarily Conan Doyle's. There is one passage which reads highly ironically today, and was almost certainly conceived in a moment of almost Maupassant bitterness. This is where "Stark Munro" argues that drunkards are Nature's way of thinning the species, in that their posterity will die out. There was no way by which the normal reader could see the irony. Although commentators have pointed to the divergence in religious views between Stark Munro and his father as autobiographical, Stark Munro's father seems to have very little in common with Charles Altamont Doyle, save possibly in a certain censorious and supercilious manner. Munro's father is a doctor, is clearly very much master of his own house, and has a considerable practice. Very oddly he tells his son, when the latter has qualified, "my practice is so entirely a personal one that I cannot hope to be able to hand over to you enough to afford a living". This really makes no sense at all: nothing could be more commonplace than a doctor's inheritance of his father's practice.

George Budd proved unable to take over his father's Bristol practice, but Dr William Budd had been invalided by a stroke for seven years, and in fact died six months before his son's graduation, by which time there was nothing left of his practice. Reginald Hoare clearly intended his son take over the Birmingham practice, and despite the fact that he, too, was invalided before his death in 1898, in this case only for four months, his son took it over successfully despite the interval of more than a year between his father's demise and his own graduation. The link here may be Waller. Old Dr Munro is not Waller: for one thing, Waller was decidedly a heterodox influence on Arthur in religious matters in the mid-seventies, although he was a strong churchman after his return to Masongill House, possibly for social reasons more than religious. But it was true that Waller's was a consulting practice and hence that Arthur could not have taken it over, in the event of Waller's returning to Yorkshire. The reference to Stark Munro's taking a post with "Dr Horton", whom his descendant Commander R.M. Ratcliff Hoare identified as Reginald Ratcliff Hoare, is preceded by Dr Munro senior stating "I know Horton, and I am convinced that I can get you the appointment". That sounds like Waller, and it would make sense, as Hoare became F.R.C.S. Edinburgh in 1879, and hence would have acquaintains in Edinburgh medical circles. On the other hand, partly, perhaps, for the pleasure of fictionalisation for its own sake, Horton is represented as a widower, practising at Merton on the Moors, Yorkshire. The patients are largely connected with the local colliery. Undoubtedly ACD picked up a good deal of detail about medical practice in the collieries: *"The Croxley Master"* testifies to that. But the collieries were a long way from mid-Birmingham.

Other fictions include Stark Munro's graduating in 1880, at the same time as Cullingworth, as opposed to the reality of Arthur's graduation in 1881, the year after Budd. Again, Stark Munro seems oddly shiftless about getting work, being fifteen months with no job at all in the first instance, whereas Arthur, as we know, hurled himself at every job opportunity he could find, and found several, before and after graduation. The Horton episode is presented as a single term of two or three months, whereas the actual period put in by ACD with Hoare before going to Plymouth was the last of a series. Stark Munro turns down a post as ship's doctor with the comment "A ship's surgeon must remain a ship's surgeon", whereas Arthur's own experience showed that a ship's surgeon certainly did not. Conan Doyle says of *Stark Munro* in *Memories and Adventures* that "there are some few incidents there which are imaginary, and that, especially, the whole incident of the case of a lunatic and of Lord Saltire in Chapter IV occurred to a friend and not to myself" but it seems likely that part of the story of the lunatic was based on the experience of dealing with Charles Altamont Doyle as his epilepsy began to reveal itself: no doubt there was an actual case in the manner he indicates also. In any case, Waller would have had fuller experience of attending Charles Doyle than did Arthur. Curiously enough, the Saltire incident is the one noteworthy case in the book where Stark Munro appears as a figure of some strength and individuality. Elsewhere we learn much of his opinions and ethics, but he exists in the work as someone to whom things happen or before whom they appear. Chapter IV, on the other hand, is written at good, forceful tilt, and sparkles with wit, irony and human drama. It is integral to the story, in that it turns on a point of honour where Stark Munro feels he has only one alternative open to him. He takes it. He is then censured by his family. Yet his parents then want him to break with Cullingworth on ethical principles of theirs. He resists. Events seem to prove them right, but there remains a lingering attraction to the greatness of Cullingworth and perhaps a thought that all might have been well had Stark Munro's mother shown some discretion and self-restraint. These lines are not given the fullest chance to work themselves out, partly because of the letters very naturally concerning themselves with Stark Munro's own private religious problems, partly because Stark Munro's mother is modelled too closely on Conan Doyle's for him to drive home the injustice of his hero being condemned for his fidelity to his code of honour and later condemned for not modelling himself on others.

For all that, he presented the Saltire episode with very charming and harmless entertainment about his mother. Stark Munro goes for an interview with a firm of lawyers "and my mother stood on a chair and landed me twice on the ear with a clothes brush, under the impression that she was making the collar of my overcoat look presentable". Then he learns he is being asked to attend the lunatic son of Lord Saltire. Conan Doyle plays very nicely with the mingled appeal of social position, financial security and sheer snobbery:

> I walked home, my dear Bertie, with a bounding heart, and the pavement like cotton wool under my feet. I found just eightpence in my pocket, and I spent the whole of it on a really good cigar with which to celebrate the occasion. Old Cullingworth has always had a very high opinion of lunatics for beginners. "Get a lunatic, my boy! Get a lunatic!" he used to say. Then it was not only the situation, but the fine connection that it opened up. I seemed to see exactly what would happen. There would be illness in the family,—Lord Saltire himself perhaps, or his wife. There would be no time to send for advice. I would be consulted. I would gain their confidence and become their family attendant. They would recommend me to their wealthy friends. It was all as clear as possible. I was debating before I reached home whether it would be worth my while to give up a lucrative country practice in order to take the Professorship which might be offered me.

It is this sort of thing which shows Conan Doyle's immensely keen eye for the dynamics of social mobility. Just as the Sherlock Holmes and the *Round the Red Lamp* stories constantly focus on the terrible danger for the young professionals that they will collapse into bankruptcy and dishonour, dragging them socially far below the working-class, here is the dream, ridiculous and mildly contemptible but utterly human, on which so many lived. It is the kind of dream Mr Collins in *Pride and Prejudice* might have had, and been a fine enough fellow withal, until he surrendered to it and became the odious toady to Lady Catherine who delighted Jane Austen's readers and disgusted her heroine. It is universal enough, with some slight alterations for place, time and profession, to be the dream of anyone seeking to advance themselves on good fortune and advantageous acquaintance, and as these, today more than ever, play a vital part in the advancement of most professionals, there is even more value to the work. It also induces its own Nemesis very nicely. Perhaps the point of the story is that Conan Doyle was much too honest to pretend he had not had some hopes of that kind of advancement, but that he was very thankful in the end he did not advance that way. When he finally achieved medical prosperity in Southsea, it was because of who he was and what he had done, not whom he had known, and the same would be true of his literary achievement, apart from some critical interventions from sympathetic fellow-Scots such as Andrew Lang.

To continue with the Saltire saga, at the moment of acceptance of post, "My father took the news philosophically enough, with some rather sardonic remark about my patient and me being well qualified to keep each other company." This again makes it clear that Munro senior has almost no relation to Charles Doyle: the remark would be unthinkable for someone in his position, unless it arose from the madman charging his audience with madness, or the drunkard denouncing drunkenness. But it is not conceived in that vein. If Waller and Arthur had been having some argument on democratic questions—and by the evidence of *Stark Munro* Arthur was now very democratic, whereas all sources agree Waller was very authoritarian—perhaps some such comment would be possible for him. Stark Munro's mother's anxiety about his wardrobe in an aristocratic household is admirably realised: "A dreadful vision of Lady Saltire looking over my things and finding the heel out of one of my socks obsessed my mother." Then:

> She was great, as we walked home, upon the grand people into whose service I was to enter. "As a matter of fact, my dear", said she, "they are in a sense relations of yours. You are very closely allied to the Percies, and the Saltires have Percy blood in them also. They are only a cadet branch, and you are close upon the main line; but still it is not for us to deny the connection." She brought a cold sweat out upon me by suggesting that she should make things easy by writing to Lord Saltire and explaining our respective positions. Several times during the evening I heard her murmur complacently that they were only the cadet branch.

This brings into excellent perspective what Mary Foley Doyle's heraldic obsessions meant in practical terms. Apart from the nonsense of her writing to Lord Saltire, the passage shows us that her emphasis on genealogy was very much the Irish stress on regal descent from centuries back entitling the speaker to consider himself any man's equal. It was not a device to curry favour with the higher social ranks, but rather one to reassure her and her people that they were as good as any lords in the land. Conan Doyle went so far with her on this, that the aristocrats who receive the kindest treatment in his pages are those of ancient but impoverished family, such as Sir Jacob Clancing in *Micah Clarke*, or Dame Ermyntrude in *Sir Nigel*: although it is perilous to make hard and fast rules for his literary genius on this as on so much else, and it has to be acknowledged that few figures in Conan Doyle's works possess an older lineage than Dr Grimesby Roylott, of Stoke Moran, whose evil fortunes were what set in motion the case of "*The Speckled Band*."

The Saltire case continues, with such nice points as Stark Munro almost shaking hands with the butler, and finding Lord Saltire much less formidable "than his retainer—indeed, I felt thoroughly at my ease with him from the moment he opened his mouth. He is grizzled, red-faced, sharp-featured, with a prying and yet benevolent expression, very human and just a trifle vulgar. His wife, however, . . . is a most depressing person,—pale, cold, hatchet-faced, with drooping eyelids and very prominent blue veins at her temples". Relations with her continue very frigid, and one comment shows how in Conan Doyle's case his medical sense of the lack of social distinction between one human anatomy and another can bite hard enough when it wishes:

> You cannot imagine a more ignorant, intolerant, narrow-minded woman than she. If she had only been content to be silent and hidden that small brain of hers, it would not have mattered; but there was no end to her bitter and exasperating clacking. What was she after all but a thin pipe for conveying disease from one generation to another? She was bounded by insanity upon the north and upon the south.

On the evidence presented she probably made her contribution to its incidence, in that she sounds a very bad case of psychological frustration, dragging Stark Munro, who has made no remark in disagreement with her, into a controversy as to whether Episcopalian clergy do not do wrong to take part in any religious service in a Presbyterian church, and forcing him in reply to a direct question to express his wish that all sects threw aside their difference on "those ridiculous doctrinal points which are so useless, and which have for so long set people by the ears".

> "I presume", said she, "that you are one of those people who would put all churches on the same footing?"
> "Most certainly", I answered.
> She stood erect in a kind of cold fury, and swept out of the room. Jimmy [the lunatic son] began to chuckle, and his father looked perplexed.
> "I am sorry that my opinions are offensive to Lady Saltire", I remarked.
> "Yes, yes; it's a pity; a pity", said he; "well, well, we must say what we think; but it's a pity you think it—a very great pity."

The point is quite nicely achieved, that in fact Stark Munro and Lady Saltire are concerned about two entirely different things: he is anxious to sweep away social bitterness arising from sectarian divisions, she is on a perpetual watch against any attempt to diminish the church establishment. It is true that the conversation is supposedly taking place in Scotland, where the established church is Presbyterian and where the monarch during residence there is constitutionally so also. It would be very difficult for anyone in that age to shut their eyes to such a situation, and Lady Saltire's quarrel would begin, not with Stark Munro, but with her sovereign lady the Queen. It is a pointer that the origin of this episode, if any, was probably in England. *The Stark Munro Letters* in any case reeks with that kind of transposition: Budd's father's practice was in Bristol, but Cullingworth's father's is in Avonmouth, stated to be in the West of Scotland. In any event, Lady Saltire will not leave the thing alone and tries, unsuccessfully, to force Stark Munro into an argument on the House of Lords. Then the mad "Jimmy", who has taken to his keeper, whispers to his mother what Lord Saltire terms "a blasphemous wish, most coarsely expressed, as to the future of the Upper House to which I have the honour to belong", and she declares this to be the result of Munro's teaching. In fact, the boy since mental illness had moved on his own volition from high and dry Tory to violent democrat. "In substance, I am bound to say", notes Stark Munro to Swanborough, "that I think his new views are probably saner than his old ones, but the insanity lies in his sudden reasonless change and in his violent blurts of speech." Lord Saltire proposes terms:

> ". . . However, I have no doubt that all may be smoothed over if you would see Lady Saltire and assure her that she has misunderstood your views upon this point, and that you are personally a supporter of a Hereditary Chamber."
> It put me in a tight corner, Bertie; but my mind was instantly made up. . . .
> "I am afraid", said I, "that that is rather farther than I am prepared to go. I think that since there has been for some weeks a certain friction between Lady Saltire and myself, it would perhaps be as well that I should resign the post which I hold in your household. . . ."

And off he goes, regretted only by the lunatic. Old Munro attaches to the incident the charitable moral "I fear that you can hardly expect to get on in the world, my boy, if you insult your employer's religious and political views at his own table".

Now, whatever the fictionalisation or borrowing from a friend's experiences in this incident, the opinions ascribed to John Stark Munro are given consistently throughout, and we are apparently to take them as Arthur's in 1881-84, especially in view of the little joke when he buys a few sticks of furniture and fixings for the first house that is his own, 1 Oakley Villas, Birchespool (i.e. 1 Bush Villas, Southsea): "As I walked through my house and viewed my varied possessions, I felt less radical in my views, and began to think that there might be something in the rights of property after all". So the Saltire incident serves to throw important light on Arthur's politics. That he subsequently became a Liberal Unionist in 1886 means nothing: he had thoroughly good and progressive reasons for opposing Irish Home Rule, in that he thought it would prevent the Irish from receiving the advancement and progress within the United Kingdom from which sectarianism could no longer debar them, and while many Liberal Unionists later became indistinguishable from the Tories with whom they allied, some, such as Boyd Kinnear, and Lloyd George, took up a position to the the the left of Gladstone. Radical Unionism, as opposed to Liberal Unionism, tends to be forgotten, if only because Kinnear was defeated, Lloyd George went back to the orthodox Liberal fold, and Chamberlain dropped his radicalism; but ACD seems clearly enough a radical throughout the 'eighties, and this holds true for the early 'nineties. Sherlock Holmes would be decidedly counted as a radical with his sneers about lords, his belief in some form of unity with the United States, his admiration for Board Schools, and his contempt for social respectability.

The Scottish and Irish dimensions in Conan Doyle take this farther than ordinary English radicalism. English radicalism would supply the loyalties

Conan Doyle celebrates in *Micah Clarke,* though it probably took a fellow-countryman of Walter Scott to employ that form of celebration. But Scottish radicalism grew in opposition to the Calvinist insistence on the importance of outward appearances, and *"The Beryl Coronet"* in which the respectable banker father automatically blames the raffish son, and which ends with Holmes most sternly rebuking him for for his injustice to the boy, captures this form of Scottish protest. If the beginning of the story really was one of Arthur recalling looking out of the bow window in Argyle Park Terrace, seeing The Meadows under snow, and some banker sliding around in it totally out of control, then the train of thought followed nicely. The class which emphasised appearances as vital to social, economic and moral stature is rendered ludicrous by the snow, and yet its ethical judgments entirely grounded on such appearances still survive the process. *The Stark Munro Letters* reflects sardonically on the significance of judgment on outward appearances in the medical profession, with the loss of custom because the doctor answers his own door. Sherlock Holmes would also testify that such judgments are nonsensical themselves in any case, since they are made on prejudice by observers who have failed to notice anything like enough data to justify coming to conclusions, and George Budd operated on the principle that by shocking and exciting the public the normal prejudices can be swept away.

If the passage is a clue to Conan Doyle's politics, it also raises another fairly consistent phenomenon: the unattractive woman who seeks to force a man who does not like her to subject himself to her will. *"The Cardboard Box"* turns on the point, with Sarah Cushing trying to seduce Jim Browner, and destroying his marriage when he will not submit; *The Parasite* turns on precisely the same point, hypnotism giving Miss Penelosa her temporary victories. Lady Saltire is, formally, not a sexually voracious figure as the others are, but in fact her desire to draw Stark Munro into conflict or enslave or expel him is directly analogous to the other cases. The particulars are given with the cool reporting one might expect from a medical man, and in any case one of Conan Doyle's great powers of narrative arose from the exceptionally lucid style he developed in description of medical cases and deduction from their progress, as exhibited in his few contributions to professional medical journals.

It seems probable there is some antecedent for these ageing vessels carrying fire under the ice. What is very problematic is where Arthur encountered them. The original case may indeed have been an argument with some aristocratic woman, probably in England. The only likely candidate is Waller's neighbour, the Countess of Bective at Underley Hall. Her husband, the Earl, was MP for Westmorland (in which shire Kirkby Lonsdale then was), having inherited it from his father, and he from his father-in-law. Waller dined regularly at Underley all of his life, and it is his only known close association with the local landed gentry. The Earl died in 1893, and Underley went to Lady Olivia, the Bectives' only surviving child, who married Lord Henry Cavendish-Bentinck. The Dowager Countess died in

1928, when her obituary in *The Times* of 27 February described her as "an enthusiast to the last, jubilant over every Conservative triumph, tragically distressed at any reverse". She had been Lady Alice Hill, daughter of the Marquis of Downshire, a landlord of vast estates in Ireland. Her obituary notes her passionate interest in Irish political questions. Her brother, Lord Arthur Hill, was an Ulster Tory MP. In blunt fact, the Hills owed much of their continuing wealth and power to the exploitation of religious sectarian hostility between Protestant and Catholic in Ulster, and their political ethos was one of official élitist conservatism actually supporting itself by a mobilisation of profound Protestant bigotry.

Lady Bective had a natural basis for hostility to ACD and his heritage. He would not have disguised his repudiation of Catholicism; he would equally have refused to associate himself with any justification of anti-Catholic bigotry especially when marshalled for political profit under the guise of principle. Her situation by the 1880s when Arthur would have first met her, was not an enviable one: she was two years older than her husband, had no male child and was now most unlikely to present the Earl with an heir, in consequence of which omission his father's title, the Marquisate of Headfort, would pass away from his line unless she should predecease him and leave the chance of succession open by means of a second and more fecund marriage. So if she had kept her husband countenance in her ancestry, she had failed to meet his needs in her posterity, and this in itself supplied a basis for bitterness. For the rest, the Doyles' name would automatically cause an Ulster Protestant Tory aristocrat to presume and discuss Catholic antecedents, any statement by Mary Foley Doyle on her own aristocratic connections would have been in danger of severe snub, and Arthur would have been bullied to accept the Protestant and Unionist cause for what he would have regarded as unacceptable reasons. Waller was respectful of title: his epic poem *Perseus and the Hesperides* published in 1893 was avowedly in answer to the urging of a titled lady, most probably the Bectives' daughter, and he was not likely to appreciate Arthur's insistence on disagreeing with the Countess on points where common ground could have been established in rejection of Home Rule, Catholicism, etc. So a disagreement between the châtelaine of Underley Hall and Waller's former protégé over dinner could well have prompted a subsequent outburst from the seigneur of Masongill House in a manner similar to that of Stark Munro's father on the Saltire episode.

All this is entirely conjectural, yet it seems extremely unlikely that Arthur was not brought to dine at Underley Hall, during a visit to Waller's: it is the one house in the locality singled out by local recollection for Waller's fidelity to its table, and he was decidedly anxious to flourish his claims to importance founded on noteworthy relationships. Again, what we know of the Downshire interests and consequent prejudices indicates a potential collision course between the two representatives of conflicting Irish strains, Protestant ascendancy and dispossessed Catholicism. Finally the elimination of Ireland as a topic in *Stark Munro* and the substitution of a general radicalism should give us no surprise: the radicalism, as stated, is clearly true, but ACD would be no more anxious to claim credit as a martyr for Irish Catholicism than he showed himself in recalling the Eddie Tulloch episode. He fought the battles of his lost religion—he would continue to do so until he forced the purging of its anti-Catholic content from the Coronation Oath to be taken by Edward VII and subsequent rulers—but he was not going to gain Catholic support thereby as he showed when he explicitly rejected any attempt to have his halting professional fortunes at Southsea assisted by his uncles' use of Catholic links.

The Saltire passage in *Stark Munro* is described by ACD as having happened to a friend, yet it seems in its social (or anti-social) side to have as autobiographical a ring as anything in the book. On the other hand, factual material, known from other evidence to be true, has an oddly contrived air. The latter is the case because in disguising to a small degree the autobiographical matter Conan Doyle had to cut out the multitude of minor characters who complicate any ordinary personal relationship, and once embarked on a fictionalisation he seems to have enjoyed laying false trails for their own sake. His various autobiographical articles for the *British Journal of Photography* in the early 1880s are full of complex and bizarre disguises, many of them much more intricate than necessary. He really liked weaving little jokes into his narrative which nobody might understand other than himself. Thus in the short story *"The Doctors of Hoyland"* Dr James Ripley is outraged to find a woman doctor establishing herself in the village, and their interview ends in a deeply humiliating experience for him:

> "It was a singular coincidence", she continued, "that on the instant that you called I was reading your paper on 'Locomotor Ataxia' in the *Lancet*."
> "Indeed", said he drily.
> "I thought it was a very able monograph."
> "You are very good."
> "But the views which you attribute to Professor Pitres, of Bordeaux, have been repudiated by him."
> "I have his pamphlet of 1890", said Doctor Ripley angrily.
> "Here is his pamphlet of 1891." She picked it from a litter of periodicals. "If you have time to glance your eye down this passage—"
> Doctor Ripley took it from her and shot rapidly through the paragraph which she indicated. There was no denying that it completely knocked the bottom out of his own article. He threw it down, and with another frigid bow he made for the door.

The interview is a deeply satisfying step in the assertion of the value of woman doctors, and indeed of their superiority to men (since with the obstacles in their way only the very best could hope to get through). But apart from the general lessons administered in the story to Dr Ripley and the reader (and it is very hard not to feel sory for him in the end when Dr Verrinder Smith chooses her profession rather than marriage to him), there is at least one little joke entirely for ACD. His own doctoral thesis deeply depended on a pamphlet of Professor Pîtres, published in 1884: indeed he had a piece of very good fortune in this regard, as Pîtres, hearing of his investigation, sent him the pamphlet. It was natural that he should have the research student's nightmare that his great piece of luck might prove a two-edged sword, in that if Pîtres were to repudiate his views and he were only to learn the fact at a doctoral oral, where would he be? Fortunately for us, he channeled the recollection of that fear into "*The Doctors of Hoyland*", but the joke of using the same authority for the unsympathetic Dr Ripley as had been the lynch-pin of his own work was too enjoyable for him to ignore. There is no record of his telling anyone about it, although he may, of course, have told his friends on the *Idler*, Jerome K. Jerome and Robert Barr, when they edited it for publication.

Hence whether or not he is being self-confessedly autobiographical, Conan Doyle has to be treated with great caution. Art, diplomacy and humour all supply motives to conceal and alter. He himself wrote, in *Through the Magic Door*, of autobiography:

> It is the most difficult of all human compositions, calling for a mixture of tact, discretion, and frankness which make an almost impossible blend. . . . No British autobiography has ever been frank, and consequently no British autobiography has ever been good. Trollope's, perhaps, is as good as any that I know, but of all forms of literature it is the one least adapted to the national genius. You could not imagine a British Rousseau, still less a British Benvenuto Cellini. In one way it is to the credit of the race that it should be so. If we do as much evil as our neighbours we at least have grace enough to be ashamed of it and to suppress its publication.

Apart from the importance of that compliment to Trollope's *Autobiography* written at a time when neither book nor author were any too popular this really is important as a critique of *The Stark Munro Letters*. Let us, for instance, turn to the incident at the close of the book on which all biographies rely: Stark Munro, now establishing himself in practice in "Birchespool", puts up a boy with brain damage due to meningitis as a resident patient, the boy dies, and Munro marries the boy's sister. This also seems to have been the pattern of his marriage to Louise Hawkins. But what is the reason for including the story? To get it out of his system? And what was it he wanted to get out? Did he have feelings of guilt or fear that he had made some blunder which caused Jack Hawkins's death? Certainly in the book Stark Munro is exceedingly alarmed when a detective calls to enquire about the boy's death and the doctor is only saved an exhumation after a neighbour doctor with whom he had collaborated initially on the case gives his testimony. Arising out of this, it might be remembered that inquests with their multi-ranging enquiries conducted without much respect to individual feelings by self-important coroners often without legal qualification of any kind, were an ugly novelty to Arthur: Scotland did not have them, and enquiries about death were handled by the local police and procurator-fiscal. *The Stark Munro Letters* says of Cullingworth:

> . . . there had been one or two coroner's inquests, which had spread the impression that he had been rash in the use of powerful drugs. If the coroner could have seen the hundreds of cures which Cullingworth had effected by that

same rashness he would have been less confident with his censures. But, as you can understand, C.'s rival medical men were not disposed to cover him in any way. He had never had much consideration for them.

And one final question comes forward on Jack's death and its consequences. In *The Land of Mist* Professor Challenger is told by the spirits of two patients of his that they had died many years ago not, as he had feared, of the new drug he had given them, but from their disease itself. This revelation is immediately preceded by a message from the spirit of his dead wife. Stark Munro is conscious of the chloral in the medicine his patient "Fred" had been taking and that any investigation of the exhumed corpse would have revealed chloral. Was one of the reasons why Conan Doyle took up spiritualism a message laying the ghost of an old fear about the death of Jack Hawkins? Is the origin some piece of gossip about Rutherford? Or is Challenger here nothing more than another manifestation of Budd, who, as the original Cullingworth, had courted some close shaves with drugs which he so readily administered, and no doubt obtained some coroners' rebukes which he would put down to professional jealousy (if the coroner were a doctor) or establishment prejudice (if he were a lawyer)? Certainly Cullingworth's freedom with drugs impresses Stark Munro for the boldness of its kill-or-cure philosophy and despite, or perhaps because of, Cullingworth's treatment of him, Stark Munro is very ready to defend his doctrines although not to practise them himself. A passage arising from perhaps the same antecedent in *The Sign of Four* seems rather more satirical:

> He was clearly a confirmed hypochondriac, and I was dreamily conscious that he was pouring forth interminable trains of symptoms, and imploring information as to the composition and action of innumerable quack nostrums, some of which he bore about in a leather case in his pocket. I trust that he may not remember any of the answers which I gave him that night. Holmes declares that he overheard me caution him against the great danger of taking more than two drops of castor-oil, while I recommended strychnine in large doses as a sedative.

The Stark Munro Letters, then, deserves attention as an interesting piece of imaginative literature, closer to real life than is customary with any but first novels (again, possibly a clue to its initial date of composition), but not necessarily as clear a guide to Conan Doyle's life as to his mind in 1881-84. That it remains a serious effort to give a character-sketch of George Turnavine Budd is indisputable, and it should be added that in its claims for his greatness it is extremely, and perhaps excessively, generous. But that character-sketch was part of a larger story, and one which goes back a very long way.

The Wallers claimed descent from Waltheof, father of Earl Godwin, whose son Harold II defended his English crown against Norway and lost it against Normandy, which puts them quite in the Grimesby Roylott class: they also made much of Richard Waller of Agincourt. The Budds claimed descent from Baldwin, who came over with William the Conqueror, but no reputable account of him exists, and the authorities have looked coldly on the claim.

For all such claims to antiquity, claims which must have been decidedly distasteful to persons to whom genealogy was a matter of high and weighty import such as Mary Foley Doyle and Bryan Charles Waller, the first we really know of George Turnavine Budd's ancestry was when the Rev. Richard Budd settled in Lower St Columb, Cornwall, in the early eighteenth century, married a lady named Turnavine, and exhibited a fanatical devotion to whist, which he played for guinea points. His son, John Turnavine Budd, took minor orders and was apparently prevented from receiving ordination in the Church of England in that he chose to anticipate the event by celebrating a marriage when he was merely a deacon. He afterwards lost his money and went blind at an early age. Of his son, Samuel Budd, Surgeon, who settled at North Tawton, Devonshire, the reputation is sufficiently mixed. Samuel had ten children, nine of them sons, and built up a splendid practice which was ultimately inherited by his sixth son, Christian. He apparently came to North Tawton with experience as ship's surgeon during the Napoleonic wars. What has entirely eluded the vigilance of scholars is his actual medical education and acquisition of medical credentials, and this despite the earnest researches of his son William's biographer Goodall. His son Richard recorded that his father was a doctor's apprentice with the future Sir Astley Cooper, with whom he shared a bed in the doctor's loft and formed a lifelong friendship; but there is absolutely no record of this, and Dr Goodall concluded that if Samuel Budd had been a friend of the great London surgeon, it did not arise from early medical collegiality. It seems quite possible he was on civil terms with Cooper: it seems an oddly specific name to invent, and reference is made in Richard Budd's account of a visit to Sir Astley's home in the late 1820s. The truth is most likely to be that Samuel Budd was not qualified as a doctor at all, but that he had obtained a very good practical training through the exigencies of naval warfare, that he won some useful acquaintance with the profession by judicious associations, and that he wisely buried himself near enough to his grandfather's country to give himself assurance, far enough from it to be discreet, and above all thoroughly remote from urban centres where questions as to his qualifications might be raised. Clearly, on the basis of his career he was much better fitted to practise than many men sporting the cream of medical distinctions.

Whatever Samuel's inadequacies in the matter of medical degree, his progeny more than made up for it. His daughter Catherine was the first-born, after which his wife presented him with: John Wreford Budd, M.D. of Cambridge, afterwards practising in Plymouth; Samuel Budd, M.D. of Edinburgh; George Budd, who was Professor of Medicine at King's, London, from 1840 to 1863, retiring to Barnstaple, Devon, in 1867; Richard Budd, who won a gold medal for his Edinburgh M.D. and practised at Barnstaple where he received in mid-September 1881 a testimonial and a portrait, from Earl Fortescue, the local magnate and patron of medicine, on behalf of his many admirers; William, the father of George Turnavine Budd, also an Edinburgh M.D., and an outstanding contributor to the development of medical knowledge in his time; Christian, his father's successor at North Tawton;

Thomas Septimus, who also was an Edinburgh M.D. but showed marked eccentricity sufficient to cause his family much anxiety, went to the United States and apparently died there soon afterwards; Charles Octavius, who practised as a wine merchant in Torquay; and his twin Francis Nonus who practised as a barrister in Bristol, and lived in a house with the pleasing title of "Batworthy".

Now, the very existence of this extraordinary range of relatives throws an entirely different picture before us. It is no surprise to find among George Turnavine Budd's ancestors and uncles a mixture of brilliance, eccentricity and contempt for orthodox procedure. What is in marked contrast to the solitary figure who seems so much thrown on his own resources in *The Stark Munro Letters* is this omnipresence of Budds from Bristol to Plymouth, their fame firmly established in Cambridge, Edinburgh and London, and their name in Devon so great that one unfortunate doctor who tried to break into the county remarked that he left it in disgust because all the inhabitants were "Buddists". Conan Doyle says in *Memories and Adventures* that Budd "came of a famous medical family, his father having been a great authority upon zymotic disease" and also mentions the athletic tradition, particularly with reference to his brother "reckoned by good judges to be about the best forward who ever donned the rose-embroidered jersey of England". That was Arthur Budd, who studied medicine in London and died young. Yet ACD left no impression that the distinguished medical family was still extant. It most certainly was: John Wreford Budd of Plymouth died in 1873, with his reputation for considerable eccentricity supposedly injuring his practice in later years (he is credited with telling women patients that if they did not obey his orders he would get into bed with them), but he left a son, also John Wreford Budd, who was a solicitor, was put on the council of the Law Society, served on the Court of Bristol University, and settled in Combe Park, Lynton, North Devon dying in 1922. Professor George Budd did not die until 1882. Dr Richard Budd, whose testimonial was presented to him the year before Conan Doyle's time in Plymouth, was still resident at Barnstaple in 1894. Charles Octavius died in 1890, Christian in 1891, and Francis Nonus in 1899. William Budd on his death in 1880 left a widow, George Turnavine's mother, who survived him for about seven years; she owned some property in her own right. The inference is simple enough. George Turnavine Budd was cut off by the family.

There are at least two possible grounds for it. One was that he ran away with a ward in chancery, as Conan Doyle records in *Memories and Adventures:* "the deed was done and all the lawyers in the world could not undo it, though they might punish the culprit". She was under age, and may have been quite young: *The Stark Munro Letters* mentions the hoodwinking of a governess, which sounds as if she was not beyond eighteen, if that. John Wreford Budd the younger, building up a reputation as a Bristol legal worthy, must have been anything but pleased at the emergence of his disreputable cousin carrying on that reputation for eccentricity that had been happily presumed buried in America with Septimus or in Plymouth with John

Wreford Budd the elder: and quite apart from the eccentricity, a cousin on the wrong side of the law was not wanted.

The second is the presumption that the episode in Bristol in 1881, when Budd was overwhelmed by his creditors and left town, ended with his relatives paying his bills and cutting him off: here again the legal cousin John is the obvious candidate. Arthur was summoned by Budd down to Bristol just before going on the *Mayumba*, and during a stint with Hoare after his graduation, and was told how impossible it was proving to keep up the style of his father's practice, that it had failed in the seven years since the old doctor's stroke and that he was being dunned by all of his tradesmen. Arthur advised him to meet his creditors and

> I heard afterwards that he assembled them, addressed them in a long and emotional speech, reduced them almost to tears with his picture of the struggles of a deserving young man, and finally got a unanimous vote of confidence from them with full consent that he should pay at his own leisure. It was the sort of thing that he would do, and tell the story afterwards with a bull's roar of laughter which could be heard down the street.

But the implication remained, after they met again in Plymouth, that the Bristol merchants were never paid. Mary Foley Doyle apparently made this one of the cardinal points in her attacks on Budd, and Arthur could only be optimistic that they would be paid, and insistent that this in any case was a matter outside of the time of his partnership.

Here *The Stark Munro Letters* offers a clue: Cullingworth tells Stark Munro a story about bringing witnesses so that when he pushed a boy into the water in order to gain a medal for saving his life and advance his reputation, they would support it with needful detail and desirable omissions, after which Mrs Cullingworth secretly shows Munro a newspaper account of Cullingworth nearly losing his own life and being hauled out of an ice-bound river unconscious, having saved an unfortunate child who would otherwise have unquestionably lost its life. Either in detail or in contour, this means that in ACD's view Budd would prefer to be thought a clever rogue than a courageous hero (passing over the possibility that he had his wife give proof of his courage or knew that she would). Certainly the Budd of Arthur's account would have preferred to present himself as the smooth orator, charming the creditors only to bilk them. In reality, he probably obtained his credit not only for the memory of his father, but also because of the high standing of his family in the locality. He was definitely trading on that: witness his conduct in going no farther afield from Bristol than the other periphery of the Budd family territory in Plymouth. In 1881 his uncle Nonus was an established Bristol barrister of fifty-seven; his cousin John Wreford an established solicitor of slightly over forty. They were almost certain to be approached if their relative fled from his financial obligations, and to protect their own standing they would probably have paid up, and furiously cut him off. Other members of the family might have been brought into the effort to save the family name.

One point which certainly indicates George Turnavine Budd had been cut off from the family is the paucity of information about him which his father's biographer, Goodall, included in his book. He mentions only what is to be found in *The Stark Munro Letters* and *Memories and Adventures*. He says that Budd left a widow and four daughters, but gives no account of their fate. He thanks one of William Budd's daughters, and her son, for use of material in their custody: according to the usage of the time, that would have normally gone to the eldest surviving son, who was George Turnavine, and thence to his descendants (in addition to George's dead brother Arthur, there had only been one other son, William, who died an infant). That George's progeny had no hand in the ownership of his father's papers again suggests a break.

On the other hand, Arthur must have known something about the relations between Budd and his family: they were famous in Devon, and as we will note he uses certain names in *Micah Clarke* which suggests he was very much aware of their existence. But it would not have been possible to allude directly to them in *The Stark Munro Letters* without danger of a court action; the most innocent allusion to family curtailment of support could become the basis of a very ugly trial, in which not only would Arthur, a wealthy and reputable public man in 1895, be mulcted, but his mother might be drawn in, and possibly, as we shall see, Waller and Hoare as well. The fact that the leading Bristol relatives were lawyers increased such a likelihood. And since ACD's reference in *Memories and Adventures* to Budd's leaving his family in bad financial circumstances implies inquiry on his part—and, from what we know of him, financial support—he probably had been in touch with Uncle Nonus or, more likely, with Cousin John Wreford of Combe Park, nearer to him in age. In fairness to the Budds who survived George, they probably would have chosen to make some provision for the reprobate's children, if only to avoid the stigma of their flesh and blood being thrown on the parish, but this did not involve acceptance in the clan, from what Goodall conveys. If the picture of Mrs Budd in *Stark Munro* be accurate, she would never have accepted resumption of diplomatic relations with her husband's enemies, even if she was forced to accept their charity.

The Stark Munro Letters and *Memories and Adventures* are absolutely clear about Budd having read Mary Foley Doyle's letters, and, as we have seen, they are dealt with in the former without reference to the correspondence which is telling the story, such that their origin would clearly seem to be what did happen, presented without artistic contrivance. It must have been galling for Budd to find himself reproached for not having paid tradesmen who had been paid, and to have Arthur prompted to enquire about their having been paid, when to have admitted the truth that they had received settlement would have been far too humiliating for him to countenance. It would have increased the rage which finally spilled out over Arthur's innocent head.

One very odd point about *The Stark Munro Letters* is the two references by Cullingworth to the father whose practice he unsuccessfully sought to revive before moving elsewhere. In the episode at Avonmouth, which is to say Bristol, he tells Stark Munro:

"You have probably heard—in fact, I have told you myself that my father had the finest practice in Scotland. As far as I could judge he was a man of no capacity, but still there you are—he had it."

For "Scotland" read "Bristol" or possibly "the West Country". And again:

"But why not conform to professional etiquette?"

"Because I know better. My boy, I'm a doctor's son, and I've seen too much of it. I was born inside the machine, and I've seen all the wires. All this etiquette is a dodge for keeping the business in the hands of the older men. It's to hold the young men back, and to stop the holes by which they might slip through to the front. I've heard my father say so a score of time. He had the largest practice in Scotland, and yet he was absolutely devoid of brains. He slipped into it through seniority and decorum. No pushing, but take your turn. Very well, laddie, when you're at the top of the line, but how about it when you've just taken your place at the tail? When I'm on the top rung I shall look down and say 'Now, you youngsters, we are going to have a very strict etiquette, and I beg that you will come up very quietly and not disarrange me from my comfortable position'. At the same time, if they do what I tell them, I shall look upon them as a lot of infernal blockheads. Eh, Munro, what?"

It is easy to see from this why not only punctilious and hierarchically-conscious Bryan Charles Waller would be appalled by Budd's views but why more relaxed men such as Hoare might be also. And such a man was dangerous from their point of view, especially in his influence on Arthur. For all of Waller's pride of ancestry which he might contrast with Budd's bogus family tree, Budd was born in the purple of medicine and Waller was finding his feet as the first generation. Budd knew the tricks of the trade from the inside, and was ruthless in his cynicism about them. No greater contrast could be found between this sort of talk and the reverential though not obsequious tone in which Waller applied for recognition for his lecturing courses by Edinburgh University in 1879, or for the place of examiner in 1881. His manner was that of one proving himself the true servant of the gods, unequalled in his fidelity to their rites. Budd talked about the gods as though they were a set of drunken old family retainers whom he would turn off without a character.

Conceding the probability of Budd speaking about etiquette as quoted, how could he talk of his father like that? It might, of course, be not his father but his uncle, John Wreford deceased in 1873 whose practice in Plymouth had preceded his own: on the other hand, from what we know of him, John Wreford the elder was about the only member of the Budd medical uncles likely to win his nephew's approval, and etiquette seems to have been as foreign to him as to George Turnavine. It could be any of the other medical uncles: the London professor, the pet of Barnstaple, the heir of North Tawton, the paternal namesake. References to them in Conan Doyle's pages would have been ill-advised: Dr Richard Budd of Barnstaple was probably still alive when *The Stark Munro Letters* was going through the press, and he might well have been the target for an outburst of this kind, especially with that testimonial being presented possibly at the very time of Arthur's visit to Bristol in response to George Turnavine Budd's cry for help. The allusion in *The Hound of the Baskervilles* to a testimonial for a Devonshire doctor may be a natural product of such a memory. All the same, it does suggest that George Turnavine Budd was if anything resentful of the memory of his father. And there was good reason for it. William Budd was one of the greatest men in medical science of his day. And on the basis of such writing of his as survives, his son George was fundamentally a self-advertising charlatan.

It was in public health that William Budd won his European reputation. The terrible cholera epidemic of 1831 apparently made a profound impression upon his youthful mind, and his researches led him to pioneer the discovery of transmission of typhoid infection by excreta, with the conclusion that control of sanitation in the sewers was vital if the disease was to be prevented from reaching epidemic proportions. Similarly he showed how infection was carried by water used for drinking, when insufficient care had been taken to isolate it from the tainted liquid of the sewers. He turned his attention to scarlet fever, and the contagion from the scales it produces. He laid down directions to cut down such dangers by smearing the skin of the patient with ointment and commenced the code of sick-room sanitation and quarantine. He published his conclusions and discoveries in the *British Medical Journal* whence they were reproduced across the world. His later years took him into the investigation of smallpox, as well as typhoid of the pig and cattle-plagues. He was a tremendous hero of the Bath and Bristol branch of the British Medical Association; however, his career had its setbacks at the start. In 1839 he put in for the Warneford prize for the best essay on fever, and it was denied him because his ideas were "too novel and startling": the principle judge, John Forbes, was made physician to the queen the following year, a fair indication to the young William Budd of the priority given to orthodoxy. Ultimately his views on Preventive Medicine triumphed, and to him is due much of the credit for turning the tide against cholera and typhoid fever, although in the case of the former he never failed to assign due credit to the anaesthetist John Snow. His practical work in 1866 demonstrated his principles fully by preventing a cholera epidemic in Bristol, a firm illustration of the value for the hygienic reformer of remaining in the provinces, where he has more capability of bending the local authorities to his will and exhibiting the truth of the conclusions he wishes to affirm. His lengthy memorial in the *B.M.J.* (17 and 31 January 1880) declared "He died undoubtedly a martyr to his work, of which the greatest part and the most exhausting was done for the public good": but it also made it clear that for some years before his death he was undergoing increasing agony in his brain. Of his son George ACD would write in *Memories and Adventures* "I understand that an autopsy revealed some cerebral abnormality" (another clue to his taking some steps for the Budds after George's death): here at least was a resemblance between father and son. On the other hand, William Budd was acknowledged to have powerful, emotive eloquence in arguing for his crusades for the prevention of contagious diseases while in private being proverbial for kindliness and gentleness, a claim not easy to make for George.

But the father at certain moments must have felt as isolated as the son.

London made the best of its opportunities for sneering at provincial learning, and when Budd declared that cattle-plague could only be stopped when it was discovered by killing all the animals infected, *The Times* entertained its readers by jocosity on "the Pole-axe Theory of Dr Budd". He succeeded: and every traveller arriving at airport or harbour today who is faced by questions from the Department of Agriculture as to his recent acquaintance with livestock, is unwittingly beholding the omnipresent effects of the courage and originality of William Budd. It must sometimes have seemed the day would never come, or that each new field would go against him however victorious the last. One of his consolations was that in London he could count on the support of one man: his old teacher, now Sir Thomas, but when they first met, simple Dr Watson.

William Budd was admitted Fellow of the Royal Society 1870, some ten years after Sir Thomas Watson, who survived him by two years although twenty years his senior. We know from *Memories and Adventures* that Conan Doyle was acquainted with the particulars of William Budd's career—indeed any sensible medical student would have to be, since his works, and especially his *Typhoid Fever,* were pre-eminent in the field. Professor George Edward Challenger had a strong look of George, not William, Budd, as well as a look of Professor William Rutherford; William Budd was tall, handsome, well-formed and hardy in appearance, where George Turnavine was shorter, more squat, with bulldog jaw, heavy thick brows, bloodshot deep-set eyes and stiff yellowish hair. But it was William and not George Budd who could justly have uttered the cry in the first great meeting in *The Lost World:*

> "Every great discoverer has been met with the same incredulity—the sure brand of a generation of fools. When great facts are laid before you, you have not the intuition, the imagination which would help you to understand them. You can only throw mud at the men who have risked their lives to open new fields to science. You persecute the prophets! Galileo, Darwin and I—"

And Arthur's need for reticence in his memoirs, and (more particularly) in *Stark Munro,* about the Budd family, meant that they do not convey how much of Budd's fascination for him was that of knowing the offspring of the great hero of Preventive Medicine. It could not fail to appeal to a boy in medicine, three of whose sisters died in youth and a fourth, Annette, his closest companion among them, fellow-explorer on photographic rambles, infant guide and protector, would die of the influenza epidemic in 1889 because no William Budd had stopped the death-march of that horror.

To be the son of a great man, however, is neither conducive to mental self-assurance nor eminence of reputation. The outer world sets for him higher standards than for anyone else, and should they be reached, ascribes it to paternal influence and training; the inner self sets even greater demands, since the inner self knows the great man to be even greater than the world concedes. Arthur had known sons of great men: his father was one. Professor Simpson, who had taught him midwifery at Edinburgh (though for his practical midwifery he had qualified with Hoare), was another: he had succeeded his father, the great Sir James Young Simpson, in his chair.

Occasionally sons of great men will remind us they can make their lives
sublime; the younger Pitt did, as Arthur knew, and as he also knew, the
younger Pitt took to drink and was dead at 46. Budd may have belittled his
father's achievement: there is a slightly icy note in the *B.M.J.* obituary of
William Budd by W. Michell Clarke, consulting surgeon to Bristol General
Hospital, "Dr Budd . . . had many children, by *some* of whom and by his most
devoted wife he was tenderly nursed until his death" (italics mine). The break
may have taken place earlier; Cullingworth hardly appears flush in the brief
glimpse of his Edinburgh days at the beginning. On the other hand, the style
of a great man emerged in Budd's table-talk, which had the largeness and
confidence an authority on many things might possess. *Stark Munro* recalls a
fascinating discussion, sounding highly authentic at least in outline, concerning Budd's ideas on inventions to revolutionise the future of warships, and it
is surely this Conan Doyle has in mind in *The Sign of Four* on the eve of the
river-chase:

> Our meal was a merry one. Holmes could talk exceedingly well when he chose,
> and that night he did choose. He appeared to be in a state of nervous exaltation.
> I have never known him so brilliant. He spoke on a quick succession of
> subjects—on miracle plays, on mediaeval pottery, on Stradivarius violins, on
> the Buddhism of Ceylon, and on the warships of the future—handling each as
> though he had made a special study of it. His bright humour marked the
> reaction from the black depression of the preceding days.

The use of the word "Buddhism", too, is suggestive, especially if we recall the
bitter jest of the victim of the Budd medical monopoly in Devon, although the
allusion to Ceylon is prompted by the lost Jim Ryan. The reaction from the
"black depression" recalls the vicissitudes of Budd's own attitudes to Conan
Doyle during Plymouth days, depending on when he had last been giving
himself the masochistic satisfaction of examining Mary Foley Doyle's latest
exercise in frank penmanship. There is an admirable juxtaposing, too, in the
sentence in *The Sign of Four* which follows the calendaring of Holmes's table-
talk:

> Athelney Jones proved to be a sociable soul in his hours of relaxation and faced
> his dinner with the air of a *bon vivant*.

There is a very pleasing touch in all those miracle plays, medieval pots,
Stradivarii, Cingalese Buddhists and warships yet to come, floating firmly
past Athelney Jones's range of scrutiny, by now entirely confined to the
oysters, the brace of grouse and the white wines. It would be trespassing on
the ground of the Sherlockians to suggest the last item accounted for Jones's
curious quietness on the voyage, and his highly unorthodox readiness to allow
Watson take over the treasure-box, but perhaps we may salute the oysters as
beloved by Waller while the future warships are acknowledged as Budd's.

One aspect of Budd's conversation, arising from his father, was clearly his
freedom in comment on the medical profession and its forms of advancement.
Waller had been ready enough with university gossip, but his attitude to
medicine had a sacerdotal quality which could be irritating to a witty,
irrevent anti-clerical like Arthur: having bid adieu to his own priesthood,

ACD was even less disposed to take seriously the priestly pretensions of others. Budd, born and reared within the shrine, with the heads of more doctors bobbing about in his immediate proximity on the genealogical table than most medical students could show within ten generations, took a delight in terming the whole profession a racket, a dilating on the "tricks of the trade". This in its way, over a long period, was as distasteful to Arthur as the status-consciousness of Waller, but in its short term it was engaging. His *Round the Red Lamp*, the medical stories published in the early 1890s, happily combined regard for the great medical traditions with a gentle sociological malice. Dr James Ripley, before the advent of his feminine rival, is introduced in *"The Doctors of Hoyland"* as "two-and-thirty years of age, reserved, learned, unmarried, with set, rather stern features, and a thinning of the dark hair upon the top of his head, which was worth quite a hundred a year to him." (The touch of mockery is not confined to medicine: it is also a wicked sideswipe at the conventional forms of introducing a romantic hero in popular fiction.) A rather less sympathetic portrait, that of the fashionable doctor attending the gout-ridden Foreign Secretary in *"A Question of Diplomacy"*, is rounded off "He bowed in the courteous, sweeping, old-world fashion which had done so much to build up his ten thousand a year". Of course these delicate ironies are in their form quite foreign to Budd's blunderbuss iconoclasm: they reflect much more the acid asides of the Edinburgh academics, and yet more than that, the sardonic manner of the senior Jesuits at Stonyhurst. But the initial impact of Budd's gossip was necessary to prepare the ground.

In addition to *The Stark Munro Letters* (perhaps resurrected from oblivion following the drawing on some of its material for *Round the Red Lamp* which in book form appeared the year before it), a further fictional portrait of Budd exists in *"Crabbe's Practice"*, published in the *Boy's Own Paper* in 1884 (and hence unlikely to be read by Budd, and not likely to be taken seriously by a court of law as a location for libel), but never reprinted until *Tales of Adventure and Medical Life* in 1922. The name is far closer than "James Cullingworth" to George Turnavine Budd: "Tom Waterhouse Crabbe". The surname, indeed, is Dickensian, in that Budd's method of walking had a jerkiness, and his advance in a boxing contest a pincer-like appearance, which suggested the crustacean. It conveys, fleetingly, a little more than its successor Conan Doyle's awareness of the father in the son: "Geniuses are more commonly read about than seen, but one could not speak five minutes with Crabbe without recognising that he had inherited some touch of that subtle, indefinable essence."

The story itself is excellent fun, and one sorrows for that mass of the English-speaking world between 1884 and 1922 which, not having read the *Boy's Own Paper*, had to live out a fairly grim history without the consolation of reading *"Crabbe's Practice"* (though as we will see, one person, not of the original audience, did see it, and he was the best person in the world who could be chosen to do so). *The Stark Munro Letters* has Cullingworth in his destitute, Avonmouth, phase, trying to think up means of building up a practice:

He was in his best form, and full of a hundred fantastic schemes, by which I was to help him. His great object was to get his name into the newspapers. That was the basis of all success, according to his views. It seemed to me that he was confounding cause with effect; but I did not argue the point. I laughed until my sides ached over the grotesque suggestions which poured from him. I was to lie senseless in the roadway and to be carried in to him by a sympathising crowd, while the footman ran with a paragraph to the newspapers. But there was the likelihood that the crowd might carry me in to the rival practitioner opposite. In various disguises I was to feign fits at his very door, and so furnish fresh copy for the local press. Then I was to die—absolutely to expire—and all Scotland was to resound with how Dr Cullingworth, of Avonmouth, had resuscitated me. His ingenious brain rang a thousand changes out of the idea, and his own impending bankruptcy was crowded right out of his thoughts by the flood of half serious devices.

Clearly some such conversation did take place in Bristol, although nothing came of it. *"Crabbe's Practice"* is the result of the writer as artist—Conan Doyle—applying his genius to the invention of the fraud as artist—George Budd. For the purpose he invents a narrator much more compliant with such schemes, as opposed to his own sturdy independence of both Budd and his critics: the narrator does ultimately object when Crabbe, having persuaded him to upset the boat in which he is rowing and feign death on his being brought to shore, and having put up a wonderful exhibition of various methods of artificial resuscitation, finally applies a galvanic battery to him:

I gave one ear-splitting yell and landed with a single bound into the middle of the room. I was charged with electricity like a Leyden jar. My very hair bristled with it.

"You confounded idiot!" I shouted, shaking my fist in Tom's face. "Isn't it enough to dislocate every bone in my body with your ridiculous resuscitations without ruining my constitution with this thing?" and I gave a vicious kick at the mahogany box. Never was there such a stampede! The inspector of police and the correspondent of the *Chronicle* sprang down the staircase, followed by the twelve respectable citizens. The landlady crawled under the bed. A lodger who was nursing her baby while she conversed with a neighbour in the street below let the child drop upon her friend's head. In fact Tom might have founded the nucleus of a practice there and then. As it was, his usual presence of mind carried him through. "A miracle!" he yelled from the window. "A miracle! Our friend has been brought back to us; send for a cab." And then *sotto voce*, "For goodness' sake, Jack, behave like a Christian and crawl into bed again. Remember the landlady is in the room and don't go prancing around in your shirt."

"Hang the landlady", said I, "I feel like a lightning conductor—you've ruined me!"

"Poor fellow", cried Tom, once more addressing the crowd, "He is alive, but his intellect is irretrievably affected. He thinks he is a lightning conductor. Make way for the cab. That's right! Now help me to lead him in. He is out of danger now. He can dress at his hotel. If any of you have any information to give which may throw light upon this case my address is 81 George Street. Remember, Doctor Crabbe, 81 George Street. Good day, kind friends, good-bye!" And with that he bundled me into the cab to prevent my making any further disclosures, and drove off amid the enthusiastic cheers of the admiring crowd.

It is a beautiful example of Arthur's sense of humour transforming pain and misfortune into laughter and charm: the Budd episode had been disappointing and humiliating, his championship of the reprobate against the advice of his own people proving woefully requited, yet already by 1884 he could take the memory and transform it into a thing of zest, speed, irony, comedy, realism and science fiction. He made it funny and iconoclastic enough to appeal to boys, although the theme of financial crises of struggling doctors hardly seems *Boy's Own Paper* material at first sight. He also adjusted his methods accordingly: being a story for boys, the actors are "Tom" and "Jack", in speaking to one another, not "Crabbe" and "Barton". The last name is chosen, incidentally, as a reference to his old friend W. K. Burton, the Professor of Engineering whose experiments in photography had drawn him along the same road: he would use the variant again in *"The Illustrious Client"*. The theme of electricity as reviving agent probably came from Burton: ACD would use it again in *"The Los Amigos Fiasco"*, published in the *Idler* in December 1892, and with variations in *Round the Red Lamp*, its argument being that an excessively strong electrical charge to administer capital punishment to a murderer would have the effect of prolonging his life and making him invulnerable to shooting and hanging. (The latter story gave Arthur a great deal of glee to write anyway: he detested capital punishment and had got into trouble when he was with Dr Elliot at Ruyton-in-Salop in August 1878 for saying "yesterday that I thought capital punishment should be abolished—a trite enough remark—, but he went into a fury, said that he would not have such a thing said in his house. I said I would express my opinions when and where I liked and we had a fine row. All right now".)

Other engaging touches include the mingling of science and the super-natural, rather at the expense of both, a further twist of the thread of that controversy which dominated his whole intellectual life: for the public clearly think he is not so much a cure as a ghost, and hence take to their heels headed by the police, the press, and the town worthies, all suitable object of scorn by medical students. Budd's own half-fantasy world is splendidly pitchforked into that of the youthful imagination, which is still close enough to belief in magic to see the iconoclasm as that of the schoolboy prank imposing on juniors who still believe in fairies. The *Boy's Own Paper* deserves credit for printing it, and its doing so is an interesting counter-argument to the critics of Victorian and Edwardian children's fiction. Barton can caper around without his trousers in front of the landlady because of the absolute innocence of the whole thing, and the story, while funny, is also highly realistic in its comments on medical practice and its economics. *"Crabbe's Practice"* was only one of several stories the *Boy's Own Paper* would publish from ACD's pen in the 1880s and there is little sign of censorship or restriction. A word must also be said for young Innes Doyle, eleven years of age when the story was written and living with Arthur in Southsea: his brother surely read it to him, as he would later read his stories to his family, and it is to Innes's appreciation and possible advice that we may owe his sureness of touch in writing for boys, and beyond them for the men and women who had not discarded the appreciative strengths of their childhood. Innes was probably the first person to take the place of Jim Ryan. Arthur Conan Doyle's most extraordinary achievement was his identification with his audience, and posterity owes a grand salute to Innes as the advance guard of that audience. It is by his apprenticeship, following Ryan's companionship, that the masterstroke which created Dr Watson was forged.

The earlier part of "*Crabbe's Practice*" throws important light on Budd's other, and more assiduously followed, methods of self-advertising. Before Barton is called to see Crabbe at Brisport, as Stark Munro is to see Cullingworth at Avonmouth, and Conan Doyle was to see Budd at Bristol "I read one most deep and erudite paper in a medical journal, entitled 'Curious Development of a Discopherous Bone in the Stomach of a Duck', which emanated from his pen, but beyond this and some remarks on the embryology of fishes he seemed strangely quiet". When they meet Crabbe asks if Barton has seen it:

> "Yes; it seemed rather good."
> "Good, I believe you! Why, man, it was a domino which the old duck had managed to gorge itself with. It was a perfect godsend. Then I wrote about embryology of fishes because I knew nothing about it and reasoned that ninety-nine men in a hundred would be in the same boat. . . ."
> ". . . You remember old Hobson at college. He writes once a year to the British Medical and asks if any correspondent can tell him how much it costs to keep a horse in the country. And then he signs himself in the Medical Register as 'The contributor of several unostentatious queries and remarks to scientific papers!' "

The ducks are in fact Crabbe's own: livestock was frequently maintained by private individuals in Victorian cities. Crabbe continues, "moodily eyeing his fowls":

> ". . . Now, there was the excitement about the discopherous bone. If Huxley or some of these fellows had taken the matter up it might have been the making of me. But they took it all in with a disgusting complacency as if it was the most usual thing in the world and dominoes were the normal food of ducks. . . ."

This reads like a good medical student joke: absurd origins for ridiculous papers published in medical journals are a perennial form of student satire. But it turns on Budd's own literary career in the learned journals, and in so doing illustrates his aims and conduct. "*Crabbe's Practice*" is presented as pure comedy, with the assumption that the rivals whom he wishes to displace are really very ignorant and he is a man of talent unfairly kept down if unorthodox in his efforts to advance himself. The portrait is shorn of Budd's darker side. There still is a hard-bitten quality to both Crabbe and Barton. Crabbe's final letter to Barton recording the success of the fraudulent resuscitation and consequent beginning of the practice reflects all the cold-blooded attitude to cases inevitable for most doctors thinking in terms of professional economics:

THE QUEST FOR SHERLOCK HOLMES

". . . I'm cutting Markham and Davidson out completely, my boy. The day after
our little joke I got a bruised leg (that baby), a cut head (the woman the baby
fell upon), and erysipelas, and a bronchitis. Next day a fine, rich cancer of
Markham's threw him up and came over to me. Also a pneumonia and a man
who swallowed a sixpence. I've never had a day since without half a dozen new
names on the list, and I'm going to start a trap this week. . . ."

But the campaign Budd waged in the medical journals, possibly beginning
before he ever met Arthur, was exceptional in its brazen character, in its
ignorance, in its capitalisation on his family name, and in its grotesque parody
of the courageous and epoch-making papers with which his father had
revolutionised public attitudes to infectious disease. They began when he was
23 or 24, and in his fourth year as a medical student, with a discussion of
"*Amyloid Degeneration*", running to a column and presented by the *British
Medical Journal* as an article, an honour for an unqualified neophyte but no
doubt accorded in compliment to the name of his stricken father and his
uncle, Professor George Budd, for he signed himself "George Budd, junior",
whereby his public would be reminded of his seniors. The best description of
it is undoubtedly Crabbe's reason for writing about the embryology of fishes
(ACD in writing "*Crabbe's Practice*" would have been taking far too great a
risk had he chosen any title for a paper like "*Amyloid Degeneration*"). It reads
as though the author selected his subject because he knew nothing about it
and assumed his audience to be in like case. The topic itself was anything but
settled in its definition. Budd's contribution was to unleash a series of
hypotheses, supported by tough assertions, a few names of authorities
apparently opposed but not directly refuted, and no actual proof based on
serious research. P. H. Pye-Smith, a Harley Street doctor, was sufficiently
nettled to reply in the *B.M.J.* of 10 May 1879 to Budd's article which had
appeared on the 3rd, and furiously scouted Budd's attempt to show
resemblance between lardacein and glycogen: he concluded by complaining
about the word "amyloid" which "will continue to mislead the unwary until
it is finally abandoned". Very far this got him. Budd, in the issue of 31 May,
returned delightedly to the charge. It gave him further free advertisement,
and he waded into Pye-Smith's pomposities, making rotund debating points,
generally dancing round his opponent's arguments and charging Pye-Smith
with failure to follow his argument or "comprehend the purport of my
paper". It was an excellent tactic. It left the Harley Street doctor looking too
stupid to understand the reasoning of the undergraduate. There was nothing
left to Pye-Smith but to abandon the controversy or be trapped in a situation
of complete lack of dignity. He chose the former. Whatever the *B.M.J.* may
have thought of it, they continued to be generous in space to the son of their
dying luminary.

Budd was then resident at Kingston-on-Thames, where he was taking
London medical courses approved for the Edinburgh degree: so that this
period is outside any continued acquaintance with Arthur. He returned to the
fray on 1 July, now claiming that recent discoveries by Dr Seegen supported
his view, conducting himself in the approved fashion of the cuckoo in the egg-

laying season. This time he was restricted to a letter. His next attempt looks like a direct attempt to capitalise on his dying father: he addressed readers of the *B.M.J.* on 2 August 1879 on household ventilation, commenting on its effects on the health of a population and the inattention it received. This time, however, he revealed a propensity for slightly dotty experiments in living which had interested Arthur in him. (Apparently in Edinburgh days he sealed up a room in his small lodgings, asserting it to be unhealthy, if *Stark Munro* is accurate: Stark Munro puts the smell of which Cullingworth complained down to cheeses in the room below.) He argued for the building of pipes with taps labelled "cold" and "hot", one giving access to the outer air, the other to the fireplace. Harley Street wisely left this alone.

On 13 March 1880 he was back with another article for the *B.M.J.* on "*The Nature of Rheumatic Symptoms*", arguing that rheumatism was "due to the accumulation of some morbid matter in the blood, and that the symptoms are traceable to an effort on the part of nature to eliminate that matter", again with nothing to suport him other than theorising. Meanwhile on 28 February 1880 he had won extensive space in *The Lancet,* once more on his old friend amyloid degeneration. *The Stark Munro Papers* seem in part borne out by this essay and its successor which appeared on 27 March 1880. Stark Munro describes Budd stealing a specimen from the Professor of Pathology and then being forced to cut it up and fry it in a frying pan—it was a waxy liver—to obtain results, none of which emerged. There is a difficulty at accurate identification: the Professor of Pathology, William Rutherford Sanders, was, like Budd's father, immobilised by a stroke at the time. Budd in his first article thanks Bryan Charles Waller "for his kindness, and for the facilities he has afforded me in making the preceding experiments". It would surely have been risking appalling trouble had this meant that it was from Waller the waxy liver had been stolen, although it would be consistent with a wholly adverse view of Budd entertained by Waller thereafter. What is more likely is that the liver was stolen from the unfortunate assistant who was filling in for Sanders, and that Waller lent his medical museum in Minto House, Chambers Street, partly at Arthur's urging. Waller's own researches were critical of Dr Dickinson, whom Budd was seeking to refute, and this might have helped. In any case the experiments were described without reference to the frying-pan although there is mention of subjection to gradual evaporation at a low heat. The experiments included argument that in treating an advanced waxy spleen alkali proved to have no effect upon lardacein, but that iodine produced a mahogany-red reaction, while experiments of Virchow which had suggested the incidence of blue spots on an affected spleen when treated with iodine and sulphuric acid were somewhat negatived when Budd found the same effect on a healthy spleen. Although this, in fact, seemed to get nobody anywhere, it is probably the origin of the meeting of Holmes and Watson when the former is making his famous "Sherlock Holmes test" for bloodstains, proof of which was achieved when the contents of the relevant vessel "assumed a dull mahogany colour". Mr Martin Dakin's comment in his *Sherlock Holmes Commentary* is apposite:

It is strange that this test is never heard of again, either in Holmes's cases or in general use. It may be that further experiment showed it not to be so universally effective as Holmes first assumed (after all, it was rather rash to claim it was precipitated by haemoglobin *and nothing else*, until he had tried everything else), and Holmes preferred to say nothing more of it.

Translating from the Sherlockian, the example reinforces the argument for a highly satiric basis to much of the Holmes stories, Budd making as great a pother about his experiments as Holmes, and with as empty an ultimate result.

Budd remained silent, and Arthur was on the *Hope*, for the next six months. He had won a little premature distinction from the *Lancet*, the pages of his papers being headed "*Dr Budd on Amyloid Degeneration*", which Waller would certainly have disapproved. But having legally graduated and illegally married, he returned to the *B.M.J.* in a letter questioning an alleged treatment of incontinence of urine, which was published on 25 September 1880, and on 16 October he argued that Esmarch's Bandage might induce death from heart failure, on the basis of a case described in the journal on the previous week. Then on 20 November 1880 he went the length of seeking to refute a recent address by the veteran surgeon Sir James Paget, shortly to become Vice-Chancellor of London University, on the relevance he had argued for the study of botany to that of pathology. (This last *apercu* of Budd's probably derived from the hatred of the botany lectures prescribed for Edinburgh University medical students which was so widely shared, but this owed less to the subject than to the personality of John Hutton Balfour, whose retirement on grounds of growing debility had been obtained in 1879.) Budd's position was becoming less and less defensible. With his father's death, the *B.M.J.* had less reason to show him kindness: the self-advertisement was becoming very blatant and the interventions increasingly egregious. Finally the storm burst, from an unexpected but very significant quarter.

Budd was restored to the regular, as opposed to the correspondence, columns, with an article on gout which appeared on 18 December 1880. On 25 December 1880 the *B.M.J.* carried a reply to him which reflected none of the compliments of the season. It came from the pen of Reginald Ratcliff Hoare, and it is noteworthy as being the only publication he seems to have produced, certainly the solitary item he listed under that head in the *Medical Directory*. It speaks all too well for itself:

> Few will be found willing to dispute Mr Budd's proposition, that there is a law of compensation between the various organs of the body; when, however, he propounds a new pathological doctrine founded upon this basis, he is perhaps a little too sanguine. Our physiological knowledge of the lymphatic system, and of its functions in our economy, is not exact enough to warrant our laying down hard and fast pathological rules in regard to it. Mr Budd's application of Chrzonszczewsky's experiment, where, after tying the ureters, he discovered urates in the connective tissue corpuscles, is extremely ingenious. He is, however, hardly justified in drawing a deduction of his own, and ignoring the interpretation put upon the fact by the eminent Russian physiologist. Chrzonszczewsky, if I remember right, considered that the experiment proved

the origin of urates from the connective tissue corpuscles; while Mr Budd
quotes it as conclusive evidence that matter is drained away into the lymph-
channels when the kidney is unable to excrete it. The corpuscles, too, can
hardly be called lymphatic, as the views of Recklinghausen are now pretty
generally accepted, which maintain that the spaces in fibrous tissue are the true
starting-points of the lymphatic vessels.

Apart from the physiological facts, we cannot see how Mr Budd can answer
certain objections to his novel theory. How is it, we would ask, that other
noxious material circulating in the blood, and requiring elimination, does not
produce the same train of symptoms? What is the subtle connection between
uric acid, in particular, and the lymphatics? If the disease be due to the
breaking down of an eliminative system, and subsequent congestion of the part,
why should one agent alone be able to produce it? In spite of objections, there
can, however, be no doubt that Mr Budd has advanced a bold and original
theory, and one capable of far wider application. Pathologists will welcome any
rational explanation founded upon a true scientific basis, and not dependent
upon pure hypothesis, or upon deductions from organic chemistry.

Budd replied with spirit: but despite his gallant attempts to keep the flag
flying this was the last publication of his known to have appeared in the
learned medical journals. It may not have been his last attempt at such:
Hoare's crushing could have ensured editorial hospitality would   go no
farther.

What were Hoare's motives for taking so drastic a step without parallel in
his career? It was not exactly a Jovian descent in terms of eminence and age:
while he had a very flourishing practice in Brimingham in contrast to Budd's
virtually extinct one in Bristol, he was now about 36 and Budd some ten
years his junior. Clearly, the determining factor was Arthur. There is a
reference in "Crabbe's Practice" to the narrator being summoned back by the
"Manchester" doctor to whom he was articled ordering his return "by the
next train". This is not particularly demanded by the story: it was clearly
advisable for the beneficiary of Crabbe's cure, supposedly unknown to him, to
clear out of town as fast as possible before, say, the boatman remembered he
had seen both of them together. Hoare and his wife certainly saw themselves
as in some respects in a parental relationship to Arthur, who was still only 21.
Budd's exploitation of the B.M.J. probably put the match to the train
of powder. It supplied the true scientific basis on which to condemn Budd for
unprofessional conduct, as opposed to inference and hearsay which was all
Hoare had hitherto in the way of evidence. Unquestionably it was done out of
an anxiety to shield Arthur from an influence deemed liable to injure his
professional standing, possibly capable of luring him into questionable
practices, certainly unlikely to give him a satisfactory association in terms of
his reputable advancement, conceivably likely to crash in ruin in which
Arthur could become involved.

If Hoare had moved to such drastic effect in public, his initiative was
almost certainly accompanied by equally formidable activity in private.
Correspondence between him and Waller seems likely, between his wife and
Mary Foley Doyle almost certain. Matters were moving rapidly to a crisis in

Edinburgh at the same time. Waller, already recognised by the University
Court as a lecturer, now applied for the post of Examiner in Pathology, and,
ironically, began to publish at frenzied speed himself, getting articles into the
Lancet on 5 and 12 February 1881 on an aspect of his dissertation and on 16
April coolly disposing of a rejoinder from the chief object of his criticism,
Professor George Johnson of King's College Hospital. He was pushing his
dissertation through the press at the same time, and in March and April he
published a brilliant lecture on Cyanosis in the *Edinburgh Medical Journal*,
moving with such haste that it retained his instruction to students about a
tour of exhibits after the lecture.

None of this was likely to endear Budd to him. From Waller's point of
view, the use of the learned journals for cheap, non-researched or in-
conclusively researched grandiloquent assertions of questionable theses was
likely to call into question the whole business of publication as a scholarly
credential. The bad articles would drive the good from consideration: an
academic Gresham's Law would apply. On 26 February 1881 the ailing
Professor Sanders died, ironically of the same disease which for so long struck
down William Budd. In fact, Waller was but one of twelve candidates for the
examinership, and his somewhat patronising printed application proved to
carry less weight than the two pages of handwritten letter from William
Smith Greenfield of London, who was appointed examiner and subsequently,
on 2 May 1881, was inducted as the new Professor of Pathology at the
Senatus Academicus. Waller was again passed over in the appointment of the
new examiner. The decision was, basically, a sound one. Waller was
impressive, if arrogant, as a learned writer, and clearly was in his element as a
lecturer, lucid, clear, comprehensive and witty in his use of analogy and
metaphor. But he would probably have been too closely identified with old
procedures at Edinburgh, and the Department of Pathology needed a new
broom. Apart from Sanders's illness, his predecessor's term had been marked
by appalling controversies with attempts by Simpson and Syme to have him
thrown out of his post for his championship of homeopathy. Greenfield
transformed the Department and its modern history dates from him. Waller
continued to practice as a recognised Lecturer with students permitted to
count his courses towards their degree, but there would have been far less
demand for his services under the new Professor than in the days of the
enfeebled Sanders. Waller's last article in the *Lancet* appeared in the summer
of 1882, and on 7 April 1884 the Court took his name off its books as a
recognised lecturer, he having ceased to teach for two consecutive sessions.
This could put the move to Masongill House as early as Autumn 1882 or, if
the Court was speaking of winter and summer sessions, early in the Spring of
1883. It was a bitterly frustrating close for a career so splendidly commenced.

So when Arthur returned from the *Mayumba* in January 1882 he found a
full-dress crisis before him, with Budd cast as Ishmael by a formidable
Birmingham-Edinburgh axis. He took service with Hoare once again. Then
came the summons from Budd to Plymouth. We cannot neglect the possibility
that the first move came from Arthur, despite his implication that it came out

of the blue. His account as initially conceived was obliged to suppress Hoare's part against Budd: indeed *The Stark Munro Letters* is definitely misleading on this point, as the book represents "Horton" as saying Stark Munro "had nothing to lose and everything to gain" by accepting Cullingworth's offer. The exact converse would be consistent with the other evidence. This is not to charge ACD with dishonesty: Hoare is fictionalised heavily as regards his practice, location and marital circumstances in the creation of Horton and in making claims for the fidelity of the Cullingworth story there is no question of its applying to Horton. In any case, Arthur clearly felt sorry for the Ishmael, so imprisoned in his ambitions, rhetoric and dreams, so cruelly beleaguered by economics and apparent ill-luck, so incapable of winning the support of respectable society. He was fascinated by Budd, claiming to the end of his days that there was genius in the man, whatever the appearance of charlatanry. This dichotomy persists in several of his portraits in which Budd supplies one element: both Holmes and Challenger are charged with being charlatans, Holmes in the initial instance by Watson, Challenger by virtually everybody. The genius Arthur recognised was William Budd's but he did not realise that; and the charlatanry was not an unfounded charge, as with Holmes and Challenger, but very much the greatest part of George Turnavine Budd.

Finally, the omnipresence of all these good people, his mother, perhaps his father, certainly the Hoares, surely Bryan Charles Waller, telling him he must have nothing to do with the wretch had exactly the reverse effect from that intended. He was not a child to be kept away from dubious companions: he had never accepted such a status, he, who had been the champion of the poor boys in Sciennes Hill Place against respectability as represented by the offspring of the Rev. Mr Tulloch. He had now returned from dangers and adventures such as none of his guardians had encountered. A whole new dimension of the history of freedom had been opened up to him by Henry Highland Garnet. Was he now to commence his own career by an acceptance of restriction on his freedom? He hated quarrelling with his friends, above all with his mother, but his sense of financial duty to his family did not mean his life was to be thrust into a bourgeois groove according to their specifications. He went to Plymouth, pursued by their very genuine if repressive anxieties.

On this showing, everybody's conduct makes sense. Mary Foley Doyle ceases to appear an alarmist charged with views on medical etiquette wholly outside her knowledge: she becomes a desperately anxious mother, deeply informed by persons whom she had every reason to trust and believe, absolutely convinced of their wisdom on the profession, and justly confident in their desire for Arthur's welfare, happiness and success. Bryan Charles Waller is, once again, status-conscious and interfering, but absolutely for altruistic motives: it was concern for Arthur much more than distaste for Budd which animated him, however it may have sounded. The Hoares again are truly benevolent and motivated by love for the boy who had entered their family and their hearts. And Arthur himself, as always throughout his life concerned for the underdog, and passionately committed to idealism and independence, is absolutely comprehensible.

But the pattern also implies a logic to the conduct of George Turnavine Budd, and a much more sinister one than is indicated by *The Stark Munro Letters*. Arthur went down to him as a champion: Budd, in all probability, had destined him from the first as a victim. Certainly Budd liked showing off, and lecturing about his theories, and raking in money from his huge intake of patients with free consultation and fees for inevitable medicine dispensed by his unqualified wife, and enjoying the contrast between his own assurance and his colleague's struggles. But *The Stark Munro Letters* actually conveys a point against its own argument. Its thesis is that Budd became hostile when he first began to read the indignant letters from Mary Foley Doyle. In fact, it portrays an ugly row on the very first day, before any letter could have arrived at all. Of course Arthur would have had letters hostile to Budd written to Birmingham by her, but these he would not have carried loosely in his jacket pocket, where Budd, as he describes it, found them when he left the jacket hanging up in the hall: they would have been in his trunk in his room, much less easily ransacked. Knowing what we do about Budd, it seems incredible that he would have welcomed with open heart a man straight from the house and family friendship of the enemy who had driven him from the public forum of his profession in such suave yet devastating fashion. Over the years he showed growing fears of conspiracy against himself, it seems ultimately resulting in a conviction that people were trying to poison him with copper to avert which he made elaborate chemical tests on every dish before he tasted it. With Arthur in his hands, he saw himself as having one of the figures in the conspiracy against him in his power, and the most vulnerable one.

It clearly mattered nothing that Arthur had been kind to him: to hurt Arthur would be to hurt Hoare, and Waller, and Mary Foley Doyle, whose critical attitude apparently had begun during Budd's Edinburgh acquaintance with her son. And the conspiracy did of course exist, though Arthur was entirely innocent of it. If Budd realised, as he probably did, that the conspiracy had first come into being in Arthur's interest, that increased the reason to ruin him. The psychiatrist might want to make something of Arthur's bearing the name of that dead brother, so admired for the looks, the scholarly promise and the athletic achievement in all of which he had during his short life eclipsed George Turnavine. The letters, when they did arrive, more than confirmed Budd's suspicions. Arthur certainly sent one letter to the Hoares from Plymouth: and he is likely to have received at least one from them. Waller might well have weighed in with a lordly and vituperative effusion. Taken together with Mary Foley Doyle's contributions, it was easy for Budd to make the correspondence his own excuse for ruining Arthur, whereas it had arisen from his decision to do so. No doubt he would tell himself that Arthur's pleasant demeanour and supposed defence of him to his detractors were what might be expected from a pupil of the Jesuits.

Pearson's close of his chapter on Budd is eminently sound: "Thus he left Plymouth, in complete ignorance of the real cause that had driven him forth, and wholly unconscious that Budd, in trying to ruin him as a doctor, had helped to make him as an author." We can indeed reinforce Pearson at one point. *Stark Munro* tells of an incident which Holmes could term somewhat too *outré* to be fictitious, apparently at the end of the first full day in Plymouth, where Cullingworth fires a dart from an airgun to hit a medal held by Stark Munro, but in fact it transfixes the holder's right forefinger. Stark Munro is quite clear that it was an accident, and no doubt the charitable Conan Doyle felt the same: I would not care to trust too heavily in the inaccuracy of Budd's aim myself, although the impulse to wound could have been born out of the moment. But the air-gun as a lethal weapon remained in ACD's consciousness, and it ultimately emerged in a most remarkable fashion.

Pearson is of course incorrect in seeing Budd as the "energy" of Holmes and the "malignity" of Moriarty; Gaboriau supplied the inspiration for part of the energy, Waller, Christison, Hoare, and Conan Doyle himself more of it, and Budd some as well. He is wholly unlike Moriarty, whose origins in John Moriarty, Thomas Kay, and certain Edinburgh academics coincide with the suave, ironic, faintly mournful and paternally rebuking style of Moriarty speech, with the deviousness heavily contributed by his namesake. On the other hand, Pearson is absolutely right in seeing in him an origin for Dr Grimesby Roylott. Roylott's autocracy, ancient Saxon lineage and impatience with servants are drawn from Waller (presumably he was somewhat less violent, although he is said to have used the stick he carried) while in height and physical description he resembles neither of them. Budd comes into it because of Roylott's readiness to exhibit his hostility, sometimes becoming actual physical hostility, notably towards Helen Stoner, Holmes and the village blacksmith, while at the same time carrying out a highly complex plot for the destruction of one of the open objects of his aversion. "*The Speckled Band*" might seem a little incredible in the mixture of subtle planning and open hostility against the victim: but it is quite consistent with Budd's performance towards Conan Doyle. Budd's presence in "*The Final Problem*", however, is entirely restricted to Holmes fixing on an airgun as a lethal weapon, so that if Budd did not give birth to Holmes, he did play a part in his resurrection: that airgun remained a loose end teasing its creator to explain it on another occasion, as indeed he did in "*The Empty House*". (Its inventor, Von Herder, is a little tribute to Johann Gottfried Herder, one of the German romantic influences on ACD at Feldkirch and beyond, after the manner of "Von Schlegel" in *The Silver Hatchet*.) Budd was in Conan Doyle's mind after Colonel Sebastian Moran fires the air-gun for the last time:

> ". . . There are some trees, Watson, which grow to a certain height and then suddenly develop some unsightly eccentricity. You will see it often in humans. I have a theory that the individual represents in his development the whole procession of his ancestors, and that such a sudden turn to good or evil stands for some strong influence which came into the line of his pedigree. The person becomes, as it were, the epitome of the history of his own family."
>
> "It is surely rather fanciful."
>
> "Well, I don't insist upon it. . . ."

As we have noted, this is inconsistent with Holmes's normal common sense, and so is the receptivity to Watson's disclaimer. It is a remarkable comment on Budd, however, and it suggests that both from himself and from enquiries after his death, ACD discovered a good deal about those remarkable ancestors and uncles. Uncle John Wreford and Uncle Septimus were two who went wrong, or at least began to act very strangely. Grandfather Samuel has some curiously dark and obscure passages in his life. Great-grandfather John Turnavine is an ominous precedent, with that uncanonical celebration of marriage and reckless profligacy.

Presumably Arthur, in his medical capacity, might have wondered about some ancestral syphilitic taint working its way out through posterity, in the form he describes so tragically about the doomed grandson of the foul old rake in "*The Third Generation*". The phrase "general paralysis" is used about William Budd's final stages by his obituarist, but this may, of course, be nothing more than a description of the victim of a stroke or series of strokes. Arthur certainly was directly influenced by Budd in his own medical studies. He also considered the question of gout in a letter to the *Lancet* on 29 June 1884. But where he differed from both Budd and Waller was in the modesty of his presentation, preferring letters to pretentious articles; and in the profundity of his findings, which came to the verge of very remarkable discoveries for medical science indeed. In the end, the hares were wholly outclassed by the tortoise.

Budd influenced Arthur, too, in his decision to maintain his independence. Budd's design had clearly been to leave him in Southsea, a bankrupt, dishonoured, discredited failure, fit only to whine his way home to his unhappy and troubled family. In any case, their departure from Edinburgh may already have been decided, and with the impending break-up of the house in Lonsdale Terrace, Arthur's choice of so unsuitable a partnership must have been particularly unwelcome. As it was, his descent into Southsea solved the problem of Innes, who could neither have been allowed to go to Budd at Plymouth, nor be easily cooped up on the estate at Masongill. The same consideration militated against Arthur's returning to the Hoares. Quite apart from Budd, he needed a separate house and by throwing him on his own resources Budd spurred him to new heights of self-reliance. Return to Hoare would have been accepting double defeat: it would be capitulation to Hoare's domination as well as admitting Budd's victory. Naturally Arthur handsomely admitted himself wrong in the matter of Budd, both in writing to the Hoares and in writing home. But fleeing back to either of them was another matter. Hence everything he could give to his profession he would, and his early enforced leisure at Southsea threw him even more into the effort to make an additional income from writing. Pearson wrote very truly indeed: on economic, quite apart from artistic grounds, Budd helped to make Conan Doyle as an author. "*The Captain of the 'Pole-Star'* " was one of the earliest fruits of his desperation.

*   *   *

Budd was the bad seed, but great was the harvest it yielded. We now go forward some twenty-odd years. It is time for cricket. ACD's team is batting, and he has batted and been disposed of by the opposing team. Now he stands at the pavilion, perhaps not quite so straight as he did in the early 1880s, but with a fine carriage and with his shoulders high, if a little rounded. His moustache is quite luxuriant, now, his hair receding a trifle on either side, though curving well forward in the centre. His Scots accent is unchanged, his manner as captain of his team a little more military after his service in the Boer War. He takes much pleasure in a slightly dramatic turn of phrase. And facing him, slightly taller, with humour and the deepest of admiration nicely blended on his long, handsome face, hair thinning despite his little more than twenty-two years, is young Wodehouse. Sir Arthur—for that is his title now— gives some final words of instruction. He has done what he can, the boy must carry on. Just for a second, for the field is not too clear at eighty years' distance, the cricket-bats look like swords.

P. G. Wodehouse interviewed Sir Arthur Conan Doyle for a magazine in 1903, and was playing cricket on his team in 1906 and presumably earlier. What follows must be deduction. It is possible to trace from Wodehouse's "*By the Way*" column in the *Globe* certain crusades where the younger man followed the lead of the elder. Conan Doyle made public war on Hall Caine's incessant self-advertisement: Wodehouse kept up a running joke in the column on the same theme, a fake almanac in 1907-08 perpetually including entries on "Hall Caine tells what he thinks of . . ." the subjects including the Pyramids, neolithic man, the drink question, the Elephant Puzzle, Jew-baiting in Russia, dangerous insects, England and the English people, jam-making, the *Yorkshire Post*, the *Daily Mail*, by-elections, trusts, pseudo-neurotics, dairy farming, higher education, the Suffragettes, party government, antiseptic surgery, horse-breeding, molluscs as food, British trade, our judicial system and Sanskrit civilisation. The entry for 19 August 1907 read: "Hall Caine tells us what he thinks of self-advertisement". Similarly, Conan Doyle made public war on *The Times* Book Club when it tried to have him surreptitiously buy author's copies of his *Sir Nigel* and sell them off to the Club. P.G. Wodehouse took up that cause too. The war on Hall Caine strayed into his *Psmith in the City* where Psmith suggests derisively that a senior bank official's hobbies must be postage stamps, dried seaweed or Hall Caine. Their alliance natually did not rule out jokes at the expense of one another. The "*By the Way*" column described Conan Doyle as "the only private detective who has been hit for six fours in one over"; and is it coincidence that "*The Bruce-Partington Plans*" published in the *Strand* of December 1908 had Holmes remarking "Suppose that I were Brooks or Woodhouse, or any of the fifty men who have good reason for taking my life, how long could I survive against my own pursuit? A summons, a bogus appointment, and all would be over"? He could hardly have written "Wodehouse": the name was becoming known, and in any case was hardly ever found outside the family and relatives of the Earl of Kimberley, of whom Pelham Grenville Wodehouse was a cousin. Rudyard Kipling always spelt Wodehouse's name as pronounced.

Richard Usborne's excellent pioneer work *Wodehouse at Work* (1961: revised and updated under the splendid title *Wodehouse at Work to the End,* 1976) pointed out that the famous rogue hero Stanley Featherstonehaugh Ukridge is partly based on Cullingworth:

> Cullingworth has a little, timid wife, Hetty, who adores him, and whom Munro (largely Conan Doyle) feels he wants to pick up and kiss. Hetty is not unlike Ukridge's Millie, who has something of the same effect on James Corcoran (largely Wodehouse). Cullingworth calls Munro "laddie". Cullingworth is always, he thinks, on the edge of riches, and always, in fact, on the edge of bankruptcy, with duns and county court summonses threatening.

Mr Usborne very rightly notes other origins: the friend described by Bill Townend whom he watched trying to run a chicken-farm, and another friend who borrowed clothes, and he could also have mentioned Robert Graves's brother, and Wodehouse's colleague on "*By the Way*", Herbert Westbrook, and, I think, Townend himself, who travelled to many of the places mentioned in connection with Ukridge including a tramp steamer (actually, in Ukridge's case, a cattle-ship). But Conan Doyle, whose work Wodehouse so revered, seems an absolutely basic influence. Even the choice of narrator's name for the Ukridge short stories first published in the early 1920s, "James Corcoran", suggests that the author's mind is not too far from the words "James Cullingworth", although there is no other identification between Cullingworth and Corky.

The Stark Munro Letters certainly indicate many points of influence on *Love Among the Chickens,* and on the short stories collected in *Ukridge.* There is Cullingworth's "open throat" mentioned at the beginning of *Stark Munro* and Ukridge described at the beginning of *Love Among the Chickens* as never able to get a collar-stud "to do its work". There is Stark Munro's advice to Cullingworth at Avonmouth to call his creditors together, and Ukridge's hilarious address to his creditors at the end of *Love Among the Chickens* when he returns to find they have already gathered together. There is the more general theme throughout the Ukridge saga of his pursuit by duns with a signal anticipation of the theme from Cullingworth even in his days of prosperity: "*Ukridge's Dog College*", first of the short stories, presents the same principle of the creditor who must not be paid even when money is in hand. Cullingworth's attempt to take on Stark Munro in boxing anticipates Ukridge's disastrous resolve to take the place of Battling Billson, his tender-hearted pugilist, in "*The Exit of Battling Billson*". Cullingworth tries to write a novel at one point whose only redeeming feature is:

> "Sir Robert tottered into the room with dry lips and a ghastly face.
> " 'My poor boy!' he cried. 'Prepare for the worst!'
> " 'Our horse has lost!' cried the young heir, springing from his chair.
> "The old man threw himself in agony upon the rug. 'No, no!' he screamed. '*It has won!*' "

Similarly, Ukridge loses an expected packet when it turns out that Battling Billson in "*The Return of Battling Billson*" was supposed to lose a boxing-match but wins it when his opponent steps on his ingrowing toe-nail. Again there is a surprise when it emerges that the victory was in fact what was not wanted.

Stylistically, also, there are comparable points. When Cullingworth says that Stark Munro had better start up again elsewhere:

> "Well, my boy", said he, "I am inclined myself to think that we should do better apart; and that's Hetty's idea also, only she is too polite to say so."
>
> "It is a time for plain speaking", I answered, "and we may as well thoroughly understand each other . . . "

Now to *Love Among the Chickens*:

> " . . .And I'll tell you another thing. I'm getting precious tired of living on nothing but chicken and eggs. So's Millie, though she doesn't say so."
>
> "So am I", I said, "and I don't feel like imitating your wife's proud reserve. . ."

Both conversations commence with a discussion of the decline in the medical practice, and of the funds in the chicken-farm, respectively. Then both novels involve the marriage having taken place after some skullduggery to deceive the forces of authority, skullduggery more intricately spelled out in *"Ukridge rounds a Nasty Corner"*. *The Stark Munro Letters* tell of Cullingworth jumping out of a house not to compromise a previous inamorata, while *"First Aid for Dora"* relates how Ukridge compromises an older flame by failure to get her *inside* a house. Or take the siege of authority to accept Cullingworth's inventions:

> " . . . What's the value of that magnet?"
>
> "A pound?"
>
> "A million pounds. Not a penny under. And dirt cheap to the nation that buys it. I shall let it go at that, though I could make ten times as much if I held on. I shall take it up with the First Lord of the Admiralty in a week or two; and if he seems to be a civil deserving sort of person I shall do business with him. It's not every day, Munro, that a man comes into his office with the Atlantic under one arm and the Pacific under the other. Eh, what?"

and then when the offer is refused:

> "As to the magnet", said he, "I'm very sorry for my country, but there is no more command of the seas for her. I'll have to let the thing go to the Germans. It's not my fault. They must not blame me when the smash comes. I put the thing before the Admiralty, and I could have made a board school understand it in half the time. Such letters, Munro! Colney Hatch on blue paper. When the war comes, and I show these letters, somebody will be hanged. Questions about this—questions about that. At last they asked me what I proposed to fasten my magnet to. I answered to any solid impenetrable object, such as the head of an Admiralty official. Well, that broke the thing up. They wrote with their compliments, and they were returning my apparatus. I wrote with my compliments, and they might go to the devil. And so ends a great historical incident, Munro—eh, what?"

The use of this in *Love Among the Chickens* is diverse:

> " . . . I got a letter from Whiteley's this morning asking when my first consignment was going to arrive. You know, these people make a mistake in hurrying a man. It annoys him. It irritates him. When we really get going,

Garny, my boy, I shall drop Whiteley's. I shall cut them out of my list and send my eggs to their trade rivals. They shall have a sharp lesson. It's a little hard. Here am I, worked to death looking after things down here, and these men have the impertinence to bother me about their wretched business. . . ."

. . .

" . . . I told them in my last letter but three that I proposed to let them have the eggs on the *Times* instalment system, and they said I was frivolous. They said that to send thirteen eggs as payment for goods supplied to the value of £25. 1s. 8½d. was mere trifling. Trifling, I'll trouble you! That's the spirit in which they met my suggestions. It was Harrod who did that. I've never met Harrod personally, but I'd like to, just to ask him if that's his idea of cementing amiable business relations. He knows just as well as anyone else that without credit commerce has no elasticity. It's an elementary rule. I'll bet he'd have been sick if chappies had refused to let him have tick when he was starting his store. Do you suppose Harrod, when he started in business, paid cash down on the nail for everything? Not a bit of it. He went about taking people by the coat-button and asking them to be good chaps and wait till Wednesday week. . . ."

But was Conan Doyle's influence on Wodehouse confined to the printed word? Were those conversations purely about cricket? Or did Wodehouse, no doubt in answer to a question as to how his writing was progressing, tell his problem about trying to break out of school fiction into an adult novel? He did. ACD, remembering his own ordeal in trying to break away from Sherlock Holmes, would naturally sympathise. Presumably Wodehouse acknowledged that he was being influenced by *Stark Munro*. At that point ACD gave him some additional facts about Budd, not included in *Stark Munro* but learned either at the time or subsequently. In particular, he would seem to have told him about the crises with relations, and the ultimate cutting off of Budd. *Love Among the Chickens* has a protracted crisis with Aunt Elizabeth; *Ukridge* has as a constant theme of the short stories the worsening of relations with Aunt Julia, who finally disowns her nephew after he sells tickets to her private Pen and Ink Club Dance to the Warner's Stores Social and Outing Club ("*Ukridge Sees Her Through*"). Trouble with aunts is of course a standard device in Wodehouse, but disowning definitely is not. It would have been natural for ACD also to mention that the surviving John Wreford Budd the younger was a solicitor, so Wodehouse should be careful: curiously enough, the revised edition of *Love Among the Chickens* (1921) alters the location from Lyme Regis to "Combe Regis", and the solicitor lived at Combe Park, but that would simply be a name lodging itself in Wodehouse's mind.

But the real proof that Conan Doyle helped P.G. Wodehouse with *Love Among the Chickens* lies in the fact that the book draws not only on *The Stark Munro Letters* but also on "*Crabbe's Practice*". It is inconceivable that Wodehouse would have stumbled across it: in trying to break out of school-story writing one does not commence research on the files of the *Boy's Own Paper* twenty years previously. He certainly did not read it at the time: he was three when it appeared. Conan Doyle was clearly fond of it, witness his very unusual act in including a story, never previously put within an anthology of his, in what he intended to be his final selection of his work in

1922. So he showed it to Wodehouse. The results are very evident. The boat-upset in *"Crabbe's Practice"* is paralleled by a boat-upset in *Love Among the Chickens*, and both are artificially contrived to achieve a major strategic result. *"Crabbe's Practice"* leaves at a slightly loose end the risk of the boatman (who has seen in each other's company the victim and the doctor before their alleged first meeting at resuscitation) remembering and squealing: in *Love Among the Chickens* disaster strikes when the boatman does squeal. The talk about the injury to Crabbe's duck, as written into a learned paper, is mildly reminiscent of the illness of Ukridge's hens: and the duck-motif is asserted at the close of *Love Among the Chickens* when Ukridge decides to start a duck farm. Crabbe's moodily "eyeing his fowls" is virtually a blueprint for Ukridge on the farm.

Even the name suggests *"Crabbe's Practice"*. The origin of Ukridge itself is unknown: my own guess would be that before Wodehouse decided it was pronounced "Ewe-kridge" he thought up a name coupling the "uk-uk-uk" of a hen with a word "ridge" as in farm. It is the conjunction of names, and the centre name, which argues for ACD's influence. "James Cullingworth" does not prompt Stanley Featherstonehaugh Ukridge. "George Turnavine Budd" does: so to a lesser extent does "Thomas Waterhouse Crabbe". In particular, "Turnavine" invited a comparably unusual middle name. Conan Doyle could have supplied this. His old Mentor, John Hill Burton, in his famous *The Book Hunter*, tells a complicated story of an antiquarian named Surtees deliberately perpetrating a bogus ballad called *"The Death of Featherstonhaugh"* with which he imposed on Sir Walter Scott who included it in his collection. Burton points out that Surtees still deserves well of posterity, in that he seems to have fed Scott the idea for *Waverley*. Featherstonhaugh was therefore associated in Conan Doyle's mind with complex, intricate and sophisticated gentlemanly crookery. The name, incidentally, is not necessarily rendered "Fanshaw" as is commonly supposed. It is also pronounced as written, and two other pronunciations exist. And with its Newcastle location it is a little unlikely to have impinged forcibly on Wodehouse from his own experience. On the other hand *The Book Hunter*, particularly around the account of the origins of *Waverley*, would naturally be a favourite work of Arthur's.

Naturally Wodehouse was to draw on many other sources than Conan Doyle for Ukridge, and they probably include other instances of works recommended to him by ACD, or at least works beloved by them both. *"Ukridge's Dog College"*, for instance, is clearly inspired in part by *"Trinket's Colt"*, one of the earliest stories in *Some Experiences of An Irish R.M.* by Edith Oenone Somerville and Martin Ross: it also involves an aunt, a nephew's theft of livestock from her, and an innocent friend implicated against his own better judgment. ACD was a great admirer of Somerville and Ross, and prized his copy of *Some Experiences* which had previously appeared in part in the *Strand* where he reigned and whither Wodehouse successfully aspired. There is one very odd connection between the popular monthlies, and the influence of ACD on *Love Among the Chickens*. In his first year of professional scrutiny of the monthlies, 1899, Wodehouse must have encoun-

tered in *Harmsworth's* a story called *"The Manoeuvres of Jerry"*. Jeremy
Garnet, the narrator of *Chickens*, is called "Jerry" very late in the story, and
to his utter delight, by Phyllis, the girl with whom he has fallen in love and
now has finally won. A strong index to the reader that she has been growing
in love for him is her interest in his two novels from the moment when he
sees her in the railway-train reading one of them. It receives fairly consistent
mention in the text; its name is *The Manoeuvres of Arthur*.

There is something very moving about the partnership of Arthur Conan
Doyle and P.G. Wodehouse arising out of the ruins of the earlier, treacherous
partnership into which Arthur was drawn by Budd. And Wodehouse reflected
its impact far beyond the Ukridge stories. *Love Among the Chickens* is in
many ways delightful in its celebration of young love, more in wonder than in
the sophistication of his subsequent work after he had begun to write for the
theatre. The revised edition has some classic work in it; but the first edition
shows immaturity and clumsiness in dealing with the first-person narrator. It
was Conan Doyle's great narrative strength, the first person, but it could not
be conferred on Wodehouse over a pint of ale, in the way that the facts in the
case of Budd's relatives or *"Crabbe's Practice"* could be. In fact, Wodehouse
was never to use it with the all-purpose confidence of Conan Doyle. In novels
he only uses it for the Wooster-Jeeves saga, apart from *Laughing Gas* (whose
action is set in motion by the same set of circumstances as the first Wooster
story anyway, *"Extricating Young Gussie"*, the cousin who has to be rescued
from a foreign adventuress being Gussie Mannering-Phipps in the story and
Egremont Mannering in the novel of twenty years later—and whose
inspiration is evidently *"The Great Keinplatz Experiment"* both in the
exchanges of personalities and the form of humour involved). In the short
stories only the Ukridge and Jeeves ones have a really credible first-person
narrator: Mr Mulliner never enters his own stories save momentarily, and the
Oldest Member, who tells the golf stories, is a shadowy individual, more a
genus loci boring his hearers and delighting his readers than a real person
especially as he (and his location) vary considerably from story to story. But
the use of first person narrative for Wooster and Jeeves is masterly, and is the
greatest of all variations on the Watson-Holmes theme.

The stories with which Wodehouse finally broke out of school, when the
school story, *Mike*, received its post-graduation sequel in the City, are also
firmly based on the Holmes-Watson method. It is not perfect: Mike lacks the
versatility and maturity of Watson, but this is compensated by his being very
firmly established by his family and himself in several books, short stories and
half of *Mike* itself before Psmith appears at all. Psmith is much closer to
Holmes than Mike to Watson, in character, and as Mr Usborne points out,
Holmes is the strongest single influence on Psmith's mode of speech. The
book *Mike* itself has several direct uses of the Holmes principle, especially
when Mr Downing, the unpopular form-master, seeks to employ it. In *Mike*'s
sequel, *Psmith in the City*, the election meeting has all the flavour of the
Bulgarian atrocity protest in *"Crabbe's Practice"*. W.W. Robson remarks to
me that there is also a firm line between *"Crabbe's Practice"* and *"The Long*

Arm of Looney Coote" in *Ukridge*, though the election meeting there also owes something to the meetings in *The Lost World:* Challenger and Ukridge, two figures partly deriving from Budd, are accused of dishonesty. Wodehouse clearly re-read *"Crabbe's Practice"* when it was published in *Tales of Adventure and Medical Life* in 1922. It is reflected in several of the *Ukridge* stories, such as the desperate set of contrivances in *"No Wedding Bells for Him"* when Corky is asked to be doctor then friend announcing bad news of Ukridge's aunt, after the manner of the acceptance of masquerade which Barton is to undergo for Crabbe. Masquerade and false identity abound in Wodehouse, but at its most vigorous *"Crabbe's Practice"* would appear to be its parent. A variant is when Ukridge and Corky meet as strangers in *"Ukridge Rounds a Nasty Corner"* just as Crabbe and Barton have to do immediately before the accident.

The *Inimitable Jeeves* was also conceived very shortly after the re-publication of *"Crabbe's Practice"* and here there is a direct link, not so much to the fake drowning, as to the story told by Cullingworth in *The Stark Munro Letters* about saving a child by first knocking him into the water: Bertie Wooster does exactly this in the story about Honoria Glossop and her brother, or at least he would have done if the child had not been a better swimmer. Something of Cullingworth, too, is evident in those moments in the Wooster saga when old, and menacingly athletic, friends turn on Bertie and threaten to disembowel him: the classic case is Tubby Glossop in *Right Ho, Jeeves* (the Glossops seem as a family Cullingworth-directed, possibly because of Sir Roderick's professional dealings with lunatics, possibly because of his medical eminence), but in that of Stilton Cheesewright in *Joy in the Morning* it is more formidable, more long-lasting, and the breach is irreparable.

If *"Crabbe's Practice"* reawakened Wodehouse's interest in *Stark Munro* and S.F. Ukridge when it reappeared (and the long interval between the two Ukridge books indicates there was need of reawakening), it is worth recalling what Wodehouse was writing about his master during the same time, specifically in his letter to Townend of 28 April 1925:

> Conan Doyle, a few words on the subject of. Don't you find as you age in the wood, as we are both doing, that the tragedy of your life is that your early heroes lose their glamour? As a lad in the twenties you worship old whoever-it-is, the successful author, and by the time you're forty you find yourself blushing hotly at the thought that you could ever have admired the bilge he writes.
>
> Now, with Doyle I don't have that feeling. I still revere his work as much as ever. I used to think it swell, and I still think it swell. Do you remember when we used to stand outside the bookstall at Dulwich station on the first of the month, waiting for Stanhope to open it so that we could get the new *Strand* with the latest instalment of *Rodney Stone* . . . and the agony of finding that something had happened to postpone the fight between Champion Harrison and Crab Wilson for another month? I would do it today if *Rodney Stone* was running now.
>
> And apart from his work, I admire Doyle so much as a man. I should call him definitely a great man, and I don't imagine I'm the only one who thinks so. I love the solid, precise way he has of talking, like Sherlock Holmes. He was

telling me once that when he was in America, he saw an advertisement in a paper: CONAN DOYLE'S SCHOOL OF WRITING. LET THE CONAN DOYLE SCHOOL OF WRITING TEACH YOU HOW TO SELL—or something to that effect. In other words, some blighter was using his name to swindle the public. Well, what most people in his place would have said would have been "Hullo! This looks fishy." The way he put it when telling me the story was "I said to myself, 'Ha! There is villainy afoot.' "

Thus the disciple on the master, and thus my reason for writing this book. It is none the worse an analysis because, like so much else, what is true of Sir Arthur Conan Doyle is also true of Sir Pelham Grenville Wodehouse.

Epilogue: Two Studies in Scarlet

". . . blow for blow, as Conan said to the devil. . . ."
            —Sir Walter Scott, *Waverley*, Chapter 22.

It is mine—the little chamber,
            Mine alone.
I had it from my forebears
            Years agone.
Yet within its walls I see
A most motley company,
And they one and all claim me
            As their own.

There's one who is a soldier
            Bluff and keen;
Single-minded, heavy fisted,
            Rude of mien.
He would gain a purse or stake it,
He would win a heart or break it,
He would give a life or take it,
            Conscience-clean.

And near him is a priest
            Still schism-whole;
He loves the censer-reek
            And organ-roll.
He has leanings to the mystic,
Sacramental, eucharistic;
And dim yearnings altruistic
            Thrill his soul.

There's another who with doubts
            Is overcast;
I think him younger brother
            To the last.
Walking wary stride by stride,
Peering forwards anxious-eyed,
Since he learned to doubt his guide
            In the past.

> And 'mid them all, alert,
> But somewhat cowed,
> There sits a stark-faced fellow,
> Beetle-browed,
> Whose black soul shrinks away
> From a lawyer-ridden day,
> And has thoughts he dare not say
> Half avowed.
>
> There are others who are sitting,
> Grim as doom,
> In the dim ill-boding shadow
> Of my room.
> Darkling figures, stern or quaint,
> Now a savage, now a saint,
> Showing fitfully and faint
> Through the gloom.
>
> And those shadows are so dense,
> There may be
> Many—very many—more
> Than I see.
> They are sitting day and night
> Soldier, rogue, and anchorite;
> And they wrangle and they fight
> Over me.
>
> If the stark-faced fellow win,
> All is o'er!
> If the priest should gain his will,
> I doubt no more!
> But if each shall have his day,
> I shall swing and I shall say
> In the same old weary way
> As before.

He seems to have written it some time during the mid-1890s, and he called it *"The Inner Room"*. It is probably more valuable in helping us to understand him than anything you have read up to now in these pages. Perhaps they may stand as some of its footnotes.

He is speaking there of an *inner* room. All this study has done is to show an outer room. I cannot speak for his mind. I believe that I know more of his early years than any biographer of his to date, and yet they have the advantage of me in this, that they all believed themselves to have known him. I cannot say I know Conan Doyle. I like him, certainly. I know, far better than any of his other biographers, how deep was the pain and loneliness from which he drew the courage and resolution which made him the great artist and the indomitable workman he was. I have never felt, in my pursuit of the mysteries of his young life, whose solutions and even whose existence he took the greatest pains to conceal, that I have been working against him. To the contrary, and without any other commitment to spiritualism, I have time and again been conscious of a great figure behind me and a finger pointing at a line on a page telling me to look again. All he asked of me was honesty, and I hope I have given him that. In addition he has, as since I first read him he has always had, my love.

There is a remarkable passage in Robert Penn Warren's novel *All the King's Men*, somewhat absurdly omitted from its early English editions, where the hero engaged in research finds he cannot know what his central subject was like, despite having read his diary, while he can be sure he knows what more peripheral figures were like. It may be illusory. When one knows less, one is convinced one knows more. Yet I believe I know Bryan Charles Waller, and Francis Cassidy, and George Renarden Kingdon, and Joseph Bell, and Robert Christison, and George Turnavine Budd. In the inner room to which I have sought to penetrate the man in the centre is the most indiscernable. I know so much about what happened to him; I can only guess at what its effect on him was.

The outer room, that room of physical reality, is another story. Here the metaphor is very relevant for us. He hungered for love, yet he also hungered to be his own man. He was surrounded by figures who wanted, in their own ways, to give him love, yet all of whom seem to have been anxious to love by possession. The one real exception in this sense is the candidate normally accredited in such cases with possessive love: his mother. Mary Foley Doyle was passionately proud of her first-born son, but the record, so far as I have been able to piece it together, is one of courageous renunciation of possessiveness. The horror at home was something it would have been so easy to visit on a son in an understandable bid for sympathy. The Jesuits' evidence is clear and stark. She tried to get him away from that horror, even to the extent of cancelling his home holidays. She let him go out, again and again, to find jobs away from home to win money, as he saw it, and to be saved from the horror, as she saw it. She would not put him into sheer escapism, and resisted his efforts to throw up his career and enter the army. But she would take any way to keep him as immune as possible from the ruin of his home: the Jesuits' choice of him for Feldkirch was clearly the result of their understanding with her. And in her anxiety not to force an adult identity on her eldest son before he was ready for it, she turned understandably to a surrogate eldest son.

It cannot have been easy for Arthur to see Bryan Charles Waller assuming the responsibility and authority of the eldest sibling. But when Waller came into the family he was a man in his early twenties, with knowledge, especially vital medical knowledge, and detachment, and assurance, and authority, all of which were vitally necessary. These were not qualities to be thrust on a teenage boy, however much he wanted them. Waller could, and no doubt did, cope. Arthur, and Annette, and the next girls, had to be got away. Then, when Arthur's break was clean and he had been protected from disastrous errors, Mary could settle down to talking heraldry, and advising him on the plot of *"The Copper Beeches"*. Arthur always loved his mother, though I think he was bewildered by her need to keep him away, and hence his love for her was partly diverted to other mother-figures: Mrs Hoare, Mrs Drummond, possibly Mrs Ryan, perhaps Catherine Burton, maybe even his future mother-in-law Mrs Hawkins. He did not have an Oedipus complex, if that cliché now means anything. In any case, a Jocasta complex is probably far more likely than an Oedipus complex, given the self-absorption of men and the altruism of women. Mary Foley Doyle was no doubt tempted in the direction of a Jocasta complex. To her eternal credit and to the eternal advantage of her son she resisted it.

Father and son never reached an accord similar to that of mother and son, and perhaps for that reason Charles Altamont Doyle emerges as possessive in a way Mary was not. The careful classification of data on Arthur's books and their reception when Charles was incarcerated need be seen as nothing more than the pride of an imprisoned father in the achievement of a son at liberty in a world now lost. But the illustrations to *A Study in Scarlet*, bad in all else but faithful in their identification of Charles Altamont Doyle's lineaments with those of Sherlock Holmes, are a different matter. How far Arthur took the implication of those drawings seriously is unknown. The lesson to ourselves is clear enough. Charles Doyle could not give his son a normal paternal affection: he did seek to possess him by seeing in himself what he took to be his son's hero-figure. But Sherlock Holmes was never an Arthurian hero.

The Jesuits also sought to possess Arthur, although more subtly and indirectly than has been assumed. Francis Cassidy has to be singled apart here: he evidently saw his work as compensating for the absence of parents, and as such sought to respond to a need for human affection. He did try to possess his young charges to the extent of giving them his own devotion to Christ and His Eucharist, but it seems to have been a possessiveness which had in it neither a personal self-aggrandisement nor a transference of self to an institution. That was all. The Stonyhurst Jesuits were more deeply implicated in the sense of institution, quite apart from their zeal for Christ. They do not really seem to have tried to draw Arthur into their ranks, as Conan seems to have feared. But they deeply wanted to make him one of the tribe of Stonyhurst conformists, and their love was sublimated into the ideal of discipline and obedience to regulations.

One healthy result of this was to make Arthur a rebel, which he became much more consciously and much earlier than James Joyce, and in certain respects the nature of the rebellion was the same: an insistence on the individual and his retention of his rights, coupled with a belief that the opinion of authority for its own sake was not enough to justify acceptance, but that the individual had to subject that opinion and its demands to his own tests on his own yardstick. Where the boys were similar was in their discovery of literature as food for the mind, and their growing reliance on it to supply the ethical dynamic which formal religion ceased to give them. Both of them had the Jesuits to thank for it that their grasp of culture was so closely allied to the training of memory, and the retention of so much literature almost *verbatim.* Conan Doyle was fortunate in being cut off from the puritanism of a local community which could constrain the options open to the Jesuit teachers in a day-school such as Belvedere, and while his open rebelliousness contrasted with Joyce's very early adhesion to silence and cunning, it opened his creative capacities earlier. Francis Cassidy above all deserves credit for his early encouragement of those capacities, and so too does the schoolboy audience for his tales, among whom James Ryan was the first disciple.

Hence literature and the making of it became for Conan Doyle the means of expressing that love he found it so hard to find. For him, as his heroes Scott and Macaulay, the business of writing was at once an economic activity and a conquest of love from his audience. Joyce never attained this: he offered an aesthetic ideal whose acceptance meant so much more to him, but in whose formulation the primary concern was always himself. The Jesuits also had the singular effect of immunising both boys from the prevailing orthodoxies of the secular world they would encounter after school. In Conan Doyle's case, he may have taken himself to have left the University as a pure materialist; but in fact materialism would never satisfy him, either as an explanation of life or as a guiding principle of behaviour. Clerical, and subsequently, academic politics he rejected; but the role of the priest and of the scholar in being potential judges where necessary—as opposed to by definition—he carried through in his own life and in his own character. He related the sacerdotal-scholastic right of ultimate intervention and judgment to performance, not to position, and hence liked to present heroes such as Sherlock Holmes, Sir Nigel and Professor Challenger who are either morally passive, when not called on to pronounce, or, as in Challenger's case, ludicrous when laying down the law outside of his proper sphere. The last tendency is even more evident with an avowedly comic figure like Brigadier Gerard, although all his heroes carry a great element of comedy; Gerard is famous for his misjudgments, but it is important that in his proper business as a soldier he very seldom makes a tactical error, however frequently he blunders as lover, decoy, spy, adventurer or diplomat. This sense of the hero as comic and heroic at once he may have first learned from Cassidy, who alone of the teachers seems to have understood the importance of respect and authority being intermingled with fun. It also owed much to his mother, whose enthusiasm with heraldry was a comic escapism if anything increasing the grandeur of her martyrdom and sacrifice in her tragic marriage.

The search for love and rebellion against possessiveness demonstrated itself most forcefully in his relations with Bryan Charles Waller, whose surviving letter to him is at once a cry for individualism and an insistence on its denial. Arthur was being summoned to the cult of the individual on Waller's terms, and those terms took possessiveness more deeply into Arthur's world than anything he had known before. Hence he fled away and found human response from Dr Reginald Ratcliff Hoare and his wife, yet possessiveness came to dominate that relationship also. At the same time it was clearly seminal, more so than it is probably possible for us to chart. It was in Birmingham, after all, that his first published writing seems to have been done, and it was Birmingham also which he honoured by making it—as "Birchespool"—the setting of so many of his early stories. Edinburgh itself supplied much, most notably when he was bringing his mind to bear on London and found his ignorance of the southern capital answered by memories of the northern.

As his coldly accurate analysis bears witness, Edinburgh University seemed to ask of him neither love nor conformity, yet he did end by being made Joseph Bell's acolyte and target for exploitation. The final irony there was supreme. It was more as an academic prop or an audio-visual aid that Bell possessed him, yet it was perhaps the most unscrupulous of all the forms of possessiveness he encountered: and it ended by Bell's being possessed, dominated and immortalised by him. That George Budd tried to take him over also is clear enough, yet Budd acted as a means of striking independence from him once more, in relation to his mother, Waller and the Hoares initially and finally from Budd himself: the object for whose cause rebellion took place ultimately demanded rebellion against itself.

As the case of Budd reminds us, all of these attempts to answer his need for love by attempts at domination were menacing to the independence of mind and will of the boy, but in retrospect the figures appear less menacing than pathetic: the tragic Charles Doyle, the neurotic Splaine, the sworn anti-modernist Kingdon, the ambitious Bell unable to fill the shoes of Syme, the domineering Waller denied his career and his children, Hoare only able to achieve publication in order to destroy, the resourceful Budd obliterated by his own short-cuts. Yet they crowded around the early years, sometimes in conjunction, sometimes in succession, now inspiring, now stifling. It was not only his need for choice among them, not of any one of them but of what part of each of them he wanted: it was also his need to make the most of them in cultural and intellectual terms.

So the conflict of the forms in that outer room plagued and galvanised him, and the boy they tried to make their Watson wove them remorselessly and inescapably into his Holmes.

Conflict and its aspects—science against spirit, masculinity against women's rights, culture against specialisation, social orthodoxy against Bohemianism, self-reassurance against autoexperiment, dignity against financial need, antiquarianism against hatred of snobbery, love against possessiveness—all played their part in the fulfilment of his creative powers. Yet it is vital to see conflict itself in combat within his mind against peace, and it was peace which produced his first great work—the tranquillity induced by the discovery of his own world aboard ship, short-lived, self-fulfilling, thrilling in its perpetual revelation of the new, thrilling also in its brushes with death whether from whales or fever, most valuable of all in the human material it presented to him without any threat to his own identity and integrity: the captains, the sailors, Henry Highland Garnet. And he finally achieved his permanent sureness of touch by finding such tranquillity in a world of his discovery and his own making when he went alone to Southsea.

Southsea also gave him the certainty of command he needed. Apart from the individual dangers, his life on board ship was clearly defined and protected as his life at Stonyhurst and Feldkirch had been, even if the protection was extended purely to his material life. While in Edinburgh, Birmingham and Plymouth his life had been shaped in forms responsive to the personalities of others—his parents, Waller, Bell, Budd—though he had ultimately had to make his own decisions, sometimes very grave and difficult ones. In Southsea, he might be partly imprisoned by economic and social constraints, but he could feel himself master of his fate in some degree. The household was his, and to it he brought his nine-year-old brother Innes, and he could choose his friends and diversions instead of having them prescribed by family patterns, or school determinants, or student norms. That he should become, at last, the man in control was also essential if he was to enter the mind of Holmes.

And then, there was another room, partly outer, partly inner. He sketched it frivolously in his *"A Literary Mosaic"* otherwise called *"Cyprian Overbeck Wells"* written around 1886, but it was as important in his formation as the selves within him and the protagonists around him. *"Cyprian Overbeck Wells"* itself is a clever little squib, describing a rather idiotic young narrator who is interested in literature. It could perhaps join the catalogue of Doyleana with probable influence on Wodehouse, since it was included by ACD in *The Captain of the "Pole-Star"* and maintained in print throughout its author's life despite its very modest origins in the *Boy's Own Paper* for 1886, and the narrator as silly ass could be a remote ancestor of Bertie Wooster:

> From my boyhood I have had an intense and overwhelming conviction that my real vocation lay in the direction of literature. I have, however, had a most unaccountable difficulty in getting any responsible person to share my views. It is true that private friends have sometimes, after listening to my effusions, gone the length of remarking, "Really, Smith, that's not half bad!" or, "You take my advice, old boy, and send that to some magazine!" but I have never on these occasions had the moral courage to inform my adviser that the article in question had been sent to well-nigh every publisher in London, and had come back again with a rapidity and precision which spoke well for the efficiency of our postal arrangements.

One of the charms about this is that it is autobiographical: the early 1880s would see many such "paper boomerangs", as Smith goes on to call them, making their way from and to Arthur, and it is cheering to see how here as elsewhere he made disappointment become transformed into humour.

But the comic possibilities of Mr Smith—and he is essentially comic in the self-revelatory fashion of Bertie Wooster, rather than merely poltroonish as is Hammond in *"That Little Square Box"*—are subordinated in the taking over of the work he is trying to write by the Great Literary Dead in contentious collaboration.

It was not the first time he had played with that sort of thing, nor would it be the last. *"The Secret of Goresthorpe Grange"*, which antedates *"Cyprian"* by a couple of years, presented a succession of ghosts according to successive recipes by Bulwer Lytton, Sir Walter Scott, Dickens, Poe and others. *"Borrowed Scenes"*, many years later, is a hilarious transposition of George

Borrow's conversation and habits into real life. *"A Physiologist's Wife"*, written towards the end of the 1880s, is a very amusing, though also touching, use of Henry James themes wickedly crowned by a highly ambiguous heroine rejoicing in the (false) name of "Mrs O'James". But *"Cyprian"* goes deeper, and reflects the tension in Conan Doyle's writing between his love of great literature, his scholarly desire to quarry it and be influenced by it, and his danger of being possessed by it. His excellent memory still left him a prey to unconscious plagiarism in these years. The problem was not particularly serious for his short stories, but for novels, to which he was constantly seeking to turn his hand in the Southsea years, it was very great. *The Firm of Girdlestone*, he reflected in *Memories and Adventures*, "was too reminiscent of the work of others": Dickens, pointed out Hesketh Pearson, supplied many tricks of style and character-depiction, Sheridan LeFanu, charged M.R. James, gave him the basis of the plot in *Uncle Silas*, and Anthony Trollope, I would argue, provided much of his method in chapter-arrangement, presentation of Bohemian life and use of themes such as gambling economics and unnatural sons. *Mr Scarborough's Family* was serialised in *All the Year Round* in 1881-82 just when Arthur was beginning to write for it and hence reading it, and the *Girdlestone* material concerning military gambling, financial disaster and the social life of their practitioners seems heavily reminiscent of it: much more remotely, Augustus Scarborough is morally as anxious to curtail his father's existence as Ezra Girdlestone proves ultimately lethal to his father's physical survival. There are obvious differences here most notably in that Mr Scarborough hates his son Augustus, while Mr Girdlestone loves his. But in the end Scarborough's hatred carries a greater justice than Girdlestone's love.

And *A Study in Scarlet*, of all Conan Doyle's works, is that one in which obligations to major literary inspiration are omnipresent. We will return to its problems, but *"Cyprian"*, composed probably within the same calendar year, diagnosed what ailed it perhaps better than the author knew.

So on the one hand, Arthur wanted to open his mind to Daniel Defoe, and Jonathan Swift, and Charles Lamb, and Henry Fielding, and Walter Scott, and Tobias Smollett, and Robert Louis Stevenson, and those other friends who moved Cyprian Overbeck Wells so rapidly from adventure to adventure and century to century: on the other, his humility was seriously inhibiting his originality. He finally faced the dilemma and crushed it in *Micah Clarke*, just after having been all but overwhelmed by it in *A Study in Scarlet*.

The 1880s were absolutely critical for Conan Doyle's literary achievement, however few his major works by comparison to those of the forty years which followed. He had "taken on board" in the years from birth to his departure from Plymouth; he would slowly "put out" when in Southsea, and the nature of the "putting out" gave him the critical experience to learn from mistakes. His life at Southsea was very full, yet the town itself supplied very little in the nature of location as we have seen Stonyhurst, Edinburgh, the *Hope*, the *Mayumba*, Feldkirch, Birmingham and (as regards at least one of its inhabitants) Plymouth do. The most obvious use of it is in the most obvious place: his tales of medical life and his *Stark Munro Letters*. But if Southsea did not particularly inspire him, even if it did stabilise and direct him, the hinterland country did. In these years his photographic and other expeditions bred in him a deep love of the Hampshire countryside, and this realised itself in giving him excellent ground for the opening sequences of *Micah Clarke* and *The White Company*. But more than that, Southsea gave him the time and the tranquillity he needed to undertake long works: his doctoral thesis, *The Narrative of John Smith* (now lost: unless that Smith is the narrator of *"Cyprian"* or that his name was later altered to John Stark Munro), *The Firm of Girdlestone*, *A Study in Scarlet* and *Micah Clarke*.

Moreover, while he was preoccupied with coming to terms with the novel form, his short story writing suffered. He built up an increasing literary income, but in his own view very few of the publications whence it originated merited survival beyond periodical publication. It is possible to pay respect to his exceptions such as *"The Man from Archangel"*, and to note some that he inexplicably ignored, such as *"The Heiress of Glenmahowley"*, but in general the frustrations over novel-writing lowered the quality of the short stories from the heights reached by *"The Captain of the 'Pole-Star' "* and *"J. Habakuk Jephson's Statement"*: *"Glenmahowley"*, in fact, is the contemporary of the latter, and *"Archangel"* follows them rapidly. What was happening was that stories like *"The Winning Shot"*, *"The Actor's Duel"* and *"Uncle Jeremy's Household"*, with much remarkable material were failing because they came to resemble novels trying to climb out of short stories or short stories conceived in novels' terms. As a result there was wastage: in *"Uncle Jeremy's Household"*, for instance, a splendidly absurd figure is established in Uncle Jeremy himself, benign, self-absorbed, fascinated by his own appalling poetry (and we know of at least one poet of Arthur's acquaintance who is unlikely to have stinted quotation from his own poetry), but he simply disappears from the plot. ACD was also having problems in moving between character and plot. *"The Man from Archangel"*, for instance, does excellent work in first presenting the Gothic misanthropic narrator, who no doubt owes something to Stevenson's Northmour in *"The Pavilion on the Links"*, but whose ferocity of repudiation of the entire planet by comparison reduces Northmour to the geniality of Squire Trelawney: then we reach the love-crisis of the tortured Russians, and while a good balance is maintained between character and plot development, in a way the narrator has become too large to be accommodated into merely one episode. One way out of that difficulty was to turn it into an advantage: Holmes and Watson became a series in a thoroughly natural way once the trouble had been taken to establish them.

But literary economics were having other difficulties. *"The Heiress of Glenmahowley"* opens on a splendidly satiric note about the Irish land war and the worthless English trippers who are having it presented as a tourist attraction, it then becomes a marvellous piece of Edgeworthian tragi-comic melodrama when the story is told of the heiress and why she was prevented from seeing any man, and finally it ends with suitable modern irony in the heiress proving neither an heiress nor unmarried. The mingling of themes is effective, the last being a very shrewd use of the Penelope theme, yet another, if somewhat unexpected, common point of literary inspiration between the two Jesuit pupils, Conan Doyle and James Joyce. But the infuriating thought remains that Conan Doyle really had materials here for an Irish novel, falling somewhere between Trollope's *The Landleaguers* and Somerville and Ross's *Naboth's Vineyard*, in time of writing as well as in theme of concern, and possessed of a finer sense of humour than is to be found in those books, masters of humour though the three were. The Penelope ending is an anti-climax, in the work of Conan Doyle if not in that of James Joyce.

Arguably Conan Doyle did not commence work on *Micah Clarke* until 1885, the year in which he presented his doctoral dissertation. He said in his contribution to the *"My First Book"* series in the *Idler* that it took him a year to research and five months to write, and in *Memories and Adventures* that it was finished early in 1888, to be followed by further boomerang treatment from publishers until it and its author were taken up by Andrew Lang. Ironically, the only one of his early long works not mentioned in *"My First Book"*, *A Study in Scarlet*, had been seen by Lang, according to the American syndicator and future magazine owner S.S. McClure, who tells in his *Autobiography* how effectively Lang aroused his interest in the young writer. But for all of its early difficulty in finding a home, *Micah Clarke* was the first book by Conan Doyle to show his arrival at literary maturity. We are safe in doubting, then, that he simply commenced work: before research there was a necessary period of reflection and gestation, of choice and rejection of theme. He had to determine the nature and period of the historical theme on which he was itching to write, whither in time and place he was to send his actual Cyprian Overbeck Wells, and under whose literary influence and on what terms of inspiration. Inevitably his choices fell on his two prime favourites, Walter Scott and Thomas Babington Macaulay, with some allowance for Charles Reade, Tolstoy and Stevenson.

Tolstoy's influence may be asserted at once, in that it was partly exhibited in the highly personal view of the battle of Sedgemoor with concentration on ordinary people rather than on the major protagonists, and partly in a bitter passage at the end of the battle whose humanity utterly destroys the view of Conan Doyle as a blood-thirsty militarist:

> Oh, war, my children, what a terrible thing it is! How are men cozened and cheated by the rare trappings and prancing steeds, by the empty terms of honour and glory, until they forget in the outward tinsel and show the real ghastly horror of the accursed thing! Think not of the dazzling squadrons, nor of the spirit-stirring blare of the trumpets, but think of that lonely man under the shadow of the alders, and of what he was doing in a Christian age and a Christian land.

The origin of Micah's outburst to his grandchildren here is, significantly, a medical one, the sight of a man whose "arm had been half-severed by a cannon-ball, and he was quietly completing the separation in order to free himself of the dangling and useless limb . . . the man, with a short nod of recognition, went grimly forward with his task, until, even as we gazed, he separated the last shred which held it, and lay over with blanched lips which still murmured the prayer":

> Surely I, who have grown gray in harness, and who have seen as many fields as I have years of my life, should be the last to preach upon this subject, and yet I can clearly see that, in honesty, men must either give up war, or else they must confess that the words of the Redeemer are too lofty for them, and that there is no longer any use in pretending that His teaching can be reduced to practice. I have seen a Christian minister blessing a cannon which had just been founded, and another blessing a war-ship as it glided from the slips. They, the so-called representatives of Christ, blessed these engines of destruction which cruel man has devised to destroy and tear his fellow-worms. What would we say if we read in Holy Writ of our Lord having blessed the battering rams and the catapults of the legions? Would we think that it was in agreement with His teaching? But there! As long as the heads of the Church wander away so far from the spirit of its teaching as to live in palaces and drive in carriages, what wonder if, with such examples before them, the lower clergy overstep at times the lines laid down by their great Master?

Like much else in *Micah Clarke*, this passage is partly induced by a reflection in Macaulay's *History*. The historian had merely commented, fairly enough, of the Bishop of Winchester's loan to the Royal army at Sedgemoor of his horses and traces to drag up the great guns whither they were needed, that "This interference of a Christian prelate in a matter of blood has, with strange inconsistency, been condemned by some Whig writers who can see nothing criminal in the conduct of the numerous Puritan ministers then in arms against the government". In so saying, Macaulay gave one of his many proofs that history was not, with him, merely a matter of the Whigs getting the best of it, but Conan Doyle's reflections, placed a little uneasily on his narrator's tongue, reveal a profundity of thought lacking in his over-complacent source.

This sense of what inspiration could be drawn from Macaulay in a spirit of acceptance but not uncritical acceptance dominates the entire book. Macaulay had said that Scott had rescued social history when the historians had excluded it; he himself wished to restore it from the realm of the historical novel to the history proper. Conan Doyle in *Micah Clarke* uses the fictional method of Scott blended in with the historical findings of Macaulay. It is idle to guess what led to the choice of theme, the ill-fated Monmouth revolt in the West Country in 1685. Much though Arthur loved Macaulay, it was the essays, not the *History*, which commanded his fullest allegiance, and even in the *History* the attempt of Monmouth is only viewed as an overture for the general revolt against James and the triumph of William. Macaulay's finest pages in the relevant chapter, his fifth, describe the savagery of the punishment inflicted on the rebels and their friends; his account of Sedgemoor is vivid, but not comparable to his set-pieces on the battles later, such as the Boyne, Steinkirk and Landen. His notes on Sedgemoor show some lack of self-assurance in describing a battle, and are the better for it, and Arthur must have derived aid and comfort from Macaulay's discussion of the impossiblity of any witness giving an accurate version of events. My impression would be that ACD determined on the Monmouth revolt for two reasons: that he had come to know Somerset however briefly from living at Plymouth, and had probably had his first sight of Taunton at that time; and that he was deeply influenced by certain contrasts and comparisons the theme suggested with Sir Walter Scott's *Waverley*. He was above all else a literary workman. He studied not only his seniors, but thought about what made them as good as they were, and in launching into historical fiction it was natural to look at the novel which launched Scott's career as a master of historical fiction. Having done these things he turned back to his Macaulay, found much there to delight him and many blanks to be filled in, and went from Macaulay to the main sources.

His approach to the Monmouth revolt is fundamentally Macaulay's save that he spends only one chapter, albeit a horrific one, in describing the Bloody Assizes. Sometimes the extent to which he follows Macaulay is uncertain. Micah Clarke as narrator is rather too tolerant for his own time, and reflects in his philosophy sometimes the liberal spirit of Macaulay, sometimes the deeper humanity of Conan Doyle. But ACD was sensible, as was Macaulay, that too much cannot be asked of the past in questions of modern liberalism, and it is only sensible to have Micah think of Judge Jeffreys as some frightful diabolic aberration in the history of English justice. We do not know if Conan Doyle realised that Jeffreys was very much a man of his time in the savagery of his conduct in court, being chiefly distinguished by his intellect; Lord Justice Scroggs was if anything worse, and Lord Justice Pemberton conducted the trial of St Oliver Plunkett with comparable brutality. One point where the Catholic-educated Arthur certainly demanded too much of his Micah was when he made him tell his grandchildren: "We can scarce credit how . . . ecclesiastics like Archbishop Plunkett . . . were dragged to death on the testimony of the vilest of vile, without a voice being raised in their behalf ". Nor is the preceding sentence "We recognise now that there are no more useful or loyal citizens in the State than our Catholic brethren" precisely what might be expected of a veteran of Monmouth's army and a son of an Ironside cornet. But Conan Doyle was doing more than writing historical fiction in *Micah Clarke*: he wanted to explain the Puritans, but in no way by justifying their anti-Catholic delusions or by furthering late Victorian anti-Catholic sentiment. If he was anachronistic, it was with profoundly moral purpose.

In his use of Macaulay, Conan Doyle is receptive, but not conservative. Perhaps the main villain of the piece in Macaulay's version (apart from Jeffreys and his Royal master) is Robert Ferguson, "the Plotter", presented as Iago to Monmouth's Othello. Conan Doyle gives him as noisy, self-important, canting, egregious, irritating, but not fundamentally bad or dishonest. This makes some sense. Micah Clarke would probably not have any great sense of Ferguson's darker qualities. On the other hand, Ferguson ultimately did flirt with Jacobitism in his later years and was sent to the Tower, and Micah Clarke would have to have been buried fairly deeply in Hampshire not to have heard of it. But from a novelist's point of view weaving and bobbing in and out of the actual narrative of events to footnote them in the light of further revelations would be foolish. Micah therefore has to be seen as a narrator remembering the Monmouth campaign vividly, but knowing little of its actual origin in Monmouth's career in the reign of his father Charles II or his plotting in exile after his uncle James's accession, nor does he really know much of politics in general. He simply says he became a soldier after escaping to the continent at the end of the revolt, and continued as such under William III when he invaded England and drove out James. In fact, one of the strengths of the book is the sense of the old man looking back and remembering event on event as they occurred, being more concerned with the events than their meaning.

Professor Weil-Nordon, in a detailed discussion of the novel, lists three points of breach with Macaulay, and they may be worth following to watch the problem of creation and reception. One is that Macaulay says Monmouth was definitely an illegitimate child of Charles, whereas Conan Doyle in text and notes (he followed Scott, rather less laboriously, in adding notes), suggested there was written proof of the legitimacy. In fact this is nonsense. Micah Clarke himself has to be vaguely conscious that Monmouth might be legitimate, although it doesn't matter too much to him since he is in the affair because of his Ironside father (to whom, presumably, all Stuarts were bastards). Conan Doyle's note quoted Sir Patrick Hume to the effect that Monmouth told him he was legitimate and hoped to be able to prove it, and he followed this by citing Monmouth's commissions from Charles of 1668 and 1673 where he appears as " our . . . natural son". Possibly Weil-Nordon did not realise that "natural" means illegitimate, but Conan Doyle clearly assumed his audience did. It was the acceptable word in his day as in that of Charles. Admittedly he does not quote Macaulay's ribald sentence on the possibility that Charles was not Monmouth's father ("A suspicious lover might have had his doubts; for the lady had several admirers, and was not supposed to be cruel to any") but that side of the question was hardly relevant to Micah Clarke and the notes do well in keeping so few in number and so close to the text.

The professor is then exercised because of a passage in which John Derrick, although a Puritan, is discovered ready to betray Monmouth's army to James's troops having been worsted in love, whereas Macaulay mentions that a Royalist lady in Bridgewater tried to warn the King's troops. In fact, the incident shows how Conan Doyle went to work with his material. First of all, the fact that one person tried to warn the King's men, and that he depicts another as doing so, counts in no way against him: it was likely enough that several persons disaffected from Monmouth, for one reason or another, might be found in Bridgewater and if they heard that a night attack was being planned, it was hardly a matter of one person holding a monopoly patent for informing. Secondly, he actually did use the story of the woman with great skill: what seems to have happened, says Macaulay, is that when the lady reached the Royal camp she was seized and raped, and fled away in horror, her story untold. Conan Doyle actually uses the theme of rape, but with remarkable skill transfers it to Monmouth's own headquarters at Taunton, rightly wishing to make the point that where soldiery were collected a formerly secure civilian population might find itself in considerable danger, however Puritan the soldiers' official leadership, and that persons wishing to perpetrate private crimes could use the disruption induced by the arrival of the soldiery to cover their guilt. The rape is foiled, and Derrick, the person responsible, then resolves on treason. The professor rightly points out that Derrick's death is also that of Stapleton in *The Hound*; and one can also show foreshadowing of *The Hound* in the pursuit of Micah and his friends by bloodhounds on Salisbury Plain. Presumably *Uncle Tom's Cabin* was the ultimate progenitor of that idea, a source ACD would have read with greater interest after meeting Garnet. But on the matter of Derrick's treachery and its source, the use of material is entirely to Conan Doyle's credit. It is an excellent example of how the artist in historical fiction allows his material to inform his imagination.

Links between *Micah Clarke* and *The Hound* make excellent sense in that Conan Doyle was very conscious in the latter book of returning to the West Country where his first historical novel had been set. Weil-Nordon rightly sees Stapleton's death as possessing more dramatic force than the original or Derrick version. The difference, he might have added, lies in Stapleton's death not being seen, and hence much more disturbing than Derrick's, which is. In the interval Conan Doyle had learned the importance of leaving his most terrible effects to the reader's imagination. Wodehouse told his friend Townend that the supreme genius of Moriarty lay in his never being confronted by Watson, so that the reader never sees him as more than a silhouette. It is the same principle.

Weil-Nordon's third charge lies in the use of the Duke of Beaufort, whom Conan Doyle represents as hedging his bets on Monmouth and sending him assurances through Micah Clarke that he will support him in the event of success; and Mr Ronald Pearsall, ever ready to fashion a gibe founded on another man's work, sneers "Doyle's own opinion of what the seventeenth century was really like led him to distort the character of a historical figure, the Duke of Beaufort. One might as well write a historical novel dealing with the nineteenth century in which Queen Victoria marries John Brown and Gladstone runs off with one of the prostitutes he rescued." In fact, Victoria may have married Brown: there is a fragment of evidence that she did. Gladstone's private life, we learn from his *Diaries,* was not in his view quite the monument of rectitude Mr Pearsall evidently presumes. As Macaulay said in that review of Montgomery which Conan Doyle thought too harsh, "So may such ill got gains ever prosper!" Actually, the painstaking Weil-Nordon rather outran himself. It is perfectly true that no evidence exists, nor is there reason to suspect any could ever appear, to show that Beaufort tried to take out insurance on a Monmouth victory. He had done well out of the Tory reaction in Charles's final years, winning his dukedom in 1682. He did not support the invasion of the Prince of Orange in 1685, but took oaths of loyalty to him with no hesitation once the new King and Queen were firmly installed and the old one an exile. Where Conan Doyle had a point, however, was that although of extreme Royalist parentage, Beaufort had been initially a Catholic, then supported Cromwell, then on Cromwell's death called for a free Parliament which facilitated the return of Charles II and thereafter was a constant Tory. Hence it was not out of character to see such a man as a judicious politician following the turn of the tide and seeking to use it to his advantage. It was not just the need to have a *deus ex machina* who by judicious blackmail on Decimus Saxon's part could save Micah Clarke, as Weil-Nordon will have it, that led Conan Doyle to show Beaufort as hostile to a Monmouth emissary in public and careful to remain in good standing with him and his master in private. It is not inconsistent with the younger Beaufort although by the time of the Monmouth episode, when he was 56, Beaufort seemed to have settled down with his family in an unswerving Toryism. It is absolutely consistent with the politics of the day in general. Macaulay's pages teem with references to noblemen and others who sought to maintain good standing with William and James before and after the revolution. Hence as a political type Beaufort is reasonably presented, and as to the fact that he himself would almost certainly never have treated with an emissary of Monmouth, there is no concealment of the fiction of what Conan Doyle is saying. Micah Clarke, the emissary who sees Beaufort, is nowhere suggested to be a real person, nor one whose career reflects real persons. No note implies any basis to the interview or its sequel. To any person familiar with the period, Micah Clarke's elderly liberalism makes it very clear that he is without foundation.

If real historical figures presented in historical fiction are only allowed to do that which they are known to have done, and not to utter a word otherwise, not even when it is consistent with their conduct at some time in their lives, there is an end to all historical fiction. Conan Doyle's trick on this occasion does an excellent service in presenting the realities of political loyalty in the seventeenth century, and it is as a symbol of that uncertain loyalty, not as a serious statement of the conduct of the actual person, that the portrait of Beaufort makes its claim. Conan Doyle was assuming that it was a profile of such loyalties, and not one of Beaufort, which his readers would ask of him.

One further point may be made on Conan Doyle's use of Macaulay. In style, he followed him carefully, though with great control. In particular he leaned not only on Macaulay's prose but also on his poetry. He clearly pondered deeply on Macaulay's "*Battle of Naseby*" allegedly by a sergeant in Ireton's regiment. He also used some of the language of the *Lays of Ancient Rome* to increase the power of his narration. He savagely underscores Macaulay's point in the *History* as to the leaders' anxiety to save themselves where the lower supporters suffered and continued to give their lives at Sedgemoor after the cowardly Monmouth had fled from the stricken field; "Grey, Wade, Ferguson, and others had contrived also to save themselves, while Stephen Timewell lay in the midst of a stern ring of his hard-faced burghers, dying as he had lived, a gallant Puritan Englishman." Curiously enough, the inspiration comes from the portrait of Tarquin in "*The Battle of Lake Regillus*":

> *There, in a dark stern ring,*
> *The Roman exiles gathered close*
> *Around the ancient king.*

But to see the novel as a whole it is necessary to turn to the other great inspiration, Scott. *Waverley* presents a view of a rising in the cause of one exiled Stuart, *Micah Clarke* a view of another in that of another. *Waverley* describes what led to the last battles fought on Scottish soil, *Micah Clarke* what led to the last battle fought on English. *Waverley* recounts the political events leading to the death of Gaelic Scotland; *Micah Clarke* tells of the last flaring-up of a culture also in its death-throes, Puritan England. Both novels are characterised by speed, power, intense preoccupation with revelation of social attitudes in dead cultures, consciousness of ambiguities and complexities of loyalty among the protagonists, wit, humour, gallantry, idiosyncrasy and sublime martyrdom. The major difference lies in the sense of time. In *Waverley* the whole story wins an additional horror by the subtitle " *'Tis Sixty Years Since*": Scott uses it primarily in two ways, firstly in that the evidence on which he bases his narrative derives in large part from oral testimony collected by himself or by trustworthy reporters, secondly in that he wishes to say that the tragedy he is describing seems that of another world and yet it is within living memory. Conan Doyle tries to capture this by the device of Micah Clarke telling his grandchildren about events apparently wholly remote from them but vital to his development. He cannot make it "sixty years since", otherwise Micah would be an octogenarian and hence naturally less credible. The vigour of the narrative itself is that of a man in excellent health, and good for a long recital each nightfall. In any case Scott's original subtitle was " *'Tis Fifty Years Since*", as his first chapters were written in 1805.

Another difference lies in the manner of narration Conan Doyle had preferred to date, that of the first person. Accordingly the ironies of Scott, which supply so much of the humour of *Waverley*, are missing from much of *Micah Clarke*. The aged Micah can see and present the humour of a situation, but if he does laugh at himself it is in a straightforward and soldierly manner. The irony that does peep out is more through character, though there is one delicious moment worthy of Scott himself, all the greater because it directly follows Micah having been strung up for hanging and reprieved in the nick of time. One of his captors, an enthusiastic play-goer, begins literally to make fun of the book's plot:

> "I desire to share the same lot and fortune as has befallen my companions in arms", I answered.
> "Nay, that is but a sullen way to take your deliverance", cried the smaller officer. "The situation is as flat as sutler's beer. Otway would have made a better thing of it. Can you not rise to the occasion? Where is she?"
> "She! Who?" I asked.

"She. The she. The woman. Your wife, sweetheart, betrothed, what you will."
"There is none such", I answered.

"There now! What can be done in a case like that?" cried he despairingly.
"She should have rushed in from the wings and thrown herself upon your
bosom. I have seen such a situation earn three rounds from the pit. There is
good material spoiling here for want of some one to work it up."

The last sentence is admirable self-mockery. The passage hits off the contrast
between Restoration gallant and Puritan idealist, and the inspiration may be
from Scott's hilarious comments in his introduction on his failure to present a
work in the style of Mrs Radcliffe, the same who moved the satire of Jane
Austen in *Northanger Abbey*. It may also be that the passage was added after
a few rejection slips complaining about the absence of a central love interest.
In fact the failure to include anything relative to Micah's marriage—we do
not even know where he met his wife—seems very deliberate. Because he is a
central figure, innocent and inexperienced but of moral firmness in contrast
to Waverley's wavering—Scott may well have chosen the name for the
quality—the love-interest is confined to a figure much closer to Waverley,
Micah's friend Reuben Lockarby.

Lockarby, unlike Micah, joins for reasons of schoolboy friendship and in
defiance of his parents, whereas his father's wish is Micah's sole reason for
supporting Monmouth. Certainly Lockarby remains true, but his attempted
murder at the hands of Derrick incapacitates him from taking part at
Sedgemoor, and so eases his return to orthodox society. In this he is helped
by a prisoner, Major Ogilvy, who proves his deliverer, much as Colonel
Talbot ultimately proves Waverley's. There is an excellent joke in the Ogilvy
portrait. So far from allowing the character to follow the situation in being
borrowed from Scott, Ogilvy would by name seem to be Scots where Talbot
was archetypally English, and Ogilvy discusses modern science with an
obsessiveness reminiscent of the antiquarianism of Baron Bradwardine, which
Talbot detests. There is certainly more than Waverley in Lockarby: he
probably owed something to memories of Jim Ryan, and as such naturally
operates as a Watson figure. Ryan's own volatility and dilettantish ways as
revealed by his library reading-lists, his change from Arts to Medicine at the
University and his ultimate dropping out, suggest further points. It was
presumably his friendship with Arthur which led to his taking up Medicine,
as Lockarby takes up Monmouth for love of Micah, and Lockarby's orthodox
Anglicanism contrasting with Micah's Puritan heritage recalls Ryan's adhesion to the Catholicism Arthur abandoned. Ultimate geographical separation
also holds true in each case, Lockarby settling down in Taunton while Micah
returns to Hampshire after his exile. They certainly must have been
patriarchs of no mean authority: each contrived that not only children but
even grandchildren should be called after the other, Lockarby at the time of
narration being grandfather to a small Micah, and Reuben being one of old
Micah's grandchildren to whom his statement is made. Lockarby is also
reminiscent of the ill-fated Ford in *The White Company*, and if they are
closely based on Ryan, he would seem to have had a splendidly irrepressible
sense of humour and irreverence to authority.

Conan Doyle faced problems of anachronism in using human material of his own acquaintance, but on the other hand it helped him to solve a difficulty which held Scott's composition back for nearly ten years: his opening. *Waverley* does not take off until several introductory chapters have been completed and the hero at last got to Scotland. *Micah Clarke* is moving by the second chapter. The father, Ironside Joe Clarke, is too stock a realisation of Macaulay's vision of the Puritans of integrity to gain momentum, and while his wife, Micah's mother, has one or two very pleasing touches which suggest a seventeenth-century version of Mary Foley Doyle, with her self-sacrifice, her resourcefulness and her peculiarly obsessive hobbies, she is but a charming detail. But in the second chapter Micah explains how the Vicar of the parish is responsible for his dismissal from school following a childish prank, and the Vicar, although never to reappear, is the overture to flesh and blood characters with whom we will be concerned:

> The Vicar, whose name was Pinfold, possessed in this manner great power in the town, and as he was a man with a high inflamed countenance and a pompous manner, he inspired no little awe among the quiet inhabitants. I can see him now with his beaked nose, his rounded waistcoat and his bandy legs, which looked as if they had given way beneath the load of learning which they were compelled to carry. Walking slowly with right hand stiffly extended, tapping the pavement at every step with his metal-headed stick, he would pause as each person passed him, and wait to see that he was given the salute which he thought due to his dignity. This courtesy he never dreamed of returning, save in the case of some of his richer parishioners, but if by chance it were omitted he would hurry after the culprit, and, shaking his stick in his face, insist upon his doffing his cap to him.

Now this is in fact an exceedingly accurate if unkind portrait of Bryan Charles Waller as his former employees recall him at Masongill. Memory and photographs are clear about the beaked nose. Everyone agrees that he was insistent on being capped by the locals and any failure to salute him was met by "Do you know who I am?" "Yes." "Yes, what?" "Yes, sir." His learning was famous in the neighbourhood, and so was his rigid churchmanship with attendance at St Oswald's, Thornton-in-Lonsdale, every Sunday. And his legs were bandy, so much so that they had to be tied together to get him in his coffin; after which exercise one of the undertaker's assistants said malevolently "there you are, you old bugger, and nobody will be raising their cap to you where you've gone". Clearly, on visits to the Masongill estate Arthur saw this side of the former family lodger, and his easy democratic manner led him to react much as the locals did. He even seemed to have picked up their fierce resentment of the whole thing. *Treasure Island* also supplied a little of the inspiration: the Vicar's tapping cane recalls Blind Pew's, and the fact that the prank which leads to Micah's expulsion from school is the cutting through of a bridge to entrap some schoolboy foes (shades of Eddie Tulloch) only to result in the immersion of the Vicar in the stream, owes something to Jim Hawkins and his mother hiding under the bridge as they hear the sound of Pew's cane. The ambiguities of Long John Silver, too, would give some incentive to the depiction of those of Decimus Saxon, and the last line on each directly invites the parallel: "Of Silver we have heard no more." "Of Saxon I have heard more than once." ("I can see him now . . ." of the Vicar also recalls the very first presentation of the old sea-dog at the "Admiral Benbow".)

But Decimus Saxon, having much work to do in the story, is much more than that. In one respect he derives from George Turnavine Budd, rather more than do the many characters Hesketh Pearson saw as the children of Budd. His name directly comes from the Budd clan, save that all of his siblings have the names of Roman ordinal numerals, and the Budd uncles only included three such—Septimus, Octavius and Nonus. Decimus Saxon's appalling relations with his brothers Quartus and Nonus support the view that George Turnavine was on bad terms with his uncle Nonus (and no doubt with "Quartus" or Dr Richard Budd of Barnstaple). Saxon's readiness to dissimulate, his hot-tempered readiness to engage in quarrel and his contempt for ethical criticism of his conduct all suggest Budd. The story is thoroughly on its way once he enters it in chapter four. But he has also very different origins. He, too, has in his enthusiasm for military theory an echo of Bradwardine's fascination with aristocratic protocol, and in his alternation between sectarian votary, freebooter, intriguer, general, quarreler, blackmailer and rescuer he recalls Fergus Mac-Ivor Vich Ian Vohr in *Waverley*, who is first presented as running an unscrupulous protection racket, then appears as noble Highland chief, then as European diplomatic intriguer, then as comrade-in-arms, then as ominous adversary, then as friend in need of rescue and finally as proud, noble and fearless martyr. With an eye on the counterparts, Conan Doyle makes Decimus Saxon the instrument of Micah's deliverance, whereas in *Waverley* it is Fergus whom Waverley tries un-successfully to save. Here again, the later book has the advantage. Although Waverley's very neutrality wins reader identification in ways Micah can not, Fergus's death throws all that follows into insignificance and the happy endings for the Waverleys and their friends seem almost insipid. Micah, if less easy to become oneself, is a central character worth seeing through to the end, partly because Saxon returns to preside over the final scene.

How Arthur and his mother, to whom *Micah Clarke* is dedicated, got over the portrait of the Rev. Mr Pinfold we do not know. It may have been by the fact that one other character shows Wallerian qualities, including "curved aquiline nose" and "flowing beard"—Sir Jacob Clancing, the old impoverished cavalier turned alchemist, whose workroom and experiments seem modelled on Waller's "surgery". Sir Jacob Clancing also remains an example of the kind of true aristocrat Conan Doyle respected, as opposed to those he ridiculed in the Holmes stories in ways reminiscent of Trollope's treatment of the aristocracy in *The Way We Live Now*. Professor Weil-Nordon will have it that in the aged Zachary Palmer, from whom Micah imbibes his theological liberalism, "*nous pouvons sentir . . . le reflet de la personnalité, de la pensée et de l'influence du Docteur Waller*", but this derives from his vision of Waller as a venerable family friend: the most one can say is that the ideas of both clearly had a common source in Winwood

Reade's *Martyrdom of Man*. The sailor Solomon Sprent is presumably from the same source as "Captain Whitehall" in *The Stark Munro Letters*. Given the prevalence of efforts to type-classify Conan Doyle as repressive Victorian it is worth saluting Solomon Sprent's description of his intended courtship in language so bristling with naval terminology that the effect is one of the purest ribaldry. It is Rabelaisian to a degree, without the slightest departure from good taste, and constitutes a splendid break from the dark atmosphere of Puritanism. Here, too, Conan Doyle's historical sense was keen: the economic significance of the sailor in the Puritan commercial empire was acute, but his manners gravely disturbed his more theologically-minded investors. One need only think of how ill the seafarer Governor Sir William Phipps sat at the end of the century with the Puritan oligarchy of witch-hunting Massachusetts.

The preacher Joshua Pettigrue comes into the journey of Micah, Lockarby and Saxon much after the manner of Gilfillan in *Waverley,* but here again a real-life original, and a formidable one, is at hand. It is hard to believe it would have escaped Arthur's notice that the American Civil War was the first conflict on a broad scale among the English-speaking peoples since the Monmouth revolt when men went to war chanting hymns, and it would have been surprising if he had not in his three days' conversation elicited some account of this aspect to the conflict from the Rev. Henry Highland Garnet. In detail Pettigrue clearly derives from the source material, but Garnet would have conveyed the sense of a holy war, and Conan Doyle was exceedingly lucky to have had the experience of hearing first-hand evidence of what that meant. Garnet's incapacity prevented his going to war, but he could testify to the effect of the "*Battle Hymn of the Republic*" on his congregation in New York and Washington, D.C. This, if Conan Doyle had it, was the one piece of oral testimony on which he could set himself alongside the methods of Scott, all the more because in Garnet's case it was far less than sixty years since.

Although much of the work in writing *Micah Clarke* was a matter of amplifying the sources, there are certain passages where great effects are achieved by magnificent compression. The news of the failure of the Argyle revolt involves a reduction of Macaulay's judgments on Argyle's aides in the attempt on Scotland, to one-liners from Decimus Saxon:

"... the Duke had trusty councillors with him. There was Sir Patrick Hume of Polwarth—"

"All talk and no fight", said Saxon.

"And Richard Rumbold."

"All fight and no talk", quoth our companion. "He should, methinks, have rendered a better account of himself."

"Then there was Major Elphinstone."

"A bragging fool!" cried Saxon.

"And Sir John Cochrane."

"A captious, long-tongued, short-witted sluggard ..."

Although Micah Clarke himself is not a Puritan, however much he values the Puritan heritage, ACD said in *Memories and Adventures* "I had always felt great sympathy for the Puritans, who, after all, whatever their little peculiarities, did represent political liberty and earnestness in religion". But he did not fail to hit out at what seemed to him the less admirable of the little peculiarities. The same Rumbold, in a letter to Joseph Clarke, adds a postscript which says volumes about the Puritan male chauvinism: "Present my services to thy spouse. Let her read Timothy chapter two, ninth to fifteenth verses." Conan Doyle left it to his readers to examine that text, but the staunch advocate of women in medicine certainly felt little sympathy with its outlawry of women teachers, insistence on female submissiveness, and insistence that Woman's true destiny lay solely in being wives and mothers. The Puritans could console themselves with the thought that for his shaft at them to sink home, his readers would have to turn to the Bible.

The stories are highly comparable when we turn to the Stuart pretenders, because Scott and Conan Doyle had very good historical sense and there was much similarity in the circumstances and character of Monmouth and Bonnie Prince Charlie. Had the authors pursued their subsequent fortunes the parallels between the cousins—for they were first cousins once removed— would have become clearer still. Charles conducted himself with far more gallantry than Monmouth when all was lost, yet the end-product was the same, a leader in flight to save his own skin, his followers doomed to the vengeance of his enemies. Initially Conan Doyle's Monmouth recalls Scott's Young Chevalier, but in fact the model is Monmouth's putative father Charles II, whence his charm probably derived. History, however, permits Conan Doyle to show the disintegration of Monmouth first into ineffectuality, then into cowardice, and he does it well. Scott pointed out that Prince Charles Edward on his campaign showed himself far better than before or after it, and certainly the long decline into debauchery and decay is not his business, but his is a little too much the Charles of legend. *Waverley* is a novel of high realism, but there is nothing in it equal to the moment of truth in *Micah Clarke:*

> "Who would have thought it of him?" cried Sir Stephen with flashing eyes, as Buyse and Saxon rode out to meet him. "What think ye now of our noble monarch, our champion of the Protestant cause?"
>
> "He is no very great Krieger", said Buyse. "Yet perhaps it may be from want of habit as much as from want of courage."
>
> "Courage!" cried the old Mayor in a voice of scorn. "Look over yonder and behold your King." He pointed out over the moor with a finger which shook as much from anger as from age. There, far away, showing up against the dark peat-coloured soil, rode a gaily-dressed cavalier, followed by a knot of attendants, galloping as fast as his horse would carry him from the field of battle. There was no mistaking the fugitive. It was the recreant Monmouth.
>
> "Hush!" cried Saxon, as we all gave a cry of horror and execration; "do not dishearten our brave lads! Cowardice is catching and will run through an army like the putrid fever."
>
> "Der Feigherzige!" cried Buyse, grinding his teeth. "And the brave country folk! It is too much."
>
> "Stand to your pikes, men!" roared Saxon in a voice of thunder, and we had scarce time to form our square and throw ourselves inside of it, before the whirlwind of horse was upon us once more. Where the Taunton men had joined us a weak spot had been left in our ranks, and through this in an instant the

Blue Guards smashed their way, pouring through the opening, and cutting fiercely to right and left. The burghers on the one side and our own men on the other replied by savage stabs from their pikes and scythes, which emptied many a saddle, but while the struggle was at its hottest the King's cannon opened for the first time with a deafening roar upon the other side of the rhine, and a storm of balls ploughed their way through our dense ranks, leaving furrows of dead and wounded behind them. At the same moment a great cry of "Powder! For Christ's sake, powder!" arose from the musqueteers whose last charge had been fired. Again the cannon roared, and again our men were mowed down as though death himself with his scythe were amongst us. At last our ranks were breaking. In the very centre of the pikemen steel caps were gleaming, and broadswords rising and falling. The whole body was swept back two hundred paces or more, struggling furiously the while, and was there mixed with other like bodies which had been dashed out of all semblance of military order, and yet refused to fly. Men of Devon, or Dorset, of Wiltshire, and of Somerset, trodden down by horse, slashed by dragoons, dropping by scores under the rain of bullets, still fought on with a dogged desperate courage, for a ruined cause and a man who had deserted them. Everywhere as I glanced around me were set faces, clenched teeth, yells of rage and defiance, but never a sound of fear or submission. Some clambered up upon the cruppers of the riders and dragged them backwards from their saddles. Others lay upon their faces and hamstrung the chargers with their scythe-blades, stabbing the horsemen before they could disengage themselves. Again and again the guards crashed through them from side to side, and yet the shattered ranks closed up behind them and continued the long-drawn struggle. So hopeless was it and so pitiable that I could have found it in my heart to wish that they would break and fly, were it not that on the broad moor there was no refuge which they could make for. And all this time, while they struggled and fought, blackened with powder and parched with thirst, spilling their blood as though it were water, the man who called himself their King was spurring over the countryside with a loose rein and a quaking heart, his thoughts centred upon saving his own neck, come what might to his gallant followers.

It seems effortless enough, but in fact it is a mesh of sensitive interthreading. One vital image is that of the dishonoured Messiah: the book abounds naturally in Puritan allusions to God, brimming at times into a ludicrous confidence in His certainty to give victory to His chosen ones. At the same time the fact that old republicans had accepted the claims of kingship of their leader is now a matter of bitter self-reproach. Ironically, the title "Sir Stephen" which Monmouth conferred on the Mayor of Taunton, is used at the very moment when the old man who had kissed the hand of the claimant now sees the speed of the departing feet of clay. Stephen Timewell would be horrified at the thought of intentional blasphemy but his bitter cry "behold your King" is a natural resort to Scripture in crisis, and in a form intended to acknowledge that he has followed a false Christ. The Puritans had an apocalyptic theological frontier and although Micah, a good soldier narrator, is moving far too rapidly with his story and is far too little a Puritan to think of it, Sedgemoor is clearly Armageddon to Timewell and Monmouth has proved the false Christ which would be one of the signs of Doomsday. The text that has torn itself from Timewell's lips is Pilate's cry to the Jews presenting the scourged and thorn-crowned Jesus "Behold your King!" (John, xix. 14). The very fact that the republicans have followed a pretended King is a reminder to them that the strange death of Puritan England is in part self-inflicted. (They were not, of course, the only republicans in the story to have dishonoured their former repudiation of monarchy: the Duke of Beaufort, in Cromwellian days, had renounced his title and married according to the republican rite, although he maintained an austerity in Restoration days which distinguished him strongly from Charles's court.) Here again, Conan Doyle is bringing out a fine parallel with *Waverley*: although the nature and action of the latter prevents our seeing comparable scenes to Sedgemoor at Culloden, which is only mentioned in passing, *Waverley* makes it clear that the rank and file died there for the clan system and the Gaelic order which perished with them, however much their chieftains might be attached to the cause of James III and VIII and the person of his son. And while Micah, like Waverley, will have a happy ending to his own story, the Puritan cause is finished. Yet Micah is infected by the apocalyptic spirit, as is made evident by his sense of Jeffreys on the bench as "The Devil in wig and gown", directing his carnival.

Hesketh Pearson did not like his subject's historical novels, but he acknowledged in Conan Doyle a master of combat description. However, this is far deeper than a rattling good yarn. Monmouth alone would make it so. Timewell, facing his doom, is as effective a transformation from a somewhat absurd provincial pedant into the symbol of a doomed cause as is Fergus Mac-Ivor Vich Ian Vohr, although in other respects neither his person nor his place in the story permits the development of a character of the magnitude of Fergus. Conan Doyle stays with Macaulay's imagery of Tarquin in *"Lake Regillus"*: Timewell's finger "which shook as much from anger as from age" derives from the exiled king

> And, if the lance shook in his gripe,
>   'Twas more with hate than age.

The use of *"Lake Regillus"* in this way reminds us that that also was an attempt to overthrow the state in favour of an unwanted claimant, and while the narrator Micah does not dishonour his cause, however contemptible he acknowledged Monmouth's flight, Conan Doyle like Walter Scott leaves the reader in no doubt that the cause was a bad one. The losers had a beautiful idealism, but it brought them to support a claimant who could not rule even if he won, Monmouth in *Micah Clarke* because of his selfishness and cowardice, Bonnie Prince Charlie (and his father) in *Waverley* because already the world had moved beyond what they understood. Both men maintained this attitude to the past in subsequent works, that deeds of honour and nobility are constantly done in bad causes, witness the comrades of *The White Company* sacrificing themselves in order to reinstate the odious Pedro the Cruel.

Conan Doyle was by now a professional of the first rank in his deployment of first-person narrative. It is not only the simplicity of Micah's narration which conveys so much of his own nature, it is also little tricks such as his mind running slightly ahead of his matter. By the time he is describing the

cannon and its consequences, his mind is naturally darting ahead to the
resistance of his poor men with their scythes, and so in reaching for a simile
to describe the slaughter caused by the cannon he automatically speaks of the
scythe of Death. He has enough Puritanism in him to sound a little like
Ireton's sergeant narrating Macaulay's "*Battle of Naseby*", although the
inversion is bitter: it is the Puritans' Stuart enemy, Charles I, whose flight is
described there

> *Fast, fast, the gallants ride, in some safe nook to hide*
> *Their coward heads, predestined to rot on Temple Bar;*
> *And he—he turns, he flies:—shame on those cruel eyes*
> *That bore to look on torture, and dare not look on war.*

But the inversion can also be sweet, for the paragraph after Timewell's last
stand describes the exquisite, Sir Gervas Jerome (also destined to supply a
name to one of the listening grandchildren), ruined financially and enlisted in
Monmouth's cause almost as a last frivolity:.

> Large numbers of the foot fought to the death, neither giving nor receiving
> quarter, but at last, scattered, broken, and without ammunition, the main body
> of the peasants dispersed and fled across the moor, closely followed by the
> horse. Saxon, Buyse, and I had done all that we could to rally them once more,
> and had cut down some of the foremost pursuers, when my eye fell suddenly
> upon Sir Gervas, standing hatless with a few of his musketeers in the midst of
> a swarm of dragoons. Spurring our horses we cut a way to his rescue, and laid
> our swords about us until we had cleared off his assailants for the moment.
> "Jump up behind me!" I cried. "We can make good our escape."
> He looked up smiling and shook his head. "I stay with my company", he
> said.
> "Your company!" Saxon cried. "Why man, you are mad! Your company is
> cut off to the last man."
> "That's what I mean", he answered, flicking some dirt from his cravat.
> "Don't ye mind! Look out for yourselves. Good-bye, Clarke! Present my
> compliments to—" The dragoons charged down upon us again. We were all
> borne backwards, fighting desperately, and when we could look round the
> Baronet was gone for ever.

One gallant did not seek a safe nook. Sir Gervas came under some literary
criticism as being rather premature: in fact his strength arises from his being
a type, amusing in the context as the fop among the Puritans, but eternal in
Conan Doyle's pantheon from medieval knight-errantry to Napoleonic
brigadiers, obsessed by what is triviality to the rest of the world and
courageous in devotion to comrades to the point of utter indifference to self.
It was a character Arthur first encountered in his mother.

Sir Gervas throws into relief one aspect of *Micah Clarke* which distinguishes it very strongly from *Waverley*, and one which animates almost all
of Conan Doyle's great writing: the chivalric quest. *Waverley* sees the course
of history as dictated by accident to an outstanding extent, and as such offers
an interesting similarity in historical thought between Sir Walter Scott and
A.J.P. Taylor. Men plan, but plans go awry, and much that happens is
affected by chance, and by plots of little men tangling up the machinations of

great ones. Waverley himself is brave, and likeable, and good at observation if not at analysis, but he is constantly borne out of his depth and his actions are dictated by events out of his control. Micah Clarke is in many ways the prisoner of events also, and accident plays a great part in what happens to him, but his actions remain largely the result of his own initial intention.

It was a Godsend to Conan Doyle that he had gone first to Plymouth and then to Portsmouth, for it led him to begin Micah's story in the Hampshire hinterland he knew, and then describe the progress of Micah and his companions to the West Country whose acquaintance he had made earlier. The advance of the comrades, their adventures on the way, and their acquisition of new recruits, are deeply in the tradition of chivalric quest. First Saxon and Micah ride out, then Lockarby catches them up, then after some delay they pick up Sir Gervas, and then they join the Reverend Joshua Pettigrue and his band. There are touches of Dumas in it, Saxon having the duplicity of Aramis, Sir Gervas the ostentation of Porthos, Micah himself the stern ethics of Athos, and Reuben the eagerness of D'Artagnan, but Conan Doyle had now far too much control over his material to imitate the fellowship of the musketeers, contenting himself with profiting by the lesson of their diversity of character and motivation. (There is also a neat reversal of *Twenty Years After* at Sedgemoor, Saxon's "Stand to your pikes, men!" when all is lost echoing Lord de Winter's "All faithful hearts with me!", only there it is the army which deserts the Stuart king.) Conan Doyle had his eye perpetually out for the irony of his chivalric theme, *Don Quixote* being as fully in his mind as Froissart in the making of Sir Nigel, Sherlock Holmes, Brigadier Gerard and Professor Challenger. In *Micah Clarke* it is explicit, as Sir Gervas points out, on his first encounter with Saxon: "But here comes a heavy tread and the clink of armour in the passage. 'Tis our friend the knight of the wrathful countenance, if I mistake not."

The chivalric theme may seem less fitted for the twentieth century, apart from children's fiction, but *Micah Clarke* certainly seems to have inspired the opening passages of the most famous invocation of it: *The Lord of the Rings*. Danger at an inn, the ambiguous travelling companion encountered en route, the pursuit (at Stonehenge, in one case, and the Barrow-Downs, in the other) by beings that are not human, the temporary sanctuary in the home of a benevolent figure interested in the quest but essentially preoccupied by personal vocation, are all common links. The inn where Micah, Reuben Lockarby and Decimus Saxon meet Sir Gervas is across a river called Brue; the inn where Frodo, Sam, Pippin and Merry meet Strider or Aragorn is in a town called Bree. Tolkien had many sources, the most famous being in ancient languages, but it is *Micah Clarke*, I think, that gets his quest moving. It is, of course, a very different chivalric quest in Conan Doyle which ends with the hero facing doom on a mountain.

The role of *Waverley* as direct inspiration for *Micah Clarke* was one singular effect on it. *Waverley*, in the strict sense, is not a historical novel at all. It is much more a novel of folk-memory. The immediacy of its events in the recent past before Scott's own life gives a deeply personal quality to it.

Scott accepts the outcome of events, but he cannot, nor does he wish to, silence the heart-cry which they give rise to in himself. He has only seen the cultural ruins left after the 'forty-five, but it is his contemplation of them and his recovery of what they once were which makes the novel one of absolute relevance to his own life, beliefs and identity. Conan Doyle, on the other hand, was driven by no such sentiment. He had an intellectual interest, all the greater because of his Catholic upbringing, in paying his tribute to the death-throes of English Puritanism and in seeing what animated the Puritan mind and heart. His Scottish birth and Irish origins increased his remoteness, as did his Catholic education: they also gave him a fine, sympathetic detachment which was of great value to him as historian. But however much he liked the people of Hampshire and the West Country, he did not confuse them with their ancestors two hundred years earlier. Even Macaulay, researching fifty years earlier, found fragments of folk-memory which would not be there for him. But because *Waverley* influenced the book so deeply and was so much dictated by the background to its time of writing, *Micah Clarke* is not absolutely historical either. If the Holmes stories represent a protest against the cold-blooded scientific indifference to individual human beings in Edinburgh medicine, *Micah Clarke* is also passionately concerned about people. In this sense it touches a profounder depth than *Waverley*. The doom of Gaelic Scotland is presented by Scott through the symbolism of the martyrdom of Fergus Mac-Ivor Vich Ian Vohr and his devoted follower Evan Maccombich. Conan Doyle presents the martyrdom of an entire people, the men of Devon (not actually strongly represented in the Monmouth rising), of Dorset, of Wiltshire and of Somerset. Neither Stephen Timewell nor any other of the major characters who die are allowed to do duty for the great mass of insurgents. Much though he loved Sir Walter as man and writer, Conan Doyle well knew them to differ in one respect: he was a democrat and his master, emphatically, was not. He admirably counterpointed the courage of Fergus against the cowardice of Monmouth; but the real parallel is between Fergus and Evan, facing death at Carlisle, and the vanquished peasants at Sedgemoor.

Micah Clarke is not as great a book as *Waverley* and its author would have indignantly repudiated any claim that it was. *Waverley* is in many respects a profoundly original historical work, *Micah Clarke* a very good piece of secondary interpretation seeking to add details to firmly established historical contours. Nor is it as great a novel. Perhaps Conan Doyle had seen so much human weakness among the major figures of his own young life—his father, Waller, Budd, even Bell—that he never liked to write about it, and Waverley himself, as a study in weakness, provides much of the strength of Scott's work. Yet *Micah Clarke* is a great book. If Conan Doyle had not shown himself capable of shooting an arrow to the mark with the precision of Sir Walter Scott, he had shown that he was the only novelist in the English language since Scott who could bend Scott's bow, and whose arrow, if not in centre target, came respectably close to it. Moreover, it was essential to his development as a short story writer. He had now shown that he could master the dimensions of a novel: what lay before him was the bringing of the same control to the short story, no longer in occasional successes, but with a consistency which made him the greatest craftsman in that form of his time. Above all he had learned to make the sources of his inspiration servants at his disposal and not masters intruding in defiance of his will. The sorcerer's apprentice had become the sorcerer.

If there had been no Mahomet, said the great Henri Pirenne, there would have been no Charlemagne. If there had been no *Micah Clarke*, there would have been no Sherlock Holmes. The assumption that Holmes and the historical novels are somehow in conflict is at bottom false. Each fed on the other, and nowhere more than here. Before *Micah Clarke*, Conan Doyle had written two or three great works. With *Micah Clarke*, he was a great writer. The historical sense he exhibited in *Micah Clarke* he brought into full play in the Holmes stories, most particularly by giving Holmes more and more the technique of a historian himself. As Sir Herbert Butterfield believed, and as Professor Adam Watson testifies in the introduction to Butterfield's posthumously published *The Origins of History*, Holmes offers the supreme example of the historical investigator.

> After Lestrade had fitted many but not all of the facts into a plausible reconstruction of the events, Holmes would engage in minuter, more detailed microscopic research, and would then meditate over all the facts for long hours until a solution emerged from them which he recognised as right. This refusal to force the facts, to suspend judgement until they offered you their own answer, the ability not to pre-judge anything, Butterfield called elasticity of mind.

It was his own work as a historian, in *Micah Clarke*, which gave Conan Doyle this supreme understanding of what historical investigation is, and hence made Sherlock Holmes in his approach to his problems the exemplar of the historian at work. The historical novels were essential to this development, since Conan Doyle needed to put that awareness of the business of historical investigation into practice continually in order to maintain his perception of the craft as revealed in Holmes. In that sense it is not that Holmes stood in the way of recognition of the historical novels that is important: it is that Holmes played a major part in writing them.

But the Holmes who helped in the writing of *Micah Clarke* was part parent and part child of the process. *Micah Clarke* would dispose, for the rest of the Holmes cycle, of the weaknesses which almost sank *A Study in Scarlet*. Control of sources ended the dangers of derivation. In *The Sign of Four*, for instance, Wilkie Collins's *The Moonstone* is an influence, as various commentators have remarked, but it is an influence at arm's length, ready to be hauled in when needed and replaced when not. There is all the difference in the world between the pursuit by the priests of the moonstone, and the ambitions of Jonathan Small, as agent of his three Sikh partners, to recover the Agra treasure. For one thing, Collins set a great gulf between the Indians and the whites: Conan Doyle, schooled by Henry Highland Garnet, redeemed the otherwise unqualified selfishness of Jonathan Small by his friendship for his Indian fellow-conspirators and for the Andaman Islander. He also played very shrewdly with the gulf Collins had fixed; Tonga of the Andamans is presented through the eyes of Watson as a figure of subhuman savagery, whereas through Small's narrative he shows a devotion as richly human as that of any medieval squire to his knight. And Small himself, a thief and a murderer, wins a stature momentarily which sets him above his captors at his success in crossing the racial lines where they have failed. He has known the humanity of his little Tonga; they have reduced him to the level of a murderous beast to be hunted down and destroyed without mercy or even conventional coroner's inquest. More importantly *The Moonstone* suggested an important means of humanising Holmes himself, showing his vulnerability by drug dependence partly inspired by Conan Doyle's autoexperimentation on nitrate of amyl in his search for cures of his patients, partly by the sufferings and resort to drugs of Ezra Jennings whose investigations provide the real solution to *The Moonstone*. But again this is judicious use of inspiration, not derivation: Professor Wallace Robson made the Jennings point to me, but most commentators, confronted with *The Moonstone*, assume the model for Holmes in its pages to be Sergeant Cuff. Hence Jennings is a source for *The Sign of Four* under sufficient control to be invisible to most observers. Cuff may have supplied the precise subject to inspire Holmes's metaphysics arising from contemplation of a rose, and he certainly is ruder to other police investigators than is found in the literature of detection to that time, but these are very minor points of influence.

Micah Clarke was probably also the turning-point in Holmes's cultural career. With the prompting of Scott and Macaulay, Conan Doyle embarked on a view of history which saw cultural awareness as indispensible to the historical investigator. It was a short step to recognise its vital necessity to Holmes, and hence the Philistine of *A Study in Scarlet* becomes the philosopher of *The Sign of Four*. We certainly cannot eliminate *Micah Clarke* from the making of *A Study in Scarlet:* the latter preceded it in writing , but the smaller book was hurried into being while the mind of the writer was preoccupying itself with the greater. This played some part in the weakness of *A Study in Scarlet*, and part in its strength. Conan Doyle's anxiety to hurry it along and get back to *Micah* gave that combination of pace and intellectual analysis which characterises all of the Holmes stories henceforward. What started as an occupational disease became an excellent standard characteristic. On the other hand, it left Conan Doyle singularly inattentive to the marks of haste, and accounts for the crudity of *A Study in Scarlet* and some of its blemishes. The early part is apparently from Watson's *Reminiscences,* despite the utter disparity of the military career handled in the briefest of compass and the case and acquaintance with Holmes handled at such length. And while the date of the first Afghan war puts the action about 1881, what on earth is Watson supposed to have been doing in the five years between then and the time of writing to justify a book of reminiscences? His stay with Holmes is apparently limited to nine months during which he has been placed on an invalid pension and after which he is to return to active service. His health is "irretrievably ruined" which is hardly likely to give him much to write of respecting the next five years. Presumably Conan Doyle was thinking of Dr Patrick Heron Watson and his unquestionably significant life, but that Dr Watson had had his unhappy military experiences and subsequent illness during the Crimean War and hence was in a good position to write reminiscences on an active career as medical researcher, practitioner and teacher by 1886 had he wished so to do. Then there is no clue as to who the author of the American chapters may be: apparently he, and not Watson, is in control of the presentation of the book. Finally the reader is returned to Watson, but this time with reference to his "Journal", although the chapter-title and the content argue for its being a resumption of the *Reminiscences*. Yet at the end Watson insists that he proposes to publish the truth: is he assuming that he will have memoirs to write in the future, or are the references to *Reminiscences* and the intrusion of an anonymous second author a literary fudge of some kind? All of this was comfortably ironed out by *The Sign of Four* and thereafter, but as it stands it is, like Dr Shlessinger's ear, jagged or torn.

And having said all this, we should also bear in mind Ronald A. Knox's structural analysis of the Holmes stories published in his *Essays in Satire*, a pioneer work of profound value for all of its Oxonian coyness and implied parables respecting Knox's pedantic sectarian controversies. If we set aside the Roman Catholic tribalism and the foolish jokes, what remains is of outstanding value. Knox identified eleven segments to *A Study in Scarlet*, each one of them critical to the story's development; and he notes that while only this case has all eleven, the same structure is essential to all the stories with the omission of some parts. He is in part following the method of textual analysis of Shakespearean drama in vogue in the late nineteenth and early twentieth century, and is parodying the use of Greek terminology beloved by that school:

> The first part is the Prooimion, a homely Baker Street scene, with invaluable personal touches, and sometimes a demonstration by the detective. Then follows the first explanation, or Exegesis kata ton diokonta, that is, the client's statement of the case, followed by the Ichneusis, or personal investigation, often including the famous floor-walk on hands and knees. No. 1 is invariable, Nos. 2 and 3 almost always present. Nos. 4, 5 and 6 are less necessary: they include the Anaskeue, or refutation on its own merits of the official theory of Scotland Yard, the first Promenusis (exoterike) which gives a few stray hints to the police, which they never adopt, the second Promenusis (esoterike), which adumbrates the true course of the investigation to Watson alone. This is sometimes wrong, as in the *Yellow Face*. No. 7 is the Exetasis, or further following up of the trial, including the cross-questioning of relatives, dependants, etc., of the corpse (if there is one), visits to the Record Office, and various investigations in an assumed character. No. 8 is the Anagnorisis, in which the criminal is caught or exposed, No. 9 the second Exegesis (kata ton pheugonta), that is to say the criminal's confession, No. 10 the Metamenusis, in which Holmes describes what his clues were and how he followed them, and No. 11 the Epilogos, sometimes comprised in a single sentence. This conclusion is, like the Prooimion, invariable, and often contains a gnome or quotation from some standard author.

Knox finds that *The Sign of Four* and "*Silver Blaze*" have ten such parts, and the other stories (his paper was first written about 1911 and includes nothing later than *The Hound* and the *Return*) omit even more of the prime factors until he reaches "*The Gloria Scott*" with only four. This makes an excellent case for the structural achievement of *A Study in Scarlet*: with all of its imperfections, it taught Conan Doyle how to set his material out, and he pursued it thereafter with a precision almost mathematical. In passing, it may be noted that Knox's ostentation with his Greek terminology, a trifle unnecessary in the translator of the New Testament, is far from irrelevant. It is he who pointed out that the "Anaskeue", in which Scotland Yard does its worst, derived from Plato's *Republic*, at the intervention of the bullying Thrasymachus on whom Socrates then makes such dreadful execution. Knox rightly identifies Thrasymachus as much closer to Athelney Jones in *The Sign of Four* and in fact Jones on this one appearance (for he largely loses identity as well as Christian name in "*The Red-Headed League*") achieves far greater presence, and certainly much finer comic capacity, than Lestrade or Gregson. If Lestrade's name is better known, it is because of the frequency of his reappearance.

A Study in Scarlet is more directly using the medical tradition of several doctors disagreeing; controversies in Edinburgh were seldom merely two-sided, as "*His First Operation*" acknowledges (and as the Challenger-Summerlee-Illingworth feuding of *The Lost World* asserts in thunder). This is not badly done, and at times achieves high humour:

> "My dear fellow", he cried, wringing Holmes' unresponsive hand, "congratulate me! I have made the whole thing as clear as day."
> A shade of anxiety seemed to me to cross my companion's expressive face.
> "Do you mean that you are on the right track?" he asked.
> "The right track! Why, sir, we have the man under lock and key."
> "And his name is?"
> "Arthur Charpentier, sub-lieutenant in Her Majesty's navy", cried Gregson pompously rubbing his fat hands and inflating his chest.
> Sherlock Holmes gave a sigh of relief and relaxed into a smile.
>   . . .
> "The fun of it is", he cried, "that that fool Lestrade, who thinks himself so smart, has gone off upon the wrong track altogether. He is after the secretary Stangerson, who had no more to do with the crime than the babe unborn. I have no doubt that he has caught him by this time."
> The idea tickled Gregson so much that he laughed until he choked.
>   . . .
> "This is a most extraordinary case", he said at last—"a most incomprehensible affair."
> "Ah, you find it so, Mr Lestrade!" cried Gregson, triumphantly. "I thought you would come to that conclusion. Have you managed to find the secretary, Mr Joseph Stangerson?"
> "The secretary, Mr Joseph Stangerson", said Lestrade gravely, "was murdered at Halliday's Private Hotel about six o'clock this morning."

On which "Gregson sprang out of his chair and upset the remainder of his whisky and water", and who shall blame him?

The satire on the rival Edinburgh doctors is at its most acute here, and Holmes's fears that his rivals will reach success before he does are eminently characteristic of the world of Joseph Bell. In this respect the Socratic antecedent—which assumes that Thrasymachus can never be right—is not achieved until *The Sign of Four*. But what is clearly derived from Plato in *A Study in Scarlet* is "the second Promenusis (esoterike), which adumbrates the true course of the investigation to Watson alone": this is Socrates answering his Glaucon (or Charmides or Phaedrus or Phaedo) who will be wrong but who is so anxious to learn, and whose questions may be conducive to eliciting the truth in ways the obstinate ignorance of Thrasymachus can not be. It is noteworthy that the increased use of Plato in stories after *A Study in Scarlet* shows once more how Conan Doyle was increasing his control. Certainly the memory of the Edinburgh rivalries remained acute, as *The Lost World*, as late as 1911, bears witness. Lestrade in *"The Norwood Builder"* is very much the rival academic jostling and bullying his opponent aside on a research controversy. But while such memories continued to provide the flesh and blood for imaginative creations, Conan Doyle recognised that his strength lay in drawing from the deeps which had dominated European culture for two millenia. There is nothing mechanical in his use of Plato: it is scientific, shrewd and skilful. Recognising that Plato offers food for both intellect and emotion, in the high powers of reasoning, and the affection between Socrates and his disciples, he makes the most of both, his highest point of achievement in this respect being the heartbroken conclusion of *"The Final Problem"* with its deliberate adaptation of the last words of *Phaedo* (which set the seal on its narrative of the death of Socrates).

There was nothing wrong with Conan Doyle's fine eye for caricature in his drawing on the Edinburgh intellectuals for *A Study in Scarlet;* as he arranged his composites of Bell and Waller and their fellows, he showed himself most emphatically the grandson of John Doyle. *A Study in Scarlet* is more caricaturish than any other Holmes story, particularly with Holmes's absurd exclusion of astronomy and literature from his awareness. Where the story was very weak was in its detective matter. It is derivative, and at times it fails to add up. This precedent was also an important one. As Edmund Wilson would later recognise, the primary importance of the Holmes stories has nothing to do with their detective content: they are literature, and that is an end of it. But the *roman policier* hardly received a new lease of life with it; indeed for this story it was no more than new bottles for old wine.

The borrowings from Poe, from Gaboriau, and from Robert Louis Stevenson and his wife are famous and blatant: it has also to be said that their influence is very strongly acknowledged. Dupin and Lecoq are discussed at the opening, not (as foolish commentary has stated) so that Conan Doyle can triumph over them but to remind readers that they are the pioneers; Gaboriau's title *L'Affaire Lerouge* is deliberately invoked in the words, *A Study in Scarlet*, a remarkable bilingual pun; the Stevensons' *"Story of the Destroying Angel"* seems consciously recalled in the chapter title *The Avenging Angels*. Where trouble arises is that conscious, if misunderstood, expression of literary obligations goes alongside apparently unconscious looting from the sources in question. Poe and the Dupin stories, Gaboriau and the Lecoq ones, each supply not only little devices and ideas, but at times Conan Doyle's Jesuit-trained memory recalled passages almost word for word. It is impossible to believe that this was deliberate. His actual use of the names of Poe and Gaboriau was virtually inviting the reading public to turn to his sources and measure the justice of Sherlock Holmes's criticisms. Mr R. F. Stewart in his . . . *And Always a Detective* goes into some detail on the borrowings from Gaboriau, and these are, in fact, more serious ones than the derivation from Poe, since Conan Doyle was consistently conscious of Poe with his sense of Dupin (and Poe) as the dilettante amateur and Holmes (and himself) as the scientific professional. In part the difference between Poe and his Dupin, and Conan Doyle and his Holmes was that of the century: the day of the gentleman scholar was over and that of the trained specialist dawning. Even by Poe's time the gentleman scholar was on his last legs: Poe and Dupin leeched on friends, Holmes and Conan Doyle paid their way.

But Gaboriau was less clearly present in Conan Doyle's mind as a classic or constant friend, and hence he was less aware of how much he had seeped up from him. Mr Stewart gives examples. Some of these are a little weak. He juxtaposes these passages from *L'Affaire Lerouge* and *A Study in Scarlet*:

I prefer to proceed without receiving any details, in order to be more fully master of my own impressions.	It is a capital mistake to theorize before you have all the evidence. It biases the judgement.

In fact, these passages are not particularly similar, and Lecoq's is rather silly. Holmes is not rejecting details—on the contrary, he wants as many as he can get and frequently says so—but he is rejecting premature theories. His remark is much closer to Bryan Charles Waller on his predecessors on the kidney or Reginald Ratcliff Hoare on George Turnavine Budd. But Mr Stewart has a better case when he is giving an example of the detective in action as opposed to conversation:

. . . he darted into the inner chamber. He remained there about half an hour; then came out running, then re-entered and then came out again; once more he disappeared and re-appeared again almost immediately. The magistrate could not help comparing him to a pointer on the scent, his turned-up nose even moved about as if to discover some subtle odour left by the assassin. All the while he talked loudly and with much gesticulation, apostrophising himself, scolding himself, uttering little cries of triumph or self-encouragement . . . the investigating magistrate began to grow [im-] patient, and asked what had become of the amateur detective. "He is on the road", replied the corporal, "lying flat in the mud."	As he spoke, he whipped a tape measure and a large round magnifying glass from his pocket. With these two implements he trotted about the room, sometimes stopping, occasionally kneeling, and once lying flat on his face. So engrossed was he that he appeared to have forgotten our presence for he chattered away to himself under his breath the whole time, keeping up a running fire of exclamations, groans, whistles, and little cries suggestive of encouragement and hope. As I watched him I was irresistibly reminded of a pure-blooded, well-trained foxhound as it dashes backwards and forwards through the covert, whining in its eagerness, until it comes across the lost scent.

It is not an entire victory for Gaboriau. The parent passage rather justifies Holmes's rude remarks about Lecoq's energy, and it does not seem to be energy as well systematized as Holmes's, which moves carefully from roadway to driveway, body to walls and floor of room. There is a clever realisation of means by which Gaboriau can be taken farther in the taking of the laughing supposition that Lecoq might sniff an odour of the assassin and transforming it into the actuality that Holmes really does sniff proof of an assassination. But Mr Stewart has some strong ground, and Conan Doyle would have been a little horrified had he realised how very close indeed his excellent memory had brought him to the original on which he was seeking to improve.

Actually, the excessive dependence on Gaboriau, unconscious though it was, proved its own Nemesis. The Gaboriau method, largely demanding at the conclusion a huge discussion of the circumstances leading up to the crime, proved a highly unsatisfactory model for Conan Doyle. In general, when the geometrical arrangement of the stories are under firm control, it works: even when the criminal's narrative is exceptionally long, as in *The Sign of Four* and "*The Cardboard Box*", its intrinsic interest justifies it. The one exception other than *A Study in Scarlet* is *The Valley of Fear,* where the two halves of the story do not totally marry, and the high science of Holmes is in over-sharp contrast to the sensationalism of the narrative founded on Douglas's account: had Douglas's own role been under greater scrutiny (and the facts as discovered would have sustained a thesis that he deliberately lured Baldwin into murderous ambush), his own narrative could have been subjected to the awkward questions it rather demands, and its original, the account by the Pinkerton detective McParlan, demanded even more. Holmes's own reproach to Watson about *A Study in Scarlet,* uttered at the beginning of *The Sign of Four,* seems a clear admission by Conan Doyle that his attempt to tie his detective narrative to a lurid plot of love and Mormonism had been a mistake: "You have attempted to tinge it with romanticism, which produces much the same effect as if you worked a love-story or an elopement into the fifth proposition of Euclid."

In any event, the Mormon sub-plot was another casualty of memory. The Stevensons' disappointing sequel to Stevenson's *New Arabian Nights, The Dynamiter,* contains a brief piece of phoney autobiography by a young lady of what Watson would call equivocal reputation, in which she alleges an upbringing in Utah among Mormons, one of whose agents destroys her father and induces the suicide of her mother, so as to obtain control of herself, although he makes no attempt to impose conjugal privileges on her. It begins with a vignette of her future father seeing her future mother in a starving group of Mormon pilgrims in the wilderness, when the future "destroying Angel" steals the blanket sheltering the lady. It is a tolerable piece of imagery, all the more because the story is not supposed to be believed by anyone including its recipient. *A Study in Scarlet* has its second part also beginning with the sheltering of a young girl, this time a very little girl, by an old man who, however, protects her with the greatest affection. This may be an acceptable emendation. A realistic note is substituted for the deliberate anti-realism of the Stevensons. The little girl, Lucy, is believable, where her Stevensonian counterpart, also Lucy, is not. The transformation of the hard-pressed pioneers from Mormons rescued by others and yet inexplicably permitted to establish their tyranny, into two survivors of a non-denominational group rescued by an enormous Mormon caravan, is consistent with the realities of the Mormon frontier. But the leaning on the Stevensons becomes really acute when the Mormon omnipresence as their victims attempt flight is depicted: all Conan Doyle has done is to move fantasy into a terrifyingly credible reality, use the menace of a descending number of days before doom announced by unseen agents, and make the Stevensons' picture that the Mormons could hear anything spoken in an empty wilderness become just plausible by transforming it into silent agents eluding the vigilance of watchers. Certainly some of his work is an improvement: the fugitives in "*The Destroying Angel*" go trembling back to doom in Utah when they find an enormous eye put up by the Mormons on the mountain across which they are fleeing, whereas Conan Doyle has them cut down on the mountains far beyond where they assume the Mormon writ will run. Yet, so close are the two accounts, that *A Study in Scarlet* launched the two most famous characters in English literature of the past century on borrowed and battered wheels. The book's obligations to his childhood favourite, Captain (Thomas) Mayne Reid's *The Scalp-Hunters*, as well as to Bret Harte's *A Waif of the Plains*, also go well beyond the justifiable. If the mature Lucy of the Stevensons becomes the adorable little orphaned girl Lucy of *A Study in Scarlet* it is to Harte we owe that transposition.

Gratifyingly enough, Conan Doyle's defender in this regard is Stevenson himself in the article on *Treasure Island* he contributed to the *Idler's* "*My First Book*" series because of Conan Doyle's earlier essay in it. Stevenson very charmingly indicts himself for plagiarism so strongly that one wonders if in addition to the really important general argument, it was his way of telling Conan Doyle he did not mind any thefts from the family cupboard to make *A Study in Scarlet*:

> . . . stolen waters are proverbially sweet. I am now upon a painful chapter. No doubt the parrot once belonged to Robinson Crusoe. No doubt the skeleton is conveyed from Poe. I think little of these, they are trifles and details; and no man can hope to have a monopoly of skeletons or make a corner in talking birds. The stockade, I am told, is from *Masterman Ready*. It may be, I care not a jot. These useful writers had fulfilled the poet's saying: departing, they had left behind them Footprints on the sands of time, Footprints which perhaps another—and I was the other! It is my debt to Washington Irving that exercises my conscience, and justly so, for I believe plagiarism was rarely carried farther. I chanced to pick up the *Tales of a Traveller* some years ago with a view to an anthology of prose narrative, and the book flew up and struck me: Billy Bones, his chest, the company in the parlour, the whole inner spirit, and a good deal of the material detail of my first chapters—all were there, all were the property of Washington Irving. But I had no guess of it then as I sat writing by the fireside, in what seemed the spring-tides of a somewhat pedestrian inspiration; nor yet

> day by day, after lunch, as I read aloud my morning's work to the family. It
> seemed to me original as sin; it seemed to belong to me like my right eye.

That is Bertrand du Guesclin coming to the aid of Sir Nigel after they have
met in combat at the tournament, and critics who have not entered the ring
have little to justify themselves. Conan Doyle in his turn could think of
Bernard Shaw pillaging Henry Higgins, Colonel Pickering and Mendoza from
Holmes, Watson and the Marshal Millefleurs, with, as Shaw stressed, far less
of the unconscious about it. In any case, whither he meant it specifically or
not, RLS is the leading witness in ACD's defence.

A Study in Scarlet was 'prentice work too in the business of the detection
itself. Gregson and Lestrade were in fact right in their implied criticism of
Holmes for not following up the trail of the hat-maker or the secretary.
Holmes never investigated the front-door lock, and had he done so would
surely have had to ask questions of the house-agent as to possession of keys,
since the lock had not been forced. That could have brought results much
faster than the cable to Cleveland, whose value would have in any case been
seriously diminished had Jefferson Hope taken the elementary precaution of
changing his name: the house-agent would have probably taken a note of the
name and number of the cabman who brought in the key to the house
dropped in his cab. Michael Dibdin, in his unpleasant and tasteless pastiche
The Last Sherlock Holmes Story, rightly points to the incongruity of Holmes
expecting Jefferson Hope to come to a house to which he had only twenty-
four hours previously sent an accomplice in highly elaborate disguise with
cunningly-laid false trails. Martin Dakin wonders why Hope should want to
retain a ring which was in fact given to Lucy Ferrier by the man who
abducted and raped her under marriage, causing her death, and whom Hope
ultimately succeeded in murdering.

Yet as against that the craftsman that was coming into full maturity with
Micah Clarke showed his prowess time and again in A Study in Scarlet. That
he was a contemporary historian, and a good one, he exhibited in his
delightful and revelatory versions of the London press at the time. If he had
much work yet to do on Holmes, he had already achieved a masterly success
with Watson. The strange mingling of realism and fantasy, high learning and
irresistible fiction, thought-provoking philosophy and delicious comedy were
already at work. In one way the ambiguities were asserted at the outset.
Watson's opening paragraphs about his service in the Second Afghan War are
factual and crisp, culminating in his account of his near-destruction at the
battle of Maiwand: yet in his "Life on a Greenland Whaler" Arthur recorded
that during the months he would in the future assign to Watson's campaign
he himself had been cut off from the world:

> When we were in whaling latitudes it is probable that, with the exception of
> our consort, there was no vessel within 800 miles of us. For seven long months
> no letter and no news came to us from the southern world. We had left in
> exciting times. The Afghan campaign had been undertaken, and war seemed
> imminent with Russia. We returned opposite the mouth of the Baltic without
> any means of knowing whether some cruiser might not treat us as we had treated

the whales. When we met a fishing-boat at the north of Shetland our first inquiry was as to peace or war. Great events had happened during those seven months: the defeat of Maiwand and the famous march of Roberts from Cabul to Candahar. But it was all haze to us; and, to this day, I have never been able to get that particular bit of military history straightened out in my own mind.

Thus the first word from Watson, apparently founded on fact, actually from events which never assumed reality in his creator's mind, enables us to see the marriage of fact and fancy which grounded the stories from the first. Conan Doyle's last words on the cycle, in his preface to the book version of the *Case-Book*, speaks of the "fairy kingdom of romance", and yet his naturalism was by then already yielding its reward in the legions who insisted Holmes and Watson must be real.

That the Holmes cycle achieved its conquest of the reading world is due to many things—the loyal Scots reviewers of *A Study in Scarlet* when it appeared in 1887 in *Beeton's Christmas Annual*, the encouragement of Andrew Lang, the prowess of *Micah Clarke*, the discovery of the ideal dimensions in the short story, the American anxiety to take up this new creation as expressed by *Lippincott's* and S. S. McClure, the advent of the *Strand* and its urgent need of good material such as would satisfy the reader of one issue yet draw him to the next, the roots in great literature such as Plato, Cervantes, Boswell and Poe while displaying its material in terms which entertain without seeming to talk down, the Bells and Christisons, Wallers and Budds, parents and teachers who gave Holmes that first note of realism lacking in Dupin and Lecoq and Prince Florizel. But the greatest achievement of *A Study in Scarlet* was Watson. ACD had worked over ten years with the first-person narrator, friendly and hostile, noble and contemptible, sublime and ridiculous. He had made his voice that of a girl choosing between admirers in "*Our Derby Sweepstakes*" and of another drawn into a hatred which became obsession and possession in "*The Winning Shot*". He had rashly tried to catch the tones of a South African prospector in "*The Mystery of Sasassa Valley*" and of an Antipodean medic in "*My Friend the Murderer*". He had been a generous if conventional bank clerk in "*Gentlemanly Joe*", and a vulgar, snobbish fortune-hunter in "*The Heiress of Glenmahowley*". He became a hypochondriac poltroon in "*That Little Square Box*" and a misanthropic philosopher in "*The Man from Archangel*". He had reached his greatest heights in an identity wholly close to his own experience, as the doctor of a whaler, in "*The Captain of the 'Pole-Star'* ", and in one absolutely remote from himself in nationality and time as an abolitionist New Englander in "*J. Habakuk Jephson's Statement*".

And now, at last, he found the voice of a man reflecting the finest if least pretentious attitudes and responses of the conventional professional world of his day, a man who was truly Platonist and squire, Boswell and Sancho Panza, author and reader, Chorus and presenter, a man who was so like ourselves with an ordinary life and conventional if humane spirit, a man differing only from the rest of the world in having a rather unusual friend.

Sources, Acknowledgments and Procedures

This biographical investigation of the making of Arthur Conan Doyle as a great writer carries within it a number of problems. It is essentially an historical exercise, endeavouring to use some of those techniques which Sir Herbert Butterfield saluted in Sherlock Holmes as true historical method, in order to elicit much which was hitherto dark. It carries its own pitfalls: I have simultaneously been seeking to explain how many of the stories came to be written, and employing the evidence they give about their author to fill in gaps in what is known of his life. To argue that a story was written as it was because of Charles Altamont Doyle's alcoholism and to seek to deduce from it what that alcoholism involved, runs the risk of conflating evidence with conclusion, but the effort had to be made. In this particular matter my work was greatly assisted by the recommendation of Mr Tom Sutcliffe, of the BBC, that I examine Professor John Carey's recent biography of John Donne. Having considered his concentration on Donne's apostasy from Roman Catholicism as a basic theme in his creative life, I looked at ACD's writing in quest of such a theme. Alcoholism leaped out at me. In presenting my conclusions in this first chapter I was influenced by Conor Cruise O'Brien's essay on François Mauriac in his *Maria Cross*. More generally, with respect to ACD's youthful Catholicism and the impact of his Jesuit education, I owed much to Richard Ellmann's magnificent biography of James Joyce, and my personal debt to these two scholars is very great. What we know of Charles Doyle's tragedy has been largely that given in *The Doyle Diary* edited and introduced by Michael Baker in 1978. I am decidedly in debt to Mr Baker, however strongly I dissent from the criticism of ACD and his mother into which his generous sympathy for Charles Doyle has led him. I have been greatly assisted on the topic of Charles Doyle's family by reading copies of letters of Charles, Richard and Henry Doyle to their father presented to the National Library of Ireland by Adrian Conan Doyle. My debt to that splendid institution, whence I have received so much education, is impossible worthily to acknowledge, most particularly to its then Director Dr Alf Mac Lochlainn, whose inspiration, ingenuity and infectious laughter are endless. Alas, its array of MSS on Irish parish registers do not include the relevant volume of Waterford marriage certificates which would have given needful information about the marriage of ACD's maternal grandparents, as this volume was lost before the registers were microfilmed for the Library, but Dr MacLochlainn gave me rich material from the Genealogical Office concerning the Foley family.

I have not wanted to repeat what is to be found in other biographies, especially where their conclusions could not be checked against their sources, most notably relating to what has been taken without quotation from the now closed Conan Doyle MSS. Carr, to whom I have been somewhat harsh in these pages, is valuable in his classification and itemisation of that collection, and I have benefited from his book's guidance on such episodes as Mary Foley Doyle's influence on *"The Copper Beeches"* where his evidence is clearly presented. On this last matter an additional word may be said. Mary Foley Doyle was probably led to the idea from a reading of Charlotte Brontë's *Jane Eyre*, whose first episodes are set in Cowans Bridge, lying between Masongill and Kirkby Lonsdale. The horrible Rucastle child may have been inspired by Jane's loathsome cousin John who appears in those first chapters. The fat, laughing Rucastle is an obvious inversion of the lean, sombre Rochester. The notion of Jane, a governess, taking the marital place of the actually living and imprisoned Mrs Rochester is echoed by Violet Hunter's being used as a substitute for the imprisoned Alice Rucastle, in both instances the substitute being unaware of the presence in the building of the original. It is noteworthy, also, that where *Jane Eyre* is extremely hostile to the imprisoned woman and sympathetic to her jailer, the feminism of Mary Foley Doyle is reflected in the reverse directing of loyalties in *"The Copper Beeches"*. The maiming of Rucastle at the close is again suggestive of the fate of Rochester. The terrain at Masongill is in any case basic to many Conan Doyle stories.

Where I have had nothing useful to add, I have not gone over much old ground. For instance, the closed collection apparently includes references to some ladies who attracted the youthful ardour of ACD. These transient involvements doubtless had their literary effects, and if the theme of the sinister enchantress in *"John Barrington Cowles"* and her male counterpart in *"The Winning Shot"* derives from a woman he loved and came to detest, the omission from an account of his early years is a serious one. But in the absence of any original evidence at my disposal, anything I could have said would have been much worse than what appears in the biographies drawing on the Conan Doyle MSS. In any case such a theme is an infrequent one, compared to the evident impact on Arthur's writing by his parents, by Waller and Ryan and Budd, and by the Jesuits and the Edinburgh Medical School. Something more could have been squeezed from literary influences: for instance the plot of *"The Noble Bachelor"* surely comes from Scott's *"Lochinvar"* with the abduction of the bride by her lost lover come uninvited to the wedding ceremony from "the West". Scott's letters and journals have been invaluable to me, and I have benefited from employing Professor Andrew Hook's Penguin edition of *Waverley*. I have been usefully provoked by some of the judgments in A. N. Wilson's *The Laird of Abbotsford* without always agreeing with it, and I owe much in this whole study to the omniverous range of reference of Philip French, producer of "Critics' Forum" where I was one of the team reviewing it. (I also warmly thank David Perry and Martin Goldman of the BBC.) The work of David Daiches and Jenni Calder on Stevenson, proved even more vigorous in its stimulus than Mr Wilson's. The late James Pope Hennessy's biography of Stevenson is much less satisfactory than their work, but it contains useful information. Barrie's *Letters* supply the text of his fraudulent Stevenson anecdote. Burke and Hare I have taken forward from my own book on them; I have tried not to repeat it, although I have included some material published in my Lothian Lecture, *Dr Jekyll and Mr Holmes*, in whose preparation for publication I was profoundly obliged to Mr Harvey Mitchell. But much is new, if only because my wits have been all too frequently sluggish: one point which only occurred to me at the page-proof stage of this book is that on Burke and Hare, ACD's *"His Last Bow"* may have been his last laugh. The German spy Von Bork and his diplomat superior Von Herling (a name ACD would have pronounced "Hareling") now seem to me to have had Burke and Hare as their godparents as far as nomenclature goes, the contrast between Von Bork's charm and his conduct being as pointed as that of Burke. Ironically Von Bork's name had struck me as oddly Hibernian from my first acquaintance with it, some thirty-five years ago.

In my quest for the details of the Doyles' family life, one which to my great surprise elicited the presence and role of Bryan Charles Waller, I owe very much to the courtesy and charm of the staff of the Edinburgh Room of the Central Branch of the Edinburgh City Libraries where I consulted the City Directories and maps. The Valuation Rolls I obtained at the Scottish Record Office where again I obtained the utmost courtesy and assistance, notably from Mr Cecil Sinclair: this was the more necessary because of the uncertainties of classification by parish. There are still some mysteries. For some years the City Directory only lists Charles Doyle at his place of work: his family are last heard of in Portobello in the early 1860s and return to its pages at Sciennes Hill Place at the end of the decade. Mr Richard Lancelyn Green discovered from letters that Arthur was staying with the Burtons at Liberton Bank (a house across the road from my own residence) but there is nothing absolutely definite about the situation, as regards length of time involved, presence of other members of the Doyle family, and so on. Professor Gordon Donaldson set me on the track of the Census at the Registrar-General's office. This was very valuable for the three relevant years, 1861, 1871, and 1881, and among other things produced the hitherto unknown Aunt Kate. The excellent and most amusing staff of this office were helpful in every inquiry, and it was from there that I obtained the details of Arthur's and his siblings' births, the deaths of his father, grandmother and some siblings, his parents' marriage and allied information. Mr Lancelyn Green obtained other relevant material for me from comparable records in London.

The Roman Catholic authorities of Edinburgh have been generosity itself towards this wayward member of their flock. Monsignor O'Grady and his fellow-priests at Cathedral House have been endless in their good nature as I rummaged through their records of baptisms. It was from here that I discovered Arthur's second name to be "Ignatius", something unknown outside the family. He told his children that he was also christened "Charles", but it seems he was mistaken on that point. The baptismal records give important information about godparents, residence and so on: the absence of childbirths during the interval, if any, between residence at Portobello and at Sciennes Hill Place prompts the thought that Charles and Mary Doyle may have separated for a time at that juncture. We do not know how long Arthur spent in Ireland during that first visit of which he gives a tantalisingly brief mention in *Memories and Adventures:* he thought it was in 1866, and while he speaks of it being "a few weeks" the possibility exists that it was longer and amounted to a temporary residence for Mary and the children. In the absence of further information, which may be forthcoming when the disputed papers are opened, no useful discussion of the point could be made.

I have been able to draw on some letters of ACD, some of which are in private keeping and not available for direct citation. Mr Richard Lancelyn Green and Dr A. E. Rodin reported to me on materials they had examined in American libraries; Dr Rodin very courteously sent me the catalogue of the letters to Dr and Mrs Hoare preserved in the Berg collection of the New York Public Library. It has not been permissable for me to see copies of these, but on one or two very important points, notably the oral with Professor Spence, Dr Rodin supplied me with vital information. On Ireland, the richest deposit known to me is the correspondence with Roger Casement in the Casement papers at the National Library of Ireland; dating from the period before World War I they indicate Conan Doyle's conversion to Home Rule, passionate support of Casement on the Putumayo as well as the Congo, work on *The Lost World* and so forth, but in more general terms they convey much about ACD's sense of his Irish and Catholic heritage. I have written a little about their relations in my essay on the Casement trial published this year in the *Transactions of the Royal Historical Society,* to whose editor I am most indebted. I am particularly grateful to my old friend Michael Foot for his discussion of this matter with me, and his delight in the courage and wisdom of Conan Doyle about the "Black" diaries ascribed to Casement. Apart from the Stonyhurst records, a couple of letters to Father Joe Keating, S.J., have been most kindly copied for me by the distinguished archivist of the Jesuit house at Farm Street, London, the Rev. Francis Edwards, S.J. for whose comments after my talk to the Royal Historical Society I was grateful.

To the National Library of Scotland my gratitude is boundless. I must first thank the Trustees for permission to reproduce illustrations from the *Strand* magazine (the serialisation of *The Lost World* and *The Poison Belt,* in vols. XLIII, XLIV and XLV, 1912-1913), as well as that of William Budd from the Goodall biography. Mr William Brown and the staff of the Reading Room have been fertile of ideas, suggestions, assistance and patience far beyond any call of duty. The same is true of their colleagues in the photographic division, and in the Department of Manuscripts where in the Blackwood collection is preserved *"The Haunted Grange of Goresthorpe".* Mr Cadell of the MSS division has given most fruitful study to this latter, and the collection in general is very valuable with its several letters from Conan Doyle throwing light on the date of composition of several of his works. I much appreciate the personal knowledge and insights on this collection placed at my disposal by my fellow-author at Mainstream, Mr Trevor Royle. The Manuscript Room at NLS also houses papers of the Chambers publishing company, and of the house of Smith, Elder. As yet the former has produced little of interest, but the latter includes the *Cornhill* roster of contributions and some correspondence from ACD notably with respect to his controversy with *The Times* Book Club on *Sir Nigel*. It seems possible that more may emerge from archives of both of these houses yet to be placed in the Library: in particular the earliest correspondence has not yet come to light.I have obviously made much use of the Library's newspaper collection, particularly for the files of the *Scotsman,* the *Glasgow Herald* and *The Times.*

Edinburgh University Library have been likewise invaluable to me, and I must thank Miss Brenda Moon, the Librarian, Mr Peter Freshwater, her Deputy, and their staff for their unfailing interest, encouragement and aid. The issue desk and reference staff have done everything I could possibly ask of them, and indeed much more, from alerting me to and providing me with a fugitive article noticed by one of them on the *Mary Celeste*, to obtaining rare material through inter-library loan. My greatest debt of all in the University Library is that incurred by me to Dr John Hall, Head of Special Collections, and his staff. Dr Hall's personal vast knowledge of student records and publications at the University was placed whole-heartedly at my disposal, and he came up with idea after idea, spurring me on with his enthusiasm and sardonic charm. To him I owe the thought of digging in records of Library borrowing. Students paid for this, and did not avail themselves of it where other material was at their disposal. Arthur apparently did not make use of it: he had Waller's library at his disposal, he lived very near the University and probably did much of his reading in the Library in part as a refuge from his father and from Waller. But James Ryan, who lodged somewhat farther from the University, was a borrower and his records tell a good deal about the variation in his interests. The matriculation records and reports on examinations were essential to assess Arthur's student career; I have found them an invaluable check on the accounts of examination in *Girdlestone,* as well as showing the student function of ACD's time with Reginald Hoare. The Court minutes throw light on the Department of Pathology in Waller's time, and the Court Papers are much richer. But the business of professorial appointment was handled by Curators of Patronage and their records do not survive to my knowledge. Appointment of Examiners and recognition of extra-mural lecturers do emerge from the Court papers, and these were also helpful regarding Waller.

The Erskine Medical Library in George Square also gave me the fullest of co-operation, and here I was enabled to comb the *Lancet, B.M.J., Edinburgh Medical Journal* and a host of pamphlets and published lectures relating to the Medical School. Necessarily some material is retained in the main

Library: John Smith Flett's manuscript memoir is in the Special Collections there, for instance. There is an accessible range of publications about various aspects of the history of the Medical School: the official history, for instance, includes some quotations from letters of former students. The *Medical Directory* and the Register of the General Council provided many clues.

In the University itself, I have very many colleagues to thank. Professor George Shepperson, William Robertson Professor of Commonwealth and American History, has been a fount of inspiration and encouragement from start to finish. Above all, his unique knowledge of the history of Africa and the United States was my salvation for the chapter on Henry Highland Garnet, and my use of Earl Ofari's study derived from his loan of that work to me with helpful pointers about its subject. Mr Christopher Fyfe identified Garnet as the unknown "Consul" mentioned in *Memories and Adventures* when I furnished him with its sparse particulars. Dr Rhodri Jeffreys-Jones aided me with many insights and all forms of assistance, and Dr Thomas J. Barron enabled me to draw on his unrivalled knowledge of Ceylon in my pursuit of James Ryan. Professor W. W. Robson, Masson Professor of English Literature, has been a most valuable critic of the entire enterprise from its inception, and provided a host of constructive and wide-ranging comments on the manuscript on reading it for the publishers. He read most of it before the Epilogue was written, and it is due to points raised by him that I embarked on a third reading of *Micah Clarke* as a result of which my understanding of it was transformed and the Epilogue took the form it has done. Above all Professor Robson's conviction of Conan Doyle's stature as a writer, and his brilliant insights on his work, were a beacon of inspiration for me. My friend Dr Roger Savage of the same department was unfailing in his receptivity to endless talk about Conan Doyle and wise advice on the business of writing. My former colleague in History, Professor V. G. Kiernan, provided fine analysis of the social implications of ACD's work. Professor K. A. Fowler, of the History Department, discussed the historical quality of the medieval novels with me, and I have benefited not only from his specialist knowledge but also from those of his fellow-medievalists Dr Angus MacKay and Dr Anthony Goodman. Mr Ray Footman, Information Officer to the University, has been endless in his own investigations of Conan Doyle material at Edinburgh, and as a result of his enthusiasm and hard work I have been given many targets for investigation. Of my medical colleagues, Mr I. B. Macleod and Dr J. S. K. Stevenson helped me greatly in conversation about their profession. If, as I have sought to show, Arthur Conan Doyle found many Sherlock Holmeses at Edinburgh, I have found even more.

I must thank the Principal of the University, Dr J. H. Burnett, for his help and interest in this book, and the Secretary, Mr Alexander Currie, for his generous encouragement of it. Of my students, I owe great debts to Mr M. J. McGrath, Mr Adam Naylor and Mr Daniel J. O'Donnell, for their excellent criticisms of theses raised with them during its development.

Turning to the Roman Catholic chaplaincy at the University, where ACD and his family once lived, I must appreciate the courtesy of the Rev. Aidan

Nichols, O.P., and the Catholic Society, for enabling me to study the house and report to them on my findings. The former Catholic chaplain and more recently former Rector, the Very Rev. Anthony Ross, O.P., now Prior Provincial of the Dominicans in Britain, cleared up many important questions about the Catholic world in Arthur's time, and gave me the confidence and guidance I needed in coming to terms with theological problems in the study. I am deeply grateful to the Library of Hawkesyard Priory where I worked during Spode House Family Week, and to our friends who share that week with us; their comments in response to my talk on ACD were most useful. The Rev. Joseph Kavanagh, O.P., firmly disposed of one doctrinal question I needed to clear up rapidly.

It will be evident that I fell very much in love with Stonyhurst College, and this is due to the unparalleled courtesy and thoughtfulness I received at all points from its staff and students. I most warmly thank for their hospitality and their aid the Headmaster, Father Bossy, S.J., the editor of the *Stonyhurst Magazine*, Father Joseph Dooley, S.J., the archivist, Father Frederick Turner, S.J., and the distinguished authority on Gerard Manley Hopkins on the staff, Mr Gerald Roberts. Father Turner placed before me the letters of ACD to Francis Cassidy, and the invaluable obituaries privately printed for the use of the Society of Jesus only, as well as many other documents and memorabilia which enabled me to reconstruct so much of what had hitherto been unknown. Father Dooley, for whom I wrote a somewhat different account of Arthur's Stonyhurst years, discovered Everard Digby's memoir of his student days. Father Bossy provided me with some excellent analysis of the nature and attitudes of the Jesuits of the time: his brother's work on which I drew is best known in his book on the English Catholics, but I received even more benefit from his article on Lancashire Catholicism printed in the collection of essays in honour of Professor Michael Roberts of which he was co-editor. Father Bossy's contribution to my work was complemented by talks about the Jesuits and their teaching with Father Paul Andrews, S.J., then Rector of Belvedere College, and subsequently with his successor, Father Bruce Bradley, S.J. Father Dooley also put me in touch with Father J. H. Crehan, S.J., who answered very many queries about Stonyhurst traditions on Conan Doyle, and his unrivalled knowledge of Herbert Thurston and his contemporaries enabled me to round out the Jesuit side of the story: I deeply regret that he did not live to see how much he had given me. As to Mr Gerald Roberts, I cannot possibly be sufficiently grateful for the good fortune which gave me his advice, wisdom and enthusiasm. Several pupils at Stonyhurst gave me much aid by their knowledge of their school's history and their independent investigations of Arthur's association with it. It was a privilege and a pleasure to lecture on him there, and a delight to walk and work within its walls. I am most grateful to correspondents who responded to my contribution to the *Magazine*, whose own early files threw much light on ACD. The Digby manuscript includes some of his drawings, and the records of student plays convey his participation and that of his colleagues. The records of admission produced very helpful comments, as well as invaluable particulars about names of his classmates.

I have many other obligations to record. My friend Mr Nicolas Barker of the British Library offered critical guidance and assistance, and I must thank the staff of his institution for their aid especially in the pursuit of out-of-way periodicals. Mr Richard Whittington-Egan has helped me time after time in chasing hares and coming to conclusions. Mr Anthony Curtis generously gave me a copy of his edition of the Raffles stories, containing a most helpful introduction. My old Mentor, Sir Rupert Hart-Davis, who first directed my activities as a literary detective, firmly placed before me the need to justify another book on Conan Doyle: I have sought to follow his principles, and I only hope he feels I have given him a satisfactory answer. Mr Alan Macdougall, formerly of the Bank of Scotland, has given both my publishers and myself most warm and enthusiastic championship and wise advice. Mr Peter Cunningham, of Stewart's Bar, was an admirable counsellor and friend, especially on the history of Rutherford's and of late nineteenth-century Edinburgh in general. Councillor Mrs Kathleen Macfie brought her deep knowledge of Stevenson to my aid, and her charm and laughter to my inspiration. Mr Peter T. Fraser has been a mainstay and prop in the quest from the first. Mr D. Martin Dakin has courteously answered my questions, and has obligingly provided in his *Sherlock Holmes Commentary* the best single volume on the subject I know. The University of South Carolina and its Library gave the subject its first glimmer of existence with the research materials they provided, and my seminar there in 1973 enabled me to investigate many of its implications for American history: my special thanks are due to Professors Robert Ochs, Robert Patterson, Edward Beardsley, to my fellow-visitor Dr Roger Highfield of Merton College, Oxford, and to Dean Willie Harriford.

Mr Michael Holroyd most generously sent me from his private collection the file of Hesketh Pearson's papers relating to his life of Conan Doyle. I only hope, in return, I have provided something of a vindication of the merits of this unjustly-traduced work, whose imperfections are far below its merits. It will be evident how much I have enjoyed debating with it, and I should also record how from boyhood I have been delighted by the verve and wit of Pearson's biographies in which, as a former actor, he sought to play the parts of his subjects.

Mr George Richardson very kindly pursued an investigation for me respecting the publication of Waller's poems. On Waller himself, my deep gratitude must be recorded to all my informants and correspondents from the Masongill country. I have had the great advantage of speaking with the present owners of Masongill House, the family of Mr William Hartley, whose aunt, Mrs Coates, gave me vivid memories of Waller and his wife from the days of tenancy under their unwelcoming rule. They also sent me to other witnesses, who were very rich in memories and observations: Mrs Kate Mitton and Mrs Violet Redhead, both of whom had been in service to the Wallers and who enabled me to build up new and important evidence about them. Mrs Mitton also recalled material she had heard from her father, the late Mr Kettlewell, head gardener on the estate, and Mrs Redhead exceedingly thoughtfully sent after me a very valuable letter indicating Waller's dietary preferences whose high points for our story were the curry and oysters. The Rev. Arthur L. Hughes, Vicar of Burton-in-Lonsdale and also Thornton-in-Lonsdale, replied very fully to my request for details of ACD's first marriage certificate, his sister's marriage to the Rev. Cyril Angell and particulars of the Waller family, and I am most appreciative of the trouble he took. Mrs Humphries, of Burton-in-Lonsdale, kindly lent my publishers the photographs of Waller and of the group before Masongill House: they form part of her private collection. Other residents whom I met included Mrs Mitton's sister, who added further recollections and aided me in my study of the churchyard and its tombs at Thornton-in-Lonsdale; the Vicar's wife at Kirkby Lonsdale, who charmingly set my mission off to a flying start; the schoolteacher near Cowans Bridge; and the officials of a mobile library who sheltered me from the elements (during which time a lady came in to borrow a book, declining *The Sign of Four* because she preferred Sherlock Holmes on television). Although it had completely eluded all students of ACD and Holmes, Mr William Mitchell had written an account of Waller in the *Dalesman* for July 1975. It is based on the recollections of the witnesses I saw myself, but it added some further details: from its theories I strongly dissent. One of the richest sources for Waller was of course the posthumous collection *Echo:* strangely, there is no copy in the British Museum (where I did inspect his homonymous relative's much poorer verse) but the National Library had a copy. I am grateful to my friends at James Thin, booksellers of Edinburgh, for their aid, especially Mr Alan Boyd, and also the manager of the antiquarian section for her hard but unavailing enquiries for a copy of *Echo*. I must also mention the value of conversation about Sherlockiana with another bookseller, Mr Michael Scott, of Fred Hanna in Dublin.

I met Dr Alvin E. Rodin, of Wright State University, at a late stage of my investigation. He entered into most useful discussion with me as to the work he is doing on Conan Doyle as a medical writer, and many of the very helpful points he communicated to me then and subsequently have enriched my study considerably. Were it not for him the information on the Spence oral, for instance, would not be there. He drew to my attention an important monograph on the licencing of vivisectors where the reproduction of a table of rejected applicants gave Waller pride of place, and he told me of a new biography of Joseph Bell, which I have not yet seen. I understand it makes some use of Dr P. H. Watson: however, my discovery of him was made independently, and Mr Ray Footman was in the field before any of us.

Other American correspondents have also been very helpful, including my former student Mr Stephen Burrington, to whose timely gift of an absurd pastiche on Holmes I owe the hint of the importance of certain German writers. Heine's significance is made clear by the doctoral dissertation, safely on deposit in the Special Collections at Edinburgh University: a brief portion of it was published in *The Edinburgh Stories of Arthur Conan Doyle* together with other work. The publishers of that volume, Polygon, are directed by Edinburgh University Student Publication Board, the inheritors of *"The Field*

Bazaar" (also included), which ACD gave to the editors of *Student* in 1896. I am deeply grateful for the work of Mr Jamie Donald in connection with that and so much else, and also to Mr Neville Moir, of the Board, and his wife Judy, of the Scottish Publishers' Association, for their support at all times.

Naturally, the roots of my interest in ACD go very far back. To my parents I owe very great thanks: my father for his admiration for Herbert Butterfield and reflections on his methods, my mother for having talked Holmes to me since my infancy (including dealing with the psychological consequences of premature reading of *"The Speckled Band"* and *"The Musgrave Ritual"*). I also owe much to my sister Mary, and our friend Conan Rafferty, for conversation on Holmes when we were children. My friend Professor Robin Winks, of Yale University, has been a most valued colleague in the use of detective fiction for historical investigation. To look to the future, my children have all made individual contributions to this book, Leila and Michael in the checking of references, Sara in the making of the index. I have to thank my mother-in-law for her eternal laughter and encouragement, and my wife, Bonnie Dudley Edwards, for everything under the sun, and over it too, I suspect.

Dame Jean Conan Doyle, OBE, has been kindness itself to me. She has provided me with innumerable clues, and has kept me on sound historical paths with the wisdom of a very enlightened academic supervisor. She has gone to the utmost trouble to help me find critical material, and she and her husband, Air Vice-Marshal Sir Geoffrey Bromet, have won the hearts of my family, colleagues, students and self for their charm and generosity. My gratitude to her father is doubled by the privilege of working with her. She was not in a position to show me the family papers, but very kindly allowed me to see pictures, memorabilia and books in her possession: of these the most important to me have proved to be the marginal writings on various personal copies of his favourite books. Scott's *Journal* proved especially fruitful in the comments it elicited from ACD. She has also been tremendously helpful in keeping me in touch with scholarship elsewhere, making me aware of new documentary finds, and placing me in touch with other scholars, and custodians of material. In addition, she has saved me from many errors. I only wish the book were worthy of the trouble she has gone to for me: of course she must in no way be held responsible for its views.

Dame Jean read the work in proof. Her cousin, Brigadier John Doyle, OBE, son of the late General Innes Doyle, has not seen it, but he also has been of outstanding aid to me and his hospitality and abundance of information and assistance were most generously placed at my disposal and at that of my research colleague, Timothy Willis, during a visit to his archives at Brockenhurst. The Innes Doyle MSS and other papers and books in his possession were a very rich source. They contain a few letters to and from ACD, memorabilia on lecture-tours, a brief but revealing journal kept by Innes Doyle in the 1890s and 1900s, and many personal items of great value. Brigadier Doyle was also enabled to draw on his recollections of his elder cousin Mary which he recalled very fully for me and which helped greatly with the period of ACD's life before his own birth, admirably supplementing the evidence in his father's diary. Thanks to his stimulus I hope I succeeded in getting the historical writings of ACD in better perspective. The copyright of the picture of Charles and Arthur is his. That of the Stonyhurst group and of ACD at Southsea belong to another private collection.

Lastly, the recipients of the dedication. Mr Colin Ian Affleck read the entire work in page-proof and disposed of countless errors and ambiguities with an Argus eye. Mr Graham Richardson read it in draft at an early stage and made some admirable and trenchant criticisms which did much to correct its vagaries, and mine, and deserved better results. Mr Timothy Willis, a son of Stonyhurst, was a brilliant research assistant there and at Brockenhurst: if there is a research equivalent to a green thumb, it is his, for long-buried secrets seemed to fly from the past into his resolute grasp. Dr Graham Sutton went very carefully over the medical chapters in manuscript, and read and judged for me the medical writings of Waller, Budd, ACD, Hoare and others, moving with unerring strength from their language to ours. Naturally he is not to blame where the cloven hoof of the layman pokes through in this discourse. And Mr Richard Lancelyn Green has done so much that the recital of his assistance should occupy as much space again of this note on sources: he has read the text, thrown out endless ideas for investigation, reported on material everywhere from auction sale-rooms to far-flung libraries, pursued the London links in problems I opened up in Edinburgh, and been so very good indeed as to let me use the material forthcoming in the works to be edited by himself and Mr John Gibson (for whose permission I am also grateful). These will include ACD's work on photography, and his uncollected short stories. I am most grateful for the charm and hospitality shown me by his parents as well as by himself. If I ever write another volume on the life of Conan Doyle, it will only be with his co-authorship. This is selfishness on my part, for he is the better scholar on Conan Doyle. I look forward, as must all students of Conan Doyle, to his and Mr Gibson's bibliography which is to appear next year. I have not troubled to include material which will be far better handled in its pages.

The imperfections of this volume are in no way to be charged to any of these admirable benefactors.

I must also express my gratitude to my publishers, who are fascinating, maddening and brilliant.

Department of History
University of Edinburgh
15 October 1982

Owen Dudley Edwards

Index

No entries occur under the names of Arthur Conan Doyle, Sherlock Holmes or John H. Watson. Double barrelled names are found under the last name, save where the name only exists hyphenated. Titles are by ACD unless otherwise indicated.

MORE ABOUT PENGUINS, PELICANS AND PUFFINS

For further information about books available from Penguins please write to Dept EP, Penguin Books Ltd, Harmondsworth, Middlesex UB7 0DA.

In the U.S.A.: For a complete list of books available from Penguins in the United States write to Dept DG, Penguin Books, 299 Murray Hill Parkway, East Rutherford, New Jersey 07073.

In Canada: For a complete list of books available from Penguins in Canada write to Penguin Books Canada Ltd, 2801 John Street, Markham, Ontario L3R 1B4.

In Australia: For a complete list of books available from Penguins in Australia write to the Marketing Department, Penguin Books Australia Ltd, P.O. Box 257, Ringwood, Victoria 3134.

In New Zealand: For a complete list of books available from Penguins in New Zealand write to the Marketing Department, Penguin Books (N.Z.) Ltd, P.O. Box 4019, Auckland 10.

In India: For a complete list of books available from Penguins in India write to Penguin Overseas Ltd, 706 Eros Apartments, 56 Nehru Place, New Delhi 110019.

PENGUIN OMNIBUS EDITIONS

THE PENGUIN COMPLETE FATHER BROWN
G. K. Chesterton

Here are all forty-nine quietly sensational cases investigated by the high-priest of detective fiction, Father Brown. Immortalized in these famous stories, G. K. Chesterton's little Norfolk priest has entertained and endeared himself to countless generations of readers. For, as his admirers know, Father Brown's cherubic face and unworldly simplicity, his glasses and his huge umbrella, disguise a quite uncanny understanding of the criminal mind at work.

THE COMPLETE TALES AND POEMS OF EDGAR ALLAN POE

The Fall of the House of Usher, *The Murders in the Rue Morgue*, *The Pit and the Pendulum*, *The Gold-Bug* – some of the most famous tales of terror, the most macabre detective stories ever written. Acknowledged master of suspense, Poe was also a poet and – as his stories of mesmerism and time travel prove – a pioneer of science fiction. In this collection, probing to the depths of the human psyche, Poe's haunted genius will chill and enthrall you.

THE PENGUIN COMPLETE STORIES AND PLAYS OF OSCAR WILDE

Widely quoted, razor-tongued craftsman of the *mot juste*, devotee of beauty and wit, parodist of affectation – Wilde was the inventor of Bunburying and a self-declared genius. This volume spans the flamboyant wickedness of *The Picture of Dorian Gray*, the bubbling comedy of *The Importance of Being Earnest*, and the stark prose of *De Profundis*. It also includes *The Ballad of Reading Gaol* and selections from Wilde's essays and letters.

THE PENGUIN BRONTË SISTERS

This volume contains three novels, differing in style, united in their emotional intensity, passionately held beliefs and creative power. In *The Tenant of Wildfell Hall*, Anne Brontë wrote the first fully sustained feminist novel with her story of the wronged wife. One of the most unforgettable love stories ever written, Charlotte Brontë's *Jane Eyre* spoke out – and still speaks out – for women struggling for personal autonomy and sexual fulfilment in a hostile society. In *Wuthering Heights*, Emily Brontë achieved a unique portrayal of the irresistible forces of sexual passion and of nature, straining against the physical confines of the world.

THE PENGUIN COMPLETE SHORT STORIES OF FRANZ KAFKA

From 'Metamorphosis' to 'In the Penal Colony', Kafka's stories create a paradoxical world where individuals faced with the absurdity of existence continue to search for the truth.

'The author who comes nearest to bearing the same kind of relationship to our age as Dante, Shakespeare and Goethe bore to theirs . . . Kafka is important to us because his predicament is the predicament of modern man' – W. H. Auden.

THE PENGUIN COMPLETE LONGER NON-FICTION OF GEORGE ORWELL

All the force of George Orwell's vision, compassion and candour went into the making of these three books. In *Down and Out in Paris and London* he brings the poor of two capitals to life with eerie intensity; in *The Road to Wigan Pier* he exposes, in a series of painfully vivid descriptions, a cruel system; and in *Homage to Catalonia* he memorably describes the bright hopes and cynical betrayals of the Spanish Civil War.